Changing Canada

*Political Economy as
Transformation*

EDITED BY
WALLACE CLEMENT
AND LEAH F. VOSKO

This book is dedicated to

RIK DAVIDSON

legendary Social Sciences editor at the University of Toronto Press.

© McGill-Queen's University Press 2003
ISBN 0-7735-2530-0 (cloth)
ISBN 0-7735-2531-9 (paper)

Legal deposit third quarter 2003
Bibliothèque nationale du Québec

Printed in Canada on acid-free paper.

McGill-Queen's University Press acknowledges the support of the Canada Council for the Arts for our publishing program. We also acknowledge the financial support of the Government of Canada through the Book Publishing Industry Development Program (BPIDP) for our publishing activities.

National Library of Canada Cataloguing in Publication

Changing Canada : political economy as transformation / edited by Wallace Clement and Leah F. Vosko.

Includes bibliographical references and index.
ISBN 0-7735-2530-0 (bound).—ISBN 0-7735-2531-9 (pbk.)

1. Canada—Economic conditions—1991– 2. Canada—Politics and government—1993– 3. Canada—Social conditions—1991–
4. Social change—Canada. I. Clement, Wallace
II. Vosko, Leah F.

HB121.A2C48 2003   971.064′8   C2002-905150-9

Typeset in 10/12 Baskerville by True to Type

Contents

Acknowledgments

This collection is dedicated to RIK Davidson, the recently retired legendary editor at the University of Toronto Press, who was so influential during the formative period of the "new" Canadian political economy tradition. Under his leadership at the University of Toronto Press, three centrally defining collections were published: Ian Lumsen's *Close the 49th Parallel, etc* (1970), Gary Teeple's *Capitalism and the National Question in Canada* (1972) and Leo Panitch's *The Canadian State: Political Economy and Political Power* (1977). These volumes have provided the springboard for much more. In the last twenty-five years, the new Canadian political economy has been marked by surges in the fields of feminist political economy, political ecology, and the political economy of race and ethnicity and by a resurgence in the Innisian tradition of political economy. The journal *Studies in Political Economy* and the two precursors to this collection published by McGill-Queen's University Press have been principal contributors to the new Canadian political economy.

Every contributor to this volume has played a pivotal role in expanding and deepening the terrain of the new Canadian political economy. We acknowledge their dedication to the field, as well as their patience and diligence in preparing this collection. We are also grateful to McGill-Queen's University Press, particularly Executive Director Philip Cercone, the Canada Research Chairs Programme and the Social Sciences and Humanities Research Council of Canada. Special thanks to Innis College, University of Toronto, and its director, Frank Cunningham, for hosting a workshop that made this project a collaborative relationship between the editors and contributors, to Susan Wessels and Kimberley Glaze for their assistance in preparing the volume for publication, to Ron Curtis for his editorial skills, and to our partners, Elsie and Gerald, for their support and encouragement. We also wish to acknowledge the untimely passing of Rodney Bobiwash, former co-ordinator of the First Nations' House at the University of Toronto, who began this project as one of our contributors.

Introduction

Fundamental to the social sciences, and to political economy in particular, is a focus on identifying social relations and scrutinizing social change. The previous volume in this series was entitled *Understanding Canada: Building on the New Canadian Political Economy* (Clement 1997). *Understanding* was the operative theme. The first volume in this series was entitled *The New Canadian Political Economy* (Clement and Williams 1989). It concentrated on the roots of the *revival* of political economy in Canada, building from the classic Innisian tradition. The present volume has as its primary theme the notion of *transformation*. It is about the engagement of political economy in changing Canada and also about changes in Canadian political economy itself. In this collection, transformation is taken to mean gaining understanding in order to promote or direct social change. It is this intellectual engagement that is our main theme – applied political economy is the way we characterize it and this means extending Canadian political economy into new domains, seeking broader audiences, and building on the renewed engagement by students of political economy in trying to understand, explain and resist the complex forces around them.

Sociologist C. Wright Mills is renowned for opening the minds of many scholars; in his justly famous *Sociological Imagination* (1959, 187) he reminds us to learn how "to translate personal troubles into public issues." As important as this advice is, it is surpassed by his thoughts on engagement and objectivity, where he appeals to scholars to strive for objectivity by being transparent about their assumptions and guiding principles as they shape their theories and methods. This appeal does not replace engagement in the public issues of the day but rather calls for informed and reasoned interventions. Canadian sociologist John Porter supports this position on values and social science research in the prologue to his last book, *The Measure of Canadian Society* (1987, 2), noting that "social scientists have to choose sides and to fashion their work with a clear idea of what their values are ... the major task of social science is to abstract from the confused flow of events perspectives which clarify and which submit some judgment about society in the light of moral principles." It is thus the responsibility of social scientists to marshal evidence and explanation so as to "help to mobilize forces of change" (3).

The various strands of the new Canadian political economy are exemplary in their efforts to mobilize political economy to advance analyses of progressive social change (including interrogating what is meant by "progressive"), always questioning dominant ideas about economy and polity and identifying contradictions and tensions in research represented as value-free. Reflecting this commitment, a primary strength of this body of scholarship is its openness to internal debate, frequently resulting in challenges to core values that often result in piercing self-critique. Like the late-1970s challenge to the gender blindness of political economy, which highlighted the narrow economism of male-stream scholarship, analyses of decolonialization, as well as race and gender relations have, for example, unsettled established strains in feminist political economy and have thereby taken transformation in a direction different from the one taken by conventional political economy (Andrew 1996; Creese and Stasiulus 1996; Jhappan 1996; Vosko 2002).

Progressive political economy, which derives from an engagement with the Marxist tradition of radical social criticism, is an important root of the self-reflexivity now shaping social science theory and method. The new Canadian political economy is motivated by values such as economic and social justice and therefore does not claim to be value-free. All theories both reveal and conceal. Since no political-analytical approach is, in fact, value-free, as researchers who are differently situated we can move closer to objectivity by being aware of our normative commitments as well as the necessarily partial nature of our vision. Thus, the new political economy strives to be self-conscious and transparent about its assumptions. This certainly does not mean that no significant differences exist within this body of thought. Many different perspectives find a place within Canadian political economy. The new Canadian political economy in its many variants is marked by particular debates, dominant modes of questioning, and specific sets of preoccupations. The common ground is informed engagement based upon research oriented towards a political economy method emphasizing contradiction and change. The common ground is defined by logic, evidence, and openness to alternative explanations – and indeed by transformation itself. Transparency includes openness about assumptions and self-consciousness about procedures, including fundamental tenets about what progressive scholarly practice entails.

POLITICAL ECONOMY AS TRANSFORMATION

Transformative behaviour – "creativity" – arises out of the contradictions which attract both the internalized heterogeneity of "things" and out of the more obvious heterogeneity present within systems. In a dialectical view, opposing forces, themselves constituted out of processes, in turn become particular nodal points for further patterns of transformative activity. Matter and non-matter, positive and negative charges, repulsion and attraction, life and death, mind and matter, masculine and feminine, capital and labour etc. are constituted as oppositions around which congeal a whole host of transformative activities that both reproduce the oppositions and restructure the physical, biological and social world. (Harvey 1996, 54)

Political economy embodies "uncommon sense." It seeks to abandon the common-sense view that certain things (e.g., capital or markets) and social and economic systems (e.g., capitalism) are irreducible rather than relational and *always* in process or flux (Ollman 1993, 11–12). Political economy aims to trouble and challenge conventional ways of framing issues, in particular, in the present era, the neoliberal paradigm and its project. From a progressive political economy perspective, objects and subjects of study taken to be fixed or static and unproblematic in the empiricist and positivist traditions of political science and neoclassical economics are conceived dialectically. They are understood as internally contradictory, opening space for analyzing profound efforts at mediation, for identifying the forces of *stability* as well as change (Picchio 1992), and ultimately for the possibility for social transformation.

Neoliberalism has become entrenched in the Canadian political space in the past decade as the dominant common-sense understanding of what is natural and inevitable in an era of economic globalization, political continentalization, and global terrorism (whether state or movement-based). It has narrowed the discourse of political, economic, and social debate, transforming what it means to be liberal, social democratic, or even progressive conservative in the twenty-first century by asserting itself against social entitlements, rights, and citizenship. Following the official state responses to the attacks of September 11th, 2001, "security" no longer invokes the social rights of citizens but the military right to curtail human rights. And it is a very particular military: American security is equated once again with the defence of the "free world" where intellectual space is narrowed to being loyal or being the enemy. The hegemon is America and its "friends," not the United Nations or even NATO (see the special issue of *Studies in Political Economy* on the politics of protest (no. 67, spring 2002)). The atrocity of 9/11 has become a justification for curbing dissent and muting the envisioning of alternatives. More than ever, it is important to promote perspectives independent of the free market economy, conservative politics, and militarism packaged as justifications that come to dominate what passes for thinking.

Inspired by developments in the new Canadian political economy, this collection is motivated to assemble the questions posed that not only trouble dominant ways of thinking and knowing but also promote alternative ways of understanding and explaining Canadian society and politics, with the aim of promoting progressive social change. As Carroll and Coburn write in their contribution to this volume, "the new political economy has never been detached from movement activism but has included in its project an explicitly activist dimension." Thus, like Clement's previous collection (1997, 4), our goal continues to be to "explain the 'economy' and market forces so that political and social interventions can direct economic processes," but our aim here is also to chart new transformative directions for the new Canadian political economy. The collection is dedicated to the promotion of emancipatory politics, to social and economic justice, redistribution, libratory struggle, human rights, and human welfare. We aim to investigate how changes in the organization or disorganization of capitalism are producing new types of transformations and forms of resistance and to move the sites of contestation into and beyond the state. Contributors to the volume recognize the often paradoxical or contradictory effects of various social forces, such as the liberating and constraining features of new communications technologies, new employment norms, and new household forms. In such cases, they seek to understand the conditions under which these forces are either liberating or constraining, always asking, for whose benefit? They also examine the limitations and possibilities of political economy as an approach to understanding social change, suggesting ways in which earlier assumptions and foci in the field itself (be they methodological or political) need to be maintained, shifted or displaced. Their aim is to extend the new Canadian political economy into new domains and simultaneously seek broader audiences.

CHANGING CANADA

The new Canadian political economy strives for transformation in the double sense – social change within society and changes to political economy itself as it develops as a tradition. This collection, in turn, is concerned with, on the one hand, what is changing Canada (e.g., the macrolevel forces associated with globalization and commoditization) and, on the other hand, what it takes to change or transform Canada (i.e., the ingredients of progressive social transformation). The leading assumption of the collection is that political economy, through its understanding of contradiction and change, can serve as a transformative tool in both scholarly work and action.

We wish to critique economic essentialism in two ways: by arguing that the "economic" itself is a social, political, cultural and ideological construct (think of the market as the paradigmatic case) and by arguing that there is no "essentialism," or sameness, in the economy, because time and space are ever-present variables for political economy. Instead, there are variations and complexities resulting from the fact that political economy as practised in Canada is an interdisciplinary hybrid. We want to know the contingencies, the possibilities and the prospects for social change – in short, transformations. But more than an attempt at understanding transformations, this collection is an exercise in disruption; it seeks to trouble conventional social science and traditional political economy.

Applied political economy is the main theme in many of the chapters in the collection. It is central in the contribution by Armstrong, Cornish, and Millar concerning pay equity and is also a feature of the chapters on childcare by Jenson, Mahon, and Phillips; the gendered rise of contingent work by Fudge and Vosko; welfare state restructuring by McKeen and Porter; municipal restructuring by Andrew; organized labour by Gindin and Stanford; ecology by Adkin; and native peoples' struggle against recolonization by Green. Applied political economy recognizes the unintended consequences and contradictions underlying specific actions and strategies; specifically, it recognizes how the strategic choices of social actors are limited by circumstance, time and space. "Applied political economy" as we use the term here is not meant to refer to a formula that is to be used on all occasions. Instead, we take it to mean the application of ways of seeing, thinking, and inquiring to practical situations and political actions. It is this intellectual engagement for which the collection strives. As the chapter by Armstrong, Cornish, and Millar reveals, on the ground, where political economy meets the courts, employers, or policymakers, there are other dominant assumptions and methods that produce different rules of evidence and argumentation and reconfigure, as well as reframe, so-called expert testimony. In their assessment of transformations taking place in the contemporary organized labour movement, Gindin and Stanford also highlight the importance of day-to-day events and struggles that reflect inherent tensions between structure and agency.

Flowing from the theme of applied political economy is the question of how popular groups challenge and engage globalization with alternative agendas of resistance. In *The Brave New World of Work*, Ulrich Beck (2000, 132) discusses the rise of "civil society international," the civil society organizations, initiatives, and networks that have evolved as alternatives to counter and, in some instances, engage with contemporary intergovernmental conferences. The actions and strategies pursued by this "new" civil society international, which transcends international borders yet whose strengths often reflect its local base, are explored here by Gabriel and Macdonald, whose contribution reveals how popular-sector groups in Canada, the United States, and Mexico have used organizing around the North American Free Trade Agreement (NAFTA) to initiate a cross-border alliance. They are also explored by Satzewich and Wong to examine new forms of international ethnic communications and by Adkin in her discussion of how to construct collective action for a democratizing political ecology. Carroll and Coburn and Keil and Kipfer also explore the activities and dynamics of popular sector groups challenging and engaging globalization, although at different levels. Through an exploration of several phases of social movement activism during the formative years of the Canadian political economy, Carroll and Coburn explore the mutual implications of social movements and political economy in terms of a dialectic of theory and practice, while Keil and Kipfer trace the roots of the new Canadian political economy's neglect of the production of urban space, pointing as does Andrew to the radical potential of urban groups.

Multiple forms (and "new" agents) of resistance represent yet another viewpoint into the applied political economy theme, especially in contributions by Kurasawa, Hollands, and Green. For example, in his contribution exploring the uneasy coexistence between the new Canadian political economy and cultural studies, which he explains on the basis of three subjects dominating the new Canadian political economy – namely, authenticity, commoditization, and dependency – Kurasawa shows how analyses of Canadian cinema, music, and culture-jamming can improve political economy's grasp of resistance. These cultural forms make visible contradictions and struggles imbedded in capitalist society, and Hollands, in his chapter, reveals their centrality to evolving youth culture(s) and, hence, to spawning engagement between "old left" actors, students, and young workers. Like Kurasawa, Green identifies the importance of documenting the activities of a wide range of agents of social change in the new Canadian political economy literature. Yet forms of resistance against colonization practised in aboriginal communities are the targets of her inquiry. Salée evaluates the transformative politics of Quebec in terms of social governance, the social economy, and the popular sector.

Several subthemes tied to applied political economy cut across the volume as well. Changes to political economy itself as it develops as a tradition are a salient thread in various contributions, but especially in those exploring welfare state restructuring, social movements, and the new urban experience. Challenges to the new Canadian political economy to adapt to dramatic social transformations make space for new forms of resistance, and marginalized actors also frame discussions throughout the volume, but especially in chapters exploring resistance, popular culture, and urban politics.

Contributors ranging from Kurasawa on popular culture to Keil and Kipfer and Andrew on the urban experience to Carroll and Coburn on social movements and Adkin on ecology express a common sentiment: the new Canadian political economy must change in response to developments in society and expand its conception of resistance. Combined with more established modes of inquiry into areas marked by accelerating commodification (see Mosco on communications), this type of renewal is necessary for deepening and enlarging the engagement between the new Canadian political economy and social-movement theory, as well as culture theory, for radicalizing political ecology, and for theorizing the urban and its counterpart, the municipal, as sites of transformation.

Challenges to the field are also evident in debates over how best to transform politics, particularly in discussions exploring the appropriate locus of political struggle – the mechanisms and strategies, as well as the methods, that the new Canadian political economy would do well to engage, as well as those demanding ruthless criticism (see the chapters by Green and Watkins). Should political economists intervene in debates over the social economy and explore the Quebec model in greater depth, as Salée's contribution suggests? Does the new anticapitalist movement provide an appropriate space for engagement as Carroll and Coburn argue? Will recent attempts to rebuild the left in Canada amount to a genuine beginning rather than short-lived experiments? If so, to reinvigorate interactions between scholars and activists, Gindin and Stanford suggest that political economists would be wise to engage more vociferously in these efforts as a means of fuelling a praxis-oriented research agenda.

At a broader level, is it time for the new Canadian political economy to reject the artificial borders that other fields of inquiry have erected around it despite its interdisciplinary core? Contributions on the North American Monetary Union (NAMU) and Canada's role in global finance and cross-border alliances under NAFTA suggest that the time for collapsing divisions between disciplines has come. The chapters by Coleman and Porter, Gabriel and Macdonald, and Helleiner effectively challenge the false boundary between the new Canadian political economy and critical international political economy.

Forceful challenges to subfields of the new Canadian political economy also emerge throughout the volume. As Satzewich and Wong illustrate, in the case of the political economy of immigration, scholars have yet to consider fully the implications of the growing internal differentiation within and between immigrant communities in Canada and its impact on political economy's understanding of the intersections of race, class, and gender relations. Along similar lines, Fudge and Vosko propose that feminist political economists renew their efforts to challenge male-stream political economists, specifically those focusing on the central institutions of the labour market, by probing more deeply the relationship between social reproduction and prevailing labour market trends. Surely, they argue, with the gendered rise of contingent work, reinvigorating unresolved debates is a more productive endeavour than reinforcing what have effectively become two solitudes in the new Canadian political economy of the labour market. Fudge and Vosko are not alone in their contention; it receives support from interventions by McKeen and Porter on welfare state restructuring, as well as Jenson, Mahon, and Phillips on childcare and Armstrong, Cornish, and Millar on pay equity, all of whose incisive analyses underscore the need for a thick feminist political economy of the supply and demand sides of the labour market.

No volume of reasonable size intended for classroom use can touch on all themes and issues germane to the expanding new Canadian political economy today, although this one attempts to survey a wide range. Just to mention health, biotechnology, strategic/peace studies, federal involvement in education, knowledge production, and training, and the so-called third sector as topics illustrates a vast range of additional issues. Students are encouraged to turn to the earlier version of this collection, *Understanding Canada*, for coverage of some topics not concentrated on here, such as manufacturing and natural resources (Clement and Williams), the changing nature of work (Phillips; Maroney and Luxton), structures and policies of the Canadian state (Albo and Jenson), law and regulation (Salter and Salter), foreign policy (Neufeld and Whitworth), regionalism (Brodie), and sports culture (Whitson and Gruneau). The present collection is intended to be as comprehensive as is reasonable, yet space limits the range of topics explored. Changing Canada – and all the tensions and contradictions that transformation entails, is a process – it is an ever-expanding scholarly endeavour, as well as an agenda for research and action.

THE COLLECTION

The chapters in this collection are organized into five sections, mainly for ease of use in discussions. Each contribution takes political economy as transformation as its central lens, several through applied approaches, and each takes seriously political economy's implicit rejection of the objectivity/value distinction, suggesting that the tradition does not pretend to be value-free, but that it is nevertheless transparent and open to challenge.

Part 1 examines political transformations, inverting the common scholarly practice of beginning at the level of the local and moving gradually to the level of the global. In this section, globalization is taken to entail the accelerating mobility of capital and the growth of international production, redistribution, and consumption and to encompass phenomena such as feminization and racialization, which are linked to the transmission of a set of value-laden goals associated with neoliberalism, goals like privatization, efficiency, competitiveness and social cohesion (Cohen 1997; Fudge and Cossman 2002). The objective of the section is three-fold. It aims to explore the relationship between globalization and the Canadian federation, highlighting the tensions and contradictions produced by this relationship (Salée); to demonstrate that globalization and the Canadian federation, both the concepts and the ideas that they embed, need to be scrutinized by the new Canadian political economy (Green and Watkins); and to illustrate the connections between transformations in society and political economy as an analytical tradition (Carroll and Coburn).

How does globalization unsettle forms of collective resistance predominating in Canada during the Keynesian era, and do the contradictory patterns and processes that it unleashes afford progressive groups opportunities as well as challenges? What does the restructuring of Canada's hybrid welfare state (Jenson, Mahon, and Phillips) mean for federal political parties and the shape of popular movement organizing? In confronting these questions, contributors to part 1 probe Aboriginal people's struggle for social justice, the politics of social change in Quebec, political reconfigurations in Canada in a time of globalization, and social movements. They ask, is the vision of the social economy emerging in Quebec viable and does it have the capacity to serve the cause of social justice or does it represent a uniquely Quebecois variation on the "third way"? What new tools must a transformative (in a normative sense) Canadian political economy embrace if it seeks to move Canada to a postcolonial state?

Mel Watkins is a kind of litmus test for Canadian political economy. Beginning with the consolidation and re-interpretation of the classic staples thesis (Harold Innis), then moving to liberal nationalism (Walter Gordon), and through the heady days of English-Canadian nationalism of the left (the Waffle), Watkins articulated the times. He has been at the core of the new Canadian political economy's revival, which, as he notes in his contribution, is not so new anymore. Watkins has led each of the two previous volumes in this series, and he leads once again, with an important viewpoint. For him, globalization is not a new phenomenon, nor is resistance to it. Rather, "the issue ... is what's new about globalization, and *how* novel is it?" In his contribution "Politics in the Time and Space of Globalization," Watkins contends that many contemporary theorists of globalization make a double error: the global economy is not "out there" for Canadians to let in, nor is there no alternative to globalization – this is not the end of politics. According to Watkins, it is imperative that the new Canadian political economy respond to this double error by returning to Innis's ideas on empire and Polanyi's conception of movement/countermovement and by calling on the Canadian left to build on the insights of these thinkers in developing a strategy for resisting globalization. In Watkins' view, a renewed NDP infused with social-movement activism – a party that is committed to social democracy rather than the third way – has the capacity to respond to this double error at the level of party politics and, therefore, offers promise in confronting the ideology of globalization.

Daniel Salée's contribution also takes a critical look at the state of the left in Canada – this time with an emphasis on Quebec. In "Transformative Politics, the State, and the Politics of Social Change in Quebec," he examines the fate of the Quebec model, finding growing weaknesses in its counterparadigmatic status in the face of globalization. Salée identifies a range of tensions and contradictions surrounding the model. For example, he recognizes the potential of Chantier de l'economie sociale, an independent but state-supported body that brings together labour and community organizations to develop social economy initiatives throughout Quebec, as a prototype for other initiatives flowing from the social-economy approach. Yet his analysis also reveals that the interest of the government in such measures and in the social economy more generally is instrumental, motivated by its perceived ability to lighten the burden on the Quebec welfare state. He finds, moreover, that although the old left has deliberately made itself an active player in the Quebec model of social economy, accepting it as the best course available for realizing its transformative agenda, support for concertation is by no means universal among left critics of neoliberalism in Quebec. Rather, various social-movement organizations, as well as the women's movement (the so-called new left), are increasingly expressing their lack of confidence, as evidenced by anti-WTO demonstrations and the emergence of groups such as the Coalition autonome populaire jeunesse, and their anxieties are sustained by repeated recessionary cycles, high unemployment rates, and a continuing fiscal crisis in Quebec.

In "Decolonization and Recolonization in Canada," Joyce Green also examines transformations taking place in the political sphere. Her subject is Aboriginal politics, and her chapter explores what she identifies as the simultaneous processes of decolonization and recolonization confronting Aboriginal people. Green argues forcefully that just at the moment when Canada has the greatest potential to move to a postcolonial relationship with Aboriginal nations, a new set of fragmenting forces is emerging as a result of increasingly complex interrelationships between federalism as a structure and a process and the escalating power of transnational capital in overriding existing arrangements at the level of the state. To explore these forces, Green traces Canada's colonial foundations and then examines the tensions raised by the growing formal recognition of Aboriginal rights in Canada, on the one hand, and transnational capital's threat to recolonize, on the other. She draws several cases to the reader's attention, including the case of the Lubicon in Alberta, the Innu in Labrador, and the larger debate around the wisdom of gas and oil development in the Canadian North, where transnational capital is playing a central role in blunting libratory impulses and rights-based political regimes by "selling the myth of economic equality via incorporation into the dominant economic and political regime." For Green the best possibilities for transcending prevailing contradictions and tensions, for constructing a postcolonial Canada whereby inequitable power relations are transformed into mutually beneficial relationships, require that Canada confront its history, understand it from the perspective of the most disadvantaged and cultivate the collective will to change institutional structures.

William Carroll and Elaine Coburn, in their chapter, "Social Movements and Transformation," further illuminate the praxis prism of the new Canadian political economy. Like Gabriel and Macdonald (in part 3), they develop a globalization-from-below thesis, but in this case the object of inquiry is the interaction between social-movement politics in Canada and the new Canadian political economy. By reviewing the evolution of the field, they suggest that Canadian political economy has drawn much of its intellectual strength from an active engagement with social movements, enabling it to reach pivotal insights on the politics of creating social change. Carroll and Coburn credit a great deal to the dialogical nature of the relationship between social movements and political economy, suggesting that it has meant, quite constructively, that Canadian political economists' knowledge claims have been provisional, yet cumulative. This tradition of interaction, therefore, creates space for interpreting growing anticapitalist social movements, drawing on the new Canadian political economy, whose tools are critical to revealing that "the 'globalization' of political economy is not simply about the impersonal forces of capital seeking to internationalize markets," as Carroll and Coburn note, but also about the "many Davids" of civil society.

Part 2 probes developments at the level of the political economy of the Canadian welfare state and its expanding margins. In "Welfare State Restructuring: Shifting Employment Norms and New Household Forms," "restructuring" is the operative term, understood as patterns and processes reflecting a tacit acceptance that the imperatives of the "new" global economy include "increased international competition between countries for investment and production, a greater emphasis on trade, and less government spending and regulation of the economy ... in other words, governments have no choice but to adapt their domestic economies, particularly the fiscal side, to the new demands of an increasingly global economy" (Bakker 1996, 3). Contributions in this section explore how welfare state restructuring is affecting households, labour markets, and communities defined by space and other affinities such as economic insecurity, age, race, and gender. Transformations taking place inside the Canadian federation are apparent not only at the level of the welfare state but also in changing employment norms, new household forms, and the restructuring of the municipal. Welfare state restructuring, however, is proving to be a contradictory – indeed, paradoxical – process. On the one hand, the Canadian state is withdrawing support for public services, downloading the cost of social reproduction onto households – and particularly onto women in households. Yet, on the other hand, it is delivering supports for care-giving in new and more targeted ways.

In part 2, as well, Wendy McKeen and Ann Porter explore the changes taking place in two central and related social policy areas located on the critical but porous boundary between production and reproduction – unemployment/employment insurance policies and family/child benefit policies. They find that while new maternity policies under EI have the potential to help some women, the trend in Canada is toward targeted benefits modeled on the American negative income-tax system, resulting in increasing pressures on women, low-income earners and the poor. Like co-contributors Jenson, Mahon, and Phillips and Fudge and Vosko, McKeen and Porter propose that the challenge to progressive policymakers as well as scholars – particularly political economists – rests on the need to recognize the value of social reproduction. Transformations taking place in Canada and other liberal welfare states call on political economists to consider new ways of organizing care-giving and income support and, in particular, to consider how these activities would be best redivided between the state, the market, and the community.

The contribution by Jane Jenson, Rianne Mahon, and Susan Phillips traces the four critical moments of transformation in debates over childcare, illustrating the depth of the challenges facing the childcare movement in the post–Canada Assistance Plan era. It also highlights the fracturing role that persisting provincial variation in childcare provision has played in the childcare advocacy movement in Canada. Where childcare policy is concerned, provincial variation has shaped the politics of social transformation in a dramatic way. The new trend, a strategy that these authors argue offers the most transformative potential, is towards coalition-based work among childcare advocates, in the face of the homogenizing elements of the Canada Health and Social Transfer and the new Social Union Framework Agreement.

Who benefits and who loses from transformations in the political economy are central questions, as well, in "Pay Equity: Complexity and Contradictions in Legal Rights and Social Processes." In this chapter, Pat Armstrong, Mary Cornish and Elizabeth Millar identify and analyze challenges in the fight for pay equity in the face of shifting interpretations of the Charter of Rights, on the one hand, and in the face of eroding employment norms, described in the preceding chapter by Fudge and Vosko, on the other hand. Unique in its standpoint, the chapter traces contradictions and tensions in the process of fighting for pay equity through three different voices – a union staff person representing 180,000 public sector workers (Millar), a labour lawyer and chair of a group successfully lobbying for pay equity in Ontario (Cornish), and an expert witness frequently called on by unions to defend pay equity, based on her knowledge of women and work and her role as professor of sociology and women's studies (Pat Armstrong). The chapter focuses on how the law shapes contradictions and tensions in women's struggles for equality and points to new and expanding axes of inequality revealed in legal struggles. In a contribution that is consistent with several other chapters in the collection, Armstrong, Cornish, and Millar also highlight the limits of struggles for equality focused on the law.

Earlier authors argue that while the Canadian state has treated childcare as a minor matter, childcare is the key to understanding the political economy of the Canadian welfare state. In their exploration of the gendered rise of contingent work in Canada, Judy Fudge and Leah Vosko come to a complementary conclusion, although their focus is social reproduction more broadly and its relationship to labour laws legislation and policy. They illustrate that the contradictions between labour market policy and equality policy have contributed to the gendered rise of contingent work and that the absence of supports for care-giving exacerbates this troubling development. They argue further that understanding recent developments in social and labour market policy demands bridging the two solitudes in the new Canadian political economy literature – the political economy of labour market institutions and feminist political economy.

The evolution of labour legislation in late twentieth century highlights the paradoxical role of the standard employment relationship and, at the same time, the new political economy's failure to link production and social reproduction. Until the mid-1970s, the extension of standard employment to more and more (largely male) workers cushioned a sizeable portion of the population from engaging in contingent work. Yet, flowing from long-standing racialized and gendered exclusions from the standard employment relationship and from the creation of equality polices that are subsidiary, rather than integral, to labour laws legislation and policies (e.g., pay and employment equity), the normative pre-eminence of the standard employment relationship laid the groundwork for growing contingency. For Fudge and Vosko, halting the rise of contingent work is possible only through a transformative feminist political economy of the labour market.

As a means of exploring fundamental changes in capitalist markets, another central theme of the collection, part 3 address issues related to international boundaries and contexts. What is Canada and how do we "know" it? How are the forces of globalization, specifically international capital and new globalized communication networks, acting on the entity Canada and how are they changing it in a North America "without borders"? Christina Gabriel and Laura Macdonald's chapter, entitled "Beyond the Continentalist/Nationalist Divide: Politics in a North America 'Without Borders,'" initiates this discussion of creative resistance with an inquiry into the changing nature of the Canada-U.S., and, to a lesser extent, the U.S.-Mexican border under globalization and in the post-9/11 era. Their chapter documents the way that the new Canadian political economy has intervened in various trade debates and advocates a new approach to transborder organizing now that NAFTA is in place, an approach based upon a popular continental alliance. Gabriel and Macdonald deploy David Held's threefold distinction between "hyper-globalists," "skeptics," and "transformationalists" to explore the new racialized, classed, and gendered ways in which borders matter in the North American context. Examining the movement of labour between nations and the movement of so-called foreign labour within nations under NAFTA, for example, they find that professionals who cross the Canada-U.S. border experience globalization and continentalization as liberating, as loosening international borders and creating supranational labour markets – the only concern of their governments appears to centre on the potential loss of human capital. Yet working class people, Mexicans in particular, experience the U.S.-Mexican border as an increasingly impenetrable wall – in their range of vision, attempts at border control to safeguard territorial sovereignty and national security abound. For Gabriel and Macdonald, this set of complex and contradictory dynamics calls for an approach to resistance that recognizes barriers to global citizenship and recognizes at the same time the weaknesses of the traditional nationalist/continentalist divide as a way of interpreting Canadians' place in North America and thereby as a suitable means for organizing collective struggles. They highlight the uncertainty about the future direction of the North American region: the terrorist attacks brought increased security integration, yet the new walls in the North American security perimeter are far from clear.

Shifting from the geography of globalization to the global finance, William Coleman and Tony Porter highlight the depth of the contradictory tendencies in Canadian capitalism under globalization, troubling dominant ideas about developments in Canada's financial sector. Their chapter asks, does Canada have an independent role in global finance and does it matter? Despite the common assumption that global markets have become so large that they are undermining the autonomy of nation states, Coleman and Porter highlight a dual tendency in the political economy of this sector. Canada is actively seeking to integrate Canadian financial conglomerates into the global economy, yet it is also working to preserve a distinctive Canadian financial centre that respects regional differences, and in this way it is strengthening its central banks.

The invisible border is also a central topic in Eric Helleiner's chapter on the North American Monetary Union (NAMU). However, change through continuity is the overriding theme of this contribution. Helleiner reveals the striking continuities in debates over a common currency, drawing a parallel between the first piece of legislation passed on this issue after Confederation – legislation that created a common currency among the provinces – and growing economic integration between the federal states of Canada, the United States, and Mexico today. Yet, in elaborating the insight that "monetary structures serve not just economic purposes, but also political, ideological and cultural ones," he also illustrates that support for the NAMU is growing due to the peculiar combination of the forces of the sovereignty movement in Quebec, financial globalization, and the dominance of neoliberal monetary policy.

According to Vincent Mosco, Canadian media conglomerates fare considerably worse under globalization than Canada's central banks. His contribution, "The Transformation of Communications in Canada," is a disturbing tale, a stark illustration of the challenges posed by new communications technologies. Mosco examines the relationship between commodification and digitization in the era of globalization, focusing on the communications business (i.e., newspapers, television, and multimedia) and reveals that digitization takes place in the context of an accelerating process of commodification, or through the transformation of use to exchange value. In the Canadian context the process has resulted in mass mergers in the communications sector, the squeezing out of independent communications outfits, and accelerating Americanization. Paradoxically, while Coleman and Porter find that Canada is seemingly preserving the uniqueness of its financial sector, despite the integration of national financial conglomerates, there are opposing tendencies towards greater integration in the communications industry – developments that threaten the vitality of this sector of the economy.

Moving to transformations on the ground, the new urban experience is the focus of part 4, where each chapter reveals the growing social and economic polarization characterizing urban centres in Canada. Caroline Andrew's chapter focuses on the progressive potential of municipal politics in several of Canada's large urban centres, with emphasis on two sets of issues: the ways in which municipal politics, in their interface with the organization of daily life, can create spaces for social justice and the relationship between municipal politics and knowledge and expertise (i.e., the question is, who has the status of the "knower"?). In "Municipal Restructuring, Urban Services and the Potential for the Creation of Transformative Political Spaces," Andrew uses two previous periods of urban reform in which the potential for progressive municipal politics was not realized – the late nineteenth century and the mid-1960s – to situate her examination of the contemporary situation. In both periods, she argues, municipal politics failed to play a transformative role, due to the perceived lack of importance of urban issues, the dominance of middle-class reform movements, the role of "expert" professional discourses, and the attractiveness of an individualized solution to suburban development.

In the present context, however, a range of contradictory tendencies are at play. On the one hand, the current wave of restructuring of urban governments by provincial governments is dominated by the neoliberal political climate of the 1990s and its preoccupation with privatization and decentralization. The debates around amalgamation articulated by the Ontario government, for example, relate to cutting costs, reducing the number of politicians, and producing municipal governments better able to compete for business in the global economy. On the other hand, some examples of progressive politics at the municipal level are in evidence. As Andrew demonstrates, safety audits in Toronto and Montreal, as well as Ottawa's Working Group on Women's Access to Municipal Services, which focuses on issues ranging from public transit to childcare, reflect a municipal politics capable of transforming knowledge production, destabilizing "expert discourses," and thereby creating new spaces for social justice. There are parallels between Helleiner's chapter and Andrew's chapter. Both look at continuities in two distinct periods and come up with similar assessments of the nature of transformation.

Like Andrew, Roger Keil and Stefan Kipfer conclude their chapter, "The Urban Experience," on a positive note, citing examples of local civil society groups forging local internationalism through their understanding of the urban as the "space between the macro-dimensions of the social order and the micro-worlds of everyday life." However, despite its optimistic conclusion, this contribution documents accelerating social and economic polarization in Canadian cities in the face of globalization and calls on the new Canadian political economy to adopt a hybrid approach – fusing critical theory and with political economy – to understanding transformations taking place in urban centres like Toronto, Vancouver, and Montreal. Keil and Kipfer argue forcefully that globalization should be analyzed not as a deterritorialized force but rather as a process or strategy refracted through urbanization. They characterize recent developments in urban settings as reflecting transnational urbanization and reveal that in the Canada this process is contributing to the emergence of the competitive city, whereby city governments mediate conflict and enforce restructuring through entrepreneurial planning, so-called diversity management and the implementation of a law-and-order policing agenda.

According to Keil and Kipfer, the rescaling of the "competitive city-region" is contributing to new social disparities in Canada. For example, they assert that one result of the class and gender bias of Canada's immigration policy is that immigrants are increasingly divided into wealthy, well-educated migrants and poorer refugees or migrants whose education levels are not recognized by Canadian institutions. In their chapter, "Immigration, Ethnicity, and Race: The Transformation of Transnationalism, Localism, and Identities," Vic Satzewich and Lloyd Wong take this observation further. The central pillar of their argument is that in the Canadian context growing transnationalism is amounting to a transformation in the political economy of immigration, making it critical for scholars to explore internal differentiation between and among immigrant communities. Satzewich and Wong suggest that these transformations present political economists with a set of challenges as well as opportunities. They identify a pressing need to pay more attention to the transnational social practices of immigrants and also to address the question, does transnationalism and transmigration affect the traditionally bounded and established nation-centred notions of citizenship and belonging?

Paraphrasing Carroll and Coburn (part 1), Satzewich and Wong suggest that

the architectonic questions about exploitation, racism, and intergroup relations that political economists once posed about immigration and race and ethnic relations continue to remain relevant ... [Yet] issues of ethnic and racial inequality, exploitation, and discrimination have become more complex as the class, ethnic, and racial composition of immigration flows to Canada has broadened ... Immigration and race and ethnic relations now occur in a context where migrants to Canada consist of men and women, workers, professionals and capitalists, first- and later-generation immigrants, producers and consumers, and national and transnational citizens.

In the face of these developments, they suggest, a challenge for political economists is to understand patterns of race and ethnic relations when members of the same ethnic or racial community occupy quite different positions within the social relations of production. They also indicate that class and gender may continue to represent the key axes fracturing transnational communities but "that proof needs to come via further research that looks beyond the boundaries of Canada." Hence, their chapter aims to trouble assumptions about the relationship between race, class, and gender that have been fundamental to debates framing the new Canadian political economy since the mid-1980s.

Several contributions to part 4 conclude by emphasizing the importance of resistance in the face of the emergence of the competitive
city-region in Canada. Part 5, "Creative Sites of Resistance," builds on
these sentiments, taking seriously the challenge to theorize the local,
as well as the national and the continental, in the face of globalization. This section concludes the collection by returning to the idea of
political economy as "uncommon sense." Each chapter in the section
applies a political economy method to challenge dominant norms,
values, and ideas and to draw lessons from a range of cultural practices reflecting agency and resistance. The chapters in this section
probe the prospects for positive transformation from four angles: in
the ecology (Adkin) and trade union movements (Stanford and
Gindin); among youth (Hollands); and in popular culture (Kurasawa). Laurie Adkin's challenging analysis of ecology is located in an
activist mode, developing a comparative political economy of the
Canadian and European contexts. In "Ecology, Political Economy,
and Social Transformation," she argues that political economy has an
important role to play in radicalizing ecology, specifically, by theorizing about collective action for a democratizing political ecology. Yet
at the same time Adkin warns that left political economy is also in
need of a futuristic vision, echoing the sentiments of Stanford and
Gindin (the next chapter). In order to be sustainable, she argues, this
vision must draw on the insights of radical ecology – for example, on
its understanding of the importance of reducing working time – especially if the goal is to advance a genuinely alternative agenda for social
transformation. According to Adkin, the project of creating an "ecological political economy" involves gradually expanding counterhegemonic struggles to develop responses to a range of deprivations and
dis-eases, from those linked to the changing conditions of employment and the growth of precariousness (Fudge and Vosko) to those
tied to increasing insecurity in subsistence (Picchio 1998) and to the
consumption and lifestyle patterns that these conditions reproduce
and reinforce.

Like Adkin, Jim Stanford and Sam Gindin also attempt to activate
debate and discussion around alternatives. In their chapter on Canadian labour and the political economy of transformation, they begin
by identifying the "(healthy) turmoil" characterizing left politics in
Canada today, evidenced by the three political projects emerging on
the left – the expansion of "civil society" groups, reflected in growing
anticapitalist movements, efforts to revive social democracy taking
place inside the New Democratic Party, and attempts to rebuild a
socialist left. They then inquire into the challenges that these parallel
movements pose for organized labour by discussing the current state

of the trade union movement and its transformative capacities in a political environment dominated by neoliberalism. Gindin and Stanford advance a highly provocative thesis – they argue that there is no homogeneity within organized labour and therefore that it is inaccurate to pose the task facing the Canadian labour movement in terms of its collective ability to form a progressive alliance. Furthermore, the process of labour's politicization requires deeper transformation-generating polarizations within the trade union movement. This thesis aims to unsettle commonplace assumptions about the necessary correlation between unity and active solidarity. If it proves to be correct, developments on the Canadian left may signal that something exciting is, in their words, "finally beginning."

Robert Hollands' chapter, "Towards a Political Economy of Canadian Youth," also calls on the new Canadian political economy to pay greater attention to culture. In this case youth culture is the target, and declining labour market prospects for young people, as well as the subtle shift in the popular discourse, which Hollands characterizes as a change from constructing youth as "having problems" to "being problems," heighten the challenge to political economy. Echoing the findings of other contributions pointing to growing contingency in the labour market and its gendered and racialized character (Fudge and Vosko) and, as Hollands emphasizes, age-based forms and expressions, Hollands argues that more accurate and contextualised information on Canadian youth is increasingly necessary to improve their prospects. The underdevelopment of youth studies in this country is evident, and it can be traced back to a wider failure to confront various conceptual issues and to a lack of adequate theorisation about youth transitions and cultures and the relationship between them. In the face of processes of welfare state restructuring that marginalize youth (McKeen and Porter), it is time for analysts to take issues confronting youth more seriously.

Through a lens that is different from the one used by other contributors to this section, Fuyuki Kurasawa's contribution also aims to trouble dominant understandings and modes of knowledge, yet his project is to enlarge and deepen existing strains of the new Canadian political economy and, more specifically, to alter the asymmetrical relationship between libratory forms of artistic expression previously marginalized in the field. "Finding Godot: Bringing Popular Culture into Canadian Political Economy" seeks to identify the sources of Canadian political economy's downgrading of popular culture and to explore possibilities for uniting these two solitudes. Kurasawa first embarks on a genealogy of Canadian political economy. Here, he examines how Innis, McLuhan, and Grant portrayed popular culture in relation to political economy – as a subordinate object of analysis, a derivative reality and/or as a transmitter of Americanization – and finds that the thematic triptych of dependency, authenticity, and commodification in the Canadian political economy tradition is the source of these unflattering portrayals of popular culture. Yet, Kurasawa rejects their depictions, using the second part of his chapter to consider popular culture as a source of change and resistance, a location of renewal and transformation for the new Canadian political economy.

Only a renewed political economy can help address some of these issues and contribute to a wider debate about political transformation in Canada society. It is our hope that students will find this collection a helpful introduction to the debate, inspiring them to challenge political economy and to change Canada in progressive directions.

REFERENCES

Andrew, Caroline. 1996. "Ethnicities, Citizenship and Feminisms: Theorizing the Political Practices of Intersectionality." In Jean Laponce and William Safran, eds., *Ethnicity and Citizenship: The Canadian Case*, 64–81. London: Frank Cass.

Bakker, Isabella. 1996. *Rethinking Restructuring: Gender and Change in Canada*. Toronto: University of Toronto Press.

Beck, Ulrich. 2000. *The Brave New World of Work*. London: Polity Press.

Clement, Wallace, ed. 1997. *Understanding Canada: Building on the New Political Economy*. Montreal and Kingston: McGill-Queen's University Press.

Clement, Wallace, and Glen Williams, eds. 1989. *The New Canadian Political Economy*. Montreal and Kingston: McGill-Queen's University Press.

Cohen, Marjorie. 1997. "New International Trade Agreements: Their Reactionary Role in Creating Markets and Retarding Social Welfare," In Isabella Bakker, ed., *Rethinking Restructuring: Gender and Change in Canada*, 187–202. Toronto: University of Toronto Press.

Creese, Gillian, and Daiva Stasiulus, eds. 1996. *Studies in Political Economy: Special Issue on Intersections*. 51: Introduction.

Fudge, Judy, and Brenda Cossman. 2002. Introduction to *Privatization, Law, and the Challenge of Feminism*. Toronto: University of Toronto Press.

Harvey, David. 1996. *Justice, Nature, and the Geography of Difference*. Cambridge: Blackwell.

Jhappan, Rhada. 1996. "Post-Modern Race and Gender Essentialism, or a Post-Mortem of Scholarship." *Studies in Political Economy* 51: 15–64.

Lumsden, Ian, ed. 1970. *Close the Forty-ninth parallel etc.: The Americanization of Canada*. Toronto: University of Toronto Press.

Mills, C. Wright. 1959. *The Sociological Imagination*. Oxford University Press: New York.

Ollman, B. 1993. *Dialectical Investigations*. New York: Routledge.

Panitch, Leo, ed. 1977. *The Canadian State: Political Economy and Political Power*. Toronto: University of Toronto Press.

Picchio, Antonella. 1998. "Wages as a Reflection of Socially Embedded Production and Reproduction Processes." In Linda Clarke, Perder de Gijsel, and Jorn Janssen, eds., *The Dynamics of Wage Relations in the New Europe*, 195–214. London: Kluwer.

– 1992. *Social Reproduction: The Political Economy of the Labour Market*. Cambridge: Cambridge University Press.

Porter, John. 1987. *The Measure of Canadian Society: Education, Equality and Opportunity*. Ottawa: Carleton University Press.

Stasiulus, Daiva. 1997. "The Political Economy of Race, Ethnicity and Migration." In Wallace Clement, ed., *Understanding Canada: Building on the New Canadian Political Economy*, 141–71. Montreal and Kingston: McGill-Queen's University Press.

Teeple, Gary, ed. 1972. *Capitalism and the National Question in Canada*. University of Toronto Press.

Vosko, Leah. 2002. "The Pasts (and Futures) of Feminist Political Economy in Canada: Reviving the Debate." *Studies in Political Economy* 68 (summer): 55–84.

PART ONE

Political Transformations

1 Politics in the Time and Space of Globalization

MEL WATKINS

The times move on. So must our means of understanding them.

We live in fresh times with stale ideologies, left, right, and centre. So too the established scholarly paradigm of Canadian political economy – created mostly in the 1970s but with roots in the writings of the first half of the twentieth century – although it has served us well in the study of Canada, it no longer suffices. Still, if we are to avoid mere fashion changes in scholarship, it must be built on rather than discarded.

The present proclaims itself, too loudly, to be the era of globalization. We need to deconstruct this new discourse of globalization and reconstruct the paradigm of Canadian political economy.

Can we then see the basis for a new politics for our new times – one transcending the mainstream, dissenting from it, willing to grapple with the profoundly complex matter of the transformation of politics amidst the robust rule of capital and, possibly, epochal shifts in technology with pervasive consequences – a politics speaking to the great gaping hole on the left of the spectrum?

What frames our discussion is the powerful thesis put forward more than half a century ago by the social historian Karl Polanyi (1944), who was writing on that great phase of "globalization" that extended from the late eighteenth to the mid–twentieth century, mostly under British auspices. Polanyi saw development under the aegis of capitalism as, on the one hand, the movement, led by capital, of technological innovation and expanding markets – in short, of economic growth – and, on the other hand, as the countermovement that is called forth and emerges out of society to protect people and their working and social and natural environments and that may include unions and socialist politics and the conservation movement. Today we have globalization led by corporate capital as movement, and as countermovement we have the array of social movements, of environmental groups, of labour organizations, of social democratic and green political parties, of anarchists – the forces against globalization simply in the service of the corporation and for genuine, democratic people's globalization, the profusion of the vehicles of protest of civil society that transcend national boundaries.

What, more precisely, is this globalization? Consider the following utterance by David O'Brien, CEO of Canadian Pacific and chairman of the powerful business lobby the Business Council on National Issues (or BCNI – of which more in a moment), renamed the Canadian Council of Chief Executives in 2001: "The global economy is at our doors. It is not a question of our deciding what we want to do; it is deciding for us."

O'Brien makes a double assertion – and a double error: first, that the global economy, aka globalization, is out there and that we must let it in – as if it is appearing for the first time and we must alter our parochial ways; second, that there is no alternative, it's all inevitable and it's apparently the end of politics – as if there was no political space and things just had to happen the way they did and there could not be, perhaps never had been, protest and dissent that influenced what happened. Of course, Mr O'Brien almost certainly believes that there is nothing here that we should fear, for it's all for our own good. He is not alone in so alleging; fulsome statements to that effect fall even more easily from the mouths of politicians than of businessmen. Pierre Pettigrew, Canadian minister of international trade, had this to say in an address to the Inter-American Development Bank in August 2000: "Globalization, quite simply, is part of the natural evolutionary process. It goes hand in hand with the progress of humanity, something which history tells us no one can stand in the way of." (Statements like this compel us to remember the dictum of Oswald Spengler, the historian of civilizations, that "Optimism is cowardice.") Yet to know anything of the past and of the political economy that has interpreted it is to know that all of this is nonsense – albeit nonsense that has to be taken seriously because of the power behind the source, the muscle behind the mouth.

Whatever globalization is, it is not new and not new to Canada, nor is resistance to it. The issue, rather, is what's new about globalization and *how* novel is it?

It was a Canadian, the media guru Marshall McLuhan who, borrowing from Wyndham Lewis, popularized the phrase "the global village" (Theall 2001). He, in turn, was building on the writings of another great Canadian scholar, the political economist Harold Innis, on communications and civilizations throughout history. (What could be more global than that?) Building on both, Ronald Deibert of the University of Toronto has recast the study of the transformation of world order in the last millennium in terms of "medium theory." (Deibert 1997). Robert Cox of York University was a seminal writer on global political economy, and Leo Panitch, of the same university, as editor of the prestigious *Socialist Register*, has published many of the important articles on globalization. Today, one of the best young writers anywhere on the roots of the reason for resistance to globalization is the Canadian Naomi Klein, author of *No Logo*. (2000). Among her insights: companies don't just brand their products, they brand us with their logos, but when companies do bad things we – the young in particular – feel betrayed and react against corporations and consumerism; it is a brilliant argument, one part pure McLuhan, one part pure Polanyi. She has called globalization "a massive rebranding campaign for imperialism." Such has been Klein's success in shaking up the political agenda that the *Economist*, the bible of big business, ran a cover story *reacting* to her thesis under the heading "Pro Logo: Why brands are good for you" (*Economist*, 8–14 September 2001). Linda McQuaig, a popular intellectual critical of the Canadian establishment and economic orthodoxy, herself goes back to Polanyi in her most recent insightful book (2001) on globalization.

The school of classic Canadian political economy, which originated in the interwar years in the first half of the twentieth century, saw what is now Canada as having been created out of Europe as a colony of trade and of settlement by massive inflows of people and of capital; in short, it saw it as the creature of what then passed for the forces of globalization. Should anyone underestimate the reality of these forces, ask the indigenous peoples of the Americas and of Africa; we've seen nothing like it since. The great writer for Canada was Harold Innis, and his encyclopedic volume *The Cod Fisheries* was properly subtitled *The History of an International Economy* (Innis 1940, 1954). And while Innis in his powerful generalizations seemed sometimes neglectful of human agency, those who worked in his shadow wrote of the politics and the protest of, for example, the prairie wheat farmers who, selling in world markets over which they had no control, helped to create the co-ops and the regulated freight rates and the Wheat Board and in due course the Co-operative Commonwealth Federation (CCF) as the precursor of the New Democratic Party (NDP); in short, they did not give up in the face of the "inevitable."

Innis believed passionately that Canada was worth studying, so much so that he insisted that imported theory was not enough and that indigenous theory was required (Innis 1956, 3); to prove his point, he then created classic Canadian political economy and was the first to articulate medium theory. But central to his writings throughout was the idea that the appropriate unit for study was neither the nation nor the world but empire; having first asserted that insight as essential to the study of Canada, he read it back into history in his later writing on media, titling his first book thereon *Empire and Communications* (Innis 1950). So it was that when the later Innis wrote on Canada in the late 1940s and early 1950s he did so, with remarkable prescience, to warn of the dangers of an American imperialism that refused to name itself, while nevertheless having little confidence himself in the willingness of Canadians to resist (Innis 1956, 407, 411). In fact, American capital and Canadian resources combined to create a great boom in the Canadian economy in the post–World War II years, though with some signs of resistance to the extent of American ownership evidenced by both the Conservative John Diefenbaker and the Liberal Walter Gordon, albeit to slight effect.

The new Canadian political economy (NCPE) emerging out of the turmoils and triumphs of the 1960s, which mingled Innis and Marx, sharpened the analysis and heightened the political hopes. It rewrote Canada – in the language of those long ago times – as an economic dependency of the metropolitan, imperialist United States, so kept by a comprador corporate elite that exercised its power in an "unequal alliance" with American capital (Clement 1977). Implicitly, sometimes explicitly, the new generation of political economists called for a popular nationalism – at its best, an alliance of English Canadian and Quebec nationalisms – that would create an independent socialist Canada. In a powerful reaction to America's crimes in Vietnam and the apparent limits of empire and in a creative achievement both politically and intellectually, the antiwar sentiment of the centre became a movement for Canadian left nationalism at the margin. In accompaniment with the NCPE and partly under its umbrella, came scholarship representing an array of popular forces – labour, aboriginal peoples, women, environmentalists, and gays and lesbians – all of which was too good to be true as, with the economy in crisis and the pie to be shared no longer growing, the forces of reaction returned with a vengeance in the 1980s and 1990s.

In spite of widespread, even majoritarian, opposition, the elites took Canada into a free trade deal with the United States in the late 1980s. The nationality of capital was deemed irrelevant – by 2001 no one cared when the Montreal Canadiens were bought by an American! –

and economic nationalism as a political force withered away in English Canada. At the national level as represented by constitutional debates, popular forces proved too strong to permit the elites to get their way (the Meech Lake Accord and the Charlottetown Accord of the late 1980s and early 1990s both failed in the face of public opposition) but too weak to compel a democratic alternative.

As the goods times, both economically and politically, played out, Carleton University's Glen Williams, in a most perceptive and pre-scient article written in the midst of the free trade debate of the late 1980s, rethought the NCPE – which was now rather long in the tooth – by going back one more time to Innis. Canada, said Williams, was neither a dependency nor an independent nation in the customary senses of those terms. Rather, "it was a lesser political, economic and cultural *region* incorporated within a succession of powerful empires." (1988, 109). It could be studied, as Innis had said, only as part of an empire – meaning now, of course, the United States.

In calling Canada a *region* (the italics are his), however, Williams may go too far. There remains a border between Canada and the United States, and while business may claim it is merely an impediment, statistical analysis shows that on a kilometre-by-kilometre basis, trade within Canada is significantly larger for the same distance than cross-border trade (Helliwell and McCallum 1995; see Gabriel and Mac-Donald in this volume on how globalization can also recreate borders, making them matter in new ways). And the "political" within political economy should warn us not to be too dismissive of the notion of national sovereignty; there is always some political space, some will to use it (Evans, McBride, and Shields 2000; Maxwell 2001); if nothing else, popular forces must sometimes be put down.

Williams should be read with the memory that Canada was created as an outpost of empire(s) and has been a nation within an empire for a century and a half. Politics in its bureaucratic, even legislative, dimension is centrally about the "management" of that imperial con-nection. The columnist Richard Gwyn has reminded us that "former U.S. secretary of state Henry Kissinger remarked in his memoirs that Canadian leaders have always had to operate within a 'very narrow margin' in their dealings with the U.S. – not looking too soft to their own voters and yet not annoying Washington too much. They had per-formed this tightrope act, Kissinger judged, 'with remarkable skill.'" (*Toronto Star*, 7 February 2001). To be praised by Kissinger, however, a person who is increasingly seen as having been a war criminal in Cam-bodia and Chile, is to be damned by decent folk.

The contemporary implication of all this remains clear. There is talk of globalization, which we must try to define more precisely, but in Canada one is really talking about how our relationship with the world is mediated through the United States. It is globalization with one most important degree of separation. Intuitively every Canadian knows this, but it is not easy for scholarship fully to incorporate it. Indeed, most Canadian scholars, particularly mainstream historians of Canada – the sort that American essayist and editor Lewis Lapham calls "dependable historians" – see no necessity to incorporate it, since the American connection is perceived as inherently a good thing, requiring Canadians only to do what they ought to be doing anyway.

There may be yet more to be learned from Innis – and McLuhan and Deibert – with respect to the breadth and depth of circumstances within which we locate any discussion of our present condition. The cumulative impact of the electronic media – the telegraph, telephone, radio, TV, and the Internet – may match that of that great technological change from which flowed modernity itself, the printing press. So understood, today's globalization, albeit going back to the telegraph, is indeed revolutionary.

As well, a perhaps more frequently encountered claim, in both mainstream and dissenting scholarship, is that we are living today in an information (or services or postindustrial) revolution that is comparable to the Industrial Revolution that first gripped Britain in the late eighteenth century and spread globally from there. (None of which necessarily makes understanding easier. When Henry Kissinger asked Chou En-lai for his views on the French Revolution, Chou is said to have replied, "Too soon to tell.")

Whatever else it may be, globalization is the latest, present stage of capitalism. That means a stew of

- Economic or corporate globalization – free trade, unlimited mobility for capital, the rights of corporations to produce everywhere and of speculators to speculate everywhere with no matching responsibilities, and the unceasing march of commodification and of privatization of public space. Jaggi Singh of Montreal's Anti-Capitalist Convergence says of corporate globalization: "It's a vision that sees everything as having a dollar value – people, the environment, the air" (*Montreal Gazette* 16 October 2000).
- Technological globalization – the wired world, the shift from the economies of scale, the mass markets, of the Fordist industrial era to the economies of scope, the niche markets, of the information economy.
- Ideological globalization – neoliberalism, the messianic message of the market leavened by fundamentalist messianic Christianity; see the utterances of George W. Bush.

- Cultural globalization – the Americanization of everything: fast food for the stomach and the mind, cultural homogenization and ethnic fragmentation (Hetata 1998), and postmodernism as the cultural analogue of neoliberalism.
- Military globalization – the American monopoly of high-tech weapons, of the weaponization of space, of the world market for arms, of the proliferation of nuclear weapons, and of selective "humanitarian" interventions (Kosovo but not Rwanda) of warlike state terrorism massively to search out and destroy stateless but very real terrorism.
- Political globalization – the International Monetary Fund (IMF), the World Trade Organization (WTO), the World Bank, and the North Atlantic Treaty Organization (NATO), on the one hand, and the lessening importance of the nation-state on the other. The implications for scholarship are profound: "The central feature of the idea of globalization is that many contemporary problems cannot be adequately studied at the level of nation-states, that is, in terms of international relations, but need to be theorized in terms of global (transnational) processes, beyond the level of the nation-state" (Sklair 1998). Profound also are the implications for democracy: the need to create it at the global level and re-create it at the local level (Rebick 2000; Cunningham 1994).
- Social globalization – the universality of capitalist inequality of wealth and income, with the homeless everywhere, on the streets of the rich countries and globally as displaced peoples, as refugees, as boat people seeking somewhere to land.
- The globalization of disease – AIDS, Mad Cow, foot-and-mouth disease, and so on, and the deterioration of public health from the IMF's so-called structural adjustment, imposed on poor countries and compelling cutbacks in government spending even on essential services.
- Following Polanyi's analysis, the globalization of dissent itself (the world-wide movement against globalization, as the new witticism puts it) from Chiapas to Seattle to Quebec City to Genoa.

The sum of all this, which is humungous, is Corporate Rule – the phrase popular with critics of the corporate agenda (Korten 1995; Clarke 1997; Dobbin 1998) – under the aegis of America, no longer as superpower but as hyperpower. Hardt and Negri (2000) encapsulate it all as Empire transcending the old imperialisms. Globalization can be understood as the political project of this ruling elite. "[T]he global free market is not an iron law of historical development but a political project" (Gray 1998, 210). Call it the project of Davos-man, of that strata of homo sapiens who assemble each year at Davos in Switzerland for the World Economic Forum – it moved to New York in 2002 to demonstrate imperial solidarity – and, between feasts, pretend to care about those who do not live in gated communities on top of a mountain of goodies; they are, of course, overwhelmingly male, literally men in suits. In 2000, however, in reaction thereto, there emerged Porto Allegre–person, men and women meeting in Brazil at a World Social Forum under the banner "Another World Is Possible." Writing in the *Nation* (22 March 2001), Naomi Klein tells us what that world could be like: "What seemed to be emerging organically out of the World Social Forum ... was not a movement for a single global government but a vision for an increasingly connected international network of very local initiatives, each built on direct democracy."

The implications for Canada as periphery-within-the-core of this world of Corporate Rule are necessarily pervasive; this paper touches only on those that seem most immediately relevant to this volume's theme of transforming politics, and not even on all of those.

The creation in the mid-1970s of the BCNI – consisting of the CEOs of the 150 largest private-sector corporations in Canada regardless of the nationality of ownership, which means that foreign-owned, meaning American-owned, firms are abundantly represented – is indicative of the cohesion of the Canadian business class and the solidifying and enhancing of its power. That greater power is *the* surest sign of globalization; conversely, the issue, for Canada and elsewhere, is not globalization per se but corporate power and the corporate agenda. In turn, its greater cohesion enabled the Canadian business class wholeheartedly to embrace globalization, meaning free trade and the end of economic nationalism, and to push for its fuller realization.

The BCNI quickly became a de facto parallel government with a committee structure mimicking that of the departments of the federal government (Langille 1987). Its greatest achievement is the selling of free trade, first the Canada-U.S. Free Trade Agreement of 1989 and then the North American Free Trade Agreement of 1994, which brought in Mexico. It can also take credit for pushing anti-inflation policies that damaged many Canadians and for insisting on cutbacks in government spending that likewise hurt many people, so as to deal with deficits. This policy was so "successful" that surpluses resulted, and it then called for dissipating these surpluses through tax cuts that would disproportionately benefit the rich, including its own members. Recently, the BCNI did its best to get the Canadian government to sabotage the Kyoto accord on greenhouse gases; while Canada, to its credit, stopped short of following the United States in repudiating the agreement, it drastically undermined it. What business wants, business mostly gets.

As the titles of the free trade agreements tell us, this is *not* globalization as global but rather globalization as continentalism. (The tendency to conflate the two was nicely demonstrated in newspaper headlines on 4 December 2000. The *National Post* told its readers that "Police fear Quebec bikers going global," while according to the *Globe and Mail*, "Bikers strengthen ties with u.s. gang." Or, again, a story about the University of Toronto law school that was headlined "Law school goes global" included a subhead explaining that "The dean of the University of Toronto's Law School wants to give it Ivy League clout to attract the best professors and students, but critics say that just means the Americanization of Canada's top program.") The object of the free trade exercise was to guarantee access for existing Canadian resource exports, aka staples, into the critical American market and to make Canadian manufacturing competitive. There was a problem, it was argued, with respect to the "efficiency" of Canadian industry, but, it was alleged, it resulted from being able to hide behind tariff barriers rather than from foreign control and the branch plant economy; eliminate the tariff and Canadian industry would become efficient and would penetrate American markets.

At worst, the Canadian economy would have trouble adjusting – meaning the Canadian business class would not have the requisite economic smarts to match its political clout – and would end up further lagging behind the American economy. At best, Canadian manufacturing would be rebuilt on an export basis, with both cross-border trade and cross-border ownership increasing – meaning, in fact, the further entrenchment of the Canadian economy within the American economy.

The result, more than a decade on, is a bite of both (Jackson 1999). The Canadian economy has been sucked into the American economy to the point that it is sometimes hard to see it even on a clear and cloudless day. Trade has both grown in importance to the Canadian economy and become increasingly concentrated with the United States; the only certain upper limit to the latter is presumably 100 percent. (One sometimes imagines that the main purpose of the much-hyped Team Canada missions to distant points – as to China in early 2001 – is to mask this elementary fact). Canada has become *less* globalized so far as trade with the world-without-the-u.s. is concerned. Foreign, mostly American, ownership of the Canadian economy, which had been in relative decline from the 1970s, surged upwards under free trade. The brute power of the transnational corporation has made the distinction between foreign and domestic capital too subtle to be relevant. The "competitiveness" of the Canadian economy has been bought in some part by a depreciating dollar and stagnating wages.

The transformation of the Canadian economy from staples-biased – or commodity-based, to use the language of currency markets – to fully mature industrially should not be exaggerated. Exports of manufactured goods overwhelmingly to the United States are offset by imports of manufactured goods from the United States; Canada still pays its way externally with the foreign exchange earned from its huge surplus in resource exports relative to imports. Thus the weakness of the Canadian dollar is mostly because commodity prices have been in one of their historic declines. As well, Canadian direct investment abroad tends to be in resource industries, particularly oil exploration and mining – where, like companies from other countries, Canadian companies consistently violate human rights while governments look the other way; certainly in this respect the nationality of capital does seem irrelevant. In trade with the so-called emerging economies, Canada tends, revealingly, as in the case of Mexico, to export food and import manufactured goods – auto parts in the Mexican case.

Incredibly, when the BCNI met in Toronto in May 2000, this trumpeter for American companies in Canada reported that 40 percent of its own members feared that their jobs would disappear as Canadian operations were incorporated into American corporate structures and the Canadian head office disappeared. As long ago as 1972, the Canadian-born economist Stephen Hymer (who died in 1974 at the age of forty) wrote, "Although the multinational corporation spreads production over the world, it concentrates coordination and planning in key cities, and preserves power and income for the privileged" (1979, 142). Going on thirty years later, the phenomenon is even more evident: "The decentralization and global dispersal of productive processes and sites, which is characteristic of the postmodernization or informatization of the economy, provokes a corresponding centralization of the control over production. The centrifugal movement of production is matched by the centripetal trend of command" (Hardt and Negri 2000, 297). Likewise, Canadian companies like Northern Telecom that succeeded in penetrating the American market found that the larger market tended to pull head office functions toward the United States. (Admittedly, some may have seen this tendency as the least of the problems associated with Northern Telecom in the early years of this century as its share prices plunged and there were massive layoffs of workers.) A 2001 study by the Conference Board of Canada found that almost half the Canadian executives interviewed in a survey said their headquarters are more than 50 percent likely to be transferred out of the country during their tenure (Conference Board of Canada 2001). When head offices close, not just the top managers lose out; in the longer run, fewer skyscrapers will be built, there will be fewer windows to clean, and so on. And u.s.-based managers of Canadian operations may be less likely to contract with Canadian service providers of everything from insurance to advertising.

The Canadian capitalist class, even as a managerial class, is apparently waning, being "hollowed-out" as activities shift to the United States. Meanwhile, sectors in which Canadian capital has long been dominant are in trouble. In retailing, the Canadian icon, Eaton's, has been taken over by Sears Canada, which is owned by Sears Roebuck of Chicago; Shoppers Drug Mart is controlled by the u.s. buyout firm Kohlberg Kravis Roberts & Co.; and Future Shop has been bought out by u.s. giant Best Buy. And Wal-Mart invades from the u.s., as does The Gap, with its discount offspring, Old Navy. No Canadian bank makes the list of the top fifty banks in the world and would not do so even if the mergers under consideration in the 1990s, which the federal government refused to approve, were permitted. This does not augur well, at least for Toronto's future as a global city, as a node of command over the shifting decentralized production of the post-Fordist world.

In the face of all this, the response of Canadian business is to call for tax cuts for the rich and the corporate – today's universal panacea – and, in general, to make Canada more competitive, more business-friendly, by mimicking American policy. In trade agreements, it's called harmonization, which sounds sweeter than it is for most Canadians who find the tax cuts illusory (taxes fall for one level of government, rise for another, or are replaced by user fees) and try to survive the waves of deregulation and privatization.

Canadian capital, which is in charge within Canada to the extent that anyone is, holds a bleak political vision: Canada can survive by becoming more like the United States, though that might be thought to negate the object of the exercise. "Two hundred big names from government, business, universities and trade associations gathered [30 May 2000] at the University of Toronto's Rotman School [of Management] and just about all anyone could do was look at the United States and salivate at that country's success" (*Financial Post* 31 May 2000). After only a bit more than a decade of free trade – which then prime minister Brian Mulroney described in 1988 as a commercial agreement that could be abrogated on six months notice – the talk on Toronto's Bay Street, which runs downhill to the waterfront and is the slipperiest of slopes, is now of North American monetary union (see Helleiner in this volume). Ironically, the annexationist tendencies of Canadian business are constrained by an American state whose manifest destiny does not require – indeed, may not even want – territorial expansion. The existence of Canada as a distinct entity on the map hinges, if only by default, on popular forces.

In the largest sense, globalization as we know it is about guarantees of corporate rights not matched by human rights. It is corporate globalization, not people's globalization; no wonder there is a backlash (see Carroll and Coburn in this volume).

Capital insists on rights of mobility between countries, but there is no similar right of mobility for people. In the so-called borderless world, borders to keep the people out have never been higher than they are now; to see the images on television of the poor and the desperate dying in their effort to enter the rich countries is to understand what an obscenity, reeking of class bias, that phrase "borderless world" is. More people have been shot trying to cross the border from Mexico to the United States – "the wall of death" – than died attempting to cross the Berlin Wall (Juniper and Wainwright 2001). In relative terms, the number of people on the move today is far less than it was in the nineteenth and early twentieth centuries. Contrast the reception that Canada accords to today's boat people from China with that offered the Irish boat people fleeing the famines of the 1840s. Or consider, for example, that in March 2001 Canadian and American police discovered a migrant pipeline from Canada to the United States across the St Clair River taking illegal immigrants into the United States via Canada. In the media Canadian police officials and then immigration minister Elinor Caplan talked feelingly about the evil smugglers who were exploiting people who risked their lives and vast sums they didn't have in the hope of living the American dream. An essential skill for an immigration minister in a rich country, whose job it is mostly to keep people out, is evidently the ability to shed crocodile tears; Bill Clinton would be perfect for the job. Nowadays the running shoes made in China have the freedom to cross borders but not the people who make them – people who earn too little where they are to be able to afford to buy them. It is, furthermore, a stunning fact that neoclassical economists have elaborated the so-called factor-price equalization theorem, according to which trade alone can equalize wages globally without factor mobility, aka migration. Putting people in their place is actually counted as a virtue of free trade. Whatever the intent of economists, one of their most theoretically and mathematically impressive theorems merely mirrors the false utopia of globalization.

Thus the ugly face of globalization, which thrives on the great gap in living standards while claiming to be solving it. "This world ... is sumultaneously equalizing and unequal: *equalizing* in the ideas and habits it imposes and *unequal* in its opportunities" (Galeano 2000, 25). "There is a vacuum at the heart of globalization. It lacks a moral dimension, a sense that there is something wrong about a system that apportions risk to those able to bear it least and that tolerates grotesque disparities in wealth" (Elliott 1999).

Canada, as an immigrant society, becomes a country of many colours – the official multiculturalism that is the good face of globalization – but that does not negate the deep asymmetry of globalization's treatment of (mostly white) capital and (increasingly nonwhite) labour – nor the reality of racism that lurks about, particularly in labour markets (see Gabriel and MacDonald this volume), nor the centuries-long maltreatment of aboriginal peoples where redress proceeds slowly but not surely. The rhetoric of globalization is inclusive; its practice is exclusive.

In a manner made familiar by Polanyi, the increasing power of capital in this era of globalization is everywhere at the expense of labour; Thatcher smashed the coal miners, Reagan the air traffic controllers. Labour has not been defeated in Canada in the same way – Mike Harris in Ontario tried without success to smash the union of goverment employees (OPSEU) – probably because the new era of corporate rule coincided in Canada with the creation, for the first time in Canadian history, of a sovereign trade union movement independent of American unions, the so-called international unions (Gindin and Stanford this volume.) In a marvelous example of Polanyi's thesis, corporate continentalism (like the Autopact) in the context of a weak and weakening American labour movement encouraged Canadian unions (like the Autoworkers) to break the ties with the American parent and go it alone, thereby feeding the popular forces of Canadian nationalism. A rejuvenated Canadian Labour Congress, in coalition with the social movements, almost stopped the Free Trade Agreement from happening.

Canada has likewise been impressive in the quality of its social movements (Barlow and Clarke 2001; again, see Carroll and Coburn in this volume). The Council of Canadians has a larger membership than any political party and increasingly acts like one in terms of its ability to respond to a full range of issues. It is the people's noncorporate, anticorporate match to the Canadian Council of Chief Executives. Often more effective than the federal NDP (not, admittedly, a hard race to win), it is that most impressive of political creations, a nationalist grouping with global reach. As such, it played an important role in derailing the Multilateral Agreement on Investment (MAI). The Council of Canadians is global – an innovative global player – in a way that Canadian business overwhelmingly is not. To be a Canadian on the left today is necessarily to be a global citizen and to protest precisely those assemblies – like the WTO when it met in Seattle and the Organization of American States (OAS) when it met in Quebec city and the G-8 when it met in Genoa – where governments, like the Canadian government, pretend to speak not only for Canadians but for billions who are, as in the case of the G-8, not entitled to any representation whatever. Under such circumstances, where the achievement of liberal democracy at the national level has simply been negated, there can be no more basic and straightforward demand than for democracy at the global level.

As a "new" country originally overrun by Europeans, the better to exploit its resources, Canada, like the United States, badly lags Europe with respect to green politics. Catharine Parr Trail wrote in the 1830s that the typical Upper Canadian farmer treated the forests "as though they were his most obnoxious enemies." Gustave Beaumont, who accompanied Toqueville to America, observed that "There is ... in America a general feeling of hatred against trees." It has been said of the present Bush administration that it bears a grudge against nature. Still, Greenpeace, which pioneered taking on corporations directly rather than lobbying governments to do so, was born in Canada. (Dale 1996; in general, see Adkin in this volume).

The second half of the twentieth century was characterized by two long periods, the first of a generalized economic boom in the 1950s and 1960s to circa 1973, the second of a generalized economic crisis from 1973 that may or may not have ended with the American boom from the mid-1990s, in which Canada was fully engaged by the turn of the millennium. (As I write in early 2002 it appears that the much-touted recession may not actually have happened, that is, neither the American nor the Canadian economy experienced two consecutive decades of negative growth.) Globalization can be seen as a phrase and a practice that emerged in that second period; if it has laid the basis for a new boom, it promises to persist along with it.

The post–World War II boom has been seen by political economists as characterized by the Keynesian welfare state of positive government with a progressive tinge. When crisis followed boom, rather than seeing this as inherent in capitalism, the powerful blamed the best of the good times (like the welfare state) for the bad times and resolved to turn back the clock. So, in sharp contrast, the crisis years are symbolized by the Schumpeterian workfare state (Jessop 1993) of private entrepreneurship, of taking government off the backs of business, of no-rights-without-responsibilities for the rest of us (though how this can be applied to children escapes me) – of allowing the full play of Schumpeter's "creative destruction" of the market at home and abroad. In short, the politics of the right are triumphant; those of the left struggle to be heard.

The discourse of politics is ideology. The ideology of globalization is neoliberalism. Inherent in the capitalist ethos – and in the mainstream economics that legitimizes and justifies capitalism, in contrast with the critique of political economy – is the emphasis on the individual and on his or her (mostly his, in fact, as patriarchy persists) self-interest that, mediated by the market, yields the public good. "Capitalism is the extraordinary belief that the nastiest of men, for the nastiest of reasons, will somehow work for the benefit of us all" (John Maynard Keynes). In fact, it has long been a problem for real people that the corporation is given the legal rights of the individual and is allowed to use the language of personal liberty; the bigger and the more pervasive the corporation, the more this matters. Today, for example, the corporation is able to use the rhetoric of "intellectual property" and the "rights" to the benefits thereof to justify monopolistic patents that appropriate the knowledge of indigenous peoples and deny cheap drugs to the sick and the dying in poor countries. (With the Cold War over, famed spy writer John le Carré's most recent novel, *The Constant Gardener*, is about pharmaceutical companies willing to sacrifice Third World people and engage in murder to protect profits. Le Carré says his subject is "the dilemma of decent people struggling against the ever-swelling tide of heedless corporate greed, and our complicity in letting the corporations get away with it.") When the times become tougher, what is implicit becomes explicit: liberalism degenerates into neoliberalism, and the pursuit of self-interest into the glorification of greed. The American economist Paul Krugman, who writes a regular column for the *New York Times*, noted in 2000 that "In today's greed-is-good business world, companies announcing lay-offs, don't try to soften the blow; they exaggerate the damage to impress financial markets with their tough-mindedness." Economics retreats into abstraction on the one hand, vulgar polemics on the other; political economy is desparately needed but rarely heeded.

Likewise, the "individual" swells up, some – a few really – so bloated that, in the famous words of Margaret Thatcher, there is no society, no room for one. The political implications are profound: "If there's no society," as the columnist Rick Salutin has written (*Globe and Mail* 22 December 2000, A17), "then there's no need for social programs, social analysis, social reform or paying debts to it. There are only individuals who at best shop and at worst murder."

The discourse of neoliberalism, the obessive insistence on the totalism of the market, is so extreme that it is difficult fully to put into practice. Modern capitalism first took form in Britain and spread most easily to English-speaking countries. Perhaps not surprisingly, neoliberalism is a disease of the body politic that thrives in English – in Britain, the United States, New Zealand, and Canada (Alberta and

Ontario) – and now (once upon a time Britain too practised the imperialism of free trade) spreads globally under American aegis.

Wherever there is capitalism, as there surely is in Canada, there is an
indigenous capacity to generate neoliberalism and associated ills;
there is no need to pretend it is merely imported. Still, as befits
Canada's neocolonial status within the American empire, free trade
agreements entrenching corporate rights – including those of the big
American corporations operating in Canada – and "compelling" harmonization with neoliberal American policies in the name of "competitiveness" enabled the neoliberalism of the metropolis to sneak in
through the back door and to permeate the premises, even though no
neoliberal government has been elected at the national level in
Canada. Nor does it seem likely that one will be; in 2001 the ideologically neoliberal Canadian Alliance, as led by Stockwell Day, imploded,
while its main media supporter, the *National Post* under Conrad Black,
was taken over by the Liberal Asper family.

Provincially, the appeal of neoliberalism to Alberta seems unsur-
prising; as in Texas, cattle (and barbed wire and cowboys and the myth
of the frontier) followed by oil (the dark greed that spouts from the
ground and tempts and dirties all it touches) provide fertile ground
for the political right. The puzzle is stodgy, Tory, terribly Canadian,
master-of-the-country, middle-of-the-road Ontario, where no one
would have imagined a decade ago that a neoliberal government
could be elected not once but twice. Its election must have been a consequence, as everything consequential is, of a conjuncture of circumstances, but free trade and the quantum leap in the imperial connection might be thought to have loomed large. It radically undermined
the east-west logic of an Ontario-centred national economy, casting
Ontario adrift, while compelling that province – where the great bulk
of the manufacturing was and is – to accept American rules of competitiveness; think of it as a local variant of economic shock therapy,
the political consequences of which are rarely pretty.

The much-debated Hartz-Horowitz thesis in Canadian politics –
both are political scientists, Louis Hartz of Harvard University and Gad
Horowitz of the University of Toronto – postulated a Tory (Progressive
Conservative) touch in the Canadian polity absent in the purer American liberal polity that, further, made possible, at the other end of the
political spectrum, an unAmerican socialism. So understood, the
swamping of Toryism in Ontario by neoliberalism did not augur well
for the prospects for the social democratic left in Ontario. Still, were
the Conservatives to be defeated by the more centrist Liberals (a distinct possibility at least as I write, Harris having been driven from
office), there might then be some room too for a party to the left,
some straw at least at which to grasp.

Ontario risks joining the other half of Central Canada going its own way in its own fashion. There is a clear and accurate understanding by the Quebec sovereignty movement that North American free trade is permissive of Quebec's independence vis-à-vis Canada (Parti Québécois 1994). Only Quebec (and Alberta) unambiguously supported free trade in 1988; for Quebec this support was in fact followed by the incredible closeness of the referendum of 1995 and the near-death experience of the country. But, again, the present is in flux. Quebec nationalism has, at least for the moment, waned. No sensible person would write it off, but Chantal Hebert, the national affairs columnist for the *Toronto Star*, makes the point that the politically active children of the sovereignists are now, like the young of so many countries, less interested in "national dynamics" than they are in opposing corporate globalization. "[T]he PQ embraced freer trade and globalization with a passion. In so doing, it accelerated the fundamental realignment that is now putting sovereignty out of its reach for the foreseeable future" (*Toronto Star* 25 June 2001).

The quintessential politics of the new era of globalization is the so-called third way. Its leading practitioner is United Kingdom prime minister Tony Blair. Faced with Thatcherism, the social democratic Labour Party countered by embracing what Blair himself called the third way, which attempts to blend the free markets of neoliberalism with the social justice of social democracy. Roy Hattersley, a former deputy leader of the British Labour Party, who is now critical of Blairism, has caustically observed: "The neo-liberals do not simply argue for the market economy. They claim that social justice is a meaningless idea and that any attempt to impose it on a free society is immoral as well as economically damaging. These two ideas – one holding social justice to be the moral imperative of civilized government and the other regarding social justice as an excuse for theft by taxation of the rich – cannot be reconciled" (Hattersley 2000, 246). Left critics claim the third way is really left-wing neoliberalism – and they are right; after all, social democracy in the Keynesian era was really left-wing Keynesianism (Przeworski 1985). That is, social democracy is hard put to be other than the left of the ruling capitalist agenda. This is said neither to reject social democracy nor to apologize for it but rather to describe and explain it. This does mean, however, that the current third way involves a definite shift to the right by the left.

But the third way is more than the new language of social democrats. When there was a global gathering of third way politicians in 2000, then American president Bill Clinton was there. So too was Jean Chrétien, who was passed over on the first round of invitations and, we're told, got Clinton to get him an invite – which is enormously revealing. It seemed that the hard-line neoliberalism of the

Thatcher/Reagan variety had given way to a softer version, though the election of George W. Bush – being somewhere between a fluke and a fix – has returned America to the hard path. Neoliberalism has truly triumphed – it can still win in its own right, and when it doesn't, the centre and the left must nevertheless accomodate to it – and it has the hallmarks of being here to stay for somewhere between a while longer and indefinitely.

The left – in the parliamentary sense of that term – is everywhere threatened with marginalization. That has certainly happened with respect to the NDP in Canada. At the federal level the NDP can hardly don the mantle of the third way, because, as we've seen, the Liberals are already there proclaiming it. The Liberal Party of Canada, after all, is one of the wonders of the political world in its ability to occupy the middle group and ooze right or left as circumstances beckon. The third way, whatever the morality of it – and from a left perspective (including that of this writer) it frankly leaves much to be desired – may make electoral sense in a two-party system where the electorate has moved right. But where the NDP has traditionally been a minority taste – at the federal level and very probably in Ontario – the third way can't work.

The NDP was born as the CCF, and, particularly in the West, it was both a party and a movement. Over time, the movement side was played down in the interest of the party side. Movements advocate and agitate on the basis of principle; parties compromise to govern or in the hope of governing. With the election of the CCF in Saskatchewan in 1944 the reality of the party and the appeal of governance much increased. Another decisive step away from a movement was the creation of the NDP in 1960, with the muscle and hard-nosed practicality of labour leaders now up-front. Add the expulsion of the left-nationalist and socialist Waffle caucus and the forces of the New Left in the early 1970s – myself included – which may have contributed to the party's inability to withstand the onslaught of the New Right and to make a firm connection with the anti-corporate-globalization forces now so much in evidence. After a third consecutive trouncing in the polls in the federal election of 2000, the federal caucus opted to make globalization *the* issue. It took a first step in the direction of making the party more of a movement again, in the hope that this would restore its relevance. It has taken the advice not of Tony Blair but of former French prime minister Lionel Jospin. After the demonstrations in Genoa in 2001 against the G-8, in which one demonstrator was killed and numerous others beaten and jailed by the police, Jospin observed: "While denouncing the violence to which a minority resorts on the pretext of renouncing the ravages of globalization, France rejoices in the worldwide emergence of a citizens' movement, in as much as it expresses the wishes of the majority of mankind better to share the potential fruits of globalization." In following Jospin's example, the NDP might likewise heed the advice of Rick Salutin, from left of the NDP: "Social movements can voice their own concerns: what electoral parties can do is voice the largely unvoiced, yet deeply felt, common concerns of voters who are isolated from each other. These are essentially separate functions. When such parties become governments, their role is less to 'encompass' vital social groups than to engage and debate with them, in fruitful conflict as much as in cooperation" (*Globe and Mail* 8 June 2001).

As I write, there is fresh ferment on the left. The NDP is going through a formal renewal process. The New Politics Initiative, led by socialist NDP MP Svend Robinson, prominent activist-feminist-communicator Judy Rebick, and CAW economist Jim Stanford (a contributor to this book; this contributor also supports it), is trying to broaden the appeal of the NDP, especially to youth, by pulling it to the left.

Let us recall the new Canadian political economy with its astute understanding of Canadian privilege and dependency that accrues from living in the full shadow of America, recall Innis on empire, and recall Polanyi on movement/countermovement.

To live at the periphery of empire is to know, to feel in one's bones, that the central political task is indeed to live with the imperial connection, to bob and weave with the shifting punches thrown from the metropolis. How has free trade, the Canadian version of globalization, the watershed event of our times, affected that exercise, that ability to manoeuvre? On the one hand, the entrenchment of a rules-based trade regime can be argued to have lessened the ability of the United States to take unilateral action in trading matters, thereby reducing Canada's economic vulnerability and increasing the space for autonomous Canadian action, as in foreign policy. On the other hand, the quantum link in the integration of the Canadian economy into the larger American economy has meant a quantum leap as well in the sheer range of Canadian vulnerability to American actions. Perhaps of equal importance, these evident facts may have so permeated our political culture that we have lost the ability to imagine that we could significantly defy American wishes. There is clearly no room here for easy optimism.

Current American politics is providing an ample testing ground, as the Bush administration repudiates the Kyoto Accord, rejects a treaty on control of small arms and a treaty on germ warfare, walks out of the 2001 United Nations conference on racism, and gives notice of pulling out of the Anti-Ballistic Missile Treaty, so that it can proceed with the National Missile Defence on the way toward the weaponization of space. These actions add to the Clinton administration's opting out of the Ottawa Treaty banning land mines and the proposed International Criminal Court. Canada has stood separate from the United States on these matters – conspicuously so on land mines, where Ottawa played an initiating role. And on things to do with nuclear weapons and with NATO we go along with U.S. power – though, to be fair, so do the rest of what are euphemistically called America's allies.

Students of Canadian political economy in the era of globalization should keep their eye on these matters to make sure there is still a Canada sufficiently distinct to merit study. They could show how the common link in these matters – from the environment to peace to human rights – is the dominant and often destructive role played by corporations, wherever domiciled, in the name of globalization. This would aid and abet political activists in their struggles against corporate capitalists pursuing narrow self-interest with slight regard for the consequences and in their own attempts to further human rights broadly conceived.

Recall Innis and McLuhan, Cox and Panitch, Deibert and Klein and McQuaig – and others unnamed – who study the world from Canada. We, as Canadians, are well positioned, not only geographically but also intellectually, to know what's going on and to inform whatever choices we – perhaps even others – make.

The beginning of wisdom and a prerequisite for scholarly and political activism is to know one's place in time and in space. So long live Canadian political economy, robust and revised and ready for action.

Then came September 11th. Everything changed, we are told. Or is it that nothing has changed – except more of the same?

Violence is endemic to empire. The novelty of September 11th is that the killing moved from the margins to the centre, which caused the empire – its centre, that is – to strike back, with all its vengeance, to demonstrate that it was still in charge and that, therefore, nothing had changed.

The number of lives lost on September 11th is, sadly, not large by the standards of other acts of violence, but it is intolerable that Americans should die. In today's global village, all lives are not equal; such is the true nature of globalization.

In the discourse of Polanyi, the movement (at its core, the American military-industrial complex) is in total command, bullying and brutal, while the countermovement (dissenting civil society) is disconbobulated and repressed.

In the analysis of Innis, Canada, already in the American embrace, is now subjected to the fullness thereof, whether it wants it or not.

Nations, we have been taught – and know in our gut – are imagined communities, constructs of the collective memory and mind. Canadians must, indeed, now be an imaginative and determined people to justify our existence.

REFERENCES

Barlow, Maude and Tony Clark. 2001. *Global Showdown: How the New Activists Are Fighting Global Corporate Rule.* Toronto: Stoddart.

Clarke, Tony. 1997. *Silent Coup: Confronting the Big Business Takeover of Canada.* Toronto: Lorimer.

Clement, Wallace. 1977. *Continental Corporate Power: Economic Elite Linkages between Canada and the United States.* Toronto: McClelland and Stewart.

Conference Board of Canada. 2001. *Restructuring in a Global Economy: Is Corporate Canada Being Hollowed Out?* Ottawa: Conference Board of Canada.

Cunningham, Frank. 1994. *The Real World of Democracy Revisited: And Other Essays on Democracy and Socialism.* Atlantic Heights, NJ: Humanities Press.

Dale, Stephen. 1996. *McLuhan's Children: The Greenpeace Message and the Media.* Toronto: Between the Lines.

Deibert, Ronald J. 1997. *Parchment, Printing, and Hypermedia: Communication in World Order Transformation.* New York: Columbia University Press.

Dobbin, Murray. 1998. *The Myth of the Good Corporate Citizen: Democracy under the Rule of Big Business.* Toronto: Stoddart.

Elliott, Larry. 1999. "A World Driven by Blind Greed." *Guardian Weekly*, 15–21 July 1999.

Evans, B. Mitchell, Stephen McBride, and John Shields. 2000. "Globalization and the Challenge to Canadian Democracy: National Governance under Threat." In Mike Bourke, Colin Mooers, and John Shields eds., *Restructuring and Resistance: Canadian Public Policy in an Age of Global Capitalism.* Halifax: Fernwood.

Galeano, Eduardo. 2000. *Upside Down: A Primer for the Looking-Glass World.* New York: Metropolitan Books.

Gray, John. 1998. *False Dawn: The Delusions of Global Capitalism.* New York: New Press.

Hardt, Michael, and Antonio Negri. 2000. *Empire.* Cambridge, MA: Harvard University Press.

Hattersley, Roy. 2000. "In Search of the Third Way." *Granta* 71: 229–55.

Hébert, Chantal. 2001. "Sovereignty Pushed to Back Burner in Quebec." *Toronto Star*, 8 September, A13.

Helliwell, John, and John McCallum. 1995. "National Borders Still Matter for Trade." *Policy Options*, July/August.

Hetata, Sherif. 1998. "Dollarization, Fragmentation, and God." In Frederic Jameson and Masao Miyashi, eds., *The Cultures of Globalization.* Durham, NC, and London: Duke University Press.

Hymer, Stephen. 1979. *The Multinational Corporation: A Radical Approach.* Papers by Stephen Herbert Hymer, edited by Robert B. Cohen,Nadine Felton, Morley Nkosi, and Jaap van Liere. Cambridge: Cambridge University Press.

Innis, Harold A. 1940. *The Cod Fisheries: The History of an International Economy.* Revised edition 1954. Toronto: University of Toronto Press.

– 1950. *Empire and Communications.* London: Oxford University Press.

– 1956. *Essays in Canadian Economic History.* Toronto: University of Toronto Press.

Jackson, Andrew. 1999. "Free Trade – A Decade Later." *Studies in Political Economy* 58: 141–60.

Jessop, Bob. 1993. "Towards a Schumpeterian Workfare State? Preliminary Remarks of Post-Fordist Political Economy." *Studies in Political Economy* 40.

Juniper, Tony, and Hilary Wainwright. 2001. "Alternative Visions That Are Worlds Apart." *Guardian Weekly*, 8–14 February.

Klein, Naomi. 2000. *No Logo: Taking Aim at the Brand Bullies.* Toronto: Knopf.

– 2001. "A Fête for the End of History." *The Nation*, 19 March, 22.

Korten, David C. 1995. *When Corporations Rule the World.* West Hartford: Kumarian Press; San Francisco: Berrett-Koehle.

Langille, David. 1987. "The Business Council on National Issues and the Canadian State." *Studies in Political Economy* 24: 41–85.

Maxwell, Judith. 2001. "Toward a Common Citizenship: Canada's Social and Economic Choices." *Reflexion*, January, Canadian Policy Research Network.

McQuaig, Linda, 2001. *All You Can Eat: Greed, Lust and the New Capitalism.* Toronto: Penguin.

Parti Québécois. 1994. *National Executive Council of Quebec in a New World.* Toronto: Lorimer.

Polanyi, Karl. 1944. *The Great Transformation: The Political and Economic Origins of Our Times.* Boston: Beacon Press.

Przeworski, Adam. 1985. *Capitalism and Social Democracy.* Cambridge: Cambridge University Press.

Radice, Hugo. 1999. "Taking Globalization Seriously," *Socialist Register.*

Rebick, Judy. 2000. *Imagine Democracy.* Toronto: Stoddart.

Salutin, Rick. 2000. "Is Morality the New politics?" *Globe and Mail*, 22 December, A17.

Sklair, Leslie. 1998. "Social Movements and Global Capitalism." In Frederic Jameson and Masao Miyoshi, eds., *The Cultures of Globalization.* Durham and London: Duke University Press.

Theall, Donald F. 2001. *The Virtual Marshall McLuhan.* Montreal and Kingston: McGill-Queen's University Press.

Williams, Glen. 1988. "On Determining Canada's Location within the International Political Economy." *Studies in Political Economy* 25: 107–40.

2 Transformative Politics, the State, and the Politics of Social Change in Quebec

DANIEL SALÉE

Previously, William Coleman and I argued that much of Quebec's evolution over the past three or four decades could be understood in terms of the development of a counterparadigm that was premised on contesting Canada's political and cultural hegemony and on continued commitment by the provincial state to social solidarity and social justice. In light of the adoption of a fairly neoliberal policy agenda by the Quebec government, however, we considered with some perplexity the future "counteracting" potential of the counterparadigm, and we noted the emerging tendency of a number of scholars, intellectuals, and activists, on the left mostly, to doubt its ability to make good on its promise of a better society (Salée and Coleman 1997).

The present chapter examines further the fate of this so-called counterparadigm and the nature of transformative politics in the Quebec context. More particularly, it explores whether it still makes sense to characterize Quebec's approach to social governance and socioeconomic development as a counterparadigm, given the rather positive image the word tends to convey as a model for social change, social justice, and social progress, and more generally, as a synonym for transformative politics. Vocal supporters and promoters of the current government take great pride in the Quebec state. They eagerly claim that its accomplishments over time amount to a credible alternative and exemplary model of social progress. In reaction to the creation of a new leftist political party, Premier Landry recently maintained that his party, the Parti Québécois, remains the only true progressive party in Quebec.

Is this self-congratulatory fervour well-founded? Can the Quebec state and its socioeconomic allies still be viewed as bearers and sources of social change? Can the Quebec experience be legitimately proposed as a possible "third way," as an inspiration to reconfigure prevailing social hierarchies and structures of governance? This chapter critically addresses these questions. The first section looks at the so-called Quebec model and why it is presented as a progressive alternative. Second, its alleged counterparadigmatic possibilities are explored and evaluated. Third, the reasons for the apparent endorsement of the Quebec model by significant segments of the progressive social and political forces are examined. Finally, the chapter assesses the prospects of an emergent alternative left in Quebec and its ability to bring transformative politics beyond the Quebec model.

THE QUEBEC MODEL: WHAT'S IN A NAME?

In Quebec, as in most Western polities, globalization, economic restructuring, the fiscal limits of the welfare state, and difficulties in maintaining the levels of social and economic achievements reached during the previous decades have opened the way to a serious reconsideration of prevailing social hierarchies, modes of socioeconomic redistribution, and patterns of institutional relations between social groups and economic stakeholders. Since the late 1990s the current Quebec government has regularly boasted that it has successfully addressed the challenges at hand by maintaining and improving on what it calls the Quebec model. In general terms, the expression evokes the state-driven approach that originated during the years of the Quiet Revolution and contributed to the modernization of Quebec society and the Quebec economy. In its latest incarnation, however, it implies, more specifically, that Quebecers believe that solidarity is a central value of their collective lives and must remain so; that the state should be actively involved in promoting economic development, along with the co-operative movement, the labour movement, and all who are committed to the social economy; that this model is unique and that it is a defining characteristic of the only francophone jurisdiction in North America; that it has been beneficial to all Quebecers and has allowed them to grow as a united political community (Authier 1999; Parti Québécois 1999).

Proponents insist that one of the key and unique features of the Quebec model is that consensus on issues of general concern is achieved in Quebec by bringing together all the stakeholders of society (state, business, unions, community organizations, women, elderly citizens, youth, immigrants and ethno-cultural minorities) to participate in defining original global public policy orientations. They take umbrage at what they see as the persistent centralist tendencies of the Canadian state, which prevent Quebecers from developing fully and jeopardize their opportunities to enhance their social and economic potential further. In fact, the notion that there is a Quebec model works as a metaphor to express the distinctiveness of the Quebec people and to show how consensual are Quebec politics and society. The government uses it to underscore how socially and politically different and united Quebecers are in dealing with contemporary socioeconomic problems and how deleterious Canadian federalism is for a jurisdiction like Quebec, which tries to adopt solutions suitable to its own circumstances. As premier Lucien Bouchard said when lashing out at critics of the Quebec model and at those who might even doubt that there is such a thing: "The battle engaged against the Quebec model is a battle against the Quebec identity ... It is an offensive to convince us to dissolve our identity in the great Canadian bath" (Authier 1999). The very idea of the Quebec model is largely an ideological tool aimed at mobilizing Quebecers against Ottawa and the Canadian federal system (though it conveniently ignores the fact that some of Quebec's socioeconomic accomplishments of the past decades benefited in varying measures from the input of the federal state and from the administrative and jurisdictional autonomy afforded the provinces by the Canadian constitution in key sectors of activity). As such, then, whether there is indeed a model of socioeconomic development that is distinctly Quebec's own is open to debate. It is in many ways a matter of perception that hinges on one's political position on Quebec's national question.

This politicization of the argument over the Quebec model obfuscates the point. In fairness, there is more to it than mere ideological fiction. Recent and ongoing research in economic sociology shows that since the 1980s the Quebec state has been regularly encouraging and even actively promoting several socioinstitutional innovations aimed at fostering local business and economic development, curtailing unemployment, and enhancing social solidarity. These initiatives rest on extensive social partnerships, usually involving the state, private corporations, unions, and the community sector. They are real, viable, and have resulted in institutional practices that tend to set Quebec apart in North America (Bourque 2000; Comeau et al. 2001; Favreau and Saucier 1996; Lévesque and Mendell 2000). In their reviews of those initiatives, scholars and experts point to various examples of Quebec's unique economic policy-making process, including the Forum pour l'emploi (Forum for Jobs), created in the late 1980s and active until 1995 as a nongovernmental body that brought together representatives from the labour movement, the private sector, and community organizations to promote joint action to fight unemployment and influence governmental economic strategy (Comeau et al. 2001, 14–15). Other examples include worker-owned investment funds, such as the Quebec Federation of Labour's Fonds de solidarité and the Confederation of National Trade Unions' Fondaction, which emerged, with the fiscal blessing of the state, as alternative sources of financing for Quebec-based, small and medium-sized, as well as social, enterprises and as significant actors in fostering employment (CRISES 2000; Mendell, Lévesque, and Rouzier 2000); the co-operative movement, whose flagship institution, the Mouvement Desjardins, a credit union founded in the early twentieth century, now ranks among the most important Canadian financial institutions; and, finally, a number of community economic development initiatives that have emerged throughout Quebec over the past decade or so and that are establishing themselves as a new employment and economic empowerment nexus for both individuals and communities (Mendell 2000).

But it is the more recent, apparent endorsement of the principles of the social economy by the Quebec state that strikes the imagination of economic sociologists and stimulates hopes of positive social and political change. There is no single definition of the expression "social economy," since it encompasses a variety of alternative social and economic practices and different theoretical visions (Lévesque and Mendell 1999; Fontan and Shragge 2000). However, a certain consensus seems to be forming within concerned circles in Quebec that principles of solidarity, autonomy, and citizenship are embodied in the operational guidelines of the social economy, which, as such, promotes the development of initiatives characterized by "a primary goal of service to members or the community rather than of accumulating profit ... autonomous management (independent of public programmes) ... democratic decision-making processes ... the primacy of persons and work over capital in the redistribution of profits; and ... operations based on principles of participation, empowerment, and individual and collective accountability" (Ninacs 2000, 133).

This understanding of the social economy emanates mainly from the Chantier de l'économie sociale (Task Force on the Social Economy), an independent but state-supported body functioning as a nonprofit corporation that brings together labour and community organization representatives and whose main objective is to facilitate the development and implementation of social economy initiatives throughout Quebec. The Chantier de l'économie sociale was originally established as one of the working groups created around the

March 1996 Conference on the Social and Economic Future of
Quebec, in preparation for the October 1996 socioeconomic summit
that was convened by the Quebec government to consult with all the
major stakeholders of civil society in order to elaborate strategies of
economic management and employment development. In addition to
business and labour leaders, women's groups and community organizations were invited to participate in the summit, thus reflecting the
government's intention to develop as wide and as inclusive a perspective as possible on macroeconomic issues.

It was generally agreed then that the government should implement
measures necessary to reach a zero-deficit situation within the following four years. Premier Bouchard maintained that this was essential
for achieving the "winning conditions" for an eventual referendum on
sovereignty. Getting the labour movement and the community sector
to agree to a zero-deficit policy was an important political victory for
the Bouchard government, for they, more than any other social and
economic stakeholders, stood to lose much in the short run from the
unavoidable cuts and restrictions to social, welfare and employment
programs such a policy would – and did – entail. In return, heeding
the political pressures from the community sector, the government
resolved to promote the development and advancement of the social
economy. It was eventually decided that the working group on the
social economy would become a more permanent body, and it was officially constituted as the Chantier de l'économie sociale in April 1999.[1]
According to current estimates, the social economy sector in Quebec
comprises 4,764 social enterprises (nonprofit organizations and cooperatives) creating 49,450 jobs and producing $4.2 billion in gross
revenue. In comparison, the mining sector accounts for $1.2 billion of
the GDP, communication for $6.6 billion, and the construction sector
for $8.2 billion (Chantier de l'économie sociale 2001, 5).

To many specialists and scholars with an interest in these issues, the
government's involvement with the social economy is an example of
the Quebec state's commitment to include civil society in economic
policy decisions, maintain social solidarity, and enhance economic
democracy without giving in to the imperatives of market competitiveness. To them, the state's willingness to support the principles and
values of the social economy and foster social economy initiatives represents a renewal of the Quebec model and a positive, enabling and
potentially more democratic reconfiguration of socioeconomic hierarchies involving the state, business, labour, and the community sector.
They see the Quebec state as playing "a new role as a partner in social
change" (Mendell 2000, 104). Though they credit the headstrong,
rear-guard battles led by the community sector and some segments of

the labour movement with this outcome, they nonetheless consider that the Quebec government should "embrace novel and more inclusive networks of governance, rather than subvert them as in the past, or contain them, as they have done until recently" (Mendell 2002, 324).

While the currently authoritative literature on the social economy in Quebec rests on prudent analyses and qualified evaluations of the situation, it lends credence to the Quebec government's claim that a fairly broad political consensus permeates Quebec society on issues of socioeconomic management and on fundamental societal priorities. It thus reinforces the idea that there is indeed a Quebec model, a distinctly Quebec way of tackling the major socioeconomic challenges of the day, and that, moreover, the model is premised on inherently transformative politics – thanks to the vitality of the community sector and the labour movement – and on the approval by the Quebec state of a forward-looking vision of social change. It shies away from openly sharing the government's political conclusions about the allegedly negative impact of Canadian federalism on the further development of the Quebec model, but in the end it provides, willingly or not, the evidence the government readily uses to proclaim that Quebec society is socially cohesive and constitutes a tightly knit, unitary political community.

CONFRONTING THE PROMISES OF THE QUEBEC MODEL AND THE SOCIAL ECONOMY

A good deal of the current discussion about transformative politics in Quebec tends to hinge on the social economy's potential ability to bring about positive social change and create the proper conditions for individual and community empowerment. The social economy and the private-public partnerships upon which many of its initiatives rest allow the current government, in particular, to project an image of itself as a benevolent social partner imbued with a deep commitment to economic justice and democracy. They infuse the Quebec state, as a result, with a much-needed moral aura of social solidarity at a time when Western liberal democratic states seem impervious to it.

To the most caustic critics of the Quebec model and of the role assigned to the social economy in its development, the whole thing is nothing but a model of economic exploitation and political domination. The state-sponsored social partnerships are demagogic smoke screens that compel labour and the community sector to buy into social, economic, and even political compromises that work in the end against their objective and class interests. The celebrated social economy, they further argue, only keeps workers and the economically marginalized in precarious economic circumstances. Even the most successful experiments in social economy remain largely local and limited in scope. They may help those involved in them break out of the vicious cycle of economic dependence, they may even strengthen community bonds and make individuals feel good about themselves, but they rarely reach beyond the people who partake in them; they hardly amount to a global, universally endorsable model of social and civic overhaul. The interest of the government in the social economy is instrumental and basically motivated by its perceived potential ability to lighten the social welfare burden of the Quebec state (by making people find their own way out of economic dependence) without questioning the logic and the process that have created the situations of glaring socioeconomic inequality in the first place. The social economy liberates the state from its previous commitments to the segments of the population that it can purportedly no longer support and saves it from having to transform or reconsider the exclusionary mechanisms at the roots of the opposition between solidarity and scarcity in capitalist economies. In a word, to a number of critics the social economy operates as an ideological tool of social cohesion that works in the end to further the agenda of the neoliberal state (Boivin and Fortier 1998; Paquet 1999; Piotte 1998).

Supporters of and academic sympathizers with the social economy take exception to this view. They argue that it misrepresents the very real possibilities for change that the social economy brings about, but most of all they feel it grossly underestimates the vitality and accomplishments of Quebec's community organizations and the popular sector more generally in fending off the neoliberal tide. As one well-informed student of the Quebec social economy puts it,

While the social economy appears to its detractors as a facsimile of Quebec Inc., this is misleading. Indeed, the social economy brings together the state, business and labour; however, the driving force was and continues to be the community sector, which has not simply joined this select club of experienced negotiators, but, without exaggeration, has turned its practice on its head. Community organizations with an impressive record of mobilisation and economic revitalisation are demonstrating another way of doing business. The negotiations under way in the social economy, as it defines itself politically and in practice, are based upon principles which fundamentally oppose the predominance of economic over social objectives ... [While the neo-liberal agenda] failed to avoid the increase in poverty, unemployment and social exclusion that characterises Quebec society today, [i]t increasingly fell to social movements and to community groups to look for alternatives to resolve this situation. (Mendell 2000, 104)

As a result, Quebec politics are a witness to "the emergence of new mechanisms which coordinate relationships between various social actors and provide new and more powerful roles for previously marginalized individuals and groups through a new cultural legitimacy ascribed to these experiences ... [The new social economy] is redefining social relations" (Mendell 2002, 331).

There is no doubt that community organizations and the activism of the social movements in Quebec have forced the issue on a number of key concerns of social and economic policy over the past decade and brought major socioeconomic stakeholders to review their traditional stance. It is usually acknowledged, for example, that the 1995 Women's March against Poverty, a mass mobilization of Quebec's women's organizations, was a turning point that led the government to reconsider its approach to unemployment, nonstandard work, and economic exclusion and influenced its decision to set up the Chantier de l'économie sociale.

Still, it remains unclear to almost every observer whether the social economy has the transformative power that many believe it to have. Some wonder whether it represents an expansion of democracy or of social corporatism or, again, whether it is part of a new mix of welfare and workfare (Favreau and Saucier 1996). Others fear that the use of the social economy by the state might be but a strategy of cooptation of progressive forces in Quebec designed to underwrite national accumulation objectives. They suggest that, far from leading to the celebrated transformation of structures of governance and enhanced democratic practices, the continued importance of traditional centres of state power in setting the parameters for the social economy indicates, on the contrary, that grass-roots action has not really weakened sites of power at the larger scale of the state (Graefe 2001). Finally, even scholars with a natural sympathy for social economy initiatives admit that not all supporters of the social economy approach necessarily share the same understanding of what it entails. They note that individuals and popular groups or organizations that readily gravitate toward social economy solutions are concerned mostly with finding the means to promote local social solidarity, empower individuals and communities, and alleviate the social costs of globalization. Their sense of the social economy clashes with the sense that emanates from private sector supporters for whom all institutional transformations of the Quebec economy must be primarily geared towards facilitating the province's international competitiveness and for whom the social economy is good insofar as it can check social fragmentation and encourage private initiative (Comeau et al. 2001, 243–4).

These divergent views of the purported benefits of the social economy reflect, in fact, the profound tension that now exists in Quebec between, on the one hand, the desire motivated by a general and politically virtuous will to enhance social solidarity – while somehow remaining true to the progressive ideals of the counterparadigm with which Quebec's process of political transformation since the 1960s has been associated in the collective imagination – and, on the other hand, the perceived urgency to respond to the call of economic globalization and its attendant focus on market competitiveness and individualism. In other words, the turn to the social economy expresses the unease of Quebec policymakers at having to choose between two sets of policy alternatives: fending off social exclusion, not succumbing to the strictly economic imperatives of the market, enhancing social justice, developing new redistributive mechanisms, and providing individuals and communities with tools of empowerment and self-fulfilment – which are all policy choices that can be costly as a matter of strict market logic and that are unlikely to satisfy the requirements of capitalist competitiveness – or adjusting economic and social policy to the demands of economic globalization, abiding by the neoliberal consensus of the political elite on the necessity of free trade, and maintaining conditions of social cohesion that can bring the majority of citizens to buy into this consensus and embrace its underlying socioeconomic premises. Simply put, the problem boils down to a choice between social solidarity and social cohesion. Though both objectives need not be mutually exclusive, they are mutually exclusive in the current conjuncture insofar as solidarity suggests a commitment to equitable distribution of collective resources, democracy, civic participation, and pluralism – and therefore a certain willingness to curtail market rules and question capitalist social relations – while cohesion implies the primacy of sociopolitical stability and the unquestioning acceptance of market structures, the existing social hierarchies, and the dominant configuration of social relations.[2] Quebec's apparent sympathy for the social economy approach indicates that policymakers have not dared to make a choice between the two and are, rather, hoping that the policy goals implicit in both can be reconciled and achieved together.

To some, this tension is useful and can even be productive, since it forces social and economic stakeholders to search for imaginative solutions (Mendell 2002). They assume that representatives of varying and competing interests are willing to work together to develop socioeconomic outcomes that are advantageous to everyone. To others, though, the government has clearly chosen sides. Public policymakers may well use the language of social solidarity, but they have opted to heed the call of market exigencies. In support of this view, they point to the government's unequivocal endorsement of the globalization discourse and the corporate agenda, to important cutbacks in social, health, and education programs, and to the ongoing institutional overhaul that re-centralizes decision-making authority in the hands of the state bureaucracy and diminishes citizen input and participation in administrative and policy-making functions. They argue that, far from being the social partner that it claims to be, a partner attentive to the needs of the community sector and the excluded, the government responds more readily to the dictates of the business sector (Pichette 2001; Ravet 2001).

Things are not necessarily as cut and dry. In reality, the government is treading a fine line between social solidarity and market competitiveness. Its sympathy for social economy initiatives and its commitment to improving the lot of the poorest segments of society are genuine: several members of the government, including Premier Bouchard himself before his resignation, are literally sold on the principles of the social economy. However, they remain captives of the cultural weight and economic dominion of market capitalism, as if it was impossible to think outside that box and impose alternative solutions that would disrupt the existing capitalist logic. The Quebec government may be tempted by the ideals of the social economy, but it has not as yet resolved to apply them in any coherent and structured way so as to fundamentally modify the dynamics of social and economic power.

For one thing, the implementation of some of the principles of the social economy has done little to improve the general economic situation of the province. A look at some socioeconomic indicators brings the limitations of the social economy and the Quebec model in general into a clearer focus. A recent economic study shows that in spite of an annual real economic growth rate of 2.1 percent since the early 1980s, Quebec's relative situation in contrast to the rest of Canada and the United States is deteriorating. Between 1981 and 1999, Quebec's real gross domestic product (GDP) increased by 45.2 percent, while the GDP in the rest of Canada increased by 64.2 percent during the same period. Quebec's GDP accounted for 24 percent of Canada's GDP in the early 1980s; by 1999 it had slipped to 21.9 percent. However, it is on the employment front, the basic plank of the whole social economy approach, that one gets a more tragic sense of the shortcomings of the Quebec model. Again, for the 1981–99 period, the total number of jobs in Quebec grew by 20.4 percent, but in comparison job creation grew by 31.3 percent in the rest of Canada, and by 33 percent in the United States. Between 1990 and 1999 the number of new (part-time and full-time) jobs increased by 6.9 percent in Quebec, but by 12.4 percent in the rest of the country and in the United States. In other words, Quebec's economy has systematically created jobs at a lower rate than the economy of the rest of Canada for the past two decades. Though Quebec comprises one-quarter of the Canadian population, it created less than one-fifth of all the new jobs in Canada between 1981 and 1990 and barely one-sixth for the period 1990–99. Similarly, inasmuch as full-time jobs alone are considered in this broad picture, it appears that they increased by 9.2 percent in Quebec, in comparison to a rate of 14.2 percent in the rest of Canada between 1981 and 1990; for the period 1990–99, they increased by only 5.2 percent, as opposed to a rate of 10.5 percent in the rest of Canada. Quebec was responsible for the creation of 18 percent of all the new full-time jobs in Canada for the period 1981–90; that proportion dropped to 13.9 percent for the 1990s. In order for Quebec to post an employment rate equivalent to that of the rest of Canada or the United States – it is currently at 55.5 percent, compared to 60.8 percent for Canada and 64 percent for the United States – at least 14 percent more jobs (that is roughly 469,000) would be needed immediately (Boyer 2001, 3–5).

It would be unfair to attribute this comparatively poor showing entirely to the failings of the social economy or the Quebec model. Several other factors contributed more significantly to this situation, among which are the particular dynamics of regional disparities in Canada, investment choices favouring some provinces for their comparative advantages rather than others, population movements, the structural obsolescence of some sectors of the provincial economy, the decentering of Montreal within the continental economy, the relative inexperience of the Quebec business class, and various deterrents to investment, including the political threat of Quebec sovereignty, high rates of taxation, a strong and activist union movement, and significant social charges to corporations.

The apparent failure of the Quebec model and the social economy to secure a stronger showing for Quebec's economy is not the most serious of their limitations. Given their ambition to enhance social solidarity and socioeconomic justice, it is more critical that the transformative potential of the social economy has not been developed to the fullest. As a counterparadigm of change and empowerment, the Quebec model fails to redress social hierarchies, no matter how hard the community sector and progressive forces try to influence the policy process. A new index of economic freedom constructed by researchers at the Canadian Centre for Policy Alternatives offers an even more explicit sense of the inability of the course pursued by the

Quebec model to effect any real transformation of the dominant socioeconomic logic. This index, dubbed EFRU (Economic Freedom for the Rest of Us) by its authors, "is intended to measure the impact of labour market conditions and government policies, rules and institutions on the economic prospect of those members of society who must work for a living" (Brown and Stanford 2000, 9). Based on fourteen different component variables that are grouped and weighted into three broad categories (employment, earnings, and equality and security),[3] the index is meant to "reflect the extent to which the members of society are able to support themselves in productive employment, receive an income which reflects their productivity and allows for an adequate standard of living, and are protected from arbitrary discrimination or dislocation on the basis of personal characteristics or economic misfortune" (Brown and Stanford 2000, 9).

The global image projected by the EFRU index with respect to Quebec is only partially positive. Quebec ranked fourth overall in 1990, 1991, and 1992 and third in the following years until 1999, when it ranked fourth again. Compared to the other provinces, then, it can be argued that Quebec figured as a leader in providing economic freedom. But a closer look tells a different, less glorious story. Quebec fared poorly on the employment subindex, ranking seventh, eighth, or ninth throughout the whole decade, and posted a very average performance on the equality/security subindex, ranking seventh in the early years of the decade, doing better in the middle years, but sliding back into sixth position by 1999. The earnings subindex saved Quebec from a more disastrous showing as the province scored near the top (second rank in 1990 and 1994 and third rank in the other years of the decade). Clearly, as the statistics presented above bear out, Quebec did rather poorly on the job creation front and was unable to improve the employment situation of Quebecers noticeably during the past decade. Thanks to its wage and social market policies, Quebec did succeed in maintaining a reasonable level of income for its population in spite of a limited amount of economic growth and job creation. Still, the province's total EFRU score was 2.6 points lower at the end of the decade than it was at the beginning; it was 1.9 points lower on the employment subindex, 0.7 point lower on the earnings subindex, and, more telling perhaps, 5.3 points lower on the equality/security subindex. This suggests, ostensibly, that the overall well-being of Quebecers who must work for a living was eroded during the decade and that the ability of the overall economic system to fend off a serious decline in earnings was dampened by a concurrent increase in insecurity and inequality.

Despite the state rhetoric of solidarity and socioeconomic justice, the conditions that would guarantee greater equity between majority and minority groups, a better access to mechanisms of economic empowerment for the excluded, and thus a fairer balance of social and economic power did not really materialize. It is true that this situation was not unique to Quebec, since every province experienced a similar deterioration, if not worse in some cases. But insofar as Quebec specifically is concerned, the statistics point in the end to the inadequacy of a model of social and economic development that government rhetoric inaccurately presents as different, distinct, better, and above all, as premised on a deep concern for social solidarity.

BETWEEN A ROCK AND A HARD PLACE?

What does all this mean from the point of view of transformative politics in Quebec? By supporting an approach to socioeconomic management that does not seem to improve the lot of the economically weaker segments of society has the Quebec left sold out or bought into a social compromise that is not paying off? Has it become irrelevant to or totally inefficient in shaping the province's social and political agenda? Is there still any hope for transformative politics in Quebec? Such questions, which are being raised lately with increasing regularity within progressive circles, implicitly challenge the ability of the Quebec left to formulate and foster the implementation of political and societal alternatives. They will seem unfair to scores of men and women who are intent on, and work hard at limiting the influence of a narrow market mentality and the onslaught of the neoliberal agenda on Quebec society. To them, much of the left's perceived failure may well be but a matter of interpretation: the fact that traditional left forces no longer seem to engage in radical and controversial action, as they did in the 1960s and 1970s, does not mean that they cannot be agents of change. The collaborationist, partnership-driven approach that has been emphasized in recent years may yield more permanent and more beneficial results in the long run than the protracted confrontations of the past. This, of course, remains to be seen, and the questions posed here are apposite, for through most of the 1990s left politics in Quebec remained in a state of relative indeterminacy. This is not to imply that it was ineffective or directionless but rather to signify that the standard progressive social and political forces that had been responsible for the sociocultural modernization of Quebec society and the "welfarization" of the Quebec state during the preceding decades were reorienting their traditional, confrontational strategies and rethinking the radical quality of their political positions.

Part of this reorientation may be attributed to the historical tendency of the left almost everywhere to become more institutionalized, more prudent, and less bent on emancipatory action as time goes on, particularly after it has had access to or has directly held power.[4] But to explain away the positional and strategic shift of the Quebec left over the past decade simply in terms of the effects of a general and seemingly unavoidable process of political institutionalization or as the result of co-optive strategies adopted by the state and corporate interests, as some readily argue (Piotte 1998), would be to miss the role played by fundamental societal and structural factors inherent to Quebec society as key explanatory elements. Indeed, the attitudinal conversion of the Quebec left is largely attributable to the internal dynamics of Quebec's political economy. Since the late 1970s, the Quebec economy has been plagued by repeated recessionary cycles, high unemployment rates, limited productivity, and a continuing fiscal crisis to which there seemed to be no end until recently. In addition, Quebec has wrestled, with mixed results, with finding a proper, profitable niche in an increasingly competitive global market. Although this kind of situation has been common and has characterized the national economy of several Western societies during this period,[5] Quebec has had a harder time at grappling with it, as the indicators of economic performance discussed above suggest.

In response, the state and the private sector have exercised significant and successful downward pressures on wages. For example, on several occasions during the first half of the 1990s state employees – over 270,000 workers – were forced through special legislation to accept wage freezes, wage reductions, and the extension of their collective agreements for up to three years in some cases. Private sector companies followed suit and imposed similar conditions. As a result Quebec's average weekly wage, which was only 2 percent lower than the national level through the 1980s, was 6.4 percent lower by 1999 (Boyer 2001, 5). These pressures on wages were accompanied throughout by constant (and at times actualized) threats of plant closures or layoffs, or by threats to move business facilities outside Quebec. Also notable were state and business-driven attempts at transforming the nature of the wage relation by blocking the unionization drives of workers in precarious job situations or by opening up the possibility of outsourcing and subcontracting, which usually tends to weaken the bargaining position of workers in unionized environments.[6]

Clearly, the Quebec working class has been on the losing side of the class struggle during the past two decades, and unsurprisingly, the labour movement has become increasingly pervaded with a sense that the state of public finance and the general economic situation have left the working class with little choice but to agree to social and economic compromises that would have been promptly and squarely denounced barely a decade earlier. Though in some ways more exhilarating and yielding appreciable gains, the hard-fought and epic struggles of the 1960s and 1970s had been waged at considerable personal and collective cost to the labour movement (Piotte 1987) – numerous long and difficult strikes followed in succession, union leaders were imprisoned, internal dissensions and turf wars divided the labour movement and the political left, the national liberation movement was reproved in several quarters, and the community sector was left with meagre resources and virtually alone to fend for itself. By the mid-1980s, the labour movement and the left in general began to feel, in the light of the changing and adverse economic conditions, that a more accommodating stance might bear more tangible and lasting results. In the end, the greater willingness of labour and the community sector to transcend their differences with the state and the business sector and eventually to collaborate with them on major social and economic policy issues derived more from a conscious attempt at coping as best as possible with the imperatives of the new structural reality without being thrown into political irrelevance than from the softening up of previous, more uncompromising political strategies, as some have hinted.

The natural, political proximity of the Quebec labour movement and of some segments of the Quebec left to the sovereignist ideology is another factor that explains, in part, the apparent strategic retrenchment of traditional progressive forces in recent years. Since the 1960s Quebec's will to political independence has generally been formulated as a left political project associated with transformative politics, socioeconomic justice, social solidarity, and cultural and national emancipation. Except on a few occasions and with the odd caveat, the Quebec labour movement, almost as a whole, has always readily endorsed the idea of Quebec sovereignty, siding with the yes forces in both the 1980 and the 1995 referendum. In 1995, in fact, the three main labour federations joined the broad progovernment sociopolitical coalition of the "partners for sovereignty" and strongly urged their respective membership to support the sovereignty bid of the government. While this position may have been politically defensible and perfectly understandable within the context of Quebec politics, it brought the institutional left closer to the government than ever before in the history of the province.[7] However, labour's endorsement of the government's position on the national question and its partnership with sovereignist forces further restricted, if only with respect to its credibility and consistency, its own ability to exercise its traditional prerogatives as a social and political critic. By allying itself with the government on the national question, the institutional left allowed itself to be not only a partner for sovereignty but also a partner in the government's social and economic endeavours. As sovereignty was defeated once more in 1995, the labour movement in particular felt compelled to engage again with the government to create "winning conditions" for another referendum. It came on board during the 1996 socioeconomic summit and agreed to a zero-deficit policy and a number of neoliberal measures supposedly aimed at guaranteeing sovereignist victory the next time around. The institutional left deliberately made itself an active player in the Quebec model – not out of desperation or fear of political irrelevance, it is fair to note, but rather with the conviction that this was the best course for the attainment of its own transformative agenda, which invariably includes Quebec's sovereignty.

TRANSFORMING POLITICS BEYOND THE QUEBEC MODEL

Is the strategy of accommodation and collaboration with the state that has seemingly been adopted by the labour movement and its affiliates in the social economy sector the only valid one for achieving true social change in Quebec? Admittedly, the approach has borne some significant fruits: the creation of the Chantier de l'économie sociale, the inclusion of the community sector in the government's consultative process, the government's stated commitment to the social economy, and the increasing, strategic convergence of the labour movement and the community sector are seen by many as fairly meaningful gains. Still, the obvious inability of the Quebec model to deliver a higher degree of economic security and equality, and thus a higher degree of social justice, now raises serious doubts in some quarters as to the appropriateness of the strategy of concerted action pursued by the traditional left, and its political self-restraint is far from being shared by all within the broad left.

Through the 1990s the women's movement and several social and economic advocacy groups never ceased confronting the government in no uncertain terms on a host of social and economic policy changes that they feared would lead to a significant decline in income security for the poorer segments of society. Despite their initial, theoretical sympathy for the sovereignty option, leaders of the Quebec Women's Federation, for example, have on several occasions voiced their dissatisfaction with governmental initiatives, distancing themselves from the prevailing sociopolitical consensus. Similarly, in recent years more radical, left-leaning groups have also engaged in actions that directly question the government's socioeconomic priorities.[8] In the fall of 1997, six hundred disaffected left nationalists met to create a new political movement, the Rassemblement pour une alternative politique (RAP), with well-known retired unionist Michel Chartrand at its head. A few RAP representatives ran in the November 1998 provincial election, with Chartrand himself opposing premier Bouchard in his own Lac St-Jean riding – to no avail, but the idea was to get their message across.[9] In November 1997, fifteen hundred representatives of more than twenty community and antipoverty groups held a parlement de la rue (street parliament) for a whole month across from the National Assembly, to denounce the government's social policies. In February 2000 a coalition of groups on the political left, the Coalition autonome populaire jeunesse (Autonomous Popular Youth Coalition) organized a parallel summit to protest the government's Youth Summit, which convened, following a familiar pattern, Quebec's major stakeholders to discuss policy solutions to youth unemployment, education, and job training. Organizers and participants at the countersummit decried the government's neoliberal policies and commitment to integrate Quebec into the global economy according to the rules proclaimed in such executive agreements as the North American Free Trade Agreement (NAFTA), the World Trade Organization (WTO) and the still tentative Free Trade Area of the Americas (FTAA). They eventually clashed with the Quebec City police force.

Recent movements of protest have also gone global. In the spring of 1998 and again in the fall of 2000, Quebec-based youth and antiglobalization organizations disrupted the Montreal meetings of the Multilateral Agreement on Investments (MAI) and the G-20. Similarly, in 2000 the Fédération des femmes du Québec (Quebec Women's Federation) initiated and organized the Women's World March, a peaceful protest aimed at sensitizing governments to the difficult socioeconomic situations of women around the world and at exposing the negative human consequences of economic globalization and the neoliberal economic policies adopted by national governments. Several other Quebec civil society groups were very heavily involved in the preparation of the People's Summit, to counter the official Summit of the Americas, held in Quebec City in April 2001 to discuss the FTAA, and they took an active part in the many antiglobalization political demonstrations surrounding the event.

Despite the variety of their actions and objectives, these and other left-inspired protest initiatives all reprove the policy choices of the Quebec government, distrust its alleged commitment to social solidarity, and condemn its emphasis on international competitiveness and blind faith in free market mechanisms. The depths of their popular support or the extent to which they will evolve into a well-organized political alternative (or even into an entirely new civic culture) are still quite unclear. But their very existence is undoubtedly shattering the image of societal consensus that the Quebec government is so eager to project; they partake of a conceptual paradigm that is basically at odds with the fundamental values and norms of civic engagement that mould the liberal democratic outlook of Quebec nationalists currently in power and the Quebec model they hold dear. To many of the individuals involved in this process of resistance, particularly those whose actions focus on transnational issues, the whole Quebec-Canada question is totally surreal and disconnected from their experience on the ground (despite the obvious link between national and transnational policy questions). In terms of federal-provincial relations, it is more than likely that they will not follow the nationalist elite in their "struggle" against Ottawa, partly in protest against the government's management of the province but also because the chronic Quebec-Ottawa imbroglio appears of limited relevance in the grand scheme of things. This is not to say that the new protest groups are inherently federalist. Many of them are not, or they simply could not care less whether the unity of the Canadian federal union is preserved or not. They are just as vehement in their critique of the Canadian state, to the extent that they consider that it too favours neoliberal policy choices. Their critique of the Quebec state therefore cannot be appreciated in terms of anti-Quebec, or antisovereignty, and pro-Canada sentiments; it operates at a broader and more general political level.

For the sovereignist political elite, this situation may translate into quite a setback in the long run. The sovereignty movement could always count on the support of a large coalition of left forces so long as the Parti Québécois donned the mantle of social democracy with some credibility. The political sovereignty of Quebec was also considered by most people on the left as a necessary step for the emancipation and empowerment of Quebec's labouring and economically disadvantaged classes. Some still believe that it is; the RAP is one example. But as the Parti Québécois no longer appears as a plausible vehicle of social change to increasing segments of Quebec's progressive social and political forces, sovereignists stand to lose natural allies. Premier Landry chided members of the new left coalition-turned-political-party in June 2001 for creating the risk that the sovereignist vote would be divided in an eventual general election. He was still upset by the defeat inflicted on the Parti Quebecois a few weeks earlier in a by-election in a Montreal riding that had regularly supported the sovereignist party since the 1970s. Although the Liberal Party representative won, the setback was largely attributed to the unexpectedly good standing of the relatively unknown new left sovereignist but independent candidate who, with nearly 24 percent of the vote, came ahead of the Parti Quebecois contender and was blamed for having split the sovereignist vote. Should this kind of outcome occur again on a wider basis, Landry's fear, of course, is that not only will the societal consensus that is so necessary for launching credible charges against Ottawa likely dwindle but any interest or support for the kind of jurisdictional battles the Quebec state has waged historically might wane irremediably and with it so too would the sanctity of the Quebec model.

Can Quebec's new left, as it were, gather enough momentum in the foreseeable future to make a difference and take progressive forces on a new path of social change and political transformation that would bring Quebec society to deal with issues of socioeconomic justice and political renewal outside the Quebec model? It is still too soon to say with any degree of certainty. Although the frustration of the new left is real, particularly among the youth, it does not yet have the organizational wherewithal to carry out sustained, systematic, and effective charges against current ways and structures. Its actions remain basically ad hoc. Political mobilization occurs mostly around very specific issues (social housing, employment equity, health care, globalization) and usually stops short of constituting a large, far-reaching, change-provoking movement of social protest. The recently created RAP has, at the time of writing, virtually no resonance within the larger population. Unless it succeeds in extending the coalition of left forces to include some of the most active and legitimate civil society organizations, it will probably not have a very significant impact. Besides, its stated commitment to Quebec sovereignty is already seen as problematic by some who continue to associate this political project with the Parti Québécois.

The most important obstacle to strengthening a new left alternative comes from the fact that the state-labour-business alliance that makes the Quebec model possible and, indeed, basically unchallenged is still quite solid. The government has been successful at maintaining an ambivalent discourse on issues of socioeconomic management and at making it credible. So long as the institutional left does not clearly attempt to debunk that discourse, so long as it does not realize that the government's neoliberal bent cancels out any theoretical commitment to social solidarity that it claims to have, chances are that the success of transformative politics in Quebec will be limited in the short run. Because the new left does not yet have much currency with the population, without a clearer engagement of the institutional left toward more fundamental change (as opposed to the Quebec model compromise), without a real questioning of the dominant logic of market capitalism, it is doubtful that significant sociopolitical change will take place.

CONCLUSION

Modern Quebec has long inspired quasi-mythical evocations in the political imagination of Canadian left political economists, principally as a site of emancipatory social and political practices. The social democratic, nationalist striving of the 1960s and 1970s, the uncompromising and forward-looking stances of the Quebec labour movement, the dynamism of the community sector, and the apparent willingness of various stakeholders to embark on innovative social and institutional experiments, as well as a general openness to advanced political ideas and social or lifestyle trends, all seemed to set Quebec apart within Canada as a unique example (one that some observers have considered with envy) of the kind of social change and political transformation progressive politics could accomplish. In some ways Quebec still works as a counterparadigm in the Canadian context: its repeated political attempts at countervailing its minority status and its efforts to seek distinctive solutions to the broad issues of social and economic management of the day are cases in point. But in recent years the counterparadigmatic edge of the Quebec model has lost some of its sharpness: Quebec is looking increasingly like a counterparadigm that may have lost touch with the meaning of social change and political transformation.

Despite the flaws and potential problems of the social economy approach and its attendant private-public partnership model, one can still recognize, at least provisionally, that they may constitute a legitimate and constructive avenue for the economic empowerment of marginalized individuals and communities and for effective social and political change. Indeed, "the extension of the social economy provides a basis for resisting the increasing hegemony of capital over society as a whole, [and] demonstrates the possibility of organising economic and social life in terms that challenge the taken for grantedness of the 'common sense' of the capital relation." Still, proponents of the social economy acknowledge that its potential cannot be fully achieved without a struggle. "For, as with any other form of organisation, there are complex, interpersonal, organisational, institutional and systemic preconditions necessary to its consolidation. In the case of the social economy these concern the scope for the re-absorption of the market and the state into an expanded civil society" (Jessop 2000, 94). Some analysts and students of the social economy argue that even

if the community sector and representatives of the socially and economically marginalized have derived some noticeable gains from partnerships with the state and the business sector in recent years, without
a strong willingness to engage politically with the state community
organizations that adopt a social economy approach "may simply end
up as cheap substitutes for diminished state engagement" (Shragge
and Fontan 2000, 137). In fact, despite the political advances of the
social economy and the community sector, nothing is guaranteed, and
as Bob Jessop aptly notes, "the re-absorption of the social economy by
the state (through dependence on state finance or co-optation)
and/or the logic of the market (due to integration into capitalist commodity chains and dependence on normal loans, etc.) is more likely
than vice versa" (2000, 94).

In the Quebec context, it is difficult to determine at this juncture
whether the left and progressive forces whose action hinges on the
social economy can stave off this re-absorption. The most important
and significant scholarship on this question may often convey the
impression that they can, but in fact, important and somewhat daunting organizational, institutional, and ethico-political preconditions
must be met for the social economy to be a credible and truly transformative alternative. As Bob Jessop also argues, the "effective coordination of institutional arrangements to produce 'structured coherence' at the micro-, meso-, macro- and meta-levels and to ensure the
dynamic complementarily of the social economy to the wider economic system" is essential. This involves at the micro-level "developing
and promoting interconnected productive organisations in order the
better to secure their economic and educational potential as social
movements"; at the meso-level, the existence of "territorial socio-political networks aiming to mobilise and develop resources, organise the
economy in a sustainable way, to offer and demand certain services
that could be largely met from the social economy, and to promote
interaction between suppliers, producers and customers"; at the
macro-level the creation of a global "framework able to make social
ends compatible with the economic functionality of social economy
within a wider society in which the market will still have a key role in
allocation and accumulation"; and, finally, at the meta-level, "the
ongoing transformation of values, norms, identities and interests so
that they support the social economy rather the commodification of
all areas of social life" (Jessop 2000, 96–7).

Does the Quebec model, with its purported reliance on the social
economy and its alleged concern for social solidarity, satisfy these preconditions? Studies that would allow objective answers to this question are still lacking. The bulk of the current literature has been

preoccupied more with documenting success stories and examples of genuine institutional innovations as a way to celebrate the transformative and creative capacity of the community sector, progressive social movements, and some segments of organized labour than with assessing whether the social economy and the Quebec model of social partnerships amount to an actual realignment of social hierarchies and a reconfiguration of the structure of political and economic power. Evidence from other jurisdictions, however, shows that the kind of state-society partnership and intersectoral collaboration that the social economy calls for does not necessarily resolve problems with regard to equity, access, participation, and democracy but indeed achieves cost reduction at the price of democracy and equity (Vaillancourt-Rosenau 2000).

In the end, the question of whether Quebec can still be hailed as a model of progressive social change and political transformation depends largely on one's expectations of change. To the men and women who work in the field and devote their lives to the advancement of socioeconomic minorities, the marginalized, and the excluded, the inroads made by social economy initiatives may not lead to a fundamental, democratic reconfiguration of societal power relations, but wherever such initiatives have been successful, the fruits of empowerment have been real, if limited or narrow in scope. The enabling of individuals or local communities may amount to nothing more than incremental, slow-paced social change, but it is better than no change at all. To others for whom genuine and significant social change and political transformation must necessarily imply the disappearance of old social hierarchies and the abandonment of the capitalist market logic as the guiding norm of social transactions, Quebec's experience with the social economy can only be a disappointing one. It is incumbent upon them to formulate an appropriate alternative and wage the battle for it.

NOTES

1 For a fuller account of the emergence and establishment of the *Chantier de l'économie sociale*, see Ninacs (2000).
2 For a full discussion of the concepts of social solidarity, see Silver (1994). On social cohesion, see Bernard (1999) and Saint-Martin (1999).
3 The fourteen variables contained within each of these categories are as follows. Under *employment* (that is, the freedom to work) are the employment rate, the index of precarious employment (part-time and self-employment), and the duration of unemployment; under *earnings* (that

is, the freedom to earn wages and salaries) are average real weekly wages and salaries, labour compensation as a share of the total provincial GDP at market prices, and the real minimum wage; under *equality* and *security* (that is, the freedom to enjoy a high degree of economic stability, fairness, and security) are the equality of income distribution measured by the top-to-bottom quintile ratio of after-tax income, the earnings gap between male and female workers, the earnings gap between hourly employees and salaried workers, the family poverty rate, real government spending on public programs per capita, real social assistance benefits, and job leavers as a share of total employment (Brown and Stanford 2000, 9–10).

4   Over a hundred years ago the German-Italian sociologist Roberto Michels observed how political parties and movements or trade unions that emerged with strong socialistic or democratic tendencies eventually become overwhelmed by organizational imperatives that set the leadership apart from the grass roots or rank and file. Leaders who at first are merely the executive organs of the collective become independent of its control and instead gain control over it. Though the external forms of democracy may be maintained, underneath, oligarchic attitudes become more and more pronounced and the original democratic or emancipatory goal that drove the organization in the first place subsides. It can be argued that the Parti Québécois is a case in point. Although it clearly embodied and represented the political aspirations of most of the Quebec nationalist and social-democratic left in its early years, it hardly did so after it had spent sixteen of the past twenty-five years in power. Although party supporters still argue that the party remains true to its leftist roots, its social and economic policies are in fact more characteristic of a neoliberal agenda than of a purely social-democratic one.

5   For a well-informed and clear discussion of this general process of economic transformation and of its impact in Canada, see the contribution of Sam Gindin and Jim Stanford in this volume (chap. 17).

6   One well publicized example of the obstacles workers in precarious employment situations meet in their attempt at getting unionized is the case of two McDonald's restaurants in the Montreal area. One in fact was shut down and demolished following a successful unionization drive. Such a reaction is meant to discourage workers in precarious employment from seeking unionization. In Quebec nearly three in four enterprises providing employment to the labour force are small or medium-size. In fact, a large proportion of the local economy is driven by this kind of economic unit. According to a March 2001 Groupe Everest survey commissioned by the National Bank and La Presse, more than 80 percent of those enterprises believe that keeping unions out of the picture is the best way to maintain healthy labour relations. This is consistent with the

pressures Quebec business is currently exercising on the government to
relax its labour code with regard to outsourcing and subcontracting.

7 The notion of the institutional left is used here as short-hand to include
the segments of Quebec's progressive forces that either collaborate with
the government, participate in the formulation of its socioeconomic policies, or adhere to a flexible, left-leaning agenda that they believe can be
accomplished within the prevailing institutional structures. The labour
movement as it is embodied in Quebec's three major union federations
stands largely as the figurehead of what I call in this chapter the institutional left.

8 For a general overview of the political emergence of what seems like a
new left in Quebec, see the dossier published in *La Presse* on 26, 27, and
28 May 2001.

9 Since then, the RAP officially became a political party, in June 2001,
changing its name (but not its acronym) to Rassemblement pour l'alternative progressiste. In June 2002, RAP joined forces with the Parti pour la
démocratie socialiste (PDS) and the Partie communiste du Québec (PCQ)
to create l'Union des forces progressistes (UFP), which is likely to run in
at least a dozen ridings in the next provincial election. The UFP stands
against giving in to neoliberal globalization and proposes extensive measures to eliminate poverty, foster gender parity in employment, reinvest
massively in public health and welfare services, achieve proportional representation in the electoral process, and promote Quebec sovereignty.

REFERENCES

Authier, Philip. 1999. "So What Is This Quebec Model?" *Gazette*, 15 June
1999.

Bernard, Paul. 1999. *Social Cohesion: A Critique.* CPRN discussion paper no. F-09.
Ottawa: Canadian Policy Research Network.

Boivin, Louise, and Mark Fortier, eds. 1998. *L'économie sociale: L'avenir d'une
illusion.* Montreal: Fides.

Bourque, G.L. 2000. *Le modèle québécois de développement.* Sainte-Foy: Presses de
l'Université du Québec.

Boyer, Marcel. 2001. *La performance économique du Québec: Constats et défis.* Montreal: CIRANO.

Brown, Amanda, and Jim Stanford. 2000. *Flying without a Net: The "Economic
Freedom" of Working Canadians in 2000.* Ottawa: Canadian Centre for Policy
Alternatives.

Chantier de l'économie sociale. 2001. *De nouveau, nous osons: Document de posi-
tionnement stratégique.* Montreal: Chantier de l'économie sociale.

Comeau, Y., L. Favreau, B. Lévesque, and M. Mendell. 2001. *Emploi, économie
sociale, développement local: Les nouvelles filières.* Sainte-Foy: Presses de l'Université du Québec.

CRISES. 2000. *Un cas exemplaire de nouvelle gouvernance.* Montreal: Fonds de solidarité FTQ.

Favreau, Louis, and Carol Saucier. 1996. "Economie sociale et développement économique communautaire: De nouvelles réponses à la crises de l'emploi?" *Economie et solidarités* 28(1): 5–19.

Fontan, Jean-Marc, and Eric Shragge. 2000. "Tendencies, Tensions and Visions in the Social Economy." In Eric Shragge and Jean-Marc Fontan, eds., *Social Economy. International Debates and Perspectives,* 1–15. Montreal: Black Rose Books.

Graefe, Peter. 2001. "Whose Social Economy? Debating New State Practices in Quebec." *Critical Social Policy* 21(1): 35–58.

Jessop, Bob. 2000. "Globalisation, Entrepreneurial Cities and the Social Economy." In Pierre Hamel, Henri Lustiger-Thaler, and Margit Mayer, eds., *Urban Movement in a Globalising Order,* 81–100. London: Routledge.

Lévesque, Benoit, and Marguerite Mendell. 1999. "L'économie sociale au Québec: Éléments théoriques et empiriques pour le débat et la recherche." *Lien social et politique* 41: 105–18.

– 2000. *La création d'entreprises par les chômeurs et les sans-emploi: Le rôle de la microfinance.* Research report submitted to the International Labour Organization. Montreal: PROFONDS-CRISES.

Mendell, Marguerite. 2000. "Local Finance in a Global Economy: Palliative or Panacea?" In Pierre Hamel, Henri Lustiger-Thaler, and Margit Mayer, eds., *Urban Movement in a Globalising Order,* 101–22. London: Routledge.

– 2002. "The Social Economy in Quebec: Discourse and Strategies." In Abigail B. Bakan and Eleanor MacDonald, eds., *Critical Political Studies: Debates and Dialogues from the Left,* 319–49. Montreal and Kingston: McGill-Queen's University Press.

Mendell, Marguerite, B. Lévesque, and R. Rouzier, 2000. *New Forms of Financing Social Economy Enterprises and Organisations in Quebec.* Paper presented at the OECD/LEED Forum on Social Innovations, International Seminar, The Role of the Non-Profit Sector in Local Development: New Trends. Washington, DC, 11–12 September. Unpublished.

Ninacs, William. 2000. "Social Economy: A Practitioner's Viewpoint." In Jean-Marc Fontan and Eric Shragge, eds., *Social Economy: International Debates and Perspectives,* 130–58. Montreal: Black Rose Books.

Paquet, R. 1999. "Les emplois de l'économie sociale: Forme de démocratisation du travail ou exploitation d'une main-d'oeuvre qualifiée." *Economie et solidarités,* 30(1): 78–94.

Parti Québécois. 1999. *Vers la souveraineté: Assurer l'avenir du modèle québécois.* Montreal: Conseil exécutif national du Parti Québécois.

Pichette, Jean. 2001. "Le refus de l'ordre global." *Relations* 668 (April–May): 12–15.

Piotte, Jean-Marc. 1987. *La communauté perdue: Petite histoire des militantismes.* Montreal: VLB.

– 1998. *Du combat au partenariat.* Montreal: Nota Bene.

Ravet, Jean-Claude. 2001. "De la Nation inc. à un projet démocratique." *Relations* 668 (April–May): 21–2.

Saint-Martin, Denis. 1999. "Variations sur le thème de la cohésion sociale." *Lien social et politiques – RIAC* 41 (spring): 87–95.

Salée, Daniel, and William Coleman. 1997. "The Challenges of the Quebec Question: Paradigm, Counter-paradigm and ...?" In Wallace Clement, ed., *Understanding Canada: Building on the New Political Economy*, 262–85. Montreal: McGill-Queen's University Press.

Shields, John, and Mitchell Evans. 1998. *Shrinking the State: Globalization and Public Administration "Reform."* Halifax: Fernwood Publishing.

Shragge, Eric, and Jean-Marc Fontan. 2000. "Workfare and Community Economic Development in Montreal: Community and Work in the Late Twentieth Century." In Pierre Hamel, Henri Lustiger-Thaler, and Margit Mayer, eds., *Urban Movement in a Globalising Order*, 123–38. London: Routledge.

Silver, Hilary. 1994. "Social Exclusion and Social Solidarity: Three Paradigms." *International Labour Review* 133(5/6): 531–78.

Vaillancourt-Rosenau, Pauline, ed. 2000. *Public Private Policy Partnerships.* Cambridge, MA: MIT Press.

3 Decolonization and Recolonization in Canada

JOYCE GREEN

INTRODUCTION

Canada in its current form is a model of how a colonial enterprise established by the fusion of commercial and state power and by the occasional application of military force has evolved to become mostly pluralistic, tolerant, democratic, and prosperous. Yet despite its successes, Canada is profoundly challenged by political and economic forces. The former threaten to reconfigure the state's sovereignty and geographic parameters; the latter, to transcend state sovereignty in profoundly undemocratic ways. At the historic juncture when Canada seems to have the most potential to move to a postcolonial relationship with Aboriginal nations, nationalist forces seek to transform Quebec from a province with a history of colonization to a sovereign state. Simultaneously, while Canada has attained constitutional maturity and, presumably, a measure of constitutional peace consequent to the repatriation of the 1867 Constitution Act and the adoption of the 1982 Constitution Act and Charter of Rights and Freedoms, the process has germinated contradictory forces of fragmentation that react against the perceived lack of democracy and recognition and the consolidations of elite domination, inherent in recent constitutional history.[1] That is, elite political practices consistent with federalism as constitutionally governed and politically negotiated relations between governments are challenged because these practices and the decisions produced by them are not, prima facie, transparent, democratic, representative, and inclusive. Nor are the superficially democratic processes that legitimate representative democracy (the "first past the post" electoral system) satisfactory to those who find themselves irrelevant within the federal electoral calculus.

Therefore, the stability historically produced by executive federalism and plurality representation is challenged and rendered unstable precisely because these practices have only a weak nexus with democracy. The new constitution has been a catalyst for a diffuse demand by several cross-cutting sectors of Canadians for democratic participation in directing the future practices and structures of the state. Finally, the tensions between federalism and democracy, between Aboriginal decolonization and elite self-preservation, and between incompatible conceptions of Canada and of Quebec are all played out in a political universe now both circumscribed and scripted by transnational capital(ists) through the force called "globalization." Part of the popular opposition to the politics of globalization is the international indigenous movement, which identifies itself as an anticolonial struggle in a contemporary phase.[2]

In this chapter I explore some of these tensions and make some prescriptions for a postcolonial political future. I show how colonialism, an imposed exploitative relationship characterised by the appropriation of others' economic, political, and cultural resources, continues in the processes of globalization. I argue that putatively libratory initiatives such as "self-government" are often constructed to incorporate Aboriginal communities in capitalist relations of production and to deny other socioeconomic visions. Advanced capitalism is essentially colonizing civil society and state sovereignty. Inherent in this critique is the proposition that the pressures the globalization of capital is placing on the state constitute a dangerous threat to citizenship, decolonization, and sovereignty.

COLONIAL FOUNDATIONS

Colonization, initiated by imperialism, forms the foundation of Project Canada. Colonization is not only about the physical occupation of someone else's land but also about the appropriation of others' political authority, cultural self-determination, economic capacity, and strategic location. That is, colonialism is a profoundly exploitative relationship to the benefit of one at the expense of the Other (Green 1995; but see also Flanagan 2000). Exploring it involves "the relationship between sovereignty, power, and identity, and how it serves to constitute the seemingly naturalized and presupposed boundaries of the modern state" (Bruyneel 1999) in ways that take capitalism and class as seriously as sociocultural identities. Aboriginal liberation is at core a challenge to the state's claim to occupy all space for sovereignty. It is grounded in prior and preeminent claims to that same sovereignty(Asch and Zlotkin 1997; Macklem 2001).[3]

Contemporary Canada, with all of its subnational governments and communities, is a consequence of that original and continuing colonial relationship. The current vision of the state, consolidated in 1867, is premised on colonialism by way of the 1869 National Policy which was itself premised on appropriation of Aboriginal lands and resources and subordination of Aboriginal peoples (Green 1995).[4]

In the classic international legal formulation of colonialism, self-determination, or decolonization, occurs when the colonizer "goes home." On this view, colonization occurred somewhere other than home, and the colonizing and colonized populations remained distinct and separable. For example, British colonial rule in India ended when Britain withdrew from governing India and Indians replaced the British in political and bureaucratic institutions. As part of this understanding, international conventions constructed the "blue-water" thesis, which held that colonialism occurred overseas from the "mother country" and that self-determination was thus not a right of the domestic or internal populations of any state. However, this formulation has subsequently been eroded, most notably by the UN Covenants' shared article 1 protection of self-determination as the basis for "legal protection of human rights" and by the international consensus on self-determination as a human right (Falk 2000, 98). Now, self-determination can also mean autonomy within an existing state; decolonization can include negotiated arrangements for such new relationships.

The colonial relationship in Canada and in other settler states is, first and foremost, between indigenous and settler populations, both of which are permanently resident in one territory. Now, in the second millennium, the objective of decolonization in Canada cannot be the eviction of the colonizer: settler populations are permanently here. Additionally, indigenous and settler people have a long history of involvement, resulting in diverse hybrid populations whose ancestry includes both (Said 1979, 1993). The populations are not only "each other" but also both, and diverse origins exist even within families. Obviously, separation of colonizer and colonized is politically and practically impossible.

Decolonization, however, is possible. Rather than separation, decolonization requires the inclusion of colonized peoples in institutions of power, the design of which in politically significant ways reflects the priorities and cultural assumptions of the colonized as well as those of the colonizer. In other words, Canadian federalism, the constitution, and public politics must reflect indigenous histories, imagination, and aspirations as thoroughly as they now reflect colonial priorities. Indeed, John Borrows (2000) argues that only "Aboriginal control of Canadian affairs" will be truly libratory. He means this not as an exclusive power eliminating other Canadians' franchise but as an expression of the primacy of Aboriginal citizenship grounded in the Aboriginal relationship with the land and committed to a viable common future.

Decolonization in the Canadian context requires, first, the understanding of the historical colonial process. Then, it requires substantive power-sharing to ameliorate the inequitable, unjust, and illegal appropriation of indigenous peoples' territories, resources, and political autonomy. Decolonization implies fundamental change in the Canadian federation, constitution, and political culture. Generating a public consensus (or "buy-in") on a decolonization project should be high on all governments' agendas, because only popular support will enable such a transformative initiative.

Colonial activity in Canada (and elsewhere) was motivated by the search for wealth for mercantile and capitalist investors and their political sponsors, and decolonization implies wealth sharing with those who had their lands and wealth appropriated. As national chief of the Assembly of First Nations Matthew Coon-Come said, "I'd like to push the issue of a redistribution of lands and resources and call upon Canada. Are they willing to allow First Nations peoples to share the wealth?" (CP 2000).

Decolonization requires structural and procedural changes. Canadian federalism, which is designed so that the national and provincial governments hold all the jurisdiction of the Crown according to the constitutional distribution of powers, must be transformed to include a third order, Aboriginal government jurisdiction.[5] This, in turn, will challenge us all to deal with overlapping jurisdictions and political interests in ways that will have to be more collaborative, less confrontational. The reality of large urban Aboriginal populations (approximately 70 per cent of Aboriginal peoples do not live on reserves) suggests that decolonization is not only about land claims settlements and "self" governments: it also requires new formulae for sharing political and economic power within mainstream communities. Fiscal arrangements that provincial and federal governments have argued about for decades will become more complex with the inclusion of Aboriginal governments and as mainstream governments confront the reality that they are obliged to provide the conditions for citizenship rights, human rights, and Aboriginal rights to their Aboriginal constituencies. Current government-corporate relations

will be transformed as Aboriginal voices participate in shaping new
paradigms of development, ones that are sometimes critical of the
shared myth of liberalism and socialism: that human development is
an ineluctable trajectory of beneficial improvement correlated with
"our" mastery and exploitation of nature.

Finally, the cultural corpus of Canada will have to change to accommodate a different relationship with Aboriginal peoples. No longer
will it be enough to romanticize or demonize "Indians": entertainment, news media, literature, and the academic canon must be transformed by the inclusion of Aboriginal perspectives, knowledge, and
respect for contemporary Aboriginal citizens, communities, workers,
and neighbours. Put bluntly, white Canada's racism must be challenged by all those who stand in solidarity against colonialism.

ABORIGINAL RIGHTS AND CANADIAN SOVEREIGNTY

Constitutional law has been a bulwark both of the colonial state and,
more recently, of Aboriginal rights. Before 1982 Aboriginal and treaty
rights were decided by the courts based on "the rules of the ruler": on
precedent, the common law inheritance from Britain, and on legislation passed by Parliament. Even with the impossible straitjacket of this
legal tradition, Aboriginal and treaty rights posed challenges to both
federal and provincial governments. A most profound challenge was
laid in the 1973 *Calder* case, in which the Nisga'a people of the Nass
River Valley in British Columbia argued their case for Aboriginal title
through to the Supreme Court of Canada. The court split, with three
justices supporting the Nisga'a claim, three denying it, and one ruling
on a technicality. However, the entire court accepted that Aboriginal
title existed and that the Crown must take account of it. The decision
signalled to the federal and provincial governments that Aboriginal
title, albeit undefined, must be taken account of. It helped create the
political conditions for the success of Aboriginal lobbying for inclusion of "existing aboriginal and treaty rights" in the 1982 constitution.

After 1982, the constitutional recognition of "existing Aboriginal and
treaty rights" (section 35 of the *Constitution Act, 1982*) elevated the
subject to a matter of constitutional significance. No longer can mainstream governments, citizens, and the media refuse to take indigenous
claims seriously. One important consequence is the 1999 Nisga'a Treaty,
negotiated between the Nisga'a Nation, the federal government, and
the then NDP government of British Columbia, a constitutionally recognized contemporary treaty with important legal, political, and economic
implications (Rynard 2000; various articles in *BC Studies* 1998–99).

Yet the 1982 constitution has not been read as decolonization by the federal and provincial governments, because the legitimacy of Canadian sovereignty, the Crown's title to land, and the Crown's claim to resources are still treated by law and politics as beyond critique. Indeed, the Supreme Court of Canada ruled in 1997 that the Crown's sovereignty has never been in any doubt (*Delgamuukw* v. *British Columbia*, SCC 1997). In treaty and land claims negotiations, the colonial governments offer to "give" Aboriginal claimants land and a measure of jurisdiction, but they do not offer to recognize preexisting Aboriginal jurisdiction, wrongly preempted by the state. And with whatever land and cash settlements they obtain, Aboriginal peoples are expected to buy into the capitalist market paradigm of development.

The colonial Canadian state, then, maintains its claim to radical title, to the full package of sovereignty, despite the reality of Aboriginal peoples whom the state has dispossessed. It also claims Aboriginal peoples as citizens, a status conferred late in the Canadian citizenship story and not always accepted by Aboriginal people. Citizenship, characterised by rights and duties and by constitutionally affirmed identities and belonging and implying autonomy and democracy (Trimble 1999) is still in need of a capacity to affirm Canadians' identities in ways that transform Project Canada into a collective imagining not structured by domination and exclusion.

THE ERA OF GLOBALIZATION

The role of the state in which citizenship is located is changing in response to the restructuring impulses initiated by the globalization of capital. At the precise moment in Canadian history when citizenship seems most inclusive, authentic, and emancipatory, the content and capacity of citizenship is being challenged by a the neoliberal ideology that provides the cultural logic for globalization. While decolonization impulses issue from Aboriginal peoples and from Quebec nationalists, recolonization impulses are also flowing from politico-economic imperatives inherent in transnational trade agreements and disciplinary mechanisms and from the raw power inherent in the instantaneous mobility of transnational capital. That is, as some Aboriginals, especially status Indians on reserves, gain a measure of autonomy in relation to the colonial state, the state itself is colonized by transnational capitalists through the mechanisms of transnational trade agreements and trade organisations. Additionally, the small accommodations achieved by some Aboriginal people are libratory within the context of historical oppression, but only marginally libratory relative to Aboriginal sovereignty before contact or relative to the aspirations articulated in the 1996 Royal Commission on Aboriginal Peoples. Finally, Aboriginal liberation on occasion resembles the ultimate in assimilation, as certain elites negotiate arrangements that effectively consolidate the institutions and ideology of the state and of contemporary capitalism into "self-government" agreements and memoranda of understanding with provincial governments.

Neoliberalism, the ideology of globalization, advocates minimalist governments whose primary objective is ensuring the conditions for profitability unimpeded by public ownership or public policy by means of regulatory regimes (Green 1996). The globalization of capital and of capitalism has resulted in controversial transformations of the Keynesian welfare state, including privatization of core pubic services and labour market deregulation (see Jenson, Mahon, and Phillips and Fudge and Vosko, this volume), creating its neoliberal descendant. Neither federalism nor the state itself are immune to neoliberal demands for the imperative of economic rationalism, even at the cost of fracturing federal processes, constitutional obligations,[6] citizenship capacity,[7] or sociopolitical coherence.[8]

The premier disciplinarian, the World Trade Organisation, which is designed to facilitate global trade and member state harmonisation with WTO trade conditions, requires member states to restrict domestic policy to the "least trade-restrictive" formulation. Commercial relations in the international arena, which are dominated by transnational corporate players, are paramount to domestic policy concerns, and governments are bound to abide by the WTO regime. For example, the WTO has ruled that Canada must scrap the Auto Pact (Scoffield and Keenan 1999) (it expired in February 2001) and that Canadian farming and dairy marketing cooperatives, marketing boards, and the Canadian Wheat Board break international trade rules (Scoffield 1999). The WTO is also considering how and when to require member states to commodify a host of public goods and common resources, including education, health care, and water.[9] The globalised economy is operating in an emerging regime of mechanisms designed to regulate not only commodities, services, and capital but, more fundamentally, states and citizens. A NAFTA tribunal, for example, has ruled in one recent case that "Canada must defy its access-to-information law," effectively prohibiting Canada from complying with its own laws to the extent of their conflict with NAFTA provisions (Chase 2002, A10). Trade and investment have become unimpeachable imperatives, guaranteed by the WTO, NAFTA, and the GATT, and no doubt by the proposed Free Trade Agreement of the Americas (FTAA).

A number of lobby groups are advocating a "common currency" with the United States. First raised by the Bloc Quebecois in early 1999 as part of the "winning conditions" for a sovereignty referendum, the notion was quickly adopted by the Business Council on National Issues[10] (now renamed the Canadian Council of Chief Executives – according to the council's website, "Building a stronger Canada economically and socially is our national mandate. Helping to make Canada and our enterprises number one around the world is our global mandate").[11] The notion was also adopted by the right-wing C.D. Howe Institute and has been raised with approval in the business and op-ed pages of the *Globe and Mail* (for example, Scoffield 2000, 2001). Adopting a "common currency" in the free trade zone of the Americas inevitably means adopting the U.S. dollar, thereby compromising other states' domestic autonomy with respect to fiscal policy and their economic sovereignty. The logic of this notion is premised on the precedence of economic, especially investment, interests over all other interests embodied in the state. In sum, state sovereignty and democratic citizenship are being redefined by global capitalism.

FEDERALISM UNDER FIRE

Federalism, of course, is an arrangement whereby the divided sovereignty of the state is exercised by two or more orders of government, each being sovereign within its jurisdictional sphere. The Canadian system of constitutional law and judicial interpretation is augmented by informal but effective political arrangements (executive and co-operative federalism) that permit continuous conversation between the various orders of government about matters of mutual concern.

Canadian federalism has permitted its constituent components to renegotiate historic assumptions, though not always easily. Initially adopted as a political compromise in response to the reality of cultural and regional diversity (Rocher and Rouillard 1999), federalism has allowed some identities to thrive, while others have been rendered forever peripheral. A process as well as a structure, federalism is a perpetual negotiation about the nature of power relations within the Canadian state and about the nature of the state itself. What it means to be Canadian, to be a Yukoner, to be an Aboriginal Canadian from northern Saskatchewan is partly defined by the federal relationship, even when that relationship is contested. This shapes not only federal relations but the content of Canadian citizenship, the Marshallian trilogy of political, social, and economic rights,[12] with a fourth component encompassing identities and civic commitments to valuing different identities and, arguably, a fifth component that is grounded in citizenship as a verb. This last component is conceived as citizenship practised as political engagement among citizens, between citizens and the state government and corporate apparatus, and between collectivities bonded by nonstate-based solidarities (such as transnational social movements) grounded in values associated with relationship within and between communities and with the ecosystem and the global village.

There is a weak nexus within Canadian federalism between governments and democracy: federalism has always been about the jurisdictional powers of governments and governments' relationships with each other. It is this privileging of governments as political agents that is challenged by citizens organised and empowered by the 1982 constitution into what Alan Cairns has called "Charter Canadians." (Trimble 1998; Cairns 1992, 63, 74, 81). The conversations about federalism and citizenship are contested formulations about values, agency, and sovereignty. These conversations, though, have the dignity of human relationship in a political context. They are conversations that cannot be held – are not relevant – in a context limited by the considerations of trade, investment, and global economic regulatory regimes.

The federal and provincial governments have been the agents as well as the subjects of federal processes. Other governments – territorial, municipal, Aboriginal – are subordinate under the current constitutional regime. Their representatives may sit at the table, but they do so at the pleasure of the first ministers. They may be consulted, but they have no right to voice, vote, or veto. Yet decisions about jurisdictional disputes, trade and international treaties; the exercise of constitutional powers; and the consolidation of neoliberal practices all profoundly affect these subordinate governments and those they represent. And while one-third of Canadians support "self-government," there is no "clear idea within the public's mind regarding what type of powers" would be held by such governments (Martin and Adams 2000) and hence no reliable public support.

The substitution of neoliberal rationales for those of the Keynesian welfare state has legitimated a reduction in federal economic support for provincial, municipal, and territorial governments, while citizen demands on those same governments have simultaneously increased, because of neoliberal governments' general retreat from funding the social safety net. The neoliberal state is less involved with the Marshallian trilogy of conditions that have come to define Canadian citizenship and arguably will become equivalently less relevant to citizens. Not all provincial governments are equally able to guarantee these citizenship minimums, a situation resulting in fragmented entitlements depending on provincial capacity to pay for services or on ideological commitment to public provision of social goods. Nor are provincial governments dedicated to protecting the conditions for national and regional diversity that initiated Canadian federalism (Rocher and Rouillard 1999, 24), much less to inclusion of Aboriginal governments. They are dedicated to their own particular interests, not to the general interest that includes diversity as a value. This suggests a structural and normative need for the federal government as guarantor of the general interest, of Canadian citizenship, and of Aboriginal and treaty rights minimums.

Aboriginal governments are finding themselves subjected to non-Aboriginal challenges to funding, accountability, and democracy. Some of these challenges are clearly motivated by ideological hostility to Aboriginal rights and to decolonization. Neoliberalism grounds arguments that (implicitly non-Aboriginal) "taxpayers" should not underwrite "special rights" for communities that are impliedly non-contributory, irresponsible, and illiberal (e.g., Cooper and Bercuson 2001). Indeed, the Canadian Taxpayers Federation (CTF) (Canada's watchdog on government spending, according to its website),[13] arguably a "special interest group" that presents itself as a broad-based public interest group, ran a prominent story in its propaganda organ, *The Taxpayer*, arguing that the Treaty 8 tax exemption for Treaty 8 band members gives preferential economic status to, potentially, "hundreds of thousands" of race-based Indians and, hence, advances inequality and economically threatens the survival of Saskatchewan (CP, 2001a,C4).

The CTF gained intervener status in the federal court case hearing the claim of Treaty 8 tax exemption; the judge characterised the CTF's views on this matter as "ill-informed, misguided and inflammatory" and "flawed or without merit" (Parker 2002, A12). Nevertheless, the CTF managed to get national news coverage of its proposition that federal money spent on First Nations is poorly spent and should go to individual Indians rather than to their band governments, which could then tax it back. The CTF also mocked the notion that there is underfunding of First Nations (CP 2001a, A9). To disseminate its views online, the CTF has set up a Centre for Aboriginal Policy Change, accessible via its website. The CTF is regularly quoted and consulted by mainstream media in Saskatchewan and elsewhere, out of all proportion to its intellectual and democratic significance, thus lending an undeserved credibility to its opinions on all manner of social and economic issues.

Recolonization propaganda such as that of the CTF uses the language of equality without regard to historic oppression. It talks of fiscal accountability without regard to the economics of colonial expropriation. It is designed not for Aboriginal consumption but for dominant white voters who support political parties and policy measures that continue to work to the advantage of colonial and capitalist interests and against Aboriginal peoples.

DECOLONIZATION OR RECOLONIZATION?

While the Canadian state mutates in regard to federalism, constitutional parameters, ideology, and the international political economy, Aboriginal governments are struggling to emerge as entities whose legitimacy and authority are as significant in respect of land and certain jurisdictions as are the two constitutional orders of government. They have the potential to transform the federal structure into a trilateral form. Section 35 of the constitution arguably recognizes and protects Aboriginal governments., although the nature, structure, and jurisdictional content of those governments is still indeterminate. It is in the process of clarification that Canada can move to decolonization or, perhaps, to recolonization. Recolonization limits citizenship capacity in favour of consumer status, while it privileges market imperatives over state sovereignty (and hence, policy autonomy) and normative claims for human needs. For Aboriginal communities recolonization involves the blunting of libratory impulses and rights-based political regimes by co-optation into nonconstitutional governmental forms (self-administration) and by selling the myth of economic equality through incorporation into the dominant economic and political regime. Decolonization involves the process of Aboriginal liberation from the oppressive colonial relationship with the state. It has taken several forms that vary in their degree of political autonomy from or incorporation into the colonial and federal state. Perhaps the best-known, but very different, governance initiatives are contemporary land claims and treaties such as exist in the Yukon and with the Nisga'a in British Columbia; and the Indian Act revision process touted by the federal government since 2000.[14]

The Yukon Umbrella Agreement between the fourteen Yukon First Nations, the federal government, and the Yukon government provides for a significant degree of political, economic, and cultural autonomy for the Aboriginal parties, on a land base that is differentiated into lands on which First Nation law is paramount, lands on which there is co-jurisdiction with the Yukon government, and lands on which Yukon jurisdiction is paramount.[15] It provides for regulatory regimes that are determined and implemented with First Nations participation. It provides for resource sharing in a variety of formulas on the different categories of lands. It preserves the Aboriginal rights of the First Nations and attracts constitutional protection. The Yukon Agreement enjoys broad and deep support among the First Nations but also in the non-Aboriginal Yukon community. Nation-specific governance regimes flow from the Umbrella Final Agreement, negotiated by each of the fourteen First Nations. As of February 2002, eight of the fourteen had completed governance negotiations (Moorcroft 2002). In the negotiation phase the government of Yukon made it a priority to build support for the agreement in the non-Aboriginal population. This, coupled with the reduced federal constitutional conflict because of Yukon's territorial status, led to a significant degree of societal consensus supporting the agreement and, arguably, supporting a decolonization initiative.

The Nisga'a Treaty Agreement in British Columbia is fraught with many more political difficulties, difficulties between the dominant colonial society and Nisga'a communities and between Nisga'a and other Aboriginal communities and organisations and difficulties within the Nisga'a Nation.[16] The treaty concludes efforts that were first begun by the Nisga'a in 1887 to have their sovereignty respected. Reviled by the federal Reform Party, the British Columbia Liberals (the government of British Columbia at the time of writing) and by the British Columbia Reform Party, the treaty is in fact considered by many indigenous peoples to be an inadequate and overly restrictive framework for developing institutions to protect inherent rights and cultural differences. While the agreement has been hailed as the positive conclusion of a century-old fight by the Nisga'a for accommodation by the colonizers, it has also been damned for its impulse towards assimilation into the colonial federal regime and, conversely, for its potential for race/ist segregation from the dominant society. It provides a land base that is less than a tenth of traditional Nisga'a territory, while acknowledging provincial control of the other nine-tenths, and it subordinates the Nisga'a to the existing federal relationship. This is consistent with the Supreme Court decision in *Delgamuukw,* (1997 153 D.L.R. (4th) at 240–1), which held that section 35 Aboriginal rights must be reconciled with Crown (that is, colonial state) sovereignty. Meanwhile, the language of equality has been invoked by the British Columbia Liberals, the British Columbia Reform Party, and the federal Reform Party (now the Canadian Alliance) to object to rights-based accommodations with First Nations. The Reform Party placed nearly five hundred (unsuccessful) amendments to the Nisga'a Treaty before the House of Commons, in what was clearly an obstructionist move. It has called the treaty "race-based apartheid," warned of the horrors of non-Nisga'a citizens being subjected to Nisga'a law, and argued that the treaty constitutes a constitutional amendment.

More prominently, the federal government's preference for Indian

Act revision has a strong whiff of recolonization to it. The minister of indian affairs is "asking" bands and the Assembly of First Nations (AFN) to participate in consultations about how to revise the Indian Act. The AFN and the vast majority of band governments have rejected the process as an ex post facto means of legitimating federal policy preferences and for failing to meet the already stated political and economic issues of band governments. Despite the AFN's snub, at the time of writing the minister insists consultation will proceed, with or without the chiefs' blessing. In doing this, the minister is refusing to accept the chiefs, speaking through the AFN, as the legitimate political representatives of First Nations people on reserves and is effectively undermining the chiefs by going directly to on- and off-reserve communities with the Indian Act initiative.

As some Aboriginal communities negotiate frameworks for exercising a measure of self-determination within Canada, others are ignored. Bands recognised in the Indian Act have been the object of federal government policy and of federal and provincial negotiations on treaties and governance agreements. Inuit people have, for policy purposes, been treated like Indians by the federal government. Status Indians who do not live on reserves are marginalised by these processes, while Metis and nonstatus Indians are utterly ignored by them. [17] Not all Aboriginal peoples benefit equally from Aboriginal and treaty rights or from state policy. For example, in *Marshall* v. *Canada* (S.C.C. 1999) the right to fish is recognised for those Mi'kmaqs who have status under the federal Indian Act membership regime.[18] Nonstatus Indians, equally inheritors of the 1760 treaty upheld by the Supreme Court, have been prevented by both state forces and status Mi'kmaqs from exercising a treaty right to fish.

Contemporary examples of tensions between decolonization and recolonization in the crucible of globalization and the context of federalism present themselves across Canada. Consider the Innu communities, whose traditional territory includes Voisey's Bay, touted as the largest nickel find in the world. Exploitation of the resource will certainly have an impact on the traditional hunting economy and unceded territory of the Innu, yet there is little evidence that the Innu are contemplated as major players for the stakes of high-paid, unionised jobs, royalties, and profits.

Canada's newest province, Newfoundland (now formally Newfoundland and Labrador) entered Confederation amidst still-unresolved controversy about the percentage of the popular vote in favour and the integrity of the process itself. Never an economic powerhouse, Newfoundland and Labrador's primary exports have been codfish and people. The codfish are nearly gone, and many younger folk are leaving the outports and communities that could not economically support them. Newfoundland's last premier, Brian Tobin, placed economic development at the top of his agenda, a priority continued by his successor, Roger Grimes.[19]

It is worth noting that the province has a poor track record for dealing with Aboriginal peoples, beginning with the genocide of the Beothuk and, more recently, the refusal to recognise the existence of the Conn River Mi'kmaqs till a few short years ago. Former premier Brian Peckford was hostile to the inclusion of Aboriginal and treaty rights in the constitution and to the definition of self-government at the four first ministers conferences held pursuant to section 37 of the 1982 constitution. Over the past few years, the misery of the Innu communities at Davis Inlet and Sheshatshiu, manifested by extremely high rates of child substance abuse, neglect, gas sniffing, and suicide, has been documented by the national media. These phenomena are a consequence of what Innu Nation president Peter Penashue has called "Canada's frontal attack" on the Innu (Penashue 2000, A15).

Newfoundland and Labrador's economic vision has included hydroelectric development and mining, both big-ticket investment projects designed for export and consumption elsewhere. The global economy seems promising within this logic. But the province's plans have come up against the equally urgent politics of Aboriginal peoples in Newfoundland. Here, two segregated communities, each united by its own cultural ethos and history, each relatively impoverished in relation to the Canadian norm yet not sharing a sense of common purpose or common future, fail to form a mutually advantageous coalition. Some analysts view Newfoundland and Labrador as peripheral to Project Canada; hence, the federal government's toleration of its stagnant economy. For Aboriginal nations, however, Newfoundland and Labrador was historically and is now a colonial oppressor, while Canada as represented by the federal government is a dubious champion.

Newfoundland and Labrador's hope for another hydro megaproject on the lower Churchill River in Labrador has been confounded by objections by the Innu Nation, just as Quebec's had been by the Cree until February 2002, when the Cree leadership agreed to support the Quebec project in return for certain commitments, including financial commitments. The traditional territories of the Innu include both Newfoundland and Labrador and parts of Quebec. The Innu have been particularly concerned about environmental impacts and the lack of land claims processes (CP, 1999a; Penashue 2000).[20]

Newfoundland and Labrador has high hopes for a world-class nickel mine near Voisey's Bay, but the Innu and Inuit have made it clear that development at Voisey's Bay would have to include land claims settlements and some formula for sharing jobs and wealth with Aboriginal communities. (The Innu apparently decided that such a formula was achieved in 2002 when an agreement was reached including provisions for Innu participation in Inco's development.) In the words of Peter Penashue, "the pace and scale of development must be compatible with our continued use of the land for traditional activities ... If these projects prove compatible with our way of life, and we can get the same rate of return that all Canadians would find fair, then perhaps the projects can proceed" (2000, A15).

The federal government was no Aboriginal ally: the Innu Nation and the Labrador Inuit Association were compelled to go to court to force the federal government to halt development of the Voisey's Bay project until land claims settlements and impact and benefit agreements were concluded.[21] They had to do so despite the conclusion of an environmental review panel under the Canadian Environmental Assessment Act that concluded that the project should not proceed without a land claims agreement in principle and impact and benefit agreements between Inco and Aboriginal peoples (Robinson 1999, B6), and despite an Innu Nation report to the Environmental Assessment Hearings into the proposed mine that concluded that it would not promote sustainable development, that its economic benefits were "overstated," and that the project might "leave a long-lasting economic burden through social disruption and potential for environmental contamination."[22] Finally, then-premier Tobin insisted that Inco should process the ore in Newfoundland, thereby creating some long-term, well-paid jobs and economic stability.

Inco became an indifferent suitor, insisting that it was more cost-effective to ship the ore to Ontario for processing. Negotiations waxed and waned with the international price of nickel. The company also reconsidered its production quotas and time frames, in order to potentially extend the working life of the mine, a matter of concern to environmentalists and Aboriginal communities (Milner 1999, B1). Still, Aboriginal people are worried that jobs and development will go to white Newfoundlanders and Labradorians only, rather than to Aboriginal communities (*Globe and Mail* 1999, A1), and there is also concern that neither Inco nor the provincial government know much about the Aboriginal people in Labrador.[23] Perhaps there will be no jobs at all: as of January 2000, the Newfoundland government broke off negotiations with Inco because the multinational could not prove the effectiveness of its proposed hydrometallurgical ore extraction technology yet insisted on an escape clause permitting it to export ore should the technology be "uneconomic" (Robinson 2000, B1). Inco

has decided to focus its attention elsewhere, citing economic considerations stemming from the provincial government's negotiating position. As of January 2001, Inco was committed to developing the Goro
nickel mine in New Caledonia, where "authorities have agreed in principle to a tax regime involving a 100% tax holiday for the first fifteen
years of production followed by a 50% tax holiday for the next five
years" (Robinson 2001, B1). In 2002, however, all parties – Inco, Newfoundland, Labrador, and the Innu – reached a compromise with measures of some satisfaction to all, aand at the time of writing, mining
development is expected to proceed at Voisey's Bay.

Meanwhile, the Innu Nation has been working on a land claim settlement with the often uncooperative mainstream governments.[24] It
tabled its land selection proposal with the governments of Canada and
Newfoundland in June of 1998 (Innu Nation 1999). However, governments are less interested in settling the outstanding debts of colonialism
than in negotiating relationships with corporate interests such as Inco.
This pattern continues elsewhere; consider the political and corporate
positioning in relation to global climate change, energy production and
consumption, and developing gas reserves in northern Canada.

Another example of simultaneous decolonization-recolonization
impulses is evident in the debate around the wisdom of gas and oil
development in the Canadian North and the routes by which such
energy would be exported to the American market. The combination
of excessive first-world energy consumption and restricted production
pushed oil and natural gas to unprecedented high prices on the international commodities markets in 2001. Despite the fragile commitments made in the embattled Kyoto Accord for reducing the production of greenhouse gases, American president George W. Bush has
indicated that the United States will neither support Kyoto nor implement public policy to reduce energy consumption. Rather, Bush looks
to expand energy production to keep prices down; to get more gas to
the lower forty-eight states, "the quicker, the better" (McKenna 2001b,
B1); and to keep consumption (and the concomitant production of
greenhouse gases) high (McKenna 2001a, B1; Nguyen 2001b, B6).
Hence, the corporate oil sector's attention is focussed on the Canadian North, both as a source of cheap energy and as a conduit for
energy for Southern markets. But the North is the territory of several
Aboriginal nations, which creates immediate conditions for the tensions between Aboriginal subsistence economies and jurisdictional
interests and for tensions with Canadian environmental policy and
Southern capitalist and non-Aboriginal interests.

There are two possible pipeline routes from the North to the American market. One, which follows the Alaska Highway from Alaska,

through Yukon, and down through Alberta, is predictably favoured by the governments of Alaska and of Yukon; the other, "over-the-top" route (supported by a consortium dominated by Imperial Oil and favoured by the Northwest Territories government) would follow the Mackenzie River Valley south (McKenna 2001a, B1). Both routes traverse Aboriginal territories and both would bring an immediate bonus of well-paid jobs and related economic spin-offs into Northern economies. Both are transit mechanisms to the United States, where, despite the apparent climatological havoc now being wreaked by greenhouse gasses,[25] there is no political will to promote energy conservation or sustainable energy alternatives.

The Mackenzie pipeline route through the Northward Territories would affect the territory of several members of the Dene Nation, the Gwich'in, and the Inuvaluit. As of late June 2001, the Sahtu and the Deh Cho communities, both Dene, were unwilling to sign on to the proposal, preferring instead to consider a rival proposal (Nguyen 2001a, B1). The differences concern the degree of benefit and risk that Aboriginal communities would have in return for making their territories available to the pipeline; they are not quarrels with the environmental, cultural, or economic implications of the pipeline. The Alaska Highway route through Yukon would involve the calving grounds of the Porcupine cariboo, to the detriment of the herd and of the Gwich'in people of Old Crow, who oppose the development.

The world of globalized capitalism drives not only colonial governments but, increasingly, Aboriginal ones. Those who would choose noncapitalist alternatives must maintain support for a vision that is at odds with the dominant culture, political ideology, and economic structure. Perhaps nowhere is this more apparent than in the case of the Lubicon Lake Cree, in Alberta. Alberta is a treaty province, where almost all First Nations are party to Treaties 6, 7, or 8. The Lubicon Lake Cree, however, have a claim against the provincial and federal governments by virtue of constitutionally recognized Aboriginal rights. Although their territory falls within the Treaty 8 territory, the Lubicon band was not approached to sign the treaty originally and has subsequently had great difficulty in getting either the federal or the provincial government to take it seriously. Now, the petroleum and forest resources on the Lubicon's traditional territory are claimed by Alberta by virtue of constitutional law, especially the Natural Resources Transfer Agreement of 1930. The Alberta economy has benefited from the government sale of the rights to exploit these resources to primarily transnational corporations. For example, the Alberta government projected for the provincial treasury a windfall of $2.8 billion above budget projections for fiscal 1999 as a consequence of rising oil and gas prices.[26] That surplus was dwarfed by the surplus for the first quarter of 2001, variously estimated by the provincial treasurer's office at $6.2 or $6.9 billion (CP 1999b, A9).

The Lubicon, however, have not been party to the Alberta government's decisions, nor have they shared in the wealth (Lennarson 2001). Despite the assumption in international law that indigenous peoples are captured by the sovereignty of the states in which they find themselves emmeshed, the United Nations Human Rights Committee (UNHRC) accepted a Lubicon Lake Cree complaint that the oil, gas, and timber "development" on their territories that was "allowed by the federal and provincial governments destroyed the Cree economic base and their ability to pursue their traditional way of life, and thus would destroy their culture" (Magallanes 1999, 256). The UNHRC found Canada to be in violation of article 27 of the International Covenant on Civil and Political Rights (which protects culture) and wrote that "Historical inequities, to which the State party refers, and certain more recent developments threaten the way of life and culture of the Lubicon Lake Band, and constitute a violation of article 27 so long as they continue." (UNHRC 1984, 29). However, while Canada argues that it has met the remedy required by the UNHRC, the Lubicon argue that in fact the remedy was tainted by gross manipulation of fact, and they view the issue as ongoing and critical (Lennarson 2001). The Lubicon may not want to lease oil exploration rights on their traditional territory, even though the government of Alberta has done so and has benefited from these leases and from oil royalties for decades. The Lubicon have never been part of the decision-making process, and they do not benefit from Alberta's booming economy. The traditional hunting and trapping economy of the Lubicon has been devastated by oil exploration and by forest "harvesting" for pulp.

CONTRADICTORY IMPULSES

Colonization defined the historical relationship between Aboriginal peoples and newcomers. The social consequence of colonialism exists in the racist cultural and legal construction of Aboriginals and Others, with little acceptance by either of hybridity. Racism has always provided justification for colonial exploitation and is deeply embedded in the structures of the colonial state. The economic and political consequences of colonialism are evident in the disparities of political and economic power between almost exclusively nonnative male elites and everyone else.

Decolonization occurs when the subordinated peoples successfully contest the conditions of their oppression. They may do so in various ways, by demanding political accommodation, such as inclusion in constitutional and federal processes; by demanding a measure of liberation, using the liberal ideology of the colonial state regarding justice and equality; or by demanding emancipation through the use of international law regarding decolonization, self-determination, and rights discourse.

Despite the call by the Royal Commission on Aboriginal Peoples in 1996 for a renegotiated relationship between Canada and Aboriginal peoples, the federal government has shown no appetite for creating and joining such a process. Rather than dealing with land/resource rights claims arising from Canada's illegitimate expropriation of Aboriginal lands, government and mainstream media focus on public policy that would attend to some of the social pathologies that are a consequence of the harms done by colonization. While also important, the second objective is no substitute for the first, though it is considerably less politically contentious.

Democracy is found in the practices of citizens in relation to public life. The popularity of democracy as an ideology lies in its potential as a shield against elite oppression and in its potential for creating political legitimacy through inclusive participation. But in Canada state policy and rhetoric are supportive of Aboriginal rights if liberation imposes no cost to the dominant society and antipathetic if the price of liberation includes sharing power and wealth. Non-Aboriginal Canadians are unwilling to use democracy to demand that the state move to the new relationship prescribed by the Royal Commission on Aboriginal Peoples. Aboriginal Canadians find themselves politically marginalised from effectively making those demands by the structural realities of the plurality electoral system and the federal constitutional order. Democracy, then, has been of little use to Aboriginal peoples as a political tool for seeking justice in the colonial state.

Canadian sovereignty is being transformed and, arguably, constrained by the power relations inherent in contemporary transnational capital and by the multilateral trade treaties and enforcement mechanisms that this state is party to. Simultaneously, subordinated peoples who are located within the state but who have never enjoyed full citizenship in it are seeking new federal arrangements, or perhaps confederal arrangements, and even separation, all of which inherently challenge the state's historic claim to sovereignty. This struggle for self-determination also occurs within a political and economic arena largely determined by globalized capitalism.

While some struggle for decolonization, other Aboriginal elites aspire to be part of the buccaneer class of capitalists. Aboriginal rights have on occasion been invoked to legitimate practices – casinos, smokeshops, offshore banking – that are about incorporation into capitalist economies, not about resisting oppression. In a related development, in Saskatchewan in February 2002 the Federation of Saskatchewan Indian Nations adopted a position opposing unionisation of workers on Indian reserves and in Indian-owned businesses, (mis)characterising unions as white and conflictual and contrary to Indian collaborative traditions, thereby dignifying violation of at least one human right by invoking Aboriginality (CBC Radio One 2002; Scott 2002).

Meanwhile, the notion of citizenship itself is being revised in ways that call on the state to be more tentative in its construction of "citizen" and more committed in providing the structural, procedural, and physical apparatus to make differentiated citizenship meaningful. The contestations of subordinated peoples also resonate in the theoretical challenges to dominant conceptualisations of what citizenship is, who holds it, and what state and citizen obligations are.

The elite capitalist class composed of transnational corporations and investment capitalists finds state boundaries problematic to the extent that they impede profit maximisation. Yet this class has power over state economies and, hence, indirectly over governments' policies and electoral success. The sultans of capital enjoy privileged access to political elites. They also have access to the mass media: they own most of it and so are opinion shapers and agenda setters for the dominant society. This is why the parameters of public debate and the consensus about the agenda for debate are so consistent across the media.[27] This is most blatantly demonstrated by CanWest Global's Izzy Asper in his preemption of editorial content and policy in his twelve major metropolitan newspapers (*Globe and Mail* 2001, A23) and in the lack of tolerance of dissent in those papers.[28]

CONCLUSION

We are witnessing a recolonization of existing states by capital/ists that is facilitated by the restructuring imposed by multilateral trade regimes and by the World Trade Organisation. This process is legitimated by neoliberal ideology and by popular culture, which is commodified by mass media. Governments are accepted as handmaidens of transnational capitalists rather than as agents for the public good. Democracy becomes a question of consumer choice and citizens become consumers.

So what are the possibilities for constructing a postcolonial Canada in which inequitable power relations are transformed into mutually advantageous, negotiated relationships? My prescription assumes the potential for cross-movement solidarities among Aboriginal, antiglobalization, ecology, feminist, and labour movements and, theoretically, even political parties. Solidarities, however, will emerge only when each movement understands its objectives to be advanced at least partially by others and articulates this understanding in politically significant ways. Solidarities are based not on romanticism nor on automatic support on all issues but on knowledge, analysis, and disciplined commitments.

First, Canada needs to confront its history, as did South Africa through its Truth and Reconciliation Commission (Nagy 2002). The commission was designed to trade criminal justice for acknowledgment, to produce accountability on the part of those who violated human rights, and to provide state-funded compensation to individuals. To produce similar accomplishments in Canada, Yasmeen Abu-Laban has suggested a Forum for a Post-Colonial Future (2001, 271). It could provide a sustainable mechanism for truth and compensatory justice, while allowing for a common postcolonial future.

Second, this history must be understood from the perspective of those who were most disadvantaged. "It is only by making the unjust consequences of their power visible to privileged groups that marginalized group perspectives can have any chance of transforming prevailing understandings of the requirements of justice" (Williams 2000, 141).

Third, there must be a collective will to change institutional structures, political processes, and economic practices to take into account both historical disadvantages and future equitable practices. This means that the formulas for federal jurisdictions, funding arrangements, political representation processes, and the commitment to the global capitalist development paradigm must all be up for reconsideration.

Fourth, citizens and elites must accept movement politics as an expression of democracy rather than reserving the role of democratic representation solely for political parties. This means that institutional political power must take into account the visions and programs of democratic movements and indigenous liberation struggles, not as "stakeholders" where numbers make it politically prudent to pay attention, but as an obligation of the state to engage its citizens.

Finally, all players must be committed to this transformation, not paternalistically, to "save" Aboriginal peoples, but for our collective Canadian political, ethical, and corporate liberation from colonialism.

NOTES

1 Since 1982 the sovereigntist movement in Quebec has consolidated its considerable political strength and agenda. Small groups of self-described separatists have (re)emerged in British Columbia, Alberta, and Saskatchewan; in the latter two provinces in early 2001. There is also substantial support in the influential Iroquois Confederacy for the proposition that confederacy members are sovereign and that Canada has no legitimate jurisdiction over Iroquois territory.

2 For example, the conference Americana Indigenismo: Indigenous Peoples, the Free Trade Agreement of the Americas, and the Fourth World was held in conjunction with the April 2001 Free Trade of the Americas talks and protests in Quebec City. The conference was "to advance the establishment of a network of resistance to the initiative by the governments of the 34 nation states who have resolved to establish a new commercial polity for the Americas in violation of the Aboriginal rights, titles and treaties of the hemisphere's Indigenous peoples." An earlier and continuing opposition movement is manifest in the Zapatista movement in Mexico, which is fighting for indigenous land rights and against the prohibitions on traditional landholding practices in the North American Free Trade Agreement.

3 For example, see the "Draft Declaration on the Rights of Indigenous Peoples, Sub-Committee on Minorities, Human Rights Committee of the United Nations."

4 The National Policy is generally considered to have had three components: tariff-regulated international, especially American, trade; immigration and settlement; and the trans-Canada railway. The last two of these initiatives, especially, could not proceed without high-level consideration of how to handle Aboriginal nations. This consideration resulted in the fourth component: Canada's Indian policies of peripheralisation onto reserves controlled by government agents, the signing of treaties as a means of gaining control of land; and the defeat and dispersal of the Metis.

5 Some scholars argue that this transformation is already occurring by means of incremental conventional constitutional change: see Prince and Abele (2001, 338). Patrick Macklem (2001) suggests that the constitutional recognition and protection of aboriginal and treaty rights provides a constitutional basis for the emergence of a third order of government.

6 An example is the mutation of the CAP (Canada Assistance Program) to the CHST (Canada Health and Social Transfer), which reduces the amount of federal funding of the social safety net.

7 Examples are the repressive and arguably unconstitutional treatment of student protesters of the APEC (Asia Pacific Economic Co-Operation) summit in Vancouver in 1998, for discussions of which see Pue (2001), and the rising incidence of child poverty in Canada, condemned by the United Nations and yet not even mentioned in the federal budget of 2000, with its $7 billion surplus.

8 For example, during a visit to Regina neoliberal economist Diane Francis called Canada over-governed and over-taxed and said that "Canada needs to reduce the size of government and it can start by getting rid of small provinces, like PEI and Saskatchewan" (Johnstone 1999, B1).

9 U.S. Trade Representative Charlene Barshefsky has been promoting the wish list of the U.S. Coalition of Service Industries for inclusion in WTO trade talks. The list includes education, health care, and social services (Saskatchewan News Network 1999, B8). More recently, the World Water Council suggested that water will be considered a commodity in future WTO talks (Mitchell 2001, A1).

10 Rand Dyck calls the BCNI "probably the most powerful" of business pressure groups in Canada (2000, 147).

11 http://www.ceocouncil.ca.

12 T.H. Marshall (1976) suggests that citizenship acquires weight, agency, and significance as it expands from political rights to social rights and then to encompass a minimum of economic rights.

13 http://www.taxpayer.com/home.htm.

14 See the Indian Affairs website at http://fng-gpn.gc.ca.

15 "Umbrella Final Agreement between the Government of Canada, the Council for Yukon Indians, and the Government of Yukon," Supply and Services Canada, Indian and Northern Affairs, catalogue no. R34-5/1-1993E, 1993; and "Umbrella Final Agreement Implementation Plan," Supply and Services Canada, Indian and Northern Affairs Catalogue No. R34-5/1-1-1993E, 1993.

16 The Nisga'a Treaty was passed by the House of Commons in December 1999. For discussion of the treaty, see Rynard (2000) and **B.C.** *Studies* 120 (1998/99).

17 This policy preference for the status landed Aboriginal populations is documented and critiqued by Cairns (2000).

18 *Marshall v. Canada* (1999) (S.C.C.) affirmed the right of Mi'kmaq people to fish for eels. This right was interpreted by the Mi'kmaq as a fishing right in general and exercised in the lobster fishery.

19 Brian Tobin resigned as Newfoundland premier in order to run in the November 2000 federal election; he won his seat and the federal Liberals won the election. He was replaced as premier and leader of the Newfoundland Liberal Party by Roger Grimes.

20 See also Peter Penashue, "Help Us to Help Ourselves." For a critique of the environmental and social implications, see *Fifty-two Percent of the Population Deserves a Closer Look: A Proposal for Guidelines Regarding the Environmental and Socio-economic Impacts on Women from the Mining Development at Voisey's Bay*, Tongamiut Inuit Annait Ad Hoc Committee on Aboriginal Women and Mining in Labrador, 16 April 1997.

21 For a useful discussion of the Labrador Inuit Association negotiations and the lack of gendered policy analysis of Inco's impact, see Archibald and Crnkovich (1999).

22 Thomas L. Green, Executive Summary of *Lasting Benefits from beneath the Earth: Mining Nickel from Voisey's Bay in a Manner Compatible with the Requirements of Sustainable Development*, prepared for the Innu Nation. www.innu.ca/green1.html.

23 Fran Williams, executive director of the Labrador Inuit Association's radio and television broadcasting society, captured this concern when she said, "these people know nothing about us or Labrador. They're always getting the Innu and Inuit confused. Yet they come here and impose their development on us like they're doing us a service" (Fouillard).

24 "The Innu Nation is the governing body of the Innu of Labrador ... [its] primary objective is to represent the Innu of Labrador in land rights (or comprehensive claims) and self-government negotiations [and it] works closely with the elected Band Councils in each community [Sheshatshiu and Davis Inlet (Utshmiassit]" *The Innu Nation*, www.innu.ca/the_innu.html).

25 For example, see noted University of Alberta scientist David Schindler's analysis, reported on by Mittelstaedt (2001, A6).

26 CP (1999, A9).

27 For a more complete discussion of this phenomenon, see Herman and Chomsky (1988, especially 1–35) and Taras (1999, 199–218).

28 Noted *Toronto Star* editor Haroon Siddiqui gave the Minifee Lecture at the University of Regina on 4 March 2002, in which he criticised CanWest's censorship impulses; Regina *Leader-Post* (CanWest Global) editors changed their reporter's story on the lecture to eliminate the censorship "hook," inciting a number of *Leader-Post* journalists to withhold their by-lines in protest; they were subsequently disciplined. In a related incident, fifty-five journalists from the *Montreal Gazette* wrote an open letter, published in the *Globe and Mail* on 11 December 2001, criticising CanWest's threats to press freedom. Most recently, respected journalist and *Ottawa Citizen* publisher Russell Mills was fired in June 2002 by the Aspers, allegedly for publishing editorial opinion critical of Prime Minister Jean Chrétien's government.

REFERENCES

Abu-Laban,Yasmeen. 2000-2001. "The Future and the Legacy: Globalization and the Canadian Settler-State." *Journal of Canadian Studies* 35: 262–76.

Archibald, Linda, and Mary Crnkovich. 1999. *If Gender Mattered: A Case Study of Inuit Women, Land Claims, and the Voisey's Bay Nickel Project.* Ottawa: Status of Women Canada.

Asch, Michael, and Norman Zlotkin. 1997. "Affirming Aboriginal Title: A New Basis for Comprehensive Claims Negotiations." In Michael Asch, ed., *Aboriginal and Treaty Rights in Canada.* Vancouver: UBC Press.

Blaut, James. 1993. *The Colonizer's Model of the World.* New York: Guilford Press.

Borrows, John. 2000. "Landed Citizenship: Narratives of Aboriginal Political Participation." In Will Kymlicka and Wayne Norman, eds., *Citizenship in Diverse Societies*, 326–42. New York: Oxford University Press.

Bruyneel, Kevin. 1999. "Politics on the Boundaries: Power, Identity, and the Presumption of Sovereignty." Paper presented to the Canadian Political Science Association Annual Meeting, Sherbrooke, Quebec, 7 June 1999.

Cairns, Alan C. 1992. *Charter versus Federalism: The Dilemmas of Constitutional Reform.* Montreal and Kingston: McGill-Queen's University Press.

– 2000. *Citizens Plus.* Vancouver: University of British Columbia Press.

Denis, Claude. 1997. *We Are Not You: First Nations and Canadian Modernity.* Peterborough, ON: Broadview Press.

Dyck, Rand. 2000. *Canadian Politics: Critical Approaches.* 3d ed. Scarborough, ON: Nelson Thomson Learning.

Falk, Richard A. 2000. *Human Rights Horizons: The Pursuit of Justice in a Globalizing World.* New York: Routledge.

Flanagan, Thomas. 2000. *First Nations? Second Thoughts.* Montreal and Kingston: McGill-Queen's University Press.

Fouillard, Camille. *Most to Lose and Least to Gain.* Accessed at www.innu.ca/vbwomen1.html.

Green, Joyce. 1995. "Towards a Detente with History." *International Journal of Canadian Studies* 12: 85–105.

– 1996. "Resistance is Possible." *Canadian Women's Studies* 16 (3).

Green, Thomas L. Executive Summary of *Lasting Benefits from Beneath the Earth: Mining Nickel from Voisey's Bay in a Manner Compatible with the Requirements of Sustainable Development*, prepared for the Innu Nation. Accessed at www.innu.ca/green1.html.

Herman, Edward, and Noam Chomsky. 1988. *Manufacturing Consent: The Political Economy of the Mass Media.* New York: Pantheon.

The Innu Nation. Accessed at www.innu.ca/the_innu.html.

Lennarson, Fred. 2001. Interview by author, Edmonton, Alberta, 28 February.

Macklem, Patrick. 2001. *Indigenous Difference and the Constitution of Canada.* Toronto: University of Toronto Press.

Magallanes, Catherine J. Iorns. 1999. "International Human Rights and their Impact on Domestic Law on Indigenous Peoples' Rights in Australia, Canada, and New Zealand." In Paul Havemann, ed., *Indigenous Peoples' Rights in Australia, Canada, and New Zealand,* 236–76. New York: Oxford University Press.

Marshall, T.H. 1976. *Class, Citizenship, and Social Development.* Westport, CT: Greenwood Press.

Martin, David, and Chris Adams. 2000. "Canadian Public Opinion regarding Aboriginal Self-Government: Diverging Viewpoints as Found in National Survey Results." *American Review of Canadian Studies* 30 (1): 79–88.

Moorcroft, Lois. 2002. Interview by author, Whitehorse, Yukon, 1 March 2002.

Memmi, Albert. 1965. *The Colonizer and the Colonized.* Translated by Howard Greenfeld. Boston: Beacon Press.

Nagy, Rosemary. 2002. "Reconciliation in Post-Commission South Africa: Thick and Thin Accounts of Solidarity." *Canadian Journal of Political Science* 35 (2): 323–46.

Prince, Michael, and Frances Abele. 2001. "Funding an Aboriginal Order of Government in Canada: Recent Developments in Self-Government and Fiscal Relations." In *Canada: The State of the Federation, 1999/2000.* Montreal and Kingston: McGill-Queen's University Press.

Pue, W. Wesley. 2001. *Pepper in Our Eyes: The APEC Affair.* Vancouver: University of British Columbia Press.

Rocher, Francois and Christian Rouillard. 1999. "The Impact of Continental and Global Integration on Canadian Federalism: We Can't Have Our Cake and Eat it Too." Unpublished paper presented to the Annual Meeting of the Canadian Political Science Association, Sherbrooke, Quebec, 6–8 June 1999.

Royal Commission on Aboriginal Peoples. 1996. Final Report. Ottawa: Supply and Services Canada.

Rynard, Paul. 2000. "Welcome In, But Check Your Rights at the Door: The James Bay and Nisga'a Agreements in Canada." *Canadian Journal of Political Science* 33 (June): 211–43.

Said, Edward. 1979. *Orientalism.* New York: Random House, Vintage Books.

– 1993. *Culture and Imperialism.* New York: Random House, Vintage Books.

Taras, David. 1999. *Power and Betrayal in the Canadian Media.* Peterborough, ON: Broadview Press.

Trimble, Linda. 1999. "Women, Public Policy, and the 'New Right': Facing the Neo-liberal and/or Neo-conservative State." Public Lecture cosponsored by the Department of Political Science and the Saskatchewan Institute for Public Policy, University of Regina.

– 1998. "Good Enough Citizens." *International Journal of Canadian Studies* 17.

Underhill, Frank. 1964. *The Image of Confederation*. Toronto: The Hunter Rose Company, for the CBC Learning Systems.

United Nations Human Rights Commission, Thirty-eighth Session. 1984. International Convention on Civil and Political Rights. CCPR/C/38/167/1984.

Weaver, Sally M. 1986. "Indian Policy in the New Conservative Government, Part 1: The Neilsen Task Force of 1985." *Native Studies Review* 2: 1–43.

Williams, Melissa. 2000. "The Uneasy Alliance of Group Representation and Deliberative Democracy." In Will Kymlicka and Wayne Norman, eds., *Citizenship in Diverse Societies*. New York: Oxford University Press, 124–51.

MEDIA

CBC Radio One. 2002. Provincial Newscast. 28 February.

Canadian Press (CP). 1999a. "Tobin Is Hopeful on Labrador Hydro Project Despite Opposition." *Globe and Mail*, 14 October.

– 1999b. "Alberta Government Expects to Reap an Extra $2.8 Billion." *Regina Leader-Post*, 30 November.

– 2000. *Regina Leader-Post*, CP-3, October.

– 2001a. "Magazine Article Said Inciting Racism." *Regina Leader-Post*, 18 June.

– 2001b. "More Dollars Not Solving Problems." *Regina Leader-Post*, 4 August.

Chase, Steven. 2001. "NAFTA Ruling Forces Canada to Break Own Law, Critics Say." *Globe and Mail*, 21 March.

Cooper, Barry, and David Bercuson. 2001. "A Warning to First Nations." *Regina Leader-Post*, 10 August.

Globe and Mail. 1999. "Tobin Tough Talk Leaves Labrador Cold as Election Nears." *Globe and Mail*, 6 February.

– 2001. "How CanWest Is Threatening Press Freedom." Signed by fifty-five journalists from the *Montreal Gazette*. 11 December.

Johnstone, Bruce. 1999. "Scrap Saskatchewan, Says Francis." *Regina Leader-Post*, 22 October.

Leader-Post Staff. 2002. "Columnist Takes Issue With CanWest Global." *Regina Leader-Post*, 5 March.

McKenna, Barrie. 2001a. "Fairbanks Sees Gold in Gas Pipeline." *Globe and Mail*, 16 July.

– 2001b. "Bush Eager to Build Pipeline." *Globe and Mail*, 18 July.

Milner, Brian. 1999. "Inco Blinks on Voisey's." *Globe and Mail*, 16 November.

Mitchell, Alanna. 2001. "Canadian Water on Tap for Future Trade Talks." *Globe and Mail*, 13 August.

Mittelstaedt, Martin. 2001. "Prairies May Become Dust Bowl, Scientist Says." *Globe and Mail*, 26 July.

Nguyen, Lily. 2001a. "NWT Pipe Dream Rises as Gas Falls." *Globe and Mail*, 16 July.

– 2001b. "Doubt Cast on NWT pipeline." *Globe and Mail,* 2 July.

Penashue, Peter. 2000. "Help Us to Help Ourselves." *Globe and Mail,* 7 December.

Perusse, Bernard, et al. 2001. "Open Letter: How CanWest Is Threatening Press Freedom." *Globe and Mail,* 11 December.

Robinson, Allan. 1999. "Native Groups Want Ruling Overturned." *Globe and Mail,* 8 September.

– 2000. "Inco at Impasse over Voisey's Project." *Globe and Mail,* 12 January.

– 2001. "Inco's Sopko to Step Down in April." *Globe and Mail,* 7 February.

Saskatchewan News Network. 1999. "WTO Talks May Include Health Care." *Regina Leader-Post,* 26 November.

Scoffield, Heather. 1999. "Canada Guilty of Dairy Subsidies: WTO." *Globe and Mail,* 14 October.

– 2000. "Economists Foresee Dollarization." *Globe and Mail,* 19 April.

Scoffield, Heather, and Greg Keenan. 1999. "Canada Told to Scrap Auto Pact." *Globe and Mail,* 14 October.

Scott, Neil. 2002. "Unions Skeptical of FSIN's Desire to Keep Unions Off Reserves." *Regina Leader-Post,* 28 February.

4 Social Movements and Transformation

WILLIAM K. CARROLL AND ELAINE COBURN

Transformation – the construction of a different future from a troubled past – has been an issue central to both Canadian political economy (CPE) and to the social movements that, particularly since the 1960s, have helped shape the terrain of politics and cultural life in Canada. Whether they develop around sexual, gendered, ethnic, class, or environmental interests, social movements are characteristically the carriers of social change, as they press for and even prefigure political, economic, and cultural transformation. So it is hardly surprising that political economy, sharing much the same interest in transformation, has been implicated in the emergence and growth of movements. This chapter argues that the new political economy has drawn much of its intellectual strength from an active engagement with social movements, which has enabled it to reach pivotal insights into the politics of transformation, in Canada and beyond. These insights, in turn, are of value to activists as they seek effective transformative strategies. In short, the fates of movements and political economy are entwined.

It is useful to think of the mutual implication of movements and political economy in terms of a dialectic of theory and practice. Viewed as theory, CPE has taken as its object the Canadian social formation – a historically specific ensemble of economic, political, and cultural relations within which human lives have been (re)produced. Although these relations have often been analyzed under the rubric of structural categories such as capital and state, Warren Magnusson reminds us that such structures are not permanent fixtures but no more than the sedimented product of past movements: "In truth, the human world is a world in movement in which the apparent fixtures are just sedimentations or reifications of earlier movements. Movements move in relation to one another, and not in relation to stable fixtures" (1997, 111).

Thus, the "object" itself – the social formation known as Canada – has been shaped and reshaped by the agency of movements. In this sense, even in its most structuralist mode political economy is inevitably a commentary on the ruling and oppositional social movements that in great part propel history forward. Consequently, with changes in the correlation of forces in which movements are active – with the rise of new movements, of new collective identities and political claims, of new political regimes and accumulation strategies – the issues, problems and even categories of political-economic analysis have shifted to accommodate new realities.

But the new political economy has been more than a theoretical reflection on the changing realities that comprise Canada. Political economy is itself a form of transformative practice – an intervention in the world. Since its revival in the politically charged era of the late 1960s, it has been a field of inquiry explicitly organized around what Jürgen Habermas has called "emancipatory interests"; that is, political economy in the sense employed here, is a *critical theory*.[1] "It stands back from the apparent fixity of the present to ask how the existing structures came into being and how they may be changing, or how they may be induced to change" (Cox 1995, 32). The new political economy has never been detached from movement activism but has included in its project an explicitly activist dimension: to contribute to the formation of a vibrant left in Canada. Given the centrality of "emancipatory interests" in that project, movements have figured explicitly in the actual formation of political-economic knowledge. Political economists have often participated in these movements and have both learned from movement activism and contributed analyses of value to that activism, so that there has been a *dialogical relation* between movements and political economy. With this dialogical relation in mind, part of our task will be to elucidate some practical lessons for movement activism that can be distilled from a reading of the new political economy.

The dialogical nature of the relation between social movements and political economy has meant that CPE's knowledge claims have had a provisional, yet cumulative, character. At its best, Canadian political economy has been open to new developments; it has been capable of reaching fresh insights yet of also conserving and building upon well-established formulations, such as Marx's critical theory of capitalism. Indeed, we will suggest that political economy's openness to and engagement with social movements have been key elements enabling it to avoid devolving into a degenerative research program. This chapter, then, highlights the cumulative character of knowledge in this field, enumerates some of its most important insights on social movements, and finally discusses the theoretical and practical challenges posed by recent globalizing tendencies, both in capital accumulation and in social-movement activism.

THREE PERIODS IN THE FORMATION OF CPE

It is helpful to distinguish three periods in the formation of contemporary political economy. During what Wallace Clement (1997, 6) has called the "classic period," stretching from the 1920s to the early 1950s, the staples thesis of Canadian economic history was elaborated in a series of penetrating studies under the intellectual leadership of Harold Innis. Although the classic tradition was for the most part detached from the movement politics of the day, by locating Canada as a staple-producing region within a North Atlantic structure of central and marginal states it developed a critical point of view on Canadian capitalism. After Innis's death in 1952 and amid the burgeoning influence of quantitative neoclassical approaches in Canadian economics departments, political economy became gradually marginalized within academe.

Sociologists point out that social-movement activism tends to ebb and flow in distinct "cycles of protest" (Tarrow 1998). In the Western capitalist democracies, this idea applies very clearly to the period from the mid-1960s through the mid-1970s, and in Canada a wave of protest during this period catalyzed the revival of political economy. It was in this crucial reformative phase that the dialogical relation between movement activism and political-economic analysis took shape. Consider, for instance, Kari Levitt's *Silent Surrender* – a seminal text in the new political economy, published in 1970. Drawing on Watkins's (1968) influential report on foreign investment in Canada, Levitt's book presents a critical structural analysis of the growing role of U.S.-based transnational corporations in Canada. Although social movements did not figure directly in Levitt's analysis, a rereading of Levitt in view of Magnusson's claims about the ubiquity of movements would discern the ruling movements, centred in the 1960s around the hegemonic American state and capitalist class, that were threatening Canadian sovereignty. If Levitt, along with other political economists of the time, analytically underplayed the role of collective agency, her work certainly made good on its practical, emancipatory intent. As Resnick has recounted, works such as Levitt's "spoke for a left nationalism percolating its way through the ranks of the University League for Social Reform, the student movement or the Waffle, and bringing together economists, historians, political scientists and others"(1977, 172). This was a politically engaged political economy, hooked into a left-nationalist movement against American imperialism that was based in great part on campuses and extended, through the Waffle, into the NDP. In this extraordinary period, Canadian political economy was reborn, absorbing the influences of contemporary movements – critiques of imperialism and class domination, left nationalism – and reframing them in more analytic terms that involved a strong dependentist strain.

THE NEW CANADIAN POLITICAL ECONOMY, PART 1: THE ARCHITECTONIC PARADIGM

Throughout the 1970s and into the early 1980s, the second phase of political economy was consolidated into a paradigm that employed an *architectonic style of analysis,* seeking to reveal underlying structures – the architecture – of power. Even when political economists were disagreeing as to the relative importance of metropolis-hinterland and capital-labour relations in shaping Canadian society, debates between dependentist and metropolitan-Marxist readings of Canada took place within a common paradigm: the goal of any analysis was to comprehend the structures of domination that shaped the everyday realities of people, to show how social domination is constituted, so that those with an objective interest in transcending it would have the conceptual tools needed to transform the architecture. Movements themselves were not directly theorized but were taken to be the political reflex of structural contradictions, particularly those involving the capital-labour relation, the relation between states and nations, and the relation between regional metropoles and hinterlands. Thus, although the major movements of the late 1960s and 1970s that inspired the revival of political economy – national movements in Canada and Quebec, regional protests, class politics – were addressed within the architectonic paradigm, there was scant space for theorizing movements in terms of the strategies, identities, and organizational forms they adopted (Carroll 1997, 5–6).

By the end of the 1970s, the cycle of protest that had begun in the 1960s had dissipated, and movement politics was in a state of relative quiescence, with two important exceptions. Environmental and feminist activism, both of which mobilized in the later stage of the 1960s protest cycle, continued to organize throughout the 1980s and provided a basis for rethinking the political economy project. By the late

1970s, feminist scholars had launched influential critiques of political economy's gender blindness and had advanced analyses that insisted on going beyond the familiar categories of class, nation, and state. In this instance we can see the pedagogical impact of the dialogical relation: not only was political economy reshaped and enriched by the feminist critique, but political-economic analysis found its way into feminist organizations, with the result that feminism in Canada developed a strong socialist-feminist current that enabled the movement to pursue a broad agenda of social justice, opening out to other movements. Doing double-duty on both sides of the dialogical relation were intellectuals who combined political-economic scholarship with feminist activism. And although the feminist scholarship of the late 1970s attended primarily to structures of patriarchy – the gendered division of labour, the domestic labour debate – and only secondarily to women's resistive agency, the continuing dialogue between feminist activism and political economy meant that by the late 1980s feminist scholars were placing analytical emphasis upon "how to make change" (Adamson, Briskin, and McPhail 1988, 7).

THE NEW CANADIAN POLITICAL ECONOMY, PART 2: THE PRAXIS PARADIGM

It was the question of *praxis*, along with the "greening" of the new Canadian political economy (Williams 1992) as the concerns of environmentalists broadened the research agenda, that served to reorient political economy, beginning in the late 1980s. In this third version of CPE, which Magnusson's perspective, quoted in our introduction, exemplifies, issues of transformation are front and centre. While incorporating the architectonic sensitivity to structures of domination, the praxis paradigm meant taking up the issues posed by movements themselves, including the challenges of dealing creatively with the inescapable reality of "difference" and of finding grounds for a unity-in-diversity among progressive movements. It also meant widening the conceptual lens to include a broader range of movements and to consider how political agency and identity are constructed, and it meant entering into vigorous political and strategic debates spurred by the intellectual movement known as post-modernism.

In this third phase, we can again see the formative role of social movements and of a new wave of movement activism in shaping CPE's agenda and analytic categories. Ironically, in setting the stage for the third wave the most important movement was not a popular-democratic protest but a top-down initiative, spearheaded by key organizations of the capitalist class and its organic intellectuals. The turn to *business activism* and the advocacy through that activism of a neoliberal political project had already begun in the 1970s as a reaction to reforms consolidated by the labour movement and social democratic parties during the protest cycle of the 1960s and early 1970s. At the international level, the Trilateral Commission emerged around the project of "restoring the discipline of capital" over society, and its influential 1975 report, *The Crisis of Democracy*, "recommended constraining democracy and enhancing the authority of 'expertise,' notably in the economic field" (van der Pijl 1998, 126). In Britain and the United States, which proved to be pivotal states in the consolidation of neoliberalism, consensus-forming groups such as the Business Roundtable adopted much the same project and were instrumental in mobilizing capital's collective interest in a market-oriented regime in which investors would be freed from state regulations, redistributive taxes, and social programs that undercut profits while weakening the market's disciplinary power over labour (Useem 1984). In Canada the movement for neoliberalism was organized by groups such as the Fraser Institute and the Business Council on National Issues (BCNI), which formed in the 1970s with dense ties to the country's leading corporations and with the goal of providing, particularly in the case of the BCNI, a unified voice for the business community on public policy issues (Langille 1987; Carroll and Shaw 2001).

In Canada neoliberalism's most important plank was a free trade agreement that, in integrating Canadian and American economies, would smuggle the Reagan revolution in by the back door (Panitch 1987) by promoting the "harmonization" of social policy and labour standards down to the levels of the minimalist American welfare state. The combination of continentalism and neoliberalism that free trade portended reasserted the relevance of left-nationalist political-economic analysis and stimulated a new wave of popular protest that reached a crescendo in the federal election of 1988, several months before Free Trade Agreement was implemented by a re-elected Tory government in January 1989. Having refined their conceptual tools during the revival of political economy in the 1970s, political economists were heavily involved in this second wave of left-nationalism, which centred around the Pro-Canada Network and the Council of Canadians (Bleyer 1997) and which continued through the early 1990s in the struggle against the North American Free Trade Agreement. Of course, the neoliberal project was more than simply a call for free trade; it comprised attacks on trade-union rights and other collective entitlements that had been secured within the welfare state. In targeting so many subordinate social interests at once, neoliberalism tended to inspire a wide-ranging popular opposition and thus a new cycle of protest. Already in 1985, *The Other MacDonald Report*, edited by two prominent political economists (Drache and Cameron 1985), brought to voice an impressive range of alternatives from a popular sector composed of a variety of critical social movements; subsequently the coalition movement politics that developed in and around such organizations as the Action Canada Network began to pose new questions of political praxis and new challenges for political economy.

Yet failure to stop the trade agreements and the continuing neo-liberal trend toward a "hollowing out" of liberal-democratic politics ultimately raised questions about the relevancy of a left-nationalist political economy and a left-nationalist politics in a rapidly globalizing world. The need for a reorientation of political economy was clearly recognized in Greg Albo's reflections on the occasion of the twentieth anniversary of the founding of the Waffle: "the tell-tale signs of a degenerative research program are evident, and the necessity of actively exploring Canadian political economy in new ways is obvious" (1990, 169). Albo pointed to the need for formerly marginal issues such as gender and environment to be included in a broadened agenda in which the contribution of the Canadian left to a new inter-nationalism would be developed.

This concern that political economy reinvent itself in tandem with developments in movement politics was shared by others. Indeed, our view is that in the late 1980s the articulation of three currents of praxis-oriented thinking enabled political economy to escape the fate of a degenerative research program.[2] Each of these currents brought new debates and analytic priorities that invigorated scholarship throughout the 1990s, and in this sense the praxicological concern can be viewed as paradigmatic to CPE's third period, which now extends into a new century.

THE POLITICAL ECONOMY OF PRAXIS 1: SOCIALIST-FEMINIST CONTRIBUTIONS

The first current flowed primarily from socialist feminism and is well represented by Linda Briskin's (1989) model of feminist practice, offered as a way of highlighting the dilemmas facing socialist feminists as they champion a radical vision of women's liberation. Briskin's was one of the first articles published in *Studies in Political Economy* (SPE) to adopt what she called the "standpoint of practice": to attend primarily to issues of political agency rather than architectonic structure. Recognizing the divisions within feminism among liberal, radical, and socialist currents and among various gendered social identities, Briskin argued that all feminist practice struggles with the dilemma between "mainstreaming" (reaching out to and transforming the everyday lives of women, at the risk of institutional cooptation) and "disengagement" (critiquing the system from a standpoint outside it, at the risk of marginalization). However, while liberal feminism gravitates toward mainstreaming and radical feminism gravitates toward disengagement, socialist-feminist politics is pulled simultaneously toward both poles of practice, creating "both a recurring strategic dilemma, as well as a potential solution to the dilemma of feminist practice – maintaining a tension between these poles" (1989, 102). Drawing on examples from feminist organizing in Canada, Briskin held that in the politics of transformation the conscious maintenance of a creative tension between mainstreaming and disengagement is preferable to closure around a unitary strategy for change. She also noted the leading role that socialist feminists had played and could continue to play in building coalitions within the women's movement to mediate identity differences and in allying with organizations outside the women's movement to build a mass heterogeneous movement for fundamental social transformation.

What Briskin's and similar analyses published in the late 1980s (e.g., Rayside 1988) signalled was a broadening of the political economy agenda to take up the question of how social movements, embedded as they are within structures, attempt to create social change. In a subsequent stream of articles published in *SPE*, this issue was pursued, often by means of detailed case studies, sometimes with an eye toward providing constructive criticism of movement praxis and increasingly with a sensitivity toward issues of knowledge as an element of political contestation.

For example, drawing on Dorothy Smith's (1987) feminist-materialist sociology, Gillian Walker (1990) underlined dangers of mainstreaming in the conceptual politics of "wife battering." In bringing experiences consigned to the private realm into the public sphere, the feminist critique of male violence had adopted the terms available in public discourse, which, however, were part of the ruling relations in contemporary society. As feminist political efforts became aligned with professional and state responses to "family violence," "aspects of the mobilization for a movement for political change got lost" (1990, 85). Work done with battered women became a site for professional and voluntary service provision, which took the place of the consciousness-raising practices that "might allow the issue to be linked with others in the wider struggle against women's oppression." In a similar vein, from the standpoint of feminist community-organizing, Sue Findlay critiqued post-1960s state administrative practices of "representing" designated groups, such as "women," through procedures such as consultation and employment equity. Noting that movement activists had taken up these practices as ways to mediate differences in power, Findlay analyzed them as mechanisms that work "to articulate community groups to the existing practices of the state," thereby pre-empting radical proposals to democratize state practices (1993, 165). Eschewing co-optive state reforms, Findlay advocated democratizing community organizations, a process contingent upon "the willingness of members of community organizations to engage in reforms that will allow them to celebrate difference and mediate conflicts of race, gender, and other differences when they occur"(1993, 166).

Case studies of the struggle over state regulation of Ontario's legal aid clinic system (Chouinard 1998) and of the impact of the women's health care movement on the restructuring of health care in Quebec (Michaud 2000) added further nuance to the relation between movements and the state. Vera Chouinard showed how legal clinics, often established in the early 1970s as work collectives autonomous from the state and run by representative community boards, created a more dispersed geography of power within the legal system and thus provided sites for challenges to the oppression of the poor on bases such as class and race (1998, 68). However, by the mid-1970s, the absence of stable funding and rising opposition from Law Society members worried about losing business to the clinics led activists to appeal to the state, whose Clinic Funding Committee assumed regulatory control and promoted a centralized structure that disembedded clinics from local control, mandated cost-effective delivery of services, and ultimately required clinics to be run in a hierarchical manner, headed by lawyers. In this way, "the politics of the clinic movement shifted away from collective justice toward an incorporated justice based on liberal visions of clinics as organizations dispensing legal services to needy individuals"(87).

In the case of the women's health care movement, whose project has been the creation of sites for alternative and holistic services based on a collective approach of learning and on the principle of the equality of all women, activists were long sceptical about participating in state structures. In 1992 the creation of seventeen regional health boards brought state recognition of women's health centres but also the entrenchment of the centres' marginal status by designating them as complementary to the medical establishment. Nevertheless, in this case the continued relative autonomy of the centres holds out the possibility of a renewal of feminist counterdiscourse and political transformation in the field of health (Michaud 2000, 44).

The feminist political economy of praxis has also taken up issues of ideological struggle around family politics. Lois Harder's (1996) study of Alberta's changing approach to "the family" in the 1990s drew on Nancy Fraser's (1995) theorization of claims-making within needs discourses in reading the Getty government's championing of the "traditional family" as an attempt to respond to feminist oppositional discourse (which had politicized gendered needs) with a "re-privatization discourse" that was meant to marginalize feminist groups. However, the unintended consequence of creating the Premier's Council in Support of Alberta's Families was to further politicize the issues raised in oppositional discourse by establishing a public forum on family politics, and the Klein government's move in 1995 to disband the council can be seen as an effort to displace the struggle between feminists and "profamily" claims-makers from the state (1996, 68).

Meg Luxton and Leah Vosko (1998) examined the successful campaign to have unpaid domestic labour counted as an economic activity in the Canadian Census, an instance of movement politics that challenges feminism to make "issues of unpaid work more integral to its political analyses and organising activities" (50). The campaign brought together groups ranging from the antifeminist REAL Women to the feminist Mothers Are Women in a struggle that recognized the relation between knowledge and power: "Campaign leaders believed that exclusion from the Census devalued and silenced unpaid women workers. Since their work is unacknowledged, their needs are not considered and unpaid workers are not consulted when social policies are under consideration" (60). The narrow focus on a single concrete issue allowed the diverse interests to remain united for the duration of the campaign, but in the aftermath the future of family politics – specifically, whether the increased visibility of women's unpaid work will strengthen a right-wing, "profamily" agenda or whether it will be taken up by feminist and labour activists in developing a progressive "family politics" – is contingent upon the political choices made by the movements themselves.

The feminist political economy of praxis has called attention to problems in relating to the state, issues of knowledge and power (often framed in terms of the construction of discourses and identities), and the ultimate contingency of political outcomes. These themes are also evident in a second influential current in contemporary political economy: the dialogue with postmodernism.

THE POLITICAL ECONOMY OF PRAXIS 2: THE DIALOGUE WITH POSTMODERNISM

With the publication in 1988 of Warren Magnusson and Rob Walker's "De-centring the State: Political Theory and Canadian Political

Economy," CPE entered into an extended dialogue with postmodern thought, a conversation that has led to its own unique insights on social movements and political agency. Drawing critically upon some postmodern thematics, Magnusson and Walker questioned the state-centricity of CPE – the tendency in modern thought to reduce politics to what revolves around the state, a tendency that thereby traps social critique within the political space established by bourgeois society. In these authors' view, the modernist inheritance of political economy, which it shares with liberal political thought, needs to be radically rethought, even temporarily "forgotten," so that new political identities, solidarities, and innovative forms of practice – characteristically the inventions of "critical social movements" – can be taken up. As the left's inability to present a coherent socialist alternative to free trade showed, in an era in which the globalization of capital is weakening state capacities to mediate between global capital and local communities, the efficacy of state-centred action is diminished. Yet the rearticulation of political space – the weakening of states as containers for politics – opens opportunities for critical social movements, whose refusal of preconstituted bourgeois political categories enables them to "break up the political spaces established by capital – especially the interiorized spaces we call our categories of political thought" (58).

Magnusson and Walker's counsel was that the left, and political economy in particular, *listen* to the ongoing practices of struggle within critical social movements: "We are suggesting ... that we allow the movements to be our teachers – that we open ourselves up to them and examine the potentials these movements are exploring, without prejudging them in terms of bourgeois/socialist categories" (1988, 61). Such listening would, in the first place, reveal the variegated nature of libratory struggles – the lack of any over-arching identity or moment of unity that can overcome all difference. These authors, then, embraced a politics of diversity, defining *critical* movements as "open and experimental" and *reactionary* movements as those that "attempt to cancel difference, and enforce closure" (60). They went on to characterize critical movements as engaged in a series of explorations:

- of new political spaces in which to act, including the local and personal spaces of civil society as well as the spaces of ecological regions and cultural networks;
- of political practices that often focus on small-scale actions, networking, lateral organization, self-transformation, and empowerment;
- of cultural horizons that foreground the politics of language and

knowledge and that reinterpret such modern dichotomies as subject and object, self and other, male and female;

- of pluralistic political communities that refuse the monolithic boundaries of states.

Finally, Magnusson and Walker offered a temporal view of critical movements, arguing that the pattern of development typically involves three stages. Movements originate in *struggles of specificity* – local, often parochial, action in response to a specific problem. As they discover that the connectedness enforced by capital precludes parochialism (that local action is already global action), these struggles of specificity may, if an issue is persistent, become *struggles of connection*. Activists may develop a more coherent sense of the interconnections between the local struggle and the global political economy; they may establish relationships with other movements and actors, some of which may span existing political boundaries. Such struggles may lead to *struggles of imagination*, as people rethink the meaning of taken-for-granted terms such as community or democracy, probing their own identities and social relations to discover practices appropriate to the reality they confront (1988, 62).

The insights in Magnusson and Walker's analysis, and of related post-modern approaches, took some time to be digested – immediate responses tended to invoke the very forms of orthodox closure that Magnusson and Walker questioned (Jenson and Keyman 1990; Helva-cioglu 1992). However, Eleanor MacDonald's (1998) engagement with postmodern theory was more productive, as it accepted the challenge of showing the relevance of a Marxist analysis to the identity commitments of such contemporary movements as feminism, antiracism, aboriginal rights, and gay and lesbian politics. Taking for granted that postmodern theory – with its rejection of determinism and essentialism, its championing of discursive strategies, and its sensitivity to difference – resonates with those who wish to break from constraining identities based in history, biology, and language, MacDonald canvassed recent Marxist for-mulations for historical-materialist perspectives on identity. Her conclu-sion emphasized the need for political economists to keep in view three interrelated "vectors" in theorizing the identities that inform practice: 1 determination (how are gendered, racialized and other identities pro-duced; "what kinds of practices, institutions, discourses and relations are productive of identities?" (1998, 17)); 2 association (how do categories of representation – black/white, masculine/feminine – reflect, yet also themselves produce, identities in their relationships with each other? (1998, 23)); and 3 intervention (how are identities invoked as strategic and normative choices, and with what effect in practice?).

Jo-Anne Fiske's study of ethno-political discourses in the Canadian Indigenous women's movement exemplifies the kind of inquiry into political struggle and the formation of new social identities that theoretical analyses such as MacDonald's enable. In constructing a political identity in the struggle for "Indian Rights," Aboriginal women had to respond to two discourses grounded in material practice: that of the state and that of their own male leadership. "The burden, hence, has been twofold: to construct an Aboriginal identity in common with male counterparts and distinct from that of Euro-Canadians, and more problematically to construct a gendered identity distinct from Non-Aboriginal femaleness" (1996, 74). Fiske's analysis criticized the state-centricity of the Aboriginal leadership, whose rights discourse has been little more than a derivative of modern Western liberalism, with the Aboriginal community consigned to a position within the state, as a third order of government. In Fiske's view, "ethnic and gender inequalities draw Aboriginal People into a discursive field not of their own making" (86), as "female leadership imagines a neo-traditional community for which essentialized womanhood stands as a metaphor," while "male leadership's goals emulate the masculine nation-state" (72).

Finally, in a study of the safety audit work done by Ottawa's Women's Action Centre against Violence (WACAV), Fran Klodawsky and Caroline Andrew (1999) returned to Magnusson and Walker's temporal model of practice to consider the progressive potential of acting locally. Their analysis indicated that although safety audits had helped empower women around the social use of space and although these struggles of specificity had partly led to connections being drawn between specific urban problems and broader feminist analysis, the transition from struggles of connection to struggles of imagination had not occurred. Klodawsky and Andrew pointed to WACAV's lack of a shared vision of its central mission, its diminishing resources in the 1990s as the threat of funding cuts obliged the group to adopt narrowly focused survival strategies, and its failure to build coalitions with other organizations as factors inhibiting the transition to struggles of imagination. Such struggles, along with struggles of connection, are integral to a third praxis-oriented perspective on social movements and political economy, to which we now turn.

THE POLITICAL ECONOMY OF PRAXIS 3:
NEO-GRAMSCIAN PERSPECTIVES

Following the 1971 publication in English of *Selections from the Prison Notebooks,* interest in Antonio Gramsci's approach to Marxism as a philosophy of praxis grew in several fields, including cultural studies, political economy, and social movement theory. In CPE, Mahon's (1984) landmark study of unequal structures of representation in the politics of the Canadian textile industry was followed in the late 1980s by research that began to probe the dynamics of hegemony and counterhegemony within which social movements are deeply implicated (e.g., Adkin and Alpaugh 1988; Carroll and Ratner 1989). In a Gramscian perspective, the concept of hegemony directs attention to the multifaceted practices and relations that exist in civil society as well as in and around the state, through which popular consent to the existing political-economic order is secured. Such consent is never permanent or absolute; and as the politics of neoliberalism and free trade illustrates, movements can be pivotal social forces both in organizing consent to the dominant order and in organizing dissent from that order – in constructing counter-hegemonic political agency.

One innovative use of this Gramscian thematic was launched by Jane Jenson (1989, 1991, 1993) in a series of papers that reflected on the specificity of the Canadian social formation and its changing universe of political discourse in the late twentieth century. Noting that in Canada the Fordist correlation of mass production and mass consumption assumed a particularly permeable, continentalist form (1989), Jenson considered the social bloc and societal paradigm that secured hegemony within a postwar development model and the new collective identities that were created through movement activism as the crises of the 1970s and 1980s destabilized that hegemony (1991). The pan-Canadian representation of a bilingual and bicultural nation, which in the postwar era had come to ideologically unify Canadians within a federal order, was first challenged by the Québecois nationalist movement. In deploying a collective identity founded on a dualistic vision of Canadian history, Quebec nationalism made claims for state power in two directions: towards the intergovernmental institutions of the Canadian state and towards the Québecois state and people (1993, 340). This collective identity could be used in mobilizing the population of Quebec behind claims made in federal-provincial negotiations, but it also brought an unintended consequence, as the political-opportunity structure was reorganized to recognize the claims of nations, ultimately in a series of constitutional negotiations. Aboriginal groups, which had refused the hegemonic project of assimilation outlined in the Liberal government's notorious White Paper of 1969 and had become mobilized into their own movement organizations in the ensuing two decades (Long 1992), were able to press national claims that amounted to "a counter-hegemonic challenge, both to pan-Canadian definitions of a bilingual country and to Québecois nationalists' representations of themselves and their claims" (Jenson 1993, 346). Jenson's analysis demonstrates that in times of crisis, when familiar, commonsensical certainties recede, a relatively powerless group can contribute to a reconfiguration of the universe of political discourse. In claiming space within that universe, Aboriginal nationalism gained resources and opportunities, but as Fiske reminds us, it was also faced with the its own dilemma as to how its communities might be imagined and constituted within the political-economic and discursive constraints of state, class, and gendered power. Jenson's own conclusions, reached in the early 1990s, continue to resonate in this new century: "the history of Québecois and Aboriginal nationalisms illustrates the importance of naming nations for social movement politics. The discourse of Canadian politics continues to be dominated, in everyday ways and from day to day, by contestation over who we are, and where we are going. Competing nationalisms exist side by side" (1993, 352).

If Jenson's interventions yielded some important insights on the role movements have played in hegemonic struggles to define the "national," another line of neo-Gramscian analysis has considered the counterhegemonic possibilities of popular-democratic and class-based movements and the problems and prospects of building solidarities across different collective identities and movement organizations and state-defined boundaries. Beginning with their study (1989) of the coalitions of social protest that formed in resistance to neoliberal restructuring in British Columbia, Bill Carroll and Bob Ratner have pursued a research program focused on the issue of how social movements have advanced counter-hegemonic politics in what Nancy Fraser has called "postsocialist" times. Carroll and Ratner have challenged the distinction that consigns organized labour to the category of an old social movement whose sensibilities are quite different from new movements such as feminism and peace activism. Their interviews with activists in Vancouver gave evidence of a labour movement increasingly open to various popular struggles, sensitive to the needs of diverse and marginalized constituencies, and capable of grasping the connections between movement activism and everyday life (1995). Their comparative findings suggest that the term "critical social movement" as defined by Magnusson and Walker may be more apposite than the somewhat spurious distinction between old and new, particularly since labour activists have increasingly been recruited from the same social categories (e.g., public servants and women) as form the constituency of new social movements (Warskett 1992).

A key issue in neo-Gramscian analysis concerns the shape and form of counterhegemonic practice. In a related study Carroll and Ratner (1996) considered whether in the practices of "cross-movement networking" and in the political sensibilities of activists one could discern a potential "counterhegemonic historic bloc" that might be constructed around a shared vision and an activist network spanning across movements. In probing activists' understanding of the nature of power, they found that most employed a "political economy" injustice frame; that is, they understood domination and injustice architectonically as structural, systemic, and materially grounded. The social network of activist organizations in Vancouver was found to be densely interconnected; in fact, nearly half the activists were involved in multiple-movement organizations spanning two or more movements, with the peace, labour, and feminist movements being particularly well connected. Moreover, across the various movements, activists who understood injustice in terms of a political-economy frame tended to be most involved in cross-movement networking, suggesting that

a political-economy injustice frame is elemental to counter-hegemonic politics: activism that pushes beyond conventional movement boundaries requires a common language and an analytical perspective that emphasizes the systemic and interconnected character of the various injustices and problems of late modernity. Viewed as a political project of mobilizing broad, diverse opposition to entrenched economic, political, and cultural power, counter-hegemony entails a tendential movement toward both comprehensive critiques of domination and comprehensive networks of activism. Cross-movement networking and the framing of injustice in political-economic terms are means by which activists elevate their politics beyond single issues and local contexts. (1996, 616)

Here we again see the dialogical relation between political economy and political agency: it is the vocabulary of political economy that informs and guides the practice of the more cosmopolitan, counter-hegemonic activists and movement intellectuals.

The neo-Gramscian perspective on social movements has been further elaborated in a host of case studies that have appeared in *SPE* since the mid-1990s. Roger Keil (1994) and Rod Bantjes (1997) have probed the precarious development of labour/environmental coalitions, whose success depends on a contingent and open process of redefining the identities and interests of workers and ecologists (Keil 1994, 28) as well as on local conditions, such as the strength of activist, coalition-building networks and the degree to which the state monopolizes the "power of constitution" of constituencies within civil society through commissions, official consultation, and the like (Bantjes 1997). Robert Hackett (2000) has traced the emerging, multifaceted media democratization movement in several countries and sees promise in building coalitions with other critical social movements whose own success increasingly depends on the democratization of communication. Kiran Mirchandani and Evangelia Tastsoglou (2000) develop a political-economic critique of the multiculturalist "tolerance" propagated in mainstream media, which otherizes subordinate ethno-racial groups as minorities to be tolerated by a Euro-North American majority. Opposing this hegemonic discourse is integrative antiracism, "an action-oriented strategy for institutional, systemic change to eradicate racism, homophobia and other interlocking forms of systemic discrimination" (64). Ruth Groff's (1997) study of the Philadelphia Unemployment Project (PUP) shows the value of an inclusive class politics that defines poor people as workers and workers as (potentially) poor people. PUP's outreach enabled strong alliances to be built with labour and within the religious community around a social-justice agenda, illustrating the importance in an era of globalizing capital of mobilizing "broad-based class movements which have repudiated narrow practices of the past" (1997, 113).

Lastly, Janet Conway's (2000) study of Toronto's Metro Network for Social Justice (MNSJ) provides further insights into the praxis of counterhegemony in the neoliberal 1990s. Rooted in 1980s coalitional struggles against the free trade agreements, the MNSJ exemplifies "a new political form that emerged over the last decade: the permanent, cross-sectoral, multi-issue social justice coalition" (2000, 45). Founded in 1992 in resistance to severe cuts to social services, the MNSJ grew in the ensuing five years to include 250 member groups and a regular activist base of 50 to 100 people. In Conway's view, what has been most distinctive is the MNSJ's strategic emphasis upon a Gramscian "war of position" – a long-term effort to transform worldviews among the working class and its allies, thereby eroding tacit consent for the status quo while nurturing "cultural dispositions hospitable to socialism" (43). Much of MNSJ's movement–building efforts were focused on a continuing campaign for economic and political literacy (EPL) that, at its peak, included community-based workshops on neoliberalism and popular-democratic alternatives to it, regular "train-the-trainer events" at which democratic pedagogies and expertise were developed, and "advancing knowledge" seminars at which activists could take their political analysis to a higher level. Although limited organizational resources and internal factional divisions cut short the EPL initiative, the MCJS's commitments to grassroots capacity-building, participatory knowledge creation, and democratic organizational development heralded "the emergence of a new political praxis in a new political era, organically embedded in the microprocesses of a social movement coalition"(65). Indeed, if the approaches to political economy that developed in the 1990s emphasized the emergent character of praxis, the massive protests that greeted the World Trade Organization (WTO) ministerial meeting in Seattle at the close of the twentieth century seemed to signal new, more global forms of praxis in a new political era.

INTO A NEW CENTURY: GLOBALIZATION AND THE POLITICAL ECONOMY OF PRAXIS

Although mass actions against corporate globalization were already visible by the mid-1990s (notably with the Zapatista insurgency in Chiapis in 1994 (Holloway 2002), the Seattle demonstrations dramatically confirmed the arrival of another protest cycle, this time oriented explicitly against neoliberal globalization and its central international institutions, including the WTO, the International Monetary Fund (IMF) and the World Bank. Following Seattle, protests against meetings of the international bourgeoisie at these and similar meetings – like the World Economic Forum of corporate leaders traditionally held in Davos, Switzerland – became routine. Washington, Windsor, Melbourne, Prague, Quebec, and Genoa were among the sites of mass demonstrations, each transformed (if only momentarily) into a symbol of the ongoing antiglobalization struggle.

Yet, the limitations of reacting to a rapidly-evolving agenda set by an organized global bourgeoisie were soon grasped by activists who sought to challenge the parameters of political debates and spaces of meetings convened by and for representatives of transnational capital. The World Social Forum, held annually in Porte Alegre, Brazil, since 2001, is the most obvious example of the recent effort by social activists to break from a reactive response to initiatives by the international bourgeoisie in order to create a proactive movement with an autonomous agenda and distinct politico-economic structures and spaces (Klein 2001). Indeed, the self-conscious transformation of existing neoliberal models is central to the new internationalism. For example, local participation in decision-making processes (e.g., through measures like the participatory community budgets integral to Porte Alegre's Social Forum) is held up in explicit contradistinction to the closed-door negotiations and top-down rule enforcement carried out by international capital and regulatory bodies like the WTO and the IMF, acting at capital's behest.

Canadian political economy has so far conceptualised this new "global peoples' movement" (Bleyer 2000, 31) by drawing on existing paradigms. For example, Ellen Gould (2000) builds on existing feminist paradigms when she suggests that by acting cooperatively, protestors implicitly reject the liberal individualist assumptions undergirding neoliberal policy and put new emphasis on collective equality rather than individual consumer "freedom." In so doing, Gould suggests that protestors confront both the (masculine) privatization of political protest and the privatization of the public commons integral to the neoliberal project, a position simultaneously challenging the processes and outcomes of "corporate-sponsored" globalization. Similarly, Bill Carroll (2001) builds on the insights of Lukacsian and neo-Gramscian analyses when he argues that disruptive protests against organizations like the WTO challenge neoliberal globalization's reified character, as well as its claim to hegemony. On the one hand, by disrupting the normal course of transnational elite planning, protests show that this form of nondemocratic globalization-from-above is not natural and inevitable but politically constructed and contingent. On the other hand, the manifestation of mass opposition challenges neoliberalism's claim to represent humanity's general interest (21). But if existing approaches have generated some helpful insights into the new internationalism, new forms of praxis suggest new problematics that will stretch and challenge established analytical approaches. We give three illustrative examples below of the new challenges confronting political economy and political activism in an era of transnational capitalism and anticapitalist protest.

First, a strength of CPE has been its ability to generate broad theoretical insights at the same time that it has remained firmly rooted within the political economy of Canada. This attention to national politics is precisely what Sam Gindin has found wanting in the movement against corporate globalization. As he argues, no internationally focused movement can sustain itself – let alone fundamentally challenge capitalism – without also sinking the deepest *domestic* roots. Any politics that is anti-capitalist must carry the fight into the national states that remain the ultimate bases of capitalism's power, and any anticapitalist politics with staying power can only evolve out of the collective experiences and struggles in workplaces, neighbourhoods, and universities and within historic communities such as nations (2002, 8).

Sinking such roots is tantamount to nurturing a "culture of resistance" that does not privilege episodic summit protest but that emphasizes, as much as anything, "decentralized antiglobalization praxis" rooted in a diversity of local struggles (Grundy and Howell 2001, 128). The ability to link the local and even the extralocal with the global is of particular importance in understanding the emergence and trajectory of the new internationalism, and it will figure heavily in any transformative strategies that might stem from such understanding.

Naomi Klein's book *No Logo* (2000) provides a good example of the insights that can be generated by analyzing the tension between local and international and the transition from the particular to the more general struggle. Klein documents how activists in the developed world who were agitating against the progressive invasion of logos in formerly public or private spaces (notably including advertisements in the stalls of university toilets!) sought new weapons in their struggle by investigating how the goods behind the logos were produced. This led, almost inevitably, to struggles in solidarity with workers in the developing world making products like Nike and Reebok athletic wear – the "other face" of the corporate project that first came to Western activists' attention as logos and advertisements were thrust in the faces of young consumers. In essence, Klein shows how the antisweatshop movement reacted to and built upon the slicing up of the commodity chain by creating what Watkins' (1963) might have called "forward and backward linkages" between local and national struggles against multinational corporations exploiting low-wage workers in the developing world. Klein's work serves as a useful reminder that a political economy of praxis can helpfully signal the interplay between political-economic structures and people's resistant political action – for example, by bringing to light the ways in which the disaggregation of production across geographically distant sites is connected to and may even act as a catalyst for the internationalisation of struggles that were formerly purely local. In so doing, political economists can build on their rootedness within the particular Canadian context to generate new insights into the linkages between local and global struggles that may inform counterhegemonic strategies evolving in the direction of "struggles of connection" and "struggles of imagination."

The second challenge for political economy echoes Magnusson's (1997) reminder that movements act and react within the context of other movements. Immediately following the protests against the WTO in Seattle, representatives of the international bourgeoisie began mobilising what Peter Bleyer (2000) has called the "corporate counteroffensive" to contain and limit the new internationalism. Reacting to the diversity of the so-called antiglobalization movement, transnational corporations have pursued divergent and sometimes contradictory strategies of exclusion, cooptation, and delegitimation, often with the aid of what Gramsci would call "organic intellectuals" acting for international capital. On the one hand, economic elites have sought to exclude protestors through heightened security measures and the retreat to inaccessible and repressive locations, a tactic exemplified by the WTO's decision to hold its 2002 ministerial in the emirate of Doha, Qater, and by the Canadian government's decision to pare down the

2002 G8 summit to fit within the remote and environmentally sensitive Rocky Mountain resort of Kanasakis.

On the other hand, the corporate counteroffensive has tried to selectively engage nongovernmental organizations in the negotiating process, in order to delimit, diffuse, and co-opt opposition, as in the World Economic Forum's recent creation of the Non-Governmental Organizations Council, now a permanent advisory fixture. Neoclassical economists have supported such efforts to co-opt the agenda of antiglobalization activists by insisting that neoliberalism is the best and maybe the only path towards a more equal world (particularly regarding prosperity in the developing world). At the same time, they have sought to delegitimate the new internationalism by insisting that participating activists represent no more than a highly contingent coalition of "special interests" holding onto unrealistic hopes of a return to the Fordist regime of the postwar years (see Becker and Becker 1996; Bhagwati 2000; Graham 2000; and the issue of the *Economist* for 29 September 2001). Taking Magnusson's observation seriously means subjecting the corporate counteroffensive and related instances of business activism to ongoing structural and discursive analysis.

Finally, political economy must address the reality that neoliberals "make history," but not exactly as they choose. The institutions of the post-war era, themselves the provisional outcomes of past social struggles, weigh heavily on neoliberal efforts to recreate a new world order and a new order in Canada. In the process new contradictions emerge, as well as opportunities for neoliberalism's opponents. For example, Coburn (forthcoming) has drawn on work by world polity scholars at Stanford University (Meyer et al. 1997) to argue that existing institutions from the postwar Fordist era, including the United Nations system and associated charters, provide important legitimating resources for transnational social movements. Actors within the new internationalism frequently draw upon existing documents like the UN Charter of Human Rights and Freedoms to make new, expanded claims about the rights of citizens world-wide to a modicum of economic, social, and cultural security. While such claims lack the enforcement mechanisms available to neoliberals, who can appeal for binding arbitration to boards like the WTO appellate dispute panel, they cannot be easily dismissed: they have normative weight around the globe, derived in part from the growing number of signatory nation-states to such treaties (including the Kyoto Summit Treaty on greenhouse gas emissions, which continues to accumulate signatories, notwithstanding the United States' withdrawal under President George W. Bush). This observation, combined with the fact that many nongovernmental organizations opposed to neoliberal globalization receive partial funding from UN agencies, serves as a reminder to both scholars and activists not to exaggerate the scale and scope of neoliberalism's victory. Neoliberalism faces at least one contradictory international trend, which is embedded within the UN system and environmental and rights charters, rather than within the WTO, the IMF, the World Bank, and investment and trade agreements. Globalization therefore has a contradictory, not a uniform, face and offers resources on both sides of the dialectic. If the new internationalism presents new challenges for political economy and for activists, however, this itself is not a novelty but a reflection of CPE's ongoing engagement with transformations – whether in political-economic structure or in progressive social activism.

We began by arguing that political economy and social movements, both of which are oriented towards what Habermas has called "emancipatory interests," have been engaged in a dialogical relationship. This relationship has enriched Canadian political economy, pushing it to respond creatively to developments within political practice and sparing it from the atrophic fate of many intellectual projects. At the same time, this dialogue has enriched social movements themselves as, for example, activists draw on political-economy frameworks to understand their own situation and to discover the transformative opportunities that inhabit specific situations. By interrogating "social facts" like ecological degradation, heterosexism, racial oppression, and speculative or casino capitalism, CPE has made an ongoing contribution to the practical work of activism, unmasking the contingent, constructed, and thus transformable nature of Canada. Political economy and social movements are entwined: the development of each has conditioned the development of both.

The central tasks in coming years will be to maintain both the dialogue with activists and the dynamic tension between political economy's commitment to progressive transformation of structure and its critical analysis of social movement praxis, including both hegemonic and counterhegemonic projects. At the same time, CPE has a potentially important role to play in the contemporary understanding of globalization as it exploits the tension between its historical attention to the particular social formation known as Canada and its critical awareness of the growing ties, among both ruling elites and challenging forces, between Canada and the rest of the world. It is in maintaining, not resolving, these tensions that CPE offers the most promise for theoretical innovation and the most useful critical distance in helping social movements realize the transformation of local and global political economies into sites of emancipated, creative human activity.

NOTES

1 Habermas (1971) contrasts three kinds of interests that are basic to the
human condition and that may guide the formation of knowledge: the
interest in controlling a phenomenon (e.g., through a technology), the
interest in understanding socio-cultural practices and texts, and the interest in emancipation. Knowledge produced on the basis of one interest
may differ markedly from knowledge produced on the basis of another.
For instance, while liberal economics takes for granted the apparent per-
manence of capitalism and is informed by an interest in control (including control by equilibrating market mechanisms), political economy prob-
lematizes the future of capitalism, and its scientific analyses are pursued
on the assumption that emancipatory change is possible and desirable.
2 In emphasizing the emergence of a praxis paradigm, we do not mean to
deny the continuing importance of architectonic analyses such as
Clement and Myles's (1994) comparative study of class and gender relations and Teeple's (2000) study of globalization and neoliberalism. Our
point is, rather, that by incorporating a praxicological concern, CPE
enriched and renewed itself, in contrast, say, to the political economy
current within American anthropology, which tended in the 1980s to be
superseded by a separate, praxis-oriented paradigm (Ortner 1984).

REFERENCES

Adamson, Nancy, L. Briskin, and M. McPhail. 1988. *Feminist Organizing for
Change.* Toronto: University of Toronto Press.
Adkin, Laurie E., and Catherine Alpaugh. 1988. "Labour, Ecology, and the
Politics of Convergence." *Socialist Studies* 4: 48–73.
Albo, Gregory. 1990. "The Twentieth Anniversary of the Waffle: Canada, Left-
Nationalism and Younger Voices," *Studies in Political Economy* 33:161-74.
Bantjes, Rod. 1997. "Hegemony and the Power of Constitution: Labour and
Environmental Coalition-Building in Maine and Nova Scotia." *Studies in
Political Economy* 54:59–90.
Becker, Gary, and Guity Nashat Becker. 1996. *The Economics of Everyday Life.*
New York: McGraw-Hill.
Bhagwati, Jagdish. 2000. *The Wind of the Hundred Days: How Washington Mis-
managed Globalization.* Cambridge: MIT Press.
Bleyer, Peter. 1997. "Coalitions of Social Movements as Agencies for Change: The
Action Canada Network." In William K. Carroll, ed., *Organizing Dissent: Contem-
porary Social Movements in Theory and Practice,* 134–50. Toronto: Garamond Press.
– 2000. "The Other Battle in Seattle." *Studies in Political Economy* 62:25–34.
Briskin, Linda. 1989. "Socialist Feminism: From the Standpoint of Practice."
Studies in Political Economy 30:87-114.

Carroll, William K. 1997. "Social Movements and Counterhegemony: Canadian Contexts and Social Theory." In William K. Carroll, ed., *Organizing Dissent: Contemporary Social Movements in Theory and Practice.* 3–38. Toronto: Garamond Press.

– 2001. "Undoing the End of History: Canada-Centred Reflections on the Challenge of Globalization." *Socialist Studies Bulletin.* 63–4: 5–31.

Carroll, William K., and R.S. Ratner. 1989. "Social Democracy, Neo-Conservatism, and Hegemonic Crisis in British Columbia." *Critical Sociology* 16(1): 29–53.

– 1995. "Old Unions and New Social Movements." *Labour/Le Travail* 35: 195–221

– 1996. "Master Framing and Cross-Movement Networking in Contemporary Social Movements." *Sociological Quarterly* 37(4):601–25.

Carroll, William K., and Murray Shaw. 2001. "Consolidating a Neo-liberal Policy Bloc in Canada: 1976–1996." *Canadian Public Policy* 27: 195–216.

Chouinard, Vera. 1998. "Challenging Law's Empire: Rebellion, Incorporation, and Changing Geographics of Power in Ontario's Legal Clinic System." *Studies in Political Economy* 55:65–92.

Clarke, Tony. 2000. "Taking on the WTO: Lessons from the Battle of Seattle." *Studies in Political Economy* 62:7–16.

Clement, Wallace. 1997. "Whither the New Canadian Political Economy?" In Wallace Clement, ed., *Understanding Canada: Building on the New Canadian Political Economy,* 3–18. Montreal and Kingston: McGill-Queen's University Press.

Clement, Wallace, and John Myles. 1994. *Relations of Ruling: Class and Gender in Postindustrial Societies.* Montreal and Kingston: McGill-Queen's University Press.

Coburn, Elaine. Forthcoming. "Interrogating Globalization: Emerging Contradictions and Conflicts." In Yildiz Atasoy and William K. Carroll, eds., *Global Shaping and Its Alternatives.* Toronto: Garamond Press.

Conway, Janet. 2000. "Knowledge, Power, Organization: Social Justice Coalitions at a Crossroads." *Studies in Political Economy* 62:43–70.

Cox, Robert. 1995. "Critical Political Economy." In Björn Hettne, ed., *International Political Economy: Understanding Global Disorder,* 31–45. Halifax: Fernwood Books.

Drache, Daniel, and Duncan Cameron. 1985. *The Other McDonald Report.* Toronto: Lorimer.

Findlay, Sue. 1993. "Forum: Reinventing the Community: A First Step in the Process of Democratization," *Studies in Political Economy.* 42:157–67.

Fiske, Jo-Anne. 1996. "The Womb is to the Nation as the Heart is to the Body: Ethnopolitical Discourses of the Canadian Indigenous Women's Movement." *Studies in Political Economy* 51:65–96.

Fraser, Nancy. 1995. "Struggle over Needs: Outline of a Socialist-Feminist Critical Theory of Late Capitalist Political Culture." In Nancy Fraser, ed., *Unruly Practices*, 161–87. Minneapolis: University of Minnesota Press.

Gindin, Sam. 2002. "Anti-Capitalism and the Terrain of Social Justice." *Monthly Review* 53(9): 1–14.

Gould, Ellen. 2000. "Siren Call from Seattle." *Studies in Political Economy* 62:35–41.

Graham, Edward M. 2000. *Fighting the Wrong Enemy: Antiglobal Activists and Multinational Enterprises*. Washington, DC: Institute for International Economics.

Gramsci, Antonio. 1971. *Selections from the Prison Notebooks*. New York: International Publishers.

Groff, Ruth. 1997. "Class Politics by Any Other Name: Organizing the Unemployed." *Studies in Political Economy* 54:91–118.

Grundy, John, and Alison Howell. 2001. "Negotiating the Culture of Resistance: A Critical Assessment of Protest Politics." *Studies in Political Economy* 66:121–32.

Habermas, Jürgen. 1971. *Knowledge and Human Interests*. London: Heinemann.

Hackett, Robert. 2000. "Taking Back the Media: Notes on the Potential for a Communicative Democracy Movement." *Studies in Political Economy* 63:61–86.

Harder, Lois. 1996. "Depoliticizing Insurgency: The Politics of the Family in Alberta." *Studies in Political Economy* 50:37–64.

Helvacioglu, Banu. 1992. "The Thrills and Chills of Postmodernism: The Western Intellectual Vertigo." *Studies in Political Economy* 38:7–34.

Holloway, John. 2002. *Change the World without Taking Power*. London: Pluto Press.

Jenson, Jane. 1989. "Different but Not Exceptional: Canada's Permeable Fordism." *Canadian Review of Sociology and Anthropology* 26:69–94.

– 1991. "All the World's a Stage: Ideas, Spaces and Times in Canadian Political Economy." *Studies in Political Economy* 36:43–72.

– 1993. "Naming Nations: Making Nationalist Claims in Canadian Public Discourse." *Canadian Review of Sociology and Anthropology* 30:337–58.

Jenson, Jane, and Fuat Keyman. 1990. "Comment: Must We All Be 'Post-Modern'?" *Studies in Political Economy* 31:141–58.

Keil, Roger. 1994. "Green Work Alliances: The Political Economy of Social Ecology." *Studies in Political Economy* 43:7–38.

Klodawsky, Fran, and Caroline Andrew. 1999. "Acting Locally: What is the Progressive Potential?" *Studies in Political Economy* 59:149–72.

Klein, Naomi. 2000. *No Logo: Taking Aim at the Brand Bullies*. New York: Picador.

– 2001. "Farewell to 'The End of History': Organization and Vision in Anti-Corporate Movements." In Leo Panitch and Colin Leys, eds., *Socialist Register 2002*, 1–14. London: Merlin Press.

Langille, David. 1987. "The Business Council on National Issues and the Canadian State." *Studies in Political Economy* 24:41–85.

Levitte, Kari. 1970. *Silent Surrender.* Toronto: Macmilla.

Long, David A. 1992. "Culture, Ideology and Militancy: The Movement of Indians in Canada, 1969–1991." In William K. Carroll, ed., *Organizing Dissent: Contemporary Social Movements in Theory and Practice*, 118–34. 1st ed. Toronto: Garamond Press.

Luxton, Meg, and Leah F. Vosko. 1998. "Where Women's Efforts Count: The 1996 Census Campaign and Family Politics in Canada." *Studies in Political Economy* 56:49–82.

MacDonald, Eleanor. 1998. "Vectors of Identity: Determination, Association, and Intervention" *Studies in Political Economy* 57:7–36.

Magnusson, Warren. 1997. "Globalization, Movements, and the Decentred State." In William K. Carroll, ed., *Organizing Dissent: Contemporary Social Movements in Theory and Practice*, 94–113. Toronto: Garamond Press.

Magnusson, Warren, and Rob Walker. 1988. "De-centring the State: Political Theory and Canadian Political Economy." *Studies in Political Economy* 26:37–71.

Mahon, Rianne. 1984. *The Politics of Industrial Restructuring.* Toronto: University of Toronto Press.

Meyer, John, John Boli, George M. Thomas, and Francisco O. Ramirez. 1997. "World Society and the Nation-State." *American Journal of Sociology.* 103(1): 144–81.

Michaud, Jacinthe. 2000. "The Restructuring of the Health Care System in Quebec: Its Impact on the Women's Health Movement." *Studies in Political Economy* 61:31–48.

Mirchandani, Kiran, and Evangelia Tastsoglou. 2000. "Towards a Diversity beyond Tolerance." *Studies in Political Economy* 61:49–78.

Ortner, Sherry B. 1984. "Theory in Anthropology since the Sixties." *Comparative Studies in Society and History* 26: 126–66.

Panitch, Leo. 1987. "Capitalist Restructuring and Labour Strategies." *Studies in Political Economy* 24:131–49.

Ratner, R.S. 1997. "Many Davids, One Goliath." In William K. Carroll, ed., *Organizing Dissent: Contemporary Social Movements in Theory and Practice*, 271–86. Toronto: Garamond Press.

Rayside, David. 1988. "Gay Rights and Family Values: The Passage of Bill 7 in Ontario." *Studies in Political Economy* 26:109–47.

Resnick. 1977. *Land of Cain: Class and Nationalism in English Canada, 1945–1975.* Vancouver: New Star Books.

Smith, Dorothy. 1987. *The Everyday World as Problematic.* Toronto: University of Toronto Press.

Tarrow, Sidney. 1998. *Power in Movement: Social Movements and Contentious Politics*, 2d ed. Cambridge: Cambridge University Press.

Teeple, Gary. 2000. *Globalization and the Decline of Social Reform.* 2d ed. Toronto: Garamond Press.

Useem, Michael. 1984. *The Inner Circle.* Oxford: Oxford University Press.

Van der Pijl, Kees. 1998. *Transnational Classes and International Relations.* New York: Routledge.

Walker, Gillian. 1990. "The Conceptual Politics of Struggle: Wife Battering, the Women's Movement and the State." *Studies in Political Economy* 33:63–90.

Warskett, Rosemary. 1992. "Defining Who We Are: Solidarity and Diversity in the Ontario Labour Movement." In Colin Leys and Marguerite Mendell, eds., Culture and Social Change, 109–27. Montreal: Black Rose Books.

Watkins, Melville. 1963. "A Staples Theory of Economic Growth." *Canadian Journal of Economics and Political Science* 29:141–58.

– 1968. *Foreign Ownership and the Structure of Canadian Industry: Report of the Task Force on the Structure of Canadian Industry.* Ottawa: Queen's Printer.

Williams, Glen. 1992. "Greening the New Canadian Political Economy." *Studies in Political Economy* 37:5–30.

PART TWO

Welfare State Restructuring: Shifting Employment Norms and New Household Forms

5 Politics and Transformation: Welfare State Restructuring in Canada

WENDY MCKEEN AND ANN PORTER

The welfare state affects the lives of all Canadians. Its activities range from providing health care and education to providing some form of income for those who are unable to support themselves because of illness or old age or because they are unable to find work. Dramatic changes have occurred in the welfare state in Canada in the last thirty years as they have elsewhere in the advanced capitalist countries, and particularly in the last decade. These changes reflect larger debates and shifts in policy that have taken place concerning the role of the state in the economy and in the provision of the social goods that are needed for daily survival, as well for individual growth and development. As governments around the world have come to accept a neoliberal paradigm, there has been a shift from the state to both the market and the family in terms of how social needs are met. This shift has had profound implications for the range of social welfare activities the state is involved in, for the nature of the programs, for how they are delivered, and for who benefits from them. Beyond this, these changes have implications for the broader goals of equity, fairness, and the quality of life that individuals may enjoy.

The concept of social reproduction is important in understanding welfare state development. Social reproduction refers to the process whereby people's basic needs are met. This process involves ensuring that people have a certain minimum to survive on, that the requirements for longer-term development and education are met, and that people are cared for or have the means to look after themselves if they are sick or unable to work. The state, the market, and a range of other

institutions, including the family, the church, trade unions, benevolent associations, and charities and food banks have, at different times,
assumed varying responsibility for ensuring that social reproduction
takes place. Both the division of responsibility between these institutions and the standards that are set for how income security is provided or care is given have been contested issues, shaped by such
factors as changing economic conditions, evolving family structures,
and federal-provincial institutional arrangements, as well as by con-
flicting ideas and political struggles.

The welfare state in Canada developed in a piecemeal and frag-
mentary fashion. Early in the century, responsibility for ensuring
human welfare was left primarily to the family and the market, as well
as to charities, religious organizations, and other associations of civil
society. During and after the Second World War, however, as the
welfare state expanded, the state assumed greater responsibility for
social reproduction. Responsibility for the provision of health, welfare
and education was assigned at Confederation to the provinces, while
the federal government was granted the major means of raising
revenue. The result has been a long history of negotiation and tensions between the different levels of government, with the provinces
establishing and administering major programs related to education,
social assistance, and health and the federal government being
involved through the funding of programs. In addition the federal
government has established programs involving the transfer of income
directly to individuals, including programs related to pensions, unemployment, child or family benefits, and, more recently, the Canada Millennium Scholarships.

There are two major questions that this chapter addresses. The first
concerns the nature and the extent of the transformation of the
welfare state in Canada. What form has this transformation taken and
what are the implications for individuals and groups within Canadian
society? The second major question has to do with the politics of
welfare state transformation. Which social forces and groups of actors
have pushed for welfare state restructuring and in what direction? A
key underlying question is how can one articulate social issues in a way
that mobilizes social forces and presents both an effective counter to
the prevailing view and the beginnings of an alternative conceptualization of the welfare state, the economy, and the household? The
chapter is divided into three sections. The first discusses theoretical
and comparative interpretations of the welfare state restructuring of
the last twenty-five years; the second section, the nature of welfare state
transformation in Canada; and the final section provides an evaluation
of the politics of welfare state transformation.

We argue that the new welfare state is characterized by an "employ-ability" model emphasizing reentry into the work force, by the shift from universality to the targeting of benefits, the creation of a tiered system of benefits, and a shift in the subject of benefits from adults (especially unemployed adults) to children. Not only has the welfare state in Canada been restructured, it has been transformed. As we show in the cases of employment insurance and federal child benefits, the transformation taking place is one from a more generous system to what neoliberals have described as a "tough love" social welfare system that aims to help welfare "dependents" kick their habit.[1] The result has been an increasingly punitive model; increased poverty, inequalities, and hardship among certain groups; and the download-ing of responsibility for meeting social needs to individuals and to the home. Furthermore, the politics of welfare state reform has shifted as progressive forces and social groups have become increasingly mar-ginalized in welfare state discussions.

WELFARE STATE RESTRUCTURING: COMPARATIVE AND THEORETICAL APPROACHES

Considerable debate has taken place concerning both the nature of recent welfare state restructuring and the underlying political forces bringing about change. Paul Pierson, drawing on findings from Great Britain, the United States, Germany, and Sweden argues that there is little evidence of welfare state dismantling. He suggests that the growth of the welfare state itself created certain vested interests ("the consumers and providers of social services") that resist change and, further, that politicians' concerns for reelection make restructuring difficult (1996, 176).

Myles and Pierson (1997), on the other hand, analyzing Canada and the United States, argue that there *has* been restructuring, indeed, that we are witnessing the consolidation of a new type of welfare state. This welfare state is characterized not by universality but by the selective targeting of benefits based on income. This type of program, they argue, is "ideally suited to the politics of austerity." It has been supported politically by a coalition of conservative critics who see these changes as a way of increasing work incentives and reducing expenditures and by liberal policy reformers who have seen it as a way of increasing benefits to the poor.

Clayton and Pontusson (1998) also argue that significant welfare state restructuring has occurred, but that the changes have not been positive. They point out that poverty and inequality have increased and that security of employment and income has diminished, while the growth of per capita social spending has failed to keep up with per capita GDP. They have further found a shift in spending from services to transfer payments, on transfers from social insurance schemes to social assistance, and they have found that the service component has been extensively reformed according to market principles, affecting both the delivery and the quality of services provided. In terms of the politics of welfare state development, Clayton and Pontusson argue that such factors as societal interests, coalitions between different sectors, and long-term mass unemployment need to be taken into account in assessing the politics of change.

While these authors raise a number of important points, we propose a somewhat different model of welfare state development. As feminist analyses have stressed, welfare states cannot be evaluated simply in terms of the relationship between states and markets. It is also critical to take into account unpaid work within the home and how it has contributed to human welfare and relieved both states and markets from this work. From this perspective, the relationship between states, markets, and *families* is critical. Ann Orloff, Julia O'Connor, Sheila Shaver, and others have insisted, for example, that from the perspective of women a key criterion in evaluating welfare states should be whether programs allow for personal autonomy and independence, or for the "capacity to maintain an autonomous household" (O'Connor 1993, 511–12; Orloff 1993; O'Connor, Orloff, and Shaver 1999, 32). With this in mind, they argue, for example, that services that relieve households of caring work and thus provide all household members with access to paid work are of fundamental importance.

Analyzing the welfare state from the perspective of the relationship between families, markets, and states provides important insights. The model, however, needs to be modified in certain important respects. First, a range of other institutions of civil society, including voluntary organizations, churches, and political advocacy groups, have also played a role in welfare state development, although the range and relative significance of these institutions have varied considerably both over time and from one region in Canada to another. The relationship between families, markets, and states was particularly critical as a key welfare state nexus in the period after the Second World War (Porter, forthcoming), but the relationhip is not necessarily a fixed one that always assumes the same importance. Welfare state development early in the century, for example, cannot be analyzed without an understanding of the role of charitable organizations both in the provision of welfare and in advocating reform. Similarly, welfare state development in Quebec cannot be understood without a consideration of the key role played by the church until at least the mid-1960s. At the same time, a consideration of alternative ways of addressing the needs of social reproduction cannot be fully explored without going beyond the family-market-state relation to look at alternative networks within the community and the ability to have a voice in shaping the policies that govern us.

Second, the criteria by which we evaluate welfare states need to be further assessed. A critical element, for example, is not simply having the income to support an "autonomous household," as suggested by scholars such as Orloff and O'Connor, but also having the ability to create the networks of support that can provide a sense of community and reduce the isolation that is often part of caring activities. It is important, in this respect, to consider various alternative, nonmarket ways to organize social reproduction. For example, the state, the community, and households could be involved in developing networks and building solidarity and a shared concern for the welfare of others.

A further criterion is related to the question of political voice, or the ability to influence the policy agenda with respect to social need. Jenson and Phillips (1996) argue that citizenship entails not only benefits but the right to be represented to and by the state. Celia Winkler (1998) suggests that in a democratic society we all have a need not only for care or to give care and for material resources obtained through income but also for a political voice that enables us to help shape the policies that govern us. These needs, she argues, are inextricably intertwined. The need for care or to give care affects one's ability to earn income and both receiving and giving care affect one's ability to participate politically.

Third, notions both of politics and of transformation need to be more centrally incorporated within our models of welfare state development. Myles, Pierson, and others tend to define political agency in fairly narrow terms as politician-constituent relations or as the activities of those who have been successful in establishing the new hegemonic, or governing, welfare state model. The feminist literature, on the other hand, often tends to present a static model of the relationship between states, markets, and families (Porter 1999). Incorporating a focus on political agency, broadly defined, is critical in providing a more dynamic model that can help assess the conditions under which change can come about. This means not only having a better understanding of the broader political-economic conditions constraining the options available and of the political forces pushing for neoliberal changes. Equally important is having a sense of the activities and effectiveness of the more marginal political coalitions and actors who may be pushing for welfare state change in other directions. In this respect, it is helpful to look not only at macrolevel trends and developments but also at struggles at the policy community level. To do so is to recognize that much of the struggle over the welfare state occurs as debates over policy – whether it be policy concerning poverty, health, or education – and usually only involves a narrow group of political actors, not the entire political community (Pross 1986; Coleman and Skogstad 1990; McKeen 2001). Actors' political choices are at least partly shaped by the specific constraints and opportunities operating within these policy contexts, and developments here contribute to the shaping of the governing regime. While the relationship between states, markets, and families provides a useful analytic model, then, it needs to be modified both to recognize the role, or potential role, of other institutions in the provision of welfare and to incorporate more centrally notions of both politics and transformation.

TRANSFORMATION OF THE WELFARE STATE: FROM A KEYNESIAN TO A NEOLIBERAL WELFARE STATE

The period from the Second World War until the mid-1970s was one of welfare state expansion in Canada, as elsewhere in the advanced capitalist countries. During the Second World War two key programs of the Canadian welfare state were introduced: Unemployment Insurance (1940) and Family Allowances (1944). This was followed in the 1960s and the early 1970s by a major expansion of welfare programs, which included at the federal level the introduction of universal health insurance, two new pension programs (the Canada Pension Plan and Guaranteed Income Supplement and the Canada Assistance Plan, providing federal-provincial cost-sharing for social assistance and social services), the extension of cost-sharing in health and education (the Established Programs Financing Act), and a significant expansion of the UI program. At the provincial level both the education and the health care systems were also expanded significantly.

The welfare state of this period contained certain key features. First, the state came to assume far greater responsibility than it had previously for social reproduction. For the first time it was acknowledged that the shortcomings of the economic system itself could result in unemployment through no fault of one's own. Consistent with the Keynesian notions that underpinned the state's approach to macroeconomic policy, it was argued that the federal government had responsibility both to ensure that unemployment remained at relatively low levels and that income security was provided for those who fell through the cracks. Welfare state programs, then, were not only considered important for social well-being, but further, because they maintained levels of income and aggregate demand, they were seen as beneficial to the economy as a whole.

Second, while the principle did not apply to all programs, there was greater emphasis on the universality of benefits granted as a right based on participation in the labour force or as part of the social rights of citizenship. Finally, this was a welfare state based on a family-wage model, where it was assumed that men would be the primary bread-winners and that women within the home would continue to play the key role in ensuring that the needs of social reproduction were met. This assumption, combined with greater state involvement meant that social welfare became more firmly centred on a core state-family-market nexus. While the period is often presented as the golden age of the welfare state (Esping-Andersen 1996), large numbers of minorities and women, especially those who were not engaged in full-time employment, were excluded from the full benefit of the welfare state and thus the welfare state itself helped sustain and reinforce structural inequalities.

By the mid-1970s this period of expansion had come to an end. As described below, a number of factors, including the growing economic crisis, fiscal pressure on the welfare state, changing labour market and family forms, and political struggles were forcing a reevaluation of the welfare state model. The restructuring was, however, an uneven process that varied considerably across sectors. Retrenchment in some programs, such as UI, began as early as 1975. Overall, even though restraint measures were introduced in a range of programs, social expenditures continued to increase through much of the 1980s (Prince 1999). It was in the 1990s that the most substantial welfare state restructuring took place. At the federal level, for example, the 1995 budget was particularly significant in both reducing expenditures and restructuring federal involvement in social policy. The Canada Assistance Plan and the Established Programs Financing Act were replaced by the Canada Health and Social Transfer, providing transfers to the provinces with fewer conditions attached but at much-reduced funding levels. At the provincial level governments have also reduced expenditures and undertaken sweeping welfare state reforms, including reforms in education, health care, and social assistance. They have included the privatization of many services, the introduction of workfare programs within social assistance programs, and the closing and restructuring of many schools and hospitals.

By the end of the 1990s a new neoliberal welfare state had been consolidated. This new welfare state model represents a transformation in a number of important respects. First, there has been a shift in underlying philosophy. Neoliberal macroeconomic ideology, which became more entrenched through the 1980s and 1990s, has had deep ramifications for the structure and design of welfare state programs. It has emphasized free market forces, a reduced role for the state, and a concern with inflation rather than unemployment. The reduction of expenditure on social programs in this period became a priority. Supply-side arguments that high unemployment was a result not of market failures but of individual behaviour, attitudes to work, and the nature of income security programs themselves further influenced the shape of welfare state programs. Rather than being viewed as beneficial to economic growth, income security programs were now seen as creating unwanted "dependencies" and "disincentives" to work. Further, it was argued that income security programs needed to be made more compatible with a changed economic environment: in particular, that they should be redesigned to further economic efficiency, international competitiveness, and labour market adjustment.[2] Concerns about social benefits or social equality were pushed to the background.

Second, social programs have been redesigned with a view to making them compatible with new economic growth models, the emphasis on individual behaviour, and the new philosophy towards dependency. This has involved an increased emphasis on incentives to remain in or to enter the labour force; the use of social programs to subsidize low-wage employment; and a shift from "passive" income support programs providing only income transfers to individuals to "active" programs encouraging reentry into the labour market.

Thirdly, there has been a shift away from the concept of universality and an increased "targeting" of benefits to the poor, who are defined in terms of family income levels. While targeting has always been the basis for provincial social assistance, it has now become the core model for the key areas of federal child benefits and old age security (Myles and Pierson 1997). Universality within the UI program has also been eroded and a "tiered" system that favours the full-time steadily employed has been created.

Finally, the relationship between state, market, and families has been reconfigured. Overall, there has been a downloading of responsibility for social reproduction from the state to both the market and the family, while at the same time there has been an increase in the numbers of other organizations of civil society, such as food banks, that are attempting to fill the needs of those who fall between the cracks. In terms of the criteria for eligibility there have been two important shifts: from the individual to the family as the basis for determining benefit eligibility and from adults to children as beneficiaries of the welfare state.

These shifts are occurring in varying degrees across a wide range of programs at both the federal and provincial levels. In order to demonstrate what these transformations have meant we draw on the experience at the federal level of the UI/EI and family/child benefits programs. Both these programs have undergone extensive restructuring in the last decade. Not only have there been changes within these programs, but there have been shifts between sectors that represent an important transformation in welfare state priorities: there has been a major withdrawal of funding from unemployment insurance (renamed employment insurance, or EI – on the name change, see below), while the areas that have been targeted the most for new welfare state expenditure have been child poverty and child benefits. Within the overall welfare state income-security structure, then, there has been a shift from adults, especially the unemployed, as the recipients of benefits to children. Further, there has been a shift from labour force status to family income as a basis for receiving state benefits.

UNEMPLOYMENT INSURANCE/EMPLOYMENT INSURANCE

Unemployment Insurance (UI) has been a key labour-market-based welfare state program, providing benefits to the unemployed according to past participation in the labour force. The UI program was one of the first of the welfare state programs to undergo substantive restructuring. A series of amendments between 1975 and 1978 was significant in that it pointed to the direction of income security reform over the next twenty-five years. It reflected the shift away from the view that unemployment could occur through market failures to a supply-side analysis focusing on individual behaviour and attitudes to work. Further, there was a growing concern not only with reducing expenditures but also with incentives for entering or remaining in the labour force, often in low-wage jobs. The stated goal of the amendments was to reduce "disincentives to work," and to "encourage workers to establish more stable work patterns and develop longer attachments to the active work force, thereby reducing their dependency on unemployment insurance," and UI was to assist in the "proper functioning of the labour market."[3] Reforms increased the penalty for those who left their employment voluntarily, increased the number of weeks needed to qualify (although the significance of UI to the regional, particularly the Atlantic, economies was recognized through the introduction of a "variable entrance requirement" dependent on the regional rate of unemployment), reduced the rate of benefit, and made it possible for UI funds to be used "in more directly productive or developmental ways." For the first time, a tiered system of eligibility was introduced in which more stringent entrance requirements were put in place for "repeat users" (people with a second claim within fifty-two weeks), "new entrants" and "re-entrants" to the labour force, as well as for part-time workers.

These themes were taken up in a much more serious way with the reforms in the 1990s, first under the Conservatives and then under the Liberals in the years between 1994 and 1997. Amendments, again, were aimed both at deficit reduction and reducing the "disincentives to work" by increasing the number of weeks of work needed to qualify, reducing the rate of benefits and possible length of time on them, and completely disqualifying anyone who quit voluntarily without just cause, refused a suitable job offer, or was fired for misconduct.

The amendments that came into effect in 1997 represent the most dramatic changes to the UI program. Most significantly, the changes constituted a major withdrawal of the social safety net for the unemployed. The proportion of the unemployed receiving UI dropped from 83 percent in 1989 to 42 percent by 1997 (Porter forthcoming). As a result of these reforms, far from being an expense, the UI program, through premiums levied, has become a major source of federal revenue. In addition, changes that make UI more difficult to obtain greatly reduce the options available to people and further encourage the growth and maintenance of low-wage, exploitative working conditions. The program name was changed from "unemployment insurance" to "employment insurance," further reflecting the increased emphasis on an active labour market program that would reduce the disincentive to work (Canada 1995). (The amount of funds provided for active reemployment measures has been small, however, and for the most part has taken the form of wage subsidies and income supplements for low-wage employment.)

Amendments have also moved the program much more decisively to a two-tier model of income security, largely as a result of the shift in the basis of eligibility from weeks worked to hours worked, along with greatly increased qualifying requirements for those working part-time (less than thirty-five hours a week), as well as for those defined as new entrants and re-entrants into the labour force.[4] Again, this change has encouraged the creation of a contingent, low-wage labour market with few alternatives. Altogether, these changes represent an erosion of universality, in that while previously, all paid occupations were insured against the risk of unemployment, now only a minority are. Those who are targeted as eligible for benefits, however, are not the poorest as defined by income but the somewhat better-off workers, those who are employed virtually full-time, for the full year, with only short spells of unemployment.

FEDERAL FAMILY/CHILD BENEFITS

Family/child benefits have been the prime area of federal government income support for families with children. They have historically comprised a mixture of universal and income-tested programs (i.e., the family allowance, the child tax exemption, and the child tax credit program). The system has been a prime target for reform for the past three decades, particularly since the mid-1980s, with measures being aimed at reducing expenditures, primarily by devaluing and eventually eliminating the universal aspect of the system (the family allowance program). The family allowance was subjected to a strategy of change by stealth through measures such as deindexation and a claw-back, such that by the late 1980s it had lost much of its value and public support. The income-tested refundable child tax credit, first introduced in 1978, gradually became the centrepiece of the system. Amidst a new concern about the issue of "child" poverty in the early 1990s, the system was rolled into a single refundable income-tested tax credit program that also provided a supplement for those with employment income. The current child benefits program, the National Child Benefit (NCB) (implemented in July 1998 and heralded as the first substantive success of the new collaborative federalism established under the Social Union Framework Agreement) provides benefits to low- and moderate income families through an income-tested tax credit, with eligibility and the amount received being based on family income as reported on the previous year's income tax form. This has also been referred to as a negative income tax (NIT) mechanism (Stroick and Jenson 1999; MacDonald 1999; Boismenu and Jenson 1998; Mahon and Phillips 2002).

Beyond the large withdrawal of funds from child benefits, there has been a fundamental change in the program's philosophy. The family allowance program, in particular, had reflected collectivist ideals – for example, recognition of the social contribution being made by parents in raising future Canadian citizens. It had reflected a sentiment both that all parents were deserving of a benefit (the principle of universality) and that the disposable incomes of those families with children and those without should be equalized (the principle of horizontal equity). These notions no longer have a place in the child benefits system. Whereas the family allowance provided a set monthly amount for all families with children, the new program is oriented primarily to children at risk (i.e., children in low- and moderate-income families). The goal, in other words, is to alleviate the poverty of parents who have failed as individuals to support themselves and their children.

State (collective) responsibility for the welfare of families has given way to the concerns expressed in the two stated goals of the NCB: to address "poverty" and, as with UI, to reinforce work incentives. Underlying these goals is the principle of maximizing private responsibility for the care of children; the state will step in only when there has been a failure of the family to provide for its own. There is a concomitant concern with ensuring that Canadians find, and remain in, employment. This turn in approach was signalled by the introduction in the early 1990s of a supplement portion available only to parents who had employment income. The NCB also serves in a more general sense to promote parents' attachment to the workforce by guaranteeing the same level of benefits to those on social assistance and those in paid work, thus ensuring that families will always be better off as a result of being in paid employment (Jenson 2000).

Child benefits have also been a primary site in which family-based rights are being asserted at the expense of individual-based ones. In the 1970s and early 1980s it was acknowledged that the family allowance was particularly important for many women in giving them a cheque "in their own name." By the early 1990s, however, as the focus shifted to "child poverty" any concern with the issue of financial independence for women was lost. Family-income testing was instituted on the grounds that it was "fairer" for "families and children."

What are the consequences of this restructuring? When one looks at the two programs, certain trends are apparent. First, welfare state restructuring has resulted in an erosion of notions of social solidarity and social equality and the downloading of responsibility for social reproduction from the state to the market, the family, and other institutions of civil society. With respect to child and family benefits policy, for example, the system is being geared to providing tax credits, mitigating against the possibility of a more collectivist, or community-based, approach to meeting child care needs (Bach and Phillips 1997, 253; Jenson and Sineau 2001). At the same time, there has been a downloading of the responsibility for the risks and costs of both unemployment and parenting to the individual and family/household, precisely at a time when those risks and costs have become greater than ever. This is exacerbated as restructuring in the areas of health, education and other social services have also increased individual and household (largely women's) responsibility for social reproduction.

Second, despite the current agenda focused on child poverty, poverty rates have been growing. Poverty increased from 13 percent to 17.6 percent of working-age Canadians between 1980 and 1996, including increases in the depth of poverty for families and the elderly, despite improvements in the economy (Durst 1999, 20, 25). The majority of the unemployed now have to rely on other family members or provincial social assistance plans (Canadian Labour Congress 2002, 3), which, even when supplemented by child benefits, are at a rate far less than they would have been receiving if the UI program was still fully in place. In addition, within the UI/EI program, rates that in the 1970s were as high as $66^2/_3$ percent of earnings are now only at 55 percent; again, leading to increases in poverty. With respect to child benefits, even with recent increases the benefit level is far from adequate for covering the real costs of raising children (Stroick and Jenson 1999; Durst 1999). In addition, with many provincial governments clawing back a portion of the benefit from welfare recipients, the new program is failing to alleviate the severe poverty of the poorest of poor families (those on welfare) or to curb the overall downward trend in welfare incomes (Pulkingham and Ternowetsky 1999; Jenson 2000; National Council of Welfare 1999).

Third, inequalities and polarization have been increasing. Changes in income security benefits clearly encourage a labour market structure where there are some "good" jobs but where there is also a large pool of low-wage, contingent work. At the same time, changes in income security provisions, such as for UI, make access to benefits more difficult to obtain for those working in that low-wage, contingent-work sector. The result, then, is growing polarization between those who have access to relatively stable jobs and UI/EI and those who are able to find only short-term, intermittent work and who have little access to state income security benefits.

Fourth, this polarization is reinforcing differences on the basis of gender, region, age, and, possibly, ethnicity. Women, for example, are both overrepresented in the short-term work category and have been disproportionately affected by the cuts to the UI program. So have young people.[5] The cuts have also had a disproportional effect on regional economies. The significance of UI/EI transfers to certain areas of Quebec and the Atlantic provinces, for example, has meant that any program changes, and particularly a reduction in income transfers, can have an especially disruptive effect. There is also considerable variation within regions, with many of the unemployed in major urban areas finding it very difficult to qualify (Canadian Labour Congress 1999).

In addition, the consequence of the increased reliance on the family for caring responsibilities combined with the assumption that women are or should be working in the paid labour force has meant that the pressures for women, especially minority women, are high. Women often experience not only increased domestic labour but a more marginal and fragile position within the labour market as the juggling of jobs, daycare, and other responsibilities becomes more difficult. Single mothers, who tend to be disadvantaged when it comes to securing material resources, experience these pressures in particularly acute ways and have become easy targets for blame as negligent parents, caretakers, and workers (Swift and Birmingham 1999). The assumption of intrafamilial sharing that is implicit in the shift to family-income based eligibility criteria has further implications for gender relations, as it limits women's independent access to benefits and encourages familial dependency. All these changes, then, make the goal for women of being able to achieve autonomy and access to an independent income seem more distant than ever.

Finally, restructuring has had negative consequences for the social citizenship status of adults and for their ability to exercise political voice. On the one hand, the implications of the growth of low-wage, contingent work and increased responsibility for unpaid care work are increasing gaps between those who have the time, energy, and resources necessary for being politically involved and those who do not. On the other hand, as Jane Jenson has pointed out, children are becoming the new deserving citizens. Increasingly, adults' entitlement to social support is based on the fact that they are attached to at least one child. A long-term consequence, as Jenson describes it, is that adults and their needs are being pushed into the political background, which is "render[ing] less visible the need for collective action by citizens mobilised to make claims and thereby use the state against all forms of unequal power" (Jenson 2000, 23).

UNDERSTANDING THE CHANGES:
THE POLITICS OF WELFARE STATE CHANGE

A key question that needs to be addressed is why the welfare state has been restructured along the lines described above and what possibilities exist for an alternative type of politics. It is often argued that, given global economic imperatives, there is no choice but to implement reforms of this neoliberal type. The politics of neoliberal welfare state restructuring cannot simply be seen, however, as imposed by the business community or global capitalism. Rather, a more complex process is at work in which various actors have responded and participated in shaping politics in a number of different arenas.

The politics of the welfare state has to be situated, first, within the context of broader political-economic and social changes taking place over the course of the postwar period that have meant that the welfare state could no longer be maintained in the form in which it had developed (nor indeed, was it particularly desirable to do so, given its shortcomings in meeting the needs of women and minorities). In particular, the growth of the service sector and of part-time, contingent work, starting as early as the 1960s, profoundly altered both the structure of the labour market and the demands being placed on income security programs that had assumed work on a full-time, year-round basis (Porter forthcoming). The massive entry of women into the labour force created additional pressures both for greater equality within state programs and for new types of programs and services to be put in place (for example, with respect to daycare). As unemployment rose and the economic crisis took hold in the 1970s, there were growing fiscal pressures on the state. Finally, the increasing pressure from the internationalization of economic activity both placed new constraints on the state and limited the effectiveness of the postwar model, based, as it was, on stimulating domestic demand (Drainville 1995; Bradford 1999; Campbell 1987).

These broad pressures alone, however, do not account for why the outcome was a neoliberal restructuring. To address this question, we have to examine the political forces at work – not only those that have pushed for a neoliberal agenda but the actual processes involved in the construction of neoliberalism as a hegemonic paradigm, keeping in mind that it involved the reaction of a range of actors, both those with power and those without.

THE CONSTRUCTION OF NEOLIBERALISM AS A HEGEMONIC PARADIGM

We argue, first, that the consolidation of neoliberalism as a hegemonic paradigm in Canada has involved both the building up of a new governing policy framework (Bradford 1999; Hall 1992) and, at the same time, the shaping of conditions that make it increasingly difficult for groups opposed to neoliberalism to mobilize an effective challenge. This has occurred in several ways.

First, the shift to neoliberalism involved an ideological struggle that was also political, that took place over more than twenty years, and that gradually came to present the paradigm of a reduced role for the state, and of free market forces and global competitiveness as the only alternative possible. This ideological shift was supported by business organizations, think tanks such as the Fraser Institute, and the Economic Council of Canada, and by the mid-1970s it was also taken up by key officials within the state. With respect to welfare state reform, reports in the 1980s, such as the Macdonald Royal Commission and the Forget Commission on Unemployment Insurance, further reinforced this view and recommended a reform of social programs in ways that would be compatible with these goals.

Second, the shift towards neoliberalism itself entailed (and, indeed, had as one of its objectives) a shift in power away from labour and other subordinate groups and a strengthening of the power of capital (Hall 1992, 100; Clarke 1987). The shift was accompanied by a direct attack on labour (seen, for instance, in the introduction in the mid-1970s of the Anti-Inflation Program, repressive labour legislation, and so on), while the abandonment of the full employment objective was critical in weakening the position and political power of subordinate groups in general. It has also entailed strategies to undermine the power and legitimacy of organizations representing marginalized social groups and progressive social movements. Such strategies have included the elimination both of state funding for advocacy groups within civil society (including women's groups) and of advisory bodies within the federal state that represented marginalized groups to the government. A range of social groups have been further marginalized by labelling them as "special interests" (Jenson and Phillips 1996; Brodie 1998).

Third, neoliberalism has entailed the attempt to build on and to reinforce divisions in the labour force and in society in ways that have undermined the notion of social solidarity and a sense of collectivity, both in society as a whole and as an underlying principle of the welfare state. The focus on individual, rather than state or collective, responsibility was a first important step away from a social solidarity model. In addition, both the ideological attack and the cuts have targeted certain groups – for example, single mothers on welfare, married women, and youth. In Ontario welfare benefits were one of the first areas to be cut under the Harris Common Sense Revolution. The notion that an unemployment rate as high as 8 percent was "natural" – a particularly critical dimension of the neoliberal paradigm – was justified by the Fraser Institute and others, in part because it was argued that the activities and attitudes of "secondary workers" – married women and youth – were pushing up the rate of unemployment. Likewise, the issue of "child poverty" has played out in ways that have been divisive, on the one hand, placing the responsibility (and blame) for child poverty onto the shoulders of "dependent" adults, especially single mothers on welfare, and on the other hand, through the eligibility criteria applied in certain programs, criteria dividing those with children from those without.

Social solidarity has been further undermined by neoliberalism's silence on the issues of social reproduction. As the state withdraws from a range of areas with respect to social reproduction, it promotes private individual and family responsibility, rather than a sense of collective responsibility for these activities. These costs, however, are disproportionately borne by women and the poor, and the lack of social provision creates new forms of inequality. The possibilities for having policies that foster the reconciliation of paid work and domestic responsibilities have become even more remote as the concerns of adults, and especially women, are being sidestepped in favour of a focus on children.

Fourth, policy-making institutions have been restructured in a way that marginalizes opposition voices. Increasingly, major social policy decisions are taking place within the Ministry of Finance as part of the budget process and with a view to meeting goals of international economic competitiveness rather than domestic well-being. Ironically, as Keith Banting notes, this change has taken place at the same time as a wide range of social policy groups have been drawn into the formal consultation process and been given a "voice" in hearings and discussion groups, with the result that "government officials and advocacy groups increasingly talk past each other" (1996, 44). Also possibly contributing to this marginalization is the shift in power in the area of social policy to intergovernmental bodies (e.g., the intergovernmental Council on Social Policy Renewal) and to new "framework" agreements such as the Social Union Framework Agreement and the National Children's Agenda. While these developments may have opened some space for citizenship engagement, they are also presenting new challenges to civil society groups – for example, presenting social issues in ways that make it difficult to mobilize around any single issue (Phillips with Echenberg 2000; Jenson and Phillips 1996; Jenson, Mahon, and Phillips, this volume).

THE SOCIAL POLICY COMMUNITY AND THE RESPONSES OF LEFT-LIBERAL ACTORS

We argue, second, that left-liberal organizations, which are often cast as insignificant players in the story of welfare state development (especially in relation to powerful neoliberal actors), also helped in the construction of the neoliberal paradigm and in ruling out alternatives. This is particularly evident in the policy terrain of federal family/child benefits, where the outcome of the struggle over the last three decades has defined key features of the neoliberal welfare state, including the shift to targeting and a focus on the issue of "child poverty." A left-liberal sector – consisting primarily of national social policy organizations such as the Canadian Council on Social Development, the National Council of Welfare, and the National Antipoverty Organization but also at times nationally focussed feminist organizations such as the National Action Committee on the Status of Women (NAC) and the now defunct Canadian Advisory Council on the Status of Women – had a powerful presence in this policy arena (McKeen, forthcoming). These organizations were largely oriented to seeking a more generous social policy system – but as a way to humanize, not dismantle, the capitalist system. Their influence, however, both in terms of defining the problems and in terms of the particular policy stances they adopted, was one of narrowing rather than broadening the issues and the scope of debate. This helped to close the space that more radical oppositional groups, for example, labour (e.g., the Canadian Labour Congress) and social-feminists (e.g., the post-1980s NAC), might have occupied. In view of the importance both of the transformations in this policy terrain and of a "policy community" perspective generally for understanding politics, we examine this influence in some detail.

A first key factor was the broad influence these organizations had in promoting the issue of poverty. While poverty is a material "fact" and, theoretically, an issue that can inspire support for either universal and solidaristic approaches to social policy or a liberal targeting model, the writing and rewriting of the poverty story in Canada has mainly coincided with and legitimated a liberal notion of social provision oriented to helping only those who have fallen through the cracks in the system – that is, targeting social benefits to those deemed truly needy. For example, in presenting social policy to deal with poverty, organizations often chose to highlight the plight of particularly "vulnerable" groups of poor (such as the elderly, single mothers, women in general, and children), an orientation that tends to embed and presuppose a liberal (targeting the poor) bias and to feed into the undermining of social solidarity and a sense of collectivity; this result has been a key part of the neoliberal paradigm.

These organizations had more direct influences as well in shaping child benefit politics. An important one was the support they gave, beginning in the later 1970s and continuing through the 1980s, to the solution of targeting. For instance, core social policy and women's groups supported the targeted (family) income-tested Child Tax Credit when it was introduced in 1978, albeit expressing some disappointment at the reduction of the universal family allowance. In the early to mid-1980s, these Ottawa-based organizations formed an alliance – a small high-profile coalition called the Social Policy Reform Group (SPRG), which backed the Mulroney government's proposal for a narrower, more targeted, child benefits system, including a diminished role for universal measures and the ideal of horizontal equity (McKeen 2001). As Myles and Pierson suggest, these organizations were lured by the promise that targeting would reduce poverty. They were also perhaps convinced that this was the best they could achieve, given the growing government and business hostility towards universality, and the narrow fiscal parameters for reform set by the Mulroney government. These were nevertheless critical moments in legitimating the neoliberal model and in marginalizing the values of universality, horizontal equity, and social solidarity and the principle of personal autonomy for women.

A second specific influence lay in their promotion of the issue of eliminating child poverty. Seizing upon the issue of child poverty, these groups have been a key force (along with international pressure) in pushing governments to adopt child-centred social policy initiatives (McKeen 2001a). While on the surface eliminating child poverty is a commendable goal, it has in a larger sense tended to serve as a convenient political cover and justification for shifting to the neoliberal goal of greater targeting. Under the Mulroney government, for example, this reorientation was accompanied by deep cuts in child benefits and the elimination of universality. While, as Jenson, Mahon, and Phillips suggest, the focus by the Liberals on child poverty and early childhood development may be opening the door in some provinces to new positive social policy initiatives, such as better programming for children and daycare, it also clearly has the potential to continue to reinforce a narrow, liberal or neoliberal orientation toward "fixing" children or attending to those deemed to be "at risk" (McGrath 1997) – the antithesis of a preventative/universal/social-solidarity model. Moreover, over the longer term, the focus on child poverty has tended to create political opportunities that are leading to a gradual displacement of the adult-centred social policy system and concept of social citizenship with one based on investing in the child (Jenson 2000; Jenson, Mahon, Phillips, this volume).

Finally, it is important to note the politics of inclusion and exclusion operating within the social policy community. For example, the exclusive status of left-liberal actors (the SPRG, especially) as the voice of progressives during the Mulroney era directly undermined the more radical messages of labour and popular sector groups – groups who generally held a broader view of social justice and were more strongly opposed to the Mulroney agenda.[6] Presentations by the latter groups in the public hearings on child benefits were easily dismissed in the face of the SPRG's moderate (supportive) position. Again, in the case of the contemporary debate on family/child benefits, the language of child poverty has been particularly problematic. Its predominantly family-centred and gender-blind construction has afforded little visibility to women as a social category and has helped to push women's issues and the women's movement out of this terrain of debate (McKeen 2001a). Moreover, efforts by women's movement actors (and their allies) to widen the focus of discussion to the broader issue of equality and to solutions based on social solidarity and universality have been perceived by both government and social policy "allies" as radical, adversarial, and irrelevant – thereby reinforcing their outsider status.

In a fundamental sense then, the process by which the neoliberal paradigm was shaped and alternatives were thwarted was not simply the result of the activities of neoliberals but at times involved mutually reinforcing strategies enacted by both neoliberal and left-liberal actors operating in both macrolevel and policy-community contexts.

CONCLUSIONS: DIMENSIONS OF WELFARE STATE CHANGE IN CANADA

The Canadian welfare state has been significantly transformed over the last thirty years. The changes represent a shift in family-market-state relations and a significant reduction in state responsibility for social reproduction. The adoption of a neoliberal paradigm emphasizing free market forces, a reduction in state expenditure, and increased individual responsibility and consumer choice has had a profound impact on the structure of the welfare state. It has been evident in the downloading of responsibility for social reproduction to the market, households, and other organizations of civil society; in the shift to a so-called tough-love philosophy and an "employability" model whereby a major function of social policy is to "encourage" people to take or to stay in employment; and in the restructuring of programs that has resulted both in targeting to the poor (for example in the area of family/child benefits) and in the privileging of an upper tier of full-time steadily employed workers (as in the changes to UI). There has been a shift in the subject of benefits from adults (especially the unemployed) to children and an accompanying overall reduction in funding available for social programs. These changes form part of a strategy that has encouraged the growth of low-wage industries.

The impact of this restructuring has been an increase in poverty, inequality, and hardship, particularly among certain groups. For women, particularly poor women, minorities, and their families the result has been increased pressures and poverty. This result is felt particularly strongly in communities where state income transfers such as UI have been a major source of revenue. The welfare state has moved further from the recognition of the interrelationship of care and work – with women disproportionately assigned to the low-wage, contingent work force and to a greater burden of unpaid care and domestic work. In design and impact, these policy shifts work against the possibility of women obtaining autonomy or independence from exploitative situations. These changes also have significant implications for political voice, as the deteriorating work and care situations have reduced the space for an individual to exercise political voice or public engagement. Moreover, as the target of social policy has shifted from adults to children, the need for adults to mobilize collectively against all forms of inequality and injustice is becoming less evident (Jenson 2000).

The process of consolidating neoliberalism as a hegemonic paradigm has involved both the construction of a new governing consensus, involving the replacement of notions of social solidarity with the ideals of global competitiveness and individual responsibility, and the creation of conditions that make it increasingly difficult to mount an effective challenge. The construction of the new consensus was not, however, simply the result of a business and conservative coalition. The activities of left-liberal social-policy and women's organizations also played an important role, particularly in the core area of family/child benefits. Their liberal reading of the poverty issue and the policy stances they adopted reinforced and legitimated a shift to targeting and the marginalization of more radical voices and visions.

Overall, the nature of the restructuring has posed serious challenges for labour, women's groups, and others in the "popular" sector. There is a need to rethink in more profound and creative ways alternatives not only to the neoliberal welfare state and the "politics of austerity" but also to the postwar Keynesian model. For example, how might we organize social reproduction/caring activities in ways that build a sense of social solidarity and address the collective responsibility for social welfare, but allow for more active political participation? Working towards an alternative conception of the welfare state in this sense requires an understanding not only of the interconnections between the organization of daily life in the family, in the labour market and through state programs but further, of the linkage between struggles in various areas, including those of women, labour, and minority groups, in the effort to create those kinds of transformative structures.

NOTES

1 "Tough love" is the term used by some Conservatives (especially in the context of the U.S. welfare debates) to describe the approach to welfare reform that aims to get people off welfare, the assumption being that it is in their own best interests to do so. For further discussion see Hirschmann (2001).

2 These views were put forward, for example, in the Macdonald Commission report and the Forget Commission on Unemployment Insurance (Canada 1985, (Canada 1986).

3 Canada, House of Commons, *Debates*, 9 November 1978, 983. For a fuller discussion of UI reforms, see Porter (forthcoming).

4 For example, whereas previously the latter groups needed the equivalent of 300 hours to qualify (twenty weeks at fifteen hours a week), they now need 910 hours – the equivalent of 26 weeks at 35 hours each (Canada 1995).

5 A federal government monitoring report, for example, found that between 1995–96 and 1997–98 new claims by women fell by 20 percent compared to 16 percent for men (Canada 1998, ii and table 2.4).

7 Interview with Bob Baldwin, Canadian Labour Congress, 7 July 1997, Ottawa.

REFERENCES

Adams, Ian, William Camerson, Brian Hill, and Peter Penz. 1971. *The Real Poverty Report*. Edmonton: M.B. Hurtig.

Bach, Sandra, and Susan Phillips. 1997. "Constructing a New Social Union: Child Care beyond Infancy?" In Gene Swimmer, ed., *How Ottawa Spends, 1997–98: Seeing Red, A Liberal Report Card*, 235–58. Ottawa: Carleton University Press.

Banting, Keith. 1996. "Social Policy." In Les Pal and Brian Tomlin, eds., *Border Crossings: The Internationalization of Canadian Public Policy*. 27–54. Don Mills, ON: Oxford University Press.

Boismenu, Gérard, and Jane Jenson. 1998. "A Social Union or a Federal State? Intergovernmental Relations in the New Liberal Era." In Les Pal, ed., *How Ottawa Spends, 1998–99: Balancing Act, The Post-Deficit Mandate*, 57–80. Don Mills, ON: Oxford University Press.

Bradford, Neil. 1999. "The Policy Influence of Economic Ideas: Interests, Institutions and Innovation in Canada." *Studies in Political Economy* 59 (summer):17–60.

Brodie, Janine. 1998. "Restructuring and the Politics of Marginalization." In Manon Tremblay and Caroline Andrew, eds., *Women and Political Representation in Canada,* 19–38. Ottawa: University of Ottawa Press.

Campbell, Robert M. 1987. *Grand Illusions: The Politics of the Keynesian Experience in Canada, 1945–1975.* Peterborough, ON: Broadview Press.

Canada. 1985. *Report of the Royal Commision on the Economic Union and Development Prospects for Canada* (Macdonald Commision). Ottawa: Ministry of Supply and Services.

– 1995. *A Twenty-first Century Employment System for Canada: Guide to the Unemployment Insurance Legislation.* Ottawa: Human Resources Development Canada.

– Human Resources Development Canada. 1998. *Employment Insurance Monitoring and Assessment Report.* Ottawa.

Canadian Labour Congress. 1999. *Left Out in the Cold: The End of UI for Canadian Workers.* Ottawa: CLC

– 2002. *Unemployment Insurance Bulletin* 4(1), February 2002; 2(1), August. Ottawa: CLC

Clarke, Simon. 1987. "Capitalist Crisis and the Rise of Monetarism." In Ralph Miliband, Leo Panitch, and John Saville, eds., *Socialist Register 1987,* 393–427. London: Merlin Press.

Clayton, Richard, and Jonas Pontusson. 1998. "Welfare-State Retrenchment Revisited: Entitlement Cuts, Public Sector Restructuring, and Inegalitarian Trends in Advanced Capitalist Societies." *World Politics* 51 (October):67–98.

Coleman, William, and Grace Skogstad. 1990. "Policy Communities and Policy Networks: A Structural Approach." In William Coleman and Grace Skogstad, eds., *Policy Communities and Public Policy in Canada: A Structural Approach,* 13–31. Mississauga, ON: Copp Clark Pitman.

Drainville, André. 1995 "Monetarism in Canada and the World Economy." *Studies in Political Economy* 46 (spring): 7–42.

Durst, Doug. 1999. "Phoenix or Fizzle? Background to Canada's New National Child Benefit." In Doug Durst, ed., *Canada's National Child Benefit: Phoenix or Fizzle?* 11–37. Halifax: Fernwood Publishing.

Esping-Andersen, Gösta. 1996. "After the Golden Age? Welfare State Dilemmas in a Global Economy." In Gösta Esping-Andersen, ed., *Welfare States in Transition: National Adaptations in Global Economies,* 1–31. London: Sage.

Haddow, Rodney.1993. *Poverty Reform in Canada, 1958–1978: State and Class Influences on Policy Making.* Montreal and Kingston: McGill-Queen's University Press.

Hall, Peter A. 1992. "The Movement from Keynesianism to Monetarism: Institutional Analysis and British Economy Policy in the 1970s." In Sven

Steinmo, Kathleen Thelen, and Frank Longstreth, eds., *Structuring Politics: Historical Institutionalism in Comparative Analysis,* 90–113. Cambridge: Cambridge University Press.

Hirschman, Nancy. 2001. "A Question of Freedom, a Question of Rights? Women and Welfare." In Nancy Hirschman and Ulrike Liebert, eds. *Women and Welfare: Theory and Practice in the United States and Europe.* New Brusnwick, NJ: Rutgers University Press.

Jenson, Jane. 1986. "Gender and Reproduction: Or, Babies and the State." *Studies in Political Economy* 20 (summer):9–46.

– 2000. "Canada's Shifting Citizenship Regime: The Child as 'Model Citizen.'" Unpublished manuscript.

Jenson, Jane, and Susan Phillips. 1996. "Regime Shifts: New Citizenship Practices in Canada." *International Journal of Canadian Studies* 14 (fall):111–36.

Jenson, Jane, and Mariette Sineau. 2001. "Citizenship in the Era of Welfare State Redesign." In Jane Jenson and Mariette Sineau, eds., *Who Cares? Women's Work, Childcare, and Welfare State Redesign,* 240–65. Toronto: University of Toronto Press.

Jenson, Jane, and Sharon Stroick. 1999. *What Is the Best Policy Mix for Canada's Young Children?* Canadian Policy Research Network, Study no. F–09.

Jessop, Bob. 1993. "Towards a Schumpeterian Workfare State? Preliminary Remarks on Post-Fordist Political Economy." *Studies in Political Economy* 40 (spring):7–39.

Little, Margaret. 1999. "The Limits of Canadian Democracy: The Citizenship Rights of Poor Women." *Canadian Review of Social Policy* 43: 59–76.

MacDonald, Martha. 1999. "Restructuring, Gender and Social Security Reform in Canada." *Journal of Canadian Studies* 34(2): 57–88.

Mahon, Rianne. 2002. "Gender and Welfare State Restructuring: Through the Lens of Child Care." In Sonya Michel and Rianne Mahon, eds., *Child Care Policy at a Crossroads: Gender and Welfare State Restructuring,* 1–277. London and New York: Routledge.

Mahon, Rianne, and Susan Phillips. 2002. "Dual-Earner Families Caught in a Liberal Welfare Regime? The Politics of Child Care Policy in Canada." In Sonya Michel and Rianne Mahon, eds., *Child Care Policy at a Crossroads: Gender and Welfare State Restructuring,* 191–218. London and New York: Routledge.

McGrath, Susan. 1997. "Child Poverty Advocacy and the Politics of Influence." In Jane Pulkingham and Gordon Ternowetsky, eds., *Child and Family Policies: Struggles, Strategies and Options,* 172–87. Halifax: Fernwood Publishing.

McKeen, Wendy. 2001. "The Shaping of Political Agency: Feminism and the National Social Policy Debate, the 1970s and Early 1980s." *Studies in Political Economy* 66 (fall): 37–58.

– 2001a. "'Writing Women Out': Poverty Discourse and Feminist Agency in the 1990s National Social Policy Debate." *Canadian Review of Social Policy* 48 (spring–summer): 19–33.

– Forthcoming. *Money in Their Own Name: Feminism and the Shaping of Canadian Social Policy, 1960s to 1990s.* Toronto: University of Toronto Press.

Myles, John. 1988. "Decline or Impasse? The Current State of the Welfare State." *Studies in Political Economy* 26: 73–107.

Myles, John, and Paul Pierson. 1997. "Friedman's Revenge: The Reform of "Liberal" Welfare States in Canada and the United States." *Politics and Society* 25(4): 443–72.

National Council of Welfare. 1999. *Welfare Incomes 1999.* Ottawa: Minister of Public Works and Government Services Canada. Catalogue no. H68-27.

O'Connor, Julia. 1993. "Gender, Class and Citizenship in the Comparative Analysis of Welfare State Regimes: Theoretical and Methodological Issues." *British Journal of Sociology* 44(3): 501–18.

O'Connor, Julia, Ann Shola Orloff, and Sheila Shaver. 1999. *States, Markets, Families: Gender, Liberalism and Social Policy in Australia, Canada, Great Britain and the United States.* Cambridge: Cambridge University Press.

Orloff, Anne Shola. 1993. "Gender and the Social Rights of Citizenship: The Comparative Analysis of Gender Relations and Welfare States." *American Sociological Review* 53(3): 303–328.

Phillips, Susan, with Havi Echenberg. 2000. "Simon Says 'Take a Giant Step Forward': Advancing the National Children's Agenda." Discussion paper prepared for the National Children's Alliance.

Pierson, Paul. 1996. "The New Politics of the Welfare State." *World Politics* 48: 143–79.

Porter, Ann. 1999. "Family, Labour Markets and the State: Dimensions of Welfare State Restructuring." Unpublished manuscript presented to the Canadian Political Science Association Meeting, Sherbrooke, June.

– Forthcoming. *Gendered States: Women, Unemployment Insurance, and the Political Economy of the Welfare State in Canada, 1945–1997.* Toronto: University of Toronto Press.

Prince, Michael J. 1999. "From Health and Welfare to Stealth and Farewell: Federal Social Policy, 1980–2000." In Les Pal, ed., *How Ottawa Spends, 1999–2000: Shape Shifting, Canadian Governance Toward the Twenty-first Century,* 151–96. Don Mills, ON: Oxford University Press.

Pross, Paul, ed. 1986. *Group Politics and Public Policy.* 2d ed. Toronto: Oxford University Press.

Pulkingham, Jane, and Gordon Ternowetsky. 1999. "Child Poverty and the CCTB/NCB: Why Most Poor Children Gain Nothing." In Doug Durst, ed., *Canada's National Child Benefit: Phoeniz or Fizzle?* 103–23. Halifax: Fernwood Publishing.

Rice, James J., and Michael J. Prince. 2000. *Changing Politics of Canadian Social Policy.* Toronto: University of Toronto Press.

Scott, Katherine. 1996. "The Dilemma of Liberal Citizenship: Women and Social Assistance Reform in the 1990s." *Studies in Political Economy* 50: 7–36.

Stroick, Sharon, and Jane Jenson. 1999. *What Is the Best Policy Mix for Canada's Young Children?* Ottawa: Canadian Policy Research Network. Study no. F–09.

Swift, Karen, and Michael Birmingham. 1999. "Caring in a Globalizing Economy: Single Mothers on Assistance." In Doug Durst, ed., *Canada's National Child Benefit: Phoenix or Fizzle?* 84–102. Halifax: Fernwood Publishing.

Vosko, Leah. 2003. "Mandatory 'Marriage' or Obligatory Waged Work: Social Assistance and the Single Mother's Complex Roles in Wisconsin and Ontario." In Sylvia Bashevsky, ed., *Women's Work is Never Done: Comparative Studies in Care-Giving, Employment, and Social Reform.* New York: Routledge: 165–99.

Winkler, Celia. 1998. "Mothering, Equality and the Individual: Feminist Debates and Welfare Policies in the USA and Sweden." *Community, Work and Family* 1(2): 1–40.

6 No Minor Matter: The Political Economy of Childcare in Canada

JANE JENSON, RIANNE MAHON,
AND SUSAN D. PHILLIPS

Canadian political economy has traditionally focused on "the big questions" such as the limits of staples-centred development, dependent industrialisation, the role of the state, the national questions, and matters of gender and race-ethnicity, often with respect to class relations. What place could childcare have among such big issues? Our claim is that childcare is not a minor matter. It is of fundamental importance for understanding the main business of the state and its relationships to society. Childcare provides a window on state-society relations at the point where concerns about public and private, state and market, and family responsibility and employment all intersect. In this respect it resonates with the rich feminist political economy literature.[1]

More specifically, over the past four decades, the transformation of labour markets and families has eroded the family form that dominated the twentieth century, that is, a male breadwinner and a housewife-mother. As a result, the traditional patterns of family labour and care-giving are under stress. In particular, it can no longer be assumed that mothers, wives, and daughters are ready, willing, and able to leave the labour force to care full-time for young children or for family members who are sick, living with disabilities, or are frail and elderly. At the same time, many states are engaged in downsizing and off-loading even their limited responsibilities for the financing and provision of care. They look to families and communities to provide the care that is needed and to pick up the slack as health services are reduced and investments in home care and childcare are not made.

Thus, the questions of who will provide care, who will pay for it, and how it will be delivered are increasingly on the agenda.[2]

The premise of this chapter is that a single program – childcare – provides an important opportunity to examine big questions such as the ongoing transformation of labour markets, families, communities, and the Canadian state. An analysis of debates surrounding childcare provision also allows us to think about prospects for progressive social transformation. Political struggles over who provides, who pays, and how to deliver childcare raise important issues of equality. As feminists have argued for decades, universally available, affordable, and high-quality childcare is indispensable to achieving equality between the sexes. Class and gender equality are simultaneously served when such childcare becomes part of a larger bundle of citizenship rights, recognising both cultural diversity and the equality of universal access, as well as acknowledging caring skills and work with decent wages and working conditions.

This chapter begins by describing some of the broad issues that the childcare issue illuminates. We then locate Canada's childcare practices in comparative perspective. Because childcare delivery is a provincial responsibility, we must look at patterns of provincial provision. The remaining sections then analyse childcare provision as part of a broader restructuring of the Canadian state and its role vis-à-vis that of families, markets, and communities. Debates about and the provision of childcare are thereby understood as a response to social transformations and as part of the struggle to transform Canadian society in the name of social justice.

CHILDCARE: THE CHALLENGE

The case for public support of early childhood education and care can be presented in different ways, with quite different consequences. Since the 1960s feminists have defined the availability of affordable and high-quality childcare as an indispensable element of any program for achieving gender equality. With or without an equality agenda, states have invested in some nonparental childcare services, as well as maternity and parental leaves, simply because it has been evident since the late 1960s that mothers of young children were the fastest-growing segment of most labour forces. [3] In recent years, preschool education has been defined as an early and critical contribution to meeting the life-long learning requirements associated with an emergent "knowledge-based economy." Increasingly, too, cost-conscious governments present early childhood education as a means of reducing future costs generated by long-term unemployment or crime. With the current drive to limit social assistance, the question of who would care for the children of lone mothers who are induced (or forced) into the labour force has become even more pressing.

As we shall see, the discourse surrounding childcare policy in Canada at various times has contained all such justifications. Neither the mix of rationales nor the leading argument has remained the same throughout the postwar years, however. The predominant way the issue is framed in any conjuncture fosters particular public policy choices, as well as constraining the range of strategic options of social forces that aim to transform social relations (Jenson 1986). The mix does not fall from the sky, of course. It is in part the result of the family forms and labour market participation patterns in place or undergoing change. A political economy analysis of childcare thus needs to begin with the pressures generated by changes to family forms and labour markets.

Many postwar welfare regimes focused on the male breadwinner and the risks and situations – unemployment, ill-health, industrial accidents, retirement, and death – that might jeopardise his capacity to support himself and his dependants. Families were fundamental to these regimes, because most care was delivered within the home and especially by housewives. Care for the frail elderly and people with disabilities, as well as care for the very young, was overwhelmingly provided as an unpaid "labour of love" by mothers, daughters, and sisters. By the 1970s, however, restructured labour markets were giving rise to "nonstandard" work (which for women very often meant part-time work), as well as the shift from industrial to postindustrial employment (Vosko 2000). Families changed with rising rates of divorce, separation and lone parenthood. Everywhere it was harder to believe that the two-parent family with a single breadwinner was the standard family form. Yet, even in recent years welfare state retrenchment has often assumed the availability of women's unpaid labour to take up the slack as services were reduced or never expanded to meet the needs. Increasingly, then, state strategies confronted the barrier posed both by women's growing involvement in paid work outside the home and by the fragility, as well as variety, of families.

Such pressures exist in most OECD countries, but in Canada, along with the United States and Scandinavia, they are most pressing. In 1999, for example, 71 percent of all women with children under sixteen were in the labour force on a full-time basis, while fully 68 percent of mothers with children under three were in the labour force (Vanier Institute 2000, 10). There has also been a significant increase in the number of lone-parent families (usually headed by a woman). Here again, Canada ranks with the United States – and not far behind the Scandinavian countries – among those with the highest labour force participation rates of lone parents (O'Connor, Orloff, and Shaver 1999, 71).

Women's rising labour-force participation rates coincided with the shift to postindustrial employment and the expansion of nonstandard employment forms – part-time and temporary work and self-employment (see Fudge and Voko, this volume). Whereas in Sweden public support for working parents, as part of a broader, well-developed welfare state, meant a pattern of service sector growth that produced many relatively secure, adequately paid jobs, in Canada, as in the United States, the postindustrial shift has coincided with the emergence of an increasingly polarised labour market (Clement and Myles 1994). Between 1970 and 1995, the share of income going to the lower- and middle-income groups declined (Jackson et al. 2000, 117). The growing gap has a pronounced generational profile as well, with young people and families concentrated more in the lower-income groups (Kapsalis, Morissette, and Picot 1999). Two incomes have thus become increasingly necessary to make ends meet, and often even they are insufficient to keep the family above the poverty line.

Such changes are clearly associated with the many signs that all families, but especially those with two employed parents and lone-parent families with a single earner, are experiencing substantial stress (Jackson et al. 2000, 85–8, 93; Vanier Institute 2000, 140–5, 154–7). Pressures come, at least in part, in the form of a lack of access to adequate services. In particular, as young families struggle in the restructured labour market, they face difficulties in finding affordable and quality childcare. This is where state policy might come in, by facilitating access to services either through direct provision or some form of subsidy. The choice of which to provide will, of course, have significant consequences for gender as well as class equality.

Whether and how states face up to the challenge is profoundly affected by the shape of the welfare regime within which childcare programs are embedded. Yet such regimes are not themselves static, especially today when structural and ideational changes are contributing to the redesign of the very contours of national states. The question now on the table is whether Canada will choose to move off its long-established trajectory as a liberal welfare regime or whether it is determined to find new ways of expressing its basic commitment to allowing market liberalism to trump social solidarity and equality.

CHILDCARE IN CANADA:
VARIANTS ON A LIBERAL WELFARE REGIME

Patterns of response to current challenges can be linked to the welfare regimes established in the postwar years and solidified in the 1960s.[4] Of the three basic welfare regimes – liberal, social democratic, and conservative – Canada's is clearly liberal.[5] The childcare policy approach Canada forged in the 1960s and 1970s fits well within this mould.[6] This statement has to be qualified in three respects, however. First, as various studies have shown, there are important intraregime variations, as well as differences across time.[7] In other words, it is not enough to say a regime is liberal. It is also important to analyse the particular forms of liberalism embedded in Canadian childcare policy and to look for any changes to these. Second, Canada "has not one ... but ten distinct provincial variants, each reflecting a particular way in which the state reinforces or undermines the market and family" (Boychuk 1998, xx). Third, while the notion of welfare regimes helps us to place Canada and, potentially, each of the provinces in a wider comparative context, it is important to bear in mind their often hybrid character. Canada's social policy contains elements of two regimes, with some social democratic forms (e.g., health care), encompassed within a dominant liberal regime (O'Connor, Orloff, and Shaver 1999, 192; see also Goodin 1999, chap. 1). Thus, although one welfare logic may predominate in a country, this does not rule out the successful introduction of reforms that embody an alternative approach. Once institutionalised, a liberal approach to childcare may be more difficult to change, but there is still space for transformation.

While the health care system forged in the 1960s bore a marked social democratic imprint, being both a universal right and publicly financed, childcare followed a different trajectory. It conformed to the dominant social-liberal logic of that era.[8] There was a clear class-based distinction in the ways childcare was financed by the public purse, as well as in the efforts of the state to structure forms of delivery and the quality of service. That is, patterns of who cared, who paid, and how the service was delivered varied significantly by class, as well as by place.

Middle- and upper-income families were to look to the market to meet their needs. Public support came only through the tax system (with the exception of limited maternity and parental leaves).[9] The deduction for a dependent spouse recognised that some families choose parental care, while the Childcare Expense Deduction (in place since 1972) permitted two-parent and lone-parent families with employed parents to deduct a portion of childcare expenses from their taxes.[10] They could choose any type of care or any provider, the only restriction being that the payment had to be receipted. Thus, "choices" about quality and form of provision were left to parents to make in relation to their capacity to pay and their decision about how much to "invest" in their children (Beauvais and Jenson 2001).

In contrast, needs-tested subsidies were provided to address the situation of lower-income families and to shape patterns of provision. From the mid-1960s to 1996, Ottawa made funds available through the Canada Assistance Plan (CAP) to subsidise childcare on a cost-shared basis with the provinces for those "in need or in danger of becoming in need." Part of Canada's "war on poverty," the childcare subsidies were intended to help families escape or avoid poverty by choosing to have two earners or by allowing lone mothers to stay in employment. As the subsidies went to the provider rather than the parent and as only some providers were eligible to receive certain subsidies, CAP had a major effect on the design of the most visible publicly financed portion of the system. In particular, it reinforced provision by nonprofit providers and centre-based care.

Neither the maintenance of distinctions between families nor reliance on the tax system to foster market-based "choice" for some and the use of restricted subsidies for others was a foregone conclusion when childcare policy was first under development. The regime was on a liberal trajectory, but struggles over policy principles, as well as design, were what shaped the specific choices that were made. Research on the struggles before and after CAP helps to illuminate why the initial policy took this narrow liberal focus, rather than moving toward a more universal design, such as was being generated in the health system, as the next section describes.

CANADA'S CHILDCARE PROGRAMS: TOWARD A NATIONAL STRATEGY?

Until the second wave of the women's movement put childcare squarely on the agenda, the dominance of the male breadwinner norm, reinforced by "expert opinion" as to the importance of maternal care, made any call for childcare almost unspeakable. The wartime nurseries, built "for the duration," were quickly closed at war's end. In the 1950s the first survey of working women, conducted by the Director of the Women's Bureau in the Department of Labour – the lone "femocrat" within the federal bureaucracy – noted the reluctance of working mothers to voice their need for childcare (Women's Bureau 1958). Articulation of the need for childcare was left to the Family and

Child Welfare Division of the Canadian Welfare Council. It became the focal point of a network of local social workers, whose softly voiced concerns scarcely disturbed the national policy discussion (Finkel 1995; Mahon 2000). Nevertheless, their take on the issue – families in need required help in arranging nonparental childcare – fit well with the liberal antipoverty thrust of CAP in the 1960s.

By the mid-1960s, the issue of affordable and accessible childcare was receiving some attention from other quarters. For example, the Fédération des femmes du Québec (FFQ) included state-provided childcare on its list of six basic demands at its founding in 1965 and continued to agitate for childcare in its brief to the Royal Commission on the Status of Women (Collectif Clio 1992, 464). The royal commission opened the way to a broader public understanding across Canada of universally accessible childcare as indispensable to achieving women's equality of opportunity. During much of the 1970s, however, while some feminists within the major parties worked to keep the issue on the agenda (Tyyska 1993), the then newly formed National Action Committee on the Status of Women (NAC) concentrated its energies on other issues (Burt 1986).

The result was that the struggle to challenge the narrow liberal orientation of CAP was initially confined to the newly enlarged and empowered ranks of femocrats within the federal government. Supported by the actions of several provinces, the latter were strong enough to secure some important changes to CAP, including widening the scope of those "in need." They were not, however, powerful enough to overcome the liberal bias deeply embedded in the social-policy establishment (Mahon, 2000). Public subsidies for centre-based regulated care – widely considered to be the best quality of care – were confined to lower-income families. Tax subsidies and market choices were offered to the rest, leaving families the "choice" of how to meet the challenge of balancing work and family responsibilities.[11]

A second major attempt to challenge the liberal limits of Canada's childcare policy was made in the 1980s. A critical step was taken at the 1982 national conference on daycare, which resulted in the formation of not one but two pan-Canadian childcare advocacy organisations.[12] The split in the movement reflected division over the issue of public support for commercial childcare (Burt 1990; Friendly 1994). The Canadian Day Care Advocacy Association (CDCAA), funded by the Women's Branch of Secretary of State, brought together local and provincial groups that had been fighting for universally accessible, non-profit childcare.[13] For the CDCAA and its supporters, childcare was an important social service, akin to education and health care, and an adequate supply of high-quality childcare could not be assured by commercial providers. The second organisation was the Canadian Child Day Care Federation (CCDCF), which included in its ranks both professional early childhood educators and commercial childcare providers (Friendly 1994).

The split might not have proved so critical if the wider political scene had not shifted during the 1980s. In the 1970s and early 1980s social liberalism was marked by feminism, as the appointment of the Abella Commission on employment equity and the Cook Task Force on Childcare suggest. Both commissions argued for universally accessible childcare provided under nonprofit auspices and did so in the name of gender equality. By the mid-1980s, however, the shift to a neoliberal agenda had begun (Timpson 2001, chap. 7). In this context, the split in the childcare advocacy community offered an opportunity to divide and conquer.

The Tory government's 1987 strategy on childcare offered to replace CAP funding with a National Childcare Act, but the proposed bill would have eliminated CAP's bias in favour of nonprofit forms of delivery and instituted "equal treatment" for commercial providers. Such a shift was clearly acceptable to the CCDCF. For the CDCAA and its allies in the women's and labour movements, however, the question of who provided care was central: quality childcare could only be guaranteed if the profit motive were removed. Unlike CAP, moreover, the new bill would have put a ceiling ($3 billion over seven years) on federal contributions. Thus, opponents mobilised against the bill, and in the face of such strong objections, the government let the draft die when it called the 1988 election. It did not bother to revive it in its second term in office.[14]

In retrospect, it may seem as if the CDCAA and its allies erred in opposing the Tory bill (White 2001). Placed in context, however, their decision to hold out for more was understandable. The shift toward neoliberalism had yet to be institutionalised. It had, moreover, given rise to a strong and growing "popular sector" coalition opposed to the Mulroney government's market-focused agenda. In this context, it did not seem unrealistic to press for an adequately funded policy that was designed to ensure universal access to quality childcare across the country.

The 1993 victory of the Liberals, whose campaign platform outlined in the Red Book included childcare on the party's reform agenda, seemed to justify the strategy of holding out for more.[15] In addition, the 1994 conference Vision for Childcare into the Twenty-first Century, which brought the two advocacy associations and researchers together with federal and provincial bureaucrats, concurred on the important point of no subsidies to commercial operators (Timpson 2001,198). As activists were soon to discover, however, times had changed. Concerns over the economy and deficit reduction came to dominate the agenda, so that the discourse about childcare was recast as support for "employability" and for turning "unproductive" individuals (mainly lone mothers on social assistance) into productive workers.[16] Within Cabinet the power struggle between ministers supporting social policy reform and a minister of finance focussed on cost-cutting was won hands down by the latter. Comprehensive social policy reform was abandoned; the 1995 budget replaced the cost-shared CAP with the block-funded Canada Health and Social Transfer (CHST), and soon after the federal government walked away from a proposal to the provinces for a national childcare initiative.

This time, opposition from childcare advocates was muted, in large part because the Chrétien government had succeeded in shutting down several routes to representation. The "women's state," which had provided important support within the federal bureaucracy and to national and provincial advocacy groups, was disbanded. Funding to organisations engaged in advocacy was cut dramatically, and their opportunity to participate in government consultations over public policy severely curtailed. Instead, the government worked to cultivate "partnerships" with select groups, the preference being for more "professional," less radical groups (Jenson and Phillips 1997).

RECASTING CHILDCARE: "INVESTING" IN CHILDREN

After abandoning its attempt at a national childcare strategy, the Liberal government turned its attention first to reducing child poverty and then supposedly to investing in children, in part by means of early childhood development programs that might, but need not, include a childcare component. Not only the focus but the form that any pan-Canadian initiative would take changed as a result of heightened sensitivities over respect for provincial jurisdiction. The federal government was no longer willing to contemplate developing a national program around federal standard-setting. Its participation focuses on collaborative strategies with the provinces under the Social Union Framework Agreement (SUFA) signed in 1999. At the same time, provincial governments, angered over federal unilateralism and the shock of CHST revenue cuts, began to develop greater co-operation in directing a reform agenda for children. The outcome of this collaboration was the National Child Benefit (NCB) and the National Children's Agenda (NCA).

The NCB, created in 1997 by agreement between the federal government and the provinces and territories (except Quebec), has the twin goals of reducing the depth of child poverty and promoting parents' attachment to the labour force. Under the NCB, a new tax benefit called the Canada Child Tax Benefit and a low-income supplement are paid by the federal government to families with dependent children, regardless of whether their income is received from social assistance, Employment Insurance, or paid employment. The intent is to break down the "welfare wall" by creating incentives for parents to take paid employment, even at minimum wage or part-time, because the earned income together with the NCB would make families better off financially than they would be on social assistance. With the federal contribution to the NCB, most provincial governments have reduced the income portion of what they pay in social assistance, so that parents receiving social assistance and the NCB do not have higher incomes than working parents receiving the benefit. The money saved in this way may be reinvested by the provinces in social services for children or paid as additional income supplements.[17] Although hailed by the participating governments as a major step toward more collaborative federalism and a big benefit to families with children, the NCB has several drawbacks from the perspective of childcare. Like CAP, the NCB still targets low-income families. So far, reinvestment has not led to sufficient expansion of the supply of quality, regulated childcare spaces.

The NCA is a broader and more general "investment strategy" born out of intergovernmental cooperation and underpinned by expert opinion and research that indicates that what happens to children in their early years has a lifetime effect.[18] Therefore, investing in the development of young children is anticipated to have positive impacts not only on children but on society as a whole in terms of both future competitiveness and money saved on subsequent ameliorative programs.

The goal of the NCA is to foster a shared vision and common understanding of children's needs and, to this end, to improve cooperation and information sharing among governments as each improves its policies and programming for children. In September 2000, an intergovernmental agreement (excluding Quebec), Early Childhood Development, provided a federal contribution of $2.2 billion over five years and set out priorities for investment in four areas: health during pregnancy, birth, and infancy; parental and family supports; early childhood development, learning and care; and community supports. Although childcare can be subsumed and may be funded under the Early Childhood Development initiative, it is explicitly given a low profile, in part because provincial governments have varying degrees of interest in making it a top priority for investment given the varying welfare-regime models that they have developed.

The federal and provincial governments have been able to effect such a significant shift in the discourse around childcare – a shift that makes the provision of quality childcare an instrument of early childhood development, rather than a means to permit parents to enter the labour force or a means of achieving greater gender equality – without much backlash, largely because the patterns of representation have shifted significantly in ways that have diluted the voices of childcare advocates. Such shifts did not occur independently of state action. Indeed, the federal government has had an active hand in reshaping political mobilisation and representation around childcare. A key change has been the rise of coalitions.

Once it became apparent that the Liberal government, elected in 1993, was not going to resume interest in a national childcare strategy for the foreseeable future, and faced with severely limited resources for advocacy activities, both childcare and antipoverty advocates realised that their strength would lie in their numbers. The discovery of the child by antipoverty activists provided an opening for many childcare advocates to align with them, resulting in the creation of a broad coalition, Campaign 2000, which represents over seventy national, provincial and community organisations. Given its antipoverty and activist roots, Campaign 2000 has tended to be seen by both governments and other advocates as quite radical. To appeal to somewhat more conservative national organisations, such as teachers and nurses federations, a second coalition (with some overlapping membership) was formed. The National Children's Alliance (NCA) which consists of thirty national organisations, including both the CDCAA (now CCCAA) and the CCCF, has the express purpose of advancing a broadly based national children's agenda.

The advantage of coalitions over associations is that they build bridges across related interests and help to enhance the legitimacy of political claims by demonstrating support across diverse actors. In coalitions, however, childcare advocates are only one voice among many, necessitating choices and compromises in setting priorities among claims. The choice made by the NCA was to follow the politics of pragmatism, that is, base its claims on a discourse around early childhood development, knowing that in the current environment this strategy stood a reasonable chance of success, whereas a tighter focus on childcare would be futile.

The politics of childcare is also being shaped to some degree by SUFA, with its emphasis on intergovernmental collaboration and public reporting of outcomes. Under the federal-provincial agreement on early childhood development, governments have agreed to report annually on investment against a benchmark of current early childhood development expenditures and activities, develop a shared reporting framework with comparable indicators, and report on outcomes. Because the funding for this initiative flows through the CHST, the provinces have complete discretion over how they spend the money, and the federal government cannot hold them directly accountable for it. Only the Canadian "public" can do so. This largely explains why the federal government has become so interested in shaping the nature of representation and in building a strong network of public watchdogs (see Phillips 2001). It has helped to institutionalise the National Children's Alliance, while marginalizing the more critical Campaign 2000, and it has provided funding to build stronger networks of local and provincial organisations under the national umbrella.[19] Ironically, intergovernmental relations that have always been closed to outside actors may have indirectly opened a new political space for civil society organisations through the back door of "monitoring accountability." Provincial variation in existing childcare arrangements and priorities under the Early Childhood Development initiative make advocacy at the front end of policy much more challenging, however, because it requires greater capacity to effectively advocate at both levels of government at once. It is to understanding these provincial differences that we now turn.

THE CHANGING CANADIAN STATE SYSTEM: PROVINCIAL VARIATIONS ON A LIBERAL THEME?

Throughout the postwar years publicly financed childcare had been on dual tracks, both of which confined family strategies for advancing gender equality to decisions by the families themselves. Without a universal, affordable, and high-quality childcare system, families were left with the hard choices about who would provide care and under what conditions. While the labour market and market incomes generated within were forcing more and more parents, especially in two-parent families, into employment, they did not have adequate support for their childcare needs. For the majority of families, decisions about the mix of parental and nonparental care, as well as about the quality of care, were left to the families themselves. If they decided to use non-parental care, they faced a childcare market dominated by informal care providers (babysitters, nannies, relatives, neighbours) and one in which high-quality, regulated and developmentally appropriate care was extremely hard to access, because of high costs and a lack of spaces. There was some public financing through the tax regime, but the amounts of the CCED deduction rarely fully covered the market prices of childcare.

The parallel track of regulated and educational care, with subsidies to providers to cover a range of costs and with care delivered primarily by nonprofit organisations, was closely tied to antipoverty and other social policy strategies. Therefore, it was easiest to access by means of subsidies than by paying full market costs. The residual design of Canada's liberal welfare regime and the powerful structuring effects of CAP had made quality childcare a program for lower-income families, both two-parent and lone-parent, who were in the labour force. In this parallel track, too, access was inadequate and spaces were never sufficient to meet demand.

After 1995 this second track began to change as the provinces undertook major reforms of social assistance. Reform processes were already under way in several provinces when Ottawa unilaterally announced in the 1995 budget that CAP would be eliminated the next year, to be replaced by reduced but less-targeted transfer payments. The provincial governments now were free to decide what to do about social policy reform and how to design the childcare component within it. The policy choices made have in some cases reinforced the liberalism of the welfare regime, while challenging it in others. Indeed, it is interesting to note a certain shift in the class effects of the regime. Social assistance reform is fostering market behaviour among low-income families, while an emerging focus on early childhood development is leading, in some provinces, to greater concern about supports for all children.

Since 1995 the design of reforms has put huge pressures on the childcare system. The liberal welfare regime in the postwar years and through the 1980s in several provinces had allowed lone parents on social assistance to opt for full-time parental care when their children were in school. For example, in Ontario (until 1996) lone mothers with a child under sixteen and living on social assistance had no obligation to seek employment. In the other provinces, the age varied, but most treated lone parents with preschool children as "unavailable" for employment. Therefore, while CAP did provide subsidies to low-income lone parents who did need childcare in order to work, large numbers of children in those families were still cared for by their parents.[20]

Through the 1990s, however, employability programs of many kinds lowered this age. Thus, the Harris government's Ontario Works program imposed the obligation to participate on all lone parents receiving social assistance when their youngest child reached school age. Manitoba and British Columbia also specify school age as the point at which lone parents must begin seeking employment. In Newfoundland and Labrador, as well as Quebec and Saskatchewan, the cutoff is at age two, while in Nova Scotia and Alberta lone parents with children older than six months are considered available for work (Beauvais and Jenson 2001, 50).

This move towards fostering labour force activity spawned a range of programs targeted at lone parents to improve their labour market skills. *All* of these programs include subsidies to help with the costs of childcare (Beauvais and Jenson 2001, 56–7). There are simply not enough spaces, however, for all the children to move into the publicly financed and regulated system. Therefore, there has been a significant diversification in the types of public financing made available to help parents with the costs of childcare. The childcare subsidies provided by employability programs are not the same type of fee subsidies that CAP made available and that all provinces (except Quebec) still provide. While ordinary fee subsidies for low-income parents may be accessed by participants in employability programs, more frequent is a subsidy made available to the parent (not the provider, as under CAP) that can be used to help cover the costs of care. This means that there are now substantial public funds available to allow the poorest parents to enter the care market, although each parent usually receives only enough to purchase informal care. Indeed, in some provinces the goal is to create new jobs by encouraging low-income women to become care providers for others.

At the same time as the National Child Benefit was being invented, greater attention began to be paid to the advantages of developmentally appropriate childcare for all children, in order to ready them for school. Under the NCB a number of provinces have used their "reinvestment funds" to create more licensed childcare spaces, while also financing unlicensed care as described above (Beauvais and Jenson 2001, 25). The National Children's Agenda, with its formal commitments to enhancing early childhood development, has enhanced the place of child development goals in the Canadian discourse on childcare. Several provincial regimes, as we will see below, have begun to institute programs that not only maintain the emphasis on licensed, nonprofit childcare but also promote its advantages for all children.

In these new programs, then, the distinctions between low-income and other families are beginning to blur. With the focus on "investing in children" implied in this model, parents' needs are also pushed to the background. All parents are considered employable, but any notion of the needs of women as parents has virtually vanished from the childcare discourse. While some announcements by the more progressive provinces may mention the goal of gender equality when they announce childcare initiatives, the norm is silence.

Another key result of the post-1995 reform process is the heightened diversity in provincial patterns of childcare provision. Even under CAP all provincial regimes were not the same. From the mid-1970s until its abolition in 1996, CAP offered two funding routes. The first (original) option was the social assistance route, based on a traditional means test. The more generous option was the "welfare services" route that required a simple income test administered through the tax system. The key difference between the two was that, while the former could be used to subsidise places for the "needy" in commercial as well as in nonprofit childcare centres, the latter made federal funds (subsidies and a share of operating costs) available only to nonprofit providers. In this way, CAP can be said to have established a bias in favour of social-liberal childcare arrangements.

Yet the federal government's influence was rather limited. It simply provided part of the financing, while the remaining public financial contributions came from the provinces. More importantly, it did not dictate provincial supply: it was up to the provinces to decide how much childcare to support, of what quality, and under what auspices.[21] This left considerable room for provincial variation in terms of the respective roles played by states, markets, families, and the voluntary or community sector. The provinces used that room to establish diverse childcare regimes and, in the post-CAP era, these differences have widened.

Childcare is a publicly provided citizenship right in only one province: Quebec. Although access to spaces has still been an issue since the major 1997 reform, childcare is a universal right of all children, no matter what the employment status of their parents is. In the other provinces, however, the situation ranges from classical to social liberalism. Alberta, Newfoundland, and, to a lesser extent, the three other Atlantic provinces, provide the strongest contrast, in that they have opted for a more classical-liberal solution that emphasises the role of markets. In all four, commercial providers play an important role in delivery.[22] Alberta's regime may be considered an "assisted" market model, in that parent fees account for a lower share of the cost than in the other four and the rate of coverage is somewhat higher.[23]

A second pattern of childcare provision places greater emphasis on the family. Thus, in Newfoundland and Saskatchewan, which offer the lowest share of regulated care spaces, parents are forced to look primarily to the family and the informal sector (care provided in the homes of neighbours, friends). A variation on this "family centred" theme arises where the predominant form of regulated childcare is family daycare, that is, where a provider takes children into her own home. Again Saskatchewan (with British Columbia) leads, with as much as 50 percent of regulated care provided by family daycare. Quebec (one-third) has also relied on such care, but its post-1997 family policy is designed to upgrade the quality of family daycare and to significantly reduce the informal sector.

Although none of the provinces has an extensive system of publicly provided childcare, in the majority of provinces the nonprofit/non-state sector provides more than half the regulated spaces. Esping-Andersen's typology of welfare regimes ignores this sector, despite the admittedly important role it plays in certain conservative and liberal regimes. The logic of welfare regimes can be extended to incorporate this sector too (Esping-Andersen 1995, 35n2). In conservative regimes, the voluntary sector may contribute to the reproduction of divisions among wage earners (the "pillarisation" of religious-ethnic groups). It can also reflect the prevalence of a form of conservative communitarianism that looks to "civil society" as a substitute for, rather than a supplement to, the state's role.[24] In liberal regimes like the United States employee benefits – restricted to those who occupy a relatively privileged position in the labour market – can include access to services provided by nonprofit organisations. Yet expansion of this sector's role in social service provision, such as childcare, has also taken place under left governments, as Brennan's (1998) analysis of Australia's childcare policy during the 1970s and 1980s documents. Here New Left ideas merge with social democratic communitarianism to create an emphasis on community-controlled but government-supported services.

In Canada, nonprofit provision is indeed highest in provinces that have had social democratic governments: Saskatchewan, Quebec, Manitoba, and Ontario. Recent developments in British Columbia suggest that it will soon join this group.[25] Whereas conservative communitarianism would leave a substantial role for charity, in more social democratic regimes the state retains an important support (financial and regulatory) function, which is crucial if parents are not going to be set against childcare providers on issues of pay and quality care. And it is the case that the state plays a stronger role in provinces where social democratic governments have left their imprint. Thus parents pay the lowest share of the costs in Quebec, Manitoba, Saskatchewan, and British Columbia.[26] In addition, it is only in Quebec, Saskatchewan, Manitoba, and Ontario that government financial support goes beyond the provision of subsidies to lower-income families to cover at least part of operating costs (an element of universalism) and/or to offer important salary enhancement grants.[27]

It would be a mistake, however, to equate forms of welfare regimes with the orientation of the dominant party. Liberal governments can introduce social democratic policies, as the federal government's inducements to nonprofit care under CAP indicate, and social democratic governments can follow liberal social-policy logic. Thus it is important to look beyond partisan politics to struggles in civil society to understand why certain childcare arrangements have emerged – and to uncover the alternatives that childcare advocates and their allies have placed on the agenda.[28]

It is also important not to reify regimes. An interesting story lies behind Alberta's "predictable" embrace of a liberal, market-oriented model. It did not start out that way. Under the Social Credit in the 1960s, the foundations of quite a different system were laid, only to be dismantled by successive Tory governments in the 1980s and 1990s.[29] And although it built on institutional foundations laid in the past, Quebec's new "$5-a-day" childcare represents a substantial break with the past, made possible by a particular convergence of forces (Jenson 2002). Conversely, the progressive aspects of Manitoba's childcare system were significantly curtailed in the 1990s, a process that had set in well before the changes to federal policy (Prentice 2000).

CONCLUSION

Childcare policy demonstrates in fundamental ways how a country or province structures its relationships among families, civil society, markets, and the state. In Canada childcare policy has been constructed within what are essentially liberal welfare regimes. Families purchase the childcare services they need in the market, which is comprised of both for-profit and nonprofit providers. The state's role has been confined either to helping low income families who cannot afford to pay market prices obtain childcare or to providing tax breaks for families purchasing care. The result of this model has been an inadequate supply of quality, regulated childcare and high market prices that even middle-income two-earner families often cannot afford. They are too often forced "to choose" informal, unregulated care.

Although this liberal label may describe the general contours of the Canadian system of childcare, it misses much of the real variation. In reality, there is not one childcare regime in Canada; there are several, ranging from the classically liberal, market-oriented system in Alberta to the social democratic one in Quebec, where childcare is defined as a universal right of all children. In recent years, as a result of federal government bloc funding and differing responses to welfare state restructuring, the variations in regimes across the provinces have grown, rather than diminished. And they can be expected to continue to evolve in different ways. The federal government maintains an important funding responsibility through its grants to provinces and tax credits to parents. Neither use of the spending power allows it to shape provincial delivery systems, however. Nonetheless, its current interest in funding early childhood development has helped to cement a triple-pronged discourse around childcare. It is presented, first, as a support for healthy child development, then as a means of investing in children for future pay-off to society, and, finally, as an instrument for fostering labour force participation by "parents." Gone from this discourse, however, is the goal of equalising gender relations and supporting women's needs.

The story of the politics of childcare in the postwar period has also been one of shifting patterns of representation and an uncanny ability by the federal government to abandon attempts at creating a national strategy without much public outcry. One reason for this, we argue, is that the federal government has had an active hand in shaping the nature of representation, supporting more conservative advocacy organisations while marginalising the more vocal critics.

So, what is the potential for a transformative politics, one in which civil society actors can succeed in building a cohesive movement for quality, affordable childcare systems in all provinces? Given the current focus on early childhood development and the reality of diverging provincial childcare regimes, transformation involves multiple routes, rather than a single path. As childcare advocates have already discovered, working in coalitions has become a necessity, even if it dilutes their voice among others interested in different dimensions of child and family policy. As provinces move in different directions, strong networks that connect childcare advocates and their allies from the local to the provincial and national levels become an essential means of learning from experience and of developing the policy capacity necessary to influence several levels of government at once. Finally, the pressures for outcome measurement created by SUFA and a broader movement for accountability by governments creates an opening to demonstrate how poorly current regimes actually work in most provinces and to mobilise broader support around new directions. In spite of these new openings, an important lesson for advocates from the history of the organised struggle for childcare in

Canada is that it has been a long one. There is no reason to believe that it will be over soon.

NOTES

1 One of the classic pieces linking inequality of the sexes in the labour market and in the home is Armstrong and Armstrong (1978). Clement and Myles (1994, part 2) put the Canadian experience in comparative perspective. For earlier overviews of feminist political economy in Canada, see Luxton and Maroney (1997).

2 These three questions, the answers to which provide a way of characterizing social policy design, are developed in Jenson (1997).

3 Jenson and Sineau (2001) map these various state goals and the intersection with the gender equality agenda for Belgium, France, Italy, and Sweden, as well the European Union. See also the volume edited by Michel and Mahon (2002).

4 The term "welfare regime" shifts the focus away from the welfare state considered in isolation, locating the state as part of a broader regime that includes labour markets, families, and, we would argue, the voluntary sector – the nonprofit organisations formed in civil society that have played and continue to play an important role.

5 The liberal regime tends to rely on a residual safety net supplemented by measures that reinforce dependence on the market. Social democratic regimes offer generous and comprehensive protection from market-generated and other risks ("decommodification") on an inclusive or solidaristic basis. Conservative regimes offer generous protection but do so in a way that reinforces status differences. The latter have tended to be the most resistant to the decline of the male-breadwinner family ("defamilialisation"). In the field of childcare, however, several conservative regimes – notably Belgium and France – break the mould (Jenson and Sineau 2001; Michel and Mahon 2002).

6 The argument is implicit in the work of Ergas (1990), Tyyska (1993) and Baker (1995). It is an explicit part of the argument in Mahon (1997); O'Connor et al. (1999); and Mahon and Phillips (2002). Note that Esping-Andersen, whose typology has come to dominant the literature on welfare states/regimes, argues that these regimes took shape not in the early or even in the postwar years, but rather in the 1960s and 1970s (1999, 4).

7 O'Connor et al. (1999) explore differences among four countries with liberal regimes, and Bergqvist et al. (1999) bring out differences among the "social democratic" Scandinavian countries.

8 "Social" liberalism blends elements of liberalism and social democracy.

While liberals place more emphasis on the individual than social democrats, social liberals recognize that individual freedom and equality
require supportive collective institutions. O'Connor et al. have incorporated a similar notion ("new liberalism") to differentiate the dominant
form of liberalism in the postwar era from its classical and neoliberal
counterparts (1999, chap. 2).

9 These leaves were inserted into the Unemployment Insurance system in
   1971 and subsequently extended. To be eligible, parents must meet the
   relatively stringent conditions of eligibility for Employment Insurance.
   The result is that less than one of every two women giving birth is eligible for a paid leave. On the fairness of the tax system, see Vincent and
   Woolley (2000).

10 Currently, parents may deduct up to $7,000 of childcare expenses for
    children under six and $4,000 for children aged seven to sixteen. They
    must produce receipts for the service.

11 As part of the Lalonde social security review in the 1970s Canada came
    close to getting the kind of social services act needed to enable provin-
    cial governments to offer universally accessible childcare, with federal
    assistance. For more on this see Haddow (1993) and Mahon (2000).

12 Held in Winnipeg, the conference grew out of the behind-the-scenes
    work of the national daycare councillor (the establishment of which
    marked one of the victories of the earlier struggle by the femocrats) and
    Status of Women Canada. See Mahon (2000, 608–9) for a brief discus-
    sion of the debate there and its impact on the earlier round of negotia-
    tions.

13 For more on the politics that forged the CDCAA (now Childcare Advocacy
    Association of Canada), see Prentice (1988), Kass and Rothman (1997),
    Martin (2001), and the provincial stories in Pence (1992). On the
    Women's Bureau as an important part of the "women's state," see Findlay
    (1987).

14 The Tories' policy was inspired not only by neoliberalism's preference
    for markets but also by New Right ideas on the importance of supporting
    traditional breadwinner families. One of the elements that was passed –
    the Child Tax Credit – offered several billion dollars of tax assistance to
    lower- and middle-income families. The money might have provided
    some relief to those who had to rely on unreceipted childcare, but it also
    provided tax relief for traditional male-breadwinner families, as REAL
    Women and the Tory Family Caucus had demanded. For more on this,
    see Phillips (1989), Teghtsoonian (1993), and Timpson (2001, chap. 7).

15 The Red Book promised to top up CAP, offering a 40-40-20 cost-sharing
    arrangement between the federal government, the provinces, and
    parents, with the latter contributing according to their ability to pay. The
    new funds would, however, be limited ($720 million over three years)

and were contingent on achieving provincial agreement and at least 3
percent growth per annum. See Bach and Phillips (1997).

16 The emphasis on employability dominated the comprehensive Social
Security Review begun in 1994. It quickly became apparent to childcare
advocates, however, that cost-cutting would overwhelm social-policy
objectives when the 1994 budget established savings targets for the
review even before it had begun its work (Doherty et al. 1998, 39).

17 On average, 31 percent of the reinvestment has gone to child and
earned-income supplements, 39 percent to childcare subsidies, 5 percent
to early childhood services, 3 percent to supplementary health benefits,
and 22 percent to other types of assistance (Federal/Provincial/Territor-
ial Ministers 1999, 23).

18 The NCA was initiated by the provinces in 1997 and officially joined by
the federal government in 1999. Attention to early childhood development received a big boost from the report of the Early Years Study, commissioned by the Harris government and published in 1999 (McCain
and Mustard 1999).

19 At the time of writing, the Alliance was in the process of deciding
whether it would undertake the task of producing independent measure-
ments of the impacts of Early Childhood Development funding on the
well-being of children and their families and was assessing how it could
promote broader citizen engagement on children's policy.

20 Part of this structuring effect of CAP is seen in the differential labour
force participation rates of women in two-parent and lone-parent families. Of married women with children under six, fully 69 percent are in
the labour force. The comparable number for female heads of lone-
parent families is 55 percent (Vanier 2000, 87).

21 Quality is clearly a complex issue that can involve basic standards (staff-
child ratios and safety and other regulations), staff qualifications and
training, and curriculum. Only Quebec has established a provincial curriculum, which is being instituted in family daycare as well, through the
Early Childhood Centres.

22 In 1998, nonprofits accounted for only 39 percent of the places in Newfoundland and Labrador, 41 percent in Alberta, 57 percent in Nova
Scotia, and 58 percent in New Brunswick. This is in marked contrast to
Saskatchewan (99 percent), Manitoba (87 percent), Quebec (86
percent) and Ontario (83 percent) (CRRU).

23 In 1998 parent fees accounted for 82 percent in Newfoundland, 73
percent in Nova Scotia, 69 percent in New Brunswick, 67 percent in
Prince Edward Island, and 54 percent in Alberta (CRRU). By 1998,
Alberta had regulated childcare spaces for 8.8 percent of children aged
12 and under – bested by Prince Edward Island with spaces for 15.4
percent, Quebec (14.9 percent), British Columbia (10.8 percent) and

Manitoba (10.55 percent) but better than New Brunswick (7.7 percent), Nova Scotia (7.3 percent) and Newfoundland (5 percent) (CRRU, 122).

24 This attitude is nicely captured in the Nova Scotia government's attitude to the nonprofit sector. It made it clear that "had the government intended to be fully responsible, it would have approached the development of childcare centres in a different manner and the centres might well have been entirely a government operation. Instead the government hoped that the involvement of community groups would bring about a commitment from these groups to assist financially on an ongoing basis" (Irwin 1992, 274).

25 In the spring of 2000, the British Columbia government announced an upper limit on childcare fees for school-aged children. The NDP has also promised to extend this to preschool children if re-elected.

26 In 1998 parents' share was lowest in Manitoba (33.9 percent) and Saskatchewan (38.3 percent), while Quebec (45.8 percent) and British Columbia (49.4 percent) required parents to pay just under half (CRRU). The situation will have changed in Quebec with the implementation of its $5-a-day program.

27 The additional shares covered by provincial governments in 1998 were 33 percent for Quebec, 21.7 percent for Saskatchewan, 21.6 percent for Manitoba, and 16.6 percent for Ontario. As Prentice documents, Manitoba's support has declined substantially over the last decade, but it was the first to introduce salary-enhancement grants under the NDP government of 1981–85. The Ontario NDP also introduced salary enhancement grants in the early 1990s, and it, like the current Quebec government, moved to substantially reduce the commercial sector.

28 The Pence (1992) volumes began to tell these stories of provincial struggles. The Prentice volume (2001) adds to these. See also Martin (2001), Prentice (1988, 2000), Lero and Kyle (1991), Jenson (2002), and Langford (1997).

29 The transformation did not happen overnight, in part because it encountered effective local resistance in key cities like Edmonton and Calgary. On local resistance, see Langford (1997). On the development of Alberta's childcare system, see Hayden (1997) and Langford (1997).

REFERENCES

Armstrong, P., and H. Armstrong. 1978. *The Double Ghetto.* Toronto: McClelland and Stewart.

Bach, Sandra, and Susan Phillips. 1997. "Constituting a New Social Union: Child Care beyond Infancy?" In Gene Swimmer, ed., *How Ottawa Spends 1997–1998: Seeing Red, A Liberal Report Card,* 235–8. Ottawa: Carleton University Press.

Baker, Maureen. 1995. *Canadian Family Policies: Cross-national Comparisons.* Toronto: University of Toronto Press.

Beauvais, Caroline, and Jane Jenson. 2001. *Two Policy Paradigms: Family Responsibility and Investing in Children.* CPRN Discussion Paper no. F–12. Ottawa: Canadian Policy Research Networks.

Boychuk, Gerard. 1998. *Patchworks of Purpose: The Development of Provincial Social Assistance Regimes in Canada.* Montreal and Kingston: McGill-Queen's University Press.

Brennan, Deborah. 1998. *The Politics of Australian Child Care: Philanthropy to Feminism and Beyond.* Revised edition. Melbourne: Cambridge University Press.

Burt, Sandra. 1986. "Women's Issues and the Women's Movement in Canada since 1970." In Alan Cairns and Cynthia Williams, eds., *The Politics of Gender, Ethnicity and Language in Canada,* 111–70. Toronto: University of Toronto Press.

– 1990. "Organized Women's Groups and the State." In W.D. Coleman and G. Skogstad, eds., *Policy Communities and Public Policy in Canada: A Structural Approach* 191–211. Toronto: Copp Clark Pitman.

Clement, Wallace, and John Myles. 1994. *Relations of Ruling.* Montreal and Kingston: McGill-Queen's University Press.

Collectif Clio. 1992. *L'histoire des femmes au Québec depuis quatre siècles.* Montreal: Le Jour.

CCRU (Childcare Resource and Research Unit). 2000. *Early Childhood Care and Education in Canada: Provinces and Territories: 1998.* http://www.childcare-canada.org/pt98/pre.html

Doherty, G., M. Friendly, and M. Oloman. 1998. *Women's Support, Women's Work: Child Care in an Era of Deficit Reduction, Devolution, Downsizing and Deregulation.* Ottawa: Status of Women Canada.

Esping-Andersen, Gøsta. 1999. *Social Foundations of Postindustrial Economies.* Oxford: Oxford University Press

Federal/Provincial/Territorial Ministers Responsible for Social Services. 1999. *The National Child Benefit Progress Report: 1999.* Ottawa: Government of Canada

Findlay, Suzanne. 1987. "Facing the State: The Politics of the Women's Movement Reconsidered." In M. Luxton and H.J. Maroney, eds., *Feminism and Political Economy: Women's Work, Women's Struggles.* Toronto: Methuen

Finkel, Alvin. 1995. "'Even the Little Children Cooperated': Family Strategies, Childcare Discourse and Social Welfare Debates, 1945–1975." *Labour/Le Travail* 36(5):91–118.

Friendly, Martha. 1994. *Child Care Policy in Canada: Putting the Pieces Together.* Don Mills, ON: Addison-Wesley.

Goodin, Robert E., Bruce Headey, Ruud Muffels, and Henk-Jan Dirven. 1999. *The Real Worlds of Welfare Capitalism.* Cambridge: Cambridge University Press.

Haddow, Rodney. 1993. *Poverty Reform in Canada, 1958–1978*. Montreal and Kingston: McGill-Queen's University Press.

Hayden, Jacqueline. 1997. "Neo-Conservatism and Child Care Services in Alberta: A Case Study." University of Toronto, Childcare Resource and Research Unit, Occasional Paper, no. 9.

Irwin, Sharon, and Patricia Canning. 1992. "An Historical Overview of Childcare in Nova Scotia." In Alan R. Pence, ed., *Canadian Childcare in Context: Perspectives from Provinces and Territories*, 269–88. Ottawa: Statitics Canada and Health and Welfare Canada.

Jackson, Andrew, and David Robinson, with Bob Baldwin and Cindy Wiggins. 2000. *Falling Behind: The State of Working Canada, 2000*. Ottawa: Canadian Centre for Policy Alternatives.

Jenson, Jane. 1986. "Gender and Reproduction, or Babies and the State." *Studies in Political Economy* 20 (summer): 9–46.

– 2002. "Against the Current: Child Care and Family Policy in Quebec." In S. Michel and R. Mahon, eds., *Child Care Policy at a Crossroads: Gender and Welfare State Restructuring*. New York: Routledge.

Jenson, Jane, and Susan D. Phillips. 1996. "Regime Shift: New Citizenship Practices in Canada." *International Journal of Canadian Studies* 14 (fall): 111–36.

Jenson, Jane, and Mariette Sineau, eds., 2001. *Who Cares? Women's Work and Welfare State Redesign*. Toronto: University of Toronto Press.

Kapsalis, C., R. Morissette, and G. Picot. 1999. "The Returns to Education and the Increasing Wage Gap between Younger and Older Workers." Analytical Studies Branch, Research Paper no. 131. Ottawa: Statistics Canada.

Kass, Jamie, and Laurel Rothman. 1997. "Still Struggling for Better Child Care: The Role of Labour in the Canadian Child Care Movement." Prepared for the Eighth Conference on Canadian Social Welfare Policy, University of Regina, 25–28 June.

Krashinsky, Michael, and Gordon Cleveland. 1999. "Tax Fairness for One-Earner and Two-Earner Families: An Examination of the Issues." CPRN Discussion Paper no. F–07. Ottawa: Canadian Policy Research Networks.

Kyle, Irene, and Donna S. Lero. 1991. "Work, Families and Child Care in Ontario." In L.C. Johnson and D. Barnhorst, eds., *Children, Families and Public Policy in the 1990s*. Toronto: Thompson Educational Publishers.

Langford, Tom. 1997. "Municipal-Provincial Conflict over Child Care in Alberta, 1966–1996." Paper presented at the annual meetings of the Canadian Political Science Association.

Luxton, M., and H.J. Maroney. 1987. *Feminism and Political Economy: Women's Work*. Toronto: Methuen.

Mahon, Rianne. 1997. "Childcare Policies in Canada and Sweden: Policy and Politics." *Social Politics* 4(3): 382–418

– 2000. "The Never-Ending Story: The Struggle for Universal Child Care Policy in the 1970s." *Canadian Historical Review* 81(4): 582–615.

Mahon, Rianne, and Susan Phillips. 2002. "Dual-Earner Familes Caught in a Liberal Welface Regime? The Politics of Child Care Policy in Canada." In Sonya Michel and Rianne Mahon, eds., *Child Care Policy at a Crossroads: Gender and Welfare State Restructuring*, 191–218. London and New York: Routledge.

Martin, Judith. 2001. "Child Care Advocacy in Saskatchewan: History, Lessons and a Reflection." In Susan Prentice, ed., *Changing Child Care: Five Decades of Child Care Advocacy in Canada*. Halifax: Fernwood.

McCain, N. Margaret, and Fraser J. Mustard. 1999. *Reversing the Real Brain Drain: The Early Years Study Final Report*. Available at http://www.childsec.gov.on.ca.

Michel, Sonya, and Rianne Mahon, eds. 2002. *Childcare Policy at a Crossroads: Gender and Welfare State Restructuring*. New York and London: Routledge.

O'Connor, Julia, Ann Shola Orloff, and Sheila Shaver. 1999. *States, Markets, Families: Gender, Liberalism and Social Policy in Australia, Canada, Great Britain and the United States*. Cambridge: Cambridge University Press.

Pence, Alan, ed. 1992. *Perspectives from the Provinces*. Vols. 2 and 2. Ottawa: Statistics Canada.

Phillips, Susan. 1989. "Rock-a-bye Brian: The National Strategy for Child Care." In K. Graham, ed. *How Ottawa Spends: The Buck Stops Where?* Don Mills, ON: Oxford University Press.

– 1991. "How Ottawa Bends: Shifting Government Relationships with Interest Groups." In F. Abele, ed., *How Ottawa Spends, 1991–92: The Politics of Fragmentation*, 235–58. Ottawa: Carleton University Press.

– 2001. "SUFA and Citizen Engagement: Fake or Genuine Masterpiece?" In A. Noel, ed. *Back to the Table: A New Social Union for 2002?* Montreal: IRPP.

Prentice, Susan. 1988. "Kids Are Not for Profit: The Politics of Child Care." In F. Cunningham, Marlene Kada, Suzanne Findlay, Alan Lenna, and Silva Lenna, eds., *Social Movements/Social Change*. Toronto: Between the Lines

– 2000. "A Decade of Decline: Regulated Child Care in Manitoba, 1989–1999." Winnipeg, MB: Canadian Centre for Policy Alternatives.

– ed. 2001. *Changing Child Care: Five Decades of Child Care Advocacy in Canada*. Halifax: Fernwood.

Teghtsoonian, Katherine. 1993. "Neo-Conservative Ideology and Opposition to Federal Regulation of Child Care: Services in the United States and Canada." *Canadian Journal of Political Science* 36(1): 97–122.

Timpson, Annis M. 2001. *Driven Apart: Women's Employment Equity and Child Care in Canadian Public Policy*. Vancouver: University of British Columbia.

Tyyska, Vappu. 1993. "The Women's Movement and the Welfare State: Child

Care Policy in Canada and Finland, 1960–1990." PHD diss. University of Toronto.

Vanier Institute of the Family. 2000. *Profiling Canada's Families* Vol. 2. Ottawa.

Vincent, Carolle, and Frances Woolley. 2000. "Taxing Canadian Families: What's Fair, What's Not." *Choices* 6:5.

Vosko, Leah F. 2000. *Temporary Work. The Gendered Rise of a Precarious Employment Relationship*. Toronto: University of Toronto.

White, Linda. 2001. "From Ideal to Pragmatic Politics: National Child Care Advocacy Groups in the 1980s and 1990s." In S. Prentice, *Changing Child Care: Five Decades of Child Care Advocacy in Canada*. Halifax: Fernwood.

Women's Bureau. 1958. *Survey of Married Women Working for Pay*. Ottawa: Government of Canada.

7 Pay Equity: Complexity and Contradiction in Legal Rights and Social Processes

PAT ARMSTRONG, MARY CORNISH, AND ELIZABETH MILLAR

"Who benefits?" is a central question in political economy. The answer to it may seem obvious in the case of pay equity, the hard-won legislative requirement to pay those working in female-dominated jobs on the same basis as those employed in male-dominated jobs. But as post-modernists and poststructuralists so often remind us, answers to Who benefits? can vary substantially. And the answers often reflect the location of the person addressing the question. Political economy tells us that the answers are not only complex and varied, depending on location, but also often expose fundamental contradictions. "Contradictions," as the term is used here, captures the notion of opposing forces, of opposites that clash, of actions that produce opposing actions, a double bind. While these clashes are often the basis of change, they may create new opposing forces that turn victories into losses and thus create the need for more change. The recognition of such contradictions can reveal how and why victories turn into losses and how what may be a victory for one group or for the present may be very different for another group or for the future.

In fact, there are no simple answers to the question of who benefits from pay equity. Not only do the multiple actors have different experiences with the processes but using the law to achieve gender equality is itself a contradictory process. Moreover, the actors are themselves caught in the contradictions generated by what is seen as a dichotomy between value-free and value-laden strategies. This chapter is an attempt to reveal some of the contradictions inherent in pay equity and to do so from the perspectives of people in three quite different locations. It is not an attempt to provide a comprehensive analysis of pay equity processes, to capture the full range of pay equity's complexity, or to represent the entire range of actors in this particular play. Nor does it offer a single, integrated view. Rather, it presents three different voices participating in the pay equity process. The purpose is to draw out some of the contradictions in this process and to do so in ways that have more general implications for theory and practice in terms of using the law to transform relations of ruling.

One player is Pat Armstrong, a professor of sociology and women's studies. Pat has served as an expert witness in cases that also involved either Elizabeth Millar or Mary Cornish. She has testified both about the need for pay equity and about the criteria for job evaluation schemes that are intended to reduce gender bias. Although significant strides have been made in the attempt to make visible and appropriately value women's work, the effort to do so is full of contradictions for academics called to be objective analysts of the process.

Elizabeth Millar, the second player, speaks from a location within the Public Service Alliance of Canada (PSAC), a union that represents 180,000 public sector workers. PSAC has been engaged in multiple battles for pay equity, including a decade-long effort to bring equal pay for work of equal value to the largest occupational group within the federal public service. As the staff member chiefly responsible for pay equity issues, Millar was central in the daily and continuing struggle to have the *Canadian Human Rights Act* applied and enforced. The major female-dominated group won not only an impressive wage increase but also back pay. Yet, as she makes clear in the second personal contribution of this chapter, the process is far from a simple victory for these women or for pay equity in general.

The final player is Mary Cornish, a labour lawyer who chaired a group that successfully lobbied for pay equity legislation in Ontario and led a number of precedent-setting cases through the legal system in that province. These cases were particularly important in challenging the traditional job evaluation plans that undermine the worth of women's work. Cornish has also successfully argued under Canada's Charter of Rights and Freedoms that in removing retroactively the right of women in predominantly female workplaces to proxy pay equity payments under the Pay Equity Act, the Ontario government was contravening the Charter. As a result of this ruling, thousands of women employed in some of the lowest-paid jobs throughout the broader public sector received significant pay increases. Nevertheless, there have been few simple gains for women, and there are contradictions in legal battles that are often difficult to see or counter.

Together, these perspectives help to map out the contradictions in this particular legal effort to improve women's pay – contradictions both for the actors and with the process of achieving equity. But they are intended to do more than draw out conclusions about this specific case. There are lessons to be learned about how pay equity can help us understand and assess efforts to establish and enforce legal rights more generally. Indeed, there are lessons to be learned not only about all struggles for legal rights but also about the importance of recognizing contradictions in our analysis of social processes.

PAY EQUITY

Pay equity, or equal pay for work of equal value, is a legal remedy designed to address only one aspect of women's unequal position in the labour force, namely, the undervaluing of women's work in predominately female jobs. Unlike employment equity, which is intended to reduce segregation in the workforce by increasing the access of women and other equity-seeking groups to white men's work, pay equity aims to ensure that neither men nor women are discriminated against in the amount they are paid for doing traditional women's work.

The long struggle for pay equity has rested on arguments both from evidence and for justice. Globally and locally, the research demonstrating a persistent and pervasive overall wage gap between women and men provided a starting point for legislative intervention. Initially, this intervention took the form of equal pay for equal work. But it quickly became obvious that the problem was not simply that some individual women were paid less for doing the same jobs as men. And even in the case of women and men doing the same work, it was easy for the employer to create differences to justify unequal wages. Much more important to the wage gap is the sex-segregation of the labour force, combined with the low value attached to work dominated by women. This link between low wages and female domination occurs regardless of the contribution to the employers' profits, the mission of the organization, or the well-being of society. In other words, there is systemic discrimination. Virtually all attempts to explain away the gap in terms of such factors as experience, job demands, work history, education, or women's ambition still left part of the gap unexplained. This unexplained gap was defined as discrimination.

The evidence on the segregation of the work force by sex, combined with the low value attached to women's work regardless of the skill, effort, and responsibility of working conditions involved in the job, was a central component in the successful demands for laws requiring equal pay for work of equal value – or what in Canada is called pay equity

(Brodie 1996; Cuneo 1990). The requirement for pay equity is quite different from laws requiring that women and men doing the same work be paid the same wages. One major difference is that women and men do not have to be doing the same, or even similar, work to be eligible. Indeed, the law is designed to address the fact that women and men do quite different work and to compare them in terms of their overall value to the organization. A second difference reflects the focus on systemic discrimination, the pervasive inequality that keeps so many women doing women's work at women's wages. With systemic discrimination as the starting point, the issue is women's work, rather than discrimination against individual women, and the job rather than the person. Unlike employment equity, which is concerned with redistributing individual workers among jobs and thus encouraging desegregation, pay equity is directed at improving the wages of those employees who work in traditionally female jobs. The point is not, for example, to allow nurses to become doctors but rather to ensure that nursing work is appropriately recognized and appropriately paid. While the laws on pay equity were based on evidence of the overall wage gap, pay equity legislation required that specific kinds of jobs be examined to determine sex segregation and job value within workplaces.

Federally, pay equity was promoted by the 1970 Royal Commission on the Status of Women. Academics, women's organizations, and lawyers were at least as important as unions in promoting this strategy, a strategy eventually enshrined in section 11 of the Canadian Human Rights Act. Section 11 defined unequal pay for work of equal value as discriminatory, but it required women in female-dominated jobs to complain to the Human Rights Commission and to establish discrimination. Section 11 is a general statement of principle, but the Canadian Human Rights Commission had the authority to issue guidelines on the law's implementation. The Equal Wages Guidelines were developed with input from Treasury Board and were publicly welcomed by it. The commission investigates complaints and seeks to settle those deemed legitimate. If the commission cannot reach a settlement, then a tribunal is organized to hear the complaint and order the settlement.

Although the legislation was not primarily the product of union demands, because of its nature it was mainly unions that had the resources to pursue complaints. Experience with this type of complaints-based legislation led the unions and other equity-seeking groups to demand proactive legislation. Ontario, for example, now has legislation that requires employers to demonstrate that they are indeed paying employees in different but comparable male- and female-dominated jobs equally.

Pay equity does not challenge the market determination of wages (Fudge and McDermott 1991). What is challenged is the failure of the market to apply the same criteria to male-dominated and female-dominated jobs. Some feminists have rejected pay equity because it fails to confront the market directly (Brenner 1987). Others maintain that pay equity indirectly contests the market by laws that limit the employer's right to discriminate and thus has implications for both gendered and class-based hierarchies (Figart and Kahn 1997). Developed in relatively good economic times, pay equity has been applied in bad ones. As a result, it is often blamed for rising male and female unemployment or denied on the grounds that employers cannot afford to pay equal wages. But the issues involved are about much more than pay and have implications for all legal remedies to inequality.

PAY EQUITY AND EXPERTS: THE VOICE OF PAT ARMSTRONG

In both complaint-based and proactive legislation, establishing inequality means first establishing male and female dominance. It also means both assessing the jobs and assessing the assessment of jobs. A case often ends up before a tribunal that operates much like a court. Not only are dominance and value in question, but so is equity itself. Because I have been conducting research on women's work since the early 1970s, I have been qualified as an expert on each of these issues.

While evidence is a matter for experts, justice is not, because the whole notion is that experts are objective and value-free: that is, the assumption is that the evidence given by experts is objective and value-free. It is this notion of objectivity that is at the heart of the contradiction for the expert witness and, indeed, pay equity itself. The model is truth without values, even though the question at the heart of pay equity concerns equal value and justice. There are several ways in which this contradiction is evident.

First, although witnesses are called to support one side in the case, they are expected to provide expert opinions on facts that are themselves assumed to be objective. Indeed, my expertise has been challenged on the grounds that, first, I have used political economy as a theoretical guide and thus, presumably, that I am biased in favour of equality; second, that I have been a witness only for human rights commissions or unions and never for employers and thus that I am biased in favour of workers and equity; and, third, that I have written articles that would seem to support pay equity. This last objection is particularly puzzling, as I am qualified as an expert witness precisely because I have written about pay equity and the law requires pay equity.

At the same time, although I have been called as a witness to present the most complete expert evidence possible based on the "facts," I am not allowed to consult other experts on such facts while I am being cross-examined on those facts. I was once challenged for talking with my husband during a break in testimony because my husband is an academic who does research in the same field. Yet one of the ways experts develop opinions is through discussions with others.

Second, at issue in most pay equity hearings is the objective measure of job content and demands. What kinds of skill, effort, responsibility, and working conditions are involved in a job and what are they worth? Social scientists have long challenged the notion that these factors are independent, easily measurable, or agreed-upon. Rather, they have argued that they are socially constructed and reflect, as well as create, value (Gaskell 1986). Markets are not the products of mysterious invisible hands but rather the result of those who have power making decisions that often directly subvert what are defined as the "objective" laws of supply and demand. Feminists have established the gendered and patriarchal nature of such constructions. What is defined as skill and the value attached to that skill are very much influenced by the gender of the person doing the work. The same is true of effort, responsibility, and working conditions. So, for example, nursing is defined as clean and safe, even though health care has the highest injury rate of all industries (Workers' Compensation Board of British Columbia 1996). Indeed, evidence on social construction and gender bias with respect to the value placed on work has been part of the argument that has led to the legislative requirement that job evaluation be free of gender bias. The effort to achieve pay equity means exposing those values at the same time as we are trying to make skills visible and valued in a different way. In other words, these factors are socially constructed and about values, but they nonetheless must be appropriately measured and valued, which implies a more objective approach.

Let's take the example of skill. Braverman (1974) analyzed skills as if they were measurable, objectively determined capacities with particular kinds of value for employers and employees. In contrast, feminist political economists such as Jane Gaskell (1986) have stressed not only the social construction of skills but also the gendered nature of what counts as skill and how these skills are valued. Ronnie Steinberg (1990) and others (Acker 1989) have demonstrated that most job-evaluation schemes fail to capture and appropriately value skills in female-dominated jobs. The legislation in several jurisdictions calls for evaluation free of gender bias. The witness is juggling these contradictory claims. On the one hand, the witness is providing evidence that skills exist that have been inappropriately captured and valued. On the other hand, the witness is providing evidence that skills are socially constructed and that value itself is a negotiated process reflecting values that denigrate women.

A fine balance is required to handle these contradictory claims. The witness must recognize that skills are simultaneously real and measurable learned capacities and that they are also defined through a negotiation process in which women lose more compared to men. It requires demonstrating that actual existing capacities can be made visible, while also acknowledging that for both women and men what gets understood as skill is a matter of definition and of power – of men and of employers. These definitions are negotiated in the context of unequal power relationships not only between employers and employees but also between women and men. The same issues arise in terms of what value is attached to these skills. The value of any skill, once made visible, is negotiated. Value is neither natural nor simply determined by objective market forces. It is, rather, as feminists are now wont to say, "both and." But this is difficult to argue in a pay equity case where the laws are based on dualities: right and wrong, correct and incorrect, biased or not, objective or value-free.

Third, the contradictions inherent in the idea of objective measures are also evident when it comes to determining gender dominance of a job category. Pay equity is based on a comparison of jobs dominated by one sex, yet the boundaries between jobs are themselves the product of power relations and values, rather than a simple reflection of natural, objectively determined divisions between duties to be done. Determining what constitutes a job in precise and practical terms is itself a challenge. On the one hand, it is necessary to have clear boundaries for the purpose of pay equity, but on the other, we recognize that boundaries themselves may be manipulated to avoid the consequences of pay equity and that they are socially constructed categories reflecting power relations. Although gender dominance may appear to be a simple matter of counting, people may be shifted around to alter the gender composition of particular jobs. One more male clerical worker may make a female-dominated job, on a straight count, a gender-neutral one. Although the Ontario legislation, for example, sets out guidelines intended to address these flexible boundaries, expert witnesses are placed in the position of having to claim firm boundaries while at the same time arguing that job determinations are socially constructed with flexible boundaries. So, for example, while nursing is traditional women's work, the addition of a couple of males in a small nursing home that employs only a few RNs might change the composition of that job to one that is not clearly female-dominated. The change, however, does not alter the association of this work with women and low value.

The importance of understanding the pay process as a negotiated one framed by unequal power relations and contradictions becomes evident as well when we look at the issue of job evaluation. Jobs must be evaluated to be compared, although there are multiple ways of performing the evaluation. As an expert witness, I have shown that traditional job evaluations are based on assessments of male-dominated work and thus fail to capture important aspects of female-dominated work. Many of the skills that women have and require, and much of the effort and many of the responsibilities and working conditions they face are invisible when the standard for what is required is male-dominated work. What is not made visible cannot be valued. Care is a critical example of a work component that has not been either captured or valued in traditional job evaluation schemes. Even in hospitals that frame their mission statements in terms of care, care is not a part of job evaluation and payment. Pay equity cases have successfully established the importance of care, and many new job evaluation schemes now include some way of assessing care work.[1] Yet the assessment of care is far from a simple victory for women's pay or for their place in the organization. Increasingly, those in male-dominated jobs are demanding that care be defined in such as way as to include components of men's jobs. Parking attendants and engineers now get credit for care. Attempts federally to develop a universal classification system that would address gender bias and apply to all jobs have failed in part because whenever components of women's work are made visible and valued, there is a corresponding demand to extend the definitions to male-dominated work. When the issue is framed as achieving job evaluation that is free of gender bias, ignoring the history of women's subordination and the power at play in the process, this result is not surprising.

To be an expert witness, I have to qualify as someone who bases her opinion on facts rather than values at the same time as I appear as a witness for one side in a disputed claim. It is this contradictory mix of fact and value that is at the heart of pay equity. But it is equally at the heart of any human rights issue before the law.

PAY EQUITY AND UNIONS:
THE VOICE OF ELIZABETH MILLAR

A complaints-based system means that only those with resources and security can afford to challenge an employer. As a result, unions have played the primary role in pursuing complaints, even though unions themselves are often in conflict about pay equity. As a staff person responsible for pay equity within the largest union representing federal employees, I have had to address not only contradictions between the employer and the union but also contradictions within both these organizations.

The union I work for is the Public Service Alliance of Canada (PSAC), which represents the majority of women who work in the federal public service. We face the federal government as employer. The 1967 Public Service Staff Relations Act created job classes that could be compared to groups outside the public service. Overt and covert discrimination, including inferior wages, different and lower pensions for women, and barriers to hiring in traditional male work and to benefits such as maternity leave and childcare services, were perpetuated rather than challenged by these comparators (Archibald 1970).

When the Canadian Human Rights Act became law in 1976, unions were themselves reinforcing practices that discriminate against women, even while they fought to increase women's wages. This contradiction reflected the legacy of overwhelmingly male-oriented union structures. Women were regarded as difficult to organize and integrate into the union; their integration was limited by meetings held in the evenings without childcare, with cigarettes and beer as the main staple, and with low priority being given to childcare and maternity leave. Over the last twenty-five years, unions have worked valiantly, with many conflicts but with great success, to integrate women into the union movement and to address women's concerns. However, twenty-five years ago the male model was the criterion for success within unions and in the workplace. Career progression was equally defined in terms of women abandoning their traditional jobs as clerks or secretaries and succeeding by entering male-dominated occupations. Although many of these issues are now being addressed, the integration of women's concerns into mainstream union activities remains a challenge.

The struggle to address women's concerns within unions is linked to another contradiction in pay equity. Unions have long adhered to the goal of equal treatment for all. Union solidarity means recognizing a common goal that benefits all members equally. Pay equity issues seem to violate this common goal because they suggest special treatment and thus are feared as divisive. Indeed, management may use pay equity to encourage division, undermining the goal of both pay equity and union solidarity. As a result, pay equity remains a source of tension within unions, especially when the employer uses pay equity as a justification for lay-offs or wage freezes.

Another contradiction relates to how wages are determined within unionized workplaces. Collective bargaining is at the centre of wage determination, yet collective bargaining has been based largely on traditional male concerns such as dirty work allowances, long-service pay, and overtime pay. Defined as equal treatment, such strategies were not seen as systemically discriminating against women who had breaks in work service, who worked in inside jobs, or who did not have the flexibility to work overtime. At the same time, demands that seemed to favour women, such as paid maternity leave, leave without pay for care and nurturing, or leave for family medical emergencies were often seen as unfair. In other words, the human right to pay equity might be bargained away through the collective bargaining process. It is partly for this reason that the Canadian Human Rights Act takes precedence over collective bargaining. This precedence means that equal pay can be determined outside the collective bargaining process, creating contradictions for both unions and employers who are accustomed to determining wages and working conditions through collective bargaining negotiations.

This point brings me to the contradictory location of the government in the pay equity process. On the one hand, the government has established pay equity as a human right and appoints the tribunal that determines pay equity issues. On the other hand, the government is an employer who resists pay equity and who hires the same lawyers as other employers to challenge both the law and its application. It also adopts strategies, such as contracting out, that were developed in the private sector as a means of undermining wage demands such as pay equity. The Treasury Board, which bargains for the government, initially argued that the law did not apply to the public service. Then the government argued that the cost was too high, a contradiction, in itself, given that the high cost of pay equity demonstrates the extent of the very discrimination the government is supposed to be committed to eliminating. While the federal government has repeatedly affirmed its support of equal pay, job-classification schemes free of gender bias, and strategies to eliminate systemic discrimination, it has also repeatedly resisted pay equity solutions in its own workplaces.

When pay equity became law, union leaders were unprepared and, like government leaders, were largely unaware of the impact pay equity would have on the workplace. Within both types of organization, however, those actually dealing with pay and job evaluation issues were very well aware of what was to come. And this division between those who understood the complex processes of pay equity and those who did not created tensions within both sides. Moreover, there were also significant differences between the thirteen unions in the federal public sector in their commitment to pay equity and in their understanding of the mechanisms involved. For example, the primarily female Library Science Group was ready when the law was introduced to seek pay equity and managed to achieve a measure of equality long before others. At the same time, many of the small, male-dominated unions were at best confused by the whole idea.

All these contradictions became particularly obvious in the case of the federal clerical and administrative workers. This major job classification covers thousands of women who do a wide variety of traditional women's work. Indeed, lumping so many women together itself reflects discrimination and contrasts sharply with the many male-dominated job classes that include a small number of men. PSAC, which was very aware that the Canadian Human Rights Act (CHRA) requires that all other existing mechanisms be exhausted, spent years trying to use both the grievance procedure and the collective bargaining process in an attempt to achieve pay equity before any formal complaints were filed with the Canadian Human Rights Commission. But Treasury Board negotiators refused to recognize the CHRA provisions. They not only contradicted the principles of equal pay for work of equal value but also derided the very concept of pay equity.

The 1984 federal election saw leaders of all political parties claiming to support equal pay for work of equal value, creating the expectation that immediate orders would be given for pay equity initiatives. But when it became apparent that no government action would follow this election promise, a complaint alleging discrimination in classification and pay was filed in December 1984 on behalf of the Clerical and Regulatory Group. A number of male-dominated jobs could have served as comparators for pay equity purposes. The one chosen for comparison was the work of the Programme Administration Group, because this work provided a logical career progression for clerks and was quite similar to clerical work.

The complaint was interrupted by a new government initiative. On International Women's Day, 1985, the then Treasury Board minister, Robert Réné de Cotret, announced a giant pay equity study that would include all male and female groups and all thirteen unions in the public service. The Public Service Alliance, with 180,000 members, and the Professional Institute, with approximately 30,000 members, were the largest unions and the only ones concerned with pay equity. The remaining unions, some tiny, some entirely male, were totally perplexed by this government initiative and the government's insistence on their participation.

The government was prepared to fund this pay equity study. Joint committees worked out terms of reference. A U.S. consulting firm was hired to determine job value using the Willis Job Evaluation scheme. Over three thousand jobs in the federal public service were selected randomly to represent male- and female-dominant groups. Begun in 1987, the study ended in 1989, not only because the task was huge but also because there were enormous conflicts among both unions and employers, as well as between them over job content and job value. Yet significant progress was made, and results released throughout the study indicated that by any measure a gap of 10 to 15 percent existed between male and female wages for work of equal value. However, the difficulties throughout the study created an atmosphere of tension, and the process deteriorated. By December 1989 the parties were still far apart, even though only a small amount of work remained to be done. The Public Service Alliance withdrew from the job evaluation process because it feared that the government would take arbitrary action that the union would be linked to if it remained.

One month later, in January 1990, these suspicions were confirmed. The Treasury Board unilaterally announced payments of approximately one thousand dollars annually to the Clerical and Regulatory and Secretarial, Stenographic, and Typing Groups. Payments would be backdated to 1985, the date the study was announced. These payments were a complete departure from past practice. The methodology chosen by the Treasury Board to support the payments had never been seen before and has not been seen since. The two-year pay equity study appeared to play no role, nor was there any indication that this extra money created pay equity. The Equal Wages Guidelines were ignored, foreshadowing an assault on the guidelines by Treasury Board and other employers. In spite of the fact that these payments did not reflect a comparison based on equal value according to the guidelines, the government presented them as meeting the requirements under the law. The consequences of this strategy were as contradictory for the government as the strategy itself. Those who thought that pay equity would never result in payments, as well as those who thought there was no problem of discrimination or need for pay equity, were silenced by the admission evident in the pay offers. However inadequate, the payments indicated that a problem did exist and that the problem required millions to fix.

The consequences were also contradictory for the unions. As a result of the government's representations and of the complex processes involved that made it difficult for members to understand pay equity, the union had an uphill battle to convince members that the government payments were a down payment that was inadequate to represent true pay equity in the public service. Members not included in the government announcement were concerned that they had been abandoned, and male-dominated sectors were particularly upset. PSAC worked overtime to convince them both that all members must work together to put pressure on the government for improved payments and that the payments were not the end of the road.

Thus began a decade of mass grievance action. A national strike in 1991 was ended when the government ordered the union back to work without attempting to resolve pay equity. All individuals had their salaries frozen for six of the next seven years, regardless of whether they earned twenty thousand or a hundred thousand dollars annually. The result was a perpetuation of the unequal pay identified in the pay equity study. During this period, the pay equity complaint filed in 1984 finally came before the Human Rights Tribunal. For six years the process was buried in legal technicalities raised by the government.

Rarely was pay equity the issue. The government challenged the study it had funded, the consulting firm it had hired, and the process it had agreed to. The study, the government alleged, was biased against men, even though management and representatives of all thirteen unions, only two of which had an interest in the pay equity issue, had agreed on the study. The government also attempted to prevent the tribunal from receiving the pay equity study results as evidence, claiming they were "privileged," and filed an action in the federal court challenging the jurisdiction of the Tribunal and the Equal Wages Guidelines. The government delayed and obstructed but did not present one management or expert witness to defend its past or current policies. During this struggle, many of those seeking pay equity lost their jobs through downsizing and contracting-out. The decade-long delay further undermined support. At the same time, thousands of women across the country, both inside and outside the union, buoyed up support and stressed the need to seek pay equity rather than partial increases.

While the tribunal was still meeting, the government tried once again to preempt pay equity. In 1997, during the Public Service Alliance Triennial Convention in Toronto, the government leaked an $800-million pay equity offer to a Toronto newspaper with no prior discussions with the union. The offer was craftily constructed with a sliding scale. Current workers would receive a much higher percentage of what was owed than older retired workers or those who had lost their jobs and left the public service. The government's intention, of course, was that only those who were current union members and thus working in the public service would be entitled to vote on this issue. Those who stood to lose most would be silenced – no voice, no vote. It was apparent that the government hoped the union membership would revolt against the leaders and demand acceptance of the offer, however flawed. A lawyer long associated with feminist causes was hired by the government to negotiate the payouts before the tribunal rendered its decision.

Once again, the union appeared to be standing in the way of wage increases for its members. This time, however, its leaders were prepared and its membership educated in the principles of pay equity. Union members exploded. More than one fax number on Parliament Hill had to be changed as union members began a campaign of attacking the government's refusal to pay women what they were worth. A media blitz followed with the government buying full-page ads in the

Ottawa Citizen urging union members to demand that their union hold a vote. It is a credit to those concerned that, regardless of the complexity of the issue, trust was developing. The union's arguments made sense to the membership, and no demand for the union to hold a vote on the offer ever took force. The contradiction of the Liberals refusing to implement a law they had introduced twenty-five years before was not lost on the members.

When the tribunal's decision finally came down, it supported a methodology that compared average male wages to women's wages. The result was that the total pay equity payments would be double those that had been offered by the Treasury Board. In addition, the tribunal ordered that the wages owed should be paid with interest. Even without compounding the interest, this brought the total owed to public service employees to approximately three billion dollars.

Treasury Board appealed the tribunal decision. Concerns for cost went out the window when, in addition to a flotilla of Department of Justice lawyers, Treasury Board paid a private Toronto law firm to fight the tribunal decision in the federal court. The appeal failed. Justice John Evans found that there was evidence of systemic discrimination, that pay equity payments were justified, and that the tribunal decision was valid. A negotiated settlement was finalized in November 2000 with the essential elements of the union position intact.

The impact of the decision, and more generally of the federal law, is contradictory. On the one hand, thousands of women received not only significant wage increases but also large retroactive payments. On the other hand, government strategies such as downsizing and privatization created a multitude of separate employers who have established new conditions of work. A complaint such as the clerical complaint that addresses a global discriminatory situation could not be launched today. The workplace is too fragmented. Individual complaints to individual employers require extensive resources, which unions, no matter how large, do not have.

Moreover, the very success of the union, along with the actual experience of fighting for pay equity, would make it difficult for PSAC to follow such a course again. Unions, unable to match government funding for the huge legal challenges they have had to face on many fronts over the past years, are loath to concentrate on an issue that seems to support only one group of members and that requires such enormous resources. A focus on gender issues gives the appearance of abandoning traditional union issues. The male model of trade unionism remains intact in many areas at the same time as one huge pay equity settlement creates the impression that the pay problem, and even systemic discrimination, has been solved.

This impression is in turn related to the contradiction between collective bargaining and achieving pay equity. Throughout the pay equity process, particularly while under pressure by the government to accept an inadequate offer, the union was criticized by the media, the government, and some members for refusing to bargain equity while holding out for a legal decision. The ludicrousness of this criticism ignored, of course, the union's attempt to bargain equity from 1977 onwards when the government absolutely refused to consider pay equity at the bargaining table. It also ignored the issue of bargaining a human right. Bargaining involves compromise and concessions. Bargaining is also subject to a vote by a wide variety of individuals, not all of whom will ever be affected and not all of whom are concerned about discrimination issues or aware of the existing problems. Unions have had to deal with this conundrum throughout their work on equity. It is a delicate balance, and one that must be recognized.

The federal government has undertaken a review of its pay equity legislation. It is doing so in the context of years devoted to developing finely tuned legal arguments against each proposal for pay equity that emphasized market forces. Millions of dollars have been spent by the government and by large corporations such as Air Canada, Bell Canada, and Canada Post to resist the implementation of the legislation. The resistance has forced unions to spend heavily in response. In spite of their massive victory on behalf of thousands of women, the unions are now less likely to mount strong resistance to negative changes in pay equity, in part because the public sector unions have lost members with the cutbacks, in part because they have so many other issues to face, and in part because the last fight over pay equity cost so much.

PAY EQUITY AND THE LAW:
THE VOICE OF MARY CORNISH

The struggle for pay equity is constant and neither begins nor ends when legislation is adopted. It is constant in part because conditions change, in part because the law gets used in particular ways, and in part because contradictions and compromises are always found in making and applying the law. As a labour lawyer who has also been active in lobbying for greater equality through legal means, I have been involved in both developing and interpreting the law. I have thus had the opportunity to participate in the process of creating legislation and in responding to the various efforts to turn these victories into losses.

In Ontario a lobby group I chaired brought together a wide range of community and professional organizations, women's groups, and unions to demand equal pay for work of equal value. Formed in 1976, the Equal Pay Coalition's strength was the breadth of the coalition pressuring for pay equity. But its weakness also came from its breadth, since the demands it could make were limited by the very diversity within the group. There were inevitable tensions within the coalition that reflected the various interests and locations of the members, and these tensions at times limited the nature of the coalition's demands. It was acknowledged that pay equity and legal remedies were only part of what was needed to achieve equality between women and men in the labour force. Employment equity measures designed to increase the access of women to male-dominated jobs was also needed. And so were other strategies, such as childcare services (see Jenson, Mahon, and Phillips, this volume). Yet efforts were concentrated on a legal remedy that would ensure that women's work is remunerated on the same basis as men's work. Participation in the coalition both reflected greater awareness of the issues in pay equity and promoted such awareness. This often meant the participants were ahead of those in the organizations they represented in terms of their understanding of and support for pay equity. Meanwhile, some feminists argued that such legal solutions were ineffective and divisive. They also maintained that pay equity supported rather than challenged the market. Instead of developing means to determine and compare value, they argued that women should just say, "Give us the money" (Lewis 1988), based on the overall wage gap.

While these lobbying efforts continued, the existing law requiring equal pay for equal work was used not only to demand the payments owed but also to reveal the limits of the legislation. Other legislation forbidding discrimination was similarly used to push the boundaries of existing laws and regulations. For example, a case involving a group of clerical workers who were employed by the Ministry of Health challenged the way the work of an entire group of women was classified. In this case, heard by the Grievance Settlement Board, we argued successfully that women's skills, responsibilities, effort, and working conditions were being undervalued in comparison to the work done by men within the same establishment (*OPSEU* vs *Ministry of Health*). In other words, we used the example of individual women to establish more systemic discrimination against a group of women. The jobs were reclassified and, as a result, all the women doing this work received pay increases.

Such cases, combined with the growing research on systemic discrimination, supported the demands of the coalition. After this long buildup of pressure, legal decisions, and evidence, the breakthrough came when the New Democratic Party made pay equity a condition of support for the minority Liberal Government elected in 1985. The economy seemed to be recovering from the recession of the early

1980s, and support was strong within sectors of the government bureaucracy and in the NDP.

The 1987 Ontario Pay Equity Act was a victory in many ways for the coalition. The legislation marked a significant departure from previous laws in both its assumptions and processes. Unlike other Canadian legislation, it explicitly recognizes systemic discrimination. Also unlike other legislation, it requires employers in the public and private sectors to examine their workplaces to determine whether or not they are paying equity wages. Although pay equity is established through a separate process that evaluates and compares male- and female-dominated jobs in a manner free of gender bias, unions must be part of the process in any unionized establishment. The search for comparators begins within the bargaining unit, but if the unit is without a comparator, the search can extend outside it. While the employers were largely successful in demanding that the comparisons be limited to particular workplaces, or what in the legislation is called "establishments," the coalition was successful in having a section included in the act requiring the government not only to examine what happened to female-dominated workplaces that had no male comparators but also to develop strategies to address them. The result of these mandated studies was the development of the proxy comparison method, which would allow comparisons across workplaces in the broader public sector.

Although the legislation was widely hailed as a victory and studied as a model, the impact was contradictory. Perhaps most importantly, the application of legislation intended to address systemic discrimination was not systematic – for many reasons, but the most important reason had to do with the process of achieving pay equity and with the role of unions. The process required, first, the determination of male- and female-dominated job classes; second, the evaluation of jobs in a manner free of gender bias; third, a comparison between male and female jobs; and, finally, the determination of equal wages. Each of these steps involved complex determinations and negotiations. As a result, significant wage gains for female-dominated jobs were most likely to be found in organizations where unions were both well prepared in and committed to the process. Female-dominated unions in the public sector were in the best position to work towards this end. In Ontario's public sector, these pay equity gains resulted in annual pay equity payments that are estimated to amount to approximately one million dollars at maturity.

The Ontario Nurses' Association, for example, fought several lengthy battles to achieve a job evaluation scheme that made the skills, effort, responsibilities, and working conditions involved in caring work visible and valued. Those taking the lead in these organizations had long been involved in pay equity issues, had possessed considerable expertise, and had been willing to invest the necessary time and money to make pay equity work for them. In the cases we took before the tribunal, we did much more than establish the gender bias inherent in two of the most popular job evaluation schemes used throughout the world. We also helped set out criteria for new job evaluation schemes that would help to positively value women's work in virtually any employment situation.[2] These women-dominated unions were able to win gender-neutral evaluation schemes that disrupted traditional hierarchies and wage relationships.

However, in workplaces where the union was not well enough informed or sufficiently interested, pay equity had quite different outcomes. In male-dominated unions, men were more likely to feel threatened by the pay equity requirement to compare their work directly with female-dominated jobs. Because such comparisons challenged not only employers but also traditional ideas held by many workers, they could easily appear as a direct threat to male wages. Traditional job evaluation schemes, applied without much opposition, often reinforced existing hierarchies, and the examination of jobs for the purposes of pay equity served to confirm existing wage relationships. As a result, significant differences were found among unionized workplaces in the impact of pay equity on wages and on existing relationships.

It was not simply the differences among unions that led to unsystematic consequences. The law applies to all workplaces, whether or not the employees are collectively organized. However, as is the case with any legal remedy, the law is only as good as its enforcement, and the enforcement depends on interpretation, resources, and application. Pay equity compliance among nonunionized workplaces was not high. The Pay Equity Commission was established to assist all workers in seeking equity, a strategy designed to address the lack of resources in nonunionized workplaces. But nonunionized workplaces were still disadvantaged by the precarious nature of employment, by the limited understanding of the very technical requirements in the law, and by the time-consuming nature of the process. With nonunionized workers relying exclusively on the limited resources of the commission, unions remained in a better position to negotiate pay equity in ways that significantly improved wages in female-dominated jobs. At the same time, the differences in bargaining strength between unionized and nonunionized workplaces often led to differences in pay equity settlements that further increased inequalities among women.

Additional inequalities resulted from the differences in workplace size. The Ontario legislation did not apply to private-sector workplaces of ten or fewer employees, and workplaces with fewer than five hundred employees were given a much longer time to comply. This extended time frame left an opening for strategies designed to avoid pay equity, including contracting out work to smaller organizations and other forms of work reorganization of the sort described by Fudge and Vosko in this volume.

Ontario's pay equity laws, which required substantial wage increases for women's work, posed a serious challenge to both the government and the corporations, encouraging restructuring moves that were often aimed at trying to avoid pay equity compliance. While pay equity alone obviously cannot explain the massive expansion in government and corporate restructuring, it is arguable that protective legislation in general can promote such responses. This kind of contradiction is common in legal remedies and thus needs to be considered when planning approaches to change.

The coalition had, to some extent, anticipated such strategies when it successfully lobbied to include a study of female-dominated workplaces in the law. The 1993 amendment that resulted from this study only par- tially responded to the coalition's concerns, however. It required some workplaces that had achieved pay equity to serve as proxy comparators for workplaces that could not do pay equity because they had no appro- priate male-dominated jobs to serve as comparators. This meant that women working in organizations such as daycare centres, home care agencies, small nursing homes, and women's shelters would be able to use the law to achieve pay equity. But this legislation applied only to workplaces in the broader public sector. No remedy was developed for employees in private sector workplaces, many of whom had obtained their work through restructuring or contracting out.

Ontario's Conservative government, elected in 1995, tried to elimi- nate even this limited protection. In its 1996 Savings and Restructuring Act, the government repealed the proxy method of comparison and directed employers to reduce by approximately 78 percent the pay equity adjustments already identified as owing. The Service Employees International Union responded with a challenge under the Canadian Charter of Rights and Freedoms. The Charter offers some protection against such government actions, but such challenges are beyond the reach of most individuals because they cost so much in time, money, and other resources. Moreover, they also involve considerable risk to the particular actors involved and to others seeking relief from govern- ment action. The unions, the law firm representing them, and the Pay Equity Coalition that was supporting them all knew when we began the case that it would be precedent-setting and that the precedent set could be damaging for women if the case was lost. However, Justice O'Leary declared the section of the act repealing proxy pay equity invalid, and the government did not appeal this decision. Proxy adjustments remain in place. So another important victory was won, albeit a victory that simply reaffirmed a previous one when the 1993 amendment was brought in. Yet this was one of the few successful challenges to the many "reforms" in Ontario that have hurt women.

However, the story does not end there. All these broader public sector workplaces that use the proxy method of comparison receive most of their funding from the government, mainly because they provide necessary services to marginalized groups. They are also heavily regulated by the government in ways that make it difficult to seek other resources, and, in any case, they have few alternative sources for funding such work. This means they cannot pay equity wages unless their pay equity adjustments are fully funded. Although the government has repeatedly promised this support, and even paid it on a number of occasions, it has now ended ongoing pay equity funding for proxy organizations. The effect is to once again rescind proxy pay equity, albeit without repealing the legislation. As it does with contracting out, the government is undermining the legislation in a way that conforms to the letter of the law but denies the intent. And once again, the union movement is responding with a Charter challenge, although this time many more unions are involved. Whatever the outcome, we can be sure that this will not be the end of the process of seeking pay equity wages.

The struggle for legislation was just the beginning of a long battle without end. Each new strategy is responded to in ways that require yet another response, as employers and governments find ways of avoiding or subverting the law.

CONCLUSION

There is no simple answer to the question of whether or not the law can be transformative. Pay equity is just one example of how feminist activists and others have used the law to transform social relations. There are many actors in this process, which has benefited greatly from a political economy analysis. And the Pay Equity Act has benefited many of those with labour market jobs, not only in terms of pay but also in terms of making inequalities transparent. However, as is the case with any remedy – legal or otherwise – the process and the results are contradictory.

Working for and with the law has taught us that the issues are necessarily complex. There is no single, right way to achieve change or a single view of success. Pay equity undoubtedly significantly improved wages for many women and some men, in a way no other approach has achieved.

But it did much more than that. It also encouraged many women to reassess their work, to examine the kinds of skills, effort, responsibilities, and working conditions involved in their jobs, and to demand recognition. This reassessment often involved men, especially in unions. Those working with the law had to develop considerable expertise, and this expertise has served them well in responding to the forces against change both within and outside their unions. Pay equity reflected and promoted some power shifts within unions and workplaces and within society as a whole as women's work was regarded in a new and more valued way. It challenged some old hierarchies in workplaces and unions.

But the victories were sometimes won at considerable cost, not only in terms of time and money but also in terms of relations within unions and other groups. Differences in wages among women have increased (Armstrong and Cornish 1997). Employers have become much more skilled at using the law to resist. More and more, the limited success of some groups in working towards pay equity is defined as a problem solved. There are demands to move on to other issues, even though many women have not yet gone through a pay equity process and many that have are now seeing their victories undermined by new strategies such as contracting-out and a refusal to fund. In some cases, the failure to understand or promote pay equity has led to a reinforcement of old hierarchies and to too much focus on legal processes, rather than on other strategies for change.

Undertaken in relatively good economic times, pay equity was often implemented in bad times. Combined with a new emphasis on market forces and deregulation, pay equity was difficult to implement in the face of mounting resistance. At the same time, however, such legislation is now often the only protection women have against the pressures of efficiency, which are defined solely in terms of profits and markets. Especially in such times, any human rights legislation has to be defended and extended as a counter to market forces.

NOTES

1 Two of the most important cases in this regard were heard in Ontario. The *Haldimand-Norfolk* (Ontario Nurses' Association 1989) and *Women's College Hospital* (Ontario Nurses' Association 1992) cases, heard by the Ontario Pay Equity Tribunal, set out guidelines that have had an impact throughout those countries adopting pay equity strategies.

2 See, in particular, Ontario Pay Equity Hearings Tribunal decisions in *Haldimand-Norfolk* (No. 6) (1991), 2 P.E.R. 105, and *Women's College Hospital* (No. 4) (1992), 3 P.E.R. 61.

REFERENCES

Acker, Joan. 1989. *Doing Comparable Worth: Gender, Class and Pay Equity.* Philadelphia, PA: Temple University Press.

Archibald, Kathleen. 1970. *Sex and the Public Service.* Ottawa: Queen's Printer.

Armstrong, Pat, and Mary Cornish. 1997. "Restructuring Pay Equity for a Restructured Work Force: Canadian Perspectives." *Gender, Work and Organization* 4(2):67–86.

Braverman, Harry. 1974. *Labor and Monopoly capital: The Degradation of Work in the Twentieth Century.* New York: Monthly Review Press.

Brenner, Johanna. 1987. "Feminist Political Discourses: Radical versus Liberal Approaches to the Feminization of Poverty and Comparable Worth." *Gender and Society* 1(4):447–65.

Brodie, Janine, ed. 1996. *Women and Canadian Public Policy.* Toronto: Harcourt-Brace.

Canada. Royal Commission on the Status of Women. 1970. *Report.* Ottawa: Information Canada.

Canada. 1977. *The Canadian Human Rights Act.*

Cuneo, Carl. 1990. *Pay Equity: The Labour-Feminist Challenge.* Toronto: Oxford University Press.

Figart, Deborah M., and Peggy Kahn. 1997. *Contesting the Market: Pay Equity and the Politics of Economic Restructuring.* Detroit, MI: Wayne State University.

Fudge, Judy, and Patricia McDermott, eds. 1991. *Just Wages. A Feminist Assessment of Pay Equity.* Toronto: University of Toronto Press.

Gaskell, Jane. 1986. "Conceptions of Skill and the Work of Women: Some Historical and Political Issues." In Roberta Hamilton and Michèle Barrett, eds., *The Politics of Diversity,* 361–84. Montreal: Book Centre.

Lewis, Debra. 1988. *Just Give Us the Money: A Discussion of Wage Discrimination and* Pay Equity. Vancouver: Women's Research Centre.

Ontario Nurses' Association vs Haldimand-Norfolk, Ontario Pay Equity Tribunal. 1989.

Ontario Nurses' Association vs Women's College Hospital, Ontario Pay Equity Tribunal, 1992.

Ontario. 1987. *Pay Equity Act.*

Steinberg, Ronnie. 1990. "Social Construction of Skill: Gender, Power and Comparable Worth." *Work and Occupations* 17(November): 449–82.

Workers' Compensation Board of British Columbia, 1996. *WorkSafe: Focus Report on the Health Care Industry.* Richmond, B.C.: Workers' Compensation Board of British Columbia.

8 Gender Paradoxes and the Rise of Contingent Work: Towards a Transformative Political Economy of the Labour Market

JUDY FUDGE AND LEAH F. VOSKO

Contingent work is growing in Canada. As early as 1990, the Economic Council of Canada observed that the growth of nonstandard employment was outpacing the growth of full-time, full-year jobs. By the mid-1990s Human Resources and Development Canada (1995) claimed that only 33 percent of Canadians held normal jobs, and recent studies confirm the rise of precarious forms of nonstandard work and their persistently gendered and racialized character (Krahn 1995; Ornstein 2000; Vosko 2001; Zeytinoglu and Muteshi 2000).

Conceived broadly, contingent work includes those forms of employment involving atypical employment contracts, limited social benefits and statutory entitlements, job insecurity, low job tenure, low wages, and high risks of ill health. In the Canadian context, vulnerable populations such as youth, women, and immigrants are over-represented in contingent work and, hence, more likely to experience the full impact of labour market de- and reregulation.[1] Surprisingly, however, political economists have yet to provide a nuanced analysis of the rise of contingent work in Canada – or a coherent set of prescriptions for change. This omission is explained partly by what remain the two solitudes in the Canadian political economy literature on the labour market. One solitude documents the attack on central labour market institutions. The other comprises feminists who call for greater theorization of social reproduction and who focus on specific features of women's labour market experiences. Despite their wide-ranging work, contributors to both strains of literature have done very little to trace the roots of the contradictory situation created by the normalization of the standard employment relationship. Consequently, neither grouping has devised the tools necessary for advancing a transformative political economy of the labour market directed at halting the spread of contingent work. To harness political economy in aid of this type of transformation, these two literatures must be bridged. The challenge is to use the paradoxical situation in the contemporary labour market – where not only women and workers belonging to equity-seeking groups confront an eroding employment norm – to move social reproduction to the centre of analysis, displace the standard employment relationship as the fulcrum of labour policy, and rearticulate calls for change in state policy and trade union strategy.

This chapter traces the evolution of labour regulation in late twentieth century Canada using gender as its central analytic lens to focus attention on the contradictory role of the standard employment relationship. To explore possibilities for transformation, it combines the insights of feminist political economy scholarship that reveal the relationship between social reproduction and labour market regulation and the insights of the literature documenting the erosion of institutions stabilizing the standard employment relationship. The discussion proceeds in three parts. The first part identifies and defines the central concepts used in the investigation. The second part reviews the two strains of political economy scholarship under consideration and advances a tentative strategy for bridging these bodies of literature based on concepts developed in the first part. The third part first examines developments in the 1970s, when cracks in the standard employment relationship became visible; it illustrates that this decade was marked by rising labour force participation among women but, at the same time, by persistent gendered and racialized exclusions from the standard employment relationship and early signs of instability in its associated regime of labour regulation. It then turns its attention to the 1980s, a phase of employment change marked by equality gains for women and minorities that were precipitated by equality rights legislation but also by growing attacks on public sector collective bargaining, cuts to unemployment insurance, and the proliferation of contingent employment. Finally, it explores developments in the 1990s, highlighting the state's gradual retreat from equality policy and its continuing deregulation of the central labour market institutions. Our conclusion gestures at a transformative feminist political economy of the Canadian labour market.

THE CONCEPTUAL TOOLS OF A TRANS-
FORMATIVE FEMINIST POLITICAL ECONOMY

Four related concepts frame this investigation of the rise and spread of contingent work: gender, social reproduction, the standard employment relationship, and the paradox. The term "gender" refers to the social processes through which cultural meanings come to be associated with sexual difference and the ways in which sexual difference forms the basis for social exclusions and inclusions and constitutes inequalities in power, authority, rights, and privileges. To a critical, but limited, extent, especially in procreation, sexual differences are material. But while sexual differences are the ontological basis of gender discourses, gender is socially constructed (Creese 1999; Lerner 1997; Scott 1986). A dimension of all social relationships, gender is the social significance attached to sexual difference, which, in turn, "structures organizations, affects social and political relationships, and becomes intrinsic to the construction of significant social categories and political identities" (Frader and Rose 1996, 22). Thus, the term "gender" refers both to historically and socially constituted relationships and to a tool of analysis used to understand how social relationships and cultural categories are constituted (Creese 1999; Frader and Rose 1996; Lerner 1997).

"Social reproduction" refers to the social processes and labour that goes into the daily and generational maintenance of the working population; social reproduction is intimately tied to gender relations. Like every other social system, capitalism imposes a specific relationship on the production of goods and services and the process of social reproduction of the population. The tendency towards the separation of the site of procreation and daily and generational maintenance (the household) from productive relations (waged work) means that social reproduction is not directly organized by employers but is typically organized in households and predominately performed by women. However, employers depend upon the performance of this work, since labour is a crucial factor of production (Muszynski 1996; Picchio 1992). This separation of production from reproduction gives rise to an essential contradiction in capitalist societies – the conflict between the standard of living of the workers (which is always historical, moral, and institutional and not determined by the price mechanism of the market exclusively) and the drive for accumulation (the need to make profits) (Cossman and Fudge 2002; McDowell 1991; Muszynzki 1996; Picchio 1992). The state's role is crucial in mediating this contradiction (Picchio 1992; Ursel 1992). As Jane Jenson (1986,

14) illustrates, "a common problem placed on the agenda of all capitalist states in the nineteenth century was the development of a healthy and disciplined labour force," and, as we argue, the maintenance of a healthy and compliant workforce has historically been a central project for the Canadian state.

To advance its legitimacy after World War II and facilitate social reproduction for limited segments of the working class, the Canadian state brokered an entente between capital and organized labour to construct the standard employment relationship (SER) through the introduction of various labour market institutions. At this juncture, the SER came to be identified with a full-time, full-year employment relationship where the worker has one employer, works on the employer's premises, and has access to social benefits and entitlements to complete the social wage, a set of features identified with this concept to date. Collective bargaining and labour market policies such as unemployment insurance (UI), workers' compensation, and public pensions grew up alongside the SER to cushion workers from unemployment and enable them to reproduce themselves and their families. As a normative model of employment, the SER was first associated with male workers in blue-collar and then white-collar work. Our emphasis on the gendered norm of the SER is critical, since it offers the bridge between the two political economy literatures.

The gendered character of the SER and the exclusions that it gave rise to generated a series of tensions in the labour market that became politically prominent in the 1970s, making the notion of the paradox an illuminating analytical tool.[2] Several recent contributions to feminist theory suggest that the notion of paradox is useful in understanding a central and irresolvable tension in women's struggle for equality – the tension between pursuing equality on the basis of sameness *or* on the basis of difference. Historian Joan Scott (1997) goes as far as claiming that the constitutive dilemma of feminism, the need both to accept and to refuse sexual difference, is a paradox. She suggests that feminists have offered (and arguably needed) paradoxes because the practice of democratic politics has equated individuality with masculinity, at times denying women, by virtue of their femininity, the ability to claim political and economic rights.

The normalization of the SER and the acceptance and reification of sexual difference implied by this employment relationship have led to a series of gendered paradoxes in social and labour market policy since the 1970s, fueling the rise of contingent work. The gendered paradox is especially sharp at present because of the legitimization of equality norms alongside the spread of contingent work. However, it has yet to be challenged in the Canadian political economy literature. A feminist political economy that bridges the insights of malestream political economists preoccupied with the erosion of central labour market institutions with those of feminist scholars examining social reproduction has the potential to transcend these paradoxes and challenge growing contingency.

BRIDGING TWO PARALLEL STRAINS
IN THE POLITICAL ECONOMY LITERATURE

Political economists studying labour market developments in Canada increasingly raise concerns over the spread of contingent work. Despite growing expressions of concern, however, there is a conceptual lacuna in the literature. This gap surrounds the role and function of the SER, and it relates partly to the divergent emphases of several strands of this scholarship.

Two strains dominate the new Canadian political economy literature focusing on the labour market. On the one hand, a substantial grouping of scholars examines the relationship between organized labour and the state (Albo 1990; Drache and Glasbeek 1992; Panitch and Swartz 1993; Russell 1991, 1995). Taking a historical approach, much of this scholarship probes the coercive character of Canada's central labour market institutions and highlights, in particular, recent efforts to deregulate the labour market and their implications for workers. On the other hand, an expanding group of feminist political economists focuses on the necessary and integral relationship between social reproduction (and, hence, gender) and production, a relationship that is under-explored in malestream political economy (Armstrong and Armstrong 1983, 1994; Luxton 1980; Fox 1980; Seccombe 1983). Scholars identified primarily with one strain frequently acknowledge the contributions of the other and even the shortcomings of earlier analyses (Panitch 2001), and yet there have been few attempts to bridge these literatures contributing to different approaches to transformation.

Implicit in the prescriptions of works revealing the biased character of central labour market institutions is the desire to shore up the prevailing (male) employment norm – to bring standard work and its associated benefits to a wider group of workers. Feminist political economists, in contrast, highlight the need to recognize the importance of social reproduction and its effects on women's position in the labour market. Still, neither literature adequately addresses the relationship between the declining employment norm, enduringly privatized social reproduction, and the persistence of highly gendered

employment relations. Scholars are beginning to link these two literatures by adding gender to the analysis of the SER and placing greater
emphasis on social reproduction, but although these linkages may
help explain the gendered rise of contingent work, these efforts are in
their infancy (Broad 2000; Duffy and Pupo 1992; Fudge and Vosko
2001a, b; Vosko 2000).

The Political Economy of Labour Market Institutions

Scholarship probing the operation of central labour market institutions owes a significant debt to Stuart Jamieson (1968) and Clare
Pentland (1968), whose work explored the operation of the industrial relations system in Canada, revealing how labour legislation in
Canada channels overt conflict away from expressions of direct
action to indirect, or diplomatic, channels such as mediation or
conciliation and grievance arbitration (Jamieson 1968, 21). Subsequently, scholars such as Albo, Finkel, Panitch and Swartz, and
Russell built on this analysis of the industrial relations system in an
attempt to cultivate a political economy of Canadian labour market
institutions. Studying the character of Canadian labour market institutions from the era of Privy Council (PC) Order 1003, Albo and
Finkel, for example, demonstrate that the "old" (i.e., post–World
War II) order of industrial relations generated an environment of
contractualism, where unions traded off wage gains and stability in
employment relations for greater managerial control. As we illustrate
elsewhere, this environment generated important gains for (male)
blue-collar workers in core segments of the economy (Fudge and
Vosko 2001a). But, beginning with PC 1003, as Russell (1991, 1995)
and Albo (1990) illustrate, workers were forced to endure significant
limits on strike activity, a highly constraining formula for union security (i.e., the Rand formula) and, as Jamieson and Pentland highlighted decades earlier, a rigid form of legalism. In advancing this literature, Fudge and Tucker (2001), Russell (1995), and others
highlight the important limitations built into Canada's collective
bargaining regime.

Panitch and Swartz (1993) build on this theme but broaden the
focus to include the public sector. They illustrate the fragility and par-
tiality of the consensus around the role of trade unions and collective
bargaining. In a similar vein, Drache and Glasbeek's (1992) examination of the state's deployment of labour law, legislation, and policy
(both provincially and nationally) reveals how "the logic of existing
institutions and structures has seriously limited workers' ability to act
as a political force"(ix).

The contributions of this literature are far-reaching. They reveal the state's often coercive role in the industrial relations system and its implications for workers in the private and public sectors, and, equally crucially, they highlight the fragility of the compromise between organized labour and capital generating the SER. Some scholars in this tradition have also begun to recognize the gendered (i.e., male) character of the SER and the exclusions that it generates. This is true of both those examining developments in the public sector (an important site of "good" jobs for women) (Panitch and Swartz 1993) and those recognizing the significance of minimum-wage policies and broader-based bargaining for the organized and the unorganized (Albo 1990; Russell 1995; see also Schenk 1995). However, despite its desire to uphold the SER and its lack of direct engagement with the feminist literature, the latter grouping has greater affinity with the feminist political economy literature, since it questions the gendered nature of labour market policies and regulatory instruments (Russell 1995) and proposes measures (e.g., shorter hours) to reshape the SER and, hence, recognize gendered contingency.

Feminist Political Economy

Following a different path, feminist political economists in Canada have a tradition of challenging orthodox political economists to take gender seriously in political economy theory and practice. Indeed, feminist political economy in Canada, much of which began with writings in the pages of *Studies in Political Economy*, as well as a number of path-breaking books in the early 1980s, may be divided into two overarching and highly complementary groupings.[3] One grouping comprises Canadian feminist scholars like Pat Armstrong, Hugh Armstrong, Marjorie Cohen, Patricia Connelly, Bonnie Fox, Meg Luxton, Martha MacDonald, Angela Miles, and Wally Seccombe, who were among the first to raise the issue of the gender-blindness apparent in political economy analysis and to raise debates over levels of analysis. Influencing debates in Canada and beyond, these scholars attempted to *gender* political economy analysis at the highest level of abstraction. They argued that political economy theory ignored a critical feature of any society, namely, how the daily and intergenerational maintenance of people was organized, and they challenged orthodoxy to take "women's work" (paid and unpaid) into account. The domestic labour debate began the discussion challenging the narrow economism of political economy theory. At first, it focused exclusively on the "women" question, but with growing research into the status of foreign domestic workers in Canadian households (Arat-Koc 1989), it also drew attention not only to concrete racialized gendered divisions in the domestic sphere but also to the race blindness of political economy theory.

The persistently gendered character of domestic labour remains central to new research in feminist political economy (see, for example, Armstrong, Cornish, and Millar in this volume; Jenson, Mahon, and Phillips in this volume; Vosko 2000). Spurred partly by Jane Jenson's important work "Babies and the State" (1986), beginning in the late 1980s and continuing to the present the emphasis shifted from theory to case studies probing how social reproduction shapes women's inequality in the labour market. Thus, the second loose grouping in Canadian feminist political economy covers the wide range of applied case studies, many of which adopt the lens of intersectionality, exploring the intersections of race, class, gender, and sexuality. To cite but a few dominant strains of analysis in the applied literature, case studies examined the significance of social reproduction for production (Luxton and Vosko 1998), the situation of marginalized workers (Warskett 1988; Fudge 1997a), the relationship between race and the international division of labour and gender (Bakan and Stasiulus 1997; Lipsig-Mumme 1983), the public sector as a domain of employment for women (Luxton and Reiter 1997; White 1990), and gendered assumptions about paid and unpaid work underpinning public policy (Cameron 1996; MacDonald 1999; Vosko 1996, 2002).

Applied works in this literature encourage the state and organized labour to develop a "family" policy sensitive to women's role in social reproduction and call on the government (as an employer) to strengthen the public sector. Calls to extend collective bargaining rights to workers in marginalized sectors of the economy, such as banking (Warskett 1988), domestic work (Fudge 1997a), homework, and temporary work (Vosko 2000) and to recognize racialization and end racism in these sectors (Creese and Stasiulus 1996) also cut across the literature. The scholarship examining the gendered assumptions of training, collective bargaining, and UI policy is especially rich. In her study of training policy, for example, Barbara Cameron (1996) illustrates how the (male) SER has served as a touchstone in training policy, examines whether it is desirable to use training to elevate women into the SER, and attempts to retheorize employer demand. Research examining the Canadian collective bargaining regime shows how it was based on a standard male employee in the primary sector, which had the effect of excluding women who worked in the labour market (Fudge 1993; Ursel 1992). Similarly, work on UI reveals how the standard/nonstandard employment distinction has served as an axis of gender distinction in this policy area (MacDonald 1999; Porter 1998; Vosko 2003).

The "new" feminist political economy literature has numerous strengths. Challenges to gender-blindness in political economy theory raise the necessary and integral relationship between social reproduction and production, and applied work reveals how the state relies on gendered notions of standard and nonstandard employment in public policy design. The problem, however, is that recommendations flowing from the feminist political economy literature have been unsuccessful at convincing trade unions and the state, as well as mainstream political economists, of the central relationship between "family politics" (and social reproduction) and labour market policy. Most contributions to this literature also fail in challenging those arguing for a particular set of strong labour market institutions to take gender relations more seriously.

Canadian political economists documenting the tenuous character of central labour market institutions and feminist political economists working towards a gender-aware political economy theory and practice have followed divergent paths. But both strains fail to advance coherent strategies aimed at halting the spread of contingent work. Devising genuine alternatives involves bridging the two solitudes by recognizing the gendered norm of the SER and giving social reproduction priority – it entails a transformative feminist political economy of the Canadian labour market. Historically, Canadian labour market institutions have divided workers on the basis of their relationship to the (male) SER. Taken as a whole, the Canadian political economy is currently at an impasse in developing strategies for transcending prevailing divisions and this calls for a new approach. The 1970s are our point of departure, because it was then that the two solitudes in the political economy literature began to take shape and cracks in the SER first became visible.

THE SER AND ESCALATING GENDERED PARADOXES IN THE CANADIAN LABOUR MARKET

The 1970s: Regulating the Labour Market under a New Commitment to Equality

Although they date back to the postwar compromise, Keynesian demand-management techniques and social welfare policies still appeared sustainable at the beginning of the 1970s. Because the Canadian economy was so dependent on the world market for prices of its exports and because it was firmly wedded to the u.s. economy for its development, the federal government had always played an active role in limiting disruptions caused by the fluctuations in the business cycle (see Helleiner in this volume). However, the key feature of the Keynesian compromise was the trade-off of productivity gains for wage increases in key economic sectors, and this trade-off was secured through collective bargaining arrangements. The problem, which became clear late in the decade, was that this trade-off was premised on economic expansion (Brodie and Jenson 1988).

The early 1970s marked the golden years of labour market regulation and the ser in Canada and saw a burst of legislation designed to promote sex equality in employment. The ser stabilized and became the model of employment against which social and labour market policies, such as ui and pension policy, were constructed. Some of its chief benefits and entitlements also extended to a growing number of male blue- and white-collar workers in the private sector and to public sector workers, where women's numbers expanded in the late 1960s and early 1970s. Collective bargaining and employment standards legislation were the two primary devices promoting the ser. Moreover, the male breadwinner norm was the lynchpin of social policy. The assumption was that the prototypical household unit was male-dominated, that subsistence for the majority of women and children was provided through indirect access to a man's wage, and that families, primarily defined as units comprising a heterosexual couple and their off-spring, provided the best care for children (Ursel 1992).

Paradoxically, as the institutions of labour market regulation were extended and strengthened and equality became an official theme of labour law and policy, an increasing proportion of employment deviated from the norm. Moreover, part-time, temporary, and casual employment did not provide wages and benefits equivalent to the ser. Women, whose labour market participation continued to increase, were over-represented in nonstandard employment relationships. This feminized employment norm grew alongside the ser. It also symbolized the shift to flexible labour as the Keynesian strategy began to run out of steam (Brodie and Jenson 1988). Productivity declined, unemployment increased, and inflation grew as the decade progressed. The Liberal government's attempt to control inflation by imposing wage and price controls in 1975 prefigured the demise of Keynesian economic policy and the triumph of neoliberalism in the 1980s.

Across Canada in the 1970s, governments strengthened and extended the institutions of collective bargaining in order to contain the widespread and frequently illegal industrial conflict that occurred in the late 1960s. Labour-friendly changes to private sector collective bargaining legislation were made in most jurisdictions. In 1977 organized labour achieved the acme of its demands when the Parti Québécois government introduced legislation that severely limited the right of employers to use temporary replacement workers in a lawful strike or lockout.

Not only were they strengthened, the institutions of collective bargaining were also extended to the public sector. By 1973 every jurisdiction in Canada provided collective bargaining rights to workers in the public and broader public sectors. Although it was modeled on private sector collective bargaining statutes, legislation designed for the public sector was inferior in several respects: it placed limitations on the right to strike and excluded a range of issues from the scope of bargaining (Fudge and Glasbeek 1995, 384–5). Despite its limitations, public sector collective bargaining legislation marked the third wave of unionization in Canada, which resulted in an increased feminization of the labour movement.

In 1971 the introduction of a new UI act broadly expanded entitlement to benefits during unemployment. Coverage was increased for most workers falling under the act, which meant an increase in maximum weekly earnings and the introduction of sickness and maternity benefits. As well, UI began to take regional disparities into account, extending the length of the benefit period in geographic areas with high unemployment, and it introduced special insurance for self-employed fishers, although it still excluded "fishermen's wives" working on the same boats from coverage (Neis 1993). The expansion of the UI system reflected the federal government's recognition that stable jobs could not be assumed and that workers required a stronger insurance system, especially in times of high unemployment. By cushioning the effects of unemployment, this system strengthened the collective bargaining regime, especially in the private sector.

Just as the institutions of industrial pluralism flourished during the 1970s, so, too, did direct government intervention. By 1970 minimum wages of general application, hours-of-work regulations, public holidays, paid vacations, and notice of termination of employment became the norm in many jurisdictions across Canada. The decade also saw a rapid expansion in the amount and kinds of legislation designed to recognize the increased labour-market participation of women and to promote equality in employment (Fudge and Tucker 2000).

The women's movement, which had pressured the federal government to establish the Royal Commission on the Status of Women in 1967, demanded legislation designed to promote sex equality in the workplace and to allow women to combine child-bearing with employment. The commission's 1970 report highlighted the pervasive nature of sex discrimination in the workplace and in government legislation and set out a blueprint for the reforms that were required. By 1973 employment protection for pregnant employees was provided, in one form or another, in the federal jurisdiction as well as in six provinces, and in 1972 UI was revised to provide for maternity benefits. The federal government ratified ILO Convention 100, requiring equal pay for work of equal value, and by the end of the decade the federal government, Quebec, and the Yukon had introduced legislation putting the principle of equal value into practice (Fudge 2002).

Not all employment growth in this period entailed the extension of the SER, however. Rather, while nonstandard employment relationships still supplemented the SER into the 1970s, their rise began to accelerate by mid-decade. Beginning in the mid-1970s, there was considerable growth in part-time work, contract work, temporary work, home-based work, self-employment, and on-call work (Akyeampong 1997; Krahn 1995). Most pronounced was the growth in part-time employment (Duffy and Pupo 1992). The feminization of the labour force and the gradual rise of nonstandard employment relationships went hand in hand. Women continued to be crowded into a small range of low-paid occupations, and the female employment norm departed significantly from that associated with men. It was also less likely to entail unionization and UI eligibility (Duffy and Pupo 1992). The policy emphasis on providing legal rights for women to obtain equality did not penetrate the deeper structural fragmentation embedded in other elements of the labour law regime (Fudge 1997b).

Although collective bargaining legislation was strengthened and extended in the 1970s, it was never able to overcome labour market segmentation. Even when the economic conditions and labour polices were the most favourable for the Canadian version of collective bargaining, fully half of the working population fell outside its scope. Not only was it perfectly acceptable for employers to oppose unionization, the technical requirements for certification made it simply too risky and too costly for all but the most determined unions to attempt to organize the private service sector or small workplaces. The unsuccessful attempt to organize bank workers, combined with a series of first-contract strikes in the late 1970s, many of which involved women workers, demonstrated that collective bargaining legislation still operated as a barrier to unionization in certain contexts (Warskett 1988; White 1993). Despite this, organized labour maintained its commitment to incremental law reform and protecting the SER.

While many women workers would benefit from the extension of collective bargaining to the public sector, the institutions of collective bargaining were vulnerable to government intervention from their inception. The Anti-Inflation Act of 1975, which imposed wage and price controls across the country, presaged the era of coercive controls, or permanent exceptionalism, that undermined collective bargaining in the public sector almost as soon as it was institutionalized (Panitch and Swartz 1993). The imposition of wage controls also prefigured a broader change in economic policy. While the federal Liberal government's embrace of fiscal conservatism was tentative in the late 1970s, neoliberal orthodoxy was given impetus by the election of Margaret Thatcher in Britain in 1979 and Ronald Reagan in the United States in 1980. Increased competition in the labour market was prescribed as the solution to the problem of declining productivity. Flexibility and deregulation became the defining themes of labour market policy in the 1980s. As men's wages fell and employment shifted from the goods-producing to the service sector, women became the exemplary flexible workers (Brodie and Jenson 1988; Drache and Glasbeek 1992). Moreover, flexibility, particularly in the form of part-time and temporary employment, was a means of accommodating women's increased labour market participation with the prevailing understanding that childcare was predominantly a private responsibility to be performed by women in families (Duffy and Pupo 1992; Vosko 2000).

There was, however, a growing recognition of the need to provide greater assistance to women who increasingly had to find sources of care outside the family. After a twenty-year hiatus, in 1966 federal provincial cost-sharing arrangements covering childcare under the Canada Assistance Plan (CAP) were re-instituted. This led to a moderate expansion of regulated facilities throughout the 1970s (Prentice 1999). Cutbacks in provincial spending on childcare in Ontario, for example, were coupled with relaxed standards for the licensing of private daycare facilities. The commodification of childcare was perfectly compatible with privatized responsibility and with efforts to bolster the SER, although it shifted the performance of this labour from women in the family to women in the market.

In its report, the Royal Commission on the Status of Women recommended both a childcare allowance and a system of universal daycare, providing the first glimmerings of a future in which men and women would participate equally in the worlds of paid work and parenting (Mahon 1997). But it did so within a normative framework that emphasized individual choice and that was not critical of the housewife/mother model of providing childcare. In 1971 the federal government introduced the income tax deduction for childcare expenses, inaugurating an enduring policy preference for demand-side strategies for supporting childcare. The regressive impact of the deduction, which provides the greatest transfer to taxpayers in higher marginal tax brackets, was moderated somewhat by the 1978 introduction of a refundable tax credit, which targeted low-income earners. Demand-side mechanisms like the tax system for delivering childcare reflect a preference for parental responsibility for children while simultaneously appearing to support family choices and without ever appearing to take a stand over what form of childcare provision is best (Prentice 1999).

Throughout the 1970s women's employment was regarded as a supplement to the male breadwinner norm. Simultaneously, there was a shift from outright condemnation of the working mother to a growing, though begrudging, acceptance (Finkel 1995, 92). Increasingly, women's labour-market earnings were necessary to compensate for the impact of the decline in men's real wages on the household economy and the breakdown of the single male breadwinner family (Rashid 1993; Fudge 2002). The dual demands on women's labour, in the market and in the household, were at the heart of the gendered paradox in this decade. The accommodation between social reproduction and production under Keynesianism through the institutionalization of the SER was under increasing stress, as evidenced by the gendered rise of contingent work.

The 1980s: Equality, the Erosion of the SER, and the Rise of Gendered Contingency

The gendered paradox of the 1970s, women's increased labour market participation, the policy emphasis on equality in employment, and the continued policy commitment to privatized childcare, which meant that women bore the burden of accommodating the competing demands of social reproduction and production for profit by means of the gendered rise of contingent work, heightened throughout the 1980s. The deep economic recession at the beginning of the decade hit especially hard in Canada's manufacturing sector. Employment in that sector shrank dramatically during the 1981–82 recession, and the general unemployment rate increased. Economic restructuring and neoliberal policies undermined the SER. In the 1980s male wages took the hardest hit since the Great Depression, men's labour-force participation rate declined, and women's plateaued (Amstrong 1996; Gunderson 1998). There was a crisis in the male-breadwinner wage, and households increasingly depended on women's labour market participation in order to maintain their standard of living (Fudge 1997b).

At the same time as the SER was both contracting and deteriorating, the state recognized the importance of women's labour market participation (Mahon 1997). Pay- and employment-equity legislation, a national and universal publicly funded childcare system, and labour standards to improve the conditions of part-time workers were recommended by a series of federally appointed commissions and task forces in the early 1980s as instruments to promote women's equality in the labour market (Cameron 1996; Mahon 1997). At the outset of the decade, it appeared that second-wave feminism, symbolized by the Report of the Royal Commission on the Status of Women and the subsequent establishment of the National Action Committee on the Status of Women (NAC), was capable of institutionalizing policies that would enable women to make substantial gains in the labour market (Vickers, Rankin, and Appelle 1993). But the rapidly restructuring economy and the (related) political collapse of welfare state liberalism brought new hardships as much as new freedoms to the majority of women. The women's labour market began to polarize much more sharply, and feminized forms of employment proliferated and increasingly were taken up by men.

Malestream political economists have ably documented how the new fiscal policy, combined with an outright assault on the public sector, undermined the strength of the Canadian labour movement and resulted in the erosion of the coverage and benefits provided by the SER (Drache and Glasbeek 1992; Panitch and Swartz 1993). They have, however, been less inclined to probe the impact of labour market restructuring on women's employment and to examine the host of policies designed to reregulate the labour market in order to improve the terms and conditions of women's employment. Moreover, with but few exceptions (Finkel 1995), malestream political economists have ignored the enduring problem of childcare, with the result that they have not analyzed how the contradictory relationship between social reproduction and production for profit creates tensions that traditional labour market institutions cannot mediate.

In the 1980s feminist political economy moved from the abstract level of theorizing – largely probing the role of domestic labour and the relationship between production and reproduction under capitalism – to exploring the distinctive dimensions of women's work through case-study research. Important research on immigrant domestic workers in Canada by Agnes Calliste (1993) and Sedef Arat-Koc (1989) revealed the racialized nature of privatized childcare in Canada, as foreign domestic workers, increasingly women of colour, were recruited under distinctive immigration regimes in order to provide live-in childcare. Other research concentrated on how the provision of childcare primarily by mothers in private homes shaped women's relationship to the labour market and the household economy. But most of the case studies concerned with women's relationship to the labour market did not focus on social reproduction. Instead, research shifted to concentrate on policies such as pay equity (Fudge and McDermott 1991) and institutions such as collective bargaining and unions (Warskett 1988; White 1990) that promote women's equality in the labour market. By the mid-1980s, legal norms of substantive equality in employment had been institutionalized, and the precise mechanisms and institutions for their implementation became the objects of study. While these case studies have made an important contribution to understanding women's distinctive relationship to the labour market, feminist political economy has failed to integrate the various focal points and link them back to the malestream political economy literature that emphasized deregulation and the decline of the SER. To accomplish this critical linkage, it is important to trace the relationship between the decline of the SER, the rise of gendered contingency, and the enduring dilemma posed by the need to care for children.

Throughout the 1980s, as the proportion of women in the labour force grew, employment standards deteriorated, wages dropped in real terms, and contingent work spread (Gunderson 1998; Rashid 1993). The feminization of labour was matched by a feminization of employment norms: employment terms and conditions that historically have been associated with women, such as low pay, poor benefits, and part-time or temporary work (Armstrong 1996; Fudge 1997b; Vosko 2000). The process of feminization (or deterioration) in the SER fuelled a backlash against substantive equality that deepened during the 1990s. All of this occurred despite the increasing calls by feminist scholars and activists for policies to address the growing crisis in social reproduction (namely, the need for universal, accessible, and good-quality childcare (Finkel 1995; Mahon 1997; Prentice 1999)), a crisis that was exacerbated by the erosion of the SER and the increased dependence of households on women's paid labour.

The call by feminist political economists (Arat-Koc 1989; Luxton and Vosko 1998) was not heeded in the malestream literature, which continued to narrowly conceptualize the central institutions of the labour market. Although scholars within the traditional Canadian political economy literature offered telling critiques of the limitations built into these institutions, they failed to appreciate the extent to which the feminist emphasis on the significance of social reproduction required a reconceptualization of the labour market and its central institutions.

The 1990s: Labour Market Deregulation and the Retreat from Equality Policy

Gendered paradoxes propelled by public policy take their sharpest expression in the contemporary labour market. In the 1990s women's wages polarized, young men lost ground, and the labour market became increasingly segmented by age, race, and immigration status, while the SER became an elusive norm for a growing number of Canadians, creating a climate that was conducive to the backlash against employment and pay equity (Bakan and Kobayashi 2000; Fudge 2002). Fueling these trends, Canadians witnessed an assault on central labour market institutions that is ongoing. For scholars concerned with advancing a transformative feminist political economy, the contradictions and tensions evident in the labour market that are prompting the spread of contingent work are very troubling. So, too, is the continued divergence in the Canadian political economy literature. Malestream political economists remain fixed on documenting the erosion of central labour market institutions, emphasizing the attack on workers' rights to bargain collectively and on their ability to express discontent. Feminist political economists recognize the force of this attack, but we remain focused on documenting the gendered nature of various policies. At the same time, the nostalgia for the SER shared by malestream political economists and much of the union movement blinds them to the significance of the spread of contingent work and women's labour in the process of social reproduction. This creates both analytic and strategic problems.

There was tremendous turmoil in the Canadian labour market in the 1990s. At the macro-level, Canada initiated and further developed bilateral and multilateral trade agreements following trends in other industrialized countries. The most significant development was the introduction of the North American Free Trade Agreement (NAFTA) and its inclusion of an accession clause to extend existing agreements to trade partners in Latin America and the Caribbean and create a new constitution for the Americas (Gabriel and MacDonald, this volume). In Canada neoliberalism included "active labour market policies" indicative of a strategy of competitive austerity (MacDonald 1999).

In the 1990s economic restructuring undermined the conditions for collective bargaining to function in the private sector and, at the same time, fuelled resentment against public sector workers and legal measures designed to achieve equality in employment. In labour policy across Canada the primacy of the market was asserted (Panitch and Swartz 1993). The institutional supports for the SER were under attack.

A dramatic decline in manufacturing – the foothold of the (male) SER – also followed corporate restructuring associated with free trade. Men at opposite ends of the age spectrum, especially those with low levels of educational attainment, were hit hardest by this decline, but women in export-sensitive manufacturing industries also lost many "good" jobs in manufacturing (Cohen 1994; Rashid 1993; Vosko 2003). More central for our purposes were the concomitant decline of the SER, the spread of contingent work (Krahn 1995; Picot and Heisz 2000) — both of which resulted in the erosion of the scope of coverage in the terms and conditions associated with the standard employment contract — and growing polarization in this period.

The contraction of the SER and the parallel growth of contingent forms of nonstandard employment heightened contradictory tendencies in the labour market. Growing income and occupational polarization, which continues to date, was foremost among them. In the late 1990s statisticians identified a correlation between polarization in earnings among Canadians and labour market poverty, especially among the young and the old (Picot and Heisz 2000). For example, a widening gap between the highest- and the lowest-earning men characterized this decade (Morissette 1997, 9). There is a clear relationship between the polarization in wages and recent trends in overtime: full-time and professional workers are working more overtime with one employer – though it is largely unpaid overtime – than their low-wage counterparts in part-time jobs, who moonlight instead of attaining overtime in their primary job (Duchesne 1997; Sussman 1998). At first glance these trends imply that women's rising labour-force participation has meant greater access to better jobs. However, greater polarization in women's wages is also taking place, with even more dramatic outcomes: while men often move into better-remunerated standard work as they proceed through the age ranks, the pattern of contingency among many women is consistent. There is a convergence of earnings between men and women under age twenty-five that is linked to declining wages among young men (Scott and Lochhead 1997, 2). But sharp gender differences in earnings remain in all age groups.

Given these trends, a new set of gendered paradoxes is evolving with the contraction of the SER. Trends in self-employment reflect this process, in which a growing percentage of today's own-account self-employed are involuntarily resorting to self-employment because of changes in firm behaviour designed to shed the costs of employment-related benefits and responsibilities. For example, women in self-employment are mainly concentrated in the own-account category and in relatively low-wage occupations such as childcare and sales.[4] As Karen Hughes (1999) demonstrates, not only are there sharp wage differences between self-employed employers and the own-account self-employed, they are compounded by gender-based differences within each category. Such trends reveal that the erosion of the SER means "hollow work" for more Canadians (Broad 2000) but also the "gendering of jobs" (Vosko 2000), whereby more jobs take on the character and conditions of work conventionally associated with "women's work" (Armstrong 1996) but income and occupational polarization between the sexes persists – polarization that is increasingly racialized (Ornstein 2000).

Although we characterize developments in the 1990s as creating a highly gendered and paradoxical situation, our identification of both the attack on central labour market institutions and the state's failure to take social reproduction into account in its labour and social policies is not new. Rather, both feminist and malestream Canadian political economists have highlighted the rapid deterioration of Canada's collective bargaining system, as well as the contradictory underpinnings of central labour market institutions, since the late 1970s. Feminist political economists have also demonstrated the exclusive character of a host of labour market policies and practices for decades. They have also challenged malestream political economy's neglect of the supply side of the labour market (i.e., social reproduction) through a range of case studies. What *is* new is how we identify the problem and potential remedies. We identify the troubling situation in the labour market as resting on the normalization of the SER and the hidden nature of the supply side of the labour market By focusing on the linkages between gender, the SER, contingency, and social reproduction, it is possible to bridge the two political economy literatures and re-vision the labour market.

CONCLUSION: TOWARDS A TRANSFORMATIVE
FEMINIST POLITICAL ECONOMY

What, then, are the central elements of a transformative feminist political economy of the labour market – one directed towards the elimination of gendered contingency? What can we learn from the gendered paradoxes that have persisted (albeit in different forms) at the
institutional and policy levels since the 1970s? Does a bifocal emphasis on changes in the central institutions of the labour market and the
heightening crisis of social reproduction – and a corresponding
attempt to bridge the two solitudes in the Canadian political economy
of the labour market literature – provide insights into what transformation entails?

The present process of transformation is riven with contradictions.
On the one hand, Canadians confront a less auspicious collective bargaining regime in both the public and private sectors and a contracting and declining social wage, and yet the SER still remains at the heart
of the operation of the core labour market institutions. On the other
hand, contingent work is spreading; indeed, the polarization of nonstandard work continues to take a gendered, racialized form (Broad
2000; Fudge and Vosko 2001b; Ornstein 2000).

Contingent work, primarily performed by women, arose to stabilize
the capital-labour accord of the postwar period, accommodate the
declining male wage, encourage women's increased labour-force participation, and maintain privatized social reproduction. However,
rather than resolving the competing demands of caring for humans
and participation in the labour market, the spread of contingent work
produced several gendered paradoxes that are best overcome by a
transformative feminist political economy of the labour market. The
first paradox is that contingent work can no longer mediate the contradiction between production and reproduction; as more people
work in the labour market to sustain household living standards, the
time that people are able to devote to social reproduction declines.
The second is that the importance of women's labour in social reproduction is becoming more visible – even garnering greater attention
from the state (Luxton and Vosko 1998). In Canada the problems
emanating from both paradoxes are illustrated by declining fertility
rates (Eichler 1997, 30), renewed but unmet demands for a national
childcare policy (Prentice 1999), and the state's limited recognition of
the crisis in its introduction of tax-based measures to assist working
people with children (Mahon 1997).

Contingency not only undermines the standard of living for working
people but also jeopardizes the ability of people to rear children, care

for loved ones (inside and outside the household), obtain self-fulfill-
ment, and contribute to the social good (Broad 2000). At this juncture, it poses a key political challenge. Trade unions and political
economists that remain focused on the "central institutions of the
labour market" fail to appreciate both the precarious character of the
capital-labour accord and the feminist critique of the sex/gender division of labour and their symbiotic relationship (Ursel 1992).

A feminist political economy that is attentive to the rise and spread
of contingent work recognizes that a profound transformation in
gender relations, the norms of employment, and social reproduction
is taking place at the dawn of the new millennium. Antonella Picchio
(1992) argues that Keynesian demand management represented the
highest mediation of the profound tension between production and
social reproduction inherent in capitalist social relations – here the
SER was hegemonic, as was the male-breadwinner norm and the
female-caretaker norm. In this period, women's work functioned as
the alternator to manage the ever-present contradiction. Our work on
the rise and demise of the SER confirms these findings in the Canadian
context. The present study points to the possibility of a new form of
mediation that hinges on contingent work and the escalating series of
gendered paradoxes leading to its rise. Under this new model, as we
have demonstrated, the feminization of employment norms means
that more workers must not only work for wages but labour under conditions consistent with those endured by women, immigrants, people
of colour, and those at the margins of the labour market without sufficient resources for social reproduction. The new employment norm
is feminized, increasing evidence points to its racialization, and care-
taking remains profoundly gendered; paradoxically, even with
women's high rates of labour force participation, the state is withdrawing further the public supports necessary to reproduce a healthy
working population.

Generalized contingency is no solution to the enduring contradiction, but neither is shoring up the SER. The way out of the impasse
reflected in the present paradox is to shift attention towards the
supply side of the labour market and to cultivate strategies around
improved childcare, education, and healthcare, as well as just immigration policies that enable workers to resist contingency. To move
forward, it is essential to force the state, employers, and trade unions
to reregulate the labour market. As we argue elsewhere (Fudge and
Vosko 2001b), nonstandard, or "flexible," forms of work need not
amount to contingent work; rather, certain forms could contribute to
the redistribution and redesign of work and workplaces. The challenge is to institutionalize forms of labour regulation (defined

broadly) that link production to social reproduction by elevating and integrating the importance of the traditionally gendered work of caring in state policy and union practice. This inevitably means breaking down the sex/gender division of labour. It necessitates a transformative feminist political economy of the labour market.

NOTES

We would like to thank Wallace Clement, all the contributors to this volume, and the Community University Research Alliance on Contingent Work. Leah F. Vosko also thanks the Canada Research Chairs Programme and the Social Sciences and Humanities Research Council (grant no. 410-2000-1362). All errors and shortcomings in the paper remain our own.

1   Indeed, as Zeytinoglu and Muteshi (2000, 6) demonstrate in their review of the literature on gender, race, class, and contingency, recent studies suggest that the intensifying "dualistic tendencies [in the labour market] … are critically affecting the most vulnerable group of workers: racial minority workers in the low income group." Recent research into temporary work (Vosko 2000), home-based garment work (DasGupta 1996), and female-dominated home-care work (Zeytinoglu and Muteshi 2000) revealing growing racialized gendered hierarchies by occupation and sector substantiates this assertion. And reports by Statistics Canada (Badgets and Howatson-Leo 1999) illustrate that this trend cuts across the economy by indicating that recent immigrants, three-quarters of whom are members of racial minorities, not only comprise a disproportionate number of workers in nonstandard work but also remain in nonstandard jobs involuntarily for extended periods.

2   In exploring the play of the SER in the Canadian labour market, the concept of the paradox resonates on various levels. At a technical level, it refers to a contradiction that cannot be resolved. More colloquially, it refers to a view that challenges orthodoxy. Fowler's *Modern English Usage* defines it as an "apparently self-contradictory statement, though one which is essentially true" or a seemingly contradictory statement that may actually be well-founded. Increasingly, the paradox is used by social scientists and humanists not only in a technical, ironic, or satirical sense but to convey complex and contradictory dilemmas, thoughts, and feelings. The paradox is capable of exposing not only opposition – i.e., a view that questions prevailing opinion – but a "position at odds with a dominant one by stressing the difference from it" (Scott 1997: 5). Duffy and Pupo (1992) titled their important study of part-time work *The Part-time Paradox* in order to capture the paradoxical nature of this solution to the problem of women having to combine waged work with household responsibilities,

highlighting the problems generated by the privatization of childcare in particular.

3   As Vosko (2002) argues elsewhere, it is also possible to consider feminist political economy in Canada as proceeding through four overlapping phases in the late twentieth century.

4   The term "own-account self-employment" is used to denote people who are in business for themselves but do not employ others, in contrast to self-employed employers, who do employ others.

REFERENCES

Akyeampong, Ernest B. 1997. "A statistical portrait of the Trade Union Movement." *Perspectives on Labour and Income* 9 (4): 45–54.

Albo, Gregory. 1990. "The New Realism and Canadian Workers," in Alain-G. Gagnon and James P. Bickerton, eds., *Canadian Politics: An Introduction to the Discipline*, 471–504. Peterborough, ON: Broadview Press.

Arat-Koc, Sedef. 1989. "In the Privacy of Our Own Home: Foreign Domestic Workers as a Solution to the Crisis in the Domestic Sphere in Canada." *Studies in Political Economy* 28: 33–58.

Armstrong, Pat. 1996. "The Feminization of the Labour Force: Harmonizing Down in a Global Economy." In Isabella Bakker, ed., *Rethinking Restructuring: Gender and Change in Canada*, 29-54. Toronto: University of Toronto Press.

Armstrong, Pat, and Hugh Armstrong. 1983. "Beyond Sexless Class and Classless Sex: Towards Marxist Feminism." *Studies in Political Economy* 10: 7–43.

– 1994. *The Double Ghetto*, 3d ed. Toronto: McClelland & Stewart.

Badgets, J., and L. Howatson-Leo. 1999. "Recent Immigrants in the Workforce." *Canadian Social Trends* (spring): 16–22.

Bakan, Abigail B., and Audrey Kobayashi. 2000. *Employment Equity Policy in Canada: An Inter-provincial Comparison*. Ottawa: Status of Women Canada.

Bakan, Abigail, and Daiva Stasiulis. 1997. "Foreign Domestic Worker Policy in Canada and the Social Boundaries of Modern Citizenship." In Abigail Bakan and Daiva Stasiulis, eds., *Not One of the Family: Foreign Domestic Workers in Canada*, 29–52. Toronto: University of Toronto Press.

Broad, Dave. 2000. *Hollow Work, Hollow Society? Globalization and the Casual Labour Problem in Canada*. Halifax: Fernwood Publishing.

Brodie, Janine, and Jane Jenson. 1988. *Crisis, Challenge and Change: Party and Class in Canada Revisited*. Ottawa: Carleton University Press.

Calliste, Agnes. 1993. "Women of Exceptional Merit: Immigration of Caribbean Nurses to Canada." *Canadian Journal of Women and the Law*, 6: 85–102.

Cameron, Barbara. 1996. "From Equal Opportunity to Symbolic Equality: Three Decades of Federal Training Policy for Women." In Isabella Bakker, ed., *Rethinking Restructuring: Gender and Change in Canada*, 55–81. Toronto: University of Toronto Press.

Cohen, Marjorie Griffin. 1994. "The Implications of Economic Restructuring for Women: The Canadian Situation." In Isabella Bakker, ed., *The Strategic Silence: Gender and Economic Policy*, 103–116. London: Zed Books.

Creese, Gillian. 1999. *Contracting Masculinity: Gender, Class and Race in a White-Collar Union, 1944–1994*. Toronto: Oxford University Press.

Creese, Gillian, and Daiva Stasiulis. 1996. "Introduction: Intersections of Gender, Race, Class and Sexuality." *Studies in Political Economy* 51: 5–14.

DasGupta, Tania. 1996. *Racism and Paid Work*. Toronto: Garamond Press.

Drache, Daniel, and Harry Glasbeek. 1992. *The Changing Workplace: Reshaping Canada's Industrial Relations System*. Toronto: Lorimer.

Duchesne, Doreen. 1997. "Working Overtime in Today's Labour Market." *Perspectives on Labour and Income* 4: 9–24.

Duffy, Ann, and Norene Pupo. 1992. *Part-time Paradox: Connecting Gender, Work and Family*. Toronto: McClelland & Stewart.

Economic Council of Canada. 1990. *Good Jobs, Bad Jobs*. Ottawa: Supply and Services.

Eichler, Margrit. 1997. *Family Shifts, Policies and Gender Equality*. Don Mills, ON: Oxford University Press.

Finkel, Alvin. 1995. "Even the Little Children Cooperated: Family Strategies, Childcare Discourse and Social Welfare Debates, 1945–1975." *Labour/Le Travail* 36: 91–118.

Fox, Bonnie, ed. 1980. *Hidden in the Household*. Toronto: The Women's Press.

Frader, Laura L., and Sonya O. Rose. 1996. "Introduction: Gender and the Reconstruction of European Working-Class History." In Laura L. Frader and Sonya O. Rose, eds., *Gender and Class in Modern Europe*, 1–33. Ithaca: Cornell University Press.

Fudge, Judy. 1993. "The Gendered Dimension of Labour Law: Why Women Need Inclusive Unionism and Broader-Based Bargaining." In L. Briskin and P. McDermott, eds., *Women Challenging Unions: Feminism, Militancy, and Democracy*, 231–48. Toronto: University of Toronto Press.

– 1997a. "Little Victories and Big Defeats: The Rise and Fall of Collective Bargaining Rights for Domestic Workers in Ontario." In Abigail Bakan and Daiva Stasiulis, eds., *Making the Match: Domestic Placement Agencies and the Racialization of Women's Household Work*, 119–145. Toronto: University of Toronto Press.

– 1997b. *Precarious Work and Families*. Working Paper for the Centre for Research on Work and Family, York University.

– 2000. "The Paradoxes of Pay Equity: Reflections on the Law and Market in Bell Canada and the Public Service Alliance of Canada." *Canadian Journal of Women and the Law* 12: 313–45.

– 2002. "From Segregation to Privatization: Equality, the Law, the Canadian State, and Women Public Servants, 1908–2001." In Brenda Cossman and

Judy Fudge, eds., *Privatization, Law, and the Challenge to Feminism.* Toronto: University of Toronto Press.

Fudge, Judy, and Harry Glasbeek. 1995. "The Legacy of PC 1003." *Canadian Labour and Employment Law Journal* 3(3–4): 357.

Fudge, Judy, and Pat McDermott. 1991. *Just Wages: A Feminist Assessment of Pay Equity.* Toronto: University of Toronto Press.

Fudge, Judy, and Eric Tucker. 2000. "Pluralism or Fragmentation? The Twentieth Century Employment Law Regime in Canada." *Labour/Le Travail* 46: 251–306.

– 2001. *Labour before the Law: The Regulation of Workers' Collective Action in Canada, 1900–48.* Toronto: Oxford.

Fudge, Judy, and Leah F. Vosko. 2001a."Gender, Segmentation, and the Standard Employment Relationship in Canadian Labour Law and Policy." *Economic and Industrial Democracy* 22(2): 271–310.

– 2001b. "By Whose Standards? Re-Regulating the Canadian Labour Market." *Economic and Industrial Democracy.* 22(3): 327–56.

Gunderson, Morley. 1998. *Women and the Canadian Labour Market: Transitions towards the Future.* Toronto: Nelson.

Hughes, Karen. 1999. *Gender and Self-Employment in Canada: Assessing Trends and Policy Implications.* Ottawa: Canadian Policy Research Network.

Human Resources and Development Canada. 1995. *A Twentieth Century Employment System for Canada: Guide to the Employment Insurance Legislation.* Ottawa: Ministry of Supply and Services Canada.

Jamieson, Stuart. 1968. *Times of Trouble: Labour Unrest and Industrial Conflict in Canada, 1900–1966.* Study Prepared for the Task Force on Industrial Relations. Ottawa: Privy Council Office.

Jenson, Jane. 1986. "Gender and Reproduction, or Babies and the State." *Studies in Political Economy* 20: 9-46.

Krahn, Harvey. 1995. "Non-standard Work on the Rise." *Perspectives on Labour and Income* 7(4): 35–42.

Lerner, Gerda. 1997. *History Matters: Life and Thought.* New York: Oxford.

Lipsig-Mumme, Carla. 1983. "The Renaissance of Homeworking in Developed Countries." *Relations Industrielles* 38: 545–67.

Luxton, Meg. 1980. *More than a Labour of Love: Three Generations of Women's Work in the Home.* Toronto: The Women's Press.

Luxton, Meg, and Ester Reiter. 1997. "Double, Double, Toil and Trouble Women's Experience of Work and Family in Canada, 1980–1995." In Pat Evans and Gerda Wekerle, eds., *Women and the Canadian Welfare State,* 197–221. Toronto: University of Toronto Press.

Luxton, Meg, and Leah F. Vosko. 1998. "Where Women's Efforts Count: The 1996 Census Campaign and 'Family Politics' in Canada." *Studies in Political Economy* 56: 49–81.

MacDonald, Martha. 1999. "Restructuring, Gender and Social Security Reform in Canada." *Journal of Canadian Studies.* 34(2): 57–88.

Mahon, Rianne. 1997. "Child Care in Canada and Sweden: Policy and Politics." *Social Politics* 4(3): 382–418.

McDowell, Linda. 1991. "Life without Father and Ford: The New Gender Order of Post-Fordism." *Transactions of the Institute of British Geographers* 16: 100–19.

Morisette, Denis. 1997. "Declining Earnings of Young Men." *Canadian Social Trends* (autumn): 8–15.

Muszynski, Alicia. 1996. *Cheap Wage Labour: Race and Gender in the Fisheries of British Columbia.* Montreal and Kingston: McGill-Queen's University Press.

Neis, Barbara. 1993. "From 'Shipped Girls' to 'Brides of the State': The Transition from Familial to Science Patriarchy in the Newfoundland Fishery Industry." *Canadian Journal of Regional Service* 17(2): 185–211.

Ornstein, Michael. 2000. *Ethno-Racial Inequality in Toronto: Analysis of the 1996 Census.* Prepared for the Chief Administrator's Office of the City of Toronto.

Panitch, Leo, and Donald Swartz. 1993. *The Assault on Trade Union Freedoms: From Wage Controls to Social Contract.* Toronto: Garamond.

Pentland, H. Clare. 1968. *A Study of the Changing Social, Economic and Political Background of the Canadian System of Industrial Relations.* Draft Study prepared for the Task Force on Industrial Relations. Ottawa: Privy Council Office.

Picchio, Antonella. 1992. *Social Reproduction: The Political Economy of the Labour Market.* Cambridge: Cambridge University Press.

Picot, Garnett. 1998. *What is Happening to Earnings Inequality and Wages in the 1990s?* Statistics Canada, cat. 11F0019MPGE, no. 116.

Picot, Garnett and Andrew Heisz. 2000. "The Performance of the 1990s Canadian Labour Market." *Canadian Public Policy* 26 (supp.):s7–s25.

Porter, Ann. 1998. "Gender, Class and the State: The Case of Unemployment Insurance in Canada." PHD diss., York University, Toronto, Canada.

Prentice, Susan. 1999. "Less, Worse, and More Expensive: Childcare in an Era of Deficit Reduction." *Journal of Canadian Studies* 34(2): 137–58.

Rashid, Abdul. 1993. "Seven Decades of Wage Changes."*Perspectives on Labour and Income* 5(2): 9–21.

Russell, Bob. 1991. "A Fair or Minimum Wage? Women Workers, the State, and the Origins of Wage Regulation in Western Canada." *Labour/Le Travail* 28:59–88.

– 1995. "Labour's *Magna Carta?* Wagnerism in Canada at Fifty." In Cy Gonick, Paul Phillips, and Jesse Vorst, eds., *Labour Gains, Labour Pains: 50 Years of PC 1003*, 177–91. Winnipeg: Society for Socialist Studies/Fernwood Publishing.

Schenk, Chris. 1995. "Fifty Years after PC 1003: The Need for New Directions." In Cy Gonick, Paul Phillips, and Jesse Vorst, eds., *Labour Gains, Labour Pains: 50 Years of PC 1003*, 193–214. Winnipeg: Society for Socialist Studies/Fernwood Publishing.

Scott, Joan. 1986. "Gender: A Useful Category of Historical Analysis." *American Historical Review* 93: 1053–73.

– 1997. *Only Paradoxes to Offer: French Feminists and the Rights of Man*. Cambridge: Harvard University Press.

Scott, K. and C. Lochhead. 1997. "Are Women Catching Up in the Earnings Race?" Ottawa: Canadian Council on Social Development. Paper no. 3.

Seccombe, Wally. 1983. "Marxism and Demography." *New Left Review* 137: 22–47.

Sussman, Deborah. 1998. "Moonlighting: A Growing Way of Life." *Perspectives on Labour and Income* 10(2): 24–31.

Ursel, Jane. 1992. *Private Lives, Public Policy: 100 Years of State Intervention in the Family*. Toronto: The Women's Press.

Vickers, Jill, Pauline Rankin, and Christine Appelle. 1993. *Politics As If Women Mattered: A Political Analysis of the National Action Committee on the Status of Women*. Toronto: University of Toronto Press.

Vosko, Leah F. 1996. "Irregular Workers, New Involuntary Social Exiles: Women and UI Reform." In Jane Pulkingham and Gordon Ternowetsky, *Remaking Canadian Social Policy: Social Security in the Late 1990s*, 256–72. Toronto: Fernwood Press.

– 2000. *Temporary Work: The Gendered Rise of a Precarious Employment Relationship*. Toronto: University of Toronto Press.

– 2002. "Phases of Feminist Political Economy in *Studies in Political Economy*: Reviving Debates, Recasting Theory." *Studies in Political Economy* 68 (summer): 55–84.

– 2003. "Gender Differentiation and the Standard/Non-Standard Employment Distinction in Canada, 1945 to the Present." In Danielle Juteau, ed., *Social Differentiation in Canada*, 44–136. Toronto and Montreal: University of Toronto Press/University of Montreal Press.

Warskett, Rosemary. 1988. "Bank Worker Unionization and the Law." *Studies in Political Economy* 25: 41–73.

White, Julie. 1990. *Mail and Female: Women and the Canadian Union of Postal Workers*. Toronto: Thompson Educational Publishing.

– 1993. *Sisters and Solidarity: Women and Unions in Canada*. Toronto: Thompson Educational Publishing.

Zeytinoglu, Isik Urla, and Jacinta Khasiala Muteshi. 2000. "Gender, Race and Class Dimensions of Non-Standard Work." *Industrial Relations/Relations Industrielles* 1: 133–67.

PART THREE

International Boundaries and Contexts

9 Beyond the Continentalist/ Nationalist Divide: Politics in a North America "without Borders"

CHRISTINA GABRIEL
AND LAURA MACDONALD

> To us, the boundary separating Canada from the United States is no more significant than the equator – just a line on maps, devoid of meaning.
>
> Jacques Maisonrouge,
> former head of IBM's European and Asian Operations

INTRODUCTION

During the so-called free trade election of 1988, the Liberal party produced a powerful political advertisement that portrayed negotiators of the Canada-U.S. Free Trade Agreement erasing the forty-ninth parallel, the line dividing Canada and the United States (Williams 1995, 33). The ad was effective because it evoked many of the fears of absorption by the richer and more powerful country to the south that have haunted Canadians since Confederation and before. Canadian political economy has similarly been haunted by the nature of the country's relationship with the United States and its impact on Canada's economic development and sovereignty. From the work of Harold Innis to the emergence of the new political economy of the 1970s and beyond, Canadian political economists have wrestled with understanding the terms and nature of our unequal relationship with the United States. Indeed, political economists have characterized national development strategies in terms of a struggle between nationalism and continentalism (McBride and Shields 1997, 141; Williams 1995). Throughout, there has been an enduring concern with the integrity and role of the Canadian nation-state and national sovereignty. These concerns have been accentuated under the pressures of globalization and the attacks of September 11, 2001 on the United States. Economic integration with the United States has progressed more rapidly than even its proponents expected, and a deeper form of integration may be on the agenda – at an April 2001 meeting of the leaders of the three countries, the leaders committed themselves to examining options to "strengthen our North American partnership." In the wake of the attacks of September 11, Canada and Mexico have been pressured to adopt more stringent border-control and security measures to address American concerns. Consequently, the prospects for an economic community may well be linked to a conception of a North American security perimeter, or Fortress America. Both conceptions are underwritten by a continental vision that embraces much more than Canada's trade with the United States.

North American economic integration poses a number of dilemmas in terms of democracy, political community, and citizenship. Citizenship status – membership within a delimited political community – has traditionally been assigned on the basis of a sovereign nation-state. But as nation-states become more interconnected, basic governing arrangements and political structures may no longer accommodate new demands. Global pressures have provided an impetus to question where and how political power is exercised – national, regional, and international. Similarly, some issues and concerns, immigration or the environment, for example, transcend the boundaries of a single state. The emergence of transnational organizations (both corporations and nongovernmental organizations) and actors is not confined within the bounds of a territorial nation-state. These trends have prompted some social theorists to rethink conceptions of citizenship and democracy. David Held, among others, has raised the possibility of a *cosmopolitan project*, stating that "in the millennium ahead each citizen of a state will have to learn to become a 'cosmopolitan citizen' as well: that is, a person capable of mediating between national traditions, communities of fate and alternative forms of life ... Political agents who can 'reason from the point of view of others' will be better equipped to resolve, and resolve fairly, the new transboundary issues and processes that create overlapping communities of fate" (Held et al. 1999, 449).

The emphasis here is on an emerging conception of multiple citizenship, as individuals will be implicated in a number of memberships, in their own communities but also in wider regions and within an even wider global order (Held et al. 1999, 449). In this chapter, we consider some of the implications of Canada's membership within a new North American community and the dilemmas these engender.

On the one hand, it has become popular to assert that borders are insignificant under the terms of globalization and increasing regional integration. Yet as we will illustrate, border dynamics within North America reveal a much more contradictory story of the opening and closing of national borders. States continue to assert and exercise sovereignty in new ways. Consequently, the assumption that the FTA would result in the erasure of national borders was fundamentally misleading. But simultaneously, there is evidence of new types of transborder relationships, identities, and alliances that do apparently suggest multiple connections and the democratization of civil society across territorial borders. Such connections have implications for the way we think about citizenship practices. We examine these contradictory trends and argue that they speak to the need to rethink the familiar continental/nationalist dichotomy that emphasizes Canada's economic dependency on the United States and to problematize the complexity of continentalism.

In the first section of this chapter, we argue that regional integration, as structured by the Canada-U.S. Free Trade Agreement (FTA) and the North American Free Trade Agreement (NAFTA), has positioned the Canadian nation-state within an emerging continental economic regime in new and complex ways. This regime transcends the familiar Canada-U.S. bilateral relation by including Mexico. But contrary to some dire predictions during the national debate on the FTA, Canada has not become the de facto fifty-first state. In fact, as discussed in the second section of this chapter, North American states have moved to open up borders to the freer movement of goods and capital and some highly skilled workers (Gabriel and Macdonald 2001). And in this respect, nation-states continue to deploy considerable power – albeit in new, contradictory, and uncertain ways – in determining who is included within and who is excluded from a national community. However, as our last section highlights, this apparently traditional exercise of sovereignty exists alongside the emergence in the 1990s of cross-border transnational alliances between popular sector organizations in Canada, the United States, and Mexico. These transnational activities illustrate some of the ways in which popular sector movements have responded to the challenges of globalization and continentalization. The emergence of cross-border actors and identities, we suggest, requires analysts to move beyond the inside-outside dichotomy (Walker 1993) to more fluid and sophisticated modes of analysis. Do these movements suggest the emergence of new identities that are global or regional in scope to complement the ties of national citizenship? Is it possible to embrace a vision of cosmopolitan citizenship? While cosmopolitan approaches may be too idealistic, with insufficient appreciation of the barriers to global citizenship, at the very least this study of changing forms of political identification in North America suggests the weaknesses of the traditional nationalist/continentalist divide as a way of interpreting Canadians' place in the continent.

PROBLEMATIZING CONTINENTALISM

Questions of economic sovereignty have been a long-standing concern within Canadian political economy as scholars attempted to understand Canada's relations with the imperial powers of France and England and, later, with the empire of the United States. From its earliest roots in the work of Harold Innis, Canadian political economy has attempted to analyze and assess the terms of Canada's position in the continental and global economy. Innis argued that Canadian economic history could be explained through the patterns of exploitation of particular resources, or staples. Once staples are extracted in a marginal or peripheral region, they are exported to more industrially advanced centres, or metropoles. Thus Canada, a white settler colony, traded staples with a series of metropoles – first France, then Britain, and then the United States – in return for manufactured goods and technology (Innis 1997, 15–26). This is very much a relational account, in which new countries developed, unequally, in relation to the existing metropole. From the 1970s, many of Innis's ideas influenced political economists' attempts to explain Canada's slow industrial development and its subordinate status vis-à-vis the United States (Drache and Clement 1985, ix–xxiv).

The nature of Canada's trading relationship with the United States came under scrutiny as it became apparent that most of Canada's imports were finished manufacturing goods from the superpower to the south. These findings prompted left nationalists to interrogate the implications of foreign ownership not only for Canada's economic performance but also for political and cultural sovereignty. Through their work they sought to document and explain Canada's relationship with the United States. Among the themes that were prominent within these explanations were the reliance on a staple-based economy, an overdeveloped financial or commercial sector, u.s. domination, and a branch-plant economy. For example, Tom Naylor (1972), in his "merchants against industry" thesis, argued that the Canadian capitalist class was dominated by a fraction of capital that was not only oriented toward the production of staples but had a vested interest in blocking the development of an independent manufacturing sector. Kari Levitt's *Silent Surrender* (1970) examined the role of American foreign ownership and the subsequent development of a branch-plant economy in accounting for Canada's dependent relationship with the

United States. Levitt argued that significant portions of the Canadian economy were controlled by American capital and that, as a result, capital generated in Canada was transferred to the United States in the form of profits, dividends, interest payments, and royalties, instead of being invested domestically. Levitt and others underscored the idea that Canadian sovereignty was imperilled because of Canada's economic integration with the United States. She argued that "the 'continentalist' orientation is fundamentally destructive of Canadian unity because it rejects the maintenance of the national community as an end of itself" (149).

Within this framework "continentalism" is used to describe "the theory of closer ties (e.g., in the form of closer trade links, energy sharing or common water use policies) with the United States" (Clarkson 1996, cited by McBride and Shields 1997, 141). Williams used the terms "continentalist" and "nationalism" to distinguish between two differing and competing visions of how our economic relationship with the United States should be managed. The continentalist vision embraced trade liberalization as a means to enhance Canadian prosperity. And in this sense "the continentalist school was unready to distinguish between Canadian and foreign-owned firms, and typically accorded the same Canadian 'corporate citizenship' to both" (1995, 29). In contrast, nationalism advocated that state power be used to promote greater Canadian control over the nature and scope of continental integration. Thus, state-directed industrial strategy would have a two-fold purpose of fostering Canadian-owned firms and securing more advantageous terms from American foreign investors. The nationalist interpretation came to the fore in the 1960s and to some extent found expression in policy developments in the 1980s.

Under Brian Mulroney's Conservative administration the continentalist vision emerged triumphant. The Conservatives negotiated the Canada–United States Free Trade Agreement. The 1988 election became known as the free trade election as continentalist and nationalist camps squared off over the ratification of the agreement. The Conservatives won the election and subsequently negotiated the North American Free Trade Agreement in the early 1990s. These trading agreements have deepened Canada's already significant integration with the United States and added on Mexico as the third member of the continental alliance. This repositioning, though, cannot be understood simply as making Canada more dependent on the United States or simply in terms of the old continental/nationalist dichotomy.

Stephen Clarkson's work offers a starting point to consider continentalism and its consequences much more carefully. Clarkson highlights a number of issues that demand an assessment of the forces that constitute a reconfiguring North American space. He argues that the neoliberal provisions of NAFTA provide for an "economic constitution" for business enterprise. For example, rights such as national-treatment provisions, which ensure that business enterprises from any country that is party to the agreement receive treatment identical to that of domestic enterprises, have given capital "extra-territorial security and so mobility" (1998, 15). The agreement also includes provisions for the establishment of bodies to adjudicate trade disputes. Clarkson also emphasizes, importantly, that competition between the member states to attract foreign investment constrains the ability of governments to pursue regulation and impose taxes, lest such measures adversely affect capital's ability to "increase their costs of operation or decrease their autonomy in deciding in which state to locate, how to operate, and whom to hire or fire" (1998, 15).

Clarkson and others have drawn attention to the fact that the reconfiguring of economic space prompted by continentalism may foster the growth of new political identities. Indeed, he has characterized newly emerging transnational organizing efforts among nongovernmental organizations (NGOs) as evidence of "continentalization from below" that may provide the impetus to create a "continental civil society" (Clarkson 2001, 513). We return to this theme, which underscores a broader process of social transformation, in the final section of this chapter. First, however, we discuss changing border-control policies in the new North America as an illustration of the broader practices at work in the region. As Clement and Vosko emphasize in their introduction to this volume, understanding political economy as transformation allows us to identify and analyze the forces of stability as well as change at work in the world. The Canada-United States border is a key example of the internally contradictory dynamics of globalization and neoliberal policies.

CONTINENTAL ECONOMIC INTEGRATION AND BORDER MATTERS

It has become popular to assert that territorial borders are insignificant or of no consequence under the terms of globalization and increasing economic integration. This is especially true in terms of the rhetoric surrounding the Canada–U.S. border, long characterized as the longest undefended border in the world. For example, a *Maclean's* magazine cover featured "The Vanishing Border" (20 December 1999), while *Time* Magazine followed with "Two Nations Indivisible" (10 July 2000). Recent popular debates on the "brain drain" also seem to emphasize the apparent ease with which Canadian workers can move to and work in the United States. Yet, as this section of this chapter demonstrates, a closer examination of border dynamics within North America reveals a number of contradictory dynamics. Under the terms of globalization and continental integration, the role of the state is changing. State power may well be eroded in some areas, but state sovereignty comes to the fore in the attempts by states to police and control their borders. These attempts have "involved both a physical reassertion of border control and an ideological redefinition of border functions" (Andreas 2000a, 2).

NAFTA has accelerated the processes of economic integration and entrenched a north-south economic orientation across the continental space. The trading agreement has facilitated the cross-border flow of goods, information, and capital. Consider for example, "that more than Cdn$1.5 billion of goods crosses the Canada-U.S. border daily ... [and that] U.S. exports to Canada accounted for 23% of total U.S. exports in 1998" (Hampson and Molot 2000, 6). Americans, in turn, have referred to Canada as "our number one trading partner with $379 billion in two way trade goods and services in 1997, which means over $1 billion in goods and services crosses the border daily" (Papademetriou and Meyers 1999, 5). While Mexico's trade with Canada is small, its border with the United States is a significant site of cross-border economic exchange. The U.S.-Mexican border has been characterized as "the busiest land crossing in the world," and "cross border trade has doubled since 1993, making Mexico the second largest trading partner of the United States" (Andreas 2000a, 4).

While the trade liberalization engendered by NAFTA has rendered borders more open to goods, services, and technology, this has taken place within a context where member nations, especially Canada and the United States, have moved to selectively secure or close borders. Consequently, increasing North American economic integration is marked by the seeming paradox of the simultaneous opening and closing of borders. Member countries are forced to address this paradox: how to control the border against threats – "illegal" migrants, low-skilled labour, and security threats – while simultaneously facilitating the movement of goods, capital, and information.

NAFTA contains detailed clauses regarding trade in services in general, including financial services, investment, intellectual property rights, and a dispute-settlement mechanism. However, unlike the European Union's framework, which contains clauses regarding the movement of labour from its inception[1], NAFTA says little about labour mobility. Far from being an oversight, this omission has been characterized as a deliberate decision. Labour mobility was seen as a "poison pill" because "granting Mexican workers freedom of entry into the U.S.

labour market was viewed as politically unacceptable and as certain to fail to gain ratification by the u.s. Congress" (Castles and Miller 1993, 95). Within Canada, it was argued, there was little discussion in the public debate about the consequences of NAFTA for either bilateral flows between Canada and the United States or for immigration more generally. Early assessments focused on the impact of the agreement on capital investment. "The potential labour market consequences of the NAFTA were, therefore, primarily seen as derived from changes in geographic preferences of the [multinational corporations] as far as investment was concerned" (Globerman 1999, 1).

Yet one supposed consequence that has garnered widespread public attention and debate in Canada is the brain drain. Increasing economic integration with the United States has prompted anxieties that skilled professional workers are seeking opportunities south of the border in large numbers. While NAFTA does not permit the free movement of labour, an exception is made for some highly-skilled professional workers, traders, and investors. In contemporary liberal economic doctrines, human capital is viewed as a way to enhance productivity and national competitiveness in the rising "knowledge economy"(see McBride 2000). Within this discourse, skilled workers are constructed as factors that enhance the "competitiveness" of nations in a "global economy," and nation-states are international actors seeking to attract and retain the best and brightest. The Fraser Institute, a conservative think tank, has argued that Canada is losing out in the face of more "aggressive competition for skilled immigrants from other developed countries including the u.s. and Australia" (cited in Foster 1998, 169). From the late 1990s these groups and others, including opposition political parties, professional associations, and the media, charged that Canada was suffering a massive brain drain. It was alleged that Canadian professionals were lured by a number of factors, including higher salaries, lower taxes, high technology, and maybe even better climate (McCarthy 1999, B3). However, the evidence and numbers surrounding the brain drain are confusing, and interventions in the debate contain highly charged rhetoric. Additionally, there is a conspicuous silence on the role Canada's immigration selection model, the points system, plays in taking skilled workers from other countries.[2] Nevertheless the brain drain issue speaks to the deeper insecurity and ambivalence many Canadian feel towards their American neighbour in the context of continental economic integration.

The brain drain debate tends to mask the fact that, as mentioned, NAFTA does not permit the free and open circulation of people across borders. There are, however, provisions for the circulation of some numbers of certain highly-skilled workers and business people on a system of temporary work permits. Under NAFTA's TN-1 visa, Canadian workers may enter the United States (and vice versa) on a temporary basis providing they satisfy the following criteria: provide documentation establishing citizenship and indicate that they are professionals in one of the categories listed in a professional-occupation schedule. In contrast to other types of temporary work visas there are no requirements for labour certification; employers do not have to demonstrate such hires will adversely affect U.S. workers; and TN visas – issued for one year – are not subject to a limit on renewals (Globerman 1999, 9).

A study of TN visas over the period from 1989 to 1996 indicates that the temporary migration of Canadian professionals to the United States has increased by approximately three to four thousand visas granted per year. In addition to the TN visa there are other types of temporary work permits that facilitate the cross-border movement of some workers. These include permits for traders, investors, and intracompany transfers. The last type of permit applies specifically to corporate executives, managers, and knowledge workers of multinational corporations who are moving between the parent company and its affiliates. There was a 70 percent increase in the number of intracompany transfers between Canada and the United States over the period from 1986 to 1996, and this increase was characterized as "strikingly close to the roughly 76 percent increase in Canadian exports to the United States over the same period" (Globerman 1999, 17–18).

The selective use of temporary work permits under the terms of NAFTA that favour highly skilled and professional workers is a response, Saskia Sassen argues, to the existence of two different sets of rules, rules governing the flow of capital and rules governing the flow of people (1998, 60). Further, this NAFTA response – temporary permits to facilitate the circulation of highly skilled and professional workers – is an example of the way in which state power is shifting. Sassen writes:

The NAFTA regime for the circulation of service workers and businesspeople has been uncoupled from any notion of migration but in fact represents a form of temporary labor migration. For both NAFTA and the GATT, the regime for labor mobility falls under the oversight of entities that are quite autonomous from governments. In some ways this is yet another instance of the privatization of that which is profitable and manageable. Like the cross-border legal and regulatory regimes for international business ... NAFTA represents the privatization of certain components of immigration policy – specifically, the high value-added (that is, persons with high levels of education, capital, or both) and manageability (those working in the leading sectors of the economy who are, hence, visible migrants and subject to effective regulations). (1998, 61)

Under the terms of NAFTA some small groups of workers – well-qualified, usually professional and skilled – are able to circulate within a continental economic space. In contrast, workers seen as low-skilled or unskilled, such as Mexican agricultural workers, gardeners, and domestic workers, are subject to intensified border controls and surveillance. This despite the fact that demand for cheap Mexican immigrant labour remains high in states such as California (Spener 2000, 131).

NAFTA has resulted in an enormous increase in the volume of goods and services crossing the Canada-U.S. border and the U.S.-Mexico border. But trade liberalization has also been accompanied by migratory pressures from the South to the North. The Immigration and Naturalization Service told the U.S. Congress in 1993 that the adoption of the agreement would necessitate the strengthening of border control (Nevins 2000, 106). A United Nations report suggested that the impact of trade liberalization on the small-scale agricultural sector would lead to higher migration pressures in the short to medium term. The report also noted that to the extent that economic growth in the long term could be sustained, these migratory pressures would be decreased (Populations Division 1997, 52). NAFTA created a common North American space for economic flows, and this is well recognized. However, U.S.-Mexico trade liberalization has also increased migratory pressures that have led to an escalation of control along territorial boundaries. It has been pointed out that the increasing attempts to police the U.S.-Mexico border not only underscore how integration has helped to increase state power in certain respects, i.e., at the border and towards unauthorized migrants, but also how it has helped to increase demands on the state for an "intensified nationalization of territory and society." The backlash against immigrants in California and immigration is an example of this process (Nevins 2000, 107).

In a similar vein, Peter Andreas has persuasively argued that "enhanced border policing has less to do with actual deterrence and more to do with managing the image of the border and coping with the deepening contradictions of economic integration" (1998-99, 592). The two-thousand-mile-long U.S.-Mexico border has become a heavily fortified barricade as a result of an attempt to control illegal immigration. In the period after 1994 the number of border patrol agents was doubled, as was the budget of the border patrol's parent agency, the Immigration and Naturalization Service. Law enforcement at the border was aided through the use of fortified fences and high-tech surveillance equipment. Agents were also heavily armed. The border became the focus of a number of high-profile policing campaigns, such as Operation Gatekeeper and Operation Hold the Line (Andreas 2000b).

While U.S. border-control policy is largely oriented towards Mexico, U.S. territorial anxieties have produced an unintended rebound effect on the management of the Canada-U.S. border. The "longest undefended border in the world" is now under stress as a result of heightened concern for territorial integrity in the United States. As well, the logic of NAFTA itself leads to a tendency for the United States to try to treat its two land borders (with Canada and with Mexico) symmetrically, rather than devising independent regimes for each. In the 1990s this logic led to a conflict between Canada and the United States over the latter's proposed section 110 of the Illegal Immigration Reform and Immigration Responsibility Act of 1996 (IIRIRA). Under the terms of the proposal all entrants to the United States would be required to register through the establishment of a "secure" entry and exit system (Ackelson 2000). Alarmed Canadian policymakers and border residents argued that the requirement would effectively shut down the border, and they called for a repeal of section 110. As a result of sustained lobbying, the section has so far been effectively delayed.

However, in 1999 U.S. fears were provoked by two high-profile events. In the summer, Chinese migrants arrived by boat off the coast of British Columbia and claimed refugee status. There were fears that many of them would try to slip into the United States. Later in the same year, U.S. immigration officials stopped a thirty-two-year-old Algerian, Ahmed Ressam, who was entering the United States at the Canadian border and discovered that his car contained bomb-making equipment and nitroglycerine detonators. Such events prompted U.S. politicians and officials to depict Canada as an open back door for terrorists and human smugglers, not to mention a source of high-grade drugs (McKenna 1999, A10; Smith 2000, A15). Canada was cast in the role of a security threat, contradicting the country's usually benign, if not invisible, image in Washington.

These unfounded U.S. perceptions of Canada as an external security threat grew dramatically in the aftermath of September 11th. Despite evidence indicating that the hijackers involved in the attacks were all in the United States legally, Canada was repeatedly linked to the attacks, with some members of the U.S. press initially – and erroneously – reporting that the hijackers had slipped into the United States from Canada. Politicians from U.S. attorney general John Ashcroft to Senator Hilary Clinton argued that Canada had to get tough on terrorists. Elements of the U.S. media echoed these calls by arguing that while Canada was a "fierce ally, [and] top trading partner," it was also a "haven for terrorists" and "staging ground [for] sleeper cells" (Ibbitson 2001, A1). The popular U.S. television show, *West Wing*, depicted terrorists entering the United States from across the (mythical) Ontario-Vermont border. These misleading views helped to coalesce concerns within the U.S. government and among the general public about the security and integrity of the Canada-U.S. border, shifting attention away from the U.S.-Mexico border, which had previously been identified as the source of threats to U.S. territory. The Office of Homeland Security was created under border czar Tom Ridge, who has coordinated discussions with both the Mexican and Canadian governments.

In contrast, concerns in Canada centred on the need to keep the Canada-U.S. border open to the free flow of goods and to minimize delays at the border by addressing American's growing lack of confidence in the northern border. Indeed, in the immediate aftermath of September 11th, the economic vulnerability of Canada became increasingly apparent, as there were long delays at key border crossings, Canadian manufacturing suffered, and border communities lost business (Simpson 2001). Within this context, major Canadian business groups, including the Canadian Manufacturers and Exporters and the Canadian Chamber of Commerce, formed the Coalition for a Secure and Trade Efficient Border. By December the coalition had provided eighty comprehensive recommendations to the government about how to speed up north-south trade without compromising security concerns (Toulin 2001). Before September 11th the business community had emphasized trade concerns and economic ties (Bliss 2001). However, in the wake of 9/11 it linked these concerns more explicitly to security threats. Provincial premiers, mayors of border communities, and pundits also called on the federal government to take action to address U.S. border concerns. The U.S. government allocated Can$9 billion to border-security measures, and it has stationed six thousand armed officials at the previously "undefended" Canada-U.S. border.

The concept of a security perimeter around North America was one measure that came to the fore as a means to address U.S. concerns regarding continental security.[3] While the concept is largely undefined, creating a security perimeter would see Canada and the United States (Mexico's position in the arrangement is ambiguous) move to cooperate and/or harmonize some elements of border security and immigration policies. In December 2001, Canada and United States signed the Smart Border Declaration, which has been characterized by business groups as a "major step toward the creation of a North American security and trade perimeter" (Alberts 2001). The declaration stated: "Public security and economic security are mutually reinforcing. By working together to develop a zone of confidence against terrorist activity, we create a unique opportunity to build a smart border ... that facilitates the free flow of people and commerce; a border that reflects the largest trading relationship in the world" (DFAIT 2001a). The declaration also included the thirty-point Action Plan for Creating a Secure and Smart Border, which included measures for border policing and for reviewing refugee provisions and visa requirements and pledges to "develop an integrated approach to improve security and facilitate trade through away-from-the-border processing for truck/rail cargo"(DFAIT 2001b).

It is important to emphasize that the perimeter concept and border concerns predate September 11th. The common perimeter idea can be linked to Canadian efforts to defuse u.s. concerns over the Ressam affair, and earlier incarnations tended to emphasize issues of traffic congestion, bureaucratic delays, and waits at border crossings. In the post-September 11th period the perimeter concept was linked much more closely to security. At one and the same time the perimeter concept addressed two differing sets of priorities: u.s. perceptions about the vulnerability of its external borders and Canadian concerns to ensure that the border remained open to trade.

These events typify the contradictory nature of current forms of political and economic restructuring taking place on the North American continent. While some forces are leading to the increased movement of goods and of some select individuals, other forces are heightening fears and insecurities in the region and leading to increased attempts to police traditional nation-state boundaries.

CONTINENTAL AND HEMISPHERIC TRANSNATIONAL ORGANIZING

The dual relaxation and reinforcement of the border exemplify the complex nature of continental restructuring that undermines the idea of the continentalist/nationalist divide as a viable framework for political action. Similarly, changes in how social movements are confronting challenges to state sovereignty provide another example of the dilemmas posed by continentalization. We argue in this section that in the initial phase, state and corporate moves to greater economic integration with the United States elicited a strongly nationalist response from civil society. Over time, however, this nationalist impulse has been tempered by recognition of the practical need to develop cross-border coalitions that span the nationalist/continental-ist divide.

We turn to the work of British political theorist David Held to help illuminate some of the implications of continentalization for citizen-ship and political action. Held's discussion of the implications of glob-alization and regionalization for political community resonates with the transformations in North America described above: "in all major areas of government policy, the enmeshment of national political com-munities in regional and global processes involves them in intensive issues of transboundary coordination and control. Political space for the development and pursuit of effective government and the accountability of political power is no longer coterminous with a delimited national territory" (2000, 424). In this context, Held argues, the growth of transboundary problems creates "overlapping communities of fate" in which the fortunes of individual political com-munities are increasingly bound together:

The assumption that one can understand the nature and possibilities of polit-ical community by referring merely to national structures and mechanisms of political power is clearly anachronistic. Accordingly, questions are raised both about the fate of the idea of the political community and about the appropri-ate locus for the articulation of the political good. If the agent at the heart of modern political discourse, be it a person, group or government, is locked into a variety of overlapping communities and jurisdictions, then the proper "home" of politics and democracy becomes difficult to locate. (2000, 424)

In response to these challenges to traditional liberal democratic models of governance delimited by the nation-state, Held supports the adoption of a model of "cosmopolitan democracy." In Held's view, since globalization is undermining existing forms of national democ-racy, an "international cosmopolitan democracy" must be created in order to specify the principles and the institutional basis for democra-tic governance within, between, and across states (cited in McGrew 2000, 413). Held and other cosmopolitans call for a cosmopolitan democratic law, which transcends national laws and extends to all in the "universal community" (414). This vision also has profound impli-cations for citizenship. As Andrew Linklater argues, a cosmopolitan approach to citizenship would involve a recognition that individuals "can fall within the jurisdiction of several authorities; they can have multiple identities and they need not be united by [national] social bonds which make them indifferent to, or enemies of, the rest of the human race" (1996, cited in McGrew 2000, 414).

While Held developed his theories largely based on the experience of the European Community, his ideas clearly have great relevance for what is happening in North America. Over time, the move toward North American integration has challenged traditional assumptions that the main focus of popular organizing should be the domestic state or domestic capital. As Ricardo Grinspun and Robert Kreklewich (1994) argue, trading agreements like the FTA and NAFTA are "conditioning frameworks" that lock in neoliberal reforms, assuring investors that future elected governments will not enact policies that retreat from these reforms. In the words of Stephen Clarkson, "As a conditioning framework, NAFTA becomes an external addition to each country's *political constitution:* it limits the power of governments; it defines rights for (corporate) citizens ... In terms of societal values, it represents an attempt to entrench the practices of neo-conservatism in the United States' neighbours and so permanently to change the balance of political forces within these two countries" (Clarkson 1998, 15–16). As a result of their powerful effects in symbolizing, extending, and entrenching neoliberal reforms, trade agreements create a powerful impetus for social movements to look beyond their borders and strike up alliances with counterparts in other countries within the region. Regional integration thus undermines traditional nationalist assumptions – while Canadian social movements have not abandoned the notion that the nation-state remains an important tool for progressive social change or the desire to protect the state from its diminution by the forces of globalization, they also are forced to pursue new continentalist strategies.

As discussed above, the political economy tradition in English Canada has long been dominated by Canadian nationalism. Nationalism has also exerted a powerful influence over popular organizing in Canada, and the campaign against the Canada-U.S. Free Trade Agreement represented the peak of this left-nationalist position. Yet, as we argue above, once economic integration has proceeded past a certain point, it undercuts the logic of the nationalist/continentalist divide as a guiding principle for political action. The complex and contradictory ways in which North American integration is simultaneously opening and closing borders have led to creative attempts by social activists to span the continentalist/nationalist divide and construct continental and hemispheric transnational social movements. The cross-border coalitions that came together in opposition to NAFTA and the Free Trade Area of the Americas (FTAA) proposal provide good examples of the challenges faced by social movements in an era of continentalization and globalization. While they were initially the outcome of the nationalists' rejection of the form of transnationalism promoted by capital, these alliances, in order to survive, have had to engage in cross-border dialogue and to develop shared alternative proposals. In the process, some of their differences have been overcome, and new, transborder identities have begun to emerge.

On the other hand, the events of September 11th have created uncertainty about the future direction of the North American region. While on the one hand, as we discuss above, the terrorist attacks have resulted in increased security integration, the nature and the position of the new walls in the North American security perimeter are not entirely clear. In particular, Mexico's attempts to win a more liberal immigration regime for Mexican migrants have been thwarted, and Mexico's importance to Washington seems to have declined (Clarkson 2002, 14). In this section we examine some of the implications of these changes for the approach of Canadian social movements to cross-border organizing. The evolution of the engagement of Canadian social movements with continentalization and globalization can be roughly divided into three phases: the fight against the FTA, the fight against NAFTA, and the post-NAFTA period.

The Canada-U.S. Free Trade Agreement

The fight against the FTA marked a watershed in state-society relations in Canada. In this period Canadian social movements embraced the left nationalist discourse and mobilized against the move by corporate Canada toward continentalization. This period was also notable because of the achievement of an unprecedented level of unity of thought and of practice in the struggle against Mulroney's free trade agenda. Civil society became polarized between two rigid and diametrically opposed ideological perspectives around issues of economic liberalization, perspectives that were based on the nationalist and continentalist positions outlined above. Before this point, Canadian social movements had been divided among themselves, and both business and popular movements were divided in their attitudes toward the United States. After business and the state moved toward a joint endorsement of the continentalist option, the formation of the Pro-Canada Network (PCN) to oppose the FTA forged a cross-class alliance unprecedented in Canadian politics, an alliance held together by the glue of economic nationalism (Ayres 1998, 42).

One important factor that precipitated this alliance was the transformation in labour-state relations in Canada. The postwar compromise around the welfare state had depoliticized labour's relationship with the Canadian state. In the context of postwar prosperity, unions had focused their struggles mostly on winning improved wages and benefits through collective bargaining (Bradford 1998, 55). From the

1950s to the early 1970s, the main representative of English-Canadian labour unions, the Canadian Labour Congress (CLC), had supported liberal, continentalist policies like the Auto Pact. This support reflected the prosperity the country had enjoyed during the 1950s and 1960s, when U.S. investment expanded, and the fact that workers had shared in the benefits of this economic model. It was only with the slowing down of postwar growth that the CLC adopted a more radical and nationalist economic doctrine.

In 1975, the Liberal government legislated wage controls after the failure of the consensus negotiations on wage and price guidelines. In response, in 1976 the CLC officially embraced a nationalist/interventionist discourse and embarked on a path toward greater political activism, through its alliances both with the New Democratic Party (NDP) and with other social movements (Smith 1992; Bradford 1998, 106). Labour was then further angered by the movement of the Mulroney government toward free trade, which was seen as removing many of the traditional tools of Keynesian economic management employed by the Canadian state to improve economic welfare and as lessening Canadian independence and sovereignty (Smith 1992, 51–4).

As well, changes in Canada in the early 1980s led to greater coordination between labour and other social organizations, such as the women's and environmentalist movements, with which labour previously had had little in common. In fact, the impetus for the development of a new "popular sector" coalition came from the women's movement, one of the most prominent of the new identity-based organizations. The National Action Committee on the Status of Women (NAC) argued that women, particularly poor and working-class women and women of colour, would be disproportionately affected by free trade, since they were more likely to work in the labour-intensive industries where jobs would be eliminated. NAC was also concerned that the burden associated with the trend toward the privatization of functions formerly performed by the welfare state would again fall disproportionately upon women. The struggle against free trade thus brought together a cross-class alliance of workers and such traditionally middle-class organizations as the Council of Canadians, united under a nationalist banner. These groups came together in the Pro Canada Network (PCN), later renamed the Action Canada Network.

Nationalist forces squared off against continentalist forces in the dramatic free-trade election campaign of 1988, which was seen as a sort of referendum on the deal Conservative prime minister Brian Mulroney had reached with President George Bush. During the campaign, the PCN orchestrated a colourful campaign against the free trade deal, challenging the political, economic, and cultural implications of what the government and business had hoped to portray as a noncontroversial technical matter. Popular support for the agreement gradually declined throughout English Canada, apart from Alberta. Nevertheless, the Conservatives won the election, partly because antifree trade votes were split between the Liberals and the NDP.

During this first period of popular sector protest against the government's free trade policies, popular movements in the United States were largely oblivious to the agreement with Canada, reflecting the traditional American view that Canada was not a threat. As a result, cross-border alliances did not develop during this period, despite some attempts by Canadian activists to spark interest in the United States in the implications of the FTA for such issues as the capacity of the state to protect the environment and labour rights. Nationalist discourses therefore remained the dominant motif in the discourse of anti-FTA campaigners during this period.

The North American Free Trade Agreement

The Mexican state's decision under President Carlos Salinas to pursue its own free trade agreement with the United States would have important implications for the nationalist discourse. The eventual decision by leaders of the three countries of North America to create a North American Free Trade Agreement (NAFTA) created the opportunity for new political strategies, based on the continentalization of the popular sector movement. While U.S. and Canadian business and the two states had become increasingly internationalized during the period leading up the FTA, such linkages were largely absent in the popular sector. Mexico's entry into NAFTA helped politicize trade policy in the United States and resulted in the formation of coalitions similar to Canada's PCN. An important actor in this period was Common Frontiers, an alliance of Canadian social movements with links to Latin America and an interest in expanding the fight against free trade continentally. Common Frontiers activists visited Mexico to discuss with counterparts there the impact they had seen of Canadian economic integration with the United States, and Common Frontiers eventually set up an office in Mexico charged with supporting Mexican activists' struggle against free trade. Trinational alliances of the anti-free trade coalitions in Canada, the United States, and Mexico emerged, and both the Red Mexicana ante el Libre Comercio (RMALC) and the U.S. Citizen's Trade Campaign borrowed from the PCN's coalition-building tactics (Ayers 1998, 128).

In addition to the coordination between the coalitions, sectoral linkages were established between groups of women, workers, environmentalists, and others in the three countries.[4] Apart from grassroots campaigns to educate and mobilize the North American public about the dangers of free trade, activists from the three countries focused their efforts particularly on lobbying the u.s. Congress, since the u.s. division of powers allowed some degree of influence over state policy. Mexican social movement activists set up an office in Washington to represent their perspective on NAFTA, since they felt they had a greater chance of affecting the outcome of the debate in Washington than in Mexico City. Transnational civil society pressures on Presidents Bush and Clinton eventually resulted in the Clinton administration's inclusion of side-agreements on labour and the environment.

The inclusion of Mexico also encouraged some members of the popular sector to reexamine their assumptions about protectionism, a key element of the nationalist strategy. Mexican anti-NAFTA activists rejected the existing form of the NAFTA agreement as being based on a neoliberal model that failed to take into account such issues as immigration, human rights, labour rights, and the environment. However, they were not opposed to the idea of a continental agreement per se, and they were in favour of opening Northern markets to Mexican exports. Interaction with Mexicans has meant that Canadian activists have gradually moved away from a defensive tactic of simply denouncing trade agreements toward more proactive efforts to develop alternative proposals in a collaborative manner with their u.s. and Mexican allies. For example, in October 1991 the trinational coalition published the *Alternative Declaration*, which proposed an alternative continental free trade agreement that included more protections for the environment and for labour. Such initiatives represent an alternative vision of a North American community, one based not on commercial transactions and profit but on social justice and equity (Bassett 2001, 50).

Post-*NAFTA* Organizing

As Stephen Clarkson suggests, transnational alliances are an important aspect of post-NAFTA popular sector politics, and debates about the future of trade and investment continue to dominate popular sector politics. In some sectors, linkages between social movements in the three North American countries have deepened. However, other government initiatives have shifted transnational social movement organizing away from a specifically North American focus. As demonstrations in Seattle in 1999 at the meeting of the World Trade Organization (WTO) and the defeat of the Multilateral Agreement on Investment (MAI) demonstrate, citizens are now demanding the right of civil society to participate directly in international negotiations on trade. The FTAA initiative and the organizing around the Quebec City Summit of the Americas in 2001 also illustrate the shift in popular sector transnational organizing.

In response to the FTAA initiative, the ties that Canadian groups established with allies in the United States and Mexico have now been broadened into hemispheric alliances, as displayed recently at the protests and the Popular Summit that accompanied the third Summit of the Americas in Quebec City in April 2001. The FTAA is an initiative to create a free trade zone comprising all the states of the Americas (except Cuba) by 2005. Common Frontiers attended the 1994 Miami Summit at which the FTAA initiative was launched as part of the delegation from the Action Canada Network. At the same time, the Organización Regional Interamericana de Trabajadores (ORIT), the International Confederation of Free Trade Unions body in the Americas, began to pay attention to the social dimension of the FTAA and began to hold labour forums at each of the trade ministers' meetings after Miami. A major ORIT demand was that these labour forums be granted equal status with the Business Forum of the Americas that is held in conjunction with the trade ministerials. By the time of the second Summit of the Americas in 1998, labour groups (pushed by the CLC and the Brazilian trade union federation, the CUT), decided to broaden the transnational coalition to create the Hemispheric Social Alliance (HSA). In part, the HSA's inclusion of nonlabour civil society actors reflects lessons learned by North American labour groups in the struggle against the FTA and NAFTA about the benefits of expanding their alliances.

The HSA includes leading social movements throughout the hemisphere, in addition to the main union federations such as ORIT, the AFL-CIO (the United States), the CUT (Brazil), and the CLC (Canada). The HSA was first formed at the Our Americas Forum, which was held in Belo Horizonte, Brazil, in May 1997 in conjunction with the third Western Hemisphere ministerial meeting on trade. The HSA declaration of intent states, "We are united by an alternative vision of an integrated hemisphere – one based on respect for human rights, cultural diversity, the environment, and reinforcement of national social development projects which raise standards and skills for all rather than down to the lowest common denominator" (Common Frontiers 1999, cited in Bassett 2001, 75).

Transnational civil society activists took heart from the defeat of President Clinton's September 1997 attempt to gain fast-track trade-negotiating authority from Congress, as well as from the defeat of the MAI initiative to establish an investment regime within the OECD. The Council of Canadians, headed by Maude Barlow and Tony Clarke, played an important role in the anti-MAI campaign, which was waged largely on the Internet. This campaign brought the Council of Canadians further into the global arena, and it was marked by an interesting shift away from the emphasis on lost jobs and economic sovereignty, which typified the anti-FTA campaign, and towards a greater emphasis on the threat to democracy and citizenship rights represented by the MAI. These themes remain an important element of post-NAFTA transnational organizing.

At the second Summit of the Americas in Santiago, Chile, in 1998, the HSA brought together the first People's Summit in Santiago, which was attended by about eight hundred social leaders from almost every country in the continent (Massicotte 2000, 5), although some countries, like those in the Caribbean, were under-represented. An HSA secretariat was established in Mexico City (it has since moved to Brazil). Although it is still weak and poorly funded, the secretariat has played an important role in organized civil society's Release the Text campaign, which challenges the secrecy of the FTAA negotiating process, as well as playing an important role in organizing the second People's Summit in Quebec City in April 2001. At each of the People's Summits, as well as during the time in between, the HSA has developed an *Alternatives for the Americas* document, which is similar to the *Alternative Declaration* of the NAFTA campaign. The document contains ten chapters and lays out an alternative vision of hemispheric integration. Some of the chapters present a critique of what is expected to come out in the official FTAA text on such areas as investment rules, while others address issues like democracy, human rights, and migration, which are unlikely to be included in an eventual FTAA. Member groups also carry out education campaigns within their own countries regarding the likely impact of an FTAA and participate in official consultations about the FTAA in countries where formal consultation mechanisms exist.

The campaigns against the WTO, MAI, and the FTAA have to some extent shifted Canadian activists' attention away from a North American focus. While ties between Canadian and Mexican activists remain fairly strong within the HSA, its ties with U.S. organizations have apparently languished a bit in recent years. The Mexican president, Vicente Fox, is heavily committed to promoting deeper forms of continental integration, including an energy agreement, greater mobility of Mexican labour within North America, and a development fund for the region (Rozental 2001). Before September 11th, President George W. Bush was fairly supportive of immigration reform to legalize Mexicans residing illegally in the U.S. and to create some type of guest-worker program. But immigration reform is now on the backburner, and the United States has continentalized its security policy by creating within its armed forces a new unified command called Northern Command (NORTH-COM) The U.S. NORTHCOM will be assigned responsibility for U.S. homeland security, and the commander of NORTHCOM will be responsible for coordinating the activities of U.S. forces in North America, including Mexico, the continental United States, and Canada (Canada 2000). As well, as we have seen, the U.S. government has engaged in extensive discussions concerning enactment of smart-border risk management systems at both its northern and southern borders. Canadian pundits Wendy Dobson of the C.D. Howe Institute and Hugh Segal of the Institute for Research on Public Policy are calling for a deepening of NAFTA or a North American Community, and some elites in all three countries favour a North American monetary union (see Helleiner in this volume). If popular sector activists wish to influence the shape of this "community," they will need to renew their trilateral ties and their vision of an alternative North American community.

CONCLUSION

The ongoing continental reconfiguration has not led, as predicted by the Liberal Party in 1988, to the erasure of national borders. Borders, as we have seen, have in fact become simultaneously more porous and stronger, while proposals for a continental security perimeter may geographically shift some of their functions away from the land to points of entry by air and sea. The impact of continental integration on the Canada-U.S. border represents some of the complexity of what is happening to the Canadian state as a result of globalization and continentalization. The increasing speed and movement of cross-border trade appears to suggest that national borders are less important. Yet increasing attempts at border control and management to safeguard territorial sovereignty against the free movement of people and to satisfy national security concerns suggest otherwise.

As we have also seen, continental integration has important implications for how Canadian civil society groups organize. As was seen in the campaigns against the FTA and NAFTA, as well as against the MAI, the WTO, and the FTAA, globalization creates powerful incentives for groups to coordinate their action across borders, and over time a dense web of transnational linkages has developed between labour, women's organizations, environmentalists, and others within the North American economic space and beyond. It is thus possible that over time, citizens of the three North American countries will develop multiple conceptions of their membership in an emerging North American community and a shared sense of destiny, as well as expanded institutions of collective governance. As Satzewich and

Wong argue in this volume, migration and the changing ethnic/racial composition of Canadian society also contribute to the formation of multiple political identities and allow us to move beyond localized and territorialized notions of community and citizenship.

Nevertheless, the cosmopolitans' profoundly liberal ideas lack sensitivity to the problems that stem not from the nation-state system but from the patterns of power and inequality that are rooted in patterns of production and the spread of multinational corporations. As well, as Craig Calhoun argues, an "attenuated cosmopolitanism is likely to leave us lacking the old sources of solidarity without adequate new ones. And cosmopolitanism without the strengthening of local democracy is likely to be a very elite affair" (Calhoun 2001, 1). From a more communitarian perspective, Calhoun also argues that "most versions of cosmopolitanism share with traditional liberalism a thin conception of social life, commitment, and belonging" (8) and that cosmopolitanism undervalues the importance of the necessarily often profoundly local nature of individuals' sense of belonging and of most democratic practice. It is thus rooted in seventeenth- and eighteenth-century European rationalism, universalism, and individualism. As many of the other chapters in this volume attest, most of the important struggles engaged in by Canadian social movements are still largely local or national in scope. The point, therefore, is not, as the cosmopolitan formulation might suggest, to replace the old nationalist ideology with a new, democratized, continentalism but rather to recognize that state boundaries and forms of political action are being transformed under the pressures of globalization in complex and contradictory ways. New ways of understanding political identity, community, citizenship, and sovereignty must therefore be developed.

NOTES

This article was produced with the support of the Social Sciences and Humanities Research Council, grant no. 410-2000-1466. The authors would like to thank Rob Aitken and Jimena Jimenez for their research assistance and Jeffrey Ayres, Leah Vosko, and Wallace Clement for their helpful comments.

1   In the Treaty to Establish the European Community, chap. 1, article 39.1, states that "Freedom of movement for workers shall be secured within the community," and 39.2 states that "such freedom of movement shall entail the abolition of any discrimination based on nationality between workers of the Member States as regards employment, remuneration, and other conditions of work and employment" (from europa.eu.int/abc/treaties_en.htm).

2 "Between 1985 and 1990 [Africa] is said to have lost sixty thousand
   professionals and to have been losing twenty thousand per year ever
   since (ACP-EU Courier 1996, 59). In recent years Eastern European
   countries have been facing the same problems. Bulgaria has been one
   of the hardest hit. In 1995 it lost more than seven thousand professors
   and researchers" (*Migration News* 4.1; cited by Stalker 2000,
   107–8).

3 The federal government introduced a number of initiatives in response to
   September 11th and concerns regarding terrorism. These included establishing a cabinet-level committee on antiterrorism, sweeping antiterrorism
   legislation, fast-tracking already proposed immigration and refugee
   changes, such as identification cards, and spending commitments concerning border security and infrastructure.

4 For an analysis of trinational women's networks, see Gabriel and Macdonald (1994). The CLC's ability to criticize the practice of labour rights in
   Mexico was initially constrained by the fact that the state-run Confederation of Mexican Workers, one of the main agents of labour repression in
   Mexico, was a fellow member of the International Confederation of Free
   Trade Unions (ICFTU). The CLC has become increasingly openly critical of
   the CTM, however, in recent years, and closer to independent Mexican
   trade unions.

REFERENCES

Ackelson, Jason M. 2000. "Navigating the Northern Line: Discourses of the
   U.S.-Canadian Borderlands." Paper presented at the International Studies
   Association Annual Meeting, Los Angeles, 15–18 March.
Alberts, Sheldon. 2001. "Accord Called Step toward North American Perimeter." *National Post,* 13 December. Accessed at http://www.nationalpost.com/
   scripts/prin...nter.asp?f=stories/ 20011213.
Andreas, Peter. 2000a. "Introduction: The Wall after the Wall." In Peter
   Andreas and Timothy Snyder, eds., *The Wall around the West: State Borders and
   Immigration Controls in North America and Europe.* Boston: Rowman & Little-
   field: 1–11.
– 2000b. *Border Games: Policing the U.S.-Mexico Divide.* Ithaca, NY: Cornell Uni-
   versity Press.
– 1998–99. "The Escalation of U.S. Immigration Control in the Post-NAFTA
   era." *Political Science Quarterly* 113(4): 591–615.
Ayres, Jeffrey M. 1998. *Defying Conventional Wisdom: Political Movements and
   Popular Contention against North American Free Trade.* Toronto: University of
   Toronto Press.
Bassett, Michael. 2001. "Challenging the FTAA Disconnect: The Political
   Economy of State-Civil Society Relations in the Free Trade Area of the
   Americas Process." MA thesis, Carleton University, Ottawa.

Bellavance, Joel-Denis. 1999. "Study Says Brain Drain Places Canada in Peril, but Not Everyone Agrees." *National Post,* 17 August, A6.

Bliss, Michael. 2001. "Attacks Hasten the End of Our Border." *National Post,* 29 September, A1.

Bradford, Neil. 1998. *Commissioning Ideas: Canadian National Policy Innovation in Comparative Perspective.* Toronto: Oxford University Press.

Brodie, Janine. 1994. *Politics on the Boundaries: Restructuring and the Canadian Women's Movement.* North York, ON: Robarts Centre for Canadian Studies, York University.

CNN. 2000. "Panel Considers Terrorist Threat on the U.S.-Canada Border." 27 January. Available online at www.cnn.com/2000/US/01/27/us.canada.border/.

Calhoun, Craig. 2001. "The Limits of Cosmopolitanism: Democracy, Inequality, and International Civil Society." Paper presented at the International Studies Association, Chicago, 23 February.

Canada. Department of National Defence. 2002. "Canada-U.S. Defence Relations, Asymmetric Threats, and the U.S. Unified Command Plan," 6 May. Accessed at http://www.forces.ca/eng/archive/speeches/2002/May02/vcd_s_e.htm, on 8 August.

Castles, Stephen, and Mark J. Miller. 1993. *The Age of Migration.* New York: Guildford Press.

Chwialkowska, Luiza. 2001. "Impossible Became Possible on September 11th." *National Post.* 11 December. Accessed at http://www.nationalpost.com/scripts/prin...nter.asp?f=/stories/20011211/.

Clarkson, Stephen. 2001. "The Multi-level State: Canada in the Semiperiphery of Both Continentalism and Globalization." *Review of International Political Economy* 8(3):501–27.

– 2002. *Lockstep in the Continental Ranks: Redrawing the American Perimeter after September 11th.* Ottawa: Canadian Centre for Policy Alternatives.

– 2001. "The Multi-level State: Canada in the Semi-periphery of Both Continentalism and Globalization." *Review of International Political Economy.* 8(3):501–27.

– 1998. "Fearful Asymmetries: The Challenge of Analyzing Continental Systems in a Globalizing World. *Canadian-American Public Policy* 35 (September): 1–65.

– 1996. "Continentalism." In *The Canadian Encyclopedia Plus.* Toronto: McClelland and Stewart.

Common Frontiers. 1999. "Hemispheric Social Alliance." 6 November. Accessed at http://www.web.net/comfront/cfhems.htm.

Canada. Department of Foreign Affairs and International Trade (DFAIT). 2001a. "The Smart Border Declaration." 12 December. Accessed at http://www.can-am.gc.ca/menu-e.asp?

– 2001b. "Action Plan for Creating a Secure and Smart Border." 12 December. Accessed at http://www.can- am.gc.ca/menu-e.asp?

Drache, Daniel, and Wallace Clement. 1985. "Introduction." In Daniel Drache and Wallace Clement, eds., *The New Practical Guide to Canadian Political Economy*, ix–xxiv. Toronto: Lorimer.

Duffy, Andrew. 2000. "Ottawa Urges U.S. to Adopt Continental Security Ring." *National Post*, 12 Januar, A1.

Foster, Lorne. 1998. *Turnstile Immigration*. Toronto: Thompson Educational Publishing.

Francis, Diane. 2001. "Border Policies Miss the Mark." *National Post Online*, 11 January. Accessed at www.nationalpost.com/search/story.html.

Gabriel, Christina, and Laura Macdonald. 1994. "NAFTA, Women and Organizing in Canada and Mexico: Forging a 'feminist internationality.'". *Millennium: Journal of International Studies* 23(3): 535–62.

– 2001. "Border Anxieties: Changing Discourses on the Canada-U.S. Border." Paper presented at the Annual Meeting of the International Studies Association, Chicago, 21–24 February.

Globerman, Steven. 1999. *Perspectives on North American Free Trade: Trade Liberalization and the Migration of Skilled Workers*. Ottawa: Industry Canada.

Grinspun, Ricardo, and Robert Kreklewich. 1994. "Consolidating Neoliberal Reforms: 'Free Trade' as a Conditioning Framework." *Studies in Political Economy* 43:33–61.

Hampson, Fen Osler, and Maureen Appel Molot. 2000. "Does the Forty-ninth Parallel Matter Any More?" In Maureen Appel Molot and Fen Osler Hampson, eds., *Canada among Nations: Vanishing Borders*, 1–23. Don Mills, ON: Oxford University Press.

Handleman, Stephen. 2000. "Two Nations, Indivisible." *Time*, 10 July, 20–7.

Held, David. 2000. "Regulating Globalization." In David Held and Anthony McGrew, eds., *The Global Transformations Reader: An Introduction to the Globalization Debate*. 420–30. Cambridge: Polity Press.

Held, David, and Anthony McGrew, eds. 2000. *The Global Transformations Reader: An Introduction to the Globalization Debate*. London: Polity Press.

Held, David, Anthony McGrew, David Goldblatt, and Jonathan Perraton. 1999. *Global Transformations: Politics, Economics and Culture*. Stanford: Stanford University Press.

Ibbitson, John. 2001. "U.S. Points the Finger due North." *Globe and Mail*, 27 September, A1.

Innis, Harold. 1997. "Conclusion From the Fur Trade in Canada." In David Taras and Beverly Rasporich, eds., *A Passion for Identity: An Introduction to Canadian Studies*, 15–26. 3d ed. Toronto: Nelson.

– 1956. "Decentralization and Democracy." In M.Q. Innis, ed., *Essays in Canadian Economic History*, 358–71. Toronto: University of Toronto Press.

Koring, Paul. 1999. "Plot Carries Trademarks of Bin Laden. *Globe and Mail*. 20 December, A3.

Levitt, Kari. 1970. *The Silent Surrender: The Multinational Corporation in Canada*. Toronto: MacMillan.

Linklater, Andrew. 1996. "Citizenship and Sovereignty in the post-Westphalian State." *European Journal of International Relations* 2(1): 77–103.

Massicotte, Marie-Josée. 2000. "Construyendo puentes en América del Norte: La emergencia de la Alianza Social Continental y sus redes transnacionales." Unpublished paper, Mexico City.

McBride, Stephen. 2000. "Policy from What? Neoliberal and Human- Capital Theoretical Foundations of Recent Canadian Labour-Market Policy." In Mike Burke, Colin Mooers, and John Shields, eds., *Restructuring and Resistance*, 159–77. Halifax: Fernwood.

McBride, Stephen, and John Shields. 1997. *Dismantling a Nation*, 2nd ed. Halifax: Fernwood.

McCarthy, Shawn. 1999. "Brain Drain Losses Hit Record, Conference Board Finds." *Globe and Mail*, 17 August, B3.

McGrew, Anthony. 2000. "Democracy beyond Borders." In David Held and Anthony McGrew, eds., *The Global Transformations Reader: An Introduction to the Globalization Debate*, 405–19.

McKenna, Barrie. 1999. "Rumbling Begins at Border, Although Officially All Is Well." *Globe and Mail*, 21 December, A10.

Molot, Maureen Appel, and Fen Osler Hampson, eds. 2000. *Canada among Nations 2000: Vanishing Borders*. Don Mills, ON: Oxford University Press.

Naylor, R.T. 1972. "The Rise and Fall of the Third Commercial Empire of the St Lawrence." In G. Teeple, ed., *Capitalism and the National Question in Canada*, 1–41. Toronto: University of Toronto Press.

Nevins, Joseph. 2000. "The Re-making of the California-Mexico Boundary in the Age of NAFTA." In Peter Andreas and Timothy Snyder, eds., *The Wall around the West*, 99–114. Boston: Rowan Littlefield.

Newman, Peter C. 1999. "The Year of Living Dangerously." *Maclean's* 20 December, 51–6.

Office of the Inspector General (OIG). 2000. *Border Patrol Efforts along the Northern Border*. Report number 1-2000-04. Accessed at www.usdoj.gov/oig/i20004/i200004.htm.

Papademetriou, Demetrious, and Deborah Meyers. 1999. "Law Enforcement Problems at the U.S.-Canada Border." Testimony before the Subcommittee on Immigration and Claims of the Committee on the Judiciary, U.S. House of Representatives, 14 April 1999. Accessed at www.ceip.org/files/PublicastLawEnforce.asp.

Policy Research Secretariat. 2000. "Policy Research Initiative." *Horizons* 3(2), August.

Populations Division, United Nations Secretariat. 1997. *International Migration and Development: The Concise Report*. New York: United Nations.

Rozental, Andres. 2001. "North America: A 2020 Vision." *Looking Ahead* 23(2): 12–14.

Sands, Christopher. 2000a. "How Canada Policy Is Made in the United States."

In Maureen Appel Molot and Fen Osler Hampson, eds., *Canada among Nations 2000: Vanishing Borders,* 47–72. Don Mills, ON: Oxford University Press.

– 2000b. "Fear and the New Frontier: A U.S. Perspective on the Canadian Border." 3(2): 8–9.

Sassen, Saskia. 1998. "The Transnationalization of Immigration Policy." In Frank Bonilla, Edwin Melendex, Rebecca Morales, and Mariá de los Angeles Torres, eds., *Borderless Borders,* 53–67. Philadelphia: Temple Press.

Simpson, Jeffrey. 2001. "How to Keep Those People Moving." *Globe and Mail,* 21 November, A10.

Smith, Lamar. 2000. "Plugging Our Porous Border." *Globe and Mail,* 24 January, A15.

Smith, Miriam. 1992. "The Canadian Labour Congress: From Continentalism to Economic Nationalism." *Studies in Political Economy* 38: 51–4.

Spener, David. 2000. "The Logic and Contradictions of Intensified Border Enforcement in Texas." In Peter Andreas and Timothy Snyder, eds., *The Wall around the West,* 115–37. Boston: Rowan and Littlefield.

Stalker, Peter. 2000. *Workers without Frontiers.* Boulder, CO: Lynne Rienner.

Toulin, Alan. 2001. "Business Group Wants Police at All Crossings." *National Post,* 3 December. Accessed at http://www.nationalpost.com/scripts/printer.asp?f=/stories/2 0011203.

United Nations Secretariat. Populations Division. 1997. *International Migration and Development. The Concise Report.* New York: United Nations.

Walker, R.B.J. 1993. *Inside/Outside: International Relations as Political Theory.* Cambridge: Cambridge University Press.

Williams, Glen. 1995. "Regions within Region: Continentalism Ascendant." In Michael S. Whittington and Glen Williams, eds., *Canadian Politics in the 1990s,* 19–39. Toronto: Nelson Canada.

Zhao, John, Doug Drew, and T. Scott Murray. 2000. "Brain Drain and Brain Gain: The Migration of Knowledge Workers from and to Canada." *Education Quarterly Review* 3 (spring). Accessed at www.statcan.ca:80/english/indepth/81- 003/feature/eq2000_vo6n3_a01_hi.html.

10 "Playin' Along": Canada and Global Finance

WILLIAM COLEMAN
AND TONY PORTER

During the 1980s and 1990s it seemed as if global financial markets had become so large and so integrated that they were fatally undermining the policy autonomy of even the most developed states. Gill and Law (1993) insightfully developed this idea by pointing to the "structural power of capital," by which they meant the ability of increasingly mobile capital to discipline states by moving abroad. Cox (2000) usefully highlighted the emergence of a *nébuleuse*, a transnational process bringing together private financial elites, finance officials, and international financial institutions to strengthen the degree to which states adjust to the needs of the global economy. The internationalization of the state, for Cox, involved the strengthening of the state's finance-related departments, but only through their integration with international financial institutions and their role in getting citizens to adjust to the imperatives of global capital.

Such processes raise the question of whether the Canadian state has an independent role to play in global finance. In this chapter, we argue that this role is being transformed but still shows some signs of independence and autonomy. The state has worked to help transform Canadian chartered banks and the Mouvement Desjardins in Quebec into full participants in global finance. The transformation goes beyond the banks themselves, however, to include the role of the state itself. The state not only supports the integration of the banks into the global financial system, but also is restructuring itself to participate in governance at the global level and to address the domestic implications of global political commitments and global market pressures.

This transformation of the state's role should not be seen to be robbing it of any capacity to act independently. To the contrary, the political initiatives of states and citizens continue to make a difference, even if they involve cross-border interactions in ways that they did not previously. Some state initiatives can involve the promotion of national financial interests in ways that do not simply involve passive adjustment to global market forces. More interestingly, however, states and citizens can still act to offset the negative effects of financial markets and powerful financial interests. Such steps can occur through domestic initiatives, collaborative efforts involving many states working together to control global finance better, and coordinated public advocacy and protest by citizens' groups focused on central sites of global authority and power.

Our chapter echoes and develops two related themes, therefore, that have been quite prominent in recent work on globalization (Woods 2000). First, the way in which state power is exercised may have changed with globalization, but state power has not disappeared. Indeed, state power has been transformed into more regulative, juridical, and internationalized forms. Second, globalization does not affect all states equally. What is clear, however, is that, however affected, states retain an ongoing importance. In Canada, this importance is linked closely to the nurturing of an autonomous banking sector that historically has had close ties both to the staples industries and to U.S. branch plants (Carroll 1986).

In this chapter, we start by presenting a general overview of Canada's role in global finance. Next, we examine successively recent developments in the political economy of finance within Canada, and then we turn to international initiatives taken by Canadian political actors. For each development we highlight the heightened constraints imposed by global finance, where these constraints exist, as well as political initiatives that do not reflect such constraints.

THE CANADIAN FINANCIAL SECTOR: STRONG NATIONALLY, CHALLENGED INTERNATIONALLY

From its origins Canada has always had a strong, internationally oriented banking sector. In the Canadian political economy, some scholars have argued that this strength signifies Canada's over-reliance on commerce relative to more productive manufacturing activities and should be seen as a weakness. In contrast, others see the prominence of Canadian banks in Canada and abroad as a sign of Canada's advanced industrial status. They argue that this prominence marks the type of central role played by finance capital in coordinating the economy and extracting revenues from abroad that is characteristic of the largest and most developed capitalist countries (on this debate see Naylor 1975; Clement 1977; Carroll 1982).

We see the character of Canadian finance as shaped not by some underlying essential and enduring relationship with Canadian capitalism as a whole but rather by ongoing and quite fluid competitive and collaborative relationships with other sectors, with competitors in global financial markets, and with political actors. Such an understanding does not imply, however, that the Canadian financial sector's international role will change completely from one year to the next. To the contrary, financial systems, with their intangible and complex transactions, rely heavily on institutional mechanisms to develop and process information, to regulate activities, and to foster trust. This institutional capacity is built over time by private firms, states, and nongovernmental actors individually and in interactions with one another. These historical processes establish identifiable trends and continuities in the relationship of the Canadian financial sector to global finance.

Table 1 draws together data on the Canadian financial sector from the last two decades of the twentieth century and enables us to highlight some of these trends and continuities. Three main themes stand out. First, Canadian banks are exceptionally strong in their dominance of traditional banking activities within Canada. Second, over the past three decades, Canadian banks have reduced significantly their activities outside North America, in order to focus on business in Canada and the United States. Third, despite the banks' domestic strength, Canadian financial firms are losing ground relative to competitors from other countries. These losses are particularly pronounced in the types of capital market activities that have become more important relative to traditional lending in recent years. We look briefly at each of these themes in turn.

First, the ongoing dominance of Canadian banks in traditional domestic activities is evident especially in their superior performance relative to the foreign banks that were granted expanded access to the Canadian market in the Bank Act of 1980 and in the Free Trade Agreement of 1988. U.S. banks, like other foreign banks, made an initial effort to break into the Canadian market but found that their subsequent performance was uneven and posed no significant threat to Canadian banks (table 1, lines 1–3). Moreover, the top-five domestic banks have steadily increased their share of total household financial assets, indicating their success not just with regard to foreign banks but with regard to other Canadian financial firms as well (line

Table 1   Profile of Changes in the International Aspects of the Canadian Financial
Sector

	1982	1987	1992	1997
Canadian banks have consolidated their control of the Canadian market despite continental free trade.				
1 U.S. direct investment in banks in Canada as a percentage of total equity of Canadian big-five banks		4.7	4.2	3.2
2 Income from U.S. direct investment in banks in Canada as a percentage of the investment		11.8	−4.7	3.2
3 U.S. direct investment in banks as a percentage of all U.S. direct investment in Canada		1.2	1.3	1.1
4 Share of all household financial assets held by Canadian big-five banks		13.8	15.9	17.5
Internationally, Canadian financial firms have retreated from global markets and focused on North America.				
5 Chartered bank loans to non-residents as a percentage of all loans	25.7	26.8	24.7	22.9
6 Canadian banks' foreign claims as a percentage of foreign claims of banks from all countries	–	3.2	1.9	2.0
7 Canada's share of global equity market capitalization (percentage)	4.0	2.6	2.3	2.3
8 Announced international equity issues: Canadian issues as a percentage of all issues	23.0	3.5	1.6	1.9
9 Share of countries other than the U.S. in total Canadian net new securities placed abroad	62.2	82.7	35.5	21.3
10 U.S. share of worldwide claims on nonresidents of Canadian chartered banks (percentage)	27.3	47.0	56.4	50.9
11 Percentage of all net new Canadian security issues placed in the U.S.	7.2	2.7	17.9	27.6
Securities transactions are growing more rapidly than banking.				
12 Household financial assets held in mutual funds as a percentage of household financial assets held in deposits	2.6	10.0	16.0	55.8
The foreign investments of Canadian firms are off-setting foreign firms' investments in Canada.				
13 Canadian foreign direct investment position abroad as percent of foreign direct investment in Canada	60.0	70.0	81.0	112.5
In some areas Canadian financial firms are lagging.				
14 TSE capitalization as a percentage of NYSE capitalization	20.8	22.4	11.8	9.7

Table 1   (continued)

	1982	1987	1992	1997
15 Number of TSE-listed companies as a percentage of number of NYSE-listed companies	53.6	73.3	53.5	46.6
16 Exports of financial intermediation services as % of trade in financial intermediation services	68.9	65.5	63.0	62.4
17 Canadian top-five banks' capital as a percentage of top-five U.S. banks' capital	44.7	57.2	58.5	34.5

Sources and notes, by line. 1 *Euromoney, The Banker,* various issues, and U.S. Department of Commerce (DOC), *Survey of Business,* various issues; 2–3 DOC *Survey of Business,* various issues; 4 Task Force (1998b) 114; 5 Nonmortgage loans, CANSIM II (Statistics Canada Data Base), table 1760016; 6 Bank for International Settlements (BIS), data at www.bis.org; 7 Securities Industry Association, *2000 Securities Industry Fact Book,* at www.sia.com; 8 BIS, first entry is for 1983; 9 CANSIM II, table 1760035; 10 First figure is for 1983, CANSIM, table 1760013; 11 CANSIM II, table 1760035; 12 Task Force (1998b), 42; 13 CANSIM II, table 3760038; 14–15 *World Stock Exchange Factbook 1998,* Round Rock TX, Meridian Securities Markets,1997; 16 CANSIM II, table 3800012; 17 Ranked by capital, *Euromoney, The Banker,* various issues. Three-year averages centred on the year specified were used for lines 1–3, 5–9, 10, 11, 13, and 16, except as noted.

4). Foreign direct investment in Canada is offset by Canadian direct investment abroad, showing again the power of Canadian finance (line 13).

Second, the reduction in the activities of Canadian financial firms outside North America is evident in

- the significant drop in loans to nonresidents as a percentage of all loans (line 5);
- the declining share of Canadian international bank activity relative to the international activities of banks from other countries (line 6);
- Canada's declining share of global equity market capitalization (line 7);
- the declining proportion of international equities that are issued by Canadians (line 8); and
- the declining percentage of Canadian securities issues placed in countries other than the United States (line 9).

These trends reflect a transformation in the strategic priorities of Canadian banks: foreign activities have become concentrated in the United States, while formerly they were more dispersed globally. This change is evident in the dramatic increases in the U.S. market focus for banks (line 10) and for securities (line 11). This decision to concentrate on U.S. markets rather than markets in other countries can be attributed to a number of factors:

- Canadian banks were burned by the international debt crisis of the 1990s.
- They responded to opportunities available from the more general post-FTA, post-NAFTA expansion of Canadian trade with the United States.
- They took advantage of the booming U.S. financial markets in the 1980s and 1990s.

Third, one of the changes in finance that has accompanied globalization is the expansion of securities-market activity relative to traditional bank lending. In traditional bank lending, deposited funds are intermediated through the bank's corporate structure to borrowers. The cost of the bank bureaucracy is offset by the value added by its capacity to monitor the creditworthiness of borrowers, which permits the bank to take on the risk of lending. As financial information has become a more widely available commodity, the competitive advantage of bank lending has declined relative to more arm's-length securities markets. Securities markets have expanded to include deep markets for short-term (under one-year) securities. These markets are often termed money markets. In securities markets, investors themselves take on the risk of lending in mutual funds or by directly financing borrowers by purchasing their bonds or stocks. Sometimes the shift from bank loans to securities markets is stimulated not by the greater efficiency of the latter but by the greater opportunity for speculation. For household assets this shift is evident in line 12 of table 1.

The speed with which a country's financial firms become involved in these new and profitable transformations in global financial markets can be a sign of their capacity to deal with them. Canadian firms have not kept pace with these changes. This feature is evident not just in the declining Canadian presence in securities markets noted in table 1 (lines 7, 8, 9) but also in the growing deficit in trade in financial services (that is, the services associated with financial transfers, not the transfers themselves, see line 16) and in the loss of position of the Toronto Stock Exchange relative to the New York Stock Exchange (lines 14, 15). In 1997 the top three underwriters of international equity and debt issued by Canadian borrowers were all American: Merrill Lynch, Goldman Sachs, and Salomon Smith Barney (McKinsey 1998, exhibit 3-1). This type of securities market activity is highly concentrated globally. These three investment banks together accounted for 33 percent of the total world-wide $1.8 trillion offerings in securities markets in 1997, and together with the rest of the top ten (none of which are Canadian), they account for 71 percent (McKinsey 1998, exhibit 4-7). The lagging of the biggest Canadian banks' capital relative to their American counterparts (line 17) is a further indication that they may have difficulty keeping up with their competitors in meeting the challenges of the current global marketplace.

The reference to speculation in securities markets highlights an ambiguity associated with the globalization of finance that is even more pronounced with currency markets. On the one hand, a strong national presence in international markets can bring benefits such as competitive opportunities for national financial firms and other national actors, including the state and the industrial firms that use their services. On the other hand, such integration exposes the national economy to dangerous levels of instability from the excessive volatility of global finance.

With regard to currency markets, an important measure of Canada's financial strength is the degree to which the Canadian dollar is used internationally. As Cohen (1998) has argued, a distinctive feature of contemporary global finance is a hierarchy of currencies in which only a select few trade outside their own borders. If a country's currency is used in international transactions, it helps to cushion that country's citizens from some international financial volatility. It can also confer a competitive advantage on national firms. The Canadian dollar plays a small, but increasing and not negligible, role in today's fast-moving markets. In 1998, u.s.$1.49 trillion worth of foreign-exchange trading occurred each day, and the Canadian dollar accounted for 4 percent of that trading, up from 1 percent in 1989 (BIS 1999, tables 2 and 3, 6–7) (on the question of the Canadian dollar, see Helleiner, this volume).

This heavy Canadian-dollar foreign exchange and derivatives trading, along with trading in international securities, accounts for another element of the transformation of the Canadian economy as a result of global finance. It can make Canadians more vulnerable to shocks, pressures, and disruptions from abroad. In the 1990s, the initial excessive drop in the Canadian dollar relative to other industrialized countries resulted from anxiety about the impact of the East Asian financial crisis of 1997 and 1998 on that region's demand for Canadian lumber, grains, and minerals. In a related development, the catastrophic drop in the value of East Asian currencies relative to the value of the Canadian dollar led to a flood of cheap steel that triggered thousands of lay-offs in North American steel firms. Such problems were a major feature of the 1990s, as the global financial system was in crisis or recovering from it through the entire decade.

This type of vulnerability can also lead to pressures on governments' fiscal and social policies. Some of the actions of the federal and provincial governments, including lowering taxes on profits from investments, reducing the intrusiveness of regulation, and introducing cutbacks in social spending may reflect these influences. Many of these types of vulnerabilities are complex and not easily measured by statistics such as those presented in table 1.

In summary, Canadian financial services corporations have remained present in global markets. Their role has been transformed, however, in that their foreign operations have become more concentrated in the United States and their presence in securities markets has not been as strong as the presence of their global competitors. Global financial linkages, including the continued presence of the Canadian dollar in global currency markets, have helped transmit crises in other parts of the globe into the Canadian real economy.

STATE TRANSFORMATION AND DOMESTIC POLICY-MAKING

Political economy theories of the state focusing on its role in the present period of globalization question arguments that posit the decline of the capacity of the nation-state. As Panitch (1997, 84–5) stresses, the premise that capital somehow escapes or overtakes the state is misleading. It overlooks how many of the dimensions of contemporary globalization are authored by states and involve states reorganizing, rather than diminishing, what they do. Accordingly, when it comes to domestic activities of the Canadian state as they bear on global finance, we can expect the transformation of the state's role to proceed in two ways. First, it will act more directly to facilitate the participation of Canadian global financial-services corporations and Canadian market arrangements in the global economy. Second, it will build up its own capacity so that it can better participate in the governance of the global financial economy, meet its commitments to that economy in Canadian territory, and respond to demands from citizens for protection from the negative effects of that economy.

We illustrate the first component of the transformation by looking at three domestic issues: market desegmentation to permit development of the universal-bank model, the "rationalization" of the organization of Canadian stock exchanges, and the creation of a regime to permit bank mergers. The reorganization and strengthening of state regulatory and supervisory capacity through the creation of the Office of the Superintendent of Financial Institutions (OSFI) illustrates well the second component of transformation.

Making Room for Universal Banks

Along with the rapid transformation evident in the explosive growth in the volume, variety, and geographic reach of transactions that has characterized financial markets since the 1960s has come a transformation in the convergence of the organizational structure of individual banks. The universal-bank model that traditionally has been present only in some countries, such as Germany, and not in other countries, such as Canada, has become the dominant form in global finance. "Universal" refers to the ability of the bank to be involved not just in taking in deposits and lending for commercial activities but in other financial activities, including short-term money-market securities, longer-term securities, derivatives, equities and equity-linked instruments like mutual funds, trusts and estates management, currency trading, insurance, and investment advising and portfolio management (Coleman 1996, 21). As noted above with regard to securities, globalization has involved the breakdown of distinctions between such activities. For example, money-market securities can serve as substitutes for short-term loans. Banks that do not have a universal structure have felt that they are at a competitive disadvantage in these new markets.

Beginning with the 1980 Bank Act, the federal government and the provinces moved systematically to create the policy room needed for the development of Canadian universal bank conglomerates by deregulating Canadian financial services markets and rewriting ownership rules. The 1980 legislation opened fully to the banks the mortgage-lending field that had previously been protected for trust and loan companies. Shortly after, the banks began to challenge the policy that prohibited them from engaging in crucial segments of securities markets. The Toronto Dominion Bank set up a discount brokerage service in 1983, while the Bank of Nova Scotia applied to the Quebec Securities Commission to set up a securities subsidiary in 1986. Bending to the pressure, in June 1987 the federal government issued amendments to the Bank Act, and the provincial securities commissions, notably Ontario, amended their own rules. These changes permitted the banks to become full players in the securities markets. The Bank Act was revised further in 1992, with two of the key changes permitting the chartered banks to set up subsidiaries in the trusts and estates management and insurance businesses. Complementary changes took place at the provincial level.

These policy changes led to a dramatic restructuring of the chartered banks into financial services conglomerates. First, they virtually absorbed the long-standing trust and loan companies. Toronto

Dominion took over Central Guaranty Trust in 1992 and merged with Canada Trust in 2000; the Royal Bank took control of Royal Trust in 1993; the Banque Nationale du Canada took control of General Trust in the same year; and the Bank of Nova Scotia took control of Montreal Trust in 1994 and National Trust in 1997. With Canada Trust merging with TD Bank in 2000, the trust-company sector has become virtually insignificant as a separate force within banking services.

In the securities field, the picture is similar. Five of the six major chartered banks acquired one or more of the larger, formerly independent, investment-dealer firms. The Toronto Dominion Bank decided to set up its own in-house securities subsidiary, which it later merged with the American firm Price Waterhouse. Subsequently, the banks took a very strong position in all aspects of securities markets. In 1996, they had 62 percent of treasury-bill auction winnings and 50 percent of Government of Canada bond auction winnings, up from 15 percent and 19 percent respectively in 1987. They accounted for 82 percent of the turnover in the secondary market for treasury bills and for 59 percent in the secondary market for bonds (Freedman 1998, 30). Bank-owned firms had about a 60 percent share of securities underwriting, 55 percent of commission revenue, and 65 percent of fixed income trading in 1997 (Task Force 1998a, 55).

Reinforcing Oligopoly: Bank Mergers

With a stronger base in the Canadian markets and a universal bank structure more appropriate for a fuller role in global markets, the banks sought next to address the issue of their size. As table 1 indicates (line 17), the capitalization of the top-five Canadian banks relative to the top-five U.S. banks (and other major OECD competitors) had been shrinking. Whereas at the start of the 1980s Canada's two largest banks, the Royal and the CIBC, normally were ranked in the top twenty in the world, they barely made the top fifty by the end of the century. Early in 1998, the Royal Bank, the largest Canadian bank, and the Bank of Montreal, the third largest, announced their intention to merge. This announcement spurred a response from their competitors, with the CIBC and TD Bank publicizing their own plans to merge.

These announcements immediately opened the door to a potentially sustained public critique of financial globalization, possibly undermining its legitimacy with Canadians (Tickell 2000). The already highly concentrated financial services sector stood to become a virtual duopoly, with severe consequences for the choice of vendors and the cost of financial services available to Canadians. Under Canadian law, any change in a bank charter requires the approval of the minister of finance. The minister at the time, Paul Martin, demurred and set up a task force to investigate the future of the financial services business in Canada.

After receiving its report (Task Force 1998b), the minister prepared new legislation designed, in part, to undermine any criticism of the building of larger Canadian financial conglomerates and to respond to opponents of the mergers. In legislation passed in 2001 that was consistent with the logic of globalization, the government opened the door to fuller participation of foreign banks in Canadian markets and in ownership of Canadian financial services firms. In doing so, however, it remained adamant that Canadian banks should still be widely held. No one shareholder could control more than 20 percent of a bank's shares. And even here the minister of finance reserved the right to examine the "suitability" of any foreign investor.

Responding to the demands of the credit union movement in Canada outside Quebec, the government also provided the legal infrastructure needed for it to set up its own bank along the lines of the highly successful cooperative Rabobank in the Netherlands, a major global player. It also furnished the credit unions with the means to integrate their activities across provincial boundaries, creating the possibility of their becoming a stronger domestic competitor with the banks. The credit unions had a very successful example to emulate in this regard, the cooperative Mouvement Desjardins in Quebec. The new legislation also provided for a financial services ombudsman to watch over the rights of consumers. Finally, with these steps taken, the government put in place a process that domestic banks could follow if they wished to merge. Bank mergers are thus to take place in a more political context, where the government can claim that it is defending Canadian consumers against the excesses of financial globalization.

Restructuring Canadian Stock Markets

Changes in the organization of Canadian stock markets provide a third example of the transformation of the state's role in the direction of facilitating the participation of Canadian firms in the global financial economy. In this example, the state's role was to permit and to endorse actions taken by the stock exchanges themselves. At issue here was whether Canadian financial services conglomerates would retain organized markets for equities and derivatives as a base for their operations or whether these markets would gradually disappear in competition with other organized markets in major global financial centres. The threat of disappearance was on the horizon. Evidence suggests that within Canada organized markets had become increasingly centred in Toronto. By the late 1990s the trading of senior stock issues had migrated largely to the Toronto Stock Exchange (TSE), with the Montreal Exchange (ME) having at best a 6 percent share of trading, compared to more than a 90 percent share on the TSE (CVMQ 1999, 14). At the same time, Toronto was losing market share to U.S. markets. Although the TSE accounted for 58.6 percent of the total North American value traded in Canadian corporate securities and the Montreal Exchange (ME) for 5.4 percent, 36 percent of the total value was now traded in the United States (TSE 1999, 6). Canada's largest companies were increasingly choosing to list their shares on the New York Stock Exchange and the NASDAQ, while continuing to trade on Canadian exchanges. In March 1999, 241 Canadian-based Toronto Stock Exchange (TSE) listed issues were traded on U.S. markets.

Canadian stock markets were already small on the world stage, accounting for just 2 percent of world stock market capitalization, compared to 48 percent for U.S. markets, 9.4 percent for Japan, and 8.5 percent for the United Kingdom. By the late 1990s, the Canadian industry concluded that it was simply too small to continue to afford interlisting of the same security on several domestic exchanges if it wished to be internationally competitive (CVMQ 1999, 9). On 15 March 1999 the Alberta Stock Exchange (ASE),the ME, the TSE, and the Vancouver Stock Exchange (VSE) announced an agreement in principle to carry out a restructuring program for Canadian equity markets. In a move that was similar to what had taken place in France, Germany, and the United Kingdom in the 1980s, Canada would have one exchange for all senior securities (the TSE), one exchange with jurisdiction over exchange-traded derivative products (the ME), and one exchange for all junior securities (a merged ASE/VSE). Hence, the ME would cease trading in senior securities and the Toronto Futures Exchange would be folded into the new Montreal-based derivatives exchange. After some initial hesitation by Quebec (Coleman 2001), all governments in Canada accepted the changes. Early in 2001, the restructuring continued when the TSE, in turn, purchased the shares of the new junior exchange in Western Canada.

Maintaining Global Commitments
through Building Domestic State Capacity

All markets are institutions whose boundaries and modes of operation are anchored in rules, norms, and the protection of private property rights. Historically, when markets existed within national boundaries, the rules, norms, and rights were set out and enforced by states. Global markets like those in financial services have grown up in the absence of a supranational state setting out the rules and norms and protecting property rights. In its place there have emerged international regimes in banking and securities markets promoting global values and norms (Porter 1993) and outlining commitments states need to make to implement the rules that are necessary for effective functioning of global markets. The building of deep global markets thus requires states to have sufficient capacity for participating in the construction of governance regimes and for ensuring that commitments made in intergovernmental forums are implemented and market disciplines are enforced (Panitch 1997, 93).

On reflection, it is also evident that the demands on state capacity will be higher for global markets than for national ones. The increased anonymity in market relations, the growing complexity of risks, and the vastly increased opportunities for speculative activities demand a more juridified, codified, rules-based approach to regulation (Lütz 2000; Moran 1991). The esoteric politics and cozy personal understandings governing domestic banking and securities markets before the current era of globalization are no longer effective for governance.

The building of regulatory capacity in Canada has taken three forms. First, the size and regulatory scope of the key agency have increased significantly, while its legal mandate has been strengthened. In the late 1970s, regulatory authority was divided at the federal level between the Office of the Inspector General of Banks, which employed thirteen persons in total (Coleman 1996, 218), and the Department of Insurance, which oversaw insurance and trust and loan companies. At the provincial level, small regulatory offices existed for trust and loan companies, insurance firms, and securities firms. In 1987, the federal government passed the Financial Institutions and Deposit Insurance Reform Act, which amalgamated the Office of the Inspector General of Banks and the Department of Insurance, establishing the Office of the Superintendent of Financial Institutions (OSFI). The superintendent assumed responsibility for chartered banks, federally chartered trust and loan companies, insurance companies, investment companies, and cooperative credit associations. As the banks assumed a conglomerate structure with significant securities markets affiliates, these too came within OSFI's purview. The new office was given considerable autonomy and expanded powers, and it quickly increased staff, reaching 390 persons by 2000 (OSFI 2000, 11). It became better equipped to introduce and enforce global rules in Canadian financial space.

Second, consistent with the pattern in other federations, such as the United States and Germany (Deeg and Lütz 2000), regulatory authority has become increasingly centralized in OSFI. With the absorption of the trust and loans sector by the chartered banks, the provinces have gradually moved out of banking regulation or contracted with OSFI to do the work (Coleman 2001).[1] The oversight of securities markets remains a provincial responsibility, but as we have seen above, these markets themselves have centralized. What is more, the dominant position in these markets enjoyed by the chartered banks gives OSFI a powerful oversight position, given its responsibilities for consolidated supervision.

Third, OSFI has devoted ever-increasing amounts of resources to its participation in international governance forums. In the late 1980s, when the first capital accord was agreed on at the Basel Committee on Banking Supervision (BCBS), the agency devoted less than one person-year to such activities. In its submission to the McKay Task Force in 1998, OSFI (1998, 5) reported devoting four person-years to international activity, which involved nine persons. In early 2001, both these figures had more than doubled again in size.[2] Nor do these figures directly convey the leadership roles played by OSFI staff. One deputy superintendent chaired the Executive Committee of the International Association of Insurance Supervisors (IAIS) and then acted as its chairman, while helping it to emerge as a coherent and energetic forum in the late 1990s. Another deputy superintendent chaired the task force at the BCBS responsible for harmonizing accounting standards across the globe. The superintendent has been a member of the Financial Stability Forum (see below) and has chaired the committee investigating the activities of offshore financial centres. These several activities illustrate Canada's integration into governance of global finance and its commitment to implementing global rules in Canadian financial space

STATE TRANSFORMATION
AND GLOBAL GOVERNANCE

As the previous section suggests, the transformation of the Canadian state's role takes two forms. First, it seeks to enhance the opportunities for profitable growth for the Canadian financial sector and for investors, through facilitating their access to global financial markets. In the transnational sphere, the state has focussed here on the liberalization of financial services in the trade regime and the creation of rules for investment such as the Multilateral Agreement on Investment. Second, it participates in the creation of a rules-based global-finance regime with the hope that it will bring sufficient stability so that Canadian firms and citizens are better shielded from global financial crises. It has increasingly been acknowledged by policymakers that these two goals are not necessarily compatible. This incompatibility is evident in the questions raised by Canadian citizens in an increasing number of direct-action protests against globalization.

Facilitating Access: Trade and Investment

States have played a key role in the transformations associated with the globalization of finance by engaging in regional and global trade negotiations aiming at liberalizing capital flows. Canada has played a prominent role in this process. By agreeing to financial services provisions in the Canada-U.S. FTA and thereby establishing a precedent for other trade negotiations, Canada contributed to the U.S.-led effort to include financial services in the Uruguay Round negotiations, which were going on at the time. Canada was an enthusiastic proponent of the Uruguay financial services provisions – not surprisingly, given the potential gains for Canadian banks from greater access to foreign markets. The WTO financial services agreement was reached in 1997, three years after the main Uruguay Round agreement. An important factor in the NAFTA negotiations has been expanded access to the Mexican market for Canadian and U.S. banks. At the time, this opportunity was seen to be lucrative, given Mexico's poorly developed banking system. Prospects dimmed, however, with the peso crisis of 1994. Since then Canadian banks' lending to Mexico has dropped relative to their international lending more generally.

More politically controversial have been Canadian government attempts in regional and global multilateral forums to create strong rules to protect the interests of investors. Although such rules had been promoted for many years on a bilateral basis (DeLuca 1994), the NAFTA agreement on investments moved this process a big step forward. It established for the first time in international law the right of private investors to engage states in a process of binding arbitration over investment disputes. Moreover, it committed Canada and Mexico, also for the first time, to use the World Bank's Centre for the Settlement of Investment Disputes, the preferred venue of the U.S. Investment provisions are to be applied to both direct and portfolio investment (Porter 1997).

The OECD has provided the other key forum for the negotiation of global rules for investment. The Canadian state traditionally has had a "somewhat schizophrenic position" (Paterson 1992, 136). It has wished to maintain some control over inflows of investment, a goal that was most evident in the Foreign Investment Review Act of 1972, while favouring the elimination of such controls in other countries in its international negotiations. In 1985 Canada was the last OECD country to become a party to the OECD's 1961 Code of Liberalization of Capital Movements (139). More recently, and partly as a result of the increased prominence of Canadian investors abroad, Canada has become a more committed proponent of investment rules. This commitment has included supporting the ill-fated negotiations for a Multilateral Agreement on Investment (MAI) at the OECD. The MAI was abandoned after vigorous resistance to it by NGOs in which Canadians were especially prominent.[3]

Admittedly, the Canadian government support for investment rules has been modified as some of their negative consequences have become widely recognized. For example, environmentalists' worst fears about the NAFTA investment provisions seemed to be verified by two controversial NAFTA cases. In the first, U.S.-based Ethyl Corporation claimed that the Canadian government had harmed it by banning the use of its MMT gasoline additive on health grounds. Facing a negative NAFTA panel ruling, the Canadian government reversed its ban and agreed to pay Ethyl $13 million compensation (Morton 1999). In the second, U.S. hazardous waste-processor Metalclad was awarded $U.S.16.7 million damages against a Mexican state government. It had reversed an initial authorization for a hazardous-waste processing facility on environmental grounds. By 2001, when the focus of negotiations on investment rules had shifted to the Free Trade of the Americas initiative, the Canadian government was declaring that a NAFTA-style investor protection process was too oriented towards the interests of investors, at the expense of certain public policy needs of the state. It had intervened to make that point in an appeal of the Metalclad case (Morton 1999; Government of Canada 2001).

Helping to Build Global Governance

One of the most significant recent transformations in global finance has been the strengthening by states of the institutions and rules that will provide a governance framework in global finance. The Canadian state has played a remarkably active role in helping to put these in place. This work has been done at the International Monetary Fund (IMF), the Group of Seven (G7), the Basel Committee on Banking Supervision (BCBS), and the International Association of Insurance Supervisors (IAIS). More recently, it has helped spearhead two organizations that have sought to reinforce further the global governance regime, the Financial Stability Forum (FSF) and the Group of 20 (G20).

The International Monetary Fund (IMF) is one of the most important institutions supporting efforts both to liberalize cross-border financial flows and to stabilize global finance. It has aggressively promoted liberalization of financial systems in developing countries, backed up by using the leverage from its own loans and by the influence of its assessments on private creditors. Such IMF policies have been widely criticized for imposing painful and misguided restructuring on developing countries. They are also seen as promoting the interests of wealthy investors and financial firms from those countries, especially the United States, that dominate the IMF due to its weighted voting scheme based on a country's financial contributions.

Canada's IMF voting share is approximately 3 percent, the eighth largest (Bank of Canada 1996, 43). Countries are organized into voting groups at the IMF, and Canada represents a constituency that includes Ireland and ten Commonwealth Caribbean countries. Canada is thereby guaranteed a position on the IMF's twenty-four-member executive board, which is responsible for the day-to-day operations of the fund, and on the parallel twenty-four-member International Financial and Monetary Committee, the most important policy-making committee. Formal authority rests in the board of governors, which meets annually, with one representative from each member.[4]

In general, Canada has supported the IMF enthusiastically, although it has taken initiatives to address some of the concerns raised by critics. During the Asian crisis, the United States and Britain were eager to press ahead with plans for altering the IMF Articles of Agreement to give it a mandate for promoting the liberalization of capital flows. Canada used its influence in the G7 to help get these plans shelved (Kirton 1999). In his speech to the IMF in the fall of 1998, Canada's finance minister, Paul Martin, emphasized the necessity to pay attention to the needs of the poorest countries and to develop a more specific "roadmap" to capital liberalization. These were hardly radical measures, given the severity of the crisis, but they were a step away from IMF orthodoxy nonetheless. Canada also initiated and promoted the idea of creating provisions for the IMF to authorize governments to halt payments to creditors during currency crises. This would strengthen the hand of states in their efforts to get the private sector to bear more of the costs of such crises. The G7 agreed to support this initiative in its April 2002 meeting, leading Martin to declare that "this is a tremendous Canadian achievement."[5]

These efforts to moderate the IMF's zeal for liberalized capital markets reflect the Canadian government's longer-standing efforts to support sectors within the IMF and the World Bank that are somewhat more attuned to the needs of developing countries. Thus, Canada has been the strongest supporter among the G-7 of the multilateral development banks (MDB), contributing the highest proportion of funds relative to its GDP and ranking third, behind the U.S. and Japan, in absolute contributions. As a result of its high level of contribution Canada is the only country with its own permanent executive directorship at all the MDBS (Culpeper and Clark 1994, 14).

The Group of Seven was created in 1975 in response to the global economic uncertainty that followed the breakdown of the Bretton Woods system. (The Bretton Woods system, which lasted from 1944 to the early 1970s, sought to provide states with autonomy in economic policy by pegging exchange rates and restricting capital mobility and providing for the International Monetary Fund to provide short-term capital when states had balance of payments problems.) In addition to the annual meetings of the G7 leaders, there are more frequent meetings at lower levels, most importantly between the G7 finance ministers and central bank governors. Despite its informal structure, with no permanent secretariat or founding treaty, the G7 plays a leading role in the governance of global finance.

To understand this role, it is important to remember from the previous section of this chapter that Canadian authorities are already very active in the building of an international banking and insurance regime. They participate in the Basel Committee on Banking Supervision (BCBS) and the International Association of Insurance Supervisors, which have become very important in formulating standards and rules for global financial markets. The BCBS has clarified the division of labour between home and host jurisdictions and established standards of regulation that are used as benchmarks in licensing foreign banks. These steps dramatically reduce the ability of banks to avoid regulations by playing one regulator off against another. Like the G7, these groupings operate informally, based on consensus, and they have secretariats provided by the Bank for International Settlements in Basel.

In early 1999, in response to the global financial crises of the previous two years, the G7 created a new organization, the Financial Stability Forum (FSF), which was designed to coordinate the various international regulatory groupings. Compared to previous Basel-based groupings, it was more politicized, both by its links to the G7 (which not only created it but gave G7 countries three representatives each, out of a total membership of thirty-five) and by taking on three controversial issues in its first year: hedge funds, offshore centres, and cross-border capital flows. The weakness of the FSF was its lack of developing-country representation, and it soon became apparent that something else was needed.

The G7's creation, later in 1999, of the G20 was an attempt to respond to this deficiency. The G20 is composed of finance ministers and central bank governors from the G7 and from twelve large non-G7 emerging-market countries, along with high-level representatives from the European Union, the International Monetary Fund, and the World Bank (Porter 2000). For the G20's first two years, the Canadian finance minister, Paul Martin, acted as its chair and the secretariat was headquartered at the offices of the Department of Finance in Ottawa. The G20 is modelled on the G7 in its informal structure, in its attempt to foster a genuine exchange of views, rather than formalized negotiations, among top policymakers, and in its focus on economic matters. Unlike the G7, however, the G20 does not meet at the level of heads of government, and this marks its secondary status relative to the G7.

The creation of a new institution with a mandate to consider key conceptual and policy-framing issues, rather than technical details associated with the implementation of policies, is very significant. The G20 includes powerful developing countries that are hardly G7 stooges, such as China, India, Indonesia, and South Africa. In the press conference following the Montreal meeting of the G20 in 2000, Martin stated that the G20 would broaden its agenda to consider the social dimension of globalization. This "Montreal consensus" will emphasize, for example, global public goods and social safety nets and move beyond the narrow focus on domestic macroeconomic matters associated with the "Washington consensus."[6] Even in the mid-1990s, it would have been hard to imagine that a high-level organization with such an inclusive agenda and membership would be created.

Summary

These several initiatives of the Canadian government at the global level are responses both to citizens' concerns and to powerful financial interests seeking a stable, rules-based global financial system. On the one side, many of the initiatives discussed above have been carried out in forums that are relatively obscure, highly technical, secretive, and inadequately representative. To some degree these undemocratic features are related to the difficulties of devising effective policy processes in the enormously large and complex policy field that exists at the global level. Certainly, these characteristics of the policy process privilege actors, including regulators and financial firms, that are unlikely to reflect the interests of citizens in general.

On the other side, Canadian citizens have been very active in protesting the negative effects of the globalization of finance, and these efforts have drawn a response from the government. As noted above, Canadian NGOs played a leading role in defeating the MAI. Grass-roots enthusiasm for a tax on financial transactions, such as the Tobin tax, led the Canadian government to consider adding it to the agenda of the Halifax G7 summit. The Finance Department and other member states, however, successfully persuaded the government to leave it off (Porter 1996; McQuaig 1998).[7] In 1999 the Canadian House of Commons endorsed a call for the Canadian government to pursue the financial transaction tax idea in international fora (Parliament of Canada 1999). Canadians have participated vociferously in the series of gatherings held to challenge globalization, including the Seattle protests in 2000 against the World Trade Organization, the 2001 Port Alegre meetings in Brazil, and the 2001 Summit of Americas meetings in Quebec City. As in other countries the government has had to respond to such challenges.

CONCLUSION:
PLAYING THE TRANSFORMATION GAME

There have been few transformations in the past quarter century that have been more dramatic than the globalization of finance. At times it has seemed as if states will be sidelined by this on-rush of change. Yet the Canadian state, like others, has not succumbed to this fate. Instead, it has become more adept at playing the transformation game. In supporting initiatives to facilitate linkages between the Canadian and the global financial systems and to strengthen and implement domestically the institutions and agreements that constitute governance in global finance, it has "played along" with dominant trends in a manner consistent with the analyses of Cox (2000) and Panitch (1997). Examples include the strengthened supervision and regulation of global financial services corporations, the opening of the domestic economy to foreign financial corporations, and support for multilateral systems of rules in international trade, in financial services, and in investment. In these respects, the Canadian state is "internationalised," as anticipated by Cox.

The Canadian state has not been passive, however, in playing the transformation game. It has taken some actions perhaps not anticipated by political economy theories of the state under globalization. By promoting the transformation of the already strong Canadian banks into even larger universal banks, the Canadian government has sought to improve their capacity to compete against foreign banks, both in the Canadian domestic market and abroad. Canadian banks have consolidated their control of the Canadian market and moved aggressively into U.S. markets, even if they, along with other Canadian financial firms, have retreated to some degree from markets outside North America, and have lagged in some of the newer types of financial activities. Domestically, the Canadian state has sought resolutely to preserve a Canadian financial centre that also respects regional differences, as the stock exchange reforms show. It initially refused mergers between large banks, whereas all other G7 countries have acquiesced. Instead, it sought to improve protections for consumers and to put in place a process for mergers that would include consumer input. On the international front, it has worked assiduously through the G20 to develop a Montreal Consensus as an antidote to the harder line neoliberal Washington Consensus. Certainly, any theories seeking to conceptualize the role of the state under globalization will need to take such multidimensional state strategies into account.

NOTES

1 Quebec is an exception to this generalization. The particularities of financial services in Quebec and the special place of the Mouvement Desjardins are discussed at some length in Coleman (2001).
2 Confidential interview, OSFI, 21 February 2001.
3 On Canada and the MAI see Smythe (1998).
4 Canada's representative is the minister of finance. On Canada's role in the IMF and the World Bank see Department of Finance (1997).
5 "G7 Backs Canada's Lending Plans," *Globe and Mail,* 22 April 2002, B1. Support was in part due to the interest of G7 governments in reducing the amount of money they have been putting into resolving international financial crises. The original six-point Canadian plan was set out in a speech by Martin to the Commonwealth Business Forum, 29 September 1998, and in his "Statement to the Interim Committee of the IMF," 4 October 1998. These are available at www.fin.gc.ca/newse.
6 October 24 press conference video at www.g20.org.
7 See also the summit documents available at the University of Toronto G8 website.

REFERENCES

Bank of Canada. 1996. "Canada and International Financial Institutions." *Bank of Canada Review* (autumn): 37–61.
Bank for International Settlements (BIS). 1999. "Central Bank Survey of

Foreign Exchange and Derivatives Market Activity in April 1998: Preliminary Global Data." Press release, May 10, available at www.bis.org.

Carroll, William. 1982. "The Canadian Corporate Elite: Financiers or Finance Capitalists?" *Studies in Political Economy* 8: 89–109.

– 1986. *Corporate Power and Canadian Capitalism.* Vancouver: University of British Columbia Press.

Clement, Wallace. 1977. *Continental Corporate Power.* Toronto: McClelland and Stewart.

Cohen, Benjamin J. 1998. *The Geography of Money.* Ithaca, NY: Cornell University Press.

Coleman, W.D. 1996. *Financial Services, Globalization and Domestic Policy Change: A Comparison of North America and the European Union.* Basingstoke, England: Macmillan.

– 2001. "Federalism and Financial Services." In Herman Bakvis and Grace Skogstad, eds., *Federalism at the Millennium.* 178–96. Toronto: Oxford University Press.

Commission des valeurs mobiliéres du Québec (CVMQ) 1999. *Decision: In the Matter of the Restructuring of Canadian Stock Exchanges.* Decision no. 1999-C-0241 (Montreal).

Cox, Robert. 2000. "Political Economy and World Order: Problems of Power and Knowledge at the Turn of the Millennium." In Richard Stubbs and Geoffrey R.D. Underhill, eds., *Political Economy and the Changing Global Order,* 25-37. 2d ed. Toronto: Oxford University Press.

Culpeper, Roy, and Andrew Clark. 1994. *High Stakes and Low Incomes: Canada and the Development Banks.* Ottawa: North-South Institute.

Deeg, Richard, and Susanne Lütz. 2000. "Internationalization and Financial Federalism: The United States and Germany at the Crossroads?" *Comparative Political Studies* 33(3): 374–405.

DeLuca, Dallas. 1994. "Trade-Related Investment Measures: U.S. Efforts to Shape a Pro-Business World Legal System." *Journal of International Affairs,* 48(1): 251–77.

Department of Finance. 1997. *Report on Operations under the Bretton Woods and Related Agreements Act,* 1997. Ottawa: Department of Finance.

Freedman, Charles. 1998. "The Canadian Banking System." Research Report. Ottawa: Bank of Canada.

Gill, Stephen, and David Law. 1993. "Global Hegemony and the Structural Power of Capital." In Stephen Gill, ed., *Gramsci, Historical Materialism, and International Relations,* 93–124. Cambridge: Cambridge University Press.

Government of Canada. 2001. "Canada to Intervene in Review of a NAFTA Tribunal Ruling Regarding an American Firm and Mexico." News Release, 16 February, no. 23, and "Outline of Argument of Intervenor Attorney General of Canada," BC Supreme Court Document, at www.dfait-maeci.gc.ca.

Kirton, John J. 1999. "Canada as a Principal Financial Power: G-7 and IMF diplomacy in the crisis of 1997–99." *International Journal* 54(4): 603–24.

Lütz, Susanne. 2000. "Die politische Architektur von Finanzmarkten." Plenary Lecture to the meeting of the German Political Science Association Congress, Politics in a Borderless World, Halle, 1–5 October.

McKinsey & Company. 1998. *The Changing Landscape for Canadian Financial Services: New Forces, New Competitors, New Choices.* Research Paper prepared for the Task Force on the Future of the Canadian Financial Services Sector. Ottawa.

McQuaig, Linda. 1998. *The Cult of Impotence: Selling the Myth of Powerlessness in the Global Economy.* Toronto: Viking.

Moran, Michael. 1991. *The Politics of the Financial Services Revolution: The USA, UK and Japan.* Basingstoke, England: Macmillan.

Morton, Peter. 1999. "Washington Cool to Rewriting Key NAFTA Clause: Canada Urged Review." *National Post*, 23 January, D9.

Naylor, R.T. 1975. *The History of Canadian Business.* Toronto: Lorimer.

Office of the Superintendent of Financial Institutions (OSFI). 1998. "OSFI's International Participation and Reliance." Submission to the Task Force on the Future of the Canadian Financial Services Sector. 20 February.

– 2000. *Report on Plans and Priorities for the Years 1999–2000 to 2001–2002.* Ottawa: OSFI.

Panitch, Leo 1997. "Rethinking the Role of the State." In James H. Mittelman, ed., *Globalization: Critical Reflections*, 83–113. Boulder, CO: Lynne Rienner.

Parliament of Canada. 1999. "Tax on Financial Transactions." *Hansard* 173, 3 February.

Paterson, Robert K. 1992. "Canadian and International Legal Regimes for Foreign Investment and Trade in Services." In A. Claire Cutler and Mark Zacher, eds., *Canadian Foreign Policy and International Economic Regimes.* 130–52. Vancouver: University of British Columbia Press.

Porter, Tony. 1993. *States, Markets and Regimes in Global Finance.* London: Macmillan.

– 1996. "International Capital Markets: Can They Be Tamed?" *International Journal* 51(4): 669–89.

– 1997. "NAFTA, North American Financial Integration and Regulatory Cooperation in Banking and Securities." In Geoffrey R.D. Underhill, ed., *The New World Order in International Finance*, 174–92. Basingstoke, England: Macmillan.

– 2000. "The G-7, the Financial Stability Forum, the G-20, and the Politics of International Financial Regulation." Paper prepared for the International Studies Association Annual Meeting, Los Angeles, California, 15 March, at www.g7.utoronto.ca/g7/scholar/index.htm.

Smythe, Elizabeth. 1998. "The Multilateral Agreement on Investment: A Charter of Rights for Global Investors or Just Another Agreement?" In Fen

Osler Hampson and Maureen Molot, eds., *Leadership and Dialogue: Canada among Nations 1998*, 239–66. Toronto: Oxford University Press.

Task Force on the Future of the Canadian Financial Services Sector. 1998a. *Competition, Competitiveness and the Public Interest.* Background Paper no. 1 Ottawa: Finance Canada.

– 1998b. *Change, Challenge, Opportunity: Report of the Task Force on the Future of the Canadian Financial Services Sector.* Ottawa: Finance Canada.

Tickell, Adam. 2000. "Global Rhetorics, National Politics: Pursuing Bank Mergers in Canada." *Antipode* 32(2): 152–75.

Toronto Stock Exchange. 1999. "Submission to the Commission des Valeurs Mobilières du Québec." 3 May.

Woods, Ngaire, ed. 2000. *The Political Economy of Globalization.* New York: St Martin's Press.

11 Toward a North American Common Currency?

ERIC HELLEINER

Although the move to free trade in Western Europe has long been accompanied by monetary cooperation, this has not been the case in North America. When the Canada-U.S. Free Trade Agreement (FTA) and the North American Free Trade Agreement (NAFTA) were created, no initiative was taken even to fix exchange rates between the three countries. Beginning in 1999, however, an active and high-level debate broke out about the need for a monetary union in the region. In Canada the issue suddenly received front-page press coverage and became the subject of Senate hearings. It has also been widely debated in Mexico, where President Vicente Fox has advocated the introduction of a North American monetary union (NAMU) in the medium-term future since his election in mid-2000. In the United States, interest in NAMU also exists, although U.S. policymakers seem to see this union taking the form of other countries adopting the U.S. dollar. Indeed, the U.S. Congress began prominent hearings in 1999 on the question of how to encourage foreign countries – particularly those in the Americas – to adopt the U.S. dollar.

Many Canadians have been surprised by the sudden emergence of the high-profile NAMU debate. When the free trade agreement with the United States was introduced in 1989, neither supporters nor opponents predicted that monetary union with the United States would follow. Scholars of Canadian political economy also seem to have been caught off guard. Although they have long studied the politics of North American trade and investment relations, much less attention has been given to the politics of North American monetary relations.¹

In this chapter, I explore the question of why NAMU has suddenly emerged on the political agenda. I highlight how the appearance of the NAMU debate in this age of free trade is in fact reminiscent of the era when Canada last entered into a free trade agreement with the United States, under the Reciprocity Treaty of 1854–66. Then as now, free trade prompted Canadian policymakers to consider closer monetary ties with the United States in order to facilitate cross-border economic transactions and to cope with growing unofficial "dollarization."² I argue, however, that support for NAMU in our era also stems from three transformations that have little to do with free trade: financial globalization, the political goals of the Quebec sovereignty movement, and a new interest in neoliberal approaches to monetary policy. The push for NAMU, in other words, is driven not only by intensified regional integration but also by other political-economic transformations at both the global level and domestic level.

This is not to say that NAMU is a project that will succeed in Canada. A second goal of this chapter is to highlight how Canada's history has been characterized by a high degree of monetary nationalism. Even in the 1850s and 1860s when the enthusiasm for closer monetary links with the United States was at its height, Canadian policymakers rejected monetary union partly on nationalist grounds, despite the popularity of monetary unions elsewhere in the world at the time. In the early years after Confederation, the consolidation of a distinct national currency then became closely tied to nation-building goals of constructing a national market and cultivating a national identity. In some circles at that time, a national currency was also seen in highly nationalist terms as a tool that could be managed actively to serve the macroeconomic needs of the nation. Canadian policymakers were initially wary of this latter idea in the late nineteenth and early twentieth century but came to embrace it with increasing enthusiasm after the mid-1930s. Indeed, in the years after 1945 the desire of Canadian policymakers to pursue activist, domestically oriented monetary management led them to distance Canada much more than most Western countries from a close monetary relationship with the United States. In the conclusion, I address the question of whether this long tradition of monetary nationalism will endure to provide a powerful force blocking efforts to transform Canada's monetary system on a more continental basis.

FREE TRADE AND CLOSER MONETARY
LINKS WITH THE UNITED STATES:
AN EARLIER EPISODE

The Canadian political economy tradition rightly prides itself on its close attention to history. The history of Canada's monetary relations with the United States, however, has not received as much attention as many other topics. It is particularly unfortunate that little attention has been paid to monetary debates at the time of Reciprocity Treaty. The manner in which free trade encouraged closer U.S. monetary links in that era provides an interesting parallel to our own times.

There was, however, one very different circumstance in that earlier era. Today the question is whether to give up the Canadian dollar in favour of a North American monetary union. Then the issue in Canada was whether to create a national currency in the first place. In the early 1850s, the Canadian colonies were formally on local "sterling" standards, but their monetary systems were in fact very heterogeneous.[3] Because the British government refused to produce currency for them, the colonies were forced to rely on a diverse collection of coins and notes issued by foreign governments, private firms, and even local municipalities. As Adam Ainslie, a banker from Galt, noted in 1855: "anything more chaotic than the currency of Canada it is hardly possible to conceive" (Province of Canada 1855, 54).

In 1853, the Province of Canada finally declared its intention to produce its own coin based on a new standard, a decision that was fully implemented five years later. This decision was prompted partly by the arrival of responsible government during the previous decade. Also important was the rapidly expanding economy of the time. As a wider market emerged, the enormous complexities associated with conducting business in the existing monetary system produced growing frustration. An increasingly pervasive and integrated capitalist economy required a modern, territorially homogeneous currency to reduce these "transaction costs." So too did the new modern fiscal system that the government introduced in the 1850s (Piva 1992).

When the case for reform was being made, the issue of Canada's monetary relationship with the United States was immediately raised. In the early 1850s, trade with the United States was expanding rapidly, and the Reciprocity Treaty was about to encourage it further. Growing trade led to increased interest in closer monetary links with the United

States. The relationship of monetary values under the existing "sterling" standard did not correspond easily with those of u.s.-dollar standard. As a result, transactions with the United States were complicated and costly for Canadian merchants.

These complications were compounded by the fact that u.s. coins had become widely used within Canada (although they were not legal tender after 1853) (Shortt 1986, 489–90, 496–7). In contemporary language, unofficial "dollarization" had been a product of closer economic integration. Indeed, many domestic bank notes began to be produced with values listed in both sterling and u.s. dollars. The u.s. dollar was also widely used as a unit of account in the private sector and even sometimes in local government. As one government report from 1855 noted,

[the adoption of the dollar standard] has taken place already in many parts of Canada; merchants keep their books, railways boards transact their business, hotel-keepers and traders make out their bills, in dollars and cents; bankers place their dollar on their notes as a regulating unit; the reciprocity treaty will greatly increase our trade with the United States, and our people are daily becoming more familiar with the [monetary] system in use there. The County Council of Lambton has recently ordered that dollars and cents shall be adopted as the system for keeping the country accounts, levying rates, etc (Province of Canada 1855, 9).

In this context, the government recognized the need to simplify the Canada-u.s. monetary relationship as part of its project of creating a new monetary order. The decision was taken to adopt a decimal-based "dollar" standard that was modeled on and directly equivalent to the u.s. system. The British government and some loyalists opposed this choice, preferring a British-style standard based on the "royal," with shillings and pounds. They had long argued that the creation of a standard similar to the standard of the United States would lead to annexation. But the decision prevailed because of the desire to facilitate trade with the United States and because dollars were already so familiar (Shortt 1964, 126; 1986, 444, 472–8, 486).[4] A survey of Canadian businesses in 1855 revealed that all supported the introduction of the u.s.-based monetary system, whereas under half of those surveyed in the early 1840s had favoured this option (Shortt 1986, 429, 491). In this way, closer economic ties with the United States led the Province of Canada to break with the British sterling standard much earlier than other British colonies.

Although the Province of Canada aligned its monetary standard with the United States, why did it not go further and create a formal monetary union during the period of Reciprocity Treaty? The question is particularly puzzling because monetary unions were all the rage in Europe and elsewhere at this time. By 1865, the Latin Monetary Union (LMU) had been created, involving France, Belgium, Switzerland, and Italy. Sweden, Norway, and Denmark also created the Scandinavian Monetary Union (SMU) in 1873–75. In 1867, a major international conference was even held in Paris to discuss the creation of a worldwide currency union. Although this proposal eventually faltered in the face of British and German opposition, it garnered a remarkable degree of support from governments, businesses, and liberal economic thinkers across the world from Europe to Asia and the Americas (e.g., Helleiner 2002).

The monetary unions being created and discussed in this period were not the kind that we think of today. The distinct national currencies of each country continued to be produced, and no new supranational currency was issued. They simply created a common monetary standard and agreed to let each member's coins circulate in the other members' territories. For the Province of Canada to have joined this kind of monetary union with the U.S. would have been quite simple. Canadian policymakers had already created a standard similar to that of the United States, and U.S. coins were already circulating widely in the country, even if they were not legal tender. Why then not formalize this situation with a "monetary union?"

In fact, Canada chose the opposite course. Instead of encouraging the domestic circulation of U.S. coins, Canadian policymakers became increasingly frustrated by their presence in the 1860s. Indeed, after Confederation in 1867 one of the top priorities of the new federal government was to rid the country of U.S. coins. In 1870–71, the government launched a massive and expensive operation to remove all U.S. currency from domestic circulation. Five million dollars worth of U.S. currency was taken out of circulation at a cost to the government of $118,000 (Weir 1903). At a time when many European countries were moving to encourage the circulation of each other's coins, why did Canada adopt the opposite policy course?

One practical reason was that the U.S. currency had lost its convertibility into gold at the beginning of the Civil War in 1860. This move prompted speculators to export large amounts of U.S. silver coinage to Canada, where the coins had long been accepted at face value (even though the value of their silver content was much less than the face value of the coins). The influx of these silver coins quickly came to be seen as a "silver nuisance" in Canada by merchants and the general public. Since these coins were no longer convertible into gold, Canadian merchants quickly realised the risk of accepting them at face value. In order to minimize their risks, many merchants began to accept the coins only at a discount (e.g., of 20 percent). The uneven use of discounts created considerable confusion and inconvenience for the general public, and the poor suffered particularly, because their wages were often paid in u.s. silver coin (Weir 1903, Shortt 1986, 558; Mercator 1867, 28; Government of Canada 1967, 178, 281; 1870, 869; 1975, 465). In these circumstances, it is easy to see why the idea of a monetary union was not popular and why the Canadian government moved quickly to eliminate u.s. coins from domestic circulation. In Shortt's (1986, 559) words: "Thus did the American Civil War result in the distinct separation of the currencies of the United States and Canada."

At the same time, the expulsion of u.s. coin was also part of the new post-Confederation enthusiasm for nation-building. As one member of Parliament, Thomas Oliver, put it in 1869, "We had heard a good deal lately about adopting a national policy, and was it not humiliating that we should be compelled to carry on the commercial transactions of the country in a depreciated foreign currency? If we were to be a nation, we should have a currency of our own" (Government of Canada 1975, 464).

Interestingly, nationalism had also played a role in undermining support for a monetary union in the 1850s, when Canada's monetary system was first being reformed. In that era, monetary reform was launched by Francis Hincks, who was an "ardent imperialist" and a leading opponent of the idea of annexation with the United States (an idea that had considerable support at the time) (Longley 1943, 441). Although he endorsed the creation of a new decimal-based dollar standard, his reasoning was practical, and he had no sentimental interest in any symbolic ties to the United States that a currency union might bring. Indeed, his main reason for wanting Canada to produce its own coin was "a matter of sentiment connected to national self-respect" (Shortt 1986, 482). By contrast, support for the smu was linked to the prominence of the "pan-Scandinavian" movement at the time, and the lmu also drew strength from the close political ties to France of its members (Helleiner 2002).

It must be noted that the Canadian government did not reject the idea of monetary unions entirely out of hand. Although it showed little enthusiasm for North American monetary union, it did endorse the initiative to create a worldwide universal coin at the 1867 Paris conference. The very first monetary legislation passed after Confederation, which created a unified currency among all the new provinces, included a clause allowing Canada to join the universal currency initiative, provided that the u.s. Congress had also made this decision (Government of Canada 1868, 114–18).

But even in this instance, the Canadian government showed little genuine enthusiasm for monetary union. Instead, policymakers had included the provision as a means to resolve an intense domestic dispute concerning the best way to merge Nova Scotia's monetary standard with that of the rest of Canada. At the time of Confederation, Nova Scotia used a distinct "Halifax" sterling standard that did not equate well with the dollar standard that the Province of Canada had introduced in 1853. Most people agreed that the new country would need a unified standard, but many Nova Scotians wanted the rest of Canada to adopt its standard rather than the other way around. This option held little appeal for policymakers in the rest of Canada, since they were now committed to their dollar standard and liked the fact that it facilitated commerce with the United States. But because Confederation was already very controversial in Nova Scotia, politicians in the rest of Canada did not want to press the issue too vigorously.

The universal currency proposal put forward in Paris in 1867 provided a way to avoid a divisive debate. If it was endorsed by the United States, that country would be adjusting its monetary standard in a way that fit well with Nova Scotia's standard. In that event, the rest of Canada would be happy to defer to Nova Scotian preferences. But if the United States refused, the rest of Canada insisted that Nova Scotia give up its distinct standard (Shortt 1986, 610; Government of Canada 1967, 358, 397–401, 411; 1975, 229–230; 1870, 447; 1871, 259–62, 303). The endorsement of the universal coin proposal thus did not stem from any great enthusiasm for currency unions but rather from the desire of government to be, in the words of the Finance Minister John Rose: "relieved from the embarrassment of making a choice between the courses" (Government of Canada 1967, 358).

THE STRENGTHENING OF MONETARY NATIONALISM

After this debate, very little was heard again about Canada's participation in monetary unions (until very recently!). In the 1870s, focus shifted instead to the task of consolidating Canada's domestic monetary system. When the u.s. Congress refused to endorse the universal coin proposal, Nova Scotia's distinctive monetary standard was assimilated with that of the rest of Canada in 1871. Old heterogeneous coins were replaced with new standardized Canadian ones, and the new federal government gained exclusive rights to issue the one-dollar and two-dollar notes that dominated note circulation (private banks retained the right to issue higher denomination notes until the Bank of Canada's creation in 1934).

These efforts to consolidate a territorially standardized and exclusive national currency were paralleled in many other countries at this time. Driving these initiatives in Canada and elsewhere was the idea that this monetary reform was a key part of building modern nation-states. In some countries, the desire to maximize seigniorage revenue for the state was an important motivation.[5] This goal was less prominent in Canada, although it had played a minor role in encouraging policymakers to expel u.s. coin in 1870–71 (Shortt 1986, 559; Weir 1903, 160). More important in the Canadian case was the goal of building an integrated national market. A single, homogeneous currency across the whole Canadian territory would dramatically reduce transaction costs for merchants as well as for the government (Helleiner 1999). Policymakers also saw the monetary reforms as supporting their efforts to cultivate a new sense of national collective identity. The new Dominion notes, for example, were decorated with key personalities from the nation's history (e.g., Wolfe, Montcalm, Cartier), an image of railways, and even an allegorical figure pointing to Canada's location on a globe (Gilbert 1998, 1999). Some politicians also argued that the experience of using a common currency would "make the people of the Dominion feel more like one people" (Mr Magill, in Government of Canada 1871, 304).

Initially, this inward-looking focus on domestic monetary consolidation and nation-building did not translate into any desire to lessen the close monetary relationship with the United States. Although the Reciprocity Treaty had ended in 1866, policymakers remained strongly committed to a fixed exchange with the u.s. dollar throughout the 1870s. As Hincks (who had once again become finance minister) put it in 1870, "we were too small a people to hope to have a Currency differing from other nations. It was especially necessary to assimilate the Currency with that of the United States" (Government of Canada 1870, 1350).[6]

By the late 1870s, however, a stronger form of economic nationalism was gaining support in Canada. In 1879 the government launched the National Policy, which introduced a high tariff designed to protect Canadian-based industry from foreign competition. Some nationalists also called at the time for this move to be reinforced by ending the convertibility of Canada's currency into gold. This latter group has received less attention in academic literature, but their views are worth outlining briefly (see Shortt 1986, 554, 708–12). Their leader was Isaac Buchanan, a very prominent Ontario industrialist and politician, who created the National Currency League to press his case for an inconvertible currency.[7] Buchanan's goal was partly to discourage foreign trade but also to allow the government to pursue a more activist monetary policy designed to maximize industrial growth.

Buchanan and the league drew inspiration from the issue of inconvertible greenbacks by the u.s. government during the Civil War, and they demanded an equivalent currency in Canada, which some called "beaverbacks." As one supporter noted, however, "there is a difference between the Canadian beaverbacker and the United States greenbacker. The greenback was issued truly for the preservation of the nation in a war which destroyed much property, while the beaverback would be issued to assist in developing the wealth and resources of Canada" (quoted in Wright 1885, 23). Buchanan (1879) made a similar case:

Canada is possessed of untold wealth in the wonderful energy of her population and in the boundless resources of her soil and forests and minerals, which only want the institution of full patriotic money to develop them ... [money] should be something capable of being expanded permanently to the extent which the wisdom of Parliament sees to be required for the full employment of the people and the development of the productive resources of the country.

Another supporter also highlighted the costs of remaining on gold in the following way: "Let those who do a foreign trade transact their own business; it is not for the mass of people to be inconvenienced – nay, impoverished, and peradventure, ruined – because the foreign liabilities of a mere fraction of the population have to be discharged in a costly metal. To an agricultural community the hard-money basis is a positive injustice" (Davis 1867, 11).

Buchanan (1880) cast his monetary proposals in highly nationalist terms. The gold standard, he argued, was "disloyal" and "unpatriotic" (not to mention "unchristian"). As he put it, "money should be a thing of, or belonging to Canada only, not of or belonging to the world." Some of Buchanan's supporters explained this argument in more detail. Here, for example, is the case made by Mr Wallace to the House of Commons in April 1882 in favour of an inconvertible currency:

If a man has $1000 in paper money, the value of which exists only in the country of its creation, while it may not be worth ten cents outside that country, he has an incentive to support its institutions, in addition to his patriotism, because he knows if the country goes down his money will be valueless. But the man with a $1000 of gold in the bank, which he knows will be taken in any part of the world, can readily withdraw it and leave his country if it should get into difficulty; he is not obliged to fight its battles." (Mr Wallace, quoted in O'Hanly 1882, 12)

With the economic depression in the late 1870s, the National Currency League attracted considerable support, especially "among the masses," but its proposals "antagonized the whole banking and financial world" (Shortt 1986, 712). Although Canadian businesses could gain from the new national tariff, abandoning the gold standard was more threatening to their economic interests, and it raised the prospect of inflation. In the end, the league's only achievement was that it encouraged the government in 1880 to extend the state monopoly of money to five-dollar notes and to reduce the required specie reserve backing for banknotes (715).

It was not until the 1930s that Buchanan's goals would begin to be realised. Although Canada did float its currency between 1914 and 1926, the cause was the war rather than a commitment to the kind of monetary activism Buchanan had proposed. When Canada again left the gold standard in 1931, it was also initially only following the lead of Britain and many other countries, all of whom were responding to the international financial crisis of the period. Within a few years, however, support for more activist monetary management aimed at reducing unemployment had grown considerably, and it played a role in prompting the creation of the Bank of Canada with a monopoly note issue in 1934. The bank was in fact created by Prime Minister Bennett, whose Conservative government had little interest in monetary activism. But he was prompted to endorse a central bank partly as a way of deflecting criticism of his inaction in addressing economic problems during the Depression (Stokes 1939, chaps. 3–4; Plumptre 1940, 162). The central bank was soon nationalized in 1936, when a Liberal government came to power that was committed to more activist monetary management.

Like Buchanan, those who supported active monetary management in the 1930s also often endorsed a floating exchange rate on the grounds that it would insulate domestic monetary priorities from an external constraint. This insulation was deemed particularly important for a country such as Canada, whose balance of payments fluctuated enormously in response to harvest conditions, commodity prices, and international capital flows (Plumptre [1932] 1964). This kind of thinking was increasingly influential in Canada during the 1930s.

While other British Dominions – such as New Zealand, Australia, and South Africa – stabilized their exchange rates after the early 1930s, Canadian policymakers allowed the exchange rate to continue to float relatively freely throughout the 1930s.

There was also a particular desire in this period to obtain a degree of monetary independence from the United States. This was true even of Bennett, who worried that New York bankers were controlling the value of the Canadian dollar, because the settlement of international balances between Canada and London was done through New York (Stokes 1939, 65; Plumptre 1940, 170). He hoped that by centralizing the gold and foreign exchange reserves of the country and by forcing private banks to hold reserves at the central bank, the central bank could regain some control of the exchange rate. Others also worried about the large influence of New York financial markets on the Canadian domestic monetary conditions. At the time, there was no domestic money market to speak of in Canada. As a result, interest rates were highly influenced by conditions in New York markets, and the new central bank was unable to exert much immediate influence over domestic monetary conditions through open market operations or discount rate changes. Analysts hoped that a floating exchange and the creation of the new central bank might finally encourage banks to keep liquid funds in Canada and thus build up a local money market independent of New York (Plumptre 1940).

The new commitment in Canada to monetary autonomy persisted into the post-1945 period. Indeed, Canada's external monetary policies were quite unique in the Western world during the period of the Bretton Woods system. While Western countries fixed their currencies to the u.s. dollar after the war, Canada remained an anomaly. Between 1950 and 1962 it was the only major country to float its currency. It then became the first Western country to move to a floating exchange rate again in 1970 and the only one not to accept the new (ultimately temporary) fixed rates agreed to in 1971 (Webb 1992).

Why did Canada break monetarily with the United States in such dramatic and unique ways throughout the early postwar years? Like Buchanan, Canadian policymakers in this period were driven by the goal of maintaining a degree of autonomy in domestic monetary policy-making. This cannot explain Canada's uniqueness, however, because most other Western governments shared the same goal. What distinguished Canada from other countries was the absence of controls on cross-border flows of financial capital. In other countries, the use of such capital controls became widespread in the postwar years and they provided the monetary insulation that Canadian policymakers sought. The Canadian government did introduce tight capital controls between 1939 and 1951, but it was wary of maintaining them by the early 1950s, particularly given its desire to attract U.S. investment. In 1951 the Canadian government abandoned capital controls and chose to rely instead on a floating exchange rate to provide monetary autonomy (Plumptre 1977, 149). The Canadian government's "monetary nationalism," in other words, was driven by the fact that it was unwilling to break Canada's financial links with the United States in the same way that other countries did in this period.

WHY THE DISCUSSION OF MONETARY UNION NOW?

Given the postwar history, it seems surprising that Canada would suddenly be engaged in a debate about monetary union with the United States. It has been, after all, the Western country that was least interested in preserving even a fixed exchange rate with the United States throughout most of the postwar period. To go from that position of monetary nationalism straight into a serious debate about monetary union is quite a leap. What explains the sudden interest in NAMU?

The most obvious answer would seem to be that the FTA and NAFTA have generated this interest. As we have seen, the last time Canada was involved in a free trade arrangement with the United States the issue of creating closer monetary links with that country also arose prominently. Two reasons were prominent then, and they have also emerged again today. First, in the mid–nineteenth century, growing economic integration with the United States encouraged widespread unofficial "dollarization." Interestingly, proponents of monetary union today suggest that a similar phenomenon is underway at the moment. They argue that before dollarization proceeds further, it would be better for Canada to push for the creation of a new North American common currency over which Canada had some control. This argument can easily be overstated in the current context. I have not yet seen comprehensive evidence demonstrating that dollarization is dramatically increasing in Canada today and it would be surprising if this was the case. In the mid–nineteenth century, dollarization was dramatic and extensive because the domestic monetary system was already chaotic. Today, Canada already has a standardized currency, and it would be much more difficult to dislodge its use in a major way given the many "network externalities" that reinforce the continued use of existing currencies.[8]

During the period of free trade in the mid–nineteenth century, the demand for closer monetary links with the United States also reflected a desire to facilitate cross-border trade by reducing international transaction costs. This desire was particularly strong among the business class involved in U.S.-Canada trade, and they provided key political support for the introduction of the decimal-based dollar standard in 1853. These businesses were most concerned with reducing transaction costs associated with exchanging national currencies and comparing prices between the two distinct currency zones.

In today's context, supporters of NAMU also argue that U.S.-Canada trade would be fostered by a reduction of these kinds of international transaction costs (Courchene and Harris 1999). But interestingly, it is less clear that the business class shares their concern. To be sure, free trade has encouraged businesses in Canada to become much more involved in cross-border trade with the United States. But there is not much evidence that they have become much more concerned about currency-related international transaction costs associated with trade between the two countries. When the Business Council on National Issues surveyed its members about their views on NAMU, for example, it found that most businesses opposed the idea (Wallace 1999, 18).[9] One source of opposition is the fact that the low Canadian dollar benefits certain parts of the business community, especially exporters. But a key reason for the longstanding disinterest in fixed exchange rates or currency union may be that so much of U.S.-Canada trade is intrafirm trade, consisting primarily of bookkeeping entries within a firm's overall accounting (Clarkson 2000).

Although microeconomic concerns about transaction costs do not appear to be driving political interest in NAMU, policymaking elites have become more concerned about the macroeconomic effects of exchange rate volatility. Their concern has been generated less by freer trade with the United States than by the dramatic growth of global financial flows. In today's atmosphere of high international capital mobility, countries with floating exchange rates have often experienced significant short-term exchange rate misalignments that have been quite costly for open economies in a macroeconomic sense. Governments have also found it increasingly difficult to maintain a credible fixed exchange rate or even a well-managed floating rate. Indeed, it is no coincidence that interest in currency unions everywhere around the world has accelerated in the wake of dramatic international currency crises during the 1990s (Helleiner 2002). In this new context, some Canadian policymakers have become convinced of the need to abandon floating exchange rates and to create an irrevocably fixed exchange rate through a currency union (e.g., Courchene and Harris 1999). Once again, however, what is interesting about this concern about exchange rate volatility is that it is responding more to the rapid growth of global finance than to the establishment of North American free trade.

Two other key explanations for the new interest in NAMU are also not directly linked to free trade. The first concerns the role of the Quebec sovereignty movement. Some of the most prominent support-ers of NAMU in Canada are Quebec sovereigntists who see it as a way of easing the path to Quebec independence. In both the 1980 and 1995 referenda on Quebec's political future, Quebec sovereigntists found themselves on the defensive on the question of the monetary future of Quebec. Many people in the province were nervous about the risk of massive capital flight and monetary instability if Quebec were to vote for independence. To counter this fear, sovereigntists insisted in both referenda that an independent Quebec would retain the Canadian dollar; indeed, in the 1995 referendum, Canada's one-dollar coin was featured as the *O* in the *Oui* signs (at least the side showing the loon, not the Queen). But this prediction was questioned constantly by fed-eralists, often with considerable success.[10] If Canada were to join a North American monetary union, many sovereigntists believe that Quebec sovereignty would be perceived to be a less risky option from a monetary point of view.

The support of Quebec sovereigntists for a North American cur-rency seems unusual when viewed in the context of most other nation-alist movements around the world in the nineteenth and twentieth centuries. Most nationalists have traditionally believed that their country must have its own national currency; the currency is in fact seen as one of the central symbols of the sovereignty of a nation-state. This sentiment did find more support in the Quebec sovereigntist movement back in the 1970s and 1980s. Today, however, in defending their support for NAMU, Quebec sovereigntists argue that the relation-ship between sovereignty and currencies has become more compli-cated. Sometimes the example of the European Union is cited in this respect. Another common argument is that global financial markets have already rendered monetary sovereignty a hollow shell. As one Bloc Quebecois member put it, a common currency is needed to counteract "unscrupulous speculators who destroy national curren-cies, thus threatening the countries' economic future and job creation efforts" (Yvan Loubier, in *House of Commons Debates*, 15 March 1999).[11]

Interest in NAMU in Quebec and elsewhere in Canada has also been driven by growing disillusionment among economists with the kinds of activist national monetary policies that became popular in the Keyne-sian age. This sentiment has emerged partly out of the experiences of inflation and partly from the rational expectations revolution in the discipline of economics over the last two decades. The latter undermined a key idea that had sustained support for activist monetary policies: the Keynesian notion that there was a long-term trade-off between inflation and unemployment. By highlighting how experiences of inflation over time may encourage people to adjust their expectations, this new economic analysis suggested that activist monetary management would simply produce stagflation. To break inflationary expectations, it argued, authorities would have to reestablish their credibility and reputation for producing stable money by a strong commitment to price stability. The perceived need for this kind of credibility and reputation has also been reinforced by the disciplining power of international capital markets (e.g., Andrews and Willett 1997).

This neoliberal monetary thinking has played an important role in encouraging alternatives to national currencies to be considered in many parts of the world. By eliminating a key macroeconomic rationale for wanting a national currency in the first place, it has made policymakers less resistant to the idea of giving these monetary structures up. In Europe, for example, the shift from Keynesian to neoliberal monetary ideas was a key precondition for the move to monetary union. Indeed, many policymakers saw currency union as a better way to achieve price stability than maintaining a national currency, because the union appeared to allow them to "import" the Bundesbank's antiinflationary monetary policy. Others also saw the EMU as a way to prevent national policymakers from pursuing "outdated" Keynesian macroeconomic policies (Gill 1998; McNamara 1998).

Many advocates of NAMU subscribe to the new monetary orthodoxy and argue that there is little to be lost in a macroeconomic sense from the abandonment of a national currency. Many also go further to argue that NAMU is a way of disciplining government policy in the macroeconomic realm. By eliminating the national currency, they can ensure that no future Canadian government can pursue the kind of activist monetary policies that became popular during and after the 1930s. As one of the more prominent advocates of a common currency, Herb Grubel, told the Canadian Senate: "I would like to have an institution that protects me against the future, when another generation of economists is rediscovering Keynesianism, or whatever threats there might be in the future" (Government of Canada 1999, 35).

The disillusionment with activist monetary policies has also often extended to the use of the exchange rate to foster macroeconomic adjustments. Many economists still defend the use of floating exchanges as a tool to foster macroeconomic adjustments in a context where wages and prices are slow to adjust or as a mechanism providing some autonomy to national policymakers who pursue price stability. But others have questioned whether exchange rate adjustments have any lasting effect on the real economy. A devaluation, they argue, may simply produce inflation if domestic citizens anticipate and react to its consequences. Its long-term impact may simply be to delay what they see as inevitable and necessary microeconomic adjustments. This view has provided a further reason for some economists and policymakers to support currency unions today. In Europe advocates of the euro have argued that it will bring "increased labour market discipline," since devaluations can no longer be used temporarily to offset higher wage demands from workers (European Commission 1990, 47). Similarly, in Canada NAMU supporters argue that the elimination of the devaluation option will have the effect of forcing manufacturers to bolster productivity or workers to moderate wage demands (e.g., Courchene and Harris 1999).

In sum, what explains the new interest within Canada in closer monetary links with the United States? The most obvious answer is that the free trade agreement has fostered this new interest, just as it did in the mid–nineteenth century. In fact, however, this explanation is not fully convincing. To be sure, the concerns about dollarization and international transaction costs that were present in the mid–nineteenth century have been raised again. But equally significant today, if not more so, are three other factors that are unconnected to free trade: financial globalization, the emergence of the Quebec sovereignty movement, and a new interest in neoliberal approaches to monetary policy.

CONCLUSION: WHAT FUTURE FOR CANADA'S NATIONAL CURRENCY?

Does this mean that Canada's national currency is about to be abandoned in favour of a common North American currency? From the history presented in this chapter, one would expect that resistance to this political project will be considerable. As I have highlighted, Canada has a long history of strong monetary nationalism. Even as far back as the first decision of the Province of Canada in 1853 to produce its own coin, the national currency has been seen not just as an economic instrument but also as a tool to serve nationalist political objectives. In the nineteenth century, these objectives included the creation of an integrated national market and the strengthening of a national identity. Increasingly important in the twentieth century also became the goal – initially put forward by Buchanan in the nineteenth century – of achieving some national autonomy to pursue domestically oriented macroeconomic policies. These nationalist objectives have ensured that the issue of North American monetary union has been largely absent from the country's political agenda and even that Canada has in fact distanced itself monetarily from the United States to a degree that was unusual in the Western world during the post-1945 years.

How strong does this monetary nationalism remain in the current era? There is some evidence that it is waning. In late 1999, a Maclean's/CBC opinion poll found that Canadians remain generally quite nationalist but are in fact almost evenly split on the question of whether Canada would benefit (44 percent) or lose out (42 percent) from having a common currency with the United States (in Quebec, support was considerably higher for a common currency). One Maclean's reporter explained this sentiment in the following way: "No doubt much of it [the considerable support for NAMU] stems from the weakened state of the Canadian dollar and a sense that Canadians are falling behind their American neighbours in material terms" (Laver 1999, 42). This explanation may indeed be accurate,[12] but this sentiment is an odd one, since it implies that abandoning the national currency would somehow raise the standard of living of Canadians. As critics of NAMU point out, this is a very controversial proposition on economic grounds.

Indeed, more generally, Canadian critics of the idea of NAMU strongly challenge the neoliberal argument that activist national monetary policies are misguided. Interestingly, such challenges today come not just from those following a Keynesian tradition of monetary thought. They also come from some neoliberals, as well as from officials in the Bank of Canada who have strongly opposed NAMU on the grounds that an independent currency is a crucial tool for national macroeconomic management. The Bank of Canada's position is particularly interesting. It may no longer defend the Keynesian ideas that were powerful in the early years after its creation, but it remains an important institution within the Canadian polity that is committed to national monetary policy autonomy.

In addition to economic arguments, the political battle over NAMU is inevitably linked to a debate over the Canada's national identity. We have seen how the push in Europe to abandon national currencies has often generated deep nationalist reaction, on the grounds that the move will undermine national identities. This reaction has encouraged some EU countries, such as the United Kingdom, Denmark, and Sweden, not to participate in the monetary union initiative. Supporters of NAMU worry about the same nationalist reaction emerging in Canada, and some have attempted to deflect the criticism by stressing that Canada could still retain nationalist images on one side of the new common coins and notes (e.g., Courchene and Harris 1999, 22). But the link between national currencies and national identities in history has gone far beyond the imagery on money. The issuing of a currency has long been seen as a symbol of sovereignty. By reducing transaction costs within a nation, national currencies have also often been seen as playing a role similar to that of a national language: they may create a sense of national collectivity by facilitating "communication" among members of the nation. As a tool of national macroeconomic management, national currencies have been seen as fostering national identities by providing an expression of national purpose. National currencies also create collective monetary experiences among citizens of the nation, experiences that may foster national identities. Finally, because trust plays such a large role in the use and acceptance of modern forms of money, national currencies have often been seen as encouraging identification with the nation-state at a deeper psychological level (Helleiner 1998).

The links between the national currency and national identity in the Canadian context have not yet been discussed widely in the NAMU debate. Economists have dominated the debate on NAMU, and they usually restrict their analyses of national currencies primarily to their economic purposes. This dominance is unfortunate, because currencies serve not just economic purposes but also many political ones, including, as we have seen, those linked to nation-building. Scholars working in the Canadian political economy tradition may have a central role to play in widening the terms of the NAMU debate beyond a narrow economic focus. The future of Canada's national currency is, after all, a central one for the future of the Canadian political economy.

NOTES

I am very grateful to the Social Sciences and Humanities Research Council of Canada for helping to fund research for this paper, as well as to Stephen Clarkson, Wallace Clement, Christine Gabriel, and Leah Vosko for their helpful comments.

1 There are some important exceptions. Clarkson (2000) has provided an excellent overview of the NAMU debate in the context of European monetary union. Cameron (1986), Webb (1992), and Williams (1994) each provide interesting analyses of different aspects of Canadian international monetary policy in the post–1945 period.

2 I use the term "dollarization" to refer to a situation in which the U.S. dollar is increasingly used as a monetary instrument within the Canadian monetary system alongside the national currency.

3 For a more detailed history of the material in this section of the paper, see Helleiner (1999).

4 Canadian policymakers were also aware that Canadian banks benefited enormously from the fact that they denominated their notes in dollars, because their notes would circulate widely in the U.S., providing a good source of profit (Shortt 1986, 428, 515, 553).

5 "Seigniorage" is a term used to describe the difference between the nominal value of money and its cost of production.

6 By "assimilate," he meant simply to make Canada's monetary standard match that of the United States.

7 Ironically, Buchanan was one of the largest importers in Canada in the period (Weir 1903).

8 For a discussion of the importance of "network externalities" in the use of currencies, see Cohen (1998).

9 There is also not a great deal of evidence that European businesses have been a major promoter of EMU because of concerns about international transaction costs, even though they are dealing with a very large number of national currencies (McNamara 1998, 37–41). In Europe the concerns about transaction costs have in fact been much more prominent in the public sector. Since the 1960s European governments have been deeply concerned about how exchange-rate volatility can disrupt the smooth functioning of the EU-wide Common Agricultural Policy (98–104). These fears provide a key explanation for Europe's strong preference for fixed exchange rates stemming back to the 1960s. In North America, no such supranational fiscal structures exist to generate the same concern.

10 It is well known that Robert Bourassa, for example, explained his own decision to remain a federalist primarily on the grounds that sovereigntists were wrong to argue that monetary union could work between Canada and an independent Quebec. For it to work in Quebec's interests, a monetary union would require political union, he argued (e.g., Bourassa 1980).

11 Lévesque (1979, 86) also made this argument in the late 1970s when defending his argument that Quebec did not need a national currency upon achieving independence.

12 Historically, nationalist identifications with a national currency in many countries have often been positively correlated with that currency's strength (Helleiner 1998).

REFERENCES

Andrews, David, and Thomas Willett. 1998. "Financial Interdependence and the State." *International Organization* 51(3): 479–511.

Bourassa, Robert. 1980. *L'unité monétaire et l'unité politique sont indissociable.* Montreal: Parti Libéral du Quebec

Buchanan, Isaac. 1879. *Proposal of a National Currency Reform League for Canada,* 28 October. Canada NA, MG 24 D14, v.108, file 070979.

– 1880. *Nothing Could Be More Practically Disloyal, Unpatriotic, and UnChristian than the Hard Money Legislation of England.* January. Canada NA, MG 24, D14, v.108, 070994.

Cameron, Duncan. 1986. "Monetary Relations in North America." *International Journal* 42: 170–98.

Clarkson, Stephen. 2000. "The Joy of Flux: What Europe May Learn from North America's Preference for National Currency Sovereignty." In C. Crouch, ed., *After the Euro.* Oxford: Oxford University Press.

Cohen, Benjamin. 1998. *The Geography of Money.* Ithaca, NY: Cornell University Press.

Courchene, Thomas, and Richard Harris. 1999. *From Fixing to Monetary Union: Options for North American Currency Integration.* Toronto: C.D. Howe Institute.

Davis, Robert. 1867. *The Currency: What It Is and What It Should Be.* Ottawa: Hunter, Rose.

European Commission. 1990. "One Market, One Money." *European Economy* 44.

Gilbert, Emily. 1998. "'Ornamenting the Façade of Hell': Iconographies of Nineteenth-Century Canadian Paper Money." *Environment and Planning D: Society and Space* 16: 57–80.

– 1999. "Forging a National Currency: Money, State Building and Nation Building in Canada." In E. Gilbert and E. Helleiner, eds., *Nation-States and Money.* London: Routledge.

Gill, Stephen. 1998. "European Governance and New Constitutionalism: Economic and Monetary Union and Alternatives to Disciplinary Neoliberalism in Europe." *New Political Economy* 3(1): 5–27.

Government of Canada. 1868. "An Act Respecting Currency." *Statutes of Canada,* 1868, 114–18.

– 1870. *Parliamentary Debates,* Dominion of Canada, 1st Parliament, 3d Session. Ottawa: Ottawa Times.

- 1871. *Parliamentary Debates*. Dominion of Canada, 1st Parliament, 4th Session. Ottawa: Ottawa Times.
- 1967. *House of Commons Debates*, 1st session, 1st Parliament. Ottawa: Government of Canada.
- 1975. *House of Commons Debates*, 2d session, 1st Parliament. Ottawa: Information Canada.
- 1999. *Proceedings of the Standing Senate Committee on Banking, Trade and Commerce, Issue 48 – Evidence*, 25 March.
Helleiner, Eric. 1998. "National Currencies and National Identities" *American Behavioral Scientist* 41(10): 1409–36.
- 1999. "Historicizing National Currencies: Monetary Space and the Nation-State in North America." *Political Geography* 18: 309–39.
- 2002. *The Making of National Money*. Ithaca, NY: Cornell University Press.
Laver, Ross. 1999. "The Need to Take Risks." *Maclean's*, 20 December.
Lévesque, René. 1979. *My Quebec*. Toronto: Methuen.
Longley, Ronald Stewart. 1943. *Sir Francis Hincks*. Toronto: University of Toronto Press.
McNamara, Kathleen. 1998. *The Currency of Ideas*. Ithaca, NY: Cornell University Press.
Mercator. 1867. *A Letter to the President of the Montreal Board of Trade on the Silver Question*. Montreal: John Lovell.
O'Hanly, John. 1882. *On Money and Other Trade Questions: Being a Review of Mr Wallace's Speech on an Inconvertible Currency*. Ottawa: C.W. Mitchell.
Piva, Michael. 1992. "Government Finance and the Development of the Canadian State." In Allan Greer and Ian Radforth, eds., *Colonial Leviathan: State Formation in Mid–Nineteenth-Century Canada*. Toronto: University of Toronto Press.
Plumptre, A.F.W. 1940. *Central Banking in the British Dominions*. Toronto: University of Toronto Press.
- [1932] 1964. "Currency Management in Canada." In E.P. Neufeld, ed., *Money and Banking in Canada*. Toronto: McClelland and Stewart.
- 1977. *Three Decades of Decision: Canada and the World Monetary System, 1944–75*. Toronto: McClelland and Stewart.
Province of Canada. Legislative Assembly. 1855. *A Decimal Currency – Weight and Measures*, third and fourth Reports of the Standing Committee on Public Accounts. Quebec: Lovell and Lamoureux.
Shortt, Adam. 1964. "History of Canadian Metallic Currency." In E.P. Neufeld, ed., *Money and Banking in Canada*. Toronto: McClelland and Stewart.
- 1986. *History of Canadian Currency and Banking, 1600–1880*. Toronto: Canadian Bankers Association.
Stokes, Milton. 1939. *The Bank of Canada*. Toronto: MacMillan.
Wallace, Bruce. 1999. "Say It Ain't So" *Maclean's*, 5 July, 14–18.

Webb, Michael. 1992. "Canada and the International Monetary Regime." In A.C. Cutler and M. Zacher, eds., *Canadian Foreign Policy and International Economic Regimes*. Vancouver: University of British Columbia Press.

Weir, William. 1903. *Sixty Years in Canada*. Montreal: John Lovell and Son.

Williams, Glen. 1994. *Not for Export*. 3d ed. Toronto: McClelland and Stewart.

Wright, M. 1885. *The "Torpedo," or Ten Minutes on the National Currency Question, "Beaverbacks."* St Catharines, ON: E.J. Leavenworth.

12 The Transformation of Communication in Canada

VINCENT MOSCO

INTRODUCTION: MILLENNIUM MERGERS

The new millennium brought fresh evidence of transformation in the communication industry. It began with the January 2000 announcement that America Online (AOL) would take over Time-Warner in the largest media merger in history. The announcement rocked the industry, because it brought together the world's largest Internet service provider with the world's largest holder of intellectual property. At that time AOL served twenty-six million internet subscribers in the United States alone, and Time-Warner had a major stake in just about every sector of the media industry, including *Time* and *People* magazines, Warner books, records, and films, Time-Warner cable, the second largest cable company in the United Sates, and Turner Broadcasting, including the CNN network.

It did not take long for Canadian media companies to follow suit. Bell Canada Enterprises (BCE), the company that owns Canada's largest telecommunications provider, Bell Canada, bought Canada's largest private broadcaster, the CTV network. Later in the year, BCE announced its intention to purchase one of Canada's two national newspapers, the *Globe and Mail*, from the Thomson Corporation, with a special interest in the Globe's online service globeandmail.com. Not to be deterred, this country's second-largest private broadcaster, the CanWest Corporation, which operates the Global television network, bought Canada's largest newspaper chain, Hollinger Corporation, including newspapers in every major Canadian city, Canada's other national newspaper, the *National Post*, and one of the country's largest web sites, Canada.com. In addition to these two blockbuster deals, another large Canadian media holder Quebecor, which enjoyed monopoly ownership of French-language print media, as well as a dominant position in the English-language tabloid press through its control over the Sun Media Corporation, made a successful bid for Groupe Vidéotron, one of Canada's largest cable television companies and a pioneer in the development of online interactive networks and services. The only one of Canada's dominant media companies not completing a major deal was Rogers Communication, which already owns the largest cable television network, the second largest wireless telephone network, the country's only national news magazine, *Maclean's*, and numerous other broadcast properties. Rogers tried unsuccessfully to purchase Groupe Vidéotron and continues to fuel rumours that it would make a bid for the only major newspaper property left without an electronic parent, the Torstar Corporation, publisher of the *Toronto Star*, whose circulation is close to that of the *Globe and Mail* and the *National Post* and which also enjoys a major presence on the internet with thestar.com.

What can a political economy approach contribute to our understanding of these developments? This chapter explores this question by considering the processes of *digitization* and *commodification* that underlie the acceleration of media concentration. It documents how these processes are leading to the formation of an integrated electronic information and entertainment services arena. In doing so, it considers the consequences for Canada of putting in place a regional and global communication regime. In essence, a political economy approach advances our understanding of the expansion of market power in the communication arena. But it also helps to explain the limitations on these developments, their contradictions, and the resistance to them. Media concentration is admittedly advanced by quite powerful processes, but these are not singular forces propelling communication in one direction alone. Digitization is not a flawless technical process, and numerous problems are slowing it down. The process of commodification is under attack from organizations defending both the private sphere, particularly the right to privacy, and the public sphere, primarily by advancing the basic human right to communicate openly and democratically. Hemispheric and global integration are slowed down by businesses that want to hold on to national and local privileges and by civil society groups that are joining labour and new social movements that have succeeded in challenging global business organizations like the World Trade Organization (WTO) and, in some instances, even forcing national governments to back off or halt liberalizing proposals. Political economy can also illuminate these undoubtedly important developments and help to distinguish between short-term setbacks and more important signs that the process of transforming Canadian communication is taking place on a genuinely contested terrain.

DIGITIZATION

Media mergers and the concentration of power that they embody are significant social developments. But while they capture a great deal of press attention, mergers are more the consequence, and arguably not the most important consequence, of other developments in communication. Among the ways to think about these developments, it is useful to focus on the relationship between two processes: digitization and commodification. Digitization refers to the transformation of communication, including words, images, motion pictures, and sounds, into a common language. It provides enormous gains in transmission speed and flexibility over earlier forms of electronic communication that were largely reliant on analog techniques (Longstaff 2000). These techniques physically mimicked communication by putting it into a form suitable for electronic processing and transmission. For example, on an analog system the voice of a telephone caller creates a series of vibrations whose characteristics are sent over a wire and, provided they are amplified at regular intervals, transmitted to a receiver. A digital system literally translates that voice signal into the familiar code of 1s and 0s, which has become the common language of electronic communication. Rather than the multiplicity of mechanical analogs that were employed to process oral, verbal, and image signals, digitization enables one language to govern practically all electronic media. The fundamentals of translating, processing, and distributing electronic communication no longer distinguish between a page of newspaper copy, a radio news broadcast, a CD recording, a telephone call, a television situation comedy, and an e-mail message. Each can be sent at high speed over various wired and wireless networks.

Adopting a common, universal language for electronic media makes digitization enormously attractive. But another characteristic produces an additional significant leap in efficiency and flexibility. Digitization processes and distributes signals in packets that vary in size depending on the nature of the network. A digital telephone network does not send out an entire voice message, as did the old analog systems, but rather, it packages the message in groups for transmission. Each group or packet is provided with a discreet digital address that identifies it before transmission. Breaking up telephone calls, or television signals for that matter, into identifiable packets enables them to be shipped over different network routes on their way to reunification at the receiving end. In effect, one piece of a telephone signal may be followed by a piece of a television signal, and another piece of that same telephone call may be sent over another network. This provides significant gains in the efficiency of communication networks, which used to become congested with traffic that could not be easily rerouted or broken up for efficient transmission. Communication is also made more effective because redundancy can be built into messages enabling multiple ways to correct for errors at the processing and distribution stages. Varieties of what is called packet switching thereby combine the universalizing tendencies of digitization with intelligent customization of communication packets to greatly expand the efficiency and effectiveness of electronic communication. Viewed in this way, digitization combines elements of generalization, by applying one process or one language to electronic communication, with customization, by packaging its "inventory" of communication into micro units that produce the most efficient flow through networks.

The enormous advance of digital over analog processing and transmission helps to explain the outpouring of work that celebrates this development in the most triumphalist and epochal language (Mosco 1998). One of the better exemplars of the genre of digital triumphalism is Nicholas Negroponte the director of MIT's world-renowned Media Lab. In *Being Digital* (1995), he argues for the benefits of digits (what computer communication produces and distributes) over atoms (us and the material world) and contends that the new digital technologies are creating a fundamentally new world that we must accommodate. In matter-of-fact prose, he gives us a modern-day prophet's call to say good-bye to the world of atoms, with its rough and limited, materiality, and welcome the digital world, whose infinitely malleable electrons are able to transcend spatial, temporal, and material constraints. According to him, the world of atoms is ending, and we all must learn to be digital.

In the world of mythology, Negroponte would be considered a *bricoleur*, someone who, following the anthropologist Claude Lévi-Strauss' use of the term, pulls together the bits and pieces of technology's narratives, to create a mobilizing story for our time (Lévi-Strauss 1987). Characteristic of the myth-maker, Negroponte provides us with a story that defies history, in that it admits of no alternative. There is no social or natural action that can stop it. As he says, "The change from atoms to bits is irrevocable and unstoppable (1995, 4). Indeed, it is all the more powerful because it is aligned with nature: "Like a force of nature, the digital age cannot be denied or stopped" (228–9).

And "It is almost genetic in its nature, in that each generation will become more digital than the preceding one (231). Negroponte's view is echoed over and over again in the popular and scholarly literature (Coyne 1999). In essence, it aligns digitization with discourses on the end of history, the end of geography, and the end of politics, to fashion a mythology of epochal transformation.

COMMODIFICATION

There is a great deal to be said for digitization, but there are numerous problems associated with leaping from this recognition to the view that the world of atoms is morphing into a virtual utopia. Political economy reminds us that one of the most important problems is the failure to recognize that digitization takes place in the context of, and greatly expands, the process of commodification, or the transformation of use to exchange value. The expansion of the commodity form provides the context for who leads the process of digitization and how it is applied. It is used first and foremost to expand the commodification of information and entertainment, specifically, to enlarge markets in communication products; deepen the commodification of labour involved in the production, distribution, and exchange of communication; and expand markets in the audiences that receive and make use of electronic communication (Mosco 1996). Digitization not only takes place in the context of powerful commercial forces; it serves to advance the overall process of commodification worldwide and its specific application to communication. The great transformation in communication is therefore better described as the mutual constitution of digitization and commodification.

There has been some scholarly attention paid to the ways in which digitization advances the general process of commodification in capitalist societies. Since the focus of this chapter is on communication, it concentrates on how these two processes work specifically in those areas encompassing the communication sector. Considering the major forms that the commodity takes in this sector, we can appreciate how digitization deepens and extends the ability to measure and monitor communication commodities. Digitization expands the commodification of communication content by extending the range of opportunities to measure and monitor and package and repackage information and entertainment. The packaging of material in the paper-and-ink form of a newspaper or a book has provided a flexible means to commodify communication. Both newspapers and books offer an adequate form in which to measure the commodity and monitor purchases.

Challenges arose in the commodification of communication when what Bernard Miège (1989) called "flow-type" communication systems arose, most importantly television. How does one package a television program for sale to a viewer? Initially, commodification was based on an inflexible system of delivering a batch of broadcast channels into the home, with viewers paying for the receiver and for a mark-up in products advertised over the air. This system did not account for differential use of the medium or make any clear connection between viewing and purchasing. It amounted to an industrial, or Fordist, system of delivering generic programming to a mass audience that was marketed to advertisers for a price per thousand viewers. Each step toward the digitization of television has refined the commodification of content, allowing for the flow to be "captured" or, more precisely, for the commodity to be measured, monitored, and packaged in ever more specific or customized ways. Early cable television improved on broadcast systems of commodification by charging per month for a set of channels. As this medium has become digitized, companies can now offer many more channels and package them in many different ways, including selling content on a per-view basis. Material delivered over television, the Internet, or some combination of these and other new wired and wireless systems can now be flexibly packaged and then repackaged for sale in some related form, with the transaction being measured and monitored by the same digital system.

In addition to expanding the commodification of communication content, the recursive nature of digital systems expands the commodification of the entire communication process. Digital systems that measure and monitor precisely each information transaction can be used to refine the process of delivering audiences of viewers, listeners, readers, movie-goers, and telephone and computer users to advertisers. In essence, companies can package and repackage customers in forms that specifically reflect both their actual purchases and their demographic characteristics. These packages, for example, of eighteen- to twenty-five-year-old men who order martial arts films on pay-per-view television, can be sold to companies that spend more for this information because they want to market their products to this specific sector with as little advertising wasted on groups who would not be interested in their product. This is a major refinement in the commodification of viewers over the system of delivering mass audiences, and it has been applied to most every communication medium today (Mosco 1996).

A similar extension of commodification applies to the labour of communication. The replacement of mechanical with electronic systems eliminated thousands of jobs in the printing industry, just as electronic typesetting did away with the work of linotype operators.

Today digital systems allow companies to expand this process. Newspaper reporters increasingly serve in the combined roles of editor and page producer. They do not simply report on a story; they put it into a form for transmission to the printed, and increasingly, electronic page. Companies retain the rights to the multiplicity of repackaged forms and thereby profit from each use. Broadcast journalists carry cameras and edit their own tape for delivery over television or computer networks. The film industry is beginning to deliver digital copies of movies to theaters in multiple locations over communications satellites, thereby eliminating the distribution of celluloid copies for exhibition by projectionists. Software is sold to customers well before it has been debugged, on the understanding that they will report errors, download and install patches and other corrections, and figure out how to work around problems. The ability to eliminate labour, combine it to perform a multiplicity of tasks, or shift labour to unpaid consumers further expands the revenue opportunities (Hardt and Brennen 1995; McKercher 2000; Sussman and Lent 1998).

TOWARD AN INTEGRATED
ELECTRONIC INFORMATION AND
ENTERTAINMENT SERVICES ARENA

The mutual constitution of digitization and commodification helps to explain the rapid integration of the communication sector and the concentration of corporate power within it.

Specifically, the adoption of a common digital language across the communication industry is breaking down barriers that once separated print, broadcasting, telecommunications and the information technology or computer data sectors. These divisions have historically been very significant, because they contained the legal and institutional marks of the particular period in which they rose to national prominence.

The print publishing industry is marked by a legal regime of free expression, limited government involvement, and local, typically family, ownership. Broadcasting and telecommunications came later, rising to prominence alongside the rise of strong nation-state authority and national production regimes. The legal system in Canada, as well as the systems in the United States and Europe, placed a greater regulatory burden on radio, television, and telephone systems, even going as far as to create publicly controlled institutions in these sectors, in order to accomplish national objectives such as reflecting a national identity and building a national market. National companies were more likely to control commercial broadcasting and telecommunications systems than was the case in print publishing. The information technology or computer data industry took off in the post–World War II era, and it embodies the trend away from nation-state regulation (except to advance the expansion of businesses) and toward control by multinational businesses. There are numerous legal and institutional struggles within this sector, but it began from the premise that, unlike broadcasting and telecommunications, the computer industry would face no public interest or public service responsibilities, no system of subsidized pricing to those who need it, no commitment to universality of access, and no expectation that national firms would be anything more than one step on the way to multinational control (Schiller 1999; McChesney 1999).

Digitization is eroding these distinctions. Newspaper copy is no longer limited to the daily press but now almost automatically becomes part of the online data business through newspaper websites and those of information businesses. Increasingly, video or audio, which would face one set of government regulations if sent out over television or radio, is also delivered through broadband computer systems that face little if any regulation. Telephone services, which continue to face government regulation or control, are also shifting to the unregulated Internet. These once-divided sectors are rapidly collapsing into one large electronic information and entertainment arena. The term "convergence" is widely used to describe this process, but it all too often is taken to imply that the outcome is a legal and institutional regime made up of an amalgam of the constituents of convergence. But the overwhelming evidence suggests that convergence in this case means the coming together of all sectors around regimes that are in place for the information technology and computer data sectors. This means little to no regulation and openness to the control of integrated transnational businesses (McChesney 1999; Schiller 1999; Winseck 1999).

*The Concentration of Power
in the Communication Business*

The combination of digitization and commodification and the growing integration of communication sectors into a consolidated electronic information and entertainment arena explains much of the unprecedented acceleration in mergers and acquisitions in this industry worldwide and in Canada. Communication systems in the United States are now largely shaped by a handful of companies, including Microsoft, AT&T, General Electric, Viacom, Inc., the Walt Disney Company, AOL–Time Warner, and the Liberty Media Corporation. There are others, including foreign-based firms like News

Corporation, Bertelsmann, Vivendi Universal, and Sony. Indeed, each of these firms has a significant transnational presence through outright ownership, strategic partnerships, and investment (www.thenation.com/bigten 2002).

The Canadian arena is even more highly concentrated, with arguably, four firms in the most dominant position. These are BCE-CTV-Thomson, Rogers–Maclean Hunter, CanWest Global–Hollinger, and Quebecor–Sun Media–Groupe Vidéotron. Arguably, this arena is more concentrated than that of the United States and, indeed, most of the developed world, for reasons that extend beyond the small number of dominant firms. Scholars and policymakers look to an independent press as a major source of diversity, particularly in a media-saturated environment that is feeling great pressures to commercialize (Bagdikian 1997). One of the fundamental distinguishing characteristics of the recently amalgamated Canadian communication industry is the integration of major newspapers within large conglomerate media based in telecommunications and television. With the *Globe and Mail* now part of the BCE-CTV family, the Hollinger group nested within CanWest Global Communications, and French language and tabloid media situated within the Quebecor chain, only the *Toronto Star* remains in relative independence. If, as some anticipate, Rogers or some other major Canadian firm succeeds in capturing Torstar, there would be no significant newspaper presence outside of conglomerate control.

Although the United States arena is arguably dominated by similar conglomerates, none of the major ones boast anything but token control over newspapers, largely because regulators in the United States have been more reluctant than their Canadian counterparts to acquiesce to such takeovers. The U.S. situation also attests to the power and resources of U.S. newspapers like the *New York Times*, the *Wall Street Journal*, and *USA Today* to resist such takeovers. Moreover, Canadian regulators have permitted telecommunications firms, particularly BCE, to build structures that integrate across monopoly and competitive markets and across production and distribution. Specifically, whereas AT&T was forced to divest itself of its local monopolies before it was permitted to enter new markets, BCE has retained control over local telephone companies and expanded into satellite, wireless, and television broadcasting (Winseck 1999). This has enabled BCE to plan for an integrated home communication system that would bring together its high-speed Internet service and satellite-delivered television system to provide homes with fully networked communication and information products that would eventually extend to monitoring and controlling all household utilities. Moreover, U.S. regulators have prohibited mergers of telecommunications and broadcasting networks. Admittedly, General Electric, Disney, and Viacom have been permitted to buy up the major u.s. television networks, but AT&T has been kept out of this market. Not only was BCE permitted to buy a television network, but Canadian regulators also approved its purchase of the largest private network in Canada, CTV, even as the company proposed to take effective control of its major national newspaper, the *Globe and Mail.* In effect, the transformation brought about by digitization and commodification is arguably more advanced in Canada than in almost any other country (Simon, 2001).

Toward a Regional and Transnational Communication Order

The transformation, however, is far from complete. Canadian communication firms, like their counterparts in the United States and elsewhere, face enormous pressures toward regional and global integration (Mosco and Schiller 2001). To promote transnational corporate communications services in general, and transnational media in particular, nationally controlled communications institutions would have to be eliminated or at least cut back, and public service principles would have to be sharply curtailed. u.s. corporate and political leaders lobbied during the 1980s and 1990s to advance these sweeping changes within broader efforts to liberalize trade and investment rules. Government actions, private economic diplomacy and pressure, bilateral negotiations between governments, and international bodies such as the World Bank, the International Monetary Fund, and the World Trade Organization all played important roles in this process. The Free Trade Agreement (FTA), which brought together Canada and the United States, and the North American Free Trade Agreement (NAFTA), which added Mexico, were prominent initiatives, and each was perceived as the start of a broader push for the liberalization of global trade and investment within the organizational context of the World Trade Organization (WTO) framework. Had the WTO's planned Multilateral Agreement on Investment (MAI) initiative not met with fierce resistance, it would have pressed even further in the same direction. Renewed attempts to revive the MAI may yet do so (Barlow and Clarke, 2001).

Regional integration has proceeded very far in Canadian communications, even in the face of regional trade agreements that are supposed to exempt the communication and cultural industries. Nortel has reoriented its successful business in the increasingly deregulated telecommunications equipment market toward its leading corporate customers in the United States, and the Thomson Corporation already held major interests in newspapers across the United States. Following passage of the 1989 Free Trade Agreement, connections between U.S. and Canadian media and communications interests tightened swiftly. Seagrams, a Canadian-based beverage company with considerable interests in U.S. petrochemicals, shifted into the leading group of U.S.-based culture conglomerates by purchasing Universal, though in 2000 Seagram sold its entertainment business to the French media conglomerate Vivendi. In 1999, Bell Canada permitted the U.S. telephone giant Ameritech to acquire a 20 percent stake in it. Rogers Communication, Canada's largest cable company and diversified holder of numerous media properties, including Canada's leading newsweekly *Maclean's*, struck a deal with Microsoft to sell a minority stake to the U.S. firm. Microsoft would use Canada's largest cable television provider to develop high-speed Internet access services. Furthermore, in August 1999 Rogers sold a one-billion-dollar stake in its mobile telephone company to AT&T and British Telecom. AT&T itself used the WTO agreement on basic telecommunications to challenge the Canadian dominance of Bell Canada, as well as government policies that had kept local telephone rates low to ensure universal access (Baxter 2000).

Even in the newspaper business, which still operated behind a wall of government protection enshrined in the Income Tax Act (which effectively limited foreign ownership of Canadian newspapers to no more than 25 percent), major newspaper companies built strategic alliances anticipating the end of such restrictions. The *Globe and Mail* made deals with Dow Jones to include a page of news directly from the *Wall Street Journal*, with AOL–Time Warner to include a section of *Sports Illustrated* magazine news, and with the *New York Times* for exclusive rights to home delivery of the Sunday edition of that newspaper across Canada. Thwarted by the Canadian government from establishing its own set of retail chains in Canada, Barnes & Noble, one of the world's largest book retailers, took a minority stake in Canada's largest bookseller, Chapters Inc.

Admittedly, both the 1989 Free Trade Agreement (FTA) and the 1993 North American Free Trade Agreement (NAFTA), which brought Mexico within the treaty, were supposed to leave the cultural industries out of the agreements. In both cases, however, liberalized trade in this sector was permitted by a notwithstanding clause that allowed retaliation against cultural protectionism through measures in other industries, by general agreements on restricting government activity, and by liberalizing trade in sectors converging with the cultural industries.

The "notwithstanding" clause permits a party to take measures of "equivalent commercial affect" when it believes that a treaty partner has unfairly restricted trade in the cultural industries. For example, when the Canadian government proposed legislative action against the u.s. export of magazines into Canada, publications that would have siphoned off Canadian advertising without adding much Canadian editorial content to existing American magazines, the United States threatened retaliation by restricting steel exports from Canada into the United States. This action fully conformed with the FTA and NAFTA treaties, in addition to containing the added challenge to a major industry in the home riding of the heritage minister. Regionalization was also permitted by treaty provisions that require governments to apply "national treatment" to each other's companies. This means that the CRTC is required to treat American companies on the same terms as they do Canadian ones, within the limitations of foreign-ownership restrictions. As a result, the telecommunications company AT&T Canada, which resulted from a partnership among Canadian telecommunications and computer firms, including Rogers and AT&T, must be governed by the same regulations that apply to fully Canadian firms.

The treaties also place strict limits on the ability of governments to establish new government or public institutions to provide services in competition with private businesses. This antimonopoly provision is particularly important in the communication industry, where the CBC is an important model for just such an organization. The treaties essentially prohibit the formation of a CBC for the age of computer communication, thereby eliminating the opportunity to create a genuine national public alternative to the growing commercialization and u.s. domination of cyberspace. Moreover, the treaties prohibit, for example, restrictions on the entry of foreign Internet service providers, like America Online and Microsoft, whose AOL Canada and MSN services are among the largest in Canada. With the merger of AOL and Time Warner, cultural products, like the content of the company's magazines, which were once regulated, now have easier access into the Canadian market through priority placement on AOL's home pages. In effect, the FTA and NAFTA limit Canada's ability to protect its own national communication industry and make it easier for regional powers like AOL–Time Warner and AT&T to expand into the Canadian market.

There are also significant global pressures to expand transnational control over Canadian communication. In fact, the World Trade Organization (WTO) has arguably played a more active role than have regional trade agreements in the communication arena. For example, the United States pursued its claim against a Canadian law restricting the presence of American magazines through the WTO, which delivered a victory to the United States. The WTO has also taken a leading role in negotiating the loosening of foreign ownership restrictions in telecommunications. With Canadian government support, it has succeeded in raising the limit from about 20 percent to just under majority ownership.

Admittedly, other powerful interests and actors continue to press for a policy of protection. For example, the Canadian magazine industry strongly resisted an end to the policy of keeping out Canadian editions of u.s.-owned magazines. But some of this protectionist sentiment was little more than a smokescreen for industrial interests, particularly those of Canadian media firms Rogers and Telemedia, which controlled two-thirds of the magazine industry. What is more significant is that a general shift in public policy has taken place. The Canadian federal Liberal Party historically supported strong national regulation of Canadian communication and cultural industries and Canadian controls over American cultural imports. Now, with a few exceptions, it has joined the side of ending domestic regulations and import controls. In May 2000 the Ministry of Canadian Heritage, which had been closely identified with nationalist policies, effectively threw in the towel by announcing a review of all foreign ownership restrictions on newspapers, radio, and television broadcasting (Scoffield and Craig 2000). Indeed, it is quite fair to say that in some areas the Canadian government blazed new ground, as in May 1999 when it fully supported the decision of its chief communication regulatory authority to formally rule against regulation of the Internet (Canada 1999). The impact of this particular policy change promised to be profound, because the Internet is beginning to overtake conventional media and telecommunications services.

Policies based on protectionism, moreover, no longer try to oppose including the culture and communication sectors of government in the general process of government-funding cutbacks. The Canadian government authorized a substantial decline in public service communication and culture, evidenced in budget cuts to the CBC and to government programs that provided subsidies to media involved in the arts and culture and to support organizations. Even as the Canadian government tried to counter the threat of u.s. magazine imports by advancing protectionist legislation, it was cutting off subsidies and thereby killing small-circulation Canadian magazines. In the same week that the WTO announced its decision to support Time Warner's bid to permit a split-run "Canadian" version of *Sports Illustrated* magazine, Atlantic Canada's best-known alternative magazine, *New Maritimes*, went out of business, mainly because it had lost its Canada Council grant. Citing budget cuts and the need to narrow its grant mandate, the council also warned the national magazine Canadian Forum that its subsidy would be lost unless it shifted focus from politics to the arts (Mosco 1997). Admittedly, some nationalist concerns reflected a genuine interest in preserving autonomy in audio-visual space, and this could even crystallize momentarily in high-level government policy proposals – such as the 1999 Canadian government effort to forge a global cultural pact among the world's threatened nations that would provide stronger protection for national cultural industries. But Canadian business was increasingly tied closely to the u.s. and global markets, and government policy could hardly avoid reconciling itself to this reality.

Contradictions and Opposition

Each of these transformational processes contains problems that range from technical glitches to outright challenges. Media concentration often does not produce the synergies that companies anticipate and sometimes results in content that fails to attract audiences. Digitization is not a flawless process, and numerous technical problems have slowed its development. What makes these processes particularly interesting for the political economist is that what appear on the surface as technical issues generally embody genuine political economic concerns. Specifically, they reveal a contradiction within the emerging neoliberal order that is particularly important for the transformation of communication. Neoliberalism is founded on the retreat of government from critical areas of social life, including the communication arena, where government historically was directly involved in the construction of infrastructure, the development of technical standards, the regulation of market access, and the direct provision of services. According to the neoliberal view, such functions are best provided by the private sector, with minimal government involvement. Aside from the ideological commitment to this perspective, neoliberalism aims to customize government functions, to tailor them to suit business needs, and thereby to avoid the problems that the vision of government as a universal, or public, space open to a wide range of contestation once provided. But the communication arena demonstrates that it is not so easy to accomplish this feat.

One of the most significant of what are typically presented as narrow technical concerns is standardization. Digitization succeeds only to the extent that common technical standards are used to harmonize the processing, distribution, and reception of digital signals. It is one thing to translate audio, video, and data streams into digital packets; it is quite another to ensure their flawless flow through global information grids. In order to accomplish this, a wide range of standards for equipment necessary to encode and decode signals and for managing the data flows through networks is essential. Achieving such agreement is normally difficult, because competitors are reluctant to cooperate, since they would have to share information that is itself increasingly valued in its own right and central to success in developing new technical systems.

Capitalism has traditionally dealt with this problem by establishing government agencies or private-public partnerships that might serve as independent arbiters of standards. For example, almost a century and a half ago, competing telegraph interests established the International Telecommunications Union (ITU), a global body made up of mainly government organizations and run on a one-nation, one-vote basis to establish global standards for the new technology. Over the years, as each new communication technology came along the ITU expanded its role specifically to set standards for the telephone, to allocate broadcasting frequencies, and eventually to specify the orbital locations of communication satellites.

However, as the number of nations grew, particularly the number of former colonial societies eager to create standards to expand widespread access and not just the profits of communication companies, conflict grew at the ITU, and core capitalist powers, led by the United States, began to consider alternatives. These included, first, political bodies, like Intelsat, a global communication-satellite organization whose rules permitted Western control, and more recently, private corporations, such as ICANN, the Internet Corporation for Assigned Names and Numbers, which essentially establishes standards for the Internet. The goal of these organizations has been to set standards to advance the interests of business but to do so without sacrificing global credibility. It has been increasingly difficult to accomplish this goal, for several reasons. Digitization is increasingly global, and the competition to dominate markets for the short term by controlling one phase of a rapidly changing technical system or for the long term by setting a critical standard (such as a computer operating system) is intensifying. Furthermore, the diversity of global interests is expanding, so that even something as seemingly innocuous as setting a national suffix for a web address becomes a political question when, to cite one particularly contentious case, it is Palestine petitioning for the designation. Moreover, should the common ".com" suffix expand to include ".union," as one public interest group proposed Private businesses hoping to depoliticize these issues by setting up U.S.-controlled private or only quasi-public standards organizations are actually only displacing the tensions and contradictions inherent in a system that would concentrate power and profit but that would aim to do so through universal markets that can achieve global legitimacy. As a result, seemingly technical questions are caught up in political economic maelstroms that, at the very least, slow the process of global technological development. But the alternative, setting up genuinely public national or international regulatory authorities invites turning this arena, widely recognized as critical to capitalist expansion, into a widely contested terrain (Lessig 2001).

This problem is evident not only in the struggle over standards; it has also marked debates about how to expand access to technology in order to build markets and about how to ensure some measure of privacy to create consumer confidence in the technology. In the early days of radio, capital felt it did not need the state to regulate frequencies. The result was chaos, as broadcasters poached each other's frequencies and the air was filled with worthless static. Business brought in government to regulate the mess, and government succeeded, but in doing so it opened this private arena to the wider public, which used the opportunity to fight for public broadcasting and the regulation of private station content. The technology has indeed changed, but the underlying political economic dynamic has not, and so the same tensions and contradictions mark the process of digitization.

Commodification is challenged by organizations defending both the private sphere, particularly the right to privacy, and the public sphere, the right to communicate in an open and democratic fashion (Klein 2000). Political economists are not alone in raising the threat to privacy and the public sphere, but their arguments are grounded more rigorously than most in a thorough critique of the commodification process. The privacy problem is often connected to the inevitable price that one pays for technological development or to the shortcomings of government oversight or of our oversight of government. Political economy significantly deepens these views by arguing that the drive to use communication, and particularly the new media of cyberspace, to expand the commodification process inevitably leads to the commodification of personal identity. The production and distribution of information about consumers and workers takes on a value related to, but distinct from, the value of their purchases and their labour. The threat to privacy is not just an offshoot of technology or a correctable oversight but is intrinsic to the commodification process. Consequently, from a political economy perspective, the fight for personal privacy is part of a wider struggle against the expanding commodity.

Among the many examples of the link between commodification and the struggle over privacy, consider a January 2001 Nortel Networks announcement of a new line of "personal content" network software that the company will sell to Internet service providers so that they will be able to package online services to suit individual preferences. The software tracks every choice a user makes on the Internet and configures the network to deliver more efficiently than ever the kinds of material the user typically selects. In essence, Nortel is adding to the value of the Internet by making it more responsive to customer profiles. But in doing so, the company makes it possible to gather, package, and share information on customer choices, thereby posing a privacy threat.

The response of one privacy activist focuses on the company's responsibility. Charging that Nortel and other network equipment suppliers are "pushing into the infrastructure a technology that can be very damaging to privacy, and in some ways shirking their responsibilities by saying it's up to the people we sell it to to implement it in suitable manner," Jason Catlett calls it "unacceptable" for Internet service providers to watch where their customers are going. Many political economists would likely share Catlett's concern but would go considerably further by seeing Nortel's behaviour as less a matter of corporate irresponsibility and more the response of a company that needs to expand the commodification of its major resource, the Internet. But even more than this, Nortel's product reflects a fundamental contradiction besetting the business of cyberspace: the conflict between the need to build consumer confidence to turn the Internet into a universal market tool and the need to commodify whatever moves over the Internet, including personal identity (Associated Press 2001). The contradiction is deepened by the opposition of the technology industry to most forms of state intervention, which, in the case of earlier technologies, would at least have created temporary ways to address the problem.

The challenge of commodification and global restructuring partly through the instrumentality of computer communication has also turned public space into a contested terrain. Political economists who have examined this issue have focused on struggles over the privatization of public space and the centrality of culture and communication in these struggles. One of the founding scholars in the political economy of communication, Herbert Schiller, laid a grounding for this work in his widely read *Culture, Inc.*, which addresses the central importance of culture in social life and the cultural turn in academic research. Schiller was committed to media research because he knew that culture was critical to democracy. Toward the end of his career, he expanded his research to examine the cultural significance of media in city streets and parks, billboard advertising, museums, libraries, and a host of other places that demonstrated for him that "a community's economic life cannot be separated from its symbolic content" and that "speech, dance, drama, music and the visual and plastic arts have been vital, indeed necessary, features of human experience from the earliest times" (1989, 31).

Schiller focused a critical eye on culture, not as a superstructural derivative of an economic base, but to demonstrate that the symbolic is not only inextricably bound to the material, it *is* material. His quarrel with academic cultural studies was based on the fear that it tended to diminish the cultural by neglecting how it mutually constituted economic, political, and social life. Naomi Klein's *No Logo* directly builds on this work by demonstrating that the years since Schiller wrote have brought about a deepening of the struggle over public space as global business is increasingly directed to the branding of physical and cultural space. Indeed, for many companies, like Nike, with the swoosh, and McDonald's, with its arches, the cultural brand is arguably a more important asset than its tangible property – a conclusion supported by the lengths these companies go to in order to protect their brands (2000, 365–96).

Klein's is one of a number of works in Canadian political economy that address the contested nature of public space in a digital age (Dyer-Witheford 1999). They share certain characteristics of traditional approaches to political economy, including significant attention to how the international division of labour provides a foundation for global production, distribution, and consumption (Sussman and Lent 1998). They also address the concentration of corporate power and the rise of transnational communication companies in the global power structure. But there are two important departures that embody new directions in the political economy of communication.

The first is a shift from the productivist emphasis in earlier research on the international division of labour to a concern for consumption and cultural reception. This change in emphasis follows from the interest in communication and culture, including advertising and marketing, but it is more than a disciplinary leaning. The focus on consumption reflects the expansion of consumer markets and the growth of popular culture, particularly in, but certainly not limited to, the developed world. More importantly, it has significant political implications, because many of the social movements that make headlines today for their opposition to global capital (e.g., the Battle of Seattle) are founded on the intimate connection between the labour practices of big companies in the Third World and their marketing, advertising, media, and branding practices in the developed world. Klein cites numerous examples covering such diverse companies as Shell, Coca Cola, Philip Morris, Nike, and McDonald's. Protests against Nike's sweatshop conditions in Viet Nam or Shell's use of a violent regime in Nigeria to quell labour opposition often take the form of attacking their marketing, branding, and other practices that amount to an assault on public space in the developed world. Of course, social movements also include trade unions in core societies, but these unions too are increasingly aligned to groups associated with consumption and branding, practices of companies that increasingly require what amounts to a corporate cultural strategy.

In addition to this broadening of political economy to encompass significant processes in addition to primary production, the political economy of communication is increasingly interested in the use of communication and information technology for opposition and resistance. The same communication technologies that are vital in building genuinely transnational businesses, especially the pieces that converge to create cyberspace, are also building global resistance movements. It is undoubtedly easy to romanticize this resistance with images of Subcommandante Marcos tapping on his laptop in a Chiapas village to inform the world about the progress of the resistance against the Mexican government. The global distribution of access to communication does move in lockstep with the global distribution of wealth. Both are deeply skewed, and the inequities, as political economists of communication have demonstrated, are arguably growing, (Schiller 1999; McChesney 1999). But as Klein and Dyer-Witheford describe, many of the major opposition movements have been based on building global solidarity and strategy through the use of communication systems. This strategy takes many forms, including direct attacks on the communication systems of transnational companies and their political organizations, such as took place in January 2001 when both Microsoft's computer networks and the servers containing private data (such as credit card information) on the participants at the World Economic Forum meeting in Davos, Switzerland, were hacked and opened (Weisman 2001; Reuters 2001). The strategy also includes, relatedly, the use of computer communications to organize an alternative to the annual Davos meeting that brought together some twenty thousand people in Porto Allegre, Brazil, for the World Social Forum, a six-day meeting whose theme, "Another World is Possible," featured social movement groups representing labour, women, the environment, minorities, and numerous other communities. This is just one of the more graphic examples of using cyberspace to advance the politics of democratic communication. The convergence of labour and consumption and the politics of citizenship, which seem to mark so much of what gets simplemindedly called the antiglobalization movement, may be the most significant form of convergence to understand today.

But maybe not. The sociologist Ulrich Beck has referred to the events of 9/11 as "capitalism's Chernobyl," because they undermined faith in neoliberalism, just as the nuclear disaster at Chernobyl undermined faith in Soviet communism (2001). One cannot be sure about undermining faith; perhaps 9/11 just tarnished the capitalist brand, but Beck has taught us enough about risk over the years to suggest that we need to think much more seriously about the vulnerabilities that follow directly from a global political economy rooted in networks of communication and transportation. The multiplication of global communication and transportation links also multiplies the number of nodes from which to attack and the number of nodes that are open to attack. Converging with this process is the tendency of neoliberalism to promote a retreat from government, which means a retreat from collective management of expanding networks at the national and international levels. As Beck perceptively concludes, "Today, the capitalist fundamentalists' unswerving faith in the redeeming power of the market has proved to be a dangerous illusion. In times of crises, neoliberalism has no solutions to offer. Fundamental truths that were pushed aside return to the fore. Without taxation, there can be no state. Without a public sphere, democracy, and civil society, there can be no legitimacy. And without legitimacy, no security. From this it follows that without legitimate forums for settling national and global conflicts, there will be no world economy in any form whatsoever." The convergence of accelerating communication and transportation networks and expanding neoliberalism poses the danger of an explosive combination. We do not know where it will lead, perhaps to sober second thoughts and support for a more democratic international politics that will diminish the threat, but perhaps we will not learn and will find ourselves facing at first regionally and then perhaps even globally what Robert Kaplan pessimistically calls "the coming anarchy" (1997, 7).

CONCLUSION

Several processes of transformation are taking place in Canadian communication. Digitization, combined with commodification, is deepening and extending opportunities for capital to turn the content, audiences, and labour of the communication industries into marketable commodities. It is advancing the erosion of barriers between communication sectors and, along with them, the legal and institutional regimes that distinguished what were once more accurately called the print, broadcasting, telecommunications, and information technology sectors. Furthermore, we can observe acceleration in the concentration of media ownership worldwide and in Canada, where four groups have managed to expand significantly the development of integrated conglomerates across the newly integrated electronic information and entertainment services arena. Even as this takes place, regional and transnational integration are rapidly taking hold in the communication industry as the FTA, NAFTA, the GATT, and the WTO turn national communication companies into regional and, indeed, global businesses.

Each of these transformational processes contains problems that range from technical glitches to outright challenges. Digitization creates numerous technical problems that slow its development. Commodification is challenged by organizations defending both the private sphere, particularly the right to privacy, and the public sphere, the right to communicate in an open and democratic fashion. Media concentration often does not produce the synergies that companies anticipate and often results in content that fails to attract audiences. Regional and transnational integration is slowed by companies wanting to hold on to national preferences and by civil society movements that bring together traditional labour and new social movement groups that have succeeded in shutting down meetings of the WTO and forcing national governments to back off from liberalizing proposals. These are undoubtedly significant developments, but it remains to be seen whether they are merely bumps in the road or whether they are likely to turn the process of the transformation of communication into a genuinely contested terrain, one that may, in the words of one labour leader, create the conditions for a "new internationalism" (Sweeney 2001). The events of September 11 have only compounded the uncertainty.

REFERENCES

Associated Press. 2001. "Nortel Unveils New Technology Tool," 30 January.

Bagdikian, Ben. 1997. *The Media Monopoly*. 5th ed. Boston: Beacon Press.

Barlow, Maude, and Tony Clarke. 2001. *Global Showdown*. Toronto: Stoddart.

Baxter, James. 2000. "AT&T Complains Telephone Regulation Thwarts Competition." *Ottawa Citizen*, 17 March, D4.

Beck, Ulrich. 2001. "Globalisation's Chernobyl." *Financial Times* (London), 6 November.

Canada. CRTC. 1999. *Final Report: New Media, Telecom Public Notice CRTC 99–14 and Broadcasting Public Notice CRTC 1999–84*, 17 May.

Coyne, Richard. 1999. *Technoromanticism: Digital Narrative, Holism, and the Romance of the Real*. Cambridge: MIT Press.

Dyer-Witheford, Nick. 1999. *Cyber-Marx: Cycles and Circuits of Struggle in High-Technology Capitalism.* Urbana, IL: University of Illinois Press.

Hardt, Hanno, and Bonnie Brennen, eds. 1995. *Newsworkers: Toward a History of the Rank and File.* Minneapolis, MN: University of Minnesota Press.

Kaplan, R. 1997. *The Coming Anarchy.* New York: Knopf.

Klein, Naomi. 2000. *No Logo.* Toronto: Knopf Canada.

Lessig, Lawrence. 2001. *The Future of Language.* New York: Random House.

Lévi-Strauss, Claude. 1987. *Anthropology and Myth: Lectures, 1951–1982.* Oxford, Blackwell.

Longstaff, Patricia F. 2000. *Convergence and Divergence in Communication Regulation.* Cambridge, MA: Harvard University Program on Information Resources Policy.

McChesney, Robert. 1999. *Rich Media, Poor Democracy.* Urbana, IL: University of Illinois Press.

McKercher, Catherine. 2000. "From Newspaper Guild to Multimedia Union: A Study in Labour Convergence." PHD diss., Concordia University, Montreal.

Miège, Bernard. 1989. *The Capitalization of Cultural Production.* New York: International General.

Mosco, Vincent. 1996. *The Political Economy of Communication.* London: Sage

– 1997. "Marketable Commodity or Public Good: The Conflict between Domestic and Foreign Communication Policy." In Gene Swimmer, ed., *How Ottawa Spends, 1997–1998,* 159–78. Ottawa: Carleton University Press.

– 1998. "Myth-ing Links: Power and Community on the Information Highway." *The Information Society* 14(1): 57–62.

Mosco, Vincent, and Dan Schiller, eds. 2001. *Continental Order? Integrating North America for Cyber-Capitalism.* Boulder, CO: Rowman and Littlefield.

Negroponte, Nicholas. 1995. *Being Digital.* Cambridge, MA: MIT Press

Reuters. 2001. "World Economic Forum Says Hackers Got into System." *New York Times,* 5 February.

Schiller, Dan. 1999. *Digital Capitalism.* Cambridge, MA: MIT Press.

Schiller, Herbert. 1989. *Culture, Inc.* New York: Oxford University Press.

Scoffield, H., and Craig, S. 2000. "Review of Media Rules to Be Broad." *Report on Business,* 3 May, B3.

Simon, B. 2001. "A Telecom Umbrella Extends Its Shadow." *New York Times,* 24 December, C3.

Sussman, Gerald, and John Lent, eds. 1998. *Global Productions.* London: Sage.

Sweeney, John. 2001. "Not a Backlash, but Birth Pangs of a New Internationalism." *International Herald Tribune,* 27 January.

Weisman, Robyn. 2001. "DOS Attacks: Internet Plague without a Cure? *Technology News,* 31 January. (http://dailynews.yahoo.com/h/nf/20010131/tc/7050_1.html)

Winseck, Dwayne. 1999. *Reconvergence.* Creskill, NJ: Hampton.

PART FOUR

The New Urban Experience

13 Municipal Restructuring, Urban Services, and the Potential for the Creation of Transformative Political Spaces

CAROLINE ANDREW

INTRODUCTION

The objective of this chapter is to examine whether there is presently potential to create transformative political spaces through municipal politics in large Canadian cities. This is both a new and an old question in Canada, and this chapter will examine the new context in which this question arises and the ways in which it has played itself out in the past.

The most novel element is the wave of municipal restructuring that has been going on in the large Canadian cities. Six of the largest Canadian urban centres (Toronto, Montreal, Ottawa and Hull,[1] Quebec, Hamilton, and Halifax) have recently engaged in or are presently in the process of municipal restructuring centred on the creation of single municipal governments covering substantial portions of the overall urbanized area.[2] In addition, Calgary and Winnipeg also have a single municipality covering their urbanized areas (Winnipeg since 1972 and Calgary through a continued process of annexations). Consequently, the basic pattern of metropolitan governance in Canada is now a single municipal government that covers a substantial portion of the urbanized area. Vancouver is an important exception, but the overall pattern is increasingly clear.

Another major new element in the analysis is the changing demographic reality of Canadian metropolitan centres, particularly in cultural terms. This question is explored more fully in the chapter by Satzewich and Wong in this volume, but it is central to an understanding of urban governance. The large cities – and particularly Toronto, Vancouver, and Montreal – have increasingly large non-white populations. Immigration is of course not new in the Canadian experience, but the changing origins of immigrants to Canada and their increasingly concentrated location in metropolitan centres create new political realities. If Canada is to find ways of meeting the challenge of ethno-cultural diversity with increased social justice, they will be found in the major cities.

And finally, globalization has to be taken into account in understanding the political challenges to be faced in the large Canadian cities. Castells' view of the network society (1996) as linking world class cities suggests a more important role for cities but also raises questions about the ways in which Canadian cities will be connected to these global city-based networks and, what is equally important, about the impact of these connections on Canadian cities.

The progressive potential of municipal politics can be seen along two dimensions. Along the first dimension, municipal politics deals with the organization of daily life and therefore raises questions about the spaces of social justice. Having to commute two hours each day because housing costs push people to the outskirts or because employment has moved to the suburbs and housing in proximity to employment is too expensive already imposes costs on certain groups in the population. Inadequate public transportation systems add another layer of inequality. Municipal government decisions about public transportation are thus social justice questions, with clear implications for gender (women use public transportation more than men), race and class (the use of public transportation by visible minorities is higher because of the interrelation of race and class) and physical ability (the disabled are highly dependent on public transportation).

Zoning is another municipal government policy tool with clear spatial equity consequences. Jane Jacob's classic, *The Death and Life of Great American Cities*, describes the vitality of mixed-use neighbourhoods, which are exceptions to the North American experience of zoning for single usage. The combination of zoning and patterns of allocation of urban services, such as parks, playgrounds, and so on, has helped to produce resource-rich neighbourhoods and resource-poor neighbourhoods. In addition, the creation of residential neighbourhoods with no services within the neighbourhood both encourages the use of the private automobile and imposes additional financial burdens on those too poor, too old, too young, or too disabled to have access to one.

Municipal politics can influence the structures of daily life. It can provide more or less daycare services; it can locate them in relation to public transportation or not; it can invest more or less in public transportation; it can invest more or less in social services or in grants to organizations providing services to seniors, to youth, to women; it can operate these grant programs in ways that encourage diversity or that ignore this question, and it can plan for pedestrians or for the private automobile. The resulting policies make a difference to the politics of the social justice of daily life. This is not high politics, but it is politics that makes a difference.

The second dimension of the progressive potential of municipal politics relates to knowledge and expertise and who has the status of "knowers." This is one of the critical dimensions of social equity and social justice in the modern world, and, as will be argued in this chapter, municipal government can be an avenue of progressive politics, in part because municipal politics deals with the issues of daily life and therefore with issues that ordinary people understand; in many cases they know that they have knowledge about these issues. For this reason it is a terrain where conflict about knowledge and the "knowers" can be more easily engaged and where technical expertise and technical experts can be challenged. It is not the only scale of politics where this can be done, but it is an arena where lived experience can make an important claim to be listened to.

The issue addressed in this chapter is whether the current context of cities in Canada – their increased importance through globalization, the rapidly changing demographic reality, and the recent political transformations – increases or decreases the two dimensions of their progressive potential. Is the municipal potential for increasing the social justice of daily life and for democratizing the status of the knower diminished or enhanced by the increased importance of urban centres and by the fact that their governing structure is more and more a single municipal government covering an important part of the urbanized metropolitan area?

The answer to this question is not simple. On the one hand, the fiscal context of the amalgamations and the fiscal context of globalization create pressures for the reduction of the public sector and therefore for a reduced scale for municipal policies. Thus, the progressive potential of municipal governments will have great difficulty being realized. But on the other hand, the political structures that are emerging in the larger Canadian cities are simpler and perhaps more understandable to the general public. If one of the reasons that municipal governments have been less than progressive is that they have been able to hide themselves from the public through complex and complicated structures, clarity may make municipal governments more visible. Municipal politics have not been seen as central to progressive political forces for numerous reasons, but certainly their complexity and lack of transparency have played a role. Simply creating amalgamated municipalities in metropolitan areas is not a solution, but it may provide an arena in which it is possible to build a more progressive politics.

The question of the progressive potential of municipal politics has been raised in earlier periods of Canadian history, and therefore one of the ways to address the present-day context is to examine past experience. The two periods of urban reform that stand out are the years from 1880 to 1920 and the 1960s. In both these periods considerable political organization and activity was articulated in the urban context. But case studies demonstrate that the potential for progressive municipal politics did not develop in these past periods of urban reform, because the most progressive aspects were removed from the municipal arena and taken up by provincial and federal governments through the gradually increasing centralization of social policy – be it education, social services, social housing or health. Left at the municipal level were questions of physical infrastructure, questions not regarded as central by progressive social forces. The perceived lack of importance of urban issues, coupled with the middle-class domination of the reform movements, the strong role of "expert" professional discourses, and the attractiveness of the individualized solution of suburban development help to explain how the potential for transformation was not realized at the municipal level. An analysis of these periods will provide a framework for examining the present situation and for determining whether or not conditions exist that might lead to different outcomes from those of the past. If the complexities of the intergovernmental distribution of responsibilities and resources have been one of the primary factors inhibiting transformative politics from developing at the municipal level during past periods of urban reform, what is the likelihood of politics playing itself out differently in the current period?

Answers lie both in understanding and in political action. Robert Alford has developed this question in his analysis of state-society relations:

Elite response to mass enfranchisement has been to establish decision-making processes that fragment policy-making authority into decentralized bureaucracies incapable of formulating, let alone carrying out, possible solutions to the problems they are charged with. This process has blurred the understanding of political processes for the mass electorate; it is now almost literally impossible to understand how decisions are made and how they could be made in more rational ways. The net result has been for many voters cynicism about politicians and withdrawal and for many leaders cynicism about ignorant voters and careerism (1975, 156–7).

Alford's solution – and the thrust of this chapter – is to argue that "social and political movements capable of both understanding and action may still arise to define and create alternative models of social, economic and political organization. Critical analysis of paradigms of state-society relations may contribute something to that understanding" (158). With a better understanding of the history of municipal politics in Canada, it is possible to envisage the kinds of structures that would be conducive to progressive politics. Does having one municipal government rather than multiple municipalities, together with regional levels, operating in the same urban space create a clearer political structure, one that can be better understood? And could this structure be an arena for progressive politics? Understanding and action are linked, in that political organization at the municipal level depends on a shared sense that important things can be changed by political action at that level. But if municipalities are to take effective action, they must have the resources that are necessary to meet their responsibilities. The shared sense of the potential for effective action also depends on the existence of a discourse that articulates this potential and justifies municipal politics as a space for progressive citizens. Unless this articulation exists, action is unlikely.

It is clear that this understanding does not currently exist; municipal politics is seen neither as a central arena for political debate nor as a central arena for political action. In addition, policy questions that could be seen as urban are not seen in that light and therefore are not linked to the specific conditions of political organizing in the large Canadian cities. Examining the ways in which Canadian political economy has thought about the urban helps to explain why this is so.

CANADIAN POLITICAL ECONOMY AND THE URBAN

In general, Canadian political economy has not given much attention to cities, to urban policy, or to space as a critical dimension of politics. It has not done so because political economy presupposes that the themes of economic production, of class, and of state action at the nation-state level are of primary importance and because mainstream Canadian political science has neglected urban government and is almost obsessively preoccupied with the federal-provincial dimension of politics. (For a different view of the same lack of attention to municipal politics, see the chapter by Keil and Kipfer in this volume).

Certainly, the increasingly abundant international literature that relates global economic restructuring to urban political action has been studied in Canada. Roger Keil, Engin Isin, and Graham Todd (see, for example, Kipfer and Keil's chapter in this book and Keil 1998; Isin 1998; and Todd 1998) have participated in the debates in this literature, sometimes with the example of Toronto and sometimes more generally. Pierre Hamel and Henri Lustiger-Thaler have written about urban social movements, again sometimes based on Montreal and sometimes more generally (Hamel 1999, 2000, in press; Lustiger-Thaler 1992). Christopher Leo (1995; Leo and Shaw, in press) has looked at Winnipeg and David Wolfe (in press; Holbrook and Wolfe 2000) has looked at innovation systems in Canada as a territorially based response to economic restructuring. Geographers have, not surprisingly, been active in looking at these links and the two collections, one by Bourne and Ley, *The Changing Social Geography of Canadian Cities* (1993), and the second edition of Bunting and Filion, *Canadian Cities in Transition* (2000), both include excellent analyses of trends in Canadian demography and their impact on urban structure in Canada. But even here there is little consideration of municipal government (although the chapter by Sancton (2000c) does deal with the municipal role), and the federal government is certainly the central focus for the analysis of state action.

Warren Magnusson is an exception, however, and his article with Rob Walker, "Decentring the State" (1998), has focussed attention on the link between social movement analysis and local political action. His book *The Search for Political Space: Globalization, Social Movements, and the Urban Political Experience* (1996) further develops the analysis of these links.

The exciting potential for a spatially sensitive political economy is that it can incorporate an understanding of the politics of daily life. Focussing on space opens up considerations of the relationships between home and work and between community work, employment, and work within the family. These relationships give rise to political questions – who pays the costs and who benefits from different spatial configurations of residence, employment, and urban public spaces. Feminist analyses have been particularly prominent on these questions; Suzanne Mackenzie's article "Building Women, Building Cities: Towards Gender Sensitive Theory in the Environmental Disciplines" (1988) links understanding and action by using historical experience to reflect on current practice. Damaris Rose (1993, 1996) looks at current empirical links between employment, residence, and urban services to reflect on the costs and opportunities for different groups within the population.

This brief overview of the literature indicates that much more needs to be done if political economy is to properly analyze space and urban realities. While the limited understanding of the importance of cities and urban politics in the literature is in part caused by the marginalization of the questions that arise within the overall Canadian research agenda, this limited understanding is, in turn, also of course a cause of the relative marginalization of an urban research agenda (Andrew, Graham, and Phillips in press). As was stated earlier, the preoccupation of Canadian political science with the federal-provincial dimension of intergovernmental relations has also played a role in the relative neglect of municipal politics. Political economy has focussed on other areas, rather than critically engaging with the mainstream tradition.

URBAN REFORM:
THE HISTORICAL EXPERIENCE

As mentioned in the introduction to this chapter, two periods in Canadian history stand out as moments when urban politics acquired national prominence and when there was significant grass-roots political activity at the urban level. During these two periods – 1880–1920 and the 1960s – the progressive potential of urban-based political activity was deflected into other channels.

Both periods were marked by rapid urban growth, which clearly provides the underlying explanation for the political activity. From the 1880s to the 1920s urban areas expanded considerably: the Canadian population changed from being one-quarter to being one-half urban, and the total number of urban Canadians increased from 1.1 million to 4.3 million (Rutherford 1984, 435). Montreal and Toronto were becoming large cities, and the waves of immigration created urban environments that were very different in social composition from earlier environments. The social conditions created in these cities were the basis for much of the political activity – union organizing and movements for public health reform and temperance, for social welfare, parks and playgrounds, ownership and control of public utilities, urban planning, and municipal government reform. Paul Rutherford's anthology of articles on urban reform, *Saving the Canadian City* (1974), brings together the writings of the reformers, with their preoccupations with neglected children, liquor and crime, the housing conditions of immigrant workers, and so on. J.S. Woodsworth, one of the founders of the CCF, wrote *My Neighbour*, in which he argued that it was the modern city that developed conditions of interdependence and collective responsibility. To quote Woodsworth, "As the city is moulding our social and political life, creating new institutions and developing a new spirit, may it not have a still wider effect on our thought and life? Surely in our laws, 'vested-interests' and 'property rights' must give way before the rights of men and the welfare of society" (in Rutherford 1974, 91).

So what happened to this urban political activity? Why did it not lead to transformative municipal politics? In part, reform movements were taken up by provincial and federal political parties and governments, and social reforms were enacted at those levels. James Struthers (1994) describes the provincial campaign for mothers' allowances, a campaign centred in Toronto but focussing on the provincial level. This same provincialization occurred in public health and in urban planning; it was the federal government that created the Commission of Conservation in 1909. "The Town Planning Branch of the Commission was set up by Thomas Adams, a noted British planner, who had a broad and social vision of town planning. And the essence of town planning is the safeguarding of the health of the community and the provision of proper homes for the people" (Artibise and Stelter 1979, 184). So in part, the progressive potential of urban political activity found expression in social reforms at the provincial and federal levels with the beginning of legislation in the areas of social services, health and education.

These reform movements were limited, however, by their middle-class domination, which has been analyzed by Mariana Valverde (1991) and Paul Rutherford (1984) and, for a later period, by Margaret Little (1998). The class composition of the reform movements led also to the very dominant role played by experts and the beginning in this period of the rise of the modern urban professionals: town planners, public health professionals, social workers. The experts were seen to have new and important kinds of knowledge about how cities worked and how to improve the living conditions of the urban population. It was their answers that were sought out, not those of the population. Indeed, the middle-class leadership pushed for political reforms that would distance the voters from urban government – by the creation of boards of control elected at large and therefore – to the reformers – less subject to pressures from particular groups of voters.

The last thread in the explanation for the failure of urban activity in the reform period to transform urban politics is the constantly available individual suburban solution: if social conditions were unacceptable in the city, residents could always choose to vote with their feet and move to the suburbs. Richard Harris (1996) describes the period before and after World War I as a time of a huge increase in home ownership in Toronto, including ownership by people of very modest incomes, through the development of the unplanned suburbs. Suburban development does allow families to improve their individual living conditions, but at high costs both to themselves in terms of family expenditures for housing and transportation and at a high social cost to those left behind in the dismal living conditions of the urban core.

The 1960s were similar to the earlier reform period in a number of ways, and certainly in the strong growth in the urban population, which led to issues about the redevelopment of the urban core as industrial development moved from the downtown. The archetypal urban conflict was the conflict in Toronto over the Spadina Expressway. Opposition to the expressway came not only from residents who would have been displaced by it but also from residents who enjoyed the urban neighbourhoods of the city centre. As in the earlier period, a number of interrelated political movements were active in the large Canadian cities in the 1960s – environmental movements, second-wave feminism, economic nationalism, participatory planning, gay and lesbian rights, antiracism, student democracy, and urban reform. The major theme of the urban movements was that cities should be places to live in as well as (or in contrast to) places to make money in. Once again, the leadership of the movements was middle-class, which in some cases led to political organizing to preserve centre-city neighbourhoods as comfortable middle-class areas, rather than to struggles to preserve a mixture of housing types and housing costs. Unlike the reforms in the earlier period, the political reforms in the 1960s were aimed not at the depolitization of local government but rather at trying to strengthen a political capacity for action. Boards of control were abolished, and advisory planning committees were replaced by committees of elected councillors.

Along with the strengthening of political control at the municipal level there was also an enormous growth in pressures for participatory democracy at the local level, which took various forms – neighbourhood planning, participatory planning, institutionalizing processes of consultation, and so on (Graham, Phillips, and Maslove 1998). At the same time the weight of the expert was growing, and municipal governments were restructuring around chief administrative officers. In other areas, such as planning, a new form of expert was developing: working with the population and doing advocacy planning became part of a new expertise.

As in the earlier period, the movement for reform was channelled into political activities at other levels of government. To some extent, Pierre Trudeau's federal election victory in 1968 was based on the support of the urban middle class, and, indeed, that victory was very clearly urban. It led to some social services legislation, and it led to federal support for cooperative and nonprofit housing, the creation of the Company of Young Canadians, various short-term employment programs that supported community-based projects, and the creation of the short-lived Ministry of State for Urban Affairs (created in 1971 and abolished in 1979). Social reforms were clearly visible at the provincial level. The Quiet Revolution in Quebec centralized health and social services, in order to introduce greater social redistribution, and in a less politically visible way, the Ontario government also created a welfare state. Public housing was taken over by the province with the creation of the Ontario Housing Corporation in 1964, and this centralization led to a considerable increase in activity. Indeed, in 1969 Ontario was absorbing 98 percent of an increasing federal public housing budget (Carroll 1990, 98). New Brunswick, with the same goals of social equality and redistribution, centralized all responsibility for education and social services, leaving municipal governments as entirely marginal players.

Progressive politics was therefore federal and provincial; the municipalities continued to argue for senior government support or for the assumption by senior government of further responsibilities. A progressive municipal strategy was articulated by FRAP (Front d'Action Politique) and the RCM (Rassemblement des Citoyens et Citoyennes de Montréal) in Montreal and by COPE (Committee of Progressive Electors) in Vancouver – in arguments for public transportation, a variety of housing types (including cooperative housing and nonprofit and public housing), and better parks and recreation facilities, particularly for the poorer neighbourhoods. But for the most part, municipal politics continued to be about support for the profitable development of private property. The suburban solution continued to exist, and Canadian cities became increasingly spread out because of very low-density suburban development. Stephen Dale's *Lost in the Suburbs* (1999) analyzes the kind of suburban political culture in which residents are preoccupied with the high costs of maintaining their standard of living while living lives that are increasingly distant from, and cut off from, the centre-city populations. This combination of individual financial constraints and no contacts with other realities creates the potential for a nasty-minded right-wing politics. The suburban political culture becomes individually oriented and focussed on reducing taxes and therefore reducing public services, which leaves the municipalities of the urban core with reduced resources, while trying to meet the needs of the increasingly poorer inner-city populations.

The growth of provincial welfare states in the 1960s and 1970s was therefore linked to the fact that municipal politics was dominated by questions of physical infrastructure that were associated with the promotion of the profitable development of private property. Social services, education, and health were increasingly provincialized. By 1973, every province had a provincial housing agency. Federal housing activity was also important in the period of the 1960s and 1970s.

However, this situation changed dramatically in the 1990s. As part of its budget-cutting exercise, the federal government moved out of social housing (Harris 2000; Carroll 1990; Klodawsky and Spector 1997). Most of the provincial governments followed this example by downloading social housing to the municipal level or simply by ending their activities in social housing. This change has been one of the factors fuelling the enormous increase in homelessness in Canada since the 1990s (Peressini and McDonald 2000).

This brief overview of the two periods in Canadian history in which urban reform issues were prominently on the public agenda but failed to develop into transformative politics gives weight to Alford's (1975) hypothesis about the ways in which fragmented and decentralized structures have obscured the processes of decision making for the mass electorate. They have done so for decision making both within municipalities and between them. The creation of specialized agencies, boards, and commissions with complex and opaque processes of decision making, particularly in the early reform period, allowed most of these structures to be controlled by middle-class professionals or by people linked to the development industry. Similarly the creation of regional governments in most of the major urban areas in Canada simply added to the complexity and the lack of transparency in local politics.

Beginning with the creation of Metro Toronto in 1954 and continuing through the 1970s, regional governments were created and took on increasingly important roles in deciding the directions, and forms, of urban development. For the most part, as Colton's book *Big Daddy* (1980) brilliantly describes for the case of Toronto, these new structures were distanced from the population and not very visible to them. The lack of democratic structures could be seen to be a continuation of the urban reforms of the early twentieth century in which close contacts between citizens and municipal decisions were seen as dangerous for efficient local decision making. Regional governments are a clear illustration of Alford's analysis of the blurring of the understanding of political processes for the mass electorate. Multiple municipalities within the same urban area were already confusing enough, but adding another, regional level further complicated the citizens' capacity to understand the processes of decision making and the locations of power. And finally, the intergovernmental network of responsibilities also fragmented their understanding of the ways to organize politically in order to solve urban problems. The greater visibility of federal or provincial activities in the social policy area, coupled with these governments' interest in maintaining direct links to their electoral base and the role of political parties in linking citizens to federal and provincial, but not municipal, politics meant that progressive concerns were moved relatively easily from the urban level to federal or provincial political arenas.

CURRENT MUNICIPAL RESTRUCTURING

If the past has been marked by failed opportunities, in part through the impact of "hyper-fractionalized quasi-subordination,"[3] what is the present situation? As was indicated at the beginning of this chapter, it is dominated by the current wave of municipal amalgamations being undertaken by provincial governments.

The current wave of restructuring is somewhat similar to the earlier period of the creation of regional governments. However, unlike the earlier period, the current period of restructuring is dominated by the neoliberal political climate of the 1990s, with its preoccupation with privatization and decentralization. The debates concerning amalgamation, particularly as articulated by the Ontario government, relate to cutting costs, to reducing the number of politicians, and to producing municipal governments better able to compete for business in the global economy. The opposition to the amalgamations was particularly strong in Toronto (Milroy in press; Boudreau 2000; Sewell; Slack 2000; Sancton 2000a) and in Montreal (Sancton 2000b). In Toronto amalgamation was opposed particularly by centre-city residents and in Montreal by suburban municipalities, particularly the Anglophone municipalities of the West Island. The opposition was fuelled by a strong sense that provincial government action was anti-democratic, that urban residents were being denied a right to self-government. But despite the strength of the opposition, the provincial discourse remained dominant, with amalgamation being associated with the possibility of lower municipal taxes and with an enhanced capacity to compete globally. Despite significant evidence that costs were unlikely to be cut unless there were significant reductions in services, the hegemonic discourse linked amalgamation to cost savings, to the elimination of duplication, and to increased efficiency.

This provincial discourse illustrates, once again, Alford's analysis of elite strategies for blurring the understanding of the political process. Arguing that taxes can be cut without services being cut simply plays on the difficulty of understanding the complexities of decision-making processes and of relating resources to responsibilities for each of the levels of decision making. The trends towards decentralization – for example, moving social housing from federal to provincial and, in many cases, to municipal responsibility – have triggered concerns in the largest municipalities about what they see as the increasingly dramatic gap between resources and responsibilities. The mayors of five of the largest cities – Toronto, Montreal, Vancouver, Calgary, and Winnipeg – have met to articulate their demands that more adequate fiscal resources be made available to the municipal level of government. The Toronto Charter, an initiative aimed at articulating a more formal space in the Canadian constitutional system for the City of Toronto, also argues for more appropriate fiscal resources to support a fuller range of municipal responsibilities.

To some extent these pressures are new, in that the major thrust of the twentieth century was municipal support for the centralization of responsibilities in federal and provincial governments. Decentralization has made the gap between resources and responsibilities all that much clearer, and the amalgamations that have occurred have heightened this awareness. In some areas the municipal reaction is still to ask for greater support (or fewer responsibilities) from other levels of government, but increasingly, the largest municipalities demand a more adequate fiscal base to support increased activities, since a lack of resources has created severe pressures on the newly amalgamated municipalities to cut expenditures and therefore services. The politics of the amalgamated cities have been more about the allocation of budget cuts than about the potential for expanded services. But the increasingly strident calls for intergovernmental fiscal justice suggest an appetite on the part of the big-city mayors for a more significant political role. And this is certainly a major change from Canadian urban politics in the twentieth century.

This shift represents a potentially important change in the dynamics of the Canadian federation. If the big cities start to want to exercise greater political direction, they can enlarge and strengthen the municipal political arena. The task is then to develop a transformative political strategy to ensure that this enhanced political space is a democratic one. Centralization to the federal or provincial level is clearly not a strategy for progressive politics at the present time in Canada. What strategies would ensure, therefore, that progressive politics emerges from decentralization?

This discussion begins with descriptions of some current examples of progressive politics at the municipal level and then, building on these examples, moves to an analysis of how to strengthen the progressive dimensions of these policies. Even though the examples are small or limited, they do illustrate the capacity of municipal governments to be inclusive, to increase social justice in a way that relates to the daily lives of marginalized urban citizens, and to be transformative in the sense of redefining the conditions of daily life and the definitions of knowledge and expertise.

The first example is the use of women's safety audits (Whitzman 1995, in press; Andrew 2000) in Toronto, Montreal, and Ottawa. This issue arose from the clear differences between men and women in their feelings of security in urban places. Women felt particularly insecure after dark and were much more likely to limit their activities for this reason. This behaviour was not seen as "natural" or incidental; rather it began increasingly to be seen as an indication of women's unequal access to urban citizenship.

Women's safety audits originated in Toronto within the Metropolitan Toronto Action Committee on Violence against Women and Children (METRAC), an organization originally funded by Metro Toronto, the then regional government. METRAC established the basic procedures for women's safety audits: a group of women or a group led by women walk around a part of the city that they know well. Using a check list, they discuss what makes them uneasy about certain areas and what could be done to reduce their feelings of unease. Recommendations for action are then formulated, and the group works with various social actors, including municipal governments, to ensure the implementation of the recommendations.

The progressive potential of women's safety audits depends on a number of factors: the extent to which the process leads to real changes, the extent to which the changes enhance women's experience and women's expertise, the extent to which the group feels empowered by the process, the extent to which diversity is integrated into the group, and the process of formulating the recommendations and the implementation of them.

The question of women's expertise is central to the safety audit process. The technique is based on the idea that those who use the city, those who know a particular part of the city, are the experts and that solutions should come from their knowledge and their lived experience. Diversity is essential, because different experiences produce different knowledge. Taking account of those who are doubly discriminated against or doubly marginalized will lead to even more effective solutions – "safer for women, safer for everyone" also applies to different groups of women. Elderly women, women of colour, disabled women – these women often feel greater unease in urban space and therefore have particular knowledge and expertise about how it functions.

When successful, women's safety audits can enhance women's sense of their own expertise and allow them to challenge the "expert" discourses of the planners and the transportation engineers. For example, safety audits of the Ottawa transit stations made it clear that the original, expert-led planning had been severely deficient in not incorporating safety concerns, and all agreed that the knowledge expressed by the women users of the transit system would have improved the planning process. As was described earlier, "expert" municipal discourses were prevalent – particularly among planners, traffic engineers, and so on. The study of a concrete area allowed a real debate between different forms of expertise and provided a genuine opening for the expertise of the users.

METRAC did a great many safety audits that have been adapted to other situations, notably in Ottawa and in Montreal. In Ottawa the Women's Action Centre against Violence (WACAV), a voluntary organization funded by the regional government, has done women's safety audits of various neighbourhoods, of the transit way, of various transportation modes, and of federal walkways. Although the City of Ottawa elaborated a policy of examining recommendations with a view to implementing them, austerity measures reduced their ability to do so, but at least a process did exist for moving from recommendations to implementation.

The City of Montreal had a staff position that was responsible for programming related to women, under the title of Femmes et villes. Much of the work of this program was done as a partnership between the City of Montreal and a coalition bringing together neighbourhood-level crime-prevention groups, neighbourhood-level women's centres, women's groups, and parts of the city bureaucracy working on issues of crime prevention and women's safety. The group, called CAFSU (Comité d'action – femmes et sécurité urbaine), is made up of about twenty associations and acts to ensure community input into the programming of the city. The position has been maintained in the newly amalgamated City of Montreal, although at the moment only the original position exists, which in the much larger territory of the amalgamated city implies a diminution of the service.

CAFSU and individual groups within CAFSU have been responsible for a number of safety audits in different neighbourhoods, recreation facilities, and so on. Again, the approach has been important, and making sure that women's agency is central to the process has been one of the clear goals of the city's program. CAFSU has recently produced a tool kit with information about women's urban safety that includes a training package emphasizing a women-centred perspective. Validating women's knowledge and women's experience are central to the success of safety audits; they are techniques not only for physical improvements to the city but also for transforming understandings of who knows and of knowledge production more broadly.

One concrete improvement to urban services and to daily life has been for the public transportation system in Montreal to initiate a night-time program whereby passengers can leave city buses anywhere along a bus route, not just at regular stops. As a result, people are less fearful about having to walk long distances from bus stops to their destinations. For women dependent on public transportation this apparently minor change creates new opportunities for participation in the city. It also accepts that users of the system understand how it best operates and that their knowledge should be included in planning and operating urban services.

Another example that illustrates the progressive potential of municipal government comes from the City of Ottawa and the Working Group on Women's Access to Municipal Services. This working group was established by the former Regional Municipality of Ottawa-Carleton in November 1999, following the adoption by the region of the International Union of Local Authorities (IULA) Worldwide Declaration on Women and Local Government. The working group was made up of representatives of community-based women's groups, of city staff, and of the women's studies programs of the two local universities.[4] It conducted interviews with twenty focus groups, largely with doubly disadvantaged groups of women, in order to reach very diverse communities across Ottawa involving refugee women, elderly immigrant populations, young visible-minority women, women with disabilities, rural women, women in emergency housing, and so on. The groups were organized around three poles related to experiences with services that had facilitated participants' lives, experiences that had been obstacles, and recommendations for change. This process associated the participants' experience with their expertise. Because it was based on the idea that as users of the city services they were experts and that policy changes should come from their recommendations, the focus-group process was empowering to women, many of whom had never been involved in municipal government.

A day-long community forum brought together participants in the focus groups with city staff. The format of the forum was intended to encourage voice, and the energy from the group participants was enormous. The combination of language interpretation services (including sign language) and cultural interpretation services created an atmosphere in which voice was central, and multiple modes of language exchange took place. The importance given to different forms of interpretation is central to creating a sense of women's expertise and women's agency.

The recommendations of the working group picked up the suggestions from the focus groups, highlighting those areas where the largest numbers of women had made suggestions or comments. A central theme was the lack of information, and particularly appropriate information, about city services. The theme of appropriate information implied issues about language and cultural sensitivity but also about delivery mechanisms, such as using community organizations and community locations to provide information. Public transportation was another crucial area for recommendations, and the extent to which good public transportation is a social justice issue was made eloquently clear. Ensuring quality service to diverse groups implies a whole series of changes: better service to the rural areas, providing information about how long passengers must wait for the next bus, making the public aware of the policy that allows them to indicate where they want to get off the bus at night, ensuring that drivers are sensitive to cultural diversity, and providing equipment that allows elderly women to enter the bus more easily. Again, these recommendations stem from the users' understanding of how the service operates and from its importance to their daily lives.

This viewpoint became clear in the recommendations about combining services and the co-location of services. Not only public transportation but also childcare and cultural interpretation were seen as services that in turn helped women access other services. The complex organization of daily life would be facilitated if these services could be combined. For instance, without childcare, women with small children have huge difficulties getting information about employment possibilities. If employment services were available along the transit way or close to good bus routes, life would be more manageable.

It was clear from the community forum that women saw these issues to be about their equal access to citizenship. Their full participation in the life of the city was hampered or facilitated by the existence of city services, by the location of these services, by the attitudes of those delivering the services, by the information available about these services, and by the complex ways in which the various services interrelated. It was also clear that women saw these services as areas of their expertise, that they felt comfortable with their knowledge of the interrelation of municipal services and their daily lives. This example is nevertheless an unfinished story – the City of Ottawa decided that the city manager's office should coordinate a review of all the recommendations and report back. The challenge is how to monitor this review and to try to maintain community pressure and community enthusiasm for pushing for implementation.

A more general conclusion concerning the larger municipalities is that progressive social movements need to apply greater and more continuous pressure on municipal governments, insisting that they should act progressively in carrying out their responsibilities. Progressive social movements should also apply greater political pressure generally, arguing that municipalities must be given the resources they require. If homelessness is to be acted on at the local level, new social housing must be provided, and a coordinated effort must be made to bring together and integrate support services of high quality for the widely diverse groups within the homeless population. This approach demands municipal governance with community leadership, which, in turn, requires adequate financial resources. If provincial or federal governments are not going to act in this area, municipal governments must be given the resources to allow them to do so.

The women's movement can play a central role in this strategy (Andrew 2001). First of all, women have real interests in pushing for the enhancement of public services, since they are still poorer than men; some groups of women, such as elderly women and single mothers, are among the poorest in Canadian society. Since the beginning of the second wave of feminism, the women's movement has focussed more on federal and provincial public services, but municipal government responsibilities are of considerable significance for women's lives.

Safety has been the major area where women's organizations have been in close contact with municipal governments, both for issues of public safety, some of which have already been discussed, and of domestic violence. In Toronto, Montreal, and Ottawa, municipal programs have operated in close contact with women's organizations in civil society (Whitzman 1995, in press; Andrew 1995; CAFSU 2000). Questions of safety have not only linked women across class and race, they have also linked areas of municipal activity, in that issues of safety come up in municipal recreation programming, public transit and transportation more generally, planning, and public health. Good public transportation is a women's issue, since women are more frequent users of public transportation and, given their greater family responsibilities, have more complex needs in relation to the transportation system.

But women's organizations are not the only social movement organizations that need to play a stronger role at the municipal level to demand greater government action and greater equity. Like the women's movement, many organizations representing racialized communities and antiracist organizations have been more interested in federal and provincial politics than in local politics, although there have been some links with municipal governments. Given the demographics of the large Canadian municipalities, municipal action will be increasingly significant, and, as a recent City of Toronto policy framework on immigration and settlement indicates, "the City's human rights, access and equity policies and programs help build a cohesive community by creating a welcoming climate, mutual respect and acceptance of diversity among all residents. The City's Economic Development Strategy identifies Toronto's linguistic and socio-economic diversity as key competitive strengths upon which the city must build" (City of Toronto 2001, 4). Again, the progressive nature of municipal policies varies considerably, but the potential is there. Antiracist public education programs, antidiscrimination policies in local housing markets, employment programs for racialized immigrants, cultural interpretation to facilitate access to social and legal services, and significant cultural programming, all these measures have transformative potential.

But these changes will not take place if political pressure is not exerted on the municipal elites. And one of the existing constraints is the lack of an articulated discourse that links municipal government to the possibility of progressive politics and of significant social change. This discourse should be centred on the relationship between space and social justice. Space is a central dimension of municipal governments. They are responsible for locating development; planning is their area of expertise. But the implications of municipal planning for social justice are not sufficiently understood or exploited. These implications are significant at the level of people's daily lives. Good public transportation can allow poor women to get to and from employment easily, and intelligently placed public services can result in women devoting less time to the basic obligations of existence. Daycare services of high quality are an essential part of a strategy for greater social equality. Local housing markets where racial discrimination was not tolerated would make people's lives easier, and so too would recreational and cultural facilities that were inclusive, participatory, and well-resourced.

These issues of social justice in daily life become much more important in the light of global trends to social polarization (Andrew 2000–2001). Since the largest pockets of the richest and the poorest citizens together occupy the centres of the big cities in Canada, the relationships between space and social justice, between space and gender, and between race and class become increasingly important. It is municipal governments who have the responsibilities and the policy tools to ensure that there is public space for debate, as well as public space within the city. But without the active participation of social movement organizations, this will not happen. If amalgamations have done nothing else, they have clarified the issues and therefore made more acute the need for action.

NOTES

1   The newly amalgamated municipality in the Outaouais region is called Gatineau. I have referred to it here as Hull only because that was the name of the central municipality on the Quebec side of the national capital region and the name used to refer to the Quebec portion of the national capital region.

2   Halifax was amalgamated in 1996, Toronto in 1998, and Ottawa and Hamilton as of 1 January 2001. The Quebec amalgamations, for Montreal, Quebec City, and Gatineau, began as of 1 January 2002.

3   This description was given by J.S. Dupré to the provincial-municipal relationship in his study for the Ontario Smith Committee on Taxation. Dupré compared the federal-provincial relationship to the provincial-municipal one. "Hyper-fractionalization" describes the fact that municipal responsibilities are fragmented among multiple agencies, boards, and commissions, as well as the municipal government as such, and that at the provincial level there are also a large number of departments, in addition to Municipal Affairs, that have direct relationships with municipalities. The quasi-subordination describes the political reality in which the constitutional position of clear subordination of municipal government is mitigated by the political strength of the municipal elites and their capacity to exert political pressure at the provincial level.

4   I was a member of the Working Group and therefore this description is clearly that of a participant observer, with all that that role implies in term of limits and opportunities.

REFERENCES

Alford, Robert R. 1975. "Paradigms of Relations between State and Society." In L. Lindberg, Robert Alford, Colin Crouch, and Claus Offer, eds., *Stress and Contradiction in Modern Capitalism*, 145–60. Lexington, KY: D.C. Heath.

Andrew, Caroline. 1995. "Getting Women's Issues on the Municipal Agenda:

Violence against Women." In J. Garber and R. Turner, eds., *Gender in Urban Research*, 98–118. Thousand Oaks, CA: Sage.
– 2000. "Resisting Boundaries? Using Safety Audits for Women." In K. Miranne and A. Young, eds., *Gendering the City*, 157–68. Lanham: Rowman and Littlefield.
– 2000–2001. "The Shame of (Ignoring) the Cities." *Journal of Canadian Studies* 35(4): 100–10.
– 2001. "Situating the Local: Between Tensions and Passions." Conference Presentation, Tenth Biennial Conference on Canadian Social Welfare, Calgary.
Andrew, Caroline, Katherine Graham and Susan Phillips, eds. In press. *Urban Affairs: Back on the Policy Agenda*. Montreal and Kingston: McGill-Queen's University Press.
Artibise, Alan F.J., and Gilbert A. Stelter, eds. 1979. *The Usable Urban Past*. Toronto: Macmillan, Carleton Library no 119.
Boudreau, Julie-Anne. 2000. *The Mega City Saga*. Montreal: Black Rose Books.
Bourne, Larry S., and David F. Ley, eds. 1993. *The Changing Social Geography of Canadian Cities*. Montreal and Kingston: McGill-Queen's University Press.
Bunting, Trudi, and Pierre Filion, eds. 2000. *Canadian Cities in Transition*. 2d ed. Toronto: Oxford.
Carroll, Barbara W. 1990. "Housing." In R. Loreto and T. Price, eds., *Urban Policy Issues*, 86–106. Toronto: McClelland and Stewart.
Castells, Manuel. 1996. *The Rise of the Network Society*. Oxford: Blackwell Publishers.
City of Toronto. 2001. *Immigration and Settlement Policy Framework*. Toronto: City of Toronto.
Colton, Timothy. 1980. *Big Daddy: Frederick G. Gardiner and the Building of Metropolitan Toronto*. Toronto: University of Toronto Press.
Comité d'action femmes et sécurité urbaine (CAFSU). 2000. La boîte à outils du CAFSU. Montreal: CAFSU.
Dale, Stephen. 1999. *Lost in the Suburbs: A Political Travelogue*. Toronto: Stoddart.
Dupré, J. Stefan. 1968. *Intergovernmental Finance in Ontario: A Provincial-Local Perspective*. Toronto: Ontario Commission on Taxation, Government of Ontario.
Graham, Katherine, Susan Phillips, and Allan Maslove. 1998. *Urban Governance in Canada*. Toronto: Harcourt Brace.
Hamel, Pierre. 1999. "La consultation publique et les limites de la participation des citoyens aux affaires urbaines." *Recherches sociographiques* 40(3): 435–66.
– 2000. "The Fragmentation of Social Movements and Social Justice: Beyond the Traditional Forms of Localism." In Pierre Hamel, Henri-Lustiger Thaler,

and Margit Mayer, eds. *Urban Movements in a Globalising World*, 158–76. London: Routledge.

– In press. "Urban Issues and New Public Policy Challenges: The Example of Public Consultation Policy in Montreal." In C. Andrew, K. Graham, and S. Phillips, eds., *Urban Affairs: Back on the Policy Agenda.* Montreal and Kingston: McGill-Queen's University Press.

Harris, Richard. 1996. *Unplanned Suburbs: Toronto's American Tragedy, 1900 to 1950.* Baltimore, MD: The Johns Hopkins University Press.

– 2000. "Housing." In T. Bunting and P. Filion, eds., *Canadian Cities in Transition*, 380–403. 2d ed. Toronto: Oxford.

Holbrook, J. Adam, and David A. Wolfe. 2000. *Innovation, Institutions and Territory: Regional Innovation Systems in Canada.* Montreal and Kingston: McGill-Queen's University Press.

International Union of Local Authorities. 1998. *IULA Worldwide Declaration on Women and Local Government.* Harare, Zimbabwe.

Isin, Engin F. 1998. "Governing Toronto without Government: Liberalism and Neoliberalism." *Studies in Political Economy* 56:169–91.

Jacobs, Jane. 1961. *The Death and Life of Great American Cities.* New York: Vintage.

Keil, Roger. 1998. "Toronto in the 1990s: Dissociated Governance?" *Studies in Political Economy* 56:151–67.

Klodawsky, Fran, and Aron Spector. 1997. "Renovation or Abandonment? Canadian Social Housing at a Crossroads." In Gene Swimmer, ed., *How Ottawa Spends*, 259–80. Ottawa: Carleton University Press.

Leo, Christopher. 1995. "The State in the City: A Political-Economy Perspective on Growth and Decay." In J. Lightbody, ed., *Canadian Metropolitics*, 27–50. Toronto: Copp-Clark.

Leo, Christopher, and Lisa Shaw. In press. "What Causes Inner-City Decay and What Can Be Done About It?" In C. Andrew, K. Graham, and S. Phillips, eds. *Urban Affairs: Back on the Policy Agenda.* Montreal and Kingston: McGill-Queen's University Press.

Little, Margaret. 1998. *"No Car, No Radio, No Liquor Permit": The Moral Regulation of Single Mothers in Ontario, 1920–1997.* Toronto: Oxford.

Lustiger-Thaler, Henri, ed. 1992. *Political Arrangements.* Montreal: Black Rose Books.

Mackenzie, Suzanne. 1988. "Building Women, Building Cities: Toward Gender Sensitive Theory in the Environmental Disciplines." In C. Andrew and B. Milroy, eds., *Life Spaces: Gender, Household, Employment*, 13–30. Vancouver: University of British Columbia Press.

Magnusson, Warren. 1996. *The Search for Political Space: Globalization, Social Movements, and the Urban Political Experience.* Toronto: University of Toronto Press.

Magnusson, Warren, and R.B.J. Walker. 1988. "Decentring the State: Political Theory and Canadian Political Economy." *Studies in Political Economy* 27:37–71.

Milroy, Beth. In press. "Toronto's Legal Challenge to Amalgamation." In C. Andrew, K. Graham, and S. Phillips, eds., *Urban Affairs: Back on the Policy Agenda.*. Montreal and Kingston: McGill-Queen's University Press.

Peressini, Tracy, and Lynn McDonald. 2000. "Urban Homelessness in Canada." In T. Bunting and P. Filion, eds., *Canadian Cities in Transition*, 525–43. 2d ed. Toronto: Oxford.

Rose, Damaris. 1993. "Local Childcare Strategies in Montreal, Quebec: The Mediation of State Policies, Class and Ethnicity in the Life Courses of Families with Young Children." In C. Katz and J. Monk, eds., *Full Circle: Geographics of Women over the Life Course*, 188–207. London: Routledge.

– 1996. "Economic Restructuring and the Diversification of Gentrification in the 1990s: A View from a Marginal Metropolis." In J. Caulfield and L. Peake, eds., *City Lives and City Forms: Critical Research and Canadian Urbanism*, 131–72. Toronto: University of Toronto Press.

Rutherford, Paul. 1984. "Tomorrow's Metropolis: The Urban Reform Movement in Canada, 1850–1920." In G. Stelter and A. Artibise, eds., *The Canadian City*, 435–55. Ottawa: Carleton University Press.

– ed. 1974. *Saving the Canadian City: The First Phase, 1880–1920*. Toronto: University of Toronto Press.

Sancton, Andrew. 2000a. "Amalgamations, Service Realignment and Property Taxes: Did the Harris Government Have a Plan for Ontario's Municipalities? *Canadian Journal of Regional Science* 23(1):135–56.

– 2000b. *Merger Mania: The Assault on Local Government*. Westmount, QC: Price-Patterson.

– 2000c. "The Municipal Role in the Governance of Canadian Cities." In T. Bunting and P. Filion, eds., *Canadian Cities in Transition*, 425–42. 2d ed. Toronto: Oxford.

Sewell, John. Local Self-Government. At www.localselfgovt.com.

Slack, Enid. 2000. "A Preliminary Assessment of the New City of Toronto." *Canadian Journal of Regional Science* 23(1):13–29.

Struthers, James. 1994. *The Limits of Affluence*. Toronto: University of Toronto Press.

Todd, Graham. 1998. "Megacity: Globalization and Governance in Toronto." *Studies in Political Economy* 56:193–216.

Valverde, Mariane. 1991. *The Age of Light, Soap and Water: Moral Reform in English Canada, 1885–1925*. Toronto: McClelland and Stewart.

Whitzman, Carolyn. In press. "The 'Voice of Women' in Canadian Local Government." In C. Andrew, K. Graham, and S. Phillips, *Urban Affairs: Back on the Policy Agenda*. Montreal and Kingston: McGill-Queen's University Press.

– 1995. "What Do You want to Do? Pave Parks?" In M. Eichler, ed., *Change of Plans: Toward a Non-Sexist Sustainable City*, 89–110. Toronto: Garamond.

Wolfe, David. 2001. "Negotiating Order: Sectoral Policies and Social Learning in Ontario." In M. Gertler and D. Wolfe, eds., *Innovation and Social Learning*. Palgrave, ON: Basing Stoke.

– In press. "From the National to the Local: Recent Lessons for Economic Development Policy." In C. Andrew, K. Graham, and S. Phillips. eds., *Urban Affairs: Back on the Policy Agenda*. Montreal and Kingston: McGill-Queen's University Press.

Working Group on Women's Access to Municipal Services in Ottawa. 2001. *Making the New City of Ottawa Work for Women*. At http://aix1.uottawa.ca/~candrew/womenhome.html.

14 The Urban Experience and Globalization

ROGER KEIL AND STEFAN KIPFER

INTRODUCTION

Canadian cities appear once again to be in crisis. Long considered different from (and superior to) their U.S. counterparts by many observers, Canadian urban regions have now entered a period of soul searching with regard to their economic viability, political governance, social justice, cultural attractiveness, and ecological sustainability. Symptomatic of this crisis are calls by municipal politicians, pundits, and business groups who claim that Canadian cities suffer from a competitive lag and must receive financial support from senior levels of government similar to the support given to the American cities. While this crisis affects all categories of cities in Canada – resource towns in the North and West, fishing outports on the coasts, agricultural communities in the prairies, as well as old industrial towns and Fordist suburbs – it is perhaps most pronounced in the largest urban centres of the country, in Toronto, Montreal, and Vancouver. These cities belong to or aspire to a special category of global or world cities. They have been more visibly transnationalized than other cities, and they indicate that previous descriptions of the urban experience of Canadian cities as expressions of colonial, North American, or Canadian pathways to urbanization may no longer be adequate.

Unfortunately, urban questions do not figure prominently in Canadian political economy. But as the French writer Henri Lefebvre suggested, the production of urban space, the expansion of the built environment, and the industrialization of agriculture have made distinctions between city and countryside a thing of the past. Toronto and Moose Jaw are less absolutely different social forms than gradual distinctions within an unevenly urbanized world. At the same time, Toronto has more in common with other global cities of its kind than with the needs of its own hinterlands. In this context, "the urban" is the central connecting link between large social orders (class, capital, the state, patriarchy, empire) and the intricate details of everyday life. While our remarks concentrate on political economy, this urban perspective fuses critical theory (the critical, change-oriented analysis of modern social life) with political economy (the socio-spatial and political construction of capitalist economies). We argue that any critique and revolution of today's global capitalism must consider the urban as a source of utopian energies. Caught between the macro-dimensions of the social order and the micro-worlds of everyday life, urban politics is no mere local affair but holds promise for general social transformation (Lefebvre 1996).

Globalization illustrates the relevance of urban research. Current discussions about globalization, restructuring, the role of the state, and resistance/opposition could benefit greatly from a more systematically spatial and urban perspective. Globalization, as we understand it in this chapter, is not an external, a-spatial/nongeographical force but a process and strategy organized through urbanization. Our approach is a critique of the common national focus of political economy. Global-city research, a term we will return to shortly, is about urban processes as multiscale phenomena rather than forces contained by national boundaries. Global-city formation occurs when urban regions are articulated with global processes such as the international financial economy, global flows of goods and people, and global cultures. In today's world these processes usually connect heightened uneven development, transnational forms of capital centralization, and new forms of migration with any given global city. Research on Canada's global cities can shed light on the "secondary imperialism" of Canada's political economy, past and present (Carroll 1989; Dua 1999). In turn, a study of urban transnationalization can provide the starting point to investigate how city building, urban forms, and spatial relations link everyday life to a number of contemporary forms of restructuring: class formation, a growing role for "culture" in economic development, the production of nature, immigration, multiculturalism, gendered and racialized forms of social polarization, and state intervention. In particular, transnational urbanization highlights how class relations are formed through segmentations of gender, race, and culture (Stasiulis 1997). In our remarks about the "competitive city," we shed light on the role of city politics in mediating conflict and enforcing restructuring through entrepreneurial planning, diversity management, and law and order. The chapter concludes with remarks about the possibility of urbanizing resistance to neoliberalism, globalization, and capitalism.

In reviewing the Canadian urban experience in this age of globalization, we rely on critical social theory and political economy. Concentrating on Canadian writing but also drawing on theoretical literatures from other contexts, we argue that critical urban research is relevant for these works. Over the years, a growing number of scholars have concerned themselves with the specifically urban aspects of political economy. Researchers studying gentrification, that is, the gradual transformation of working-class neighbourhoods by real estate investment and professional middle-class or elite residents, have demonstrated that urban social geography and the built environment must be taken into account if one wants to analyze class formation (see Ley 1996; Caulfield 1994; Rose 1996). Economic geographers have shown how urban research helps one understand how labour markets and class relations are organized spatially and are segmented along lines of gender and race (see Arat-Koc 1999; Preston and Giles 1997; Aguiar 2000). Feminist and queer research has pointed to the relationship between gender inequality, patriarchal notions of sexuality and domestic life, and suburbanization and the design of urban form (See Werkerle 1984; Werkerle and Peake 1996; Ingram et al. 1997). Analysts of racism have demonstrated that multiculturalism can be understood as new form of racialization connected to new urban geographies of migration, racialized images of the city, the formation of urban social movements, and conflicts over land-use and housing (Koyabashi 1993, Abu-Laban 1997; Mitchell 1993; Croucher 1997; Siemiatycki and Isin 1998). Urban theorists have alerted us to the connections between new urban forms (waterfront redevelopments, edge cities), capitalist restructuring, local politics, and shifts in societal relationships with nature (Keil 1995; Hartmann 1996; Keil and Graham 1998; Desfor and Keil 1999; Adkin this volume). And research on social movements, municipal politics, and the "local state" explains how state institutions are organized spatially (Magnusson 1996; Keil 1998b; Wekerle 1999; Andrew this volume; Kipfer and Keil 2002).

Surprisingly, though, urban research is still treated as a secondary field. Even though 23.9 million Canadians, or 80 percent of the country's population, lived in urban areas in 2001, and even though 64 percent of the country's population lived in twenty-seven census metropolitan areas with populations over one hundred thousand people (Statistics Canada 2002), urban research is still bracketed from the main currents of critical social theory and political economy as the domain of specialists (urban planners or architects) or as a mere sub-field where general research questions are applied to the more concrete local level. The new Canadian political economy (NCPE), for example, is still privileging the national over the urban question. Its persistent focus on the nation-state as the main unit of analysis (Mac-Donald 1997) has meant that urban questions have continued to be eclipsed by the supposedly larger and only superficially spatialized questions of class, gender, race, region, state, and development.[1] A central mediating dimension of social life – the production of urban space – has not been given adequate attention within the NCPE.

There are three major reasons for this oversight and the relegation of urban research to an afterthought of critical social theory. First, Canada resembles countries such as the United States, Australia, and England, whose dominant national ideologies were built on images of nature uncontaminated by all the evils associated with the city: individualism, sin, deviance, politics, and protest. Ideologically, Canada was formed as empty wilderness, as a resource-rich expanse, or as a stunning North-Country inhabited by rugged pioneers. But ironically, the nonurban imagination of Canada as a frontier and a site of conquest of nature and aboriginal peoples is a product of urbanization (Wallace and Shields 1997) and the flip-side of the expansion of Canada's metropolitan core (Careless 1989). As the super-profits of the resource and agricultural economies flowed into the urban centres of the country in past centuries, little attention was paid to the specific conditions of urbanization. As Canadian cities became the built environment of the rural surplus and the container of the industrial proletariat set free from the countryside or attracted through immigration, they remained enigmatic themselves. The development of the Canadian West and North as mere resource economies and deindustrialization in the Atlantic East under Canada's national policies nurtured a common antiurban bias, a bias against the urban and industrial core of Ontario and Quebec generally and Toronto specifically. In metropolitan Canada itself, much city-building since Victorian times has kept antiurban desires alive by promising an escape from the city in low-density suburbs and lush central-city areas.

Second, the nation-state focus of the NCPE can be traced to the centrality of the national question in the English-Canadian and Quebec left. While in France, Germany, and the United States, the new left (and subsequent academic debates) had an explicit connection to the urban struggles of the 1960s, Canada's new left was much more strongly shaped by the perceived necessity to build alliances across regionalist divides. For the original proponents of the NCPE, socialism in Quebec and Canada could be achieved only by breaking the stranglehold of U.S. imperialists and their English-Canadian allies. In English Canada, left national and nationalist tendencies have recently been revived by the struggle of public-sector workers and autoworkers against the conservatism of American-based "international" unions in the Canadian labour movement, the campaign against free trade in 1987, and protectionist currents in struggles against globalization. Left and social movement debates in Quebec continue to be shaped by the national question, even after the Parti Quebecois has taken increasingly entrepreneurial and conservative turns. In Montreal the national question still has a formative, if complex, relationship to left and to progressive city politics (Sancton 1983b; Chorney and Molloy 1993).[2]

Third, the national orientation of left politics in Canada is itself partly a result of Canada's comparatively weak and aborted urban revolutionary tradition (Chorney 1981). Even if one does not share the view that the forces of urbanization, commodification, and fragmentation perpetually undermine the prospects for a revolutionary urban politics, it is clear that one aspect of urban politics – local and municipal politics – has been rather circumscribed in the Canadian context. The arenas of local and municipal politics in Canada have been captured above else by an essentially bourgeois "politics of property" (Sancton 1983a) and narrow, seemingly technical concerns of public administration (Andrew, this volume). This has meant that left and radical social movements in Canada's largest cities – Montreal, Vancouver, Toronto, Winnipeg – have been overshadowed by modest, "progressivist" reform currents centred on segments of the new middle class (Magnusson 1996, 199–206). Even in Montreal the rise of the Montreal Citizen Movement to power in the 1980s took place at the expense of the left currents that shaped what was Canada's most promising progressive local political formation in the 1970s.[3]

URBANIZATION, POLITICAL ECONOMY, AND GLOBALIZATION

Too many notions of globalization have treated it as an inexorable process or an awe-inspiring product of corporate power that imposes itself on everyday life from the outside, as it were. These notions of globalization tend to work with aspatial notions of capitalism and political economy that make globalization appear as a force removed from territory. Materialist approaches to urban studies and critical urban political economy provide a corrective to this dominant perspective.

Urban political economy, as understood here, is at once a specific subset of the larger tradition of political economy and a very particular theory in the field of urban studies that deals explicitly with local and community power.

The first approach to urban political economy is based on the neo-marxism and neoweberianism in urban studies in the 1960s and 1970s. It presents the process of urbanization as a constitutive part of the overall process of capital accumulation in space: the "creative destruction" of built environments depended on, but was also productive of, the expansion of capital's temporal and spatial reach. This intensely uneven process is historically and geographically specific and congeals in so-called spatial fixes of real and concrete built environments, which are thought of as conducive to the accumulation process at a given point. As time proceeds, the social, spatial, political, and other arrangements represented by a spatial fix become themselves an obstacle to accumulation and to the functioning of the capitalist city. The built environment is being fully or partly destroyed – examples are urban renewal or deindustrialization – to make space for yet another spatial fix (Harvey 1989a). These processes occur with the active participation of political and social actors who help shape the specific pathways of urban development in the face of general pressures (Keil 1998).

The other, more specific use of urban political economy as applied in this paper challenges traditional notions of community power as either elitist or pluralist. Between the 1970s and 1980s, a new breed of research on "urban regimes" and "growth machines" emerged that came to be called political economy, in summary fashion. Critiquing both the naïve democratic idealism of liberal urban theories and the rigidities of a certain Marxist class analysis (which in its crudest forms just derived urban issues from the larger social contradictions), urban political economists of this generation sought to understand the meso- and micro-level processes through a thick analysis of the governing coalitions and growth machines of individual cities. During the restructuring of major capitalist economies in the past decades and in the context of globalization, this approach has largely influenced work in the field of urban studies. Recently, there have been attempts to re-embed regime and growth-machine theory into neomarxist frameworks of regulation theory and state theory (Jonas and Wilson 1999; Lauria 1997).

On the basis of this work, the relationship between globalization and urbanization has now been studied extensively (Sassen 1994). Urbanization is no longer understood simply within the confines of national city systems (Brenner 1999). Rather, transnational urbanization has become a central subject of stxudy (Smith 2001). One dimension of transnational urbanization is tied to the formation of a network of world cities, or global cities (on this literature see Sassen 1994; Knox and Taylor 1995). Global cities are major urban centres of corporate control and destination points of transnational migration. They are also basing points for a new transnational imperialism (globalization) that is driven by states, capitalist interests, and multinational institutions. Global-city research demonstrates that globalization – transnational movements of capital and labour – is far from a deterritorialized process but depends on "spatial fixes" (such as global cities) for production or corporate control. Globalization is not nonterritorial but rather is a multiscale process that occurs through urbanization. Global-city research is also a fruitful way of analyzing the racialization and gendering of class relations in our world, not only because in many European and American global cities, social restructuring is tied to the new imperialism of transnational finance capital and the settlement of non-European immigrants but also because the contemporary global/urban imperial order connects to previous colonial and imperial histories (King 1990). Current forms of socio-spatial polarization and segmentation build on preexisting "racial urbanisms" (Nightingale 2001), as well as on gendered forms of class and ethnic segmentation (Marcuse and Von Kempen 2000; Abu-Lughod 1998).

Extending global-city research to questions of urban politics suggests that globalization is both a contradictory urban process and a project with discursive and ideological dimensions. Global cities are not simply places with many transnational headquarters but places of rich social and political contradiction where actors struggle on several scales of the globalization process. They are the products of "glocalization" processes and different forms of urban politics rather than the "footprints" of some abstract and removed force of globalization (see Keil 1998a; Keil and Ronneberger 2000; Kipfer 1995, 2000). Municipal politics is one aspect of urban politics, that helps to inscribe, modify, and regulate the processes and projects of globalization in urban space. Local states, growth coalitions, and regimes mediate social conflict, link transnational finance and real estate with local and regional city building projects, reinforce or moderate processes of spatial segmentation, and shape the way in which transnational migrants become political actors. Local social movements have often played an active role in the process of globalization by rebelling against the forces of postwar urbanization and resisting or reforming processes of global urbanization (Keil 1998b; Kipfer 1995, 2000).

CITIES IN CANADA:
CANADIAN, NORTH AMERICAN, OR GLOBAL?

Debates centred on the nation-state in comparative political sociology and political economy have had a significant influence in Canadian urban political economy. Debates between English–speaking students of Innis and Marx on the status of Canada within the world economy have framed critical Canadian urban studies in national terms. Staples theory, in particular, has been very influential in Canadian urban political economy (Stelter and Artibise 1982, 1984; McCann and Smith 1991). Refining this framework, Stelter has analyzed urbanization as a product of national political and economic systems refracted through the city-building practices of urban elites. While Stelter traces the origins of Canadian urbanization to the world economy and French and British imperial policies of military administration, staples extraction, and settlement, his main interest is in the formation of a city system contained by a national bourgeoisie, the Canadian nation-state, and a series of national policies. Stelter traces the formation of the Canadian city system to the transition from the mercantile and entrepot cities of the early colonial period and the commercial cities of the nineteenth century to the expanding industrial cities of the late nineteenth and early twentieth century and, since World War II, to the "corporate city" (1982, 1984). Until the interwar period, Montreal was at the core of this national city-system as Canada's major commercial and industrial city and undisputed bourgeois metropolis (Germain and Rose 2000).

Even though Stelter's periodization resembles the periodization established for the American case (Gordon 1978; Abu-Lughod 1998), his account of Canada's national urban system serves as the basis for distinguishing between Canadian and American urbanization. Canada's cities have a more persistent downtown-elite presence, a more stunted industrial base, and a more restricted jurisdictional role than their American counterparts, due to their mercantile and commercial stages of urbanization and the long-lasting policy of the British colonial authorities of emphasizing the military and staples-exporting role of cities, which delayed and restricted municipal autonomy to preempt a second American revolution (Stelter 1982, 1986). Later, Goldberg and Mercer (1986) criticized a perceived "indiscriminate application of American-based ideas about cities and urban policy to a Canadian setting" in the 1950s and 1960s. Canada's more collective, interventionist political culture and its more developed welfare state can explain why the country's cities tend to have a more compact urban form, more resilient central business districts, more populous and diverse inner-city neighbourhoods, and less racialized relationships between inner cities and the suburbs than do their American counterparts.

These formulations resemble "urban myths" about Canadian urbanization (Filion 1999; Croucher 1997). The most important of these myths suggest that the Canadian city represents a type of urbanization that is different from and superior to the American city, which is defined by "red-lining," inner-city ghettoization, and rampant suburbanization (Jacobs 1993). (American banks practise red-lining when they draw an imaginary red line around a neighbourhood to declare it out of reach for credit for investment in commercial or residential properties. It was widely used in the 1960s and 1970s and led to widespread dilapidation of entire inner-city blocks. It was often associated with other racist and exclusionary practices in urban planning and development.) Comparing the supposedly benign – ethnically harmonious, peaceful, compact – Canadian city to the dystopian American city, these urban myths provide an important reservoir of images for national-identity formation. While sustaining national identities, these myths have often been produced in locally specific contexts. Descriptions of Toronto as "a city that works," "New York run by the Swiss," and "a multicultural mosaic," and images of Vancouver as a hippie "urban village" on the Pacific Rim (Ley et al. 1992) and a "North American model for developing innovative forms of inter-municipal cooperation" (Sancton 1999, 1) were sustained by civic reform currents that have shaped the planning discourse in Canadian cities since the late 1960s. Notions of Montreal as a Quebec capital or a cosmopolitan Euro-American metropolis grew out of competing views on the national question in Quebec, views that tried to distinguish the city from English Canada or from the rest of urban North America (Germain and Rose 2000; Sancton 1983b).

Despite many differences between American and Canadian cities, it is questionable whether the Canadian city exists as a distinct type of urbanization. There are important differences between Canada's major urban regions (Filion 1999). From a global perspective, differences between American and Canadian cities appear more partial and historically contingent than absolute and generic. Canadian urbanism appears to be less a distinct type than a variation of a similar North American pattern of "frontier" development that occurred as an extension of empire and white colonial settlement in a postfeudal context and a highly ethnicized and spatially segmented form of class formation. In the realm of municipal politics, Canadian cities represent the propertied politics of growth, development, and home ownership that has historically dominated American cities

(Sancton 1983a; Garber and Imbroscio 1996). Rooted in British colonialism and early twentieth-century reform movements (Isin 1995; Weaver 1979; Gunton 1982), the municipal level of politics is the one that comes closest to its American counterpart (Price 1995). Tightly constrained by provincial governments, which have played a more significant role within Canadian federalism than American states in their federal system, Canadian municipalities lack the "home-rule" status of many American cities (Andrew 1995; Isin 1995). But as in the United States, local politics has been defined in Canada by nonpartisan, business-friendly politics, the weakness of local socialism, ethnic and class segmentation enforced by zoning, and a high degree of dependence on property tax revenues (Sancton 1983a; Magnusson 1983a).

One risks missing these similarities if one deduces urban and local questions simply from observations of a supposedly static national political culture. Moreover, restricting comparative studies to the national level has the disadvantage of underemphasizing the cross- or transnational connections that link social processes (such as urbanization) in different national contexts. After World War II, for example, Canada's "permeable Fordism" (Jenson 1989) led to a distinct automobile-centred, suburban complex of a production-consumption nexus that was in fact the core of the country's economy. While the Canadian welfare state started to diverge from its American counterpart in the 1960s and Toronto became the only North American metropolis with a partly successful regional government, the Fordist period of urbanization in Canada expressed the permeability of Canadian Fordism with regard to American influence (Jenson 1989). As exemplified by Toronto, large urban regions were the points of integration of the American with the Canadian economies. The post–World War II period invited comparisons of Canadian and American cities: the predominance of automobile-based suburbanization, inner-city slum clearance and renewal, a liberal welfare state, modest and targeted public housing programs, federal mortgage-insurance programs, and until the 1960s, white-only immigration policies that sustained the mass-consumerist sprawl of single-family-home subdivisions as the basis of the Fordist economy.

In retrospect, one might suggest that Fordist urbanization, the corporate city, and continentalization in postwar Canada laid the groundwork for processes of restructuring and globalization in the period after 1975. Yet we are currently experiencing a departure from this binational, continental pathway of development. Globalization has become the overwhelming force in the restructuring of the Canadian urban system. With increasing globalization, Canadian provinces and economic regions "were becoming less linked to each other than they were to other parts of the world" (Robinson and Simeon 1994, 384). The notion of permeable Fordism is now replaced by another notion that we think captures the current Canadian reality of "glocalized" states: Canada has moved from permeable Fordism to porous post-Fordism. Instead of the metaphor of permeability, which suggests an osmotic process along bilateral interfaces (here mostly with the United States), porosity captures the many points of entry for external matter into a given thing. Once vulnerable to physical intrusion along its long borders and coasts, Canada has now become open to the world through the ubiquitous "pores" of its entire society. Urban regions have become particularly relevant openings to transnational capital flows, migration, and cultural influences of all kinds.

The rising power of cities in the national and global economy has led to demands to create further subnational and subprovincial political institutions and structures. Proponents of changing relations of power between the federal government, the provinces, and the cities nowadays are pointing out that Canada's federalism has outlived its usefulness in a largely urban, globalized society, where urban regions need to be autonomous and strong to be able to compete with other urban regions – sometimes called city states – in other parts of the world. Others have argued that cities in this global age also need more flexibility to deal with the tremendous social and cultural problems that come with the territory of globalization (Wolfe 1997). The reopening of autonomous city-regions has also called into question the national identity as provinces now appear as generic region-states in competition with other North American cities (Courchene 1998).

The discourse on city-regions and region-states indicates that globalization realizes itself through concrete material and discursive processes and projects such as urbanization. We have now entered the era of "transnational urbanization," in which urban regions situate themselves in transnational, rather than national, urban systems. Three cities are aspiring to this elusive role as part of the second tier of global cities: Toronto, which consolidated its position as Canada's major centre of finance capital in the 1970s and 1980s (Todd 1995); Vancouver, which during the last three decades has been rapidly transformed into Canada's major regional centre within Pacific networks of capital and migration flows (Ley et al. 1992); and Montreal, which after decades of economic stagnation is now "reinternationalizing" as a Quebec metropolis (Germain and Rose 2000). Driven by a shift of capital to finance, a growing centralization of capital (Carroll 1989;

Stanford 1999; SPE 2000) and a further concentration of key economic sectors – headquarters, financial markets, producer services, high-tech districts – in selected urban areas (Semple 1996), global-city formation heralds a new level of uneven development and disarticulation of the Canadian political economy (Todd 1995; Brodie 1990). While global-city formation builds on previous rounds of continentalization and corporate concentration, it also signals a growing disassociation of core urban growth from regional and national hinterlands.

Canada's global cities are secondary and tertiary building blocks in the new imperialism of global finance capital and transnational class networks (Carroll 1989; Dua 1999). They embody and organize the forces of the centralization and financialization of capital that connect Canada to the new world order. In turn, Toronto's current status as a major global centre for mining, finance and the major basing point for Canadian financial, mining, and real estate conglomerates builds on imperial histories that articulate Canadian banking history with the Caribbean and the Canadian staples economy with the world-wide interests of Canadian mining capital. Also, the presence of non-European migrants in Toronto, Vancouver, and Montreal reflects Canada's historical ties with colonial and postcolonial labour migration (Stasiulis 1997). This is the case for migrants from former British colonies in the Caribbean and Asia (in Toronto and Vancouver) and for newcomers from the former French colonies of Haiti, Lebanon, North Africa, and Vietnam (in Montreal).

URBAN POLITICAL ECONOMY IN CANADA AT THE BEGINNING OF THE TWENTY-FIRST CENTURY

Having established the theoretical importance of the urban for political economy and the empirical weight of urbanization in the larger historical-geographical narrative of Canadian nation-building and political economy, we will now move on to name some of the most important lenses through which urban political economy research may be most fruitfully pursued. We propose to make an urban perspective central to the social theories commonly aligned with the field of political economy.

Bourgeois Urbanism

Urbanism shapes how ruling-class and middle-class elites frame their identities. Today "global urbanism" is integral to the formation of transnational class networks. In Canada, the re-formation of a globally oriented corporate service- and high-tech-based ruling class is tied more than ever in the Canadian imagination to urban centres. Reminiscent of their counterparts in European cities, Canadian elites are increasingly presenting themselves as urban. Canadian elites never abandoned the inner city, but the current recolonization is a partial reversal of earlier trends toward building the bourgeois utopia in the suburbs. While there is a tension, clearly, between this renewed tendency to gentrify the city core and competing exurban elites, this new trend also goes beyond the traditional left-of-centre middle-class reformism Canadian cities were used to. Instead, the new urbanity of certain elite factions is quite compatible with the continued colonization of the rural countryside by wealthy urban fugitives in their pursuit of gated communities in proximity to luxury "rural" entertainment such as golf courses. The "re-embourgoisement" of the city (Ley 1996) goes hand in hand with the tendency of Canadian capital to reinvest its resource-based super-profits in real estate and the built environment. This tendency corresponds well with the increased movement to sanitize and control inner city spaces as they become the site for staging global elite culture and spectacle.

The Culturalization of Urban Political Economy

An important elite strategy in Canadian cities is the redefinition of the city – once looked at as a rational container of technocratic corporate management and efficient state service delivery – into a site of cultural opportunity and spectacle. This "culturalization" of economic development (Harvey 1989a; Zukin 1995) signals a growing commodification of the everyday, which is transforming the originally oppositional claims to urbanity, centrality, difference, and the festival into demarcated spaces of market control, gentrified living, and diversified conspicuous consumption. As more well-to-do urbanites relocate into the condominium towers and lofts of Toronto, Montreal, and Vancouver, as well as into the newly rehabbed Victorian neighbourhoods close to the central business districts, culture becomes an important medium through which the city is made into a continuous entertainment event. While cloaked in populist references to diversity, community art, and decentralization, urban culture has in fact become a prime field of global-city dreams. Serving international tourists and urban elites with festivals, entertainment complexes, branded heritage sites, waterfront shopping, fibreglass moose, and other spectacles becomes the main pursuit of urban cultural policies from Victoria to Halifax. And while under duress due to the weakness of the Canadian dollar, professional sports franchises have turned select inner cities into festival places of testosterone-filled, glitzy entertainment industries. This sports, arts, and culture strategy has polarizing effects across the city system. Winnipeg, Quebec City, and, lately, Vancouver have lost teams, while Toronto is attracting ever more. In individual cities, public recreation and school sports are cut and swimming pools are closed while corporate sports events are heavily subsidized.

The Spatialization of Capitalist Growth

An important counterweight to the rediscovery of the (inner) city as a space of work, residence, pleasure, and even "nature" by elite and middle-class segments is the continued sprawl across the countryside of Canada's large urban centres. Along the Fraser River in the outskirts of Vancouver, into the Oak Ridges Moraine north of Toronto, to the North and the South of the Island of Montreal, in the capital region across from the Ottawa greenbelt, in the Calgary-Edmonton corridor but also in the vicinity of smaller boomtowns such as Kitchener-Waterloo or Quebec City, Canada's metro-regions experience an expansion of their built-up areas in contiguous swaths and insular configurations. In some way this development replicates the Fordist push for mass working-class and middle-class housing. Mass-produced "doghouse" subdivisions continue to eat up prime farmland in the most populous centres of the country. These new suburbs are also now the ports of entry for new waves of non-European immigration.

The exurban "blubber belts" of wealthy homeowners expand around golf courses, conservation areas, and gated communities that mirror the exclusivity of the downtown condominium culture of secluded middle-class communities. Parallel to the cultural attractiveness of the inner city and located on ravines and often on sensitive ecological areas on waterfronts, coasts, and watersheds, these exclusive exurban developments are sold through the medium of "nature" (Keil and Graham 1998). As the suburbs push into more and more fragile ecosystems, the political economy of urbanization (the big pipes, the freeways, the garbage dumps) produces ever more unsustainable patterns of growth. After the "natural" limits of this development were beginning to bear the marks of fatal risks (Walkerton), new "smart-growth" and "new urbanist" strategies were devised by enterprising elites to stem potential dangers. The political economy of ecological modernization in the exurbs has its counterpart in "green" strategies for inner-city waterfronts and wetlands, and in Toronto, in a "green" Olympics bid and a downtown golf course. Squeezed between the bourgeois "glamour zones" of downtown and exurbia (Young 2000), the postwar suburbs are transformed into parts of the racialized "inner city."

Shifting Images of the Urban Region

The shifting images of the urban region take two interconnected but distinct forms that replace the previously dominant image of the metropolis: the regional city and the transnational city. The claim for global competitiveness is now built on the larger urban region. Rather than constructing the urban image of Canada's large cities from their historical cores or Fordist metro-regions, the image of the competitive city-region reduces the old city cores to one among possibly many growth poles of economic and residential developments. The implications of this rescaling are potentially dramatic for the political economy of Canadian urbanization and implicitly, then, of the nation. Rather than being viewed as cores of regionally or nationally constructed hinterlands, the cities now appear as almost denationalized nodes of a global economy, whose flows of capital, people, and information dissolve the traditional spatial arrangements of urban regions.

The Transnationalization of the Urban Experience

Central to the transnationalization of the urban experience in Canada are new forms of migration. While Canadian cities have always been immigrant cities, migration has become fully globalized since the Canadian state abandoned its white-only immigration policy in the 1960s. Most immigrants now come from non-European places, to the extent that in a number of municipalities in the Toronto and Vancouver area, where most new migrants settle, non-White residents have become the majority. As a result of the class and gender bias of immigration policy towards male professionals and investors, immigrants are bifurcated into wealthy, well-educated newcomers (often from Europe but also from other regions) and poor refugees or deskilled professionals whose education levels are not recognized.

Canadian-born residents and new migrants are tied into transnational elite networks and labour markets. As Canadian urban elites become more place-conscious, they also are increasingly tied into complex global networks and hierarchies of economic interdependencies. Traditional urban ruling classes have long tied their fortunes to the North American marketplace and increasingly to the entire world. In addition, Canadian cities are magnets for large-scale investments in the built environment by international investors. Toronto is an entrepot city of the Indian and Chinese middle-class diaspora. Tied through clusters of new Chinatowns and other ethnic enclaves to similar spaces in other parts of the world, the new transnational elites of Toronto, Vancouver, and Montreal are changing the face of wealth and power in this country. On the other end of the social scale, new immigrant working classes are closely connected through communities that appear local yet are connected transnationally to far away sender-countries in Asia, Africa, Latin America, and Eastern Europe.

New Social Disparities

Both in the self-description and identity of urbanites and in the common perception of today's urban society, difference is increasingly marked in cultural terms. This culturalization of social distinctions is driven by a growing commodification of difference, whereby nonwhite bodies (athletes, pop stars) and elements of non-European culture (cuisine, music, clothing style, interior design) are reified and re-colonized into objects of consumption (Gilroy 2000). In major cities such as Toronto and Vancouver, which have become international symbols of multiculturalism, this process is very advanced. In comparative terms, Canadian multiculturalism still embodies the utopian promise of postracial human relationships. Local multiculturalism policies are often invoked to compare the dystopia of American cities with the "ethnic harmony" of Canadian cities (Croucher 1997). Yet multiculturalism as policy and as commodified everyday life represents a new form of "differentialist" racism that draws distinctions between people less on the basis of (constructed) biological differences than on the basis of (imputed, essentialized) cultural traits. Read as a new form of racism, multiculturalism displaces racialized social conflicts (over employment, policing, land-use) onto a tamed cultural level.

Social Polarization and Fragmentation

Capitalist restructuring and neoliberal policies have a produced social polarization between social classes. But class relations have become both more polarized *and* more complex – culturalized, racialized, gendered, and segmented. First, class polarization is often reified through multiculturalism and the commodification of difference. Second, social polarization is profoundly gendered and racialized (Stasiulis 1997). The growing gap is experienced disproportionately by women, nonwhite Canadians, and new immigrants, who are most affected by a "creeping economic apartheid" of poverty, unemployment, and casualized labour markets (Galabuzi 2001). Third, social polarization is mediated through uneven spatial development.

Social polarization is most pronounced in global cities because labour markets are polarized between high-level occupations in producer services (finance, real estate, insurance, consulting, advertising, law, media, entertainment) and low-paid, nonunionized jobs in hotels, restaurants, security, cleaning, and manufacturing sweatshops. It is in the latter category that a disproportionate number of nonwhite residents, new immigrants, and women work in precarious jobs that are highly segmented according to race, gender, and ethnicity (Friedmann and Wolff 1982; Sassen 1994). In Toronto, polarized labourmarkets and flexible part-time work is experienced disproportionately by nonwhite residents and new immigrants, particularly women (see Todd 1995; Aguiar 2000; Preston and Giles 1997; Ornstein 2000).

Social polarization is refracted through spatial segmentation. This is, of course, not new. Just as the growing gap builds on and complicates Canada's highly racialized and gendered history of class formation (Bourgeault 1983; Abele and Stasiulis 1989), gendered separations of work and residence and the segregation of urban space according to class and ethnicity have helped to form Canadian urbanism. Canada's histories of colonial conquest, slavery, indentured labour, and labour-market segmentation have been enshrined in apartheid on aboriginal reserves, segregated black neighbourhoods (Clairmont and Magill 1987), and racially policed Chinatowns (Anderson 1991).

Divisions between elite enclaves, gentrified areas, middle-class suburbs, ghettos, ethnic neighbourhoods, and working-class areas have intensified. While this is the case not only in global cities (Marcuse and Van Kempen 2000), the forces that accentuate spatial segmentation – real estate cycles, gentrification, and a shortage of affordable housing – tend to be most acute in such cities. Many Canadian cities are experiencing higher inequality between and within neighbourhoods and new forms of racialized residential segregation. But in the rapidly globalizing, deindustrializing, and gentrifying cities of Toronto and Vancouver, spatial inequality and racialized segregation are starkest, if also perhaps more complex than in previous periods. In these cities, racialized residential segregation is less about large-scale, concentrated ghettoization than about forms of micro-segregation that occur between and within neighbourhoods (and sometimes buildings) across urban regions. In Vancouver and Montreal but particularly in Toronto, where inner-city gentrification, the suburbanization of poverty, and the dispersal of immigrant settlement to the suburbs is most pronounced, spatial segregation and racialized segmentation are increasingly stark in the inner suburbs (see Ley and Smith 2000a, b; Fong and

Shibuya 2000; Kazemipur and Hall 2000; Myles, Picot, and Pyper 2000; Lee 2000).

The Competitive City

Globalization has remade the social geographies of states (Keil 1998b; Brenner 1999). But states have actively facilitated and enforced the conditions for transnational capitalism. The "competitive city" (Kipfer and Keil 2002) has been instrumental in mediating conflict associated with transnational urbanization and reorganizing the social and moral landscape of the contemporary urban order. As a form of governance defined by political coalitions, bureaucratic structures, policy patterns, and visions of the city, the competitive city cements and codifies the previously described processes of bourgeois urbanism, culturalization, spatialization, rescaling, polarization, and fragmentation. In the competitive city, local policy priorities are subordinated systematically to the imperative of making cities competitive locations for investment, export, tourists, and elite residents. These forms of competitiveness take place both regionally (between suburban and central cities) and continentally (between comparable cities in North America).

Competitive city politics is multidimensional. Entrepreneurial planning and economic development strategies (Harvey 1989b) try to maximize exports and business investments. The result is fiscal austerity for redistributive programs (social housing, public recreation, local transit) and privatization strategies that erode and reorganize the public sector along corporate lines. Meanwhile, law-and-order campaigns try to make cities safe and clean for the re-colonizers of the city and for the purpose of intercity competition. These racialized campaigns stimulate fear of crime and disorder and build a "revanchist" consensus against particular target groups such as nonwhite youth, panhandlers, squeegees, gays and lesbians, and radical protesters (Smith 1996). In Toronto, for example, aggressive target policing is 'reclaiming' public space for property owners, tourists, and condo-dwellers and helping to demarcate gentrified areas, tourist attractions, and business districts from skidrow, public housing, and poor neighbourhoods.

Competitive city governance and urban entrepreneurialism are new ways of regulating transnational urbanization In the Toronto, Vancouver, and Montreal of the last two decades, this entrepreneurialism has underscored restructuring by helping to transform industrial zones, expand central business districts, and gentrify inner-city areas. While contradictory (Andrew, this volume), local-state restructuring has facilitated local strategies to consolidate the competitive city.

CONCLUSION:
RESISTING GLOBALIZATION

In its focus on processes framed by nation and nation-state, Canadian political economy has so far shown little interest in urban questions. Yet urban research has a lot to contribute to a better understanding of contemporary social processes. Current urban theory and political economy suggest that urbanization is a central dimension of globalization and transnationalization. Focusing on globalizing and global cities means abandoning nation-state-centred approaches to Canadian urban studies while foregrounding the imperialist dimensions of the Canadian political economy. In turn, transnational urbanization can provide the starting point to investigate how city building, urban forms, and spatial relations connect everyday life to a number of contemporary forms of restructuring. This is most acutely the case in global cities. Transnational urbanization mediates culturalized, racialized, gendered, and spatially segmented forms of class formation. As one component of transnational urbanization, competitive city politics helps sustain the capacity of neoconservative forces to entrench their rule by becoming "champions of urbanity" (Beauregard 1999).

What are the possibilities for urbanizing the resistance against globalization? To be sure, competitive city politics has meant rolling back the achievements of social movements, which had managed to modify the direction of urban restructuring with neighbourhood preservation, citizen participation, environmental restoration, cooperative housing, multicultural school curricula, and the creation of queer neighbourhoods (see note 1). The competitive city builds on the retreat of progressive and left forces. However, from the protests against the World Trade Organization in Seattle in 1999 to the demonstrations against the Free Trade Area of the Americas in Quebec City in 2001, antiglobalization movements, which have longer but not well-recognized histories, have achieved global publicity now even in the advanced capitalist world. At the time of this writing, even the aftershocks of 9/11 have not been able to wipe out the spaces created by these movements.

What are the urban dimensions of the antiglobalization movements? If contemporary globalization projects are bound up with the realities of global urbanism and competitive city strategies, an alternative to actually existing capitalism cannot ignore the urban as a terrain of engagement. Recent protests can be seen as utopian glimpses into a different, postcapitalist urban world even in the absence of explicit urban perspectives. For a day or two at a time, they have turned urban space into liberated zones that are intense, if short-lived, ruptures of the routines of everyday life. But antiglobalization protests have also proven a fertile ground for preexisting or newly emerging urban groups (Y Basta, Reclaiming the Streets) to break out of isolation and establish a more transnational stature. Next to an interest in situationism, anarchism, and related radical urbanisms, there is some recognition among those groups that a challenge to deepening commodification cannot stop short of questioning how the production of urban space is organizing everyday life. Moreover, some Canadian antipoverty groups, labour locals, and groups concerned about police violence realize that anticapitalist strategies must resonate in neighbourhoods to have a lasting impact.

Unfortunately, links between organized protesters, and, for example, nonwhite residents and migrants in Northern cities have been rather limited (Martinez 2000). These limitations attest to the need for deepening linkages between the segmented and demarcated worlds of the everyday and the networks of organized activism. In the absence of these links, there is a danger that the new activism will reproduce the hierarchies and dissociations that sustain global urbanism and the competitive city. The fledgling internationalism (of transnational coalition-building) could benefit from a deeper, local internationalism (produced by possible strands of solidarity in globalizing city regions). This would mean embedding activist networks in urban everyday spaces that are increasingly integrated into transnational networks and that have given rise to new claims to "the right to the city" (Kofman 1998). Such "local internationalisms" would certainly broaden and radicalize existing local networks of left and progressive forces, whose social and spatial bases have been too narrow to present a challenge to competitive city politics.

NOTES

Thanks to the editors and Karen Wirsig for helpful comments on earlier drafts.

1 On the tendencies in the NCPE, see the pages of *Studies in Political Economy* and the volumes edited by Clement and Williams (1989), Panitch (1977), Jenson et al. (1993), and Clement (1997).
2 Similar tendencies have shaped the politics of Aborginal self-determination. Long (1992) has argued that in their quest to advance the cause of self-determination against the legacy of White conquest, many Aboriginal leaders have resorted to forms of "ideological protectionism" and spiritual nationalism. These problems must of course be seen in a longer context,

where Aboriginal Canadians were written out of Canada's history of frontier development or, alternatively, relegated to a decorative and exotic part of the Canadian wilderness. In this imperial context of conquest and apartheid on marginal reserves, the idea or urban Aboriginals appears as an oxymoron (Peters 1996).

3   On Montreal, see Sancton (1983b), Ruddick (1992), Hamel (1991), Chorney (1981); Thomas (1997), Germain and Rose (2000). On Vancouver, see Gutstein (1983) and Ley et al. (1992). On Toronto, see Magnusson (1983b), Caulfield (1994), Wekerle (1999), Stasiulis (1989), Kipfer and Keil (2002).

REFERENCES

Abele, Francis, and Stasiulis, Daiva. 1989. "Canada as a 'White Settler Colony': What about Natives and Immigrants?" In Wallace Clements and Glen Williams, eds., *The New Canadian Political Economy*, 240–77. Montreal and Kingston: McGill-Queen's University Press.

Abu-Laban, Yasmeen. 1997. "Ethnic Politics in a Globalizing Metropolis: The Case of Vancouver." In Timothy Thomas, ed., *The Politics of the City: A Canadian Perspective*, 77–96. Scarborough, ON: Nelson.

Abu-Lughod, Janet L. 1998. *New York, Chicago, Los Angeles: America's Global Cities.* Minneapolis and London: University of Minnesota Press.

Aguiar, Luis. 2000. "Restructuring and Employment Insecurities: The Case of Building Cleaners." *Canadian Journal of Urban Research* 9(1): 66–93.

Anderson, Kay. 1991. *Vancouver's Chinatown: Racial Discourse in Canada, 1875–1980.* Montreal and Kingston: McGill-Queen's University Press.

Andrew, Caroline. 1995. "Provincial-Municipal Relations: Or Hyper- Fractionalized Quasi-Subordination Revisited." In James Lightbody, ed., *Canadian Metropolitics: Governing Our Cities*, 137–60. Mississauga, ON: Copp Clark.

Arat-Koc, Sedef. 1999. "Gender and Race in 'Non-Discriminatory' Immigration Policies in Canada: 1960s to the Present." In Robinson and Dua, eds., *Scratching the Surface: Canadian Antiracist Feminist Thought*, 207–36. Toronto: Women's Press.

Beauregard, Robert A. 1999. "The Politics of Urbanism: Mike Davis and the Neo-Conservatives." *Capitalism, Nature, Socialism* 10(3):40–5.

Bourgeault, Ron. 1983. "The Indians, the Metis, and the Fur Trade: Class, Sexism, and Racism in the Transition from "Communism" to Capitalism." *Studies in Political Economy* 12:45–80.

Brenner, N. 1999. "Globalisation as Reterritorialisation: The Re-Scaling of Urban Governance in the European Union." *Urban Studies* 36(3):431–51.

Brodie, Janine. 1990. *The Political Economy of Canadian Regionalism.* Toronto: Harcourt Jovanovich.

Careless, J.M.S. 1989. *Frontier and Metropolis: Regions, Cities and Idenities in*

Canada before 1914. The Donald C. Creighton Lecture 1987. Toronto: University of Toronto Press.

Carroll, Bill. 1989. "Neoliberalism and the Recomposition of Finance Capital in Canada." *Capital and Class* 38:15–38.

Caulfield, Jon. 1994. *City Form and Everyday Life: Toronto's Gentrification and Critical Social Practice.* Toronto: University of Toronto Press.

Chorney, Harold. 1981. "Amnesia, Integration and Repression: The Roots of Canadian Urban Political Culture." In Michael Dear and Alan Scott, eds., *Urbanization and Urban Planning in Capitalist Society,* 535–63. New York: Methuen.

Chorney, Harold, and Andrew Molloy. 1993. "Boss Politics in Montreal and Quebec Nationalism, Jean Drapeau to Jean Doré: From the Pre-modern to the Post-modern." In Alain G. Gagnon, ed., *Quebec: State and Society,* 64–79. Scarborough, ON: Nelson.

Clairmont, Donald, and Dennis William Magill. 1987. *Africville: The Life and Death of a Canadian Black Community.* Rev. ed. Toronto: Canadian Scholars' Press.

Clement, Wallace, ed. 1997. *Understanding Canada: Building on the New Canadian Political Economy.* Montreal and Kingston: McGill-Queen's University Press.

Clement, Wallace, and Glen Williams, eds. 1989. *The New Canadian Political Economy.* Montreal and Kingston: McGill-Queen's University Press.

Courchene, Thomas. 1998. *From Heartland to North American Region State: The Social, Fiscal and Federal Evolution of Ontario.* Toronto: Faculty of Management, Centre for Public Management

Croucher, Sheila. 1997. "Constructing the Image of Ethnic Harmony in Toronto, Canada: The Politics of Problem Definition and Nondefinition." *Urban Affairs Review* 32(3): 319–47.

Desfor, Gene, and Roger Keil. 1999. "Contested and Polluted Terrain." *Local Environment* 4(3): 333–52.

DiGaetano, Alan, and John S. Klemanski. 1999. *Power and City Governance: Comparative Perspectives on Urban Development.* Minneapolis, MN: University of Minnesota Press.

Dua, Enakshi. 1999. "Canadian Anti-Racist Feminist Thought. Scratching the Surface of Racism." In Enakshi Dua and Angela Robertson, eds., *Scratching the Surface: Canadian Antiracist Feminist Thought,* 7–34 Toronto: Women's Press.

Dua, Enakshi, and Angela Robertson. 1999. *Scratching the Surface: Canadian Antiracist Feminist Thought.* Toronto: Women's Press.

Filion, Pierre. 1999. "Les mythes urbains au Canada." In *L'avenir municipal: Dynamiques québecoises et canadiennes.*

Fincher, Ruth, and Jane M. Jacobs, eds. 1998. *Cities of Difference.* New York and London: Guildford.

Fong, Eric, and Kumiko Shibuya. 2000. "The Spatial Separation of the Poor in Canadian Cities." *Demography* 37(4):449–59.

Friedman, John, and Goetz Wolff. 1982. "World City Formation: An Agenda for Research and Action." *International Journal of Urban and Regional Research* 6(3): 309–44.

Galabuzi, Grace-Edward. 2001. *Canada's Creeping Economic Apartheid: The Economic Segregation and Social Marginalisation of Racialised Groups.* Toronto: Centre for Social Justice.

Garber, Judith A., and David L. Imbroscio. 1996. "'The Myth of the North American City' Reconsidered: Local Constitutional Regimes in Canada and the United States." *Urban Affairs Review* 31(5): 595–624.

Germain, Annick, and Damaris Rose. 2000. *Montreal: The Quest for a Metropolis.* Chichester, England: John Wiley.

Gilroy, Paul. 2000. *Against Race: Imagining Culture beyond the Color Line.* Cambridge: The Belknap Press of Harvard University Press.

Goldberg, Michael A., and John Mercer. 1986. *The Myth of the North American City: Continentalism Challenged.* Vancouver: University of British Columbia Press.

Gordon, David. 1978. "Capitalist Development and the History of American Cities." In William Tabb and Larry Sawers, eds., *Marxism and the Metropolis,* 25–63. New York: Oxford University Press.

Gunton, Tom. 1982. "The Origins of Planning." *City Magazine* 6(1): 27–36.

Gutstein, Donald. 1993. "Vancouver." In M. Magnusson and A. Sancton eds., *City Politics in Canada,* 189–221. Toronto: University of Toronto Press.

Hamel, Pierre. 1991. *Action Collective et Democratie Locale: Les mouvements urbains montrealais.* Montreal: Presses de L'Université de Montreal.

Harvey, David. 1989a. The Urban Experience. Oxford: Basil Blackwell.

– 1989b. "From Managerialism to Entrepreneurialism: The Transformation in Urban Governance in Late Capitalism. *Geographiska Annaler Series B.* 71B(1): 3–18.

Ingram, G.B., Anne-Marie Bouthillett, and Yolanda Retter, eds. 1997. *Queers in Space: Communities, Public Places, Sites of Resistance.* Seattle: Bay Press.

Isin, Engin F. 1995. "The Origins of Canadian Municipal Government." In James Lightbody, ed., *Canadian Metropolitics: Governing our Cities,* 51–91. Toronto: Copp Clark.

Jacobs, Jane. 1993. "Foreword." In John Sewell, *The Shape of the City: Toronto Struggles with Modern Planning,* ix–xii. Toronto: University of Toronto Press.

Jenson, Jane. 1989. "'Different' but Not 'Exceptional': Canada's Permeable Fordism." *Canadian Review of Sociology and Anthropology* 26(1): 69–93.

Jenson, Jane, Rianne Mahon, and Martin Bielefeld, eds. 1993. *Production, Space, Identity: Political Economy Faces the Twenty-first Century.* Toronto: Canadian Scholars' Press.

Jonas, Andrew E.G., and David Wilson, eds. 1999. *The Urban Growth Machine: Critical Perspectives Two Decades Later.* Albany, NY: SUNY Press.

Kazemipur, A., and S.S. Halli. 2000. "Plight of Immigrants: The Spatial Concentration of Poverty in Canada." *Canadian Journal of Regional Science* 22(2):66–79.

Keil, Roger. 1998a. *Los Angeles: Globalization, Urbanization, and Social Struggles.* Chichester, England: John Wiley and Sons.

– 1998b. "Globalization Makes States: Perspectives of Local Governance in the Age of the World City." *Review of International Political Economy.* 5(4): 616–46.

Keil, Roger, and John Graham. 1998. "Reasserting Nature: Constructing Urban Environments after Fordism." In Bruce Braun and Noel Castrer, eds., *Remaking Reality: Nature at the Millenium,* 100–25. New York: Routledge.

Keil, Roger, and Klaus Ronneberger. 2000. "The Globalization of Frankfurt am Main: Core, Periphery and Social Conflict." In Peter Marcuse and Ronald van Kempen, eds., *Globalizing Cities: A New Spatial Order?*228–48. Oxford: Blackwell.

Keil, Roger, and Douglas Young. 2001. "A Charter for the People? The Debate on Municipal Autonomy in Toronto." Unpublished paper, York University, Toronto

King, Anthony. 1990. *Global Cities: Postimperialism and Internationalization.* London: Routledge.

Kipfer, Stefan. 2000. "Whose City Is It? Global Politics in the Mega-City." *Cityscope* 1(1): 13–17.

– 1995. "Globalization, Hegemony, and Local Politics: The Case of Zurich, Switzerland." In Joszef Böröcz and David A. Smith, eds., Westport, *A New World Order? Global Transformation in the Late Twentieth Century,* 181–99. Westport, CT, and London: Praeger.

Kipfer, Stefan, and Roger Keil. 2002. "Toronto Inc.: Planning the Competitve City in the New Toronto." *Antipode.* Forthcoming.

Knox, Paul, and Peter Taylor, eds. 1995. *World Cities in a World System.* Cambridge: Cambridge University Press.

Kofman, Eleonore. 1998. "Whose City? Gender, Class, and Immigrants in Globalizing European Cities." In Ruth Fincher and Jane M. Jacobs, eds., *Cities of Difference,* 135–51. New York and London: Guildford.

Koyabashi, Audrey. 1993. "Multiculturalism: Representing a Canadian Institution." In Duncan Ley, ed. 205–31. Place/Culture/Representation. London and New York: Routledge.

Lauria, Mickey, ed. 1997. *Reconstructing Urban Regime Theory: Regulating Urban Politics in a Global Economy.* Thousand Oaks, CA, London, New Delhi: Sage Publications.

Lee, Kevin. 2000. *Urban Poverty in Canada.* Ottawa: Canadian Council on Social Development.

Lefebvre, Henri. 1996. *Writings on Cities.* Translated by Elenore Kofman and Elizabeth Lebas. Oxford: Basil Blackwell.

Ley, David. 1996. "The New Middle Class in Canadian Central Cities." In Jon

Caulfield and Linda Peake, eds., *City Lives and City Forms: Critical Research and Canadian Urbanism.* Toronto: University of Toronto Press.

Ley, David, Daniel Hiebert, and Geraldine Pratt. 1992. "Time to Grow Up? From Urban Village to World City, 1966–91." In Graeme Wynn and Timothy Oke, eds., *Vancouver and Its Region*, 234–66. Vancouver: University of British Columbia Press.

Ley, David, and Heather Smith. 2000a. "Relations between Deprivation and Immigrant Groups in Large Canadian Cities." *Urban Studies* 37(1): 37–62.

– 2000b. "Immigration and Poverty in Canadian Cities: 1971–1991." *Canadian Journal of Regional Science*, 22(2): 38–55.

Long, David. 1992. "Culture, Ideology, and Militancy: The Movement of Native Indians in Canada, 1969–91." In William Carroll, ed., *Organizing Dissent: Contemporary Social Movements in Theory and Practice*. Toronto: Garamond.

Macdonald, Laura. 1997. "Going Global: The Politics of Canada's Foreign Economic Relations." In Wallace Clement, ed., *Understanding Canada: Building on the New Canadian Political Economy*. Montreal and Kingston: McGill-Queen's University Press.

McCann, Larry, and Peter J. Smith. 1991. "Canada Becomes Urban: Cities and Urbanization in Historical Perspective." In Trudi Bunting and Pierre Filion, eds., *Canadian Cities in Transition*, 69–99. Toronto: Oxford University Press.

Magnusson, Warren. 1996. *The Search for Political Space.* Toronto: University of Toronto Press.

– 1983a. "Introduction: The Development of Canadian Urban Government." In M. Magnusson and A. Sancton, eds., *City Politics in Canada*, 3–57. Toronto: University of Toronto Press.

– 1983b. "Toronto." In M. Magnusson and A. Sancton, eds., *City Politics in Canada*, 94–139. Toronto: University of Toronto Press.

Marcuse, Peter, and Ronald van Kempen, eds. 2000. *Globalizing Cities: A New Spatial Order?* Oxford: Blackwell.

Martinez, Elizabeth. 2000. "Where Was the Color in Seattle? Looking for Reasons Why the Great Battle Was So White." *ColorLines* 3(1): 18–23.

Mitchell, Katherine. 1993. "Multiculturalism, or the United Colors of Capitalism." *Antipode* 25:4.

Murdie, Robert. 1996. "Economic Restructuring and Social Polarization in Toronto." In John O'Loughlin and Juergen Friedrichs, eds., *Social Polarization in Post-Industrial Metropolises*, 207–33. Berlin and New York: Walter de Gruyter.

Myles, J., G. Picot, and W. Pyper. 2000. "Neighbourhood Inequality in Canadian Cities." Working Paper no 160. Ottawa: Statistics Canada, Business and Labour Market Analysis Division.

Nightingale, Carl. 2001. "The World Travels of Racial Urbanism (or Some New Ways of Asking Whether American Ghettos Are Colonies)." Manuscript. University of Massachusetts, Amherst.

Ornstein, Michael. 2000. *Ethno-Racial Inequality in the City of Toronto: An Analysis of the 1996 Census.* City of Toronto: Access and Equity Unit.

Panitch, Leo, ed. 1977. *The Canadian State: Political Economy and Political Power.* Toronto: University of Toronto Press.

Peters, Evelyn. 1996. "'Urban' and 'Aboriginal': An Impossible Contradiction?" In Jon Caulfield and Linda Peake, eds., *City Lives and City Forms: Critical Research and Canadian Urbanism.* Toronto: University of Toronto Press.

Preston, Valerie, and Wenona Giles. 1997. "Ethnicity, Gender, and Labour Markets in Canada: A Case Study of Immigrant Women in Toronto." *Canadian Journal of Urban Research* 6(2): 135–59.

Price, Trevor. 1995 "Council-Administrative Relations in City Government." In James Lightbody, ed., *Canadian Metropolitics: Governing Our Cities.* Mississauga, ON: Copp Clark.

Robinson, I., and R. Simeon. 1994. "The Dynamics of Canadian Federalism." In J.P. Bickerton and A.-G. Gagnon, eds., *Canadian Politics*, 2d ed., 366–88. Peterborough, ON: Broadview Press.

Rose, Damaris. 1996. "Economic Restructuring and the Diversification of Gentrification in the 1980s: A View from a Marginal Metropolis." In Jon Caulfield and Linda Peake, eds., *City Lives and City Forms: Critical Research and Canadian Urbanism.* Toronto: University of Toronto Press.

Ruddick, Susan. 1990. "The Montreal Citizens' Movement: The Realpolitik of the 1990s." In Mike Davis, Steve Hiatt, Marise Kennedy, Susan Ruddick, and Michael Sprinker, eds., *Fire in the Hearth: The Radical Politics of Place in America*, 287–317. London: Verso.

Sancton, A. 1999. "Differing Approaches to Municipal Restructuring in Montreal and Toronto: From the Pichette Report to the Greater Toronto Services Board." *Canadian Journal of Regional Science* 22(1,2): 187–99.

– 1983a. "Conclusion: Canadian City Politics in Comparative Perspective." In M. Magnusson and A. Sancton, eds., *City Politics in Canada*, 291–317. Toronto: University of Toronto Press.

– 1983b. "Montreal." In M. Magnusson and A. Sancton, eds., *City Politics in Canada*, 58–93. Toronto: University of Toronto Press.

Sassen, Saskia. 1994. *Cities in the World Economy.* Thousand Oaks, CA: Pine.

Semple, Keith. 1996. "Quaternary Places in Canada." In John Britton, ed., *Canada and the Global Economy* 352–79. Montreal and Kingston: McGill-Queen's University Press.

Siemiatycki, Myer, and Engin Isin. 1998. "Immigration, Diversity, and Urban Citizenship in Toronto." *Canadian Journal of Regional Studies* 20(1,2): 73–102.

Smith, Michael Peter. 2001. *Transnational Urbaniism: Locating Globalization.* Malden and Oxford: Blackwell.

Smith, Neil. 1996. *The New Urban Frontier: Gentrification and the Revanchist City.* London: Routledge.

Stanford, Jim. 1999. *Paper Boom*. Toronto: Lorimer.

Stasiulis, Daiva. 1997. "The Political Economy of Race, Ethnicity, and Migration." In Wallace Clement, ed., *Understanding Canada: Building on the New Canadian Political Economy*. Montreal and Kingston: McGill-Queen's University Press.

– 1989. "Minority Resistance in the Local State: Toronto in the 1970s and 1980s." *Ethnic and Racial Studies* 12(1): 63–83.

Stelter, Gilbert. 1986. "Power and Place in Urban History." In Gilbert Stelter and Alan Artibise, eds., *Power and Place: Canadian Urban Development in the North American Context*. Vancouver: University of British Columbia Press.

– 1984. "The Political Economy of Early Canadian Urban Development." In Gilbert Stelter and Alan Artibise, eds., *The Canadian City: Essays in Urban and Social History*, 5–38. Ottawa: Carleton University Press.

– 1982. "The City-Building Process in Canada." In Gilbert Stelter and Alan Artibise, eds., *Shaping the Urban Landscape. Aspects of the Canadian City-Building Process*, 1–29. Ottawa: Carleton University Press.

Stelter, Gilbert, and Alan Artibise, eds., 1982. *Shaping the Urban Landscape: Aspects of the City-Building Process*. Ottawa: Carleton University Press.

Studies in Political Economy (SPE) 2000. "Capitalism, Crisis, and Finance: A Forum on *Paper Boom* by Jim Stanford." *Studies in Political Economy* 62: 123–68.

Statistics Canada. 2002. *2001 Census Data*. Ottawa: Statistics Canada.

Thomas, Timothy. 1997. *A City with a Difference: The Rise and Fall of the Montreal Citizen's Movement*. Montreal: Vehicule.

Todd, Graham. 1995. "Going Global in the Semi-Periphery: World Cities as Political Projects, the Case of Toronto." In Paul Knox and Peter Taylor, eds., *World Cities in a World System*, 192–212. Cambridge: Cambridge University Press.

Wallace, Iain, and Rob Shields. 1997. "Contested Terrains: Social Space and the Canadian Environment." In Wallace Clement, ed., *Understanding Canada: Building on the New Canadian Political Economy*, 386–408. Montreal and Kingston: McGill-Queen's University Press.

Weaver, W. 1979. "Tomorrow's Metropolis Revisited: A Critical Assessment of Critical Reform in Canada, 1890–1920." In G.A. Stelter and A.F.S. Artibise, eds., *The Canadian City: Essays in Urban History*. 393–416. Toronto: Macmillan.

Wekerle, Gerda. 1999. "Gender Planning as Insurgent Citizenship: Stories from Toronto." *Plurimondi* 1(2): 105–23.

– 1984. "A Woman's Place is in the city." *Antipode*. 16(3): 11–19.

Wekerle, Gerda, and Linda Peake. 1996. "New Social Movements and Women's Urban Activism." In Jon Caulfield and Linda Peake, eds., *City Lives and City Forms: Critical Research and Canadian Urbanism*. Toronto: University of Toronto Press.

Wolfe, David. 1997. "The Emergence of the Region State." Paper prepared for the Bell Canada Papers 5, The Nation State in a Global Information Era: Policy Challenges. John Deutsch Institute for the Study of Economic Policy, Queen's University, Kingston, Ontario.

Young, Douglas. 2000. "Caught between the Glamour Zones." Unpublished manuscript, Urban Studies Program, York University, Toronto.

Zukin, Sharon. 1995. *The Cultures of Cities.* Oxford: Blackwell.

15 Immigration, Ethnicity, and Race: The Transformation of Transnationalism, Localism, and Identities

VIC SATZEWICH AND LLOYD WONG

INTRODUCTION

Immigration flows to Canada have always varied in terms of ethnicity, race, gender, and class. However, one of the striking features of late twentieth- and early twenty-first-century migration patterns is their diversity. Contemporary migration flows not only involve the movement of unskilled workers who fill undesirable, low-wage jobs that are hard to fill with domestic labour; they also involve the movement of highly skilled professionals and technical workers who fill well-paying and socially desirable jobs, and this all occurs essentially in urban labour markets, where most immigrants are destined. These flows also contain a significant proportion of individuals and households with large amounts of capital, cash, and other economic resources. These immigrants tend not to sell their labour power for wages and salaries, but rather they tend to occupy the other end of the labour-capital relationship. Both men and women migrate, as they did before, but more women are now migrating as primary applicants than was the case twenty or thirty years ago. In the not-too-distant past, the flow of what state officials deemed as "desirable" immigrants was mainly made up of white people from the United States, Britain, and Europe. Now, the United States and Europe provide Canada with less than 30 percent of all immigrants in any year, with the balance coming from Asia, the Caribbean, South and Central America, and Africa. While Canada could at one time have been legitimately described as a white-settler colony (Abele and Stasiulis 1989; Stasiulis and Jhappan 1995), this is no longer a completely apt description of the country. Indeed, the list of countries that now constitute the top ten sources of immigrants to Canada likely has Mackenzie King rolling over in his grave.

Because of the diverse backgrounds of immigrants to Canada, the labour market experiences of ethnic groups, which now consist of multiple generations and combinations of generations, are more complex now than they were when sociologists like John Porter (1965) wrote about the relationship between ethnicity and social class in the 1960s. Patterns of inequality between ethnic and racialized groups still exist and can be illustrated using various measures and techniques, but those patterns are complicated and do not lend themselves to simple generalizations. Class, gender, and generational inequalities may arguably be just as large and as socially significant within particular groups, as are inequalities between groups. Furthermore, access to elite positions is more open now than it was in the past, and while there is still room for improvement, Canada has come a long way in accepting a more diverse array of Canadians into positions of power and influence (Black 2000; Black and Lakhani 1997).

The social interactions that immigrants and ethnic communities have with their countries of origin or with their ancestral heritage have also changed. The old paradigm of immigrant integration, which assumed that international migrants broke radically with their ancestral homes to start life afresh in their new homelands, has given way to social science perspectives that emphasize the links that immigrant and ethnic communities retain and cultivate with families, institutions, and political systems abroad. In other words, the social practices of immigrants and ethnic groups seem increasingly to reflect a transnational approach to social life and citizenship.

These transformations in the sources, backgrounds, class locations, social practices, and orientations of immigrants and ethnic groups present political economists with new opportunities, challenges, and conceptual problems. In particular, political economists now need to pay more attention to, among other things, the growing significance of the transnational social practices of immigrants and the growing social and economic polarization within and among immigrant and ethnic communities. In this chapter, we begin to address these challenges by focusing on the contradictions and countervailing tendencies associated with globalization, the rise of the transnational practices of immigrant and ethnic communities, and the processes of differentiation within those communities. We argue that the continuities and discontinuities accompanying transnationalism amount to a transformation of the political economy of immigration, race, and ethnicity.

CANADIAN IMMIGRATION POLICY
AND GLOBAL POLITICAL ECONOMY

The fundamental influence of political economy on the regulation and control of international migration was established by the early work of Castles and Kosack (1973). Their structural political economy approach contrasted with long-standing voluntaristic theories of human agency. With the emergence Froebel, Heinrichs, and Kreye's work on the new international division of labour, it became clear that the global capitalist economy was constituted by the integration of human and material resources with specific spatially distant economic formations and transformations now commonly referred to as globalization (Gardezi 1995, 2). As a theory of development, the new international division of labour's argument that there is a world market for labour power was similar to Marx's reserve-army thesis regarding flexible sources of labour. These conceptualizations of flexible labour continue to be relevant to contemporary world migration. While the phenomenon of "runaway shops" has moved many industrial production sites to places where cheap labour is located, there are now large movements of professional, skilled, and unskilled labour into industrialized, developed countries such as Canada, the United States, and many other European countries.

Thus, while in the past the "reserve army" consisted essentially of unskilled or semiskilled workers, today it also consists of highly skilled and technical workers. For example, there are substantial migrations of skilled workers in high-tech industries from China and India into the United States and Canada. These migrations are facilitated by state rules and regulations that in many cases fast-track their entry. These immigrants are viewed by the state as "value-added" immigrants, in an economic model of immigration in which discussions consistently focus on the issues of the "returns" from immigration. In the 1990s there was a ratcheting up of Canadian policy to place greater emphasis on economic (independent) immigration and, within this class of immigration, greater emphasis on specific human capital requirements such as education, language (English and French), and occupational skills. This policy focus coincided with neoliberal restructuring in the 1990s; it is described by Simmons (1999) as a form of "designer" immigration. The trend towards specifying the desirable human capital that immigrants should possess continues in the early twenty-first century. The recently passed Bill C-11, the Immigration and Refugee Protection Act, has dramatically increased the selection-criteria points allotted for education, language ability, and experience, and increased the pass mark from seventy to seventy-five points.

While state motives in the area of immigration are sometimes obfuscated by claims that immigration is about promoting diversity as a value in and of itself, diversity is really the by-product of the continuing link between immigration and the Canadian state's strategy for economic development. Historically, the exigencies of nation building, defined primarily in terms of economic development, were the main factors in forming Canada's immigration policy. It was economic determinants that shaped Canadian immigration policy during the first century, utilizing a "tap-on and tap-off" regulatory system (Dirks 1995, 13).

However, immigration is about more than simply recruiting immigrants as a source of labour for an expanding economy. Immigration can also be viewed even more directly as part of a regime of capital accumulation. The creation of the Canadian business immigration program in the late 1970s emphasized capital transfers linked with migration, particularly for immigrants coming under the investor category. Other business immigrants (entrepreneurs and the self-employed), as well as nonbusiness immigrants, cumulatively transfer significant amounts of capital into Canada. For example, recent data indicate that in the year 2000 the total amount of financial capital that all immigrants to Canada declared they had in their possession was Can$1.1 billion. Moreover, the declared net-worth of business immigrants (investors, entrepreneurs, and the self-employed) to Canada in 1999 was Can$4.1 billion (Citizenship and Immigration Canada 2001), of which, the Canadian state assumes, at least a portion would be patriated.

At the same time, immigration is also an important aspect of state formation. Postwar immigration to Europe and North America cannot be understood purely in economic terms. Since immigrants are not just commodities, considerations of rights must be acknowledged (Hollifield 1992). Since immigrants are not only workers but also potential future citizens, immigration is inherently linked with the issue of citizenship (Bloemraad 2000). Citizenship entails a complex mix of rights, obligations, and appropriately defined subjectivity (also known as "identity"), and the evaluation of the social capacities of potential immigrants plays at least some role in shaping immigration flows. What is being invoked here, by means of immigration policy, is a normative conception of citizenship, insofar as citizenship is not just a legal status but also entails a sense of expectations about appropriate behaviour and attitudes.

With increasing economic globalization, the role of borders is diminishing somewhat, as supranational agencies increasingly set agendas for trade and the flow of goods and capital. Organizations like the World Bank, the International Monetary Fund, and the European Union and accords such as the North American Free Trade Agreement (NAFTA) seek to construct a global neoliberal contextual space to regulate transnational flows of capital, trade, people, and culture (Guarnizo and Smith 1998). Nevertheless, the nation-state still remains the site of power for the regulation and control of the flow of people. Indeed, as Coleman and Porter (this volume) point out in their analysis of the Canadian state's role in the regulation of financial markets, state power has not disappeared from the twenty-first century social landscape. At the same time, the work of many supranational agencies and organizations, in conjunction with national governments, often increases migration pressures. The World Banks' involvement in the Canada–Costa Rica debt-for-nature swaps (investments) has led, for example, to depopulation and the dispossession of indigenous peoples' land in Costa Rica, thus creating migration pressures (Isla 2000).

Since the 1960s a growing politicization of immigration has influenced the formation of policy. There are growing signs of turbulence and contestation as political events, both domestic and international, unfold. While both domestic and international politics affect the development of immigration policy and control, there are now increasing international pressures to harmonize various states' immigration policies. The pressure for increasing the militarization and policing of Canadian borders and for harmonization of u.s.-Canadian immigration and regulatory regimes is a collective reaction that is intended to increase security and preserve First World citizenship by building regional fortresses (e.g., Fortress Europe, Fortress North America). More than ever before, industrialized nations are now facing increasing global migration pressures as global economic and income disparity and employment insecurity increases (Dirks 1997; Simmons 1998a).

Pressure to militarize Canadian borders existed before the dramatic events of September 11, 2001. However, within a few months of those events, the Canadian state rapidly and fundamentally adopted a militarization agenda for the short and medium term. There was an immediate special allocation of federal funds ($280 million) for policing, security, and intelligence (to the RCMP and the Departments of the Solicitor General, Citizenship and Immigration, Canada Customs, and Transport Canada). While the initiatives are too numerous to list completely, they included fast-tracking a permanent resident card for new immigrants; intensified security screening of refugee claimants; increased detention and deportation capacities; increased staffing at ports of entry; redeployment of over two thousand RCMP officers to national security duties; and enhanced technological upgrading and new equipment related to national security. In December 2001 a "conjunctural month" for post–September 11 events in Canada, the controversial Anti-Terrorism Act (Bill C-36) was passed, the 2001 federal budget, dubbed the "security" budget, was delivered, and the Canada-U.S. Smart Border Declaration, along with the Joint Statement on Cooperation on Border Security and Regional Migration Issues, was announced. Bill C-36 will undoubtedly affect the militarization of Canadian borders and Canadian space, due to the increased powers and tools of investigation provided to law enforcement agencies, which provide for potentially serious infringements on civil liberties and increased racial profiling. In the United States the first post–September 11 budget nearly doubled homeland security expenditures to $37.7 billion, of which $10.6 billion is for securing America's borders. Similarly, Canada's 2001 federal budget provides for $7.7 billion (over five years) for new security measures, of which $1 billion is for improving the screening of entrants to Canada; $1.2 billion is for border-related measures such as technology and equipment and multiagency integrated border enforcement teams; $1.6 billion is for policing and intelligence; and the rest is for emergency preparedness, military deployment, and air security (Department of Finance 2001). The Canada-U.S. Smart Border Declaration and the Joint Statement on Cooperation on Border Security and Regional Migration Issues are bilateral agreements that make a commitment toward what is perceived as more efficient management of the mutual border and overall security.

The call for a continental approach to the harmonization of Canadian and U.S. immigration policy has come primarily from the United States, and it was made well before the events of September 11. Privately held discussions between respective departments occurred, but discussions also occasionally took place in public, where there were open admissions of the behind-the-scenes maneuvering. For example, at the Fifth International Metropolis Conference, held in Vancouver in November 2000, an international panel of immigration ministers discussed openly the need for greater harmonization of Canadian and U.S. immigration policy. More recently, in June 2001, the newly appointed U.S. ambassador to Canada, Paul Cellucci, called for the two countries to move toward greater convergence of immigration policy, thus allowing for a "perimeter" security concept that would lead to a more open Canada-U.S. border, since both countries would have the same rules (Trickey 2001). However, the events of September 11th made ontological security issues (that is, security at a basic, individual level) a fixation for the Canadian state because the high levels of anxiety at the time and because of the fairly high levels of mass support for a "war on terrorism" and for the notion of a Fortress North America. The latter would entail a North American security perimeter and a convergence and harmonization of immigration policy.

While continentalist forces had already been pressuring for the harmonization of immigration policy, September 11th sharpened the notion of a Fortress North America. Barring further events similar to September 11th the real driver for the regionalization of North America in the longer term will continue to be the economic forces marked out by the geographic boundaries of NAFTA. Nevertheless, the events of September 11th instantly created a bilateral process between Canada and the United States that greatly facilitates the future convergence and harmonization of immigration policy, perhaps leading to a migration regime encompassing both countries' national immigration law and regulations. The step in this direction comes not from the Anti-Terrorism Act nor from the Immigration and Refugee Protection Act (which was crafted well before September 11th) but from the Canada-U.S. Smart Border Declaration and the Joint Statement on Border Security and Regional Migration Issues. They promise collaboration between the two countries on developing compatible immigration databases; reviewing refugee/asylum processing; visa policy coordination; integrated border enforcement teams; and developing common biometric identifiers in migration documentation.

While these measures are at the level of regulations and border control rather than of general immigration policy, they still exert pressure toward convergence and harmonization. At the more general level of immigration policy, Canada and the United States are similar in certain ways. Both countries, for instance, have category-based "classes" of immigrants that are based on the family, the labour market (skills and employment), and refugee status. At a more specific level of immigration regulation and control, the differences between the two countries are readily apparent: the United States has a far greater number of restrictive, inadmissible criteria and a much lower per capita limit on the number of immigrants who will be accepted. For example, while the United States accepted annually approximately three to four times the number of immigrants accepted by Canada in the 1990s, its population was approximately ten times that of Canada. Thus, convergence and harmonization will most likely put pressures on Canada to move toward a more restrictive immigration policy. In contrast, as recent demographic census data for 2001 indicate, the growth in the Canadian population now relies more on immigration than natural births. While other authors in this volume address whether a continentalist Fortress North America makes Canada more *or* less secure and what it means for Canadian sovereignty in foreign policy, the question that arises here is, what will it mean for Canadian sovereignty over immigration? Equally important are questions of how the political economy of migration would play out? Given recent forces of neoliberal restructuring, a Fortress North America will likely produce a restrictive overall immigration policy, but at the same time it will be flexible enough to be able to bow to pressure from capital (both large and small business) for access to global labour.

In addition to this "upward" continentalist pressure on Canada's national immigration policy, there are also "downward" pressures. For example, many of the provinces and territories continue to negotiate federal-provincial accords related to the management of immigration. These accords include provincial nominee programs that provide provinces with the ability to expedite the immigration process for a certain number of "designer" immigrants whom they view as important for local and provincial economies. Thus, within-country immigration policies and programs continue to be sites of contestation (Harrison 1994, 1996), and the number of social groups that influence, or hope to influence, immigration policy and administration has multiplied (Sharry 2000). The power that federal bureaucrats exercise in the policy-making process cannot be underestimated (Veuglers 2000; Simmons 1998b), nor can the influence of ethnic and NGO lobbying (Sharry 2000). While it is difficult to determine whether the rise in popularity of the Reform Party/Canadian Alliance was solely responsible for the shifts in emphasis regarding immigration regulation and control in the mid-1990s (Kirkham 1998), it is clear that the party's repeated expression of concerns over bogus refugees, illegal immigrants, and the entry of too many family-class immigrants into the country and over the apparently negative economic consequences of poorly planned immigration flows has found some resonance among Canadians more generally and among the national Liberal and Conservative Parties more specifically.

This politicization of immigration contributes to the increasing turbulence and uncertainty of migration. International migration operates not only within the context of national and regional regulations but also at a global level, where migration pressures arise. As such, borders are porous yet at the same time restrictive, and herein lies the contradiction of globalization. In contrast to economic and cultural globalization, where there is an almost unrestricted flow of capital, currency, goods, and ideas, the flow of people across national borders is heavily restricted. As Gabriel and Macdonald (this volume) point out, in the context of NAFTA and an emerging continental economic regime, North American states have opened up borders with respect to capital, goods, and selective movements of highly skilled labour and business persons, but they have also increasingly restricted the movement of other people generally. As Papastergiadis puts it, "One clear reminder of the contradictions of globalization is that despite the relative free transfer of capital and ideas, there is no nation which is encouraging mass migration. The patterns of migration in the age of globalization have become more complex and covert as policies on immigration are more selective. No nation-state has deregulated border controls. On the contrary, there is an increasing linkage between immigration control and military defense" (2000, 82).

Thus, the control and militarization of borders is increasingly emphasized in the politicization of Canadian immigration policy, which also serves to counter any moral panic or public discourse regarding the "invasion" of Canada by illegal refugees and immigrants. Moreover, given increasing U.S. security concerns and the long, relatively "undefended" Canada-U.S. border, Canadian immigration policy is under close scrutiny and attack by U.S. politicians, who view it as lax and as allowing easy access for terrorists and drug dealers wishing to enter the United States through Canada (see Gabriel and Macdonald in this volume). Thus, the Immigration and Refugee Protection Act is portrayed as fresh policy that tightens up illegal movements across Canada's borders.

In moving beyond the new international division of labour thesis, a more apt theoretical concept for explaining international migration is Mittelman's "global division of labour and power thesis." This thesis refers to the manifestation of power both physically and socially (2000, 55). On the international stage Canada remains a small country that is heavily dependent on international trade, foreign investment, and immigrant labour. Thus, the Canadian response to recent trends in globalization has been to play up the positive effects of immigration (Simmons 1998a), while at the same time attempting to demonstrate strength in patrolling borders. With the contraction of the welfare state and expanding neoliberalism, immigration policy in Canada increasingly focuses on economic immigration. To that end, immigration is inextricably linked to economic globalization and global capitalist development. The expansion of global capitalism and the internationalization of capital have produced migrant transnational practices and transnational communities.

TRANSNATIONALISM

Transnationalism in Canada

Over the past decade the paradigm of transnationalism has emerged to characterize processes of immigrant settlement, adaptation, and integration, particularly in Britain and the United States. To this extent it has supplemented and in some cases challenged traditional theories of migration and immigrant adaptation. Immigrants are increasingly characterized not as being uprooted but rather as maintaining multiple links to their homeland through developed networks, activities, patterns of living, and ideologies that span national borders (Basch, Schiller, and Blanc 1994, 4). These linkages are referred to as transnational social spaces; in these spaces the bridging functions of social capital are manifest. Transnational social spaces include social ties, positions in networks and organizations, and the organization of networks that span geographically and internationally distinct places (Faist 2000, 197).

In Canada, Winland (1998) has pointed to the challenge the transnationalism paradigm presents to current scholarship, in which the notions of ethnic identity have traditionally been understood in terms of bounded and essentialized notions of ethnicity. Transnationalism allows for conceptual openings that move beyond theoretical and ethnographic frameworks developed around localized notions of bounded ethnic and immigrant communities such as the circulation of ethnic/cultural meanings and the global identity of politics (556). While Winland's concern relates to ethnic identity, transnationalism can be conceptualized more abstractly and also more concretely. At a more abstract level, while the Canadian nation can be thought of as an "imagined community" (Anderson 1991, 7), in spite of immense regionalism, diversity, and inequality, when that imagination moves beyond borders, transnational communities can also be conceived of as imagined communities. However, in contrast to Anderson's thesis, transnational imagined communities do not contribute to the emotional and mental formations of nationalism but rather impede such formations. Yet like nationalism, transnationalism is aided by media forms through advances such as satellite television.

At a more concrete level the practice of transnationalism includes the informal and formal daily institutional practices of many people in ethnic and immigrant communities. In this sense these transnational communities are also very much "encountered communities," and their transnational practices can be measured at an empirical level. In Canada this empirical research is just beginning, and the findings are likely to reveal diversity in the extent of transnationalism between and among particular groups. What is evident, however, is that transnationalism and transnational communities do exist and that they are a common phenomenon most evident in the large urban and cosmopolitan cities of Canada. As Cohen (1997, 174–5) states, "What nineteenth-century nationalists wanted was a 'space' for each 'race,' a territorialization of each social identity. What they have got instead is a chain of cosmopolitan cities and an increasing proliferation of sub-national and transnational identities that cannot easily be contained in the nation-state system." In the postcolonial world the "empire has struck back" by pluralizing the former colonizing countries (Winant 2000, 170), and this process has been most dramatic in the metropole. Toronto, Montreal, Vancouver, and Calgary approach what Sassen (1991) calls global cities. In these cities there are considerable simi-larities with other global cities in terms of their increasing diversity and cosmopolitanism and their location within the circuits of capital, commodities, service, and people.

As in the United States and Britain, there are many transnational communities that intersect geographically with Canada. The 1996 Census of Canada enumerated hundreds of ethnic groups defined by their ancestry. Two large non-European ethnic groups in Canada that form part of significant transnational communities are the Chinese and South Asians. In the late 1990s there were nearly one million Chinese and three-quarters of a million South Asians in Canada, most of whom lived in Canada's larger cities, which are among the most multicultural in the world. Immigrants make up 42 percent of Tor-onto's population, 35 percent of Vancouver's, 20 percent of Calgary's and 18 percent of Montreal's (Statistics Canada 2000).

While transnationalism is often characterized as being manifest in the first-generation of immigrants, this pattern may be changing. Recent research by Heibert (2000) in Vancouver suggests that among second-generation Chinese-Canadian youth there is an emergence of hybrid identities, cultural reflection, and a reevaluation of identity as the number of Chinese immigrants to the city increases and as the degree of transnationalism deepens. Other examples of transnational-ism in second and later generations can also be found. During the civil wars in the former Yugoslavia, some second-generation Serbs and Croats returned from Canada to participate in the military battles that were purportedly fought to help defend their ancestral homelands (Winland 1997; Bissoondath 1994, 119–20). The collapse of the Soviet Union and the rise of independent states has also presented various Eastern European ethnic groups with new opportunities to interact with their European "homelands." Small numbers of second- and third-generation members of the Ukrainian diaspora, for instance, have returned to Ukraine and are participating in various aspects of social and institutional development there (Ignatieff 1994; Satzewich 2002).

Transnational practices involve people's transactions with place of "origin" and can be analyzed and measured at various levels (Van Hear 1998, 242). Financial transfers with ancestral homelands, transnational ethnic business, and the ethnic media are important indicators of transnational practices. Remittances are a vital part of the financial transactions that take place within transnational ethnic networks. For some countries, such as the Philippines and Mexico, remittances are integral to domestic economies and help some families blunt poverty. Remittances by individuals in transnational communities in Canada are extensive, although specific data are not readily available. Recent u.s. data reveal that annual remittances from the United States are in the tens of billions of dollars (u.s.$29.6 billion in 1996). These remittances, moreover, further "transnationalize" social, cultural, economic, and political life within transnational communities (Vertovec 2000).

Recent research by Wong and Ng (1998) on ethnic businesses found that approximately one-half of Chinese immigrant entrepreneurs in the Vancouver area are engaged in transnational business practices, thus contributing to transnational financial transactions as well as to cultural and social ones. This transnationalism often relies on family networks and extensive transmigration. Chan has argued that spatially dispersed Chinese families constitute strategic nodes and linkages in an ever-expanding transnational field in which a new Chinese identity is emerging (1997, 195). Over the past decade or so a new Chinese diaspora has emerged, with transmigrants having "hypermobility" through transnational networks (1994, 320). Since 1998 the People's Republic of China has become the leading source of immigration to Canada, as a result of rapid industrialisation and a burgeoning population. This immigration is sustaining the Chinese transnational community and financial transfers by means of transnational entrepreneurship and remittances.

The ethnic media is pervasive in the large cities of Canada. Films, videos, television, newspapers, and radio provide a nexus of instant transnational communication to sustain members of transnational communities. For the Indian and Chinese transnational communities the ethnic media includes Bollywood (India's transnationally distributed film industry based out of Bombay); satellite television stations; radio stations and programs in Toronto, Vancouver, and Calgary; and newspapers available online and in hardcopy. The impact of the ethnic media in Canada can be measured by advertising revenue. Li and Li (1999, 56) estimate that the advertising revenue in three major Chinese newspapers in Toronto (*Ming Pao, Sing Tao*, and the *World Journal*) stood at over $34 million in 1996. Their research shows that the contest for revenue from the middle- and upper-class immigrants from Hong Kong and elsewhere, who are of course also consumers, is being fought out between ethnic entrepreneurs and so-called mainstream businesses. For the latter, forays into advertising in ethnic news-papers are, as Mosco (this volume) suggests, consistent with the more general effort on the part of corporations to appeal to and make their commodities and services attractive to a more diverse range of com-munities. They also reflect the corporations' increasing departure from traditional Fordist models of advertising, which sought to create and lure an undifferentiated mass of consumers. Li and Li's work on this dimension of the ethnic economy also points to what scholars such as Kurasawa (this volume) and Caroll and Coburn (this volume) identify as an underdeveloped element in political economy, namely, the role and social significance of consumption.

While the examples just mentioned pertain to Asian transnational communities, transnational-oriented media are also significant to many non-Asian groups. For example, satellite television is also popular among European and African transnational communities (Karim 1998, 9), where sporting and daily news events are consumed. Grescoe (1995, as cited 1998 in Karim) has noted that in Vancouver the total circulation of forty-six ethnic newspapers is larger than the combined circulation of the two main English-language newspapers. Thus, the cultural and social flows through ethnic media in Canada provide a high level of contact and exposure to the "other" home for news and entertainment.

In addition, various forms of Internet communication, including discussion groups that focus on social and political issues in the ances-tral homeland, have exploded over recent years. For instance, there are at least thirteen Internet sites that link Ukrainians in Ukraine with Ukrainians in the diaspora (Melnyk 1997, 7). Shortly after it was founded in 1997, one such site, the InfoUkes Internet site, began to record over fifteen thousand "hits" per day. Since then, discussion groups have dealt with topics such as Ukrainian politics, culture, eco-nomics, history, genealogy, and sports (5–9). It is clear that the Inter-net and the nearly instantaneous communication that it allows consti-tutes yet another link between individuals dispersed among various diaspora locations and their respective homelands.

In summary, social processes and institutions such as financial trans-actions and ethnic media constantly facilitate and negotiate the chang-ing conceptions of home and of citizenship for members of transna-tional communities. While the discussion here has focussed on selected transnational communities, the documentation for commu-nities that have not been mentioned, such as the Caribbean, Greek, Italian, Croatian, and Burmese communities, is also growing in Canada. Moreover, it should be noted that the phenomenon of transnationalism is very heterogeneous, involving elites, the highly skilled, and temporary low-wage guest-workers such as impoverished Mexican agricultural workers (Basok 1999), illustrating the diversity of transborder actors (see Gabriel and Macdonald, this volume).

Implications of Transnationalism for Citizenship and Social Identity

Does transnationalism and transmigration affect the established, traditionally bounded and nation-centered notions of citizenship and belonging? The evidence is mixed. In some readings, transnational practices may lead to the formation of hybrid identities and a decrease in attachment to a particular state and to bounded notions of citizenship. At the same time, however, some evidence suggests that certain identities have become reinfused with essentialized understandings of group membership and boundaries.

According to Albrow (1996, 93) the transnational practices and deterritorialized social identities of many international migrants provide a challenge for nation-states, because old identities are relativized and destabilized and new hybrid entities are created. These new hybrid and multiple identities involve the deterritorialization of social identity, which challenges the nation-state's claim of making exclusive citizenship a defining focus of allegiance and fidelity, in contrast to the reality of overlapping, permeable, and multiple forms of identity (Cohen 1997, 157). At this level there is resistance to the hegemony of the nation-state. And there are now doubts as to whether the nation-state can remain as the basis and reference point of citizenship. For some authors working with the transnational approach, it is no longer possible to assume that there is a one-to-one relationship of state and territory in an era of globalization and transnationalism (Jacobsen 1997).

Moreover, the state now competes with nonstate actors and organizations for loyalty and allegiance, including diasporic or multilocal forms of allegiances. Appadurai (1996) points out that states do not compete very well in such a marketplace of loyalties. Often, specific nation states are competitors with each other as dual and multiple identities increase pressure for dual and multiple citizenship. Since many newly industrializing countries depend on remittances and investments made by transnational migrants, they facilitate these capital flows back into their countries by passing laws that allow for dual citizenship. Moreover the countries of origin often encourage their citizens abroad to naturalize and participate in the receiving nation, which is a marked departure from earlier times when they were considered as defectors and automatically lost their original citizenship (Portes 1999, 476). Dual loyalties intertwine with dual citizenship and potentially contribute to economic transnationalism, as well as political mobilization.

Despite the considerable evidence for the link between transnationalism, the development of hybrid identities, and dual loyalties, there is also evidence of countervailing tendencies. In a pattern not unlike Kurasawa's argument (this volume) that "the interplay of sameness and difference is what defines Canadian popular culture in relation to the forces of the market and those of the American empire," it is important to recognize that the structural conditions that lead to the creation of fluid, hybrid, and deterritorialized identities may also be responsible for identities becoming more fixed, permanent, and infused with essentialist and primordial understandings of self and other (Satzewich 2000; Jhappan 1996). This new form of ethnic and racial primordialism is evident in some of the literature on the social construction of "whiteness" (Bonnett 1999; Hartigan 1999). Furthermore, as Floya Anthias (1998, 567) puts it in the context of studies of diaspora consciousness, "whilst, at one level, there is evidence that the cultural and identity choices of individuals and groups are becoming broader through migration and transnational movement, there is also evidence of the growth of ethnic fundamentalisms."

Even when identities are recognized as socially constructed and malleable, there is evidence of trends that question the prevalence of hybridity and dual loyalties. Howard-Hassmann argues that despite – or perhaps because of – the policy of multiculturalism, there is an increasing willingness on the part of Canadians to identify their ethnicity as Canadian and to affirm their social and political allegiance to Canada. Among English-speaking, non-Aboriginal Canadians, she claims there is an ethnic Canadian identity and that that identity can be both empirically measured and delineated. For Howard-Hassmann, English Canadian ethnicity consists of a bundle of characteristics that includes shared territory, language, religion, and common norms and values. She does not deny the reality of certain cultural and attitudinal differences among Canadians of different ancestry and origin, differences such as what food is served on certain occasions or how one mourns one's dead. However, she argues that these are all part of the normal "small differences" that exist within subcultures in most societies. Among other things, she points to social surveys that indicate that when given a choice, Canadians have strong inclinations to identify themselves as ethnically Canadian (Howard-Hassmann 1999, 531; Boyd 1999; Kalbach and Kalbach 1999).

Howard-Hassman's argument is relevant not only because it raises questions about the prevalence and pull of hybrid identities but also because it questions the common-sense view that the federal government policy of multiculturalism promotes disloyalty to Canada (Bissoondath 1994). In her view, the policy of multiculturalism encourages private, individual choices of identity, and, paradoxically, such a policy encourages identification with Canada and Canadian citizenship.

This argument is not uncontested (Abu Laban and Stasiulis 2000), but the point is that there are strong grounds to believe that even in a society that promotes multiculturalism and even in the context of a globalized world in which transnational ties seem to be assuming ever greater importance, ethnic identities are not necessarily becoming destabilized, and social and political loyalties and attachments to multicultural states like Canada are not necessarily being undermined. Clearly, questions about the material grounding of identity need to be subject to further analysis.

POLITICAL ECONOMY
AND SOCIAL DIFFERENTIATION

Social scientists have documented increases in the frequency and density of the transnational practices of immigrant and ethnic communities; they have analyzed the varying factors that shape immigration policies, and they have recognized the complexity of contemporary immigration flows. The recognition of these processes and transformations has led to renewed questions about how to understand the diversity of immigrant, ethnic, and racial community life. Many commentators acknowledge that social research needs to be sensitive to integrating gender, race/ethnicity, and class (Agnew 1996). Arguably, it is within the framework of political economy that class, gender, and other forms of diversity within immigrant and ethnic communities can best be understood.

Political economists may be able to move debates about immigrant and ethnic and racial diversity forward by returning to one of political economy's traditional strengths, which is its ability to recognize that in many aspects of social life there is an artificial separation between economic and noneconomic processes. While the dangers of economic reductionism are well known, it is nevertheless the case that even superficially noneconomic processes have economic implications. Political economists have, for instance, always recognized that Canadian immigration has been inextricably linked both to broad national macroeconomic considerations and to particular labour markets. They have also recognized that even apparently noneconomic aspects of immigration have profound implications for economic development and for labour markets.

For instance, the popular discourse regarding Canadian immigration policy distinguishes two broad types of immigration categories: economic and humanitarian. Economic immigration is defined through the independent class of immigrants, which includes skilled workers and business immigrants; humanitarian immigration is defined in terms of the family class and refugees. Over the past decade, Canada and the United States have proportionately increased so-called economic immigration. However, even though humanitarian immigration is often counterposed to the more "beneficial" economic immigration (Kirkham 1998), the former does help resolve labour problems in certain sectors of the economy.

Employers in economic sectors characterized by low wages, menial and undesirable jobs that many native-born workers are reluctant to accept continue to face labour-recruitment and retention problems. The workers include, among others, building and house cleaners, garment workers, agricultural labourers, and ethnic restaurant and supermarket workers. Many who occupy these low-wage jobs came to Canada under the broad rubric of humanitarian immigration in the family class or as refugees, but they nevertheless fill important niches within segments of urban labour markets. For example, Aguiar (2000) found that many building cleaners in large Canadian cities are Portuguese immigrant women who have come under the family class and who face employment insecurity. Moreover, since the 1980s many people of colour, a large proportion of whom are women, have come to Canada under humanitarian immigration categories and are destined for nonstandard and contingent work.

As Fudge and Vosko (this volume) point out, the standard employment relationship (SER) continues to be eroded in Canada, and this erosion occurs in gendered and racialized contexts. For example, over the past decade, as workplace restructuring and SER attrition occurred, there was a major shift in the Canadian garment industry as sweatshops moved into the homes of immigrant women who turned to home working. Roxanna Ng's research on Chinese immigrant women garment workers in Toronto finds that the public and private spheres are merged as these women cope with the demands of paid work and family responsibility in the same physical space (1999, 12). She situates this phenomenon in globalization and in the "recolonization" of Chinese women as the forces of continental trade agreements, such as NAFTA, deepen the exploitation they experience (2001).

With respect to economic immigration destined for a specific segment of the labour force, the case of Filipina and female Caribbean domestic workers, who come to Canada under the Live-In Caregiver program, illustrates the links between immigration, social reproduction (see Fudge and Vosko this volume), racialization, and gender relations in the context of an international division of labour. Detailed historical documentation of the Canadian state's regularization and regulation of domestic labour since the 1940s has been conducted by Daenzer (1993) and Schecter (1998), although earlier domestic movements did occur in Canada as early as Confederation, when migrant Chinese men worked as "houseboys." Similarly, Black female domestic workers migrated from Guadeloupe to Montreal and Quebec City in the early 1900s (Mackenzie 1988). Earlier research on the movements of foreign domestic workers in Canada exposed their tenuous and exploitive status in Canada (Silvera 1989; Calliste 1991; Arat-Koc 1989, 1992; Macklin 1994). More recent work focuses on the actual processes of placement and racialization (Bakan and Stasiulis 1995; Arat-Koc 1997) and on resistance and the negotiation of citizenship rights (Stasiulis and Bakan 1997a, 1997b; Bakan and Stasiulis 1997; Fudge 1997). In the case of Filipina domestic workers, participatory and policy-oriented research has emerged resulting in proposed short- and long-term policies dealing with the dilemma of this form of labour migration (Grandea 1996).

Once they occupy gendered and racialized low-wage sectors of the secondary labour market, it is difficult for many immigrants, regardless of their immigration class, to escape. They often lack the necessary education and language skills in English or French. Many professionals and skilled workers who have come to Canada as economic immigrants under the independent class also often find themselves in the secondary labour market due to a lack of Canadian recognition of their skills and credentials (Basran and Zong 1998; Krahn et al. 2000), and the consequences of this underemployment are no less significant than they are for so-called noneconomic migrants.

Recent economic transformations may lead to increasing diversity within immigrant and ethnic and racial communities in other ways as well. The decline in manufacturing jobs in Canada and the erosion of the SER means that opportunities for upward mobility for more recent cohorts of immigrants are often tied to self-employment or to entrepreneurship within an ethnic economy. This situation is somewhat akin to earlier times in Canada when entrepreneurship was chosen by groups like the Chinese because of blocked mobility in the labour market. There is some evidence to suggest that entrepreneurship within an ethnic economy and the related formation of transnational economic enterprises offers opportunities to immigrants of modest backgrounds to escape dead-end menial jobs and make their way into the middle class or petite bourgeoisie (Portes 1999, 471).

It is, moreover, possible to view such forms of ethnic entrepreneurship and economic transnationalism as instances of resistance and liberation. Portes et al. claim that "grass-roots transnationalism has the potential of subverting one of the fundamental premises of capitalist globalization, namely that labour stays local, whereas capital ranges global. By availing themselves of the same technologies that make corporate strategies possible, transnational entrepreneurs not only deny their own labour to would-be employers at home and abroad but also become conduits of information for others" (1999, 227).

Since transnationalism itself is tied to the logic of capitalism and since the transnational enterprise of ordinary nonelites is fuelled by the dynamics of capitalism, it may have greater potential than other alternative strategies as a form of individual and group resistance to dominant structures (Portes 1999, 227–8). Guarnizo and Smith (1998, 5) point out that the political influence of working-class movements has waned as global capitalism has advanced and that new social actors, such as transnational immigrant entrepreneurs who are neither self-consciously resistant nor very political, become invested with oppositional possibilities, so that entrepreneurial practices amount to an expression of popular resistance. These transnational actors may try to recapture a lost sense of belonging by recreating imagined communities and engaging in processes of subaltern identity formation that produce narratives of belonging, struggle, resistance, or escape. In this sense they utilize transnational practices and social spaces to counter their lack of relevant social capital, their social exclusion, and their subsequent social marginality. Portes (1999) and Portes et al. (1999, 230) suggest that in time, transnational entrepreneurship may become the normative path of adaptation chosen by groups seeking to escape the fate of cheap labour.

The conceptualization of transnational entrepreneurship as a form of resistance and liberation may, however, reflect only one side of the dialectic of class and gender relations. Framing entrepreneurship within an ethnic economy or transnational entrepreneurship as instances of grass roots resistance to globalization or as mechanisms to escape limited labour market opportunities may be appropriate for particular classes and genders within ethnic communities. But the liberation, freedom, and resistance experienced by employers and small-business owners may not resonate among the immigrants and members of ethnic communities who find themselves at the other end of the employer/employee relationship. While the warm ties of ethnicity may soften some of the more exploitative aspects of the relationship between wage-labour and capital in small-business environments and the ethnic economy, the ties of ethnicity may also facilitate what political economists used to call the super exploitation of immigrant and minority workers (Castles and Cossack 1973; Bolaria and Li 1988).

Some evidence from the United States, for instance, puts a different spin on immigrant entrepreneurship and immigrant employment within the ethnic economy. It suggests that immigrant workers who are employed by co-ethnics in ethnic small businesses may become caught in a modified version of what Norbert Wiley (1967) called an ethnic mobility trap (Sanders and Nee 1987). Lin's (1998) analysis shows, for instance, that Chinese immigrant women are an important part of the labour force in the garment, restaurant, and retail trade sectors of New York's Chinatown. But this kind of employment is often an economic dead end; it may prevent the acquisition of English-language skills or other dominant language skills, and it may preclude the acquisition of other labour-market skills that can be parlayed into upward mobility. Thus, while transnational entrepreneurs and employers within the ethnic economy may enjoy the liberation that owning a business entails, that same entrepreneurship may help solidify the social and economic marginalization experienced by less privileged members of ethnic and racial groups.

The two-sided, and contradictory, nature of employment and small-business ownership within ethnic economy is part of a larger problem of how to understand social inequality within immigrant and ethnic and racial groups (see, for example, Satzewich and Wotherspoon 2000). Even though one of John Porter's original aims in *The Vertical Mosaic* (1965) was to introduce class into the analysis of ethnic inequality (see Liodakis, 2002), much of the recent research on ethnic and racial inequality in Canada tends to place class in the background and to focus instead on ethnic and racial group differences in occupation, education, earnings, and socioeconomic status (Lian and Matthews 1998; Li 1998). That research tends to be somewhat inconclusive about whether Porter's vertical mosaic continues to provide an accurate depiction of Canadian society. Some commentators have suggested that the image of Canada as a vertical mosaic is a gross exaggeration (Darroch 1979; Winn 1985; Davies and Guppy 1998), while others argue that certain patterns of inequality point to the existence of a modified form of the vertical mosaic. For instance, after controlling for variations in earnings due to various structural and human capital variables, that data shows that visible-minority immigrants tend to earn less income than their white immigrant counterparts (Li 1998; Satzewich and Li 1987; Boyd 1992), and there are still significant differences in occupational status between ethnic and racial groups (Lautard and Guppy 1999).

Political economy needs to undertake more research, however, on the inequalities that exist within ethnic and racial categories and to examine whether they are as socially significant as the between-group differences that have been the subject of so much Canadian research. Regarding gender, Lautard and Guppy (1999, 246) note, for instance, that "the gendered division of labour is more marked than the ethnic division of labour. That is, men and women tend to be clustered in "sex-typed" jobs more often than members of specific ethnic groups are concentrated in 'ethnic-linked' jobs." In a different context, Boyd (1992, 298) finds that Canadian-born visible-minority women tend, on average, to earn more than Canadian-born, nonvisible minority women. In both cases what that research points to is a complicated picture of inequality and social mobility that cannot be captured by simplistic models of ethnic and racially based social inequality. Paying more attention to social class and gender differences may not unlock all the puzzles about ethnic and racial inequality in Canada. But a renewed interest in social class may lend important insights into the understanding of the diverse experiences of immigrant and ethnic groups.

Furthermore, while class differentiation within ethnic and racial groups can be documented empirically, more research is needed on whether class and gender differences affect patterns of ethnic community leadership, the social, political and economic priorities that ethnic organizations establish for themselves, and the ways in which members of ethnic groups interact with one another. These rather traditional questions about the continued importance of class and gender continue to be important even though a number of fundamental transformations in immigration and ethnic and racial relations have occurred.

CONCLUSION

In many ways, the continuities and discontinuities associated with the rise in transnational practices and identities and the growing socioeconomic differentiation within immigrant and ethnic communities has raised the bar for political economists who do research in the areas of immigration and race and ethnic relations. The research of those who work in the areas of immigration and race and ethnic relations has identified key issues and trends that are part of the changed political economy of Canada. Many of what Carroll and Coburn (this volume) call "the architectonic questions about exploitation, racism, and intergroup relations that political economists once posed about immigration and race and ethnic relations continue to remain relevant." Clearly, the kinds of transformations in patterns of immigration and of ethnic and racial relations that have been noted in this chapter do not negate the continuing importance of some of the questions that political economists once posed in these areas. Issues of ethnic and racial inequality, exploitation, and discrimination have become more complex as the class, ethnic, and racial composition of immigration flows to Canada has broadened. However, one of the challenges for political economy is to understand not only the political and economic, but also the entwined social, cultural, and transnational forms of immigration and race and ethnic relations. Immigration and race and ethnic relations now occur in a context where migrants to Canada consist of men and women, workers, professionals and capitalists, first- and later-generation immigrants, producers and consumers, and national and transnational citizens. In this context, a related challenge is to understand patterns of race and ethnic relations when members of the same ethnic or racial community occupy quite different positions within the social relations of production. This may simply be another way of saying that it is important to understand the interplay, and intersection of ethnicity, race, class, and gender, but all too often the calls for this kind of analysis have fallen short of what is needed.

At the same time, the transformations associated with the rise of transnational practices, identities, and social relations mean that the political economy of race, ethnicity, and immigration must continue, both theoretically and empirically, to broaden its lens to include the issues of transnational citizenship and identity. Class and gender may continue to be the trump cards that fracture transnational communities, but that needs to be demonstrated with further research that looks beyond the boundaries of Canada.

REFERENCES

Abele, Frances, and Daiva Stasiulis. 1989. "Canada as a 'White Settler Colony': What about Natives and Immigrants?" In Wallace Clement and Glen Williams, eds., *The New Canadian Political Economy*, 240–77. Montreal and Kingston: McGill-Queens University Press.

Abu Laban, Yasmeen, and Diava Stasiulis. 2000. "Constructing 'Ethnic Canadians': The Implications for Public Policy and Inclusive Citizenship, Rejoinder to Rhoda Howard-Hassmann." *Canadian Public Policy*, 26(4): 477–87.

Agnew, Vijay. 1996. *Resisting Discrimination: Women from Asia, Africa, and the Caribbean and the Women's Movement in Canada.* University of Toronto Press.

Aguiar, Luis. 2000. "Restructuring and Employment Insecurity: The Case of Building Cleaners." *Canadian Journal of Urban Research* 9(1):64–93.

Albrow, Martin. 1996. *The Global Age*. Stanford, CA: Stanford University Press.

Anderson, Benedict. 1991. *Imagined Communites*. Revised ed. New York: Verso.

Anthias, Floya. 1998. "Evaluating Diaspora: Beyond Ethnicity?" *Sociology* 32(3):557–80.

Appadurai, Arjun. 1996. 'Sovereignty without Territoriality." In P. Yaeger, ed., *The Geography of Identity*, 40–58. Ann Arbor, MI: The University of Michigan Press.

Arat-Koc, Sedef. 1989. "In the Privacy of Our Own Home: Foreign Domestic Workers as Solution to the Crisis in the Domestic Sphere in Canada." *Studies in Political Economy* 28:33–58.

– 1992. "Immigration Policies, Migrant Domestic Workers and the Definition of Citizenship in Canada." In Vic Satzewich, ed., *Deconstructing a Nation: Immigration, Multiculturalism and Racism in '90s Canada* 229–42. Halifax: Fernwood Press.

– 1997. "From 'Mothers of the Nation' to Migrant Workers." In Abigail Bakan and Daiva Stasiulis eds., *Not One of the Family: Foreign Domestic Workers in Canada*, 53–79. Toronto: University of Toronto Press.

Bakan, Abigail, and Daiva Stasiulis. 1995. "Making the Match: Domestic Placement Agencies and the Racialization of Women's Household Work." *Signs: Journal of Women in Culture and Society* 20(2):303–35.

– 1997. "Foreign Domestic Worker Policy in Canada and the Social Boundaries of Modern Citizenship." In Abigail Bakan and Daiva Stasiulis, eds., *Not One of the Family: Foreign Domestic Workers in Canada*, 29–52. Toronto: University of Toronto Press.

Basch, L., N. Schiller, and C.S. Blanc. 1994. *Nations Unbound: Transnational Projects, Postcolonial Predicaments, and Deterritorialized Nation-States*. Langhorne, PA: Gordon and Breach Science Publishers.

Basok, Tanya. 1999. "Free to Be Unfree: Mexican Guest Workers in Canada." *Labour, Capital and Society* 32(2):192–221.

Basran, Gurcharn, and Li Zong. 1998. "Devaluation of Foreign Credentials as Perceived by Non-White Professional Immigrants." *Canadian Ethnic Studies* 30(3): 6–23.

Bissoondath, Neil. 1994. *Selling Illusions: The Cult of Multiculturalism in Canada*. Toronto: Penguin.

Black, Jerome. 2000. "Ethnoracial Minorities in the Canadian House of Commons: The Case of the Thirty-Sixth Parliament." *Canadian Ethnic Studies* 32(2):105–14.

Black, Jerome, and Aleem Lakhani. 1997. "Ethnoracial Diversity in the House of Commons: An Analysis of Numerical Representation in the Twenty-fifth Parliament." *Canadian Ethnic Studies* 29(1):1–21.

Bloemraad, Irene. 2000. "Citizenship and Immigration: A Current Review." *Journal of International Migration and Integration* 1(1):9–38.

Bolaria, B. Singh, and Peter Li. 1988. *Racial Oppression in Canada*. 2d ed. Toronto: Garamond Press.

Bonnett, Alastair. 1999. "Constructions of Whiteness in European and American Anti-Racism." In R. Torres, L. Miron, and J. Inda, eds., *Race, Identity and Citizenship: A Reader* 208–18. Oxford: Blackwell Publishers.

Boyd, Monica. 1992. "Gender, Visible Minority and Immigrant Earnings Inequality: Reassessing an Employment Equity Premise." In Vic Satzewich, ed., *Deconstructing a Nation: Immigration, Multiculturalism and Racism in '90s Canada*, 279–321. Halifax: Fernwood.

– 1999. "Canadian, Eh? Ethnic Origin Shifts in the Canadian Census." *Canadian Ethnic Studies* 31(3):1–19.

Calliste, Agnes. 1991. "Canada's Immigration Policy and Domestics from the Caribbean: The Second Domestic Scheme." In J. Vorst ed., *Race, Class, Gender: Bonds and Barriers*, 136–68. Toronto: Garamond Press.

Castles, Stephen, and G. Kosack. 1973. *Immigrant Workers and Class Structure in Western Europe*. Oxford: Oxford University Press.

Chan, Kwok B. 1994. "The Ethnicity Paradox: Hong Kong Immigrants in Singapore." In R. Skeldon, ed., *Reluctant Exiles?* 308–21. Armonk, NY: M.E. Sharpe.

– 1997. "A Family Affair: Migration, Dispersal, and the Emergent Identity of the Chinese Cosmopolitan." *Diaspora* 6(2):195–213.

Citizenship and Immigration Canada. 2001. *Special Tabulations from Data Warehouse Extracts*. Ottawa: Statistics Canada.

Cohen, Robin. 1997. *Global Diasporas*. Seattle, WA: University of Washington Press.

Daenzer, Patricia. 1993. *Regulating Class Privilege*. Toronto: Canadian Scholars' Press.

Darroch, Gordon. 1979. "Another Look at Ethnicity, Stratification and Social Mobility in Canada." *Canadian Journal of Sociology* 4(1):1–25.

Davies, Scott, and Neil Guppy. 1998. "Race and Canadian Education." in V. Satzewich, ed., *Racism and Social Inequality in Canada*, 131–55. Toronto: Thompson Educational Publishers.

Department of Finance. 2001. *The Budget in Brief: 2001*. Ottawa: Department of Finance Canada.

Dirks, Gerald. 1995. *Controversy and Complexity*. Montreal and Kingston: McGill-Queen's University Press.

– 1997. *Intensifying Global Migration Pressures: Causes and Reponses*. Toronto: Robert F. Harney Professorship and Program.

Faist, Thomas. 2000. *The Volume and Dynamics of International Migration and Transnational Social Spaces*. Oxford: Clarendon Press.

Fudge, Judy. 1997. "Little Victories and Big Defeats: The Rise and Fall of Collective Bargaining Rights for Domestic Workers in Ontario." In Abigail Bakan and Daiva Stasiulis, eds., *Not One of the Family: Foreign Domestic Workers in Canada*, 119–45. Toronto: University of Toronto Press.

Gardezi, Hassan. 1995. The Political Economy of International Labour Migration. Montreal: Black Rose Books.

Grandea, Nona. 1996. Uneven Gains. Ottawa: North-South Institute and the Philippines-Canada Human Resource Development Program.

Guarnizo, Luis, and Michael Smith. 1998. "The Locations of Transnationalism." In M. Smith and L. Guarnizo eds., 1–34. *Transnationalism from Below*, New Brunswick: Transaction Publishers.

Harrison, Trevor. 1994. "Class, Citizenship, and Global Migration: The Case of the Canadian Business Immigration Program." Paper presented at the annual meeting of the Canadian Sociology and Anthropology Association, Calgary, 10–13 June 1994.

– 1996. "Class, Citizenship, and Global Migration: The Case of the Canadian Business Immigration Program, 1978–1992." *Canadian Public Policy* 22(1):7–23.

Hartigan, John. 1999. "Establishing the Fact of Whiteness." In R. Torres, L. Miron, and J. Inda, eds., *Race, Identity and Citizenship: A Reader*. Oxford: Blackwell Publishers.

Heibert, D. 2000. "Cosmopolitanism at the Local Level: Immigrant Settlement and the Development of Transnational Neighbourhoods." Working Paper Series no.00–15. Vancouver, Vancouver Centre of Excellence – Research on Immigration and Integration in the Metropolis.

Hollifield, James. 1992. *Immigrants, Markets, and States: The Political Economy of Postwar Europe*. Cambridge: Harvard University Press.

Howard-Hassmann, Rhoda. 1999. "Canadian as an Ethnic Category: Implications for Multiculturalism and National Unity." *Canadian Public Policy*. 25(4):523–37.

Ignatieff, Michael. 1994. *Blood and Belonging: Journeys into the New Nationalism*. Toronto: Penguin Books.

Isla, Ana. 2000. "Downplaying Ecological Stress: Debt-for-Nature Swaps." Available online at http://www.oise.utoronto.ca/~femres/downplay.htm. [19 March 2001].

Jacobsen, David. 1997. "New Frontiers: Territory, Social Spaces, and the State." *Sociological Forum* 12(1):121–33.

Jhappan, Rhada. 1996. "Post-Modern Race and Gender Essentialism or a Post-Mortem of Scholarship." *Studies in Political Economy* 51:15–64.

Kalbach, Madeline, and Warren Kalbach. 1999. "Becoming Canadian: Problems of an Emerging Identity." *Canadian Ethnic Studies* 31(2):1–16.

Karim, K.H. 1998. "From Ethnic Media to Global Media: Transnational Communication Networks among Diasporic Communities." Transnational Communities Working Paper Series. Available online at http://www.transcomm.ox.ac.uk/working_papers.htm – 21 January 2001.

Kirkham, Della. 1998. "The Reform Party of Canada: A Discourse on Race, Ethnicity and Equality." In V. Satzewich, ed., *Racism and Social Inequality in Canada*, 243–67. Toronto: Thompson Educational Publishers.

Krahn, Harvey, Tracey Derwing, Marlene Mulder, and Lori Wilkinson. 2000. "Educated and Underemployed: Refugee Integration into the Canadian Labour Market." *Journal of International Migration and Integration* 1(1):59–84.

Lautard, Hugh, and Neil Guppy. 1999. "Revisiting the Vertical Mosaic: Occupational Stratification among Canadian Ethnic Groups." In Peter Li, ed., *Race and Ethnic Relations*, 219–52. 2d ed. Don Mills, ON: Oxford University Press.

Li, Peter. 1998. "The Market Value and Social Value of Race." In V. Satzewich, ed., *Racism and Social Inequality in Canada*, 115–30. Toronto: Thompson Educational Publishers.

Li, Peter and Yahong Li. 1999. "The Consumer Market of the Enclave Economy: A Study of Advertisements in a Chinese Daily Newspaper in Toronto." *Canadian Ethnic Studies* 31(2):43–60.

Lian, Jason, and Ralph Matthews. 1998. "Does a Vertical Mosaic Still Exist? Ethnicity and Income in Canada, 1991." *Canadian Review of Sociology and Anthropology* 35(4):461–81.

Lin, Jan. 1998. *Reconstructing Chinatown. Ethnic Enclave, Global Change.* Minneapolis, MN. University of Minnesota Press.

Liodakis, Nikolaos. 2002. *"The Vertical Mosaic Within."* PHD diss. Department of Sociology, McMaster University.

Mackenzie, I.R. 1988. "Early Movements of Domestics from the Caribbean and Canadian Immigration Policy: A Research Note." *Alternate Routes* 8:123–43.

Macklin, Audrey. 1994. "On the Inside Looking In: Foreign Domestic Workers in Canada." In Wenona Giles and Sedef Arat-Koc, eds., *Maid in the Market*, 13–39. Halifax: Fernwood Publishing.

Melnyk, Andrew. 1997. "InfoUkes."*Forum: A Ukrainian Review* 97 (fall):5–9.

Mittelman, James. 2000. *The Globalization Syndrome.* Princeton, NJ: Princeton University Press.

Ng, Roxanna. 1999. "Homeworking: Home Office or Home Sweatshop?" Available online at http://www.oise.utoronto.ca/depts/sese/csew/nall/99HWAR~1.htm [15 June 2001].

– 2001. "Recolonizing Chinese Women in Canada: The Experience of Garment Workers in Toronto." In ISSCO, ed., *Proceedings I: The Fourth International Chinese Overseas Conference*, 76–84. Taipei: ISSCO and ISSP Sun Yat-Sen Institute for Social Sciences and Philosophy, Academia Sinica.

Papastergiadis, Nikos. 2000. *The Turbulence of Migration.* Cambridge: Polity Press.

Porter, John. 1965. *The Vertical Mosaic.* Toronto: University of Toronto Press.

Portes, Alejandro. 1999. "Towards a New World – The Origins and Effects of Transnational Activities." *Ethnic and Racial Studies* 22(2):463–77.

Portes, Alejandro, Luis Guarnizo, and Patricia Landolt. 1999. "The Study of Transnationalism: Pitfalls and Promise of an Emergent Research Field." *Ethnic and Racial Studies* 22(2):217–37.

Sanders, Jimy, and Victor Nee. 1987. "Limits of Ethnic Solidarity in an Enclave Economy." *American Sociological Review* 52:745–73.

Sassen, Saskia. 1991. *The Global City: New York, London, Tokyo.* Princeton, NJ: Princeton University Press.

Satzewich, Vic. 2000. "Whiteness Limited: Racialization and the Social Construction of Peripheral Europeans." *Histoire sociale/Social History* 23(66): 271–290.

– 2002. *The Ukrainian Diaspora: Looking Back, Looking Forward.* London: Routledge.

Satzewich, Vic, and Peter Li. 1987. "Immigrant Labour in Canada: The Cost and Benefit of Ethnic Origin in the Job Market." *Canadian Journal of Sociology* 12(3):229–41.

Satzewich, Vic, and Terry Wotherspoon. 2000. *First Nations: Race, Class and Gender Relations.* Regina, SK: Canadian Plains Research Centre.

Schecter, Tanya. 1998. *Race, Class, Women and the State.* Montreal: Black Rose Books.

Sharry, Frank. 2000. "NGOs and the Future of the Migration Debate." *Journal of International Migration and Integration* 1(1):121–30.

Silvera, Makeda. 1989. *Silenced.* 2d ed. Toronto: Sister Vision.

Simmons, Alan. 1998a. "Economic Globalization and Immigration Policy: Canada and Europe." *Contemporary International Issues* 1(1)1–15. Available online at http://www.yorku.ca/research/cii/journal/issues/vol1no1/article_2.html [20 October 1999].

– 1998b. "Racism and Immigration Policy." In Vic Satzewich, ed., *Racism and Social Inequality in Canada* Toronto: Thompson Educational Publishers.

– 1999. "Economic Integration and Designer Immigrants: Canadian Policy in the 1990s." In M. Castro, ed., *Free Markets, Open Societies, Closed Borders? Trends in International Migration and Immigration Policy in the Americas* 53–69. Miami: North-South Press.

Stasiulis, Daiva, and Abigail Bakan. 1997a. "Regulation and Resistance: Strategies of Migrant Domestic Workers in Canada and Internationally." *Asian and Pacific Migration Journal* 6(1):31–57.

– 1997b. "Negotiating Citizenship: The Case of Foreign Domestic Workers in Canada." *Feminist Review* 57:112–39.

Stasiulis, Daiva, and Radha Jhappan. 1995. "The Fractious Politics of a Settler Society: Canada." In Daiva Stasiulus and Nira Yuval-Davis, eds., *Unsettling Settler Societies,* 95–131. London: Sage Publications. 95–131.

Statistics Canada. 2000. "Statistical Profile of Canadian Communities." Available online at http://ceps.statcan.ca/english/profil/PlaceSearchForm1.cfm [11 May 2000].

Trickey, M. 2001. "U.S. Ambassador Seeks Better Immigrant Ties – More Consistency Is Called for in Rules Determining Who Gets into Canada, U.S." *Vancouver Sun,* 30 June 2001, A12.

Van Hear, N. 1998. *New Diasporas.* Seattle, WA: University of Washington Press.

Vertovec, Steven 2000. "Rethinking Remittances." Plenary lecture at the Fifth International Metropolis Conference. Vancouver, BC, November 2000.

Veuglers, Jack. 2000. "State-Society Relations in the Making of Immigration Policy during the Mulroney Years." *Canadian Review of Sociology and Anthropology* 37(1):95–110.

Wiley, Norbert, 1967. "Ethnic Mobility and Stratification Theory." *Social Problems* 15:147–59.

Winant, Howard. 2000. "Race and Race Theory." *Annual Review of Sociology.* 26:169–85.

Winland, Daphne. 1997. "Contingent Selves: The Croatian Diaspora and the Politics of Desire." Paper presented at the annual meetings of the American Sociological Association, Toronto, Ontario.

– 1998. "Our Home and Native Land? Canadian Ethnic Scholarship and the Challenge of Transnationalism." *Canadian Review of Sociology and Anthropology* 35(4):555–77.

Winn, Conrad. 1985. "Affirmative Action and Visible Minorities: Eight Premises in Quest of Evidence." *Canadian Public Policy,* 11(4):684–700.

Wong, Lloyd, and Michele Ng. 1998. "Chinese Immigrant Entrepreneurs in Vancouver: A Case Study of Ethnic Business Development." *Canadian Ethnic Studies* 30(1):64–85.

PART FIVE

Creative Sites of Resistance: Ecology, Labour, Youth, and Popular Culture

16 Ecology, Political Economy, and Social Transformation

LAURIE ADKIN

[T]he greens have one great advantage over the reds: they come later. The Green paradigm takes off from its own distinctive base, but this includes a theoretical and practical critique of the paradigm of the Left. It is a principle of hope developing in a mold that is similar – but not the same. It is the principle of hope recast.

Lipietz 2000a, 72

Ecological thought offers political economy a blueprint for a radically transformed model of development that is relevant to multiple contexts and territorial levels of collective action: local, regional, national, and international. From work on sustainable livelihoods for local communities to bioregional planning to proposals for the regulation of global trade and investment, ecological science and green economics are making important contributions to programs of reforms and their guiding principles. Indeed, no other body of thought has offered a comparable opportunity to left political economy to renew itself as a counterhegemonic discourse with enormous transformative potential. Although not all variants of environmental discourse are socially progressive, the implications of ecological principles and critiques more often than not call into question the raison d'être of capitalist accumulation. Political or social ecology, which seeks to understand the relationships between human social organization and environmental crises, constitutes a radical critique of the hegemonic model of development and its current globalization and acceleration. Around the world, youth, in particular, are keenly concerned with the foreseeable consequences of this model: widening global inequalities, ecological destruction, a potentially irreversible erosion of the conditions for a good and meaningful life.

While in the 1970s the European new left grasped the transformative potential of ecology for political economy and effected a synthesis of the concerns of alternative social movements in the form of the green parties, in North America a comparatively weaker left continues to search for a new agenda – for alternatives to social democracy. This is not to say that the social democratic left in Europe has been eclipsed by the new green movements, that the latter have not undergone, to some extent, a process of institutionalization since the 1980s, or that the green parties do not face daunting obstacles to their agendas for cultural and structural change. There is little question, however, that the European greens have advanced much further in the directions of radicalizing ecological thought and in developing far-reaching programs for environmentally sustainable, socioeconomic transformation than have the social democratic parties of Europe or North America. Ecological modernization is now squarely on the agenda of political institutions at national and European levels.[1] The challenge for European green movements is to sustain and deepen the egalitarian orientation of blueprints for ecological restructuring such as that designed for Germany by the Wupperthal Institute (Sachs et al. 1998). Intellectuals with roots in the new left and the alternative social movements have played an important part in constructing such programs.

In North America only the United States Green Party has recently presented a comparable challenge to the status quo "progressive" party and to the status quo political system.[2] The Canadian greens have only a marginal cultural and political presence. Meanwhile, left intellectuals and social movement activists in Canada maintain an ambivalent engagement with the New Democratic Party (NDP). Many socialists are critical of what they consider to be the NDP's lack of "any serious commitment to taking on business, never mind harbouring notions of one day actually transforming capitalism" (Gindin 1998, 13). Yet such criticisms by socialists of the NDP are rarely expressed in ecological terms. Instead, much of the debate about the NDP reiterates the "old left" opposition of social democracy to socialism,[3] while for the European new left, socialism has been replaced by such concepts as radical democracy or political ecology as identifiers of the counter-hegemonic project.

While ecological thought has hugely transformative potential for political economy in ways that will be sketched very briefly below, political economy also has an important role to play in radicalizing ecology. For ecological modernization to become more than a set of technical principles for more resource-efficient industrial design, for example, such principles must be articulated to a democratizing political project. Ecology, as I will discuss in more detail in this chapter, may be viewed as a primarily scientific discourse utilizing such core ontological concepts as "ecosystem," "habitat," and so on and offering explanations for such phenomena as global warming, or species extinction that emphasize the effects of human activities on environmental systems. While there is substantial scientific consensus that such problems exist and substantial consensus regarding the measures necessary to curb or eliminate them, the social, political, and economic strategies associated with such measures vary greatly. It is for this reason that in the following discussion, I characterize ecology as a highly contingent discourse. From the techno-authoritarian scenarios offered by the survivalists, or neo-Malthusians, to the democratic, humanist, and ecocentric solutions called for by ecofeminists, social ecologists, or deep ecologists, a range of philosophical and political discourses seeks to interpret the meaning of the global environmental crisis and its relationship to human nature and to the hegemonic model of development.

Political economy is one such discourse, with roots in Marxism. Yet the marriage of Marxist political economy and ecology has been as unhappy as the marriage of Marxism and feminism. The architectural project of constructing a single, over-arching ecological political economy is problematic in the same ways as fixing the meaning of "political ecology." Political economy's traditional tendencies toward economic and class reductionism, the assumption of a nation-state framing of political struggles (and, in the Canadian context, a nationalist framing), its acceptance of much of the productivist model of economic growth, and the difficulties of the approach in linking diverse social struggles are among the reasons why many commentators today believe that political economy itself must be transformed (Adkin 1994; O'Connor 1988; Lipietz 2000a). But what is at stake is more than the greening of political economy: ecological political economy must be articulated to democratic struggles and their underlying assumptions about the good life.[4] In other words, we need to address the question of how to construct collective action for a *democratizing* political ecology. Moreover, the problem of how to mobilize collective action for political-ecological reforms requires that we identify the philosophical underpinnings and the historically and culturally specific contexts of such projects.

ECOLOGICAL THINKING ABOUT
ALTERNATIVES

In the 1970s ecologists introduced evidence of natural limits to the exploitation of resources, the dumping of wastes, and the industrial growth and consumerism underpinning the Fordist era of development (entailing fossil-fuelled mass production for mass markets in the industrialized societies). These limits referred to the absorptive capacities of the earth and its atmosphere, to its finite resources, to the irreversibility of certain forms of destruction (of wilderness, biodiversity, the poisoning of soils and water systems by, for example, radioactive contamination). Ecologists also introduced such concepts as bioaccumulation, ecosystem, and carrying capacity, and they raised questions about scarcity and human population growth. With regard to the exploitation of nature and the applications and objectives of science and technology, political ecology asks us to exercise the principle of prudence, to moderate hubris with humility in the face of scientific uncertainty, and to interrogate anthropocentrism.[5]

The first photographs of the "blue planet" – seamless, fragile, finite, and whole – contributed to a shift in popular consciousness towards a global framing of environmental and other issues. This framing neatly obscures, of course, the very real political boundaries that organize the planet's human population. While there may be finite limits to growth imposed by nature (even taking into account technological innovations), the question of who gets what share of the resources available is not a scientific or environmental question per se but a political one – one having to do with relationships of power.

Ecological arguments challenge neoclassical economics in profound ways, beginning with the rejection of the belief in unlimited economic growth. The ecological economist Herman Daly refers to the idea of sustainable growth as an "impossibility theorem." In biophysical terms, the economy is an open subsystem of a finite and closed ecosystem: "The growth of the economic subsystem is limited by the fixed size of the host ecosystem, by its dependence on the ecosystem as a source of low-entropy inputs and as a sink for high-entropy wastes, and by the complex ecological connections that are more easily disrupted as the scale of the economic subsystem (the throughput) grows relative to the total ecosystem. Moreover, these three basic limits interact" (Daly 1996, 33).[6]

Ecologists transpose the concept of carrying capacity – the maximum population of a given species that an ecosystem can support in perpetuity (Dryzek 1997, 23) – to the global level, and they modify the concept by defining human carrying capacity not in terms of a maximum population but in terms of "a maximum 'load' that can safely be imposed on the environment by people" (Woollard and Rees 1999, 32). Human load is a function not only of population but also of average per capita consumption. William Rees and his collaborators have developed the now famous concept of ecological footprint, defined as "the total area of productive land and water required continuously to produce all the resources consumed, and to assimilate all the wastes produced by, a specified human population, wherever on Earth that land is located" (Woollard and Rees 1999, 32). According to their calculations, "the total land required to support present levels of consumption by the average Canadian is *at least* 4.3 hectares, including 2.3 hectares for carbon dioxide assimilation alone (Wackernagel and Rees 1995). Thus, the per capita ecological footprint of Canadians is almost three times their 'fair Earthshare' of 1.5 hectares. (There are only about 1.5 hectares of ecologically productive land for each human on Earth.)" (32–3).

Thus, "if everyone on Earth lived like the average Canadian or American, we would need at least three such planets to live sustainably" (Wackernagel and Rees 1995, 13).[7] Such demonstrations of limits to growth are now widely accepted among ecologists, even if mainstream economists continue to ignore both their existence and their implications.

Ecologists also challenge the sustainability of the linear processes of capitalist-productivist economies, in which we move from resource extraction and depletion to the production of wastes. These processes are contrasted with the cyclical processes of nature, which produce no waste and which are self-replicating. Third, the natural rhythms of life and regeneration (including climatic rhythms) are said to be threatened by the incessant acceleration of economic processes driven by technological innovations and growth imperatives (Sachs et al. 1997). Fourth, ecologists argue that the expansion of global trade is antithetical to sustainable development, as explained by Herman Daly:

Countries in which natural capital has become the limiting factor ... seek to appropriate whatever natural capital remains in the international commons, and to trade for natural capital with those less developed countries still willing and able to supply it. Trade makes it possible for some countries to live beyond their geographic carrying capacity by importing that capacity – natural capital – from other countries. And this tendency in individual countries tends to push the world economy to grow beyond its optimal scale relative to the containing ecosystem. Since the initial introduction of trade eases environmental constraints relative to total economic self-sufficiency, or autarky, it creates the illusion that further trade will continue to ease those constraints. But the benefits of moving from no trade to some trade cannot be generalized to the proposition that more trade is better than less trade. And – of course – all countries cannot be net importers of natural capital. (1996, 149)

Ecosystem sustainability as a foundation for local and regional economies has been proposed as an alternative to the presently centralized economies that are gobbling up the ecological carrying capacities of "distant elsewheres" and contributing to global inequality (M'Gonigle 2000; Rees 1992; Wackernagel and Rees 1995). Ecologists argue for the reorientation of economic development to the goals of maximal reduction of energy and material throughputs for local self-sufficiency – as opposed to export-orientated trade competition (Pierce and Dale 1999; Perkins 2000) – and for consumption norms that recognize "enoughness" (Sachs 1989).

Most ecologists, while calling for an "efficiency revolution" in our use of resources and in our production of wastes, also recognize that efficiency gains may be rapidly eaten up by growth in consumption.[8] They therefore call for a concomitant "sufficiency revolution." The challenge of reducing consumption in the North – of transforming cultural perceptions of happiness and well-being – was dramatically illustrated by the economic hysteria triggered in the aftermath of the attacks in the United States on September 11, 2001. President Bush appealed to Americans to do their patriotic duty to support the United States economy by maintaining consumer spending. In this discourse, consumption became not only an unquestioned good but a civic duty! In an economy in which 65 percent of GDP is derived from consumer spending, it is not hard to see how radical is the change entailed in calling for a reduction of consumption – or how powerful the predictable opposition.

In Canada a coalition of left economists lobbied the federal government to "take immediate fiscal and monetary actions to stimulate employment growth and restore consumer and business confidence" in the wake of September 11, warning of the danger of "zero or negative growth for the final two quarters of 2001 and into 2002."[9] Similar policy recommendations were made in the Canadian Centre for Policy Alternatives' *Alternative Federal Budget 2000*. Nowhere in these classically Keynesian proposals was there any consideration of the ecological implications of such a strategy or of ecological proposals for economic restructuring and job creation.

Here again, traditional political economy in Canada remains peculiarly indifferent to the body of green thought that in Europe is providing the only real alternatives to liberal-productivism. Many general directions for a transition to an ecologically sustainable economy were summarized in the Wuppertal Institute's study *Greening the North: A Post-Industrial Blueprint for Ecology and Equity* (Sachs et al. 1998):

- shifting from linear to cyclical production processes;
- orientating technological innovation toward the maximization of the productivity of resources, rather than toward the maximization of the productivity of labour;
- shifting taxation bases from the taxation of labour to the taxation of resource use;
- promoting "sufficiency" as a good life, rather than consumerism;
- deceleration rather than acceleration of economic processes and transportation norms;
- reducing the distances over which economic inputs and goods are transported;
- shifting from a fossil fuel-based economy to alternatives (solar, biomass, and conservation)

In addition, European greens have linked ecological objectives to the reduction of work time and unemployment, a strategy now being implemented in France and debated at the European level.[10]

There is, however, some evidence that the Canadian left is starting to integrate ecological thought into its political discourse. In the last federal election, for example, the New Democratic Party was the only party (whose campaign was covered by the media) to mention the environment, and environmental concerns seem to be important at the grassroots level of the party – mainly among youth.[11] Green budget initiatives are attracting the attention of many members of the scientific community as well as activists in the social movements.[12]

Finally, political ecologists argue that structural adjustment policies that compel Third World countries to pillage and export every available natural resource in order to repay debts are ecocidal not only for future development prospects in the South but also for the populations of the North (as a consequence, for example, of accelerated climate change). The developmentalist ideology and policies of international financial institutions and development agencies have also been challenged by the emergence of sustainable development perspectives in the wake of the Brundtland Commission Report (WCED 1987) and the United Nations Conference on the Environment and Development (UNCED 1992; United Nations Commission for Sustainable Development 2002), not to mention the spectacular debacles of various World Bank–funded "development" projects. To some extent new concerns – such as the relationship between ecological sustainability and gender equality – have penetrated development thinking and policies in the 1990s.

ECOLOGY AS POLITICS:
A HIGHLY CONTINGENT DISCOURSE

A thermodynamic definition of "sustainability" (Daly 1991) may help us to understand why fossil-fuelled economies must be converted to a "solar strategy" and may entail many consequences for existing economic arrangements (investment strategies, markets, and so on). Yet whether or not sustainability is articulated to a democratic project of social transformation and what philosophy of human needs informs its political and social agenda are questions that will be resolved only (and never definitively) by the discursive struggles of a multitude of different actors.

As many authors have pointed out, the Brundtland Commission's definition of "sustainable development" (development that "meets the needs of the present without compromising the ability of future generations to meet their own needs" (WCED 1987, 8) has been highly susceptible to such interpretations as the World Bank's ("Sustainable development is development that lasts" (Sachs 1993, 10)) or to being equated with environmental management. Big business had no difficulty endorsing *Our Common Future*'s reaffirmation of faith in the inventive potential of capitalism, science, and technology, as well as the market, to solve environmental problems (Welford and Starkey 1996; Tokar 1997). One Canadian CEO of a major mining corporation (Roy Aitken of INCO) thanked the commission for "creating an intellectual climate within which industry could move" (Adkin 1992, 137). The World Business Council for Sustainable Development, formed in 1990, was a key player in the subsequent United Nations Conference on the Environment and Development (UNCED) and processes leading up to it (Elliott 1997, 126–7). The Business Council represents about 130 of the world's largest corporations, including 3M, Du Pont, Shell, Mitsubishi, ALCOA, and British Petroleum (Dryzek 1997, 128). The interpretation of sustainable development (SD) that has become predominant in international institutions, government, and business circles emphasizes technological modernization and downplays equity issues. The content of development itself has been largely preserved from critical examination. John Dryzek describes SD as "a rhetoric of reassurance": "We can have it all: economic growth, environmental conservation, social justice; and not just for the moment, but in perpetuity. No painful changes are necessary" (1997, 132).

By the end of the twentiethth century, neoliberal discourse had largely succeeded in defusing the threat to liberal-productivism posed by the environmental movements of the 1970s and 1980s. It did so in a number of ways that are too complex to describe in detail here. Market discipline eroded the opportunity structures both for social movement activism and for alliances between labour movements and other social movements and, perhaps most of all, ecologists. There has been a trend toward the professionalization of environmental organizations and the adoption of an environmental-management approach linked to technological modernization, productivity improvements, and technical expertise and divorced from transformative social projects. Many environmentalists have been persuaded that market mechanisms offer the only achievable gains for environmental objectives. Indeed, most ecologists accept the pragmatic case for such measures as ecological tax reform and tradable pollution permits. However, such reforms are often not linked to social equity issues. For example, we can predict that increasing the cost of fossil fuels will stimulate greater efforts to conserve energy, and will make "soft energy" alternatives and public transport more "economical." At the same time, in the absence of subsidies to low-income households for retrofitting and other transitional costs, poorer groups will be much harder hit by such reforms than higher income groups.

The responses of the Alberta Conservative government, the Alberta New Democratic Party, and the Pembina Institute, an environmental research institute based in Alberta, to the spike in energy prices that occurred in Canada in 2001 provide some insight into the failures of both the left and environmentalists when it comes to mobilizing broad public support for an ecological program of reforms. The governing Conservatives sought – with relative success – to defuse public discontent with radically increased fuel bills on the eve of a provincial election by issuing about five billion dollars' worth of energy "rebates" to each resident of the province. (The government was able to do this because of the windfall revenues received from oil and gas royalties.) Households' abilities to absorb the increases were not taken into account (everyone received the same amount, regardless of income), and no investment was made in the development of alternatives to fossil fuels. The priority of the NDP's proposals was to ensure long-term, low-cost natural gas prices for Albertans. This plan had the virtue of arguing that a cap on home-heating natural gas rates should be financed by an increase in royalty rates. However, no mention was made of energy conservation or of a strategy to promote the development and implementation of alternative energy sources. Nor was there any attempt to take into account existing income inequalities among Albertans. Consequently, neither ecological nor social equity objectives were adequately addressed. The Pembina Institute published its "Smart Electricity Policy for Alberta," which outlined very credible initiatives aimed at conserving energy, improving energy efficiency, and increasing the use of low-impact renewable energy – all for a fraction of the cost of the energy rebates dished out by the Klein government. However, this plan included no measures to help low-income groups adjust to higher energy costs or to the costs of transition to alternative energy sources. Here again, the equity criterion of sustainable development was inadequately addressed.

Overall, environmentalists in Canada have not been very successful in building alliances with other actors in the social movements. However, there is evidence that new coalitions are being constructed that include unions, environmental nongovernmental organizations (ENGOs), antipoverty organizations, and other social actors. We see the outlines of such coalitions in the mobilizations against the neoliberal Harris government in Ontario during the 1990s, in the "movement unionism" of the Canadian Auto Workers Union (CAW) (Adkin 1998a, 2002), and in the recent antiglobalization protests (see the appendix to this chapter). Less evident is alliance-building between environmentalists and First Nations, in which struggles for self-governance are linked to demands for environmental justice.[13] Some initiatives indicate the potential for stronger connections between First Nations and political ecologists. In the 1980s environmentalists developed an ongoing dialogue with the First Nations bands in Clayoquot Sound, British Columbia, connecting land claims with opposition to the logging practices of multinational forestry companies.[14] More recently, the Pembina Institute has established working relationships with a number of First Nations to develop the planning and implementation of end-use energy efficiency, low-impact renewable energy, and green hydrogen.[15]

CONCEPTUALIZING COLLECTIVE ACTION

Although the sketch I have provided of some of the existing signposts for an ecological political economy is incomplete, it suggests that we do already have many insights regarding what needs to be done in order to shift our societies toward a new, ecologically sustainable future. However, it is equally evident that the transformative potential of this knowledge is by no means assured. Whether ecological knowledge will substantially subvert and redirect the hegemonic model of development – in any part of the globe – will be determined by the struggles of social actors. And it is here that we confront very difficult questions regarding the possibilities for, or ways of conceptualizing, collective action from various starting points (including the territorial ones already mentioned: local, regional, national, and international).

In thinking about collective action as a political sociologist trained in comparative methodology, I tend not to think in purely metaphysical terms or in terms of international state-systems but in terms of comparisons between spatially and temporally delimited local, regional, or national cases. I find it quite impossible to conceptualize collective action (for an ecological political economy or any other project) at a universal level of abstraction and have instead sought to ground my thinking in specific contexts. For example, we could discuss collective action in relation to proposals to reform the international trade and financial regimes, as well as environmental regulatory regimes, proposals aimed at instituting new rules that will permit more ecologically sustainable and equitable development choices. In the following section I outline in very broad terms some of the emerging possibilities for a global discourse of ecological political economy – its agenda of reforms, the actors likely to advance this agenda, and their possible collective identities. Yet this is only one of the directions in which our question regarding collective action departs. My own work has focused on the Canadian and European contexts of these problems, and it is to these regional, national, and local contexts that I will subsequently turn.

Global Political Ecology:
Universal Citizenship or Global Apartheid?

The level of global political ecology is without doubt the most complex and difficult level at which to mobilize collective action or to construct new (global) identities, given the existing political organization of the world's population by nation-states and these states' various international associations and commitments. Yet there is evidence that consensus may eventually be constructed in support of reforms aimed at countering the neoliberal, patriarchal, and racist-imperialist orthodoxies that have deepened both social inequalities and the ecological crisis. For example, calls have been growing for the democratization of the structures of international financial institutions (the World Bank

404 Creative Sites of Resistance

and the IMF) and a restructuring of their functions and mandates. Some have characterized the environmental or "environment and development" conferences and accords of the last two decades as an emerging framework of international environmental regulation (its considerable inadequacies notwithstanding). Elmar Altvater observes that

As a result of global communications and global networks, nation states and the diplomats representing national governments are losing their monopoly in shaping international relations. "Civil society" is in the process of becoming internationalized and transnationalized ... The threat to the natural environment has led, on the one hand, to "new concerns" ... and, on the other hand, to international networks which are growing into organizational forms. In the meantime, NGOs have taken on important tasks in the negotiation of international agreements, particularly in the realm of environment and development. (1998, 35)

Important actors in this regard, as Altvater argues, are the international NGOs, which are linked to coalitions and social movements in countries around the world and are working in such areas as environmental protection, human rights, third world development, and gender equality. Not only do the international conventions in these areas have regulatory effects, but the campaigns leading up to their establishment alter the terrain of discursive struggles, for example, regarding the legitimacy of decisions made by local governments and other actors (e.g., corporations, development agencies, unions).

This view of NGOs is supported, though perhaps lamented, by the *Economist* (1999), which offered this assessment of the growing importance of NGO and citizens' "disruption" of "global governance" in the wake of the November-December 1999 Seattle events:

The battle of Seattle is only the latest and most visible in a string of recent NGO victories. The watershed was the Earth Summit in Rio de Janeiro in 1992, when the NGOs roused enough public pressure to push through agreements on controlling greenhouse gases. In 1994, protesters dominated the World Bank's anniversary meeting with a "Fifty Years is Enough" campaign, and forced a rethink of the Bank's goals and methods. In 1998, an ad hoc coalition of consumer-rights activists and environmentalists helped to sink the Multilateral Agreement on Investment (MAI), a draft treaty to harmonise rules on foreign investment under the aegis of the OECD. In the past couple of years another global coalition of NGOs, Jubilee 2000, has pushed successfully for a dramatic reduction in the debts of the poorest countries.

The NGO agenda is not confined to economic issues. One of the biggest successes of the 1990s was the campaign to outlaw landmines, in which hundreds of NGOs, in concert with the Canadian government, pushed through a ban in a year. Nor is it confined to government agendas. Nike has been targeted for poor labour conditions in its overseas factories, Nestle for the sale of powdered baby milk in poor countries, Monsanto for genetically modified food. In a case in 1995 that particularly shocked business, Royal Dutch/Shell, although it was technically in the right, was prevented by Greenpeace, the most media-savvy of all NGOs, from disposing of its Brent Spar oil rig in the North Sea.

In short, citizens' groups are increasingly powerful at the corporate, national, and international level.

As the blue planet image suggests, ecology, like humanism, is evocative of universal identities (global citizenship, humankind) that supersede nationalist identities and constructions of human conflicts. Some observers have argued, for example, that a universal conception of citizenship based on the discourse of human rights is increasingly being invoked in struggles around the territorial authority of nation-states over their citizens (Soysal 1994). The international campaign against the Multilateral Agreement on Investment (MAI) has been led by a diverse network of organizations in which environmental organizations have figured prominently. In this case, governments are being called upon not to cede to multinational corporations their sovereign powers to regulate the terms of investment within their territories. While this campaign therefore views nation-states as necessary bulwarks against the predations of highly mobile global finance capital and the interests of multinational corporations, it also seeks to identify grounds for solidarity among "peoples" around the world – to construct, if you like, an international (citizens') common front against the imperialist ambitions of international capital.

However, as we know, international environmental campaigns, and various forms of environmentalism (most notably, neo-Malthusian) may also link environmental concerns to societal discourses that are neither solidaristic nor democratic. They may construct understandings of human nature that differ little from that of Hobbes, and indeed, the view that "human nature is fatally flawed" by incapacity for foresight, by greed, or uncontrollable drives is often expressed in environmentalists' explanations of environmental destruction and third world poverty and may be articulated to racist, Eurocentric, and authoritarian discourses.

Environmentalism may also turn a blind eye to the global inequities of resource exploitation, seeking to "green" capitalist economies in the North while the highly polluting basic industries are relocated to the South. This is precisely the danger signalled by Wolfgang Sachs (1992), who argues that environmentalism in the North may ultimately opt for a strategy of "containment," in which "the negative consequences of the over-exploitation of resources and sinks in the 'South'" are confined in order "to perpetuate the accumulation model, mode of regulation, and cherished life style of the privileged industrialized countries in the North." That is, "affluent societies try to secure their access to resources and sinks, but must ensure that others make the necessary sacrifices to stay within the recognized limits of global ecosystems" (Altvater 1998, 32–3). Altvater warns against an emerging "global apartheid": "The principle of equality of needs, wants and rights for all human beings in the world is being replaced with another one: the principle of rationing limited resources of highly utilized and partly over-burdened ecosystems (resources and sinks). One part of humanity is assigned a large ration while another part gets only a small ration" (33).

Ken Conca traces the discursive construction in the 1990s of environmental degradation, population, and scarcity problems in Third World countries as "national security threats" to the United States and the creation of "environmental security initiatives" within the Departments of State, Defence, and Energy, the intelligence agencies, the Environmental Protection Agency, and major research foundations (1998, 41). He warns that "there is a real danger that mainstream American environmentalism – politically adrift and increasingly reluctant to engage underlying structures of power – will converge with a foreign-policy establishment that can see the global South only as failed states or emerging markets" (45).

Thus, environmental discourse may help to construct an egalitarian conception of universal citizenship, or it may contribute to the institutionalization of a new form of global apartheid. The lesson we should draw from this is the determining importance of the discursive struggles that seek to articulate ecological knowledge to other elements of political discourse.

We Are Always Thinking and Acting Locally and Globally Simultaneously

It is often said that in building coalitions for a project of social change, we need to start from where we are – from a knowledge of a place, its social configuration, political economy, cultural characteristics, natural resources, and so on. And if we reflect on our daily practice as critical intellectuals, this is what we do when we intervene in local, provincial, or national debates. In this sense there is a tremendous fluidity in the territorial crossings of our interventions. Many of the actors in these conflicts (unions, environmental organizations, corporations) exist organizationally and function at multiple levels (local, provincial, national, international). At issue is not whether certain conflicts are local and others are global (or national, and so on), but how we cast our net when trying to interpret the meanings of these conflicts and suggest alternatives for their resolution. I have difficulty conceiving of any "local" conflict involving environmentalists that is not enmeshed in a complex web of political, economic, and juridical relationships that will be referred to in explanations of the conflict, that will be called upon as resources by the antagonists in the conflict, and that will play a role in determining the possible outcomes of the conflict.

Almost any ongoing conflict involving environmentalists, workers, communities, corporations, and governments would serve as an example here. A handful that comes to mind within Alberta alone includes multinational companies' logging, pulp, and paper operations in the northern boreal forest, the expansion of oil extraction from the tar sands, the provincial government's Special Places policy and Natural Heritage Act (introduced in 1999), oil and gas well drilling and exploitation in provincial parks, and the proposed coal mine on the border of Jasper National Park.[16] None of these conflicts or the webs of actors involved in them are in any way purely local, although intervention in them does, of course, call for local knowledge.

The problem of collective action for radical social change, therefore, lies not in what has been represented as the fragmentation of the central social conflict, for example, class struggle (which established a hierarchy of priorities) into a multitude of single-issue struggles or identities. Nor does it consist of the disintegration of a national (political) project into localized struggles or identities. The problem of collective action lies in transforming the *meanings* of social conflicts in such a way that the commonalities, or affinities, among different subordinate subject-positions become evident to their participants. For example, the conflict opposing mine workers and environmentalists in the case of the proposed coal mine near Jasper National Park needs to be reinterpreted by all actors as a collective problem of developing sustainable livelihoods. The resolution of this problem requires a major renovation of the bodies concerned with planning and governance, entailing both their democratization and a change in their relationship to the private sector.[17]

The territorial problem of collective action (should coalition-building efforts be focused locally (urban-based), regionally or provincially, nationally, or globally?) is a problem mainly in regard to a particular understanding of politics and of power and this perspective's territorial and reductionist framing of the central political struggle as one opposing nation-states to global capital. Within some segments of the Canadian left, at least, the restoration of national (state) sovereignty vis-à-vis global capital has been seen to depend on a renaissance of nationalist identity, which is mobilized largely in opposition to a globalization agenda (or something similar) that in Canada is frequently conflated by left-nationalists with Americanism or Americanization (Laxer, 2000). There is, in any case, some other identity or set of values that is said to be antithetical/threatening to Canadian values, traditions, or interests.

Why is this strategy of collective action problematic for a project of democratic political ecology? First, the construction of nationalist (Canadian) identity (as the collective identity of a broad-based social movement) necessarily rests upon a binary opposition (us/them) that is both hierarchical (our values are better than their values) and falsely homogenizing (it obscures important internal differences on the axes of class, race, gender, region, political orientations, and so on). Second, the left-nationalist discourse attributes the central-agency role to the state or to the elites who direct state policy and whose performance is judged in relation to how well or how poorly they are seen to be defending the national interests. Note that different interpretations of "national interests" may be advanced in relation to globalization pressures. Both neoliberals and social democrats, for example, have adopted policies aimed at enhancing economic competitiveness. Success in this game is measured by macroeconomic criteria such as rates of GNP, investment, or exports. They render women's unpaid domestic and other labour invisible, disregard ecological sustainability concerns, and reinforce a worldview that pits workers in one country against workers in other countries. Third, the national (people)/global (capital) opposition leaves no room for an ecological critique of consumerism and of all the many ways in which we as individuals are implicated in the reproduction of cultural and social norms and practices that perpetuate inequality and environmental degradation. Ecology – like feminism – brings together the individual and collective dimensions of social and cultural change. The enemy is not reducible to multinational capital or foreign states. Change must occur on multiple levels – apart from the formal political realm of electoral competition and parliamentary politics.

The rejection of nationalist identity as a mobilizing discourse is not equivalent to rejecting the importance of states' regulatory roles (either in regard to domestic regulation or to international regulatory regimes). Oppositional struggles for a liveable world need, however, to be interpreted as democratic struggles, in order to build the most inclusive solidarities possible. We can talk about democratizing political institutions to enhance participatory citizenship, meaningful decision making for communities, or solidarity with groups/communities elsewhere without laying claim to particular values or orientations as national ones that set us apart from "less civilized" nations elsewhere. We can defend particular visions of the good life without claiming that these visions are what define us as a nation and differentiate us from other nations.

Democratic Struggle, In All Directions

My conceptualization of collective action as a gradual and expansive form of counterhegemonic struggle that seeks to link together (and thereby to radicalize and transform) diverse forms of struggle against inequality, oppression, deprivation, and disease by means of democratic discourse does not imply a "working out" from a logic that is rooted solely in ecological knowledge, nor does it imply a picture in which ecology is at the centre of a web. It is not ecology per se that provides the meaning of all the other struggles to which we wish to connect ecology but the way in which ecology is articulated to these other struggles (e.g., struggles for social justice, or gender equality, or antiracism). Likewise, the political meaning (or identity) of ecology is transformed by its innumerable and shifting articulations to other such elements of discourse. What it means to be an ecologist (or, for that matter, a feminist) is determined by the connections established between a view of appropriate and desirable human-nature relationships and an underlying philosophy of human needs and of justice. This philosophy is necessarily a partial perspective, rooted in a situated knowledge (Haraway 1991). We need to draw on this knowledge in order to grasp the possibilities for articulating ecological goals to an agenda of social, economic, and political reforms in particular contexts.[18]

In my work on the problem of political ecology and collective action in the Canadian context, I have argued that ecologists need to articulate their struggles to those of other subjects in ways that construct shared understandings of a good life (its essential conditions) and that it is only through the examination of their relationships that the meaning of various struggles are transformed and radicalized and their commonalities discovered. Such initiatives will not lead far in the absence of interlocutors, of course. Movement-building is a long-term commitment that may need to begin with deconstructing stereotypes or putting aside historical grievances, and this process can succeed only when there is a willingness to acknowledge the relationships of power and privilege that have too often been represented as mere differences or as natural or as having origins outside the relationship itself. Clearly, for those who enjoy privileged-subject positions, there must be incentives (negative or positive) to engage in such disarming. Likewise, for those who occupy subordinate positions in these relationships, there must be grounds for trust. In my experience, it is through the work of coalition-building itself that such transformations – such discursive shifts – become possible (which is not to say that they always happen). It is when the old categories constructing opposing or different interests give way to new constructions of conflict that new solutions or alternatives also become thinkable.

Let us focus for a moment on some possible linkages between ecological goals, unemployment, gender inequalities, and other social conditions widely characteristic of North American and Western European societies today. In these societies, I would argue, substantial majorities are experiencing – though from different subject positions – deprivations and dis-ease that are linked to the changing conditions of work (including acceleration and intensification effects, the just-in-time workforce), insecurity of subsistence, and the consumption and lifestyle patterns that these conditions (along with the influence of the corporate media and other factors) reproduce and reinforce. Given this reading of how and why people are suffering (and its underlying philosophy of the good life), I find many useful, practical answers to the above questions in the debates and programs of the European green movements, which have had to develop responses to all of these developments. In the program of the French greens, for example, a very persuasive case is made for reforms that advance the principles of egalitarianism, or solidarity, individual freedom, and ecology (Lipietz 1989, 1993, 1996; Les Verts 1995, 1999).

The proposal to reduce work time and to increase free (or leisure, or self-directed) time is put forward as, simultaneously, a (partial) solution to unemployment, an improvement in the quality of life for those employed, an egalitarian way of redistributing gains in productivity and wealth-production, a condition for redressing the unequal sexual division of domestic labour, and a condition for changing consumption norms that underpin excessive resource exploitation and waste production. I would add to this list the possible implications for the social opportunity structures for involved and participatory citizenship: people who have more free time and greater security of subsistence are more likely to participate in a whole range of social, cultural, and political activities.

More free time would create at least the potential for individuals to substitute their own labour-power for purchased services and goods (e.g., for house repairs, gardening, and cooking); it would allow more involvement in activities that *require* time (playing with children, visiting elderly parents, exercise, recreation, socializing with friends, learning, and so on); it would reduce the necessity of reliance on high-speed and private modes of transportation. In other words, more free time makes more possible the delinking of our ways of living from commodity, transportation, and communication circuits (everything from fast food, to how we get to work, to things we buy as substitutes for giving time) that consume energy through-puts.

This is not to say that some of the activities we choose to pursue with our free time will not also entail the purchase of goods or services or that the reduction of work time alone will be sufficient to reorientate consumer choices in "ecological" directions. This dimension of the argument needs to be understood in conjunction with other aspects of the agenda of economic and social reforms being proposed (e.g., the concomitant reduction in income for the highest-earning groups, some form of minimum guaranteed universal income, and the creation of a "third sector" of socially and environmentally useful labour (Lipietz 2000b)) and with other elements of the ecological agenda (e.g., the transition from fossil-fuel and nuclear forms of energy to conservation and other alternatives; the redesign of cities) in order to appreciate the complexity of the possible outcomes of increasing free time. This agenda of economic and social reforms provides, at least, a framework for achieving the kind of "sufficiency" revolution that Sachs and others have argued is necessary not only for greening the North but for reducing global inequalities in resource consumption.

The expansion of economic blocs whose mode of regulation is orientated toward an egalitarian growth of free time and security of subsistence (through increased employment and minimum universal income) also has important implications for the global regime of capitalist accumulation. The neoliberal model promotes export-led growth and competition for markets based (in large part) on the reduction of labour costs. Lipietz refers to the possible reduction in domestic demand for imported goods that will function as a kind of "quiet protectionism" (market-determined rather than state-regulated). In ecological and global justice terms, reduced consumption (of imports) in the OECD economies will correspond to a reduced drawing on the "carrying capacities of distant elsewheres," and it will reduce the demand that is fuelling the pillage of Third World countries' resources by multinational corporations. How and whether such changes translate into opportunities for a reorientation of production within Third World countries toward meeting the needs of the majorities and the goal of gender equality, toward ecologically sustainable forms of economic activity, and so on, will of course be determined by the struggles within those countries, as well as by the struggles to reform the priorities and the representative structures of international economic and political institutions.

This is, of course, a very incomplete picture of the kinds of proposals that have been made by political ecologists, and there is no space here to enter into a discussion of their claims or even of the assumptions about conceptions of happiness and well-being that underpin them. Clearly, these proposals do stem from a particular interpretation of the ways in which the majorities in the OECD countries are experiencing (more precisely – suffering from) many aspects of their living conditions. This interpretation draws not only on various kinds of statistical documentation (medical, sociological, and so on) that provides evidence for particular characterizations of these experiences but also on simply listening to the ways in which many individuals are experiencing their lives and reflecting on our own "life worlds." This interpretation therefore also expresses (more or less explicitly depending on the author and the approach) a philosophy of the good life – of our needs and desires as members of these societies, differently situated in important ways but interconnected insofar as we are all implicated in certain social relationships, institutions, and regulatory frameworks that discipline, circumscribe, and direct our options and choices. This underlying philosophy of the good life and the agenda of reforms that derives from it lead us to certain conclusions regarding the agency for such a social project. In identifying the social subjects who have the greatest stakes in the realization of such an agenda, we are at once struck by their heterogeneous subject positions and hence by the different ways in which these subjects may be persuaded to support such an egalitarian ecological agenda of reforms.

CONCLUSIONS

Political ecology provides important directions for the radical restructuring of local and global economies, restructuring away from the imperatives of capitalist accumulation and towards the goals of meeting human needs within ecologically sustainable parameters in an egalitarian fashion, and with respect for the rights of other species to flourish on this planet. While environmentalism has been fighting a rearguard action since the 1980s against the worst excesses and depredations of industrial and consumer capitalism, radical green movements and parties have developed impressive, comprehensive programs for societal transformation. There are many signs that mass support for such programs exists and may be mobilized. Ecological discourse has played a central role in recent mobilizations against neoliberal globalization (see appendix) – mobilizations that are constructing coalitions between diverse social subjects.[19]

There is no return to the social democratic formulae of the post–World War II era. Left political economy needs the futuristic vision and insights of radical ecology if it is to offer a truly alternative agenda for social change. At the same time, ecology must be articulated to diverse democratic struggles in order to prevent its articulation to a project of global apartheid that supports the greening of capitalism in the North at the expense of environmental degradation elsewhere and deepening social injustice. Political economy's egalitarian commitments – its insights into the logic of capitalist accumulation – are critically important to ensuring a radical future for ecological discourse.

APPENDIX: RECENT MOBILIZATIONS AGAINST NEOLIBERAL GLOBALIZATION

May 1998	Anti-MAI protest in Montreal, Quebec
July 1999	Protests against IMF in Ankara, Turkey
August 1999	Protests against IMF policies in Ecuador
September 1999	Protests against IMF policies in Columbia
	Alternatives to the APEC Agenda forum in Auckland, New Zealand
December 1999	The battle of Seattle during the WTO ministerial meeting
February 2000	Protest against the World Economic Forum in Davos, Switzerland
	Antiglobalization protest in Bangkok, Thailand, during UNCTAD conference
May 2000	Protests during Asian Development Bank meeting, Thailand
June 2000	Protest in Calgary, Alberta, during World Petroleum Congress
	Antiglobalization festival in Millau, France[20]

July 2000   Protest in Windsor, Ontario, during Organization of American States (OAS) meetings

August 2000   Protest against the World Economic Forum, Melbourne

September 2000   People's Summit in New York City, paralleling the Millenium Summit of world leaders

Prague protests against the IMF and World Bank during these organizations' fifty-fifth annual summit

October 2000   Antiglobalization events during the meeting of World Bank and IMF officials and central bankers from nineteen countries (the G20), in Montreal, Quebec

April 2001   Second People's Summit of the Americas held parallel to the OAS Summit of the Americas and in opposition to the proposed Free Trade Area of the Americas (FTAA), Quebec City

Protests against the IMF and the World Bank, Washington, DC

July 2001   Protests against the G8 meeting, Genoa, Italy

September 2001   Antiglobalization protests in Washington, DC

November 2001   Protests in Ottawa against the IMF, the World Bank, and the G20

International Day of Protest against the WTO organized by the Common Front on the WTO, with participation from the International Confederation of Free Trade Unions (ICFTU), Ottawa

Protests in New Delhi organized by the Indian People's Campaign against the WTO during WTO meetings in Doha, Qatar

December 2001   Protests against the World Economic Forum in New York City

February 2002   World Social Forum held in Porto Alegre, Brazil, organizing resistance against neoliberalism, militarism, and war and for peace and social justice (A third World Social Forum is planned for Porto Alegre in 2003.)

April 2002   Mobilization for Global Justice, Washington, DC, during World Bank and IMF meetings

Forum on corporate globalization, Utica, New York

June 2002   G6B People's Summit held in Calgary to parallel G8 summit at Kananaskis, Alberta

Global Justice Action Summit held in Missoula, Montana

Protests held in Oslo, Norway, around World Bank Summit

October 2002   Hemispheric Social Alliance/Alianza Social Continental (ASC) against the FTAA, days of resistance, Quito, Ecuador, 27 October–1 November

November 2002   ASC Assembly against the FTAA, Havana, Cuba

NOTES

1 "Ecological modernization" (EM) is a contested concept, having both techno-corporatist (Hajer 1995) and (potentially) "reflexive" (Beck 1992; Mol 1995) "strong" (Christoff 1996) or democratic variants. Like the concept sustainable development, EM has become associated, predominantly, with the "greening" of capitalism. EM incorporates industrial ecology design principles aimed at replacing linear production processes with cyclical ones, reducing waste, increasing efficiency, and so on. The incentive for business to adopt more stringent environmental standards and to innovate is enhanced competitiveness and profitability, as well as the exploitation of new market niches. EM has been most extensively implemented in corporatist regulatory contexts (Northern Europe) and has been most resisted in the United Kingdom, Australia, New Zealand, and North America (Weale 1992). Green movements in Europe seek to marry the technical advances of EM to a more radical social and cultural project, such as that outlined in Sachs et al. (1998). For a discussion of EM as a discourse, see Dryzek (1997, 137–52).

2 The U.S. Green party is not, however, universally viewed as progressive on every front, and Nader's presidential campaign was much criticized by feminist and black activists for splitting the progressive vote in the November 2000 U.S. presidential elections. Notably, the great majority of black (particularly black female) voters did not vote for the Nader-LaDuke ticket but for the Gore-Lieberman ticket. Likewise, there remains a significant divide between the environmental-justice movements (with roots in race and class-defined struggles) and the predominantly white, middle-class environmental NGOs. See Bullard (1993, 1994); Harvey (1999).

3 A debate about the NDP as a vehicle for socialist transformation and proposed alternatives was published in the left magazines *This Magazine* and *Canadian Dimension* between 1998 and 2000.

4 I refer here to struggles for equality, understood as freedom from unwarranted discrimination; for autonomy, understood as respect for difference (or freedom from unwarranted assumptions of sameness in relation to some pseudo-universal norm); and for deepened and broadened participation by individuals and groups in decisions about the direction of society (vis-à-vis states, elites, corporations, and other institutional actors).

5 The principle of prudence is also referred to as the precautionary principle, summarized by Dryzek (1997, 139) as the belief that "scientific uncertainty is no excuse for inaction on an environmental problem. Thus, if there are good reasons for thinking a problem may be serious, then it will be addressed, even in the absence of scientific proof."

6 Note that Daly also identifies four "ethicosocial limits" to growth in this work: the depletion of the natural capital available to future generations; the human take-over of the habitats of other species, leading to their reduction or extinction; the declining welfare benefits of aggregate growth; and the "wrecking of the moral and social order" by uncontrolled growth (1996, 35–7).

7 Wackernagel and Rees' estimate may be conservative. The Wupperthal Institute study (Sachs et al. 1998, 3) calculates that if the entire global population discharged as much CO_2 as the average German, humanity would need *five* planets for nature to be able to process these emissions.

8 Some ecological economists are calling for a "factor 10 economy": the need for material growth to alleviate poverty in the Third World means that there must be a corresponding reduction in the material and energy intensity of goods and services. Specifically, the material intensity of consumption in industrialized countries should be reduced by a factor of up to ten to accommodate growth in the Third World. It is estimated that a factor 10 economy could be achieved through strategies of industrial ecology, fiscal and taxation policy, and other measures.

9 The letter, co-ordinated by the Canadian Centre for Policy Alternatives, was addressed to Prime Minister Chretien, Finance Minister Paul Martin, and the governor of the Bank of Canada, David Dodge. It was signed by about 130 left academics and dated 2 November 2001.

10 The Loi Aubry, named for the Socialist minister for employment and solidarity Martine Aubry and passed in 1998, establishes a statutory thirty-five hour work week to take effect between 1 January 2000 and 1 January 2002, depending on the type of establishment. The law allows for flexibility in the methods negotiated in each workplace to reach this target and offers certain financial incentives to employers to effect reductions in work time, while increasing employment. The reduction of work time was part of the electoral accord agreed upon between the Socialists and Les Verts prior to the 1997 legislative elections. At the Luxembourg EU summit on employment in November 1997, the Green group in the European Parliament called for a medium-term objective of a thirty-hour week, limits on overtime, a shift in taxation from employers' labour contributions to taxes on nonrenewable energy sources, waste, and pesticides, and the creation of a new "public employment sector." For more information about reduction of work time initiatives in Europe, see Hayden (1999).

11 In the fall 2000 platform prepared for the federal elections, the NDP (2000), incorporated a number of policy positions that reflect a significant degree of responsiveness to the concerns of the environmental movement, including some green economics (in areas of investment and

fiscal policy, transportation, and trade). There is also a mention of the goals of "access to leisure and sufficient flexibility to balance work and family life," hinting at a reduction of work time policy (a key component of the European greens' agenda for reducing unemployment and restructuring consumption), although no specific policy is set out in this regard. (Summaries of the party's policies may be found at its website at http://www.ndp.ca/. The NDP was also the only party to introduce environmental concerns into the campaign debates, although in a relatively marginal way. The campaign tended to focus on criticisms of the ruling Liberal Party's corruption or incompetence. The NDP's critique of the Liberals for representing the interests of big business made little reference to an alternative "sustainable development" agenda of reforms.

12 For more information about green budget initiatives in Canada, visit the websites of the International Institute for Sustainable Development (http://www.iisd.org/economics/gbr/), the National Round Table on the Environment and the Economy (http://www.nrtee-trnee.ca/), and the Pembina Institute (http://www.pembina.org/green/default.htm).

13 Native peoples in Canada have suffered terribly from the environmental degradation of their lands by mining, logging, and industrial pollution. Of many cases that could be mentioned here, two examples must suffice: the poisoning of the Dene of Great Bear Lake, NWT, by exposure to uranium ore and contamination of waterways by uranium tailings at Port Radium between 1932 and 1960 (Nikiforuk 1998) and the toxic chemical contamination by surrounding industries of water, soil, fish, and game that provided subsistence to the Mohawk of the Akwesasne reserve, which straddles the U.S.-Canadian border between northern New York, eastern Ontario, and western Quebec (Schell and Tarbell 1998).

14 For more information on the history of the conflicts of Clayoquot Sound, see the website (http://sitka.dcf.uvic.ca/CLAYOQUOT/).

15 The First Nations involved include Selkirk First Nation, Pelly Crossing, Yukon; Vuntut Gwitchin First Nation, Old Crow, Yukon; Kikino Metis Nation, Kikino, Alberta; Xeni Gwet'In First Nation, Nemiah Valley, British Columbia; Oweekeno Nation, Rivers Inlet, British Columbia; Gitga'at Nation, Hartley Bay, British Columbia; Hupacasath First Nation, Port Alberni, British Columbia.

16 A critical review of Bill 15, the Natural Heritage Act of Alberta, may be found on the website of the Environmental Law Centre, at www.elc.ab.ca.

17 A recently published analysis of this conflict is Urquhart (2001).

18 In terms more familiar to a comparativist, the objective is to develop middle-range theories of counterhegemonic political ecology and its potential agency, rather than a universal theory of social agency or stages of societal development.

19 An estimated fifty thousand protestors gathered in Seattle, representing diverse groups from many different countries: Philippine indigenous peoples, Canadian public health care defenders, French farmers, environmentalists, large trade unions (including representatives from more than one hundred countries), human rights organizations, citizens' organizations for "fair trade," Indian opponents of "bio-piracy," women's activists, and many others. Over fifteen hundred organizations from nearly one hundred countries signed a declaration (set up on-line by Public Citizen, a consumer-rights group) demanding no further trade liberalization until the social and environmental impacts of existing agreements have been fully assessed (Weissman 1999; *New Internationalist* 2000).

20 The McDonald's restaurant chain has become a symbol of the cultural values embedded in neoliberal globalization. In France, opposition to the fast-food industry takes the form of rejection of "la malbouffe." In Italy, there is a "slow food" movement. In the central French town of Millau in August 1999, 300 farmers and supporters, including the leader of the Farmers' Confederation of France, José Bové, carried out a peaceful dismantling of a McDonald's outlet under construction. Ten activists, including Bové and two members of the Verts, were charged with vandalizing property; Bové was sentenced to three months in prison – a sentence that was promptly appealed. The second trial began 30 June 2000 and was greeted by a huge demonstration of support for the accused. Tens of thousands of people converged on Millau for an "anti-globalization festival." Bové has become the symbolic leader of a revitalized antiglobalization movement in France.

REFERENCES

Adkin, Laurie E. 2002. "The Rise and Fall of New Social Movement Theory?" In Abigail Bakan and Eleanor MacDonald, eds., *Critical Political Studies*. Montreal and Kingston: McGill Queen's University Press.

– 1998a. *The Politics of Sustainable Development: Citizens, Unions, and the Corporations*. Montreal and New York: Black Rose Books.

– 1998b. "Ecological Politics in Canada: Elements of a Strategy of Collective Action." In Roger Keil, David V.J. Bell, Peter Penz, and Leesa Fawcett, eds., *Political Ecology: Global and Local*, 292–322. London and New York: Routledge.

– 1994. "Environmental Politics, Political Economy, and Social Democracy in Canada." *Studies in Political Economy* 45 (fall): 130–69.

– 1992. "Counter-hegemony and Environmental Politics in Canada." In William K. Carroll, ed., *Organizing Dissent: Contemporary Social Movements in Theory and Practice*, 135–56. 1st ed. Toronto: Garamond Press.

Altvater, Elmar. 1998. "The New Global Order and the Environment: Defining the Issues." In Roger Keil, David V.J. Bell, Peter Penz, and Leesa Fawcett, eds., *Political Ecology: Global and Local*, 19–45. London and New York: Routledge.

Beck, Ulrich. 1992. *The Risk Society: Towards a New Modernity*. London: Sage.

Bullard, Robert D., ed. 1993. *Confronting Environmental Racism: Voices from the Grassroots*. Boston: South End Press.

– ed. 1994. *Unequal Protection: Environmental Justice and Communities of Color*. San Francisco: Sierra Club Books.

Christoff, Peter. 1996. "Ecological Modernisation, Ecological Modernities." *Environmental Politics* 5: 476–500.

Conca, Ken. 1998. "The Environment-Security Trap." *Dissent* 45(3): 40–5.

Daly, Herman E. 1996. *Beyond Growth: The Economics of Sustainable Development*. Boston, MA: Beacon Press.

– 1993. "Sustainable Growth: An Impossibility Theorem." In Herman E. Daly and Kenneth E. Townsend, eds., *Valuing the Earth: Economics, Ecology, Ethics*, 267–73. Cambridge, MA: MIT Press.

– 1991. *Steady-State Economics*. Washington, DC: Island Press.

Dryzek, John. 1997. *The Politics of the Earth (Environmental Discourses)*. Oxford: Oxford University Press.

Economist. 1999. "The Nongovernmental Order," 11 December.

Elliott, Lorraine. 1997. *The Global Politics of the Environment*. New York: New York University Press.

France. Commissariat Général du Plan. 1993. *L'économie face à l'écologie*. Paris: Éditions la Découverte/La Documentation Française.

Gindin, Sam. 1998. "The Party's Over," *This Magazine* 32(3): 13–15.

Hajer, Maarten A. 1995. *The Politics of Environmental Discourse: Ecological Modernization and the Policy Process*. Oxford: Oxford University Press.

Haraway, Donna. 1991. "Situated Knowledges: The Science Question in Feminism and the Privilege of Partial Perspective." In Donna J. Haraway, ed., *Simians, Cyborgs, and Women: The Reinvention of Nature*, 183–201. New York: Routledge.

Harvey, David. 1999. "The Environment of Justice." In Frank Fischer and Maarten A. Hajer, eds., *Living with Nature*, 153–85. Oxford: Oxford University Press.

Hayden, Anders. 1999. *Sharing the Work, Sparing the Planet*. Toronto: Between the Lines Press.

Laxer, Gordon. 2000. "Surviving the Americanizing New Right." *Canadian Review of Sociology and Anthropology* 37(1): 55–75.

Les Verts. 1999. *Réinventer L'Europe (programme des Verts pour les élections européennes du 13 juin 1999)*. Paris: Les Verts.

– 1995. *Oser l'écologie et la solidarité (plateforme de Dominique Voynet pour l'élection présidentielle de 1995)*. Paris: Les Verts (March).

Lipietz, Alain. 2000a. "Political ecology and the future of Marxism," *Capitalism, Nature, Socialism* 11(1): 69–85.

– 2000b. Rapport relatif à la lettre de mission du 17 septembre 1998 adressée par Madame Aubry, Ministre de l'Emploi et de la Solidarité à Alain Lipietz, sur l'opportunité d'un nouveau type de société à vocation sociale. Vol. 1. Paris: CEPREMAP.

– 1996. *La Société en Sablier: Le partage du travail contre la déchirure sociale.* Paris: Editions la Découverte.

– 1993. *Vert espérance (L'avenir de l'écologie politique).* Paris: Éditions La Découverte.

– 1989. *Choisir l'audace.* Paris: Editions la Découverte.

M'Gonigle, Michael. 2000. "A Dialectic of Centre and Territory: The Political Economy of Ecological Flows and Spatial Relations." In Fred P. Gale and R. Michael M'Gonigle, eds., *Nature, Production, Power: Towards an Ecological Political Economy*, 3–16. Cheltenham, England; Northampton, MA: Edward Elgar.

Mol, Arthur P.J. 1995. *The Refinement of Production: Ecological Modernization Theory and the Chemical Industry.* Utrecht: Van Arkel.

New Democratic Party (NDP). 2000. *Priorities Paper.* Ottawa, 17 October.

New Internationalist. 2000. "WTO Shambles in Seattle," issue 320, January–February.

Nikiforuk, Andrew. 1998. "Echoes of the Atomic Age: Cancer Kills Fourteen Aboriginal Uranium Workers." *Calgary Herald*, 14 March. Available online at http://ccnr.org/deline_deaths.html.

O'Connor, James. 1988. "Capitalism, Nature, Socialism: A Theoretical Introduction." *Capitalism, Nature, Socialism* 1: 11–38.

Perkins, Patricia E. 2000. "Equity, Economic Scale and the Role of Exchange in a Sustainable Economy." In Fred P. Gale and R. Michael M'Gonigle, eds., *Nature, Production, Power: Towards an Ecological Political Economy*, 183–94. Cheltenham, England; Northampton, MA: Edward Elgar.

Pierce, John T., and Ann Dale, eds. 1999. *Communities, Development, and Sustainability across Canada.* Vancouver: University of British Columbia Press.

Rees, William E. 1992. "Ecological Footprints and Appropriated Carrying Capacity: What Urban Economics Leaves Out." *Environment and Urbanization* 4(2): 121–30.

Sachs, Wolfgang. 1993. "Global Ecology in the Shadow of 'Development.'" In Wolfgang Sachs, ed., *Global Ecology: A New Arena of Political Conflict.* London and New Jersey: Zed Books.

– 1992. "Von der Vereitlung der Reichtümer zur Verteilung der Risiken." *Universitas* 9: 887–97.

– 1989. "A Critique of Ecology: The Virtue of Enoughness." *New Perspectives Quarterly* (spring):16–19.

Sachs, Wolfgang, Susan George, Ivan Illich, and Andrew Ross. 1997. "Slow Is Beautiful." *New Perspectives Quarterly* 14(1): 4–10.

Sachs, Wolfgang, R. Loske, M. Linz, et al. 1998. *Greening the North: A Postindustrial Blueprint for Ecology and Equity.* London: Zed Books.

Schell, Lawrence M., and Alice M. Tarbell. 1998. "A Partnership Study of PCBs and the Health of Mohawk Youth: Lessons from Our Past and Guidelines for Our Future." *Environmental Health Perspectives Supplements* 106(3): 833–40.

Soysal, Yasemin Nuhoglu. 1994. *Limits of Citizenship: Migrants and Postnational Membership in Europe.* Chicago: University of Chicago Press.

Tokar, Brian. 1997. *Earth for Sale: Reclaiming Ecology in the Age of Corporate Greenwash,* Boston: South End Press.

United Nations. Commission for Sustainable Development. 2002. *Implementing Agenda 21* (Report of the Secretary-General). United Nations Economic and Social Council, E/CN.17/2002/PC.2/7, 19 December.

United Nations. Conference on the Environment and Development. 1992. *Report of the United Nations Conference on Environment and Development.* Rio de Janeiro, 3–14 June 1992. Vol. I, Resolutions Adopted by the Conference. United Nations Publication, sales no. E.93.I.8, and Corrigendum.

Urquhart, Ian. 2001. "Blindspots in the Rearview Mirrors: Livelihood and the Cheviot Debate." In Roger Epp and Dave Whitson, eds., *Writing Off the Rural West: Globalization, Governments, and the Transformation of Rural Communities,* 127–44. Edmonton: University of Alberta Press.

Wackernagel, Mathias, and William Rees. 1995. *Our Ecological Footprint.* Gabriola Island, BC: New Society Publishers (New Catalyst Bioregional Series).

Weale, Albert. 1992. *The New Politics of Pollution.* Manchester: Manchester University Press.

Weissman, Robert. 1999. "Democracy Is in the Streets." *Multinational Monitor* 20(12): 24–9.

Welford, Richard, and Richard Starkey, eds. 1996. *The Earthscan Reader in Business and the Environment.* London: Earthscan Publications.

Woollard, Robert, and William Rees. 1999. "Social Evolution and Urban Systems: Directions for Sustainability." In John T. Pierce and Ann Dale, eds., *Communities, Development, and Sustainability across Canada,* 27–45. Vancouver: University of British Columbia Press.

World Commission on Environment and Development (WCED). 1987. *Our Common Future.* Oxford: Oxford University Press.

17 Canadian Labour and the Political Economy of Transformation

SAM GINDIN AND JIM STANFORD

INTRODUCTION

The trade union movement constitutes a central feature in the overall constellation of organizing social change in Canada. Unions reflect a large and relatively well-organized membership: close to four million Canadians are represented under collective bargaining provisions of one form or another, or about 30 percent of all paid workers. Compared to most popular organizations, unions are relatively stable and well-funded. And since they organize workers at the point of production, unions carry unique potential to exert concrete economic pressure that can be levied in the direct private interests of union members, as well as in the pursuit of broader social and political goals.

But to what extent can the labour movement be expected to act as an agent of far-reaching social transformation? (We imagine transformation as going beyond simply asking for a better deal from capital and capitalism to demanding and enforcing some form of structural change in property relationships that would democratize and socialize economic processes.) Trade unions under capitalism have traditionally reflected a dual character, serving to advance workers' demands for better treatment (both inside and outside the workplace), while also containing the militancy and activism of their members.[1] Both the traditional faith of Marxists that labour was destined to serve as the agent of revolution and the subsequent reaction by "new social movement" theorists dismissing labour as an actively progressive force overlooked the contingent nature of the process of moving beyond capitalism. The possibility of building a new society is neither inevitable nor preordained; it depends on all kinds of economic, political, and historical factors. Because of labour's central location in the capitalist order, our radical hopes depend particularly on the development of the political capacities of the working class. If the working class, with all its flaws and complex diversity, is not there, then ultimately social transformation won't happen.

> Without labour's material resources, without labour's organizational capacity and unique ability to affect the economy (while others protest, labour can shut down capital's life-lines in production and services), without the radicalization of working people and without a working class with a *universal* sense of social justice – without all of this no movement can sustain hopes of transforming the world. (Gindin 2002, 9)

Three particular political developments over Canada's past quarter century are useful starting points for coming concretely to grips with the potentials of, and barriers inherent in, labour's role in transformation. First, there has been a shift of leadership within progressive oppositional struggles from formal party politics to coalitions of extra-parliamentary forces, prominently including labour itself. Second, there has also been a shift over time and through consecutive campaigns and struggles in the ideological orientation of this broad opposition movement. And finally and more recently, there have emerged a number of parallel political projects aimed at developing a new politics on Canada's left – one that could unite progressive labour more closely with other mobilized social forces.

As the so-called postwar Golden Age ended and capital's search for a renewed political-economic project settled upon a neoliberal orientation, labour's official political arm – the New Democratic Party (NDP) – began a long descent into marginalization. Major cracks in the relationship between the NDP and the labour movement opened up when the NDP (including elected provincial governments) supported wage controls in the mid-seventies. Later the NDP was uncertain in opposing free trade, ineffective in responding to the attack on the welfare state, and then staggered and demoralized by electoral setbacks in the 1990s. Meanwhile, the labour movement was increasingly taking independent initiatives in partnership with loose and evolving social coalitions to act on the major issues of our times. Even by the time of the free trade debate, it was already clear that the main opposition was not in Parliament but in the streets. Later, during the historic Days of Action protests against the Harris government in Ontario (in which several Ontario cities were essentially shut down by rotating one-day general strikes), people did not even ask why this remarkable political initiative was coming from labour and its coalition partners – rather than from the party whose raison d'être was supposedly to specialize in and lead progressive politics. A profound and exciting change in the location of left political leadership seemed to have taken place.

In its early stages, this broader oppositional constituency was rather conservative in the traditional sense of opposing change and maintaining what was. In the fight against free trade, this conservativism was commonly expressed in a romanticized vision of Canada's past and present. By the mid-1990s, however, the populist nationalism of the free trade campaigns was unevenly evolving into a focus that was internationalist, that identified corporate freedoms as undermining democratic freedoms, and that began to link a democratic orientation to an anticapitalist one. As evidenced in more recent struggles against globalization (such as the historic events in Quebec City in April 2001), this new radicalism also reflected a generational change in the movement's energy. The positive legacy of these protests has been the combativeness, cultural rebelliousness, organizational abilities, and anticapitalist/anti-imperialist orientation of a new youth and student movement.

In the wake of the continued weakness in the NDP and its alienation from emerging nonelectoral struggles and movements on the left, there is now a (healthy) turmoil in left politics. Greg Albo (2002) has described the emergence of three distinct political projects on the left: the expansion of nonelectoral protest movements in civil society (represented most forcefully at present in the antiglobalization campaigns); efforts to revive a more ambitious and movement-connected form of social democracy; and initial efforts to rebuild a socialist left with the explicit goal of moving beyond capitalism. Potential support for and engagement with each of these projects on the part of Canadian labour will be an important factor influencing the future trajectory of Canadian social change.

The first of these three tracks – the protest movements of civil society – reflects a general alienation from formal and electoral politics and aims to challenge state power from without. It is not interested in entering the state or capturing state power. The second strand, a revitalized and more movement-connected social democracy,[2] accepts the necessity of addressing state power, yet still expresses faith in the state as an entity that can be "captured" for progressive purposes – so long as the right people are elected. A more critical understanding of the state's inherent and structurally biased role within capitalism has yet to be developed among most of these supporters of a renewed social democracy.

The third view, influenced by traditional Marxist approaches, agrees with the fundamental importance of addressing state power but sees current state institutions as historically developed and fundamentally capitalist in nature; this state has, for example, particular hierarchical capacities to effect change from above but lacks the institutional capacities to support a more collective and democratic administration of our lives. This "rebuilding the left" movement (sometimes referred to as a structured movement against capitalism, or SMAC) consequently sees its project as developing a left politics aimed not only at taking state power but also at radically transforming the state as part of a broader effort to transform social and economic structures.[3]

Each of these three projects is in transition, because – given the nature of the present moment, both in Canada and internationally – each is necessarily experimental and unstable. That is, each confronts or will soon confront questions around which there is no ready answer and around which internal divisions exist. At present there seems to be a unique opportunity for these projects to operate in parallel fashion with relatively friendly relations and even some informal division of tasks. Over time, however, these currently separate projects – each of which has, to varying degrees, enlisted support from individual labour activists and labour organizations – will eventually have their own splits and overlaps, raising the issue of new alliances and new formations.

In addressing these issues and challenges from the perspective of labour's role, the task facing the labour movement is often posed in terms of its collective ability to form a progressive alliance with other social movements. What this formulation obscures, however, is that there is no homogeneity within labour (nor within the other social movements, for that matter) and that the process of labour's further politicization will in fact require further polarizations and divisions within the labour movement as these differences are manifested and grappled with. A myriad of ongoing debates and divisions within labour already amply attests to the contested terrain that lies ahead – including divisions over the continuing acceptance by some unions of significant bargaining concessions (like the trend toward longer-term collective agreements), ongoing disputes over organized labour's relationship to the NDP, and the expulsion from the Canadian Labour Congress in 2000, subsequently reversed, of the largest private sector union in Canada, the Canadian Auto Workers (nominally sparked by the CAW's alleged "raiding" of members from a U.S.-based union, but actually reflecting many deeper political and organizational disputes).

Without hoping for or celebrating divisions in the labour movement, it must nevertheless be recognized that apparent unity never automatically implies active solidarity. The American labour movement, for example, demonstrated great unity once its left opposition had been destroyed in the Cold War, but few would celebrate its dynamism. Any process of labour radicalization will inevitably be uneven, implying major differences and internal struggles as that radicalization occurs. Links between organized labour and the various political projects identified above are therefore not likely to occur through direct ties to labour, but rather through processes of political mediation that bring like-minded sections of each constituency together. New organizational structures will need to develop, structures that can operate within the openings that have emerged thanks to recent struggles. These structures will work to build new understandings, new relationships, and new ways of undertaking new kinds of political tasks.

Consider, for example, the political openings created by the Ontario Days of Action.[4] It is hardly adequate to lament that a remarkable series of actions faded into a whimper because of the labour bureaucracy or labour divisions. As relevant as those factors were, they are part of the terrain; the more important question is why the left could only complain about but had no capacity to influence these developments. Why, for example, couldn't the left build on the momentum of the Days of Action to recruit initially hesitant unions and locals to a more activist and militant political orientation? Why, after incredible local coalitions were built to successfully organize these unprecedented actions, could the left not provide leadership to help those coalitions evolve and continue their work after the Days were over?

The problems inherent in the left's relationship with organized labour and the contingency of labour's role in evolving struggles was perhaps never symbolically clearer than in the Quebec City protests of April 2001. By bringing tens of thousands of workers out, labour (and especially labour in Quebec) showed its potential power. But by leading them on the infamous "march to nowhere" (a long parade away from the summit site to an isolated and deserted parking lot), organized labour raised questions about its ability to effectively use that potential. There were enough workers in that march – workers of every generation – who will take up the challenge of radicalizing their own unions, but this is not only a problem of labour. The students and others who played such an inspiring role in Quebec will also have to ask – together with the left more generally – how to orient their focus, their demands, and their structures with the aim of integrating Canadian labour more solidly into their future campaigns.

This chapter will discuss the current state of Canada's labour movement and its potential transformative capacities in the context of the corresponding development of the broader political and economic environment facing the Canadian left. The first section reviews Canadian labour's uneven response to the challenges posed by the erosion of the postwar Golden Age political economy and the subsequent period of neoliberal restructuring. The second section considers the implications of the present economic conjuncture for the traditional efforts of the labour movement to extract incremental gains and improvements (at the bargaining table and more broadly) from capital. Even the successful pursuit of this traditional reformist role for organized labour will require a far-reaching reinvention of the movement's standard practices. The final section briefly considers the prerequisites and possibilities for the labour movement, in the context of the aforementioned developments in the broader left, to pursue a more transformative political and economic vision.

BEYOND GOLDEN-AGE TRADE-OFFS

The postwar institutionalization of labour relations in Canada (as in other developed capitalist economies) explicitly cemented the leading economic role of private employers and capital in return for an enhanced ability to bargain over the proceeds of the resulting economic growth. This trade-off was fully consistent with the politics of social democracy, which in Canada (as elsewhere) was the official political expression of the labour movement. While postwar Canadian capitalism was vibrant and growing, during the three decades of the so-called Golden Age, Canadian unions and their members seemed to do well by this formula.[5] Union membership grew dramatically and so did the militance of union members. Important concessions were extracted (often only after tremendous and sometimes violent struggles) from individual employers and from the economic system as a whole. These victories included higher incomes (average real earnings doubled in Canada in a generation), an extension and formalization of workplace rights (including significant progress in health and safety protection), and the construction of a broader network of regulations and social policies that more generally underwrote the economic security of working people.

In the mid-1970s, however, when the dynamic of capitalist accumulation began to sputter, the mutuality of this institutionalized arrangement began to break down.[6] The further development of the labour movement and economic progress for workers (unionized or not) ran into a brick wall of slower investment, a consequent slowdown in economic and productivity growth, increased intensity of competition between firms (including international competition), and the retrenchment of public sector programs and activities. Since unions had never tried to develop the capacity to independently challenge the economic leadership of private firms – and in particular to conceive of mechanisms through which the dominant role of private investment in initiating production could be supplemented and eventually replaced by alternative channels of accumulation – the slowdown left the labour movement naturally on the defensive, trying with varying degrees of success to preserve victories won in earlier, more vibrant times.

All of this must of course be placed in the context of Canada's unique economic integration with the United States, the imperial leader in capitalism's drive to implement the social changes subsequently identified with neoliberalism and globalization. Among other things, this integration tied Canada to the most deregulated and unequal labour market in the industrialized world. It results not only in the strong continentalist pressures facing Canadian firms and, through them, their workers. For the labour movement, it is also reflected in the fact that most private-sector union members actually belong to u.s.-based unions. The labour movement's choices about how to respond to the broad u-turn in economic conditions were thus bound up with the corresponding issues of both overall Canadian sovereignty and the autonomy and democracy of Canadian unions.

After two decades of neoliberal restructuring, the Canadian labour movement finds itself in a complex and uneasy state of affairs. Business has won obviously important victories in reshaping the political and economic environment in its favour, with negative implications for workers and their unions. The industrial relations playing field has been tilted and structured in a more business-friendly direction. Macroeconomic policy explicitly abandoned the postwar commitment to full employment, and instead – led by anti-inflation monetary authorities – began to proactively manage the labour market, with the aim of maintaining a certain desirable margin of long-run unemployment. Meanwhile, the network of public programs and services that both underwrote the economic security of working households and supplemented the consumption possibilities offered by their private money incomes came under sustained pressure for both fiscal and political reasons.

Despite this process, the Canadian labour movement – while certainly on the defensive – has not been routed. Canada is one of only a handful of countries in which the unionization rate (and therefore the organizational base of the labour movement) did not substantially decline during the 1980s and 1990s – although private sector unionization has been declining, and, combined with the contraction of public sector employment, this decline is now pulling down overall unionization. Many unions still demonstrate a punchy stubbornness in continuing to wage tough battles for recouping past losses and concessions in collective bargaining and for organizing unorganized workers into new unions in a wide array of industries. Strike frequency, which declined dramatically in Canada between the 1970s and the 1990s, has more recently shown some sign of a moderate rebound.

The structural dependence of the Canadian economy on the United States also informed the emergence of a firmer and eventually more radical and internationalist movement – a movement rooted in organized labour and other constituencies – against the free trade agreements and other manifestations of globalization. It became increasingly clear as North American integration proceeded that the possibility of establishing a "national capitalist" regime of Canadian accumulation rooted in an alliance between domestic property owners and an interventionist state was evaporating. Virtually all major businesses operating in Canada, including those owned by Canadians, became globally (or at least u.s.-) oriented, and the economic base for the former liberal nationalist project disappeared. Thanks to this experience, Canadian labour activists and other progressives were alerted to the dangers of corporate globalization before their comrades in most other countries. More importantly, they have become more likely to express their concerns with an internationalist, anticorporate bent. It has become abundantly clear to most Canadian progressives that empowering and protecting private domestic firms is not the answer to globalization (since those companies have been at least as likely to undermine or lay off their Canadian workers as any foreign multinational). What are required, rather, are forms of regulated accountability for private companies and investors of any national stripe; this suggests a more internationalist and anticapitalist politics on the part of the antiglobalization campaigners.[7]

THE LABOUR MOVEMENT
IN A "GRIM ECONOMY"

There are some indications that the neoliberal program has at least partially restored the vitality of profit-led accumulation in Canada. Business profits, investment, and job creation strengthened markedly in the latter 1990s, generating rising real incomes for the first time in two decades and contributing to a dramatic recovery in public finances. Yet the overall system remains vulnerable to external shocks and crises, and even at the best of times its profitability remains unspectacular, its sustainability uncertain. To the extent that an internally consistent regime of capitalist accumulation has indeed been restored in Canada, it certainly does not look like another Golden

Age. The institutions of labour market regulation and redistribution in Canada are presently too weak for continued economic growth to have as strong a positive impact on living conditions for the majority of Canadians as was the case in earlier decades; and at any rate, the extent of that growth will be strictly controlled by central bankers still vigilant for any upsurge in the demands of labour – whether organized or not. We might call this regime (to the extent that it has been coherently established) a "grim economy": accumulation and growth will occur, but continuing strict limits are imposed on wages, labour activism, and public programs.

Perhaps the two-decade-long neoliberal restructuring of Canada's economy and the subsequent and incomplete revitalization of private capital accumulation has restored some economic and political space for the pursuit of labour's traditional reformist (or "economist") goals – effected through efforts to extract concessions from individual employers, as well as initiatives to reconstruct the broader network of social protections. Even the unsure vitality that Canada's increasingly business-dominated economy began to demonstrate by the late 1990s was sufficient to open up room for some Canadian unions to shift to a more offensive position – aiming to win back some of the concessions extracted by business during the preceding two decades and capture a share of the productivity gains implied by a renewal of business investment and economic expansion. In some sectors revitalized productivity growth and business profitability, combined with sustained union mobilizing capacity, translated into significant economic gains for workers.[8] In others, like education and health, the sheer frustration of public sector workers, coupled with understaffing resulting from past government policies, produced historically unparalleled militancy on the part of teachers, nurses, and other public sector trade unionists.

But progress of this sort will hardly be typical across the broader labour movement, for various reasons. In the first place, the profitability and productivity demonstrated by technology-intensive, export-oriented manufacturing sectors is not representative of the economic conditions experienced by most Canadian businesses. Continuing fiscal constraints in the public sector – where over half of all Canadian union members are employed – will make it difficult for most public sector unions even to recoup the concessions extracted by employers in the 1990s (when most public sector workers had their wages frozen, resulting in real wage cuts averaging 10 percent), let alone to share in the fruits of a new era of growth and prosperity.

In addition, the labour movement's internal struggles became more intense as the period of neoliberal restructuring drew to a close. Traditional jurisdictional lines within the labour movement, which had informally allocated workers in particular sectors or industries to corresponding sector-based unions, broke down in the face of several factors: stagnation in total union membership, cross-sectoral union mergers, and a more aggressive, competitive approach to organizing new members. (These factors, common in other industrialized countries, were accentuated in Canada, where the structure of unions was distorted by their American branch-plant roots: in spite of its much smaller population, Canada had as many unions as the United States, thanks to the often-small Canadian branches of U.S. unions.) Unions effectively came into direct competition with each other – both in their efforts to organize brand-new members, as well as in representation contests associated with the restructuring of various private sector and public sector workplaces.[9]

There were profound differences within the labour movement over how to respond to neoliberalism. These broader conflicts included controversies over concession bargaining, corporatist relations with business, the constitution of the CLC (especially in its effective prohibition of disaffected union members' right to change unions), and labour's respective relationships with the NDP and grass-roots movements for social change. Most private sector unions (including all major private sector unions except the CAW) organized an explicit caucus in the late 1990s (the so-called Pink Paper Group) to wield a focused moderating influence at conventions of the CLC and its provincial federations. Meanwhile, when action-oriented resolutions were passed at these same conventions, they were often simply ignored by federation leaders or else effectively vetoed (through nonparticipation or more active opposition) by key private sector affiliates. By the late 1990s, Canada's labour centrals – the CLC and its provincial federations – had lost the effective ability to sponsor united campaigns and other initiatives.

Where rank-and-file militancy was sustained, a space was created for building a more mobilized, radicalized, and creative movement. But in the absence of a socialist current within the unions with a longer-term perspective on building working class capacities, that space was not occupied. Labour's commitment to broader initiatives – like the one-day workplace shutdowns organized as part of the Ontario Days of Action – was never complete and always contested. And even relatively successful campaigns did not translate into a more lasting and secure commitment to ongoing labour-community activism.

It is ironic, therefore, that just as the economic pendulum may be swinging back – unsteadily and unpredictably – toward a position that might allow for a resumption of forward reformist progress on the part of Canadian labour, the labour movement itself may be largely incapable of seizing the opportunity. Rank-and-file members of many unions are not engaged in union education or mobilizing initiatives; to many workers, unions are at best a service organization. And union structures have yet to adequately adapt to an economic and political environment requiring more flexibility and accountability than in the past. Yet even to win modest, reformist bargaining gains in the context of a grim economy, in which both competitive pressure and direct policy (by the central bank and other state institutions) tightly constrain the forward progress of labour, will require a far-reaching rejuvenation of union activity, starting at the level of the individual members whose loyalty has been sorely tested by the widespread passivity of many unions through the past two decades.

In other words, unions and union activists need to "think big" just to preserve the labour movement's capacity to win incremental, reformist gains for Canadian workers. Given the continued hostility of the economic and institutional environment, unions will have to become more activist, more democratic, and more radical just to rebuild their ability to fight for a better share of continued business-led expansion – let alone to fight for more fundamental, more transformative changes in Canada's economy and society. The axes along which this process of change will need to occur include the following.

Organizing the Unorganized

Union density in the public sector has been stable in Canada, but the public sector has been shrinking as a share of total employment. Meanwhile, unionization in private sector industries has been slowly slipping, falling below 20 percent by the end of the 1990s. Organizing success has been held back by numerous factors, including subtle but important changes in labour law (in areas such as card-check certification and other organizing procedures), sophisticated employer resistance, the broadly antiunion and individualistic influence of the mass media and popular culture, and an often-justified skepticism among many workers that joining a union can genuinely improve their working lives.[10] All this has made the already uphill struggle to organize new union members even harder.[11] The recognition that unions need to organize or die is relatively widespread in the labour movement, even among otherwise conservative unions, and the expenditure of resources on organizing drives has been significant. The results of these efforts, however, have so far been generally discouraging. Despite some efforts to be more systematic, more creative, and more representative in organizing drives; despite experiments such as the use of grass-roots and volunteer organizers (rather than professional organizing staff), community-rooted organizing campaigns (in which numerous employers in particular neighbourhoods or communities are targeted with integrated union drives), and the adoption of certification procedures that side-step existing hostile legal requirements;[12] and despite an increased sensitivity to the changing colour of the Canadian labour force and efforts to find and map communities of new immigrants – despite all of this, unions are losing many more organizing campaigns than they are winning.

If economic and labour market conditions continue to improve in coming years, then perhaps these exciting organizing initiatives may finally bear fruit. But the most significant breakthroughs in union organization have historically come in waves and at moments of broader social conflict and mobilization. Perhaps the most important thing unions can do to rejuvenate their organizing possibilities is to contribute to building a wider oppositional movement and hence facilitate a change in the broader social climate. In other words, perhaps it is only in the context of a movement that extends beyond unions, but includes unions that are concretely participating in, if not leading, struggles against every kind of oppression and every attack on the quality of our lives, that we can really anticipate the long-sought explosion of workers organizing *themselves* into unions.

Mobilizing the Organized

The demobilization of already unionized workers during the era of concession bargaining has been at least as important as the erosion of union penetration in explaining the decline of union power in Canada. Too many unions accepted corporate demands during the period of neoliberal restructuring (including wage and other concessions, long-term contracts, and the creation of shallow structures of "cooperation" in the workplace). Too many union leaders viewed the project of mobilizing their members with cynicism and discomfort and even as a threat rather than an asset; hence, they acted consciously to reduce the expectations and demands of their members, rather than to legitimate and give organizational expression to those expectations and demands. The creation of a demoralized, inactive, and often explicitly hostile membership base is the long-run consequence of the backward march of many Canadian unions. This is an environment that is ripe for change – a progressive, activist shift in the policies and practices of those unions, it is to be hoped, but potentially an anti-union backlash ending in widespread decertification. Transforming unions into centres of working class life – vehicles, for example, for struggling over not just wages but issues like education reform or environmental degradation – is a way to consolidate the role of the union among all its members and a step towards the most important lesson of all: that fighting back can make a difference.

In some cases, union leaders are starting to address the need for a turn-around in the nature of unionism. But in general this change will require pressure – if not a revolt – from below. Given all the difficulties in organizing such a challenge to entrenched leadership and institutions, such revolts cannot be successful unless local activists establish horizontal links across locals and communities and call on resources from elsewhere in the broader progressive movement (including ties to activists in other unions and contacts with sympathetic academics). Indeed, even where union leaders support a more forceful membership mobilization, such local activism can take better advantage of the openings provided and constructively push progressive leaders further.

A Progressive Bargaining Agenda

Collective bargaining must clearly address the direct economic and workplace concerns of union members, but it can also address the labour movement's strategic considerations – such as linking up to organizing strategies, building labour's community base, raising political concerns, and generally building the capacities of the union and its members. Supplementing traditional goals of higher incomes for unionized workers with broader demands for inclusion, balance, and equality (through measures such as employment equity and affirmative action) can be part of demonstrating a commitment to improving the conditions of traditionally excluded groups of workers, as well as being an aid in organizing. Fighting outsourcing can be a way of proving that it is the union, rather than employers, that is defending community jobs. Putting childcare on the bargaining agenda sets the stage for a political campaign to consolidate any such gain through improvements in public programs. Negotiating paid time off for union education programs can be an effective way to enhance access to ongoing education for union members – and if those programs are union controlled, they can also serve an important union-building function.

Initiatives to redistribute working time are an especially important priority for a progressive bargaining agenda. Working time can be reduced in a myriad of ways, including limits on overtime, enhanced vacations, early retirement, and expanded parental and educational leaves.[13] It is not just a matter of sharing existing jobs to reduce unemployment (though working overtime when others are laid off is a particular affront to solidarity). More importantly, retrieving and controlling more of our own time is a precondition for developing ourselves as fuller human beings with time to participate within the union, the community, and in politics. The redistribution of work time also allows for more equal sharing of paid work, and flexibility over our time is essential to both a richer and more egalitarian family life (all the more so since neoliberalism has created a worsening time crunch on families striving to supply more paid labour time in order to maintain or expand their consumption). Capturing productivity gains in the form of time off, rather than wages and consumption, can also be seen as a progressive environmental measure (especially in developed countries).

Internal Democracy and Accountability

The issue of the accountability of unions and union leaders to their dues-paying membership cannot be separated from the challenge of mobilizing those dues-paying members more effectively. A healthy union demonstrates the highest level of rank-and-file activity during the process of collective bargaining, which involves union members in designing the bargaining agenda, electing the bargaining committee, supporting collective actions (including strikes) in support of that agenda, and then subjecting any agreement ultimately reached to the strong test of membership ratification. In this process, which members of democratic unions "own" more than any other sphere of their unions' activity, unions correspondingly enjoy the greatest level of active support from their members. [14] It is hard to imagine rank-and-file union members becoming more actively involved in any struggle, whether in collective bargaining or in other arenas, unless and until unions become more participatory, democratic, and accountable. This process of democratization will be fought on numerous different fronts: from efforts to restore active and autonomous decision making at the local level, to developing meaningful cross-community and cross-sectoral labour forums, to the continuing need for greater autonomy (or complete independence) for the Canadian sections of international unions, to procedures allowing badly served union members more choice over their representation. Simply expanding the range of struggles the labour movement takes on can also be seen as enhancing democracy within the movement: active struggles tend to place democratic questions on the agenda, because they necessitate bringing new people in, debating and explaining issues and strategies, and concretely learning how to participate in change.

Rebuilding Labour's Political Voice

Canadian union leaders have expended great energy on debates over the labour movement's relationship to the NDP – with some unions expressing deep criticisms of that party and attempting to carve out a more independent political role and others expressing more dogged support for it. Yet it has become abundantly clear that the official proclamations of union leaders, whether loyal to the NDP or not, have negligible impact on the broader political preferences and expressions of union members. Trade union members no longer generally express particularly progressive electoral opinions (if they ever did) – at least not in response to the ways left-versus-right questions are conventionally asked. And even within relatively strong and well-mobilized unions, stewards and other rank-and-file leaders do not conduct the intense consultation and educational activities that are essential if union members are to become effectively and collectively engaged in broader political struggles and campaigns.

Debates over rebuilding labour's political voice will have to confront the depth of the alienation within labour and across Canadian society from formal politics. Polls consistently show a popular desperation for getting some control over one's life – isn't this what politics should be all about? Yet the kind of empty politics offered by conventional parliamentary processes has no appeal – all the more so since globalization appears to be further restricting the scope of parliamentary decision making. A related problem is that any such rebuilding of labour's political voice will have to address the depth of the worldwide crisis in social democracy; recent attention to the NDP's electoral failures obscures the more profound failures of vision (and the subsequent betrayals) of social democratic parties that have been electorally successful. The present absence of any radical socialist current within the trade union movement means that the range of alternative policies and politics being considered will be limited. Any "new politics" for Canadian labour will have to have as its ambition a radical change in political culture: changing the popular sense of what is possible and how politics is conducted. It is impossible to imagine unions playing the critical role this demands, unless there is also a corresponding and perhaps prior change in union attitudes and assumptions – particularly a change in perspective regarding the collective potentials of workers, both in democratically administering a new world and in developing the political capacities to get there.

Linking with Other Struggles

Many Canadian unions have been relatively open to efforts to build coalitions and sponsor other joint activities with the broader social change community.[15] These generally constructive relationships, however, have not been uncontested. Some conservative union officials, like traditional social democratic leaders, tend to view the independent politics and democratic practices of the grass-roots social movements as constituting more of a challenge than an opportunity. On the other hand, many progressive trade unionists are anxious to recapture some of the creative energy and moral authority that presently characterizes the work of other social movements such as the antiglobalization campaign, the student movement, and the antipoverty community. The September 11 events and their aftermath have placed new strains on the links between unions and this broader community of activists; some segments of labour have seemed to pull back from coalition-type work in the face of the more hostile political climate that existed after September 11, just as those broader struggles (such as the antiglobalization struggles) were facing a particularly challenging moment. The struggle within labour to strengthen and develop the links to other community campaigns will obviously need to continue.

An interesting idea regarding the links between labour and other community struggles emerged during the period (2000–2001) when sanctions were imposed by the CLC on the CAW and CAW activists were consequently barred from labour council participation. The CAW prepared to establish community action groups that would be set up as an alternative to the official labour councils but that would include representation for broader community participation. The focus of these bodies would be internal and external education and solidarity support – including, in a spirit of nonsectarianism, support for any struggles involving affiliates of the official labour councils. The subsequent resolution of the dispute between the CLC and the CAW meant that these alternative councils were not established; perhaps, however, that model of labour-community organizing should instead be considered as an alternative to be generalized among the labour movement as a whole.

In all of these ways, the labour movement will need to go through a process of dramatic and wrenching internal change just to rebuild its capacity to effectively wrest a share of potential economic gains from a resurgent capitalism – and this assumes that Canadian capitalism *is* at least somewhat resurgent in the wake of its episode of neoliberal restructuring. It seems, then, that there can be no business as usual for the labour movement. Failing this far-reaching revitalization, unions

can look forward to a rather pessimistic future of declining membership, eroding credibility with their remaining members, and continuing marginalization in the broader social and political milieus.

TOWARD A TRANSFORMATIVE VISION FOR LABOUR?

Revitalizing labour's traditional reformist role might seem like an ambitious enough goal. But recent developments on Canada's left, which
have variously involved portions of organized labour, indicate that the
labour movement might ultimately be able to set its sights even higher
– aiming to accomplish more in the long run than simply rebuilding
the capacity to demand a fairer deal from a capitalist system whose
authority and leadership is taken for granted. Several developing projects on Canada's left suggest an ongoing potential for revitalizing a
more ambitious anticapitalist and transformative constituency, one in
which labour would need to play a central role. As noted above, these
projects include the widening activism of extraparliamentary protest
movements in civil society (such as the antiglobalization movement and
the campaigns against the war in Afghanistan and new security legislation that were mobilized in the wake of the September 11 events);
efforts to reignite a more militant and movement-connected social
democracy in the wake of the deep crisis in the NDP; and efforts in
several cities to organize a more explicitly socialist "structured movement." After two decades of neoliberal restructuring and the consequent reinforcement of the dominant economic and political power of
business in society, these and other important voices are now going
beyond simply challenging the most painful and inhumane consequences of that restructuring to once again challenge the legitimacy of
a social system so dominated by the wealth and greed of the few. This
transformative vision is far from being mapped in detail, and indeed
the process of defining both a thorough-going critique of modern capitalism and the key elements of an alternative will be a long one – and,
it is to be hoped, a participatory and empowering one, too.

Despite this long-run optimism, we must, however, be honest. At
present one cannot speak of a transformative project within the labour
movement. The movement remains defensive. Its confidence remains
shaken by the hostile political-economic environment of neoliberalism, and it has yet to articulate a thorough critique of neoliberalism.
In fact, if anything, the labour movement has not been defensive
enough, in the sense of militantly defending its past gains. The issue,
however, is not to wait for renewed labour militancy and then place
larger transformative issues on the agenda. Rather, issues such as what

kind of political organization or what kind of party workers need must be raised alongside and in interaction with the more immediate task of mobilizing more defensive struggles. For this to happen, left activists within the labour movement need to develop independent organizations and networks extending across individual unions to raise fundamental issues and challenge their respective unions. At the same time, nonlabour activists within the various progressive streams need to develop a better understanding of the centrality of labour to any serious strategy for progressive social change and to find ways of talking to and working with labour activists that reflect the contingent but essential nature of organized labour's relationship to that process of social change. Close cooperation between left activists in various unions and their colleagues in other social movements will be required to foment and nurture a more far-reaching political stance within organized labour.[16]

Honesty about our real situation need not imply cynicism about our future prospects. Great hope is inspired in witnessing workers being infected by – rather than alienated from – the energy and direct action techniques of the antiglobalization protestors, even by the confidence with which they have raised the banner of anticapitalism. There seems to be a growing understanding – taught so well by capital itself – that free trade agreements are primarily about protecting property rights against any democratic intervention, that a deepening of democracy and equality are barriers to capital accumulation and therefore enemies of capitalism, and that capital cannot live without stealing what was once held in common (things like health, education, water) and commodifying, for the purposes of profit, every aspect of our lives. Recent history has encouraged a creeping challenge to capital's authority, now that it has gotten everything it demanded but failed to deliver on its promises. In this context, even the frustrating confusion among left activists – union and nonunion alike – about what to do next is positive. This confusion at least finally acknowledges that what we've being doing is inadequate and so sets the stage for debates – real debates – on what needs to be done. As painful as it is to be at such an early stage, it would truly be exciting to think that something is finally beginning.

NOTES

1 See the papers in Gonick, Phillips, and Vorst (1995) for a consideration of the labour movement's complex and contingent role in the Canadian context.

2 The New Politics Initiative, launched in 2001 by a collective of progressives within the NDP and in nonparty social movements, represents one expression of this stream; see Davies et al. (2001) for a founding statement, and www.newpolitics.ca for ongoing discussions.

3 See Gindin (1998) for an initial expression of this view and the web page of *Canadian Dimension* magazine (www.canadiandimension.mb.ca) for a compendium of subsequent discussion.

4 Conway (2000) discusses the unique experience of the Ontario Days of Action, highlighting (among other factors) the surprising but ultimately incomplete and troubled cooperation between sections of the labour movement and other social movements.

5 While this so-called Golden Age brought about substantial improvements in both private and public living standards for most Canadian workers, the benefits of this expansionary period were obviously distributed in an unequal and uneven fashion. Within Canada women, immigrant workers, and aboriginal people all experienced this Golden Age rather differently than the largely white, male "core" workforce, and in developing countries, of course, the postwar expansion had a rather less optimistic face than it had in the First World.

6 The economic and political factors leading to the breakdown of the postwar regime and the subsequent neoliberal response have been discussed and analyzed by many progressive scholars. The work of Brenner (1998) has sparked a lively and controversial new instalment of this ongoing discussion; among the numerous responses to Brenner, see especially the articles contained in two special editions of *Historical Materialism*, (issues 4 and 5, 2000) for a sampling of this discussion. Stanford (1999, chaps. 7–9) attempts to describe the economic dimensions of the post–Golden Age U-turn in Canada. The chapter in this volume by Watkins (chap. 1) further discusses the various political constraints and opportunities presented by the neoliberal legacy in Canada.

7 The chapter by Watkins in this volume (chap. 1) further explores the implications of a globalized political economy for left-wing political strategies in Canada.

8 For example, the CAW's major auto contract of 1999 – which provided for annual wage gains of 3 percent on top of inflation indexation and even more generous improvements in pensions and other non wage benefits – was probably the richest major collective agreement signed by a Canadian union in a quarter-century and could be interpreted as a signal of the potential return to a more optimistic and effective era of trade unionism. But this same industry also demonstrates the perpetual instability of the neoliberal era; within three years of the signing of that contract, Canadian auto assembly had plunged by over 20 percent and several assembly and parts plants were facing closure.

9　When bargaining units are amalgamated to form larger and more coherent units, any union that was represented in the initial environment has the right to compete for overall representation.

10　Yates (2000) surveys and analyzes some of these rather pessimistic results.

11　Riddell (2001) provides startling empirical evidence of the negative impact on certification success rates of the elimination of card-check certification procedures in Canada.

12　Some sections of the Hotel Employees and Restaurant Employees' union have experimented with efforts to force employers to voluntarily recognize unions through community pressure and consumer boycotts, instead of working through cumbersome and antiunion official certification processes. The grass-roots Justice for Janitors organizing drives by the Service Employees International Union in the United States similarly press employers to directly recognize unions, in actions that are completely separate from the official certification process. In a similar vein, the CAW tried numerous innovative tactics to force antiunion auto parts giant Magna International to voluntarily recognize a new union at a seat-making plant in Windsor where the union had majority support – including linking the issue to the CAW's collective bargaining at Daimler-Chrysler (the company that purchases the seats from Magna). The CAW ultimately achieved voluntary recognition at Magna, but only after agreeing that no strikes would occur during the first two collective agreements at the plant.

13　Hayden (2000) provides a useful overview of union efforts on this issue, both in Canada and internationally.

14　This is why the trend to long-term collective agreements (led by conservative private-sector unions, which have accepted employer demands for contracts of six years or even longer) is so destructive of the internal functioning of these unions. When the most important and most demo-cratic activity within the union occurs only every six years (or even less frequently), then internal union activity and democracy will inevitably decline. For a survey of the trend toward long-term agreements and a discussion of the dangers posed to the labour movement, see Murnighan (1998).

15　The chapter in this volume by Carroll and Coburn (chap. 4) explores dimensions of recent extraparliamentary social and political activism in Canada.

16　An interesting analogy in this regard is provided by the cooperative effort of feminists inside the labour movement and those in other feminist organizations to push the labour movement toward more progressive positions and actions on a wide range of women's issues (including traditional economic issues such as pay equity, noneconomic issues such as reproductive freedom, and organizational issues such as equity and representation for women within unions). Feminist trade unionists have benefited from the knowledge and solidarity of their sisters in other constituencies; in the meantime, the broader women's movement has benefited mightily from the labour movement's adoption of feminist principles and demands – not least because of unions' potential power to realize some of those demands directly through collective bargaining.

REFERENCES

Albo, Greg. 2002. "Neo-liberalism, the State and the Left: A Canadian Perspective." *Monthly Review* 53(12):46–55.

Brenner, Robert. 1998. "The Economics of Global Turbulence." *New Left Review* 229 (May–June):1–265.

Conway, Janet. 2000. "Knowledge, Power, Organization: Social Justice Coalitions at a Crossroads." *Studies in Political Economy* 62 (summer): 43–70.

Davies, Libby, Svend Robinson, Murray Dobbin, Louise James, Judy Rebick, and Jim Stanford. 2001. "After the Labour Pains, a New NDP?" *Globe and Mail*, 22 November, A27.

Gindin, Sam. 1998. "The Party's Over." *This Magazine* November–December, 13–15.

– 2002. "The Terrain of Social Justice." *Monthly Review* 53(9): 1–14.

Gonick, Cy, Paul Phillips, and Jesse Vorst, eds. 1995. *Labour Gains, Labour Pains: Fifty Years of PC 1003*. Halifax: Fernwood.

Hayden, Anders. 2000. *Sharing the Work, Sparing the Planet: Work Time, Consumption, and Ecology*. Toronto: Between the Lines.

Murnighan, Bill. 1998. *Long-Term Agreements: The New Concession*. Research Department, Canadian Auto Workers.

Rebick, Judy. 2000. *Imagine Democracy*. Toronto: Stoddart.

Riddell, Chris. 2001. "Union Suppression and Certification Success." *Canadian Journal of Economics* 34(2): 396–410.

Stanford, Jim. 1999. *Paper Boom: Why Real Prosperity Requires a New Approach to Canada's Economy*. Ottawa: Canadian Centre for Policy Alternatives and James Lorimer.

Yates, Charlotte. 2000. "Staying the Decline in Union Membership: Union Organizing in Ontario, 1985–1999," *Relations Industrielles/Industrial Relations* 55(4): 640–74.

18   Towards a "Cultural" Political Economy of Canadian Youth

ROBERT HOLLANDS

INTRODUCTION

While there are individual books on Canadian youth in selective fields and while studies of young people are found scattered among an array of academic journals and government publications in Canada, the Canadian literature in stark contrast to well-established theoretical and empirical bodies of literature in the United Kingdom (Furlong and Cartmel 1997) and the United States (Epstein 1998; Males 1996), not to mention a burgeoning interest in young people in Scandinavia (Fornas and Bolin 1995) and Australia (White 1999). Paradoxically, this lacuna belies a growing concern in Canada over the future of its younger generation. The subtle shift from the young "having prob-lems" to them "being problems" is undergirded by a long history of youthful "moral panics" (Tanner 1996) making the need for more accurate and contextualised information on Canadian youth more necessary than ever before. The underdevelopment of youth studies in this country can be traced back to a wider failure to confront various conceptual issues, a lack of adequate theorisation of youth transitions and cultures and the relationship between them, and an unhelpful obsession with some of the so-called peculiarities of the Canadian case (Brake 1985). The purpose of this chapter is to begin to show how a renewed political economy can help address some of these issues and contribute to a wider debate about political transformation in Canada society.

None of this means there is a lack of material pertaining to youth in Canada, nor should it imply that there are no relevant theoretical traditions with which to analyse this age group. Indeed, a number of important books and articles were published in the 1990s focusing on issues like education, training, and the labour market (Krahn and Lowe 1999; Anisef and Axelrod 1993; Ashton and Lowe 1991), interrupted transitions (Cote and Allahar 1994), and school dropouts (Tanner, Krahn, and Hartnagel 1995), as well as books and articles charting young people's engagement in deviance and criminal activity and including the study of youth cultures (O'Bireck 1996a; Tanner 1996; Winterdyk 1996). There is also a wealth of statistical material on young people in Canada buried in numerous government publications and reports (see Statistics Canada 1989, 1994). Three contributions towards advancing our understanding of Canadian youth are Kostash (2000), Bibby (2001), and Tyyskä (2001). Yet notwithstanding gaps in the literature, a major difficulty has been a failure to confront some of the wider theoretical issues and sociopolitical processes underlying the study of youth from the perspective of a transforming political economy.

What exactly is a political economy approach to youth and how might its constituent elements help analyse what is happening to Canada's younger generation? This approach would seek to situate young people's economic, political, and cultural position within a modified historical-materialist, feminist, and cultural analysis (Clement 1996; Mahon 1993; Connelly and Armstrong 1992). In essence, it would seek to provide a theoretical perspective that was concerned to analyse the relationship between a particular socially constructed age stage, an economic mode of production and reproduction (capitalist-patriarchy), and the socio-spatial and cultural forms of life this combination engenders (Hollands 1998). Clearly, one important aspect of this approach involves setting out young people's distinctive economic position in capitalism, while remaining acutely aware of the effect social divisions like class, gender, ethnicity, and locality have for different subsections of youth. Another central element of this approach concerns critically evaluating a range of political and ideological interpretations of the generation issue. Finally, there is a crucial need to examine how and in what ways modern forms of capital reorganisation and regulation have begun to alter traditional youth transitions, cultures, and identities and to assess the relevance of these changes in terms of political resistance and conformity. First however, such a perspective needs to tackle the surprisingly difficult task of actually defining Canadian youth.

DEFINING YOUTH AND CANADIAN YOUTH

One of the fundamental hurdles to overcome in this field of study concerns the problem of actually defining youth. While the problem is not distinctively Canadian, there are some national considerations. One particular difficulty is the way in which government statistics are collected. For instance, the Statistics Canada publication *Youth in Canada* (1994) contains information on only the fifteen-to-nineteen-year-old cohort. This contrasts markedly with the previous (1989) publication, which provides data on the fifteen-to-twenty-four-year-old grouping, a fact that makes comparisons between the groups difficult. Furthermore, due to the effect of the Young Offender's Act, 1984, statistics on crime figures refer to the, yet again, different age group of twelve to seventeen years. This is not to argue for a pure age-chronology definition of youth but rather to call for data that is consistent in a national-historical context as well as internationally comparative.

The problem of confining a definition of Canadian youth to a purely demographic grouping, however comparable, raises yet more difficulties. Historical and anthropological research (Schlegal and Berry 1991) reminds us that adolescence is very much a social construct that is contingent on a wide variety of economic factors and circumstances, cultural traditions, and historical variations. In preindustrial agrarian Canada, children would have moved quickly from childhood into the adult world of farm labour and domestic work without experiencing much of what we understand today as youthfulness (Sutherland 1976). The advent of schooling in Canada – first secondary schools, then the expansion of university education – and the postwar development of teenage youth cultures in advertising and the media were instrumental in shaping and extending this "liminal" phase (Bibby and Posterski 1985). More recently, many Western industrial countries, including Canada, are having to come to terms with the extension of youthfulness at both the bottom and top end of the age range, with children being exposed to youth culture earlier and adult transitions being delayed later. The impact of high unemployment and a shifting labour market, changing orientations to marriage and family life, and the spread of a more global and accessible consumer culture directed at children, youth, and, increasingly, young adults are all important factors here (Cote and Allahar 1994). Many European countries now utilise the age range of fifteen to twenty-four to refer to youth, while in Canada a common statistical age extends to twenty-nine years. Consequently, one needs to be careful in assuming any fixed age definition, to be aware of the elastic nature of the category of youth, and to understand how it is continually being defined and redefined in economic, social, and cultural terms.

A further warning concerning simple statistical definitions of Canadian youth is the problem of treating a given age cohort as a unified and homogeneous entity. While there may be some common experiences that separate young people from the rest of the population – whether it be leisure lifestyles or higher than average unemployment rates – it is imperative to recognise that relations like class, gender, ethnicity, sexual orientation, disability, and locality all act to differentiate the general category of youth. This is particularly important with respect to historical and even contemporary assertions that often link youthfulness to images of male – specifically, troublesome male – behaviour while ignoring the different experiences and social position of young women. Furthermore, a quick perusal of the Canadian literature reveals that there are fewer sociological studies of youth from different ethnic backgrounds in Canada, not to mention a dearth of contemporary material on the life-world of aboriginal youth (Ratner 1996).[1] There are also few studies of gay and lesbian youth in Canada, and there is little sociological work on adolescence and disability. Community-based or locality studies rarely appear to highlight the specific position of young people, and there are few comparative sociological studies of youth across Canada outside of the purview of relatively uncontextualised government reports. Finally, there has been little explicit discussion and theorisation of youth and class in Canada outside of the standard procedure of differentiating young people by their parental occupational category. None of this means that we cannot continue to speak of a general category labelled "Canadian youth" or to use statistical material relating to this category; it simply means that we need to be aware of the combined effect these social relationships have for various subsections of young people.

PROBLEMS THEORISING
CANADIAN YOUTH

Theory helps to interpret, order, and indeed generate social facts that eventually make their way into the public realm. This is particularly important in the study of youth, due to the historical weighting given to biological and psychological explanations of adolescence, many of which still find expression in everyday life, institutional practices, and social policies. The role of a renewed political economy in this regard, then, would be to challenge the "naturalism" of much of the discourse surrounding youth as a period of "trouble and strife," and to help locate adolescent social problems within a wider economic, domestic, and cultural context.

Yet previously, political economy was often part of the problem rather than a solution. Two of the key historical reasons underlying the underdevelopment of youth studies in Canada are, first, a general over-reliance on imported sociological theories (from either the United States or the United Kingdom) and, second, a failure to adequately develop a political economy of youth in Canada that brings together structural and cultural analyses. With regard to the first point, one could advance a strong argument that much of the early work on Canadian youth took its cue from two classic theories from the United States – the Chicago School and structural functionalism.

The influence of the urban theories and studies of Robert Park and his associates in the interwar period was such that the approach of the Chicago school was literally synonymous with North American sociology (for their influence on Canadian sociology, see Shore 1987). The ecological approach, with its emphasis on the social environment as a cause of deviance and its focus on delinquency and gangs, gave rise to a whole set of American-based subcultural theories of youth developed in the 1950s by scholars such as Cohen, Miller and Cloward, and Ohlin. While these latter studies did raise some interesting issues about class relations and to some extent about class cultures, the primary emphasis taken up in the Canadian context with regard to youth was the Chicago School's concern with social equilibrium and reform and its focus on male forms of delinquency.

These concerns are reflected in some of the early historical Canadian material on youth, and they continue to influence and inform current thinking on this issue. Although not acknowledged directly, the Big Brother–sponsored research, *Street Gangs in Toronto* (Rogers 1945), borrowed heavily on the methodology and the social environment perspective of deviance offered by the Chicago School. Over fifty years later, Ellis and Dekeseredy's (1996) textbook on the sociology of deviance contains a whole chapter on street gangs, and the authors refer to research that uses a version of an ecological perspective (see Lee 1992). A number of government reports and sociological studies of youth in Canada have continued to utilise the "gang model" (Matthews 1993; Pearcy 1991), and Webber's (1991) study of young Canadian runaways reproduces the Chicago School's historical fascination with vagrants, hobos, and urban street culture. Besides equating youthfulness with deviance and social problems, the ecological approach implies an acceptance of the status quo and social reform, rather than seriously questioning the economic and political dimensions of urban divisions and inequality.

A second influential tradition that can be traced historically in the Canadian literature has been the application of more functionalist models of understanding youth. While this approach has appeared quite liberal in orientation, seeing adolescent energy and experimentation as a resource, there is an underlying emphasis on maintaining social equilibrium. Some short historical examples drawn from a series of reports on the state of Canadian youth suffice to make this point. For example, Blodwen Davies' democratically titled treatise, *Youth Speaks Its Mind* (1943), while embroidered with the language of freedom, tolerance, and negotiation, is directly concerned with incorporating youth and maintaining consensus and stability in Canadian society during a time of crisis (i.e., World War II). Similarly, the document *Its Your Turn* (Committee on Youth 1971), which is a report to the Secretary of State, while constructing Canadian youth as a participating force and valuable resource in coping with a changing society, had a clear intention to assimilate young people into society through a wide range of admittedly progressive-looking policy recommendations.

Criticisms of this consensus model of society in general came from various quarters in Canada, from political movements as well as from academia. Ironically, elements of the critique also emanated from young people themselves, although, surprisingly, there has been little documentation of the generational aspect of the sixties counterculture (Kostash 1980), the student movement, the development of the New Left (the Waffle movement) (Roussopoulos 1970), and civil rights and women's liberation movements in Canada (Fitzgerald et al. 1982). On the academic side, particularly important in the challenge to functionalism were the recovery and development of a Canadian political economy tradition, the advancement of feminist perspectives, the later adoption and engagement with European Marxist perspectives, and the development of cultural studies in Canada. An equally significant but somewhat different academic response to both the grand theorising of functionalism and the political analyses of Marxism and feminism was a move towards the sanctity of quantitative positivism and the building of middle-range, empirically-based theories. All these factors influenced the direction of Canadian sociology, and hence all have important implications for the development of youth studies in Canada.

Surprisingly, the historical weight of traditional concerns in political economy appears to have weakened its application to the analysis of Canadian youth. Initially, this seems a curious omission by any standards, considering the centrality of the student movement in the creation of the Canadian Left (Roussopoulos 1970; Loken 1973) and young people's role as "objects" of government policy (Committee on Youth 1971), not to mention their crucial location in the economy with respect to the transformation of the labour market. Yet, with the exception of a small number of important studies in this field (i.e., Krahn and Lowe 1999; Ashton and Lowe 1991), youth has been curiously absent in the political economy literature. As Clement (1988, 24) laments: "A further feature too seldom examined with respect to class is age. Particularly noteworthy is the high unemployment amongst young people, but also the nature of the work they do experience. Increasingly they are being marginalised into part- time, non-union, low skilled jobs."

The failure to recognise youth as an important dimension of political economy is perhaps due to a larger problem this perspective has had with respect to theorising culture. As Brym (1989, 3) argues in his book *From Culture to Power*, political economy was formed partly in opposition to a socio-cultural perspective concerned with issues of authority, inequality, and state intervention in Canada, and it sought instead to focus on "how social structural features of Canadian society, such as the distribution of power, affect economic, political and ethnic behaviour largely *independently* of the influence of culture" (my emphasis).

This is not to say that there has been no concern with cultural analysis within this tradition (see chap. 19, by Kurasawa, in this volume). However, as Whitson and Gruneau (1996) have argued, much of the early work conducted here was either limited to studies of cultural dependency and underdevelopment or to specific institutional analyses of the media as purveyors of a dominant class ideology. While it may not be surprising to find that historically the study of popular forms of culture has been somewhat absent in political economy, there is also a relatively weak tradition concerned with exploring contemporary working class cultures and communities.[2] Analyses of Canadian youth transitions and youth cultures taken together are almost wholly absent (see Krahn and Lowe 1999 for a very tentative beginning here).

Canadian feminism, while having a connection with the student movement in Canada (Kostash 1980), grew both in tandem with and partly in response to the development of the Canadian left and the rise of the political economy perspective (Connelly and Armstrong 1992). Again, surprisingly, the movement's youthful dimensions and origins appear to have been largely ignored, perhaps in part because the "first wave" of feminism felt compelled to resist analyses of an age dimension in favour of the solidarity of sisterhood. Fox notes an academic trend whereby in the early seventies Canadian feminist sociologists were concerned to document gender inequality and gender bias in studies and theories, while by the mid- to late seventies they were proposing the wholesale reconstruction of "malestream" sociology. She also mentions that Canada has had a stronger tradition of socialist-feminist debate than many countries (see in Brym and Fox 1989, 122).

This history might help to partially explain why feminist concerns with youth in Canada have been somewhat underdeveloped (although see Kostash 1987), as does the subjects' obvious association with maleness. First, the early trend concerned with gender bias in the literature may have implied somehow that gender was simply another variable to be measured. Women and young women simply had to be added to the sample, without reconstructing the theory or recognising their different experiences. Second, and perhaps more important, were the limits imposed by traditional Marxist concerns on the scope of feminist critique. For example, even if feminists reversed and overturned some of the political economy categories when applying them to women, they also inadvertently replicated some of the traditional caveats. So while feminists counterposed reproduction to production, private spaces to public spaces, the domestic household and community to the workplace, and gender to class, they also tended to reproduce political economy's lack of concern with culture and generation (although see Luxton 1980).

Unsurprisingly then, there has been a major divide between political-economy-based studies of youth transitions in Canada and cultural-studies-based analyses of youth identities and styles. What analysis of youth culture there is in Canada (Brake 1985; Baron 1989; Tanner 1981, 1996) has been either directly or indirectly influenced by a United Kingdom cultural studies perspective developed at the Centre for Contemporary Cultural Studies (Hall and Jefferson 1976), at the expense of attempting to combine this approach with a perspective more closely tied to political economy. A failure to differentiate between different types of cultural analyses even within the Centre for Contemporary Cultural Studies (cccs) tradition (Hall 1992), and the assumption that such a perspective could simply be mapped onto an analysis of Canadian youth has stunted, rather than helped to develop, the study of youth culture here. Rather than seeing how differences in the Canadian situation called into question the applicability of the subcultural perspective more generally, commentators used its poor fit to justify a lack of Canadian youth styles (Brake 1985). However, the development of a more indigenous Canadian cultural studies that combines elements of the political tradition of the Centre of Contemporary Cultural Studies (cccs)

(Davies 1995; Fortier 1995) with existing Canadian traditions and institutional realignments (see Straw 1993), including political economy, signals some promising starting points for analysing youth in Canada.[3]

A final influence on the theoretical underdevelopment of youth studies in Canada has been a tendency to use large-scale quantitative studies (see Bibby 2001) and sophisticated statistical operations to produce middle-range theories. While part of this tradition may have been a response to the abstract theoreticism of functionalism and the power of empirically oriented government-funded agencies like Statistics Canada to contour research, the result is that while there is a lot of empirical material available on Canadian youth, there are few general theories with which to interpret this mass of information. Furthermore, studies of youth in Canada tend to be compartmentalised into certain areas like employment or education or deviance or leisure, each employing their own specific literature or sets of mid-range theories with little cross-referencing to other areas or use of more general theoretical paradigms.

THE "PECULIARITIES" OF CANADIAN YOUTH: A "NEW" POLITICAL ECONOMY TO THE RESCUE?

Related to the general problem of theorising Canadian youth are a number of more specific 'peculiarities' that have supposedly hindered youth studies, particularly at the cultural level. In brief, they are Canada's more differentiated class structure, which makes youth styles and groupings harder to identify; the greater geographical dispersion and regional isolation of Canadian youth; more ethnic diversity among young people in Canada; and a lack of Canadian national identity, including young people's proximity to and susceptibility to the influence of American popular culture. This section, looks critically at each of these areas in turn and suggests how political economy might help to address some of the issues that arise in each case.

Youth and Class in Canada

Research on youth in Canada has tended either to ignore class as a social relationship with respect to generation, to see it simply as an empirically dependent or independent variable based on occupational scale or educational achievement, or to compare class subcultures with their European (usually their United Kingdom) counterparts, finding them deficient in some manner. Curiously, Brake, in his early ground-breaking work on Canadian youth culture (1985) unconsciously reiterates some of these themes, to the extent that he contributes to some of the myths about the Canadian class structure. For example he states that "Canada is a country which prides itself on being a land of opportunity, where the class barriers of the old country no longer hinder social advancement ... a modest rise in terms of affluence, generationally, with a consequent lack of polarisation in class terms (wealth like poverty is discreetly disguised in Canada) has defused and muted class struggle" (148).

While this quote does not in itself do justice to Brake's own more complex position, the implication is that Canadian youth experience classlessness. Youth is, as he goes on to argue, "appropriately rewarded for its commitment to industry, thrift and discipline" (150), while failure is individualised and pathologised (i.e., street kids are seen as deviants). While neither of these statements is inherently wrong, they do of course require empirical proof, which Brake himself does not provide. This approach leaves little room to observe, or even look for, any forms of class experience or signs of resistance among young Canadians.

There are, then, according to Brake few, if any, examples of contemporary youth rebellion in Canada. This is especially the case in comparison to the emergence of working-class youth subcultures in England (Hall and Jefferson 1976). Again, to quote Brake, "Youth cultural studies are scarce, in Canada perhaps because the cultures lack the dramatic socially visible forms that they take in Britain and the U.S." (1985, 152). Unfortunately, this means that either youth culture in Canada becomes uninteresting or derivative or that the "borrowed" cultures that do exist are analysed according to British subcultural standards and ultimately found wanting.

There have been attempts to utilise British-based class cultural models and to apply them to Canadian youth subcultures (in addition to Brake, see Baron 1989; Davis 1994; Tanner 1996). However, one should not be surprised when they do not yield a good fit. The implication is that the subcultural model is without fault even in its own terms, an assumption that has been criticised from its earliest beginnings (see the chapters by Frith and Corrigan and McRobbie and Garber in Hall and Jefferson 1976). Ironically, much of the recent work on youth cultures in the United Kingdom emphasizes the fragmented character of style rather than class-based subcultural identity (Redhead 1993; Thornton 1995).

A transforming political economy perspective would begin to approach the issue of youth and class in Canada by first asking how the younger generation is actively being used in restructuring the neoliberal economy and, second, by asking how transformations here might be reflected in the changing cultures of young people. It is the case that youth make up a disproportionate percentage of workers in the low-skilled, low-paid service sector (Krahn and Lowe 1999; Statistics Canada 1994) and have largely borne the brunt of flexible working practices and a decline in real wages (Myles, Picot, and Wannel 1988). With respect to making up a "reserve army of labour," young people have the highest unemployment rate in Canada (Statistics Canada 1994). Correspondingly, statistics show that young Canadians are considered one of the most deprived social groupings, with over two-thirds falling into the "poor" category (National Anti-Poverty Association 1995).

Yet, with the exception of a handful of studies of street kids, runaways, and juvenile delinquency, there are surprisingly few comprehensive analyses of the lives of the ordinary young urban poor in Canada (Glenday 1996). There would appear to be a clear class divide between the cultures, life-worlds, and destinations of young Canadians heading to university and those who are simply hoping to finish high school and get a job (O'Bireck 1996b). Differences and inequalities created here affect and influence youth experiences not only in the production sphere (i.e., their experiences of work opportunities) but also with respect to consumption patterns as well. And while there may not be as many examples of class-based youth cultures in Canada exhibiting "dramatic socially visible forms," there are significant economic, social, and lifestyle differences that are created in, and through, class relations (O'Bireck 1996b).

Regional Difference and the Urban/Rural Divide

Aspects of the debate about youth and class are reinforced by the geographic dispersion of young people in Canada. Regionalism, aided by a strong provincial government structure, and the urban/rural dichotomy all play an important part in the creation of differential youth opportunities and the production of diverse Canadian youth identities. Because they live in one of the largest countries in the world with a relatively small population scattered over large geographical distances, it is indeed difficult to generalise about Canadian youth. Yet at the same time, the pattern of this dispersal is a "spacial referent" for the geographical mapping of class and ethnic divisions, which clearly help to limit opportunities for whole sections of Canadian youth.

There is a history of regional and/or community studies in Canada to draw on here, studies looking largely at one-industry towns (Lucas 1971) or regions based on one main natural resource (Clement 1981). Yet with minor exceptions, the role that youth play, either economically or domestically, in these communities has rarely been examined. One attempt to examine how mobile multinational capital has sought to incorporate young people still in the school system into its workplace ethos comes from Bryan Palmer's (1994) study of Goodyear's move into a small southeastern Ontario town. While acknowledging the importance of gaining youth support for corporate capital, Palmer unfortunately does not examine small-town youth culture, particularly in relation to any notion of resistance.

This failure to study generation and locality, in conjunction with the differentiating effect of regionalism, works to create a second pecu-liarity of Canadian youth, according to Brake (1985), namely the lack of a national youth culture. Canadian youth culture has supposedly been less discernible and less political than its English and u.s. coun-terparts. Compared to their counterparts in England, with the punk phenomenon and in the United States with rap and hip hop culture, Canadian youth have apparently never had a national youth culture – only regional peculiarities and a borrowing of styles from elsewhere. Additionally, societal responses to what little youth culture there has been is localised – for example, concerns about swarming gangs of middle-class youth in downtown Toronto, squeegie kids in Montreal, or grunge culture in Vancouver – and hence that youth culture lacks national exposure and government attention. Regionalism, then, is seen to blunt the political potential of youth movements and styles on a national level. Brake also goes on to suggest that youth cultural style is more prevalent in larger metropolitan areas than in small towns and rural areas. The assumption is that youth cultural styles in Canada are stymied by greater geographical distances and thereby remain rela-tively underdeveloped or confined to a particular city.

From a "spatially aware" political economy point of view (Mahon 1993), it is important to stress here that whereas large geographical distances between places may once have led to the cultural isolation of youth, the effects of media, improved transportation, and information technology have all effectively worked to close these gaps. The Marxist geographer David Harvey (1989) has referred to this process as time-space compression, while Giddens (1990) mentions the related phe-nomenon of what he calls the disembedding and reembedding of social relations across space. In other words, the globalisation of fast-food outlets, TV, music, films, and magazines means that increasingly youth are being exposed to many of the same cultural symbols wher-ever they live.

Still, it is important to recognise that this global culture will be consumed and appropriated by different subsections of youth in different localities in different ways (Featherstone 1990) and that this may in fact heighten local identities and regional differences, rather than having just a homogenising effect. Youth may appropriate what is relevant or develop parallel or different cultural responses in this context. In this sense, difference comes not so much from geographical distance and isolation, which has been effectively reduced, but from the need to construct and rework local identity in the context of globalisation. Geographical isolation becomes less of a distinguishing characterisation of Canadian youth, with young people across the globe generally becoming simultaneously more homogenous and more differentiated at the same time.

These same points apply to the somewhat tenuous urban/rural distinction. Again, the distance between Canadian cities would appear to be less significant considering the increased mobility of young people today and improved communication networks. One would also expect a reduction in the isolation of rural youth due to their increased exposure to urban, as well as global, cultural forms through travel and the media. This, again, is not to say that different Canadian cities will not produce different expressions of youth culture, but it is to say that there will be a greater distribution and knowledge of these cultures elsewhere. There continues to be a small-town and rural youth culture in parts of Canada, which re-creates itself in the context of country music, sports (ice hockey and baseball), and drinking (for a general analysis of masculinity in a northern Ontario town, see Dunk 1991; for the role of ice hockey, see Gruneau and Whitson 1993). Yet the very forms of culture this rural life-world appropriates are increasingly themselves products of the global media (i.e., Country Music Television, Molson's beer, and so on), mixed with national and local products and traditions.

Ethnic Diversity among Canadian Youth

The "problem" created by greater ethnic diversity in Canada, according to Brake, is that it once again complicates the production of a national youth culture. Such diversity, he suggests "undermines a collective consciousness of what are objective class problems," while "consecutive waves of immigration have assisted in dispersing any historical sense of class war" (1985, 148–9).

Ironically, while Brake mentions the potential for ethnic youth cultures to develop in Canada and possibly challenge the status quo (161), he quickly goes on to argue that these cultural forms are often "inauthentic." That is, they are expressed only at a surface level, rather than being derived from indigenous ethnic culture. The only significant ethnic youth cultural movement Brake mentions is the Quebec student movement, which, he argues, was radicalised through its association with the separatist movement. Yet how this example relates to Brake's concern with youth and class resistance remains unclear in his discussion. Rioux (1966), on the other hand, argues that Quebec youth culture, with its idealism, desire for wider social change, and youthful enthusiasm, actually helped to fuel separatism.

While one might initially have some sympathy with Brake's neo-Marxist analysis, any attempt that seeks to engulf ethnicity under the concept of class is problematic when it comes to understanding and analysing Canadian youth in all its diversity. First, it ignores the ethnic dimension of the concept of class itself in Canada (Clement 1988). It also fails to accept that although racism may be closely connected to economic factors, ethnic discrimination has other dimensions. Finally, it inadvertently contributes to the construction of ethnic youth as "other," caught not only in the middle of a confusing age transition but also in a culture gap (see Ratner 1996). Consequently, there is a tendency, although not so much in Brake's own work, to visualise immigrant or ethnic youth in Canada within a social-problem discourse.

For instance, while there have been few contemporary sociological studies of aboriginal youth in Canada, the vast majority have tended to focus around the "problem" of assimilation. Emphasis has been placed on lack of achievement in education and work and problems relating to welfarism, crime, drug use, and suicide (Sutherland 1992a), rather than on racism, cultural genocide, or the destruction of traditional employment opportunities through economic change (Condon 1987). Furthermore, this social-problem perspective is reinforced through government agencies and published documents, not to mention sensationalised through the mass media. Far less attention and analysis is given to the formation of aboriginal youth organisations and empowerment projects, for instance (although see McKenzie and Morrissette 1993). Another example of this negative approach, is the extensive coverage given to the violence and gang behaviour of immigrant youth in Canada. In their analysis of Canadian media coverage of gangs, Fasiolo and Leckie (1993) note that the most frequently cited type was the Asian gang. Previous research in the 1970s focused on Vietnamese gangs, with more contemporary research centring on Chinese youth (Lee 1992) and the Asian community (Dubro 1992).

The polarisation of studies of ethnic and immigrant youth in Canada into an unhelpful dichotomy of authentic culture versus societal assimilation ignores diversity within such groups and over-looks as well the spaces where cultural forms between different groups overlap. It is noteworthy that Aboriginals in Canada comprise over fifty distinct nations, with different social, cultural, and political traditions, living on over six hundred reserves spread across a vast country. While there may be some common points of reference here (e.g., the effect of racism), the life chances and cultural life-world of aboriginal youth are very diverse. The position of indigenous groups, not to mention immigrant youth, with respect to how they fit between their culture and mainstream white Canadian life, is extremely varied.

The main point here is that ethnic diversity in Canada does not make the country unique or peculiar with respect to youth studies. Ironically, ethnic diversity does not appear to have hindered the devel-opment of youth studies in the United States, where there have been numerous studies of immigrant youth, ranging from the early work of the Chicago School to studies of Chicano gangs (Munoz 1989). In the United Kingdom there have also been attempts to come to terms with the relationship between white nationalism and black youngsters (Gilroy 1987), and there have been studies of links between black culture and white youth (Jones 1988). Undertaking studies of the interaction and circulation of mainstream and ethnic youth cultures is a taking-off point, rather than an obstacle, for Canadian youth studies.

Canadian Youth, "Borrowed" Styles,
and Cultural Hegemony

A final peculiarity of Canadian youth relates not only to its supposed lack of national culture and identity but to its unashamed borrowing of youth cultures from different contexts. As Brake (1985, 145, 152) explains, Canadian youth cultures "are usually based on the styles of a borrowed tradition" and hence "tend to be derivative, and insuffi-ciently large to form a sense of moral outrage." As such, Canadian youth culture is seen to be bland, purely stylistic, passive, and devoid of any real social meaning.

There are a number of problems with this assertion. First, the notion of authenticity is problematic. While it still might be possible to distinguish between levels of originality, postmodern theorists have forcefully argued that much of contemporary youth culture is a global and circular reworking of past styles and different tradi-tions. The revival of aspects of youth cultures from the 1960s in the

1990s is a case in point. Redhead (1993) has argued that rave culture in the United Kingdom adopted elements of sixties counterculture, such as long hair, the use of drugs, and casual dress, combined it with aspects of gay dance culture and the DIY (do-it-yourself) ethos of punk, and topped it off with an infusion of computer-aided music technology.

In addition to this postmodern critique, there is also a strong political economy argument that might be made against an authenticity discourse. In essence, which group of youths in any country or city in the world today is not exposed to American popular cultural hegemony? The answer would appear to be very few. MTV is a truly global phenomenon now, but even in the earlier postwar period, American popular culture in the form of music and movies was making its way across the world. It should not be forgotten that one of the important roots of English Teddy boy culture came from the importation of "white" R&B (i.e., Elvis and Gene Vincent). The origins of punk music have also been questioned, as U.S. groups like the New York Dolls, the Ramones, and Velvet Underground predated acts like the Sex Pistols in the United Kingdom. Similarly, the wide appeal of gangsta rap and hip hop outside its origin in black ghettos, that is, its appeal in the suburban United States, not to mention its adoption by white middle-class British youth, is also testimony to the global circulation of Afro-American culture. Baseball caps, baggy trousers, and U.S. sport shirts are as likely to be found on British campuses as they are in Canada today.

Canadian youth have been viewed by Brake (1985) as being passive in their acceptance of American mass culture and as possessing no popular cultural traditions themselves. The notion of passivity, which is inherent in theories of mass culture and which ironically originated in the United States in the 1950s and, to some extent, in dependency theory in Canada (Teeple 1972), replicates aspects of the neo-Marxist Frankfurt School's cultural analyses. All these perspectives have been weakened by the development of more sophisticated theories that suggest that the production and consumption of culture is a much more differentiated, complex, and active process (Hall 1980) than was first thought. In fact, youth cultures have been seen as particularly good examples of cultural appropriation and resistance (Hall and Jefferson 1976; Hebdige 1979). It is more likely the case that Canadian youth – already a differentiated group, as we have seen – have both selectively appropriated and refused elements of American popular culture and that their identities and cultures are the products of a mixture of class, ethnic, gender, and regional factors and products of how they create their own indigenous culture in and through the active consumption of global products and the rejection of certain elements of U.S. corporate popular culture (Klein 2000).

CONCLUSION: STUDYING CANADIAN YOUTH – CHALLENGE OR OPPORTUNITY?

The main task of this chapter has been to start to develop a set of adequate theoretical parameters and a viable research agenda that would begin to advance youth studies in Canada from a new political economy perspective. In summary, a number of processes have contributed to the underdevelopment of our understanding of Canadian youth. At the broadest level, it has been suggested that the trajectory of sociology in Canada from "culture to power" (Brym and Fox 1989) has tended to ignore generational issues even with respect to notions of class, employment, community, and the household. Studies of youth subcultures and lifestyles have been even further marginalised in Canadian political economy and in feminism and have instead relied too heavily on imported cultural-studies models. Additionally, a strong positivistic tradition and a concern with quantitative data that produces middle-range theories has resulted in youth studies being compartmentalised and fragmented. Finally, a government-led research agenda focusing on facts rather than interpretation, on social problems as opposed to possibilities, and on consensus rather than social change and real empowerment has skewed youth studies towards selected studies of employment, education, and deviance.

Fortunately, however, none of these problems are inevitable or immutable. One of the biggest pluses in Canada is the continuing development of a political economy perspective, as this volume demonstrates. A transformed Canadian political economy provides a set of theoretical tools and concepts with which to rework notions of class and generation and to analyse the changing nature of youth labour markets and the service economy, not to mention to begin to understand issues of regional and spatial inequality. In conjunction with feminism, it also has the potential to begin to illuminate the link between gender, the labour market, and household relations and the role youth play in this interaction. Canadian political economy has also increasingly become concerned with the issue of ethnicity, and more recently, popular culture (again, see Kurasawa's contribution in this volume).

The link between a political economy of youth transitions and emerging youth cultures can start to be forged. The question of whether Canadian youth are beginning to rebel against the lack of opportunities and the collapse of traditional transitions (Krahn and Lowe 1999) or whether they are simply becoming popular "folk devils" in an emerging spiral of moral panics (Tanner 1996) provides a starting point. Either scenario clearly threatens the potency of the liberal hegemony, which has historically held young people in Canada in check. One possible result is that, rather than rebelling, the young will instead retreat into and develop new "cultures of avoidance" to such a degree that the adult world will be unable to penetrate their style and inner logic. Grunge, rave, and slacker cultures are often held up as examples of these retreatist subcultures. There is surely a connection between the stripping away of real youth opportunities and the increasing insularity of many contemporary youth cultures (see Ferguson 1994). At the same time, it might be argued that a subsection of young Canadians are actually at the political forefront of the antiglobalisation and anti-free-trade movement (Klein 2000).

To argue for the development of a Canadian youth studies under a renewed political economy banner is not a call for the creation of a new inward-looking subdiscipline. The study of youth must draw from a range of disciplines and approaches and be in dialogue with theories and empirical studies developed elsewhere. At the same time, it needs to work from its strengths in political economy and feminist analysis and to further develop its own cultural approach. It should also be remembered that the category of youth is not just about young people: it is a social construction that is often held up as a barometer for assessing the quality of our whole society and the direction it is moving in. One would hope that the development of Canadian youth studies would feed back into a more general debate and analysis about how political economy can contribute to the future transformation of Canada's neoliberal society.

NOTES

A version of this paper was first presented in the Canadian Youth session of the International Sociological Association (ISA) World Congress held in Montreal from 26 July to 1 August 1998. Thanks to session organisers Madeleine Gauthier and Diane Pacom, who invited me and made valuable comments on that earlier paper. I would also like to acknowledge Leah Vosko and Wally Clement's insightful editorial comments on an earlier draft of this paper. A special thanks to Wally for initiating my interest in developing Canadian youth studies when I was a visiting professor at the Institute of Political Economy at Carleton University in 1996.

1   There appears to be less material on French-Canadian youth in the litera-
    ture, although this may simply be due to its subordinate status within
    Canadian sociology (see Maheu and Juteau 1989) or to English writers'
    reluctance or inability to consult the relevant literature. Regarding arti-
    cles that exist on other ethnic youth in Canada, there is a skewing towards
    a deviancy perspective (see Fasiolo and Leckie 1993; Dubro 1992), while
    studies of youth and racism are rarer (see James 1990 though). Studies of
    aboriginal youth again tend towards a social-problem perspective (for
    example see Gfellner 1994; Fisher and Janetti 1996), while studies of pos-
    itive action by Native youth themselves are less available (but see McKen-
    zie and Morrissette 1993).

2   In fact, one of the main attempts to address this issue has come not from
    political economy but from radical social history. Bryan Palmer's work, in
    particular his writing on contemporary Canadian working-class experi-
    ence and culture, is most notable in this regard (see Palmer 1992). While
    Palmer's work does contain a section on Canadian youth, it focuses again
    around a somewhat unhelpful use of a "mass culture" perspective, and
    evolves into the role young workers played in labour unrest in Canada in
    the 1970s, rather than looking into the cultural dimension. Also see
    Palmer (1994).

3   It should also be noted that there is some emerging work on postmod-
    ernism and youth in Canada (see Pacom 1998, for example). While I
    continue to have reservations about the short-comings of postmodern
    theory generally, I do believe that this perspective has made and will con-
    tinue to make a valuable contribution to Canadian youth studies. Unfor-
    tunately, I do not have room in this paper to engage in a dialogue with
    this developing perspective.

REFERENCES

Anisef, Paul, and Paul Axelrod, eds. 1993. *Transitions: Schooling and Employment in Canada.* Toronto: Thompson Educational Publishing.

Ashton, David, and Graham Lowe, eds. 1991. *Making Their Way: Education, Training and the Labour Market in Canada and Britain.* Milton Keynes, England: Open University Press.

Baron, Steve. 1989. "The Canadian West Coast Punk Subculture: A Field Study." *Canadian Journal of Sociology* 14(3): 289–316.

Bibby, Reginald. 2001. *Canada's Teens: Today, Yesterday, and Tomorrow.* Toronto: Stoddart.

Bibby, Reginald, and Donald Posterski. 1985. *The Emerging Generation.* Toronto: Irwin Publishing.

Brake, Mike. 1985. *Comparative Youth Culture: The Sociology of Youth Cultures and Youth Subcultures in America, Britain and Canada.* London: Routledge.

Brym, Robert, and Bonnie Fox. 1989. *From Culture to Power: The Sociology of English Canada*. Toronto: Oxford University Press.

Clement, Wallace. 1981. *Hardrock Mining: Industrial Relations and Tecological Changes at INCO*. Toronto: McClelland and Stewart.

– 1988. *The Challenge of Class Analysis*. Ottawa: Carleton University Press.

– ed. 1996. *Building on the New Political Economy*. Montreal and Kingston: McGill-Queen's University Press.

Committee on Youth. 1971. *It's Your Turn: A Report to the Secretary of State by the Committee on Youth*. Ottawa: Information Canada.

Condon, Richard. 1987. *Inuit Youth: Growth and Change in the Canadian Arctic*. New Brunswick, NJ: Rutgers University Press.

Connelly, M. Patrica, and Pat Armstrong. 1992. *Feminism in Action: Studies in Political Economy*. Toronto: Canadian Scholars' Press.

Cote, James, and Anton Allahar. 1994. *Generation on Hold: Coming of Age in the Late Twentieth Century*. Toronto: Stoddart.

Davies, Blodwen. 1948. *Youth Speaks Its Mind*. Toronto: The Ryerson Press.

Davies, Ioan. 1994. *Cultural Studies and Beyond: Fragments of Empire*, 331–50. London: Routledge.

Davis, Scott. 1994. "In Search of Resistance and Rebellion amongst High School Dropouts." *Canadian Journal of Sociology* 19(3): 331–50.

Dubro, James. 1992. *Dragons of Crime: Inside the Asian Underworld*. Markham, ON: Octopus.

Dunk, Thomas. 1991. *It's a Working Man's Town*. Montreal and Kingston: McGill-Queen's University Press.

Ellis, Desmond, and Walter Dekeseredy, eds. 1996. *The Wrong Stuff: An Introduction to the Sociological Study of Deviance*. Scarborough, ON: Allyn & Bacon Canada.

Epstein, Jonathon. 1998. *Youth Culture: Identity in a Postmodern World*. Oxford: Blackwell.

Fasiolo, Raffaele, and Steven Leckie. 1993. *Canadian Media Coverage of Gangs: A Content Analysis*. Ottawa: Department of Solicitor General of Canada, Intergovernmental Affairs.

Featherstone, Mike. 1990. *Global Culture: Nationalism, Globalisation and Modernity*. London: Sage.

Ferguson, S. 1994. "Kurt Cobain: The Comfort of Being Sad," *Utne Reader* 64: 27–9.

Fisher, Linda, and Hannele Janetti. 1996. "Aboriginal Youth in the Criminal Justice System." In John Winterdyk, ed., *Issues and Perspective on Young Offenders in Canada*, 237–56. Toronto: Harcourt Brace.

Fitzgerald, Maureen, Connie Guberman, and Margie Wolfe. 1982. *Still Ain't Satisfied: Canadian Feminism Today*. Toronto: Women's Educational Press.

Fornas, J., and G. Bolin, eds. 1995. *Youth Cultures in Late Modernity*. London: Sage.

Fortier, Mark. 1995. "From Cultural Studies to Cultural Studies in Canada: A Review Essay." *University of Toronto Quarterly* 64(4): 557–66.

Furlong, Andy, and Fred Cartmel. 1997. *Young People and Social Change*. Buckingham, England: Open University Press.

Gfellner, Barbara. 1994. "A Matched Group Comparison of Drug Use and Problem Behaviour amongst Canadian Indians and White Adolescents." *Journal of Early Adolescence* 14(1).

Giddens, Anthony. 1990. *The Consequences of Modernity*. Cambridge: Polity Press.

Gilroy, P. 1987. *There Ain't No Black in the Union Jack*. London: Hutchinson.

Glenday, Dan. 1996. "Mean Streets and Hard Times: Youth Unemployment and Crime." In Gary O'Bireck, ed., *Not a Kid Anymore: Canadian Youth, Crime and Subcultures*. Toronto: Nelson.

Gruneau, Richard, and Dave Whitson. 1993. *Hockey Night in Canada: Sport, Identities and Cultural Politics*. Toronto: Garamond.

Hall, Stuart. 1980. "Encoding/Decoding." In Stuart Hall, ed., *Culture, Media, Language*, 128–38. London: Hutchinson.

– 1992. "Cultural Studies and Its Theoretical Legacies." In Larry Grossberg, Cary Nelson, and Paul Treichler, eds., *Cultural Studies*, 277–94. New York: Routledge.

Hall, Stuart, and Tony Jefferson. 1976. *Resistance through Rituals: Youth Subcultures in Post-War Britain*. London: Hutchinson.

Harvey, David. 1989. *The Condition of Postmodernity*. Oxford: Basil Blackwell.

Hebdige, D. 1979. *The Meaning of Style*. London: Methuen.

Hollands, Robert. 1990. *The Long Transition: Class, Culture and Youth Training*. London: Macmillan.

– 1995. *Friday Night, Saturday Night: Youth Cultural Identification in the Post-Industrial City*. Newcastle: University of Newcastle.

– 1998. "Crap Jobs, Govvy Schemes and Trainspotting: Reassessing the Youth Employment and Idleness Debate." In Jane Wheelock and John Vail, eds., *Work and Idleness: The Political Economy of Full Employment*, 99–115. London: Klewer Academic Press.

James, C. 1990. *Making It: Black Youth, Racism and Career Aspirations in a Big City*. Oakville, ON: Mosaic.

Jones, Simon. 1988. *Black Culture, White Youth: The Reggae Tradition from JA to UK*. London: Macmillan.

Klein, Naomi. 2000. *No Logo*. London: Flamingo.

Kostash, Myrna. 1980. *Long Way from Home: The Story of the Sixties Generation in Canada*. Toronto: James Lorimer.

– 1987. *No Kidding: Inside the World of Teenage Girls*. Toronto: McClelland and Stewart.

– 2000. *The Next Canada: In Search of Our Future Nation*. Toronto: McClelland and Stewart.

Krahn, Harvey, and Graham Lowe. 1999. "School to Work Transitions and Postmodern Values: What's Changing in Canada?' In Walter Heinz, ed., *From Education to Work: Cross-National Perspectives*. Cambridge: Cambridge University Press.

Lee, C. 1992. *The Dilemma of New Canadian Youth: A Discussion Paper*. Report prepared for the Asian Youth Task Force, Vancouver.

Loken, Joel. 1973. *Student Alienation and Dissent*. Scarborough, ON: Prentice Hall.

Lucas, Rex. 1971. *Minetown, Milltown, Railtown: Life in Canadian Communities of Single Industries*. Toronto: University of Toronto Press.

Luxton, Meg. 1980. *More than a Labour of Love*. Toronto: Women's Press.

McKenzie, Brad, and Larry Morrissette. 1993. "Cultural Empowerment and Healing for Aboriginal Youth in Winnipeg." In Anne-Marie Mawhiney, ed., *Rebirth: Political, Economic and Social Development in First Nations*. Toronto: Dundern.

Maheu, Louis, and Daniella Juteau. 1989. "Special Issue on Quebec Sociology." *Canadian Journal of Sociology and Anthropology* 26(5): 363–93.

Mahon, Rianne. 1993. "The 'New' Canadian Political Economy Revisted: Production, Space and Identity." In Jane Jenson, Rianne Mahon, and M. Bienefeld, eds., *Production, Space, Identity: Political Economy Faces the Twenty-first Century*. Toronto: Canadian Scholars' Press.

Males, Mike. 1996. *The Scapegoat Generation: America's War on Adolescents*. Monroe, ME: Common Courage Press.

Matthews, Frederick. 1993. *Youth Gangs on Youth Gangs*. Ottawa: Department of the Solicitor General.

Miles, Anglea Rose, and Geraldine Finn. 1989. *Feminism in Canada: From Pressure to Politics*. 2d ed. Montreal: Black Rose Books.

Munoz, Carlos. 1989. *Youth, Identity, Power: The Chicano Movement*. London: Verso.

Myles, John, G. Picot, and T. Whannel. 1988. *Wages and Jobs in the 1980s: Changing Youth Wages and the Declining Middle*. Ottawa: Statistics Canada Research Paper Series N.17.

National Anti-Poverty Association. 1995. *Poverty in Canada: Some Facts and Figures*. Ottawa: National Anti-Poverty Association.

O'Bireck, Gary. 1996a. *Not a Kid Anymore: Canadian Youth, Crime and Subcultures*. Toronto: Nelson.

– 1996b. "Preppies and Heavies in Bigtown: Secondary School Experiences." In Gary O'Bireck, ed., *Not a Kid Anymore: Canadian Youth, Crime and Subcultures*. Toronto: Nelson.

O'Grady, Bill. 1997. "Psychological Health and Youth: Unemployment in Rural Canada, A Case for 'Generation x'?" *British Journal of Education and Work* 9(2).

Pacom, Diane. 1998. "Towards a Theoretical Evaluation of the Sociology of

Youth." A paper presented in the session Spotlight on Candian Youth, International Sociological Association World Congress, Montreal, Canada, 24 July.

Palmer, Bryan. 1992. *Working Class Experience: Rethinking the History of Canadian Labour.* Toronto: McCelland and Stewart.

– 1994. *Goodyear Invades the Backcountry: The Corporate Takeover of a Rural Town.* New York: Monthly Review Press.

Pearcy, P. 1991. *Youth Criminal Gangs in BC.* A report prepared for the Ministry of the Solictor General, Canada.

Ratner, R.S. 1996. "In Cultural Limbo: Adolescent Aboriginals in the Urban Life-World." In Gary O'Bireck, ed., *Not a Kid Anymore: Canadian Youth, Crime and Subcultures.* Toronto: Nelson.

Redhead, Steve, ed. 1993. *Rave Off: Politics and Deviance in Contemporary Youth Culture.* Aldershot, England: Avebury.

Rioux, Marcel. 1966. "Youth in the Contemporary World and in Quebec." *Our Generation* 3–4: 5–19.

Rogers, Kenneth. 1945. *Street Gangs in Toronto: A Study of the Forgotten Boy.* Toronto: The Ryerson Press.

Roussopoulos, Dimitrios, ed. 1970. *The New Left in Canada.* Montreal: Our Generation Press.

Schlegal, Alice, and Herbert Berry. 1991. *Adolescence: An Anthropological Inquiry.* New York: Free Press.

Shore, Marlene. 1987. *The Science of Social Redemption: McGill, the Chicago School and the Origins of Research in Canada.* Toronto: University of Toronto Press.

Statistics Canada. 1989. *Youth in Canada: Selected Highlights.* Supply and Services Canada.

– 1994. *Youth in Canada.* Ottawa: Statistics Canada.

Straw, Will. 1993. "Shifting Boundaries, Lines of Descent: Cultural Studies and Institutional Realignment." In Valda Blundell, John Shepard, and Ian Taylor, eds., *Relocating Cultural Studies: Developments in Theory and Research.* London: Routledge.

Sutherland, Neil. 1976. *Children in English Canadian Society: Framing the Twentieth Century Consensus.* Toronto: University of Toronto Press.

Sutherland, Neil, Jean Barman, and Linda Hale. 1992a. *Contemporary Canadian Childhood and Youth: A Bibliography.* Westport, CN: Greenwood.

– 1992b. *History of Canadian Childhood and Youth: A Bibliography.* Westport. CN: Greenwood.

Tanner, Julian. 1981. "Pop Music and Peer Groups: A Study of Canadian High School Student's Responses to Pop Music." *Canadian Review of Sociology and Anthropology* 18(1): 1–13.

– 1996. *Teenage Troubles: Youth and Deviance in Canada.* Toronto: Nelson.

Tanner, Julian, Harvey Krahn, and Timothy Hartnagel. 1995. *Fractured Transitions from School to Work: Revisiting the Dropout Problem.* Toronto: Oxford University Press.

Teeple, Gary, ed. 1972. *Capitalism and the National Question in Canada.* Toronto: University of Toronto Press

Thornton, Sara. 1995. *Club Cultures: Music, Media and Subcultural Capital.* Cambridge: Polity Press.

Tyyskä, V. 2001. *Long and Winding Road: Adolescents and Youth in Canada Today.* Canadian Scholars' Press.

Webber, Marlene. 1991. *Streetkids: The Tragedy of Canada's Runaways.* Toronto: University of Toronto Press.

White, Rob. 1999. *Australian Youth Subcultures: On the Margins and in the Mainstream.* Hobart: Australian Clearing House for Youth Studies.

Whitson, Dave, and Richard Gruneau. 1997. "The (Real) Inegrated Circus: Political Economy, Popular Culture and 'Major League' Sports." In Wallace Clement, ed., *Building on the New Political Economy,* 359–85. Montreal and Kingston: McGill-Queen's University Press.

Winterdyk, John, ed. 1996. *Issues and Perspective on Young Offenders in Canada.* Toronto: Harcourt Brace.

19 Finding Godot? Bringing Popular Culture into Canadian Political Economy

FUYUKI KURASAWA

"What do we do now?"
"Wait for Godot."
    Samuel Beckett

INTRODUCTION

Economy or culture? Such are the stark and highly misleading alternatives that still appear to present themselves to most scholars working in Canadian intellectual circles today. Though for distinct reasons to be addressed below, this condition echoes conditions found elsewhere in the Western world, where the fields of political economy and cultural studies have experienced an uneasy coexistence. Studied stances of mutual ignorance or suspicion have prevailed, the two parties turning their backs to each other or eyeing each other across meticulously tended fences behind which nominally distinct objects of analysis (capitalism and popular culture) are jealously guarded. Prejudices abound on rival sides, as unhelpful labels of crude materialism and textual idealism, of structuralism and voluntarism, of Marxism and postmodernism, have become common currency.[1]

It comes as no surprise, then, that popular culture has yet to feature prominently within the mainstream of Canadian political economy, despite the appearance of important studies of popular cultural industries in Canada – notably in the case of music (Berland 1991; Berland and Straw 1995; Straw 1993b, 1996; Wright 1991), film (Armatage et al. 1999; Dorland 1996; Madger 1993) and professional sports (Donnelly 1988; Gruneau and Whitson 1993; Whitson and Gruneau 1997).[2] Many commentators have already lamented this state of affairs, to the extent that it has now become well-trodden ground. In fact, a contribution to the previous incarnation of this collection declared, in a manner requiring neither revision nor qualification, that "almost all political economy perspectives have dealt with popular culture in a perfunctory way. There has been very little sustained analysis, and much of what exists is static and pessimistic and reduces matters of culture solely to economic and technological determinants" (Whitson and Gruneau 1997, 360)[3] Efforts to establish a dialogue across the divide have since been made, yet old habits die very hard indeed.

We thus find ourselves in a rather curious predicament. Since its revival three decades ago, Canadian political economy has demonstrated an exemplary capacity for openness and self-critique. A reflexive spirit of questioning and reinvention, born out of the approach's interdisciplinary origins, has enabled it to regularly incorporate several emerging intellectual currents and substantive developments. Undeniably, as earlier surveys of the field have demonstrated (Clement 1997a; Clement and Williams 1989; Jenson et al. 1993), this spirit of renewal has been one of the sources of Canadian political economy's continued vitality.[4] Yet popular culture continues to be a distant and infrequently visited land, for if few political economists would deny that capitalism is (among other things) a cultural process – and fewer still that modern culture is capitalist – how many place the complex, reciprocal structuring of capitalism and popular cultural forms at the centre of their analyses without reducing one to the other? Although not presuming to resolve such a problem, this chapter claims that the benefits of bringing popular culture into Canadian political economy are considerable. Critical interpretations of popular culture can not only complement but also enrich political economic understandings of social life. At the same time, an invitation to take a popular-culture turn should not be mistaken for a Trojan horse, a ruse aiming to subject political economy to the dominion of cultural studies. Quite clearly, the former cannot (and should not) jettison its specificity by being collapsed into the latter; the point, as some authors have already understood, is to actively seek out points of intersection that are likely to enlarge the traditional scope of political economy while side-stepping both economistic and culturalist reductionisms.

An antireductionist stance of the sort proposed here calls for a theoretical perspective positing a dialectical process of horizontal interpenetration and articulation between the economic and cultural spheres of social life, in contrast to the more commonly presumed vertical and unidirectional determination of culture by economy (e.g., in the base/superstructure model). Accordingly, Canadian political economists can avoid the tendency to treat popular culture as ideology, or, to be more precise, as an ideological veil or manifestation of more fundamental economic, political, or social relations. While always already interacting with other domains of social reality, cultural sites and actors do not simply reflect them, since popular culture mediates and shapes capitalism to the same extent that it is fashioned by it.[5] More generally, research in the human sciences can and should eschew the Scylla of economic determinism and the Charybdis of cultural fetishism – that is to say, a conceptualization of popular culture that presents it as operating independently of capitalist forces. By envisaging the mutual constitution of economy and culture, this chapter aims to contribute to nurturing the meeting ground between a more robustly materialist cultural studies and a more culturally attuned political economy.

Before doing so, however, I would like to revisit Canadian political economy's legacy in order to grasp how it has conventionally viewed popular culture. Three representations of the latter have prevailed: it has been viewed as a marginal object of analysis (best left to other fields of inquiry), a derivative reality (an epiphenomenon determined by capitalist logic or dominant groups), and an invading force (a transmitter of Americanization). The consequent marginalization of popular culture is sustained by a thematic triptych that, I claim in the first part of this chapter, is present at the core of Canadian political economy: dependency, authenticity, and commodification.

Aside from the theoretical claims above, I would argue that greater attention to popular culture can broaden Canadian political economy's understanding of transformation. For arguably, it is on and through the terrain of popular culture that the contradictions and struggles imbedded in capitalist society become most striking. Being a perpetually contested and dynamic reality, popular culture harbours certain forms of social creativity that are not wholly captive to what, paraphrasing Habermas, can be termed the colonization of the lifeworld by economic and administrative subsystems. Popular culture never exists outside capitalist dynamics as such, nor is it inherently and completely captured by them. Instead, it is most convincingly perceived as a field of power upon which multiple groups and forces act to accelerate, subvert, or partially escape from the tripartite condition of dependency, authenticity, and commodification. Thus, the second part of the chapter considers popular culture as a potential source of resistance and socio-political change by way of Canadian cinema and music as well as an emerging kind of activism known as "culture jamming."

This chapter is therefore intended to be simultaneously retrospective and prospective, for it seeks to identify the sources of the secondary status of popular culture within the discourse of Canadian

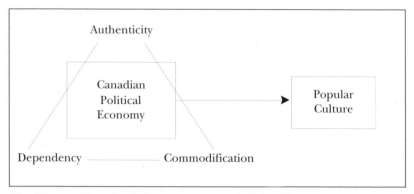

The Elision of Popular Culture in Canadian Political Economy

political economy, as well as a few reasons for and possibilities of engagement with the former as a site of transformation. Much like other intellectual endeavours, Canadian political economy can best renew itself by knowing from where it has come and by indicating some of the directions towards which it is heading.

THE CONSTITUTION OF A DIVIDE

Before the call to incorporate popular culture within Canadian political economy can be heeded, a question must be addressed: how and why did the divide between this field of knowledge and popular culture come to be constituted in the first place? Two general explanations can be brought to bear on such a query. The best-known line of argument underlines Canadian political economy's privileging of capitalist production over other spheres of social action – an implicit economism brought out by feminism a few decades ago (Luxton and Rosenberg 1986; Maroney and Luxton 1987). Another answer can be found in the tradition's macro-societal bias, which promotes analysis of social institutions (patriarchy, racism, and capitalism operating through the state, the factory, or the home) while neglecting micro-societal phenomena occurring through social interactions in everyday life. Nevertheless, above and beyond these two tendencies, popular culture's minor status for Canadian political economy can be attributed to the particularities of the human sciences' development in English Canada, the enduring legacy of which should be briefly discussed.

More precisely, as illustrated in the diagram, I would contend that Canadian political economists' casting of popular cultural forms of expression as inconsequential, derivative, or invasive has been brought about by the articulation of three themes shaping English Canadian discourses on culture that have already been mentioned: dependency, authenticity and commodification. At issue here is not whether such ideas are compelling or misleading in and of themselves but rather how they are affecting Canadian political economy's capacity and willingness to analyze popular culture as a potential site of transformative politics in contemporary society.

A Genealogy of Canadian Political Economy

Like much else in English Canadian intellectual life, the roots of the triptych of dependency, authenticity, and commodification can be traced back to Harold Innis. As is widely recognized, his early works in Canadian economic history pioneered the influential staples theory of economic growth. Writings such as the magisterial *Fur Trade in Canada* (1999 [1930]) identify dependency as the defining feature of Canadian economic development: the extraction and export of a series of primary resources (fish, fur, lumber, wheat, and minerals) determines how Canada, as a peripheral territory, is inserted within the networks of the British and American economic empires. According to Innis, the impetus for the expansion or contraction of different sectors, as well as for the transition from one staple product to another, is largely determined by the core's external dynamics. Thus, a historical situation of dependent development characterizes the Canadian economy, whose driving forces have always been located beyond its own borders (Innis 1999; Mahon 1993).

The theme of dependency provides the crucial link between Innis's earlier writings in Canadian economic history and his later interest in communication. Whether in the area of goods or information, Innis highlights the asymmetrical structure of transnational socioeconomic flows. By contrast to the liberal conception of the market as a neutral plane of exchange, Canadian culture is a space defined by its reliance upon and colonization by the American empire (Berland 1995; Innis 1952). Innis's neglect of popular culture can be seen to result directly from his highly original thesis – namely, that the stability of a civilization requires an equilibrium between spatial and temporal means of communication. Popular culture constitutes both the principal cause and the effect of three key trends viewed with suspicion in his writings. In the first instance, because it expresses a marked preference for "new" audio-visual media (television, radio, and so on), modern civilization contains a clear spatial bias privileging geographical scope over historical depth. As Innis would see it, this countertemporality is geared toward the ephemeral and superficial rather than the continuous and essential; tradition, the lynchpin of national authenticity, is thereby eroded. Second, Innis contends that audio-visual media are animated by centripetal forces that, buoyed by broadcasting technology, promote centralization (even monopolization) of the means of communication. Finally, his later work also laments rampant commercialism, especially evident in the increasing reliance on entertainment and advertising in the public domain. Popular culture epitomizes the confluence of all three of these developments for Innis, who thereby identifies it as an utterly nefarious outgrowth of *Pax Americana*. In addition to perpetuating and consolidating Canada's subordination, popular culture's assimilationist logic erodes the "authentic" European roots of Canadian high culture (Innis 1951, 33, 60, 64, 82–7; 1952, 2; 1972, 169–70).[6]

Another pivotal figure in the split between political economy and popular culture in Canada is Marshall McLuhan, whose thinking provides an interesting contrast to that of Innis. McLuhan's gradual distancing from his predecessor's theories of communication mirrors the eventual marginalization of political economy in his own writings and, consequently, the culturalist thrust of much of his later work. McLuhan's earliest book, *The Mechanical Bride* (1951), represents a rich, quasi-semiotic critique of American print advertising.[7] Specifically, the book scrutinizes the manipulation of the public's emotional and psychic needs in order to promote corporate interests as well as the sale of goods and services. Like Innis, McLuhan identifies American popular culture with popular culture tout court, yet his study does establish some of the bases for a political economy of communication. Unfortunately, this connection is severed in his subsequent (and much more widely read) work, where the fusion of technology and communication generates an increasingly metaphysical prophetism open to recuperation by the forces he describes. Political economy eventually becomes a noticeable blind spot in McLuhan's framework, whose critical thrust is correspondingly blunted (Kroker 1984, 79–82; McLuhan 1962, 1964). Further, his stance inadvertently sidelines popular culture, which is treated as a passive container or by-product of the process of technologically mediated communication rather than an object of study with noncommunicative dimensions – that is to say, where the communicative dimension is formed by social actors evolving in the arena of popular culture. McLuhan's famed declaration that "the medium is the message" (1964, 23–35) is emblematic of this problem: what becomes determinant is not the content of the communicative act but the technological media through and by which it is carried. Popular cultural forms of expression are thereby reduced to the role of receptacles for the circuits of information that fill them.

Aside from Innis and McLuhan, George Grant represents the other *éminence grise* whose reflections on the triumvirate formed by dependency, authenticity, and commodification have most influenced Canadian political economy's neglect of popular culture. Heavily indebted to Heidegger's (1993 [1954]) warning about the "enframing" essence of technology, Grant's critique of "technological civilization" is powerfully combined with his argument about the loss of Canadian national sovereignty vis-à-vis the United States. Grant thereby considers technology to be the vehicle through which the invasion of modernizing and homogenizing processes that are undermining the distinctive fabric of the Canadian nation-state and people can occur (1969, 63–9, 1982 [1965]). From such premises follow Grant's disregard for popular culture, which he believes to symbolize Americanism, technological rationality, and unbridled commercialism – in other words, the very tendencies working to erode all traces of an indigenous, European-based civilization in Canada. Popular cultural forms constitute the negation of Arnoldian "sweetness and light" (Arnold 1932), appealing instead to the lowest common denominator and destroying the authenticity of Canadian traditions by blunting the possibility of a distinctive collective memory and imaginary.

Grant's writings are perhaps the most eloquent expression of a wider current of English Canadian cultural nationalism, which has itself contributed to the peripheral status of popular culture within the field of Canadian political economy. Whether of a more conservative or progressive bent – the two tendencies uneasily allied in Red Toryism – cultural nationalists have argued that the protection and promotion of an authentic, independent Canadian culture is imperative in light of the ongoing threat of Americanization. The enormously influential Massey Report, one of the urtexts of postwar cultural nationalism, famously tied the country's survival to its sovereignty in matters of culture:

The American invasion by film, radio and periodical is formidable ... [A] vast and disproportionate amount of material coming from a single alien source may stifle rather than stimulate our own creative effort; and, passively accepted without any standard of comparison, this may weaken critical faculties. We are now spending millions to maintain a national independence which would be nothing but an empty shell without a vigorous and distinctive cultural life. We have seen that we have its elements in our traditions and in our history; we have made important progress, often aided by American

generosity. We must not be blind, however, to the very present danger of permanent dependence. (Royal Commission 1951, 18)[8]

I would contend that cultural nationalism has developed three distinctive positions vis-à-vis Canadian popular culture, all of them producing a distinct ambivalence toward the latter. In the first instance,
popular cultural forms in Canada are implicitly equated with or
believed to be irredeemably absorbed, penetrated, and contaminated
by a more powerful, commodified, and lowbrow American mass
culture.[9] Consequently, Canadian popular culture is considered
tainted by Americanism and commercialism, which are themselves
perceived to be viral forces against which "we" must be immunized
(Angus 1997, 38; Gruneau 1988, 13–6; Gruneau and Whitson 1993,
23–5). To this extent, cultural nationalists strive to secure the distinctiveness of Canadian identity by appealing to highbrow culture, which
is assumed to be less vulnerable to the seductions of the greenback
than its lower variants; one thinks here of the arts and letters, the work
of Emily Carr or Jean-Paul Riopelle, of Émile Nelligan or Margaret
Atwood.

Second, given that Americanization is perceived to be predominantly an urban phenomenon – most particularly one affecting cities
in close proximity to the forty-ninth parallel – a Romantic strand of
cultural nationalism locates the heart and soul of the nation in a
mythologized ruralism (McKay 1994). Regionalism and the Great
North are seen as the repositories of an authentic Canadianness, the
sources of truly distinctive popular cultural forms rooted in places
that the American behemoth has not yet conquered or indeed where
it has forgotten to tread (Crean 1976). The third stance is what Angus
(1997, 38–9) has termed English-Canadian nationalism's cultural-
policy discourse, whereby popular culture is reduced to state-sponsored cultural industries. Accordingly, the problem of the former's
paucity or weakness is resolved through the formulation of public
policy with a corporatist intent. Whether it be in television, radio,
music, cinema, or publishing, popular culture becomes a matter of
industrial production, to be simultaneously stimulated and protected
by public infrastructure as well as state regulations and incentives
(public broadcasting, tax shelters, Canadian-content rules, and so
on).

Undeniably, each of cultural nationalism's three positions has
advanced valid points about American control and ownership of
English Canadian popular culture and about the richness and depth
of regional cultures, as well as the importance of public funding of
national cultural institutions. At the same time, cultural nationalists

have been less successful in engaging with the complex realities of contemporary Canadian popular culture, whose varied expressions interact with the phenomena of Americanization and commodification without ever being reducible to them. Further, the multicultural and urban dynamics fuelling the diversity and multiplication of popular cultures in Canada defy any pastoral longing for a singular, authentic, or stable identity. Having been present since the dawn of the national imagined community, the visions created by Aboriginals, francophone Québécois, and people of colour resist being synthesized into a central essence of Canadianness. By contrast, escaping convenient categorizations bounded by the nation-state, the interplay of sameness and difference is currently redefining Canadian popular culture in relation to the forces of the market and those of the American empire (Gruneau 1988, 15–16; Manning 1993, 28; Walcott 1997, 53–69).

The Political Economy of Popular Culture

Regardless of how prevalent cultural nationalism's three stances have been, the problem for Canadian political economy is made even more daunting by the fact that its analyses of popular culture have, for the most part, been predisposed to adopt an economistic logic. What lurks behind such work is an implicit base/superstructure model, which represents cultural activity as derived from or entirely determined by supposedly more fundamental dynamics shaped by capitalist relations and forces of production. Needless to say, crude versions of materialism strip the domain of culture of any sort or degree of independence vis-à-vis the political and economic spheres of Canadian society. In addition, Canadian political economists have been inclined to adopt an instrumentalist vision of popular culture. For instance, John Porter's and Wallace Clement's social stratification approach has highlighted the high degree of concentration of media control and ownership, as well as the significant overlap between media and socioeconomic elites in the country (Clement 1975, 270–343; Porter 1965, 457–90).[10] In such analyses, the mass media is portrayed as a mere ideological tool functioning to promote the interests and worldviews of elite groups.

   Political-economic studies of particular cultural sectors (film, media, and so forth) have also shown themselves prone to instrumentalism. Popular culture becomes what Dallas Smythe (1982) tellingly terms a "consciousness industry," a set of ideological institutions supporting American imperialism and capitalism by manipulating or distracting the "masses." Together, foreign domination and the functional requirements of profit-generation seal the fate of popular culture in Canada, which must by its very nature serve to perpetuate the reproduction of unequal domestic and continental structures of power (Pendakur 1990; Smythe 1982). Hence, like economism, instrumentalism denies Canadian popular culture its own raison d'être in relation to exogenous social processes.[11]

Canadian Popular Culture and the Possibilities of Resistance

In the previous section I argued that despite its many insights, the thematic triad of dependency, authenticity and commodification has been responsible for Canadian political economy's peripheralization of popular culture. The failure to acknowledge the reciprocal constitution of economic and cultural domains has been compounded by a reluctance to consider popular culture as a potential site of resistance to and transformation of the processes embodied in this triad. Nevertheless, an alternative vision of popular culture can be advanced by incorporating a newer body of scholarship found at the crossroads of Canadian political economy and cultural studies, as well as by underlining emerging practices and possibilities taking shape within contemporary social life.

The Globalization of Canadian Cinema and Music

The familiar narrative of Canadian film history is one of precarious survival in the shadow of Hollywood, a survival largely made possible by public policies and the creation of institutions such as the National Film Board of Canada, as well as by the establishment of provincial and federal funding bodies (e.g., Telefilm Canada, the Société générale du cinéma, and the Canada Council). Thus, direct and indirect state involvement has been aimed at sustaining a viable domestic cinematic industry that, though not directly competing with its American counterpart, could at least reflect some of the specificities of Canadian identity (Adams 2002; Madger 1989, 1993; Dorland 1998). Conventionally, filmmaking has followed one of two mutually exclusive and competing trajectories, in accordance with a high/low cultural divide: the production of films that may have attempted to reflect the Canadian experience, yet had little commercial ambition or success (for instance, the distinguished tradition of documentary excellence); and the production of highly formulaic, generic, or derivative movies aimed squarely at the American market (e.g., a rash of eminently forgettable, commercial English Canadian films produced in the late

1970s and early 1980s). Well captured by the Hollywood North label, the latter trend has seen a substantial proportion of the domestic film industry absorbed by or integrated into the U.S. studio system.[12]

While not completely overturning the fundamentals outlined above, a few notable trends within the Canadian film industry have recently destabilized the rigid opposition between authenticity and commercialism (or, put differently, between highbrow art and lowbrow entertainment). On the one hand, as the Hollywood North moniker implies, Canada has become an increasingly popular location for shooting American blockbusters, because of its comparatively low production costs, geographical proximity, and plentiful pools of skilled labour. Almost always serving as stand-ins or substitutes for a specific or generic U.S. city, Toronto, Montreal and Vancouver are frequently used as backdrops for such films. Any local or national distinctiveness must be purged, and any trace of Canadianness must be erased or masked to protect the illusion of American authenticity. In this scenario, Canada becomes a simulacrum of its Southern neighbour, an empty signifier with an American referent, or even a virtual America.

On the other hand, the globalization of Canadian cinema has fostered more promising developments. International circuits of film financing and distribution are enabling Canadian filmmakers to establish certain collaborative ventures with partners not wholly captive to the Hollywood studio system. For instance, organizations such as Canal + (France) and Channel Four Films (Great Britain) have opened the way to interesting possibilities that, though still embryonic and modest, could not even have been contemplated a generation ago. The Canadian film festival circuit has become an important venue for the screening of domestic movies while serving as a market for international distributors. At the same time, following in the footsteps of a pioneer like Claude Jutra, the national and global visibility of Canadian cinema has been bolstered by the critical acclaim (and the modest commercial success) of the works of established directors such as Denys Arcand, Patricia Rozema, François Girard, and Atom Egoyan, as well as those of a group of young francophone Québécois filmmakers (e.g., Denis Villeneuve, Philippe Falardeau, and André Turpin) dubbed part of the French New Wave by the English-Canadian media, in homage to their postwar Parisian colleagues (Tremblay 2002). Most importantly, a critical mass of creative talent is thereby taking root.

The growing cultural syncretism of domestic films must also be taken into consideration. In the past decade or so, a number of movies (Clement Virgo's *Love Come Down*, Deepa Mehta's *Bollywood/Hollywood*, and Mina Shum's *Double Happiness*, for instance) have begun exploring the pluralism of a contemporary Canadian identity informed by transnational cultural flows (Banning 1999; Walcott 1997, 53–69). What might have previously appeared as the overwhelming dominance of American popular culture is now being moderated by the diasporic reinvention of Canadian society – a diaspora reflected in such cinematic works. Like other cultural influences from the Caribbean, Africa, Asia, and South America, Americanization is filtered, reinterpreted, and ultimately "nativized" in a creolized national imaginary (Manning 1993). Obviously, this is not to disavow the continued fragility of a Canadian film industry living in the shadow of the Hollywood juggernaut. Nor is it intended to hold up existing instances of more multiculturally astute movies as paragons of critical, cross-cultural pluralism.[13] Nevertheless, what recent scholarship suggests is the burgeoning of a space of pluralism and partial openness where the iron grip of dependency, authenticity, and commodification is complicated by and through popular culture. Madger's (1993, 250) apt conclusion to his study of the Canadian cinematic industry goes in the same direction: "We have to stop the search for some romantic and overarching common cultural bond. Instead, we need public support for cultural production to explore the manifold and contradictory ways in which we exist as social beings in our everyday lives. Against all odds, the best of Canadian cinema has done just that."

Similar transformations are affecting the Canadian popular music industry. Obviously, the conventional flow of Canadian bands and singers south of the border, emblematized in the 1960s by the American absorption of the Yorkville folk scene (Neil Young, Joni Mitchell, and others), continues virtually unabated today; one need only think of the phenomenal commercial success of a string of female singers in the past decade (e.g., Céline Dion, Sarah McLachlan, Alanis Morissette, Nelly Furtado, and Shania Twain). The Canadianness of these performers is open for debate, for their rebranding commonly involves a delocalization that converts them into generic products saleable on u.s. and international markets. Given that such acts frequently by-pass the Canadian subsidiaries of major music labels to sign directly with their American head offices, the dominance of multinational music corporations is merely reinforced (Berland and Straw 1995, 341; Brown 1991).

On the other hand, a series of interesting developments are taking place at the edges of the commercial music industry. The mainstreaming of alternative music (or, interpreted differently, the fragmentation and collapse of the mainstream sound) has enabled a number of independent Canadian musicians to find larger audiences both domestically and overseas. Internet technology has also opened up distribution channels that may by-pass the major labels' heavily centralized and hierarchical systems. And finally, authenticity has been dealt a serious blow by the creolization of forms of music created elsewhere, yet whose meaning and uses have been reinscribed by Canadian artists. For instance, the Montreal-based group Loco Locass, whose *Manifestif* CD was released in 2000, self-consciously uses rap – a form of creative protest invented by inner-city African-American youths – to defend and promote the French language in Quebec. Probably best emblematized by Ashley MacIsaac, the so-called East Coast sound has reinvented the Maritimes' Celtic musical heritage by crossing it with grunge and hip hop; the fiddle, the sampler, and the electric guitar have met in a manner that confounds the apparent divide between tradition and modernity. Another fascinating case in point is bhangra, a hybrid musical style that combines Punjabi folk music with reggae, hip hop and techno. With cities in the United Kingdom, Toronto and Vancouver have become its global epicentres.

Culture Jamming: Resisting Commodification

If contemporary Canadian cinema and music have begun to reflect a more diverse, syncretic civil society, new forms of transformational politics have crystallized in and around the sphere of consumption. Like other fields of academic knowledge, Canadian political economy has lagged behind such developments; it has not been long since Veblen's trail-blazing *Theory of the Leisure Class* was rediscovered and elaborated upon to formulate the underpinnings of a cultural and economic sociology of consumption (Baudrillard 1970; Bourdieu 1984; Ritzer 1999; Slater 1997). Additionally, political economy's productivist bias has prevented it from considering how struggles around consumptive issues regularly spark wider challenges to the capitalist social order. Best captured by the phrase "culture jamming," an innovative form of anticonsumerist activism that skilfully employs popular culture has emerged as a privileged site of resistance.

In effect, culture jamming strives to disrupt the smooth, highly aestheticized flow of consumerist images, so as to provoke a reaction against it and broaden both the meaning of and the possibilities for human existence. Thus, its theoretical discourse is a heady and eclectic mix of, *inter alia*, McLuhan, Guy Debord, Roland Barthes, E.F. Schumacher, and Herbert Marcuse. Kalle Lasn, founding editor of Vancouver-based *Adbusters* – the flagship magazine of this movement – does not mince words:

We're a loose global network of media activists who see ourselves as advance shock troops of the most significant social movement of the next twenty years.

Our aim is to topple existing power structures and forge major adjustments to the way we live in the twenty-first century. We believe culture jamming will become to our era what civil rights was to the '60s, what feminism was to the '70s, what environmental activism was to the '80s. It will alter the way we live and think. It will change the way information flows, the way institutions wield power, the way TV stations are run, the way the food, fashion, automobile, sports, music and culture industries set their agendas. Above all, it will change the way we interact with the mass media and the way in which meaning is produced in our society. (Lasn 1999, xi)

These lofty aims are geared towards putting into question the corporate control and ownership of the productive apparatus through a politicization of everyday consumptive activities and, in turn, a struggle against the commercial monopolization of the means of communication. Because it represents the most pervasive manifestation of the latter phenomenon, advertising has been one of the preferred targets of culture jammers.[14] Hence, subversion of the profoundly commodified culture of late capitalist North America has constituted anticonsumerism's preferred modus operandi. From the simple defacing of billboards to the inversion of their intended message by way of cut-and-paste editing, from "subvertisements" parodying a brand's image and slogans to "uncommercials" promoting anticonsumerist causes (such as Buy Nothing Day), the objective has been similar: to turn commodification against itself. Ironic pseudo-mimesis thereby strives to corrupt the intended meaning of commercial messages and images by revealing the absurdity or less palatable facts connected to the products they promote (e.g., fashion and anorexia, smoking and cancer, running shoes and sweatshop labour). In this manner, the original relationship between signifier and signified, a relationship upon which branding depends for its effectiveness, is disrupted; one is confronted not with the aestheticized lifestyles portrayed in advertising but rather with the actual human and environmental consequences of capitalist production and consumption (Klein 2000, 279–309; Lasn 1999). Mediatized guerrilla warfare is thus put to use to counter the public sphere's commercialization. Borrowing Debord's (1992 [1967]) situationist language, one could describe this kind of activism as a series of *détournements* interrupting the incessant spectacularization of capitalist society, the commodified re-presentation of all that surrounds us.

Having dealt with the theme of commodification, I would like to briefly discuss how culture jamming enables us to reconceptualize the notions of dependency and authenticity. The Media Foundation, one of the nerve-centres of culture jamming and the publisher of *Adbusters*, may be located in Vancouver, yet it does not preoccupy itself with questions of Canadian economic sovereignty or national identity per se. Mimicking the spread of popular culture itself, a deterritorialized and decentralized network of culture jammers has come to personify the Think globally, act locally slogan. If anything, then, the Media Foundation's situation of geographical in-betweenness – on the edge yet not completely of the American empire – is perceived as a perspectival and strategic advantage. Nonetheless, culture jamming is far from being blind to the corrosive effects of Americanization: it reserves its most stinging critiques for the "American way of life," that bloated and profoundly anomic lifestyle peddled by u.s.-based corporations and media conglomerates around the world (Lasn 1999, xii–xiv, 59–71). Thus, rather than the territorial imperialism of a specific nation-state, what is denounced is the homogenization and commodification of popular cultures by global, albeit American-led, consumer capitalism. Accordingly, culture jamming conceives of authenticity not as a matter of national essence but as a sense of "real" existence drawing from one's belonging to and participation in despectacularized and decommodified communities.

Why have anticonsumerist politics captured the imagination of a newer generation of radical activists? While the question has been extensively tackled in Naomi Klein's celebrated *No Logo* (2000), it should be considered here in light of its implications for Canadian political economy's understanding of transformative sociopolitical action. I would contend that culture jamming represents an experiential outgrowth of contemporary life in North American societies, which are thoroughly saturated by the logic, aesthetics, and, increasingly, the ethics of rampant commercialism. And although a great deal of hyperbole surrounds the claim of a recent shift from production to consumption as the primary site for the formation of identity, it nevertheless remains the case that consumptive activities have become prominent as forces of socialization and modes of cultural expression today. Indeed, given the rise of part-time and precarious employment in the lower rungs of the tertiary sector (retail, fast food, and so on), one can argue that even in the workplace, productive labour appears to merely serve and be subsumed under consumption. If individuals view themselves more and more as consumers, the manifestations of their political subjectivities cannot but follow suit. And yet, *contra* older models oriented toward the creation of consumer rights groups and protection agencies, culture jamming rejects the very premises of consumerist society – namely, the indecently crass belief in correlating purchasing power and personal happiness, to say nothing of the faith in the line of direct causation between them.

Furthermore, culture jamming constitutes a significant process of political empowerment, enabling this newer generation to partially redefine their sociocultural surroundings by contesting the incessant commodification of public space. Rebelling against the roles of passive spectators and loyal brand followers foisted upon them by capital, anti-consumerist activists have become political actors able to mobilize and capitalize upon their own experiences as targets of the incessant barrage of corporate images and messages. Weaned at the bosom of late capitalism, its children have learnt their lessons well; now media-savvy and brand-conscious because possessing high levels of popular cultural capital, they decode, criticize, and invert the meaning of marketing and advertising campaigns, while using their representational devices, techniques, and products against corporate behemoths. Hence the potency and significance of subversion of this kind, which appropriates the means of the capitalist market yet diverts them towards the realization of opposite ends.

None of this is to claim that culture jamming is a panacea for radical politics in the twenty-first century. By trying to beat commodification at its own game, activists may unwittingly be captured by it, since subversive strategies always risk being recuperated by the existing social order. Indeed, one of the keys to capitalism's resilience remains its daunting capacity for cannibalistic cooptation, that is, for blunting the cutting edge of critical social movements, incorporating them within itself, and ultimately recommodifying them as extensions of its ubiquitous logic.[15] How, then, does anticonsumerism avoid becoming yet another brand, made all the more commercially appealing by its rebellious image? At least two directions can be imagined. On the one hand, culture jamming can retain its role as a political avant-garde that, through constant strategic movement, attempts to invent new lines of flight from the grasp of global capital or to remain a subcultural gadfly living within the belly of the corporate beast. On the other hand, it can strive to convert anticonsumerism into a more affirmative politics of transformation that, in addition to reinscribing the meaning of existing corporate marketing and advertising campaigns, can sustain public discussion of alternative sets of practices and modes of thinking. For the latter scenario to be realized, culture jamming's anarcho-environmentalist ethos will need to be more explicitly articulated to and developed in the direction of broadly based struggles for social justice and economic redistribution at home and abroad. Therefore, the challenge ahead consists of spearheading an effective counterhegemonic formation composed of decentred and plural networks of social movements advancing a progressive vision of the good society.

CONCLUSION

At the dawn of the twenty-first century, popular culture still remains a vast and relatively unexplored territory for Canadian political economy. The foundations and subsequent elaborations of this tradition may have yielded tremendously insightful studies of Canadian society, but the persistent preoccupation with dependency, authenticity, and commodification has produced three stock interpretations of Canadian popular culture: as a peripheral entity outside the scope of political economy, as a derivative ideological reality whose internal processes are dictated by economic necessities, and as an invading American juggernaut sweeping away or contaminating the Canadian body social. None of these depictions is likely to make popular cultural manifestations hubs of Canadian political economy's preoccupations or to prompt us to examine them as complex entities through which processes of domination and resistance unfold. Cinema, music, and culture jamming are but three instances of the dynamism, ambiguity, and significance of popular culture for theorizing social transformation today.

Bringing popular culture into Canadian political economy does not demand that the edifice upon which the human sciences have been constructed in this country be abandoned but rather that this edifice be revised in light of a cultural materialism that analytically entwines culture and economy. Moreover, as an expanding literature in Canadian cultural studies demonstrates, the renewed interest in popular culture can partly be accommodated by engaging with other fields of knowledge. For the purposes of future research, I would suggest that three distinctive traditions of thought are particularly suggestive: the cultural wing of the Frankfurt School, notably Walter Benjamin's (1973, 1978; Buck-Morss 1989) and Siegfried Kracauer's (1947, 1998) analyses of daily life in Weimar Germany and interwar Paris; the Birmingham School of cultural studies, whose progenitors and subsequent practitioners have demonstrated how and why popular cultural expressions should be taken seriously;[16] and, finally, a French brand of cultural sociology loosely connecting authors such as Henri Lefebvre (1968, 1991) and Pierre Bourdieu (1984), who have excelled at pointing out how the apparently mundane aspects of social life are simultaneously a reflection of and influence upon forms of power in capitalist society.

Exploring and applying the perspectives of other schools of thought can only act as a prelude to what still remains to be done. I have argued that it is time for Canadian political economy to embark upon a popular cultural turn, to investigate what Marshall Berman (1999) lyrically calls "the signs in the street" through which the social world is being transformed before our very eyes. Yet it should hastily be added that the search for an alternative view of popular culture should not be confounded with a pseudo-populist idealization of all its forms of expression, which would be misleadingly portrayed as inherent moments of total refusal of the existing social order. Instead, I have suggested that popular culture be more productively viewed as a contested terrain that is neither immune to the dynamics of commodification and domination nor completely captured by them. It offers potential resources and spaces for individual and collective creativity in the formation of a politics of resistance in everyday life.

Such a view of popular culture beckons towards a rethinking of Canadian political economy's conception of transformation. Indeed, in the Western world reflection on the horizons and aims of politics has been an ongoing process in the aftermath of May 1968 and in the midst of globalization. By now, the argument is familiar: political action does not always or even necessarily take place through formal parties in and around the institutional arena of the state, for civil society has become the privileged locale for social movements of all sorts. Moreover, a latent faith in the revolutionary model of sociopolitical change – itself based upon the ideals of a sudden, permanent, centralized and total overturning of the social order – has tended to blind many observers to other expressions of struggle within contemporary society. Today, transformation may just as likely stem from the proliferation of temporary, contingent, fluid, and multiple struggles being waged in response to the vast and ever more rapacious webs of global capitalism (Jameson 1991; Hardt and Negri 2000). Clearly, no pure outside exists in Canada vis-à-vis the realities of *Pax Americana* and socioeconomic globalization. Nevertheless, we should not abandon the task of reflecting upon how popular culture can enable individuals and communities to negotiate and redefine the realities of dependency, authenticity and commodification in surprising ways.[17] Rather than wait for Godot's interminable coming, we should create him ourselves. For those who know how and where to search, he is to be found in the cracks of ordinary life, dwelling in the most unexpected places.

NOTES

Research for this chapter has been made possible by an SSHRC Postdoctoral Fellowship (756-2000-0316). For their comments and suggestions, I would like to thank Wallace Clement, Janine Marchessault, Brian

Singer, Leah Vosko, Lorna Weir, and the anonymous reviewers for McGill-Queen's University Press.

1 For instance, see the polemical exchange between Garnham (1995) and Grossberg (1995) published in *Critical Studies in Mass Communication*. For an effort to reconcile the two paradigms, see Harp (1991).

2 For comprehensive overviews of the situation of various Canadian cultural industries, see Dorland (1996), Berland (1995), Davies (1995, 164–7), Morrow (1991) and Straw (1993a) provide accounts of the origins and development of the field of cultural studies in Canada. In Quebec intellectual circles, the situation is different in two respects. First, in part as a result of francophone Québécois' distinctive linguistic, political, and geographical situation, a sociology of culture incorporating analyses of popular cultural manifestations has existed as a major current of scholarship since the early works of Marcel Rioux and Fernand Dumont. Mostly due to the strength of such a cultural sociology, the Anglo-American wave of cultural studies has not been significantly felt in Quebec. For English-language overviews and commentaries on the francophone Québécois sociology of culture, see Dandurand (1989), Fournier (1987), Dorland and Kroker (1985), Morrow (1991, 155–6), Nielsen and Jackson (1991), and Weinstein (1985)

3 Angus (1997, 35) explains that "[t]his separation and opposition is by no means necessary, but it becomes unavoidable when political economy is interpreted reductionistically and culture is defined in opposition to economy." See also Gruneau (1988, 12–18), Magder (1989, 278), and Morrow (1991, 160).

4 "Feminism, environmentalism, and cultural studies have 'challenged' political economy over the past decade. Political economy has not repelled these challenges so much as it has been transformed by them, to become richer and more interdisciplinary" (Clement 1997a, 16).

5 Hence, it is not a matter of the Althusserian moment of over-determination (guarded by the famed "in the last instance" caveat) but of an ongoing process of mutual determination in every instance.

6 The highbrow, or elitist, bias of Innis's conception of culture has been noted by Berland (1995) and Madger (1997, 341).

7 Semiotics can be defined as the study of signs and sign-systems produced in and through communication; some of its better-known practitioners include Roland Barthes and Umberto Eco. While McLuhan never explicitly subscribed to semiotics, his early work reveals commonalities with it to the extent that he treats advertising slogans and products as signs to be decoded and given meaning.

8 On the continuing significance of the Massey Report, see, inter alia, Taylor (2002), Magder (1993, 248), and Berland (1995, 515–17). On English Canadian cultural nationalism and identity, see Atwood (1972),

Crean (1976), Frye (1971), Innis (1952), Lumsden (1970), and more
recently, Saul (1997). For a stimulating collaboration combining
English-Canadian and Quebec nationalisms, see Crean and Rioux
(1983). The most profound meditation on the roots and prospects
for a progressive English Canadian postnationalism is found in Angus
(1997).

9   The viral and masculinist metaphors are deliberate here, since
Canadian culture is often portrayed as a vulnerable, female body
requiring protection from a masculine American aggressor (Berland
1995, 522–4).

10 The categorization of Porter's and Clement's work as instrumentalist is
found in Hackett (1988, 84) and Magder (1989, 284).

11 McKay's (1994) rich study of the invented tradition of the folk motif in
Nova Scotia over the course of the twentieth century stands as an exception to this instrumentalist tradition. The concept of the folk is shown to
have been produced at the intersections of popular culture and political
economy, without reducing the former to an appendage of the latter.

12 Most commonly, Canadian actors and directors have elected to take a
third route, namely to move to Hollywood in order to pursue their
careers. Discussion of such a trend would take us beyond the scope of
this chapter.

13 Indeed, Virgo's and Shum's films tend to rely too readily on self/Other
binaries juxtaposing "mainstream" (and modern) Canadian culture to
"minoritarian" (and traditional) non-Western cultures.

14 For critical interpretations of advertising, see Leiss et al. (1997) and
Williams (1980).

15 For instance, *Adbusters* temporarily ceased publishing "subvertisements,"
which were believed to have lost their critical function. Recently, a video
game entitled "State of Emergency" was released for the Sony Playstation
2; players must use characters who are members of the so-called
Freedom Movement to violently combat the iron grip of The Corporation over a fictional Capitol City (MacDonald 2002). On the paradoxes
and dangers of the cooptation of anticonsumerism more generally, see
Klein (2000, 296–302).

16 The Birmingham School's British ancestry goes back to Richard Hoggart
(1957), E.P. Thompson (1980), and Raymond Williams (1958). Stuart
Hall is its most influential founding figure, whereas Paul Gilroy (1993a,
b; 2000) is among the most interesting contemporary thinkers to have
emerged from it. On Hall's work and legacy, see Morley and Chen
(1996).

17 For discussion of numerous instances of popular resistance in the
Maritimes, see McKay and Milsom (1992).

REFERENCES

Adams, James. 2002. "The Greatest Movies You've Probably Never Seen." *Globe and Mail*, 2 February 2, R1, 8.

Angus, Ian. 1997. *A Border Within: National Identity, Cultural Plurality, and Wilderness*. Montreal and Kingston: McGill-Queen's University Press.

Armatage, Kay, Kass Banning, Brenda Longfellow, and Janine Marchessault, eds. 1999. *Gendering the Nation: Canadian Women's Cinema*. Toronto: University of Toronto Press.

Arnold, Matthew. 1932. *Culture and Anarchy*. Cambridge: Cambridge University Press.

Atwood, Margaret. 1972. *Survival: A Thematic Guide to Canadian Literature*. Toronto: Anansi.

Banning, Kass. 1999. "Playing in the Light: Canadianizing Race and Nation." In Kay Armatage, Kass Banning, Brenda Longfellow, and Janine Marchessault, eds., *Gendering the Nation: Canadian Women's Cinema*, 291–310. Toronto: University of Toronto Press.

Baudrillard, Jean. 1970. *La société de consommation*. Paris: Denoël.

Benjamin, Walter. [1955] 1973. *Illuminations*. Hannah Arendt, ed.; Harry Zohn, trans. London: Fontana.

– [1955] 1978. *Reflections*. Peter Demetz, ed.; Edmund Jephcott, trans. New York: Shocken.

Berland, Jody. 1991. "Free Trade and Canadian Music: Level Playing Field or Scorched Earth?" *Cultural Studies* 5(3): 317–25.

– 1995. "Marginal Notes on Cultural Studies in Canada." *University of Toronto Quarterly* 64(4): 514–25.

Berland, Jody, and Will Straw. 1995. "Getting Down to Business: Cultural Politics and Policies in Canada." In Benjamin D. Singer, ed. *Communications in Canadian Society*, 332–56. Toronto: Nelson Canada.

Berman, Marshall. [1984] 1999. "The Signs in the Street." In *Adventures in Marxism*. London: Verso.

Bourdieu, Pierre. [1979] 1984. *Distinction: A Social Critique of the Judgement of Taste*. Cambridge, MA: Harvard University Press.

Brown, Laurie. 1991. "Songs from the Bush Garden." *Cultural Studies* 5(3): 347–57.

Buck-Morss, Susan. 1989. *The Dialectics of Seeing: Walter Benjamin and the Arcades Project*. Cambridge, MA: MIT Press.

Clement, Wallace. 1975. *The Canadian Corporate Elite: An Analysis of Economic Power*. Toronto: McClelland and Stewart.

– 1997a. "Introduction: Whither the New Canadian Political Economy?" In Wallace Clement, ed., *Understanding Canada: Building on the New Canadian Political Economy*, 3-18. Montreal and Kingston: McGill-Queen's University Press.

– ed. 1997b. *Understanding Canada: Building on the New Canadian Political Economy*. Montreal and Kingston: McGill-Queen's University Press.

Clement, Wallace, and Glen Williams, eds. 1989. *The New Canadian Political Economy*. Montreal and Kingston: McGill-Queen's University Press.

Crean, S.M. 1976. *Who's Afraid of Canadian Culture?* Don Mills, ON: General Publishing.

Crean, Susan, and Marcel Rioux. 1983. *Two Nations*. Toronto: Lorimer.

Dandurand, Renée B. 1989. "Fortunes and Misfortunes of Culture: Sociology and Anthropology of Culture in Francophone Quebec, 1965–1985." *Canadian Review of Sociology and Anthropology* 26(3): 485–532.

Davies, Ioan. 1995. *Cultural Studies and Beyond: Fragments of Empire*. London and New York: Routledge.

Debord, Guy. [1967] 1992. *La société du spectacle*. Paris: Gallimard.

Donnelly, Peter. 1988. "Sport as a Site for 'Popular' Resistance." In Richard Gruneau, ed., *Popular Cultures and Political Practices*, 69–82. Toronto: Garamond.

Dorland, Michael, ed. 1996. *The Cultural Industries in Canada: Problems, Policies and Prospects*. Toronto: Lorimer.

– 1998. *So Close to the State/s: The Emergence of Canadian Feature Film Policy*. Toronto: University of Toronto Press.

Dorland, Michael, and Arthur Kroker. 1985. "Introduction: Culture Critique and New Quebec Sociology." In Michael A. Weistein, ed., *Culture Critique: Fernand Dumont and New Quebec Sociology*, 7–37. Montreal: New World Perspectives.

Fournier, Marcel. 1987. "Culture et politique du Québec." *Canadian Journal of Sociology* 12(1–2): 64–82.

Frye, Northrop. 1971. *The Bush Garden: Essays on the Canadian Imagination*. Toronto: Anansi.

Garnham, Nicholas. 1995. "Political Economy and Cultural Studies: Reconciliation or Divorce?" *Critical Studies in Mass Communication* 12(1): 62–71.

Gilroy, Paul. 1993a. *Small Acts: Thoughts on the Politics of Black Cultures*. London: Serpents Tail.

– 1993b. *The Black Atlantic: Modernity and Double Consciousness*. Cambridge, MA: Harvard University Press.

– 2000. *Between Camps: Nations, Culture and the Allure of Race*. Harmondsworth, England: Penguin.

Grant, George. [1965] 1982. *Lament for a Nation: The Defeat of Canadian Nationalism*. Ottawa: Carleton University Press.

– 1969. *Technology and Empire*. Toronto: Anansi.

Grossberg, Lawrence. 1995. "Cultural Studies vs. Political Economy: Is Anybody Else Bored with this Debate?" *Critical Studies in Mass Communication* 12(1): 72–81.

Gruneau, Richard. 1988. "Introduction: Notes on Popular Culture and Political Practice." In Richard Gruneau, ed., *Popular Cultures and Political Practices*, 11–32. Toronto: Garamond.

Gruneau, Richard, and David Whitson. 1993. *Hockey Night in Canada: Sport, Identities and Cultural Politics*. Toronto: Garamond.

Hackett, Robert. 1988. "Remembering the Audience: Notes on Control, Ideology and Oppositional Strategies in the News Media." In Richard Gruneau, ed., *Popular Cultures and Political Practices*, 83–100. Toronto: Garamond.

Hardt, Michael, and Antonio Negri. 2000. *Empire*. Cambridge, MA: Harvard University Press.

Harp, John. 1991. "Political Economy/Cultural Studies: Exploring Points of Convergence." *Canadian Review of Sociology and Anthropology* 28(2): 206–24.

Heidegger, Martin. [1954] 1993. "The Question Concerning Technology." In David Farrell Krell, ed., *Basic Writings*, 311–41. 2d ed. New York: HarperCollins.

Hoggart, Richard. 1957. *The Uses of Literacy*. Harmondsworth, England: Penguin.

Innis, Harold A. [1930] 1999. *The Fur Trade in Canada*. Toronto: University of Toronto Press.

– [1950] 1972. *Empire and Communications*. Toronto: University of Toronto Press.

– 1951. *The Bias of Communication*. Toronto: University of Toronto Press.

– 1952. "The Strategy of Culture." In *Changing Concepts of Time*. Toronto: University of Toronto Press.

Jameson, Fredric. 1991. *Postmodernism, or, the Cultural Logic of Late Capitalism*. Durham, NC: Duke University Press.

Jenson, Jane, Rianne Mahon, and Manfred Bienefeld, eds. 1993. *Production, Space, Identity: Political Economy Faces the Twenty-first Century*. Toronto: Canadian Scholars' Press.

Klein, Naomi. 2000. *No Logo: Taking Aim at the Brand Bullies*. Toronto: Knopf Canada.

Kracauer, Siegfried. [1930] 1998. *The Salaried Masses: Duty and Distraction in Weimar Germany*. London: Verso.

– 1947. *From Caligary to Hitler: A Psychological History of the German Film*. Princeton, NJ: Princeton, University Press.

Kroker, Arthur. 1984. *Technology and the Canadian Mind: Innis/McLuhan/Grant*. Montreal: New World Perspectives.

Lasn, Kalle. 1999. *Culture Jam: The Uncooling of America*. New York: Morrow.

Lefebvre, Henri. [1947] 1991. *Critique of Everyday Life*. Vol. 1. John Moore, trans. London: Verso.

– 1968. *La vie quotidienne dans le monde moderne*. Paris: Gallimard.

Leiss, William, Stephan Kline, and Sut Jhally. 1997. *Social Communication in Advertising: Persons, Products and Images of Well-Being*. 2d ed. London and New York: Routledge.

Lumsden, Ian, ed. 1970. *Close the Forty-ninth Parallel etc.: The Americanization of Canada*. Toronto: University of Toronto Press.

Luxton, Meg, and Harriett Rosenberg, eds. 1986. *Through the Kitchen Window: The Politics of Home and Family*. Toronto: Garamond.

MacDonald, Gail. 2002. "Click Here to Smash Capitalism." *Globe and Mail*. 2 March, R5.

McKay, Ian. 1994. *The Quest of the Folk: Antimodernism and Cultural Selection in Twentieth-Century Nova Scotia*. Montreal and Kingston: McGill-Queen's University Press.

McKay, Ian, and Scott Milson, eds. 1992. *Toward a New Maritimes*. Charlottetown, PEI: Ragweed.

McLuhan, Marshall. 1951. *The Mechanical Bride: Folklore of Industrial Man*. New York: Vanguard Press.

– 1962. *The Gutenberg Galaxy: The Making of Typographic Man*. New York: New American Library.

– 1964. *Understanding Media: The Extensions of Man*. New York: New American Library.

Magder, Ted. 1989. "Taking Culture Seriously: A Political Economy of Communications." In Wallace Clement and Glen Williams, eds., *The New Canadian Political Economy*, 278–96. Montreal and Kingston: McGill-Queen's University Press.

– 1993. *Canada's Hollywood: The Canadian State and Feature Films*. Toronto: University of Toronto Press.

– 1997. "Public Discourse and the Structures of Communication." In Wallace Clement, ed., *Understanding Canada: Building on the New Canadian Political Economy*, 338–58. Montreal and Kingston: McGill-Queen's University Press.

Mahon, Rianne. 1993. "The 'New' Canadian Political Economy Revisited: Production, Space, Identity." In Jane Jenson, Rianne Mahon, and Manfred Bienefeld, eds., *Production, Space, Identity: Political Economy Faces the Twenty-first Century*, 1–21. Toronto: Canadian Scholars' Press.

Manning, Frank E. 1993. "Reversible Resistance: Canadian Popular Culture and the American Other." In David H. Flaherty and Frank E. Manning, eds., *The Beaver Bites Back? American Popular Culture in Canada*, 3–28. Montreal and Kingston: McGill-Queen's University Press.

Maroney, Heather Jon, and Meg Luxton, eds. 1987. *Feminism and Political Economy: Women's Work, Women's Struggles*. Toronto: Methuen.

Morley, David, and Kuan-Hsing Chen, eds. 1996. *Stuart Hall: Critical Dialogues in Cultural Studies*. London and New York: Routledge.

Morrow, Raymond A. 1991. "Introduction: The Challenge of Cultural Studies to Canadian Sociology and Anthropology." *Canadian Review of Sociology and Anthropology* 28(2): 153–72.

Nielsen, Greg M., and John D. Jackson. 1991. "Cultural Studies, a Sociological Poetics: Institutions of the Canadian Imaginary." *Canadian Review of Sociology and Anthropology* 28(2): 279–98.

Pendakur, Manjunath. 1990. *Canadian Dreams and American Control: The Political Economy of the Canadian Film Industry*. Detroit, MI: Wayne State University Press.

Porter, John. 1965. *The Vertical Mosaic: An Analysis of Social Class and Power in Canada*. Toronto: University of Toronto Press.

Ritzer, George. 1999. *Enchanting a Disenchanted World: Revolutionizing the Means of Consumption*. Thousand Oaks, CA: Pine Forge Press.

Royal Commission on National Development in the Arts, Letters and Sciences. 1951. *Report* [Massey Report]. Ottawa: King's Printer.

Saul, John Ralston. 1997. *Reflections of a Siamese Twin: Canada at the End of the Twentieth Century*. Toronto: Penguin.

Slater, Don. 1997. *Consumer Culture and Modernity*. Cambridge: Polity Press.

Smythe, Dallas W. 1981. *Dependency Road: Communications, Capitalism, Consciousness, and Canada*. Norwood, NJ: Ablex.

Straw, Will. 1993a. "Shifting Boundaries, Lines of Descent: Cultural Studies and Institutional Realignments." In Valda Blundell, John Shepherd, and Ian Taylor, eds. *Relocating Cultural Studies: Developments in Theory and Research*, 86–102. London and New York: Routledge.

– 1993b. "The English Canadian Recording Industry since 1970." In Tony Bennett, Somin Firth, Lawrence Grossberg, John Shephard, and Graeme Turner, eds., *Rock and Popular Music: Politics, Policies, Institutions*, 52–65. London and New York: Routledge.

– 1996. "Sound Recording." In Michael Dorland, ed., *The Cultural Industries in Canada: Problems, Policies and Prospects*, 95–117. Toronto: Lorimer.

Taylor, Kate. 2002. "Marking the Birth of a Nation's Cultural Life." *Globe and Mail*, 6 April, R1, 14.

Thompson, E.P. [1963] 1980. *The Making of the English Working Class*. Harmondsworth, England: Penguin.

Tremblay, Odile. 2002. "Paysages cinématographiques." *Le Devoir*, 9–10 February, G3.

Veblen, Thorstein. [1899] 1953. *The Theory of the Leisure Class*. New York: New American Library.

Walcott, Rinaldo. 1997. *Black Like Who? Writing Black Canada*. Toronto: Insomniac Press.

Weinstein, Michael A. 1985. *Culture Critique: Fernand Dumont and New Quebec Sociology*. Montreal: New World Perspectives.

Whitson, David, and Richard Gruneau. 1997. "The (Real) Integrated Circus: Political Economy, Popular Culture, and 'Major League Sport.'" In Wallace Clement, ed., *Understanding Canada: Building on the New Canadian*

Political Economy, 359–85. Montreal and Kingston: McGill-Queen's University Press.

Williams, Raymond. 1958. *Culture and Society, 1780–1950*. Harmondsworth, England: Penguin.

– 1980. "Advertising: The Magic System." In *Problems in Materialism and Culture: Selected Essays*, 170–95. London: Verso.

Wright, Robert. 1991. "'Gimme Shelter': Observations on Cultural Protectionism and the Recording Industry in Canada." *Cultural Studies* 5(3): 306–16.

Contributors

LAURIE E. ADKIN is Associate Professor of Comparative Politics in the Department of Political Science at the University of Alberta. She is the author of *The Politics of Sustainable Development: Citizens, Unions, and the Corporation* (Montreal, New York, and London: Black Rose Books 1998), a major study of conflicts around environmental regulation in Canada that focuses on the strategies of unions, corporations, citizens' groups, and environmental NGOs in the petrochemical and automobile sectors. Her current areas of research include political ecology movements in Europe and social movement theory.

CAROLINE ANDREW is Professor of Political Science at the University of Ottawa. Her areas of research include municipal politics, urban development, and women and politics. She is currently Dean of the Faculty of Social Sciences at the University of Ottawa.

PAT ARMSTRONG is Professor of Sociology and Women's Studies at York University and co-author of such books on health care as *Heal Thyself: Managing Health Care Reform*; *Wasting Away: The Undermining of Canadian Health Care*; *Universal Health Care: What the United States Can Learn from Canada*; *Vital Signs: Nursing in Transition*; and *Take Care: Warning Signals for Canada's Health System*. Most recently, she co-edited *Unhealthy Times*, a book on the political economy of health. She has also published on a wide variety of issues related to women's work and to social policy and has served as Chair of the Department of Sociology at York University and Director of the School of Canadian Studies at Carleton University.

WILLIAM CARROLL is Professor of Sociology at the University of Victoria, where he also participates in the interdisciplinary graduate program in Cultural, Social and Political Thought. Currently Sociology Editor of the Canadian Review of Sociology and Anthropology, his books include *Corporate Power and Canadian Capitalism* (UBC Press 1986), *Organizing Dissent: Contemporary Social Movements in Theory and Practice* (Garamond Press 1997), and *Global Shaping and Its Alternatives* (co-edited with Yildiz Atasoy; Garamond Press, 2002). William Carroll was Fellow in Residence at the Netherlands Institute for Advanced Study in the Humanities and Social Sciences when this chapter was written. The Institute's terrific support for this work is gratefully acknowledged.

WALLACE CLEMENT is Chancellor's Professor at Carleton University.

ELAINE COBURN is a Canadian PHD student in the Department of Sociology at Stanford University. She is currently living in France, where she is finishing her doctorate, which focuses on the antiglobalization protests that took place in Seattle, Washington, at the end of 1999.

WILLIAM D. COLEMAN holds the Canada Research Chair in Global Governance and Public Policy at McMaster University. He is currently directing a major collaborative research project on "globalization and autonomy" sponsored by the Social Sciences and Humanities Research Council of Canada

MARY CORNISH is a senior partner with the firm of Cavalluzzo, Hayes, Shilton, McIntyre & Cornish. She is well known for her work as a human and women's rights advocate and as co-founder of Ontario's Equal Pay Coalition, which persuaded the Ontario Government to enact pay equity laws. She has written, advised, presented, litigated and lectured on sex discrimination issues throughout her career. Her publications cover topics ranging from women's health in the workplace to the difficulties of union organizing faced by women, as well as broad and ongoing work on pay equity. She has also been counsel in many precedent-setting cases in the field of labour law, human rights, and pay and employment equity, including the successful 1997 SEIU Local 204 Charter challenge, which restored the pay equity rights of over 100,000 Ontario women.

JUDY FUDGE teaches employment and labour law at Osgoode Hall School, York University. She is co-author, with Eric Tucker, of *Labour before the Law: The Legal Regulation of Workers' Collective Action in Canada, 1900 to 1948* (Oxford University Press 2000) and co-editor, with Brenda Cossman, of *Privatization, Law and the Challenge to Feminism* (University of Toronto Press 2002). She has published widely on the legal regulation of women's work, gendered employment norms, and precarious employment.

CHRISTINA GABRIEL is Assistant Professor in the Department of Political Science and Pauline Jewett Institute of Women's Studies, Carleton University. She is the co-author, with Yasmeen Abu Laban, of *Selling Diversity: Immigration, Multiculturalism, Employment Equity and Globalization* (Broadview Press, 2002). Her research interests include citizenship and immigration, gender and politics, and globalization. Her current research project examines the politics of continental economic integration in the areas of immigration and border control policies in North America.

SAM GINDIN holds the Packer Chair in Social Justice in the Department of Political Science at York University.

JOYCE GREEN is Associate Professor of Political Science at the University of Regina and Senior Fellow at the Saskatchewan Institute of Public Policy for 2002–3.

ERIC HELLEINER is Canada Research Chair in International Political Economy at Trent University. He is author of *States and the Reemergence of Global Finance* (Cornell 1994) and *The Making of National Money: Territorial Currencies in Historical Perspective* (Cornell 2003), as well as co-editor, with Emily Gilbert, of *Nation-States and Money: The Past, Present and Future of National Currencies* (Routledge 1999).

ROBERT HOLLANDS lectures in youth studies and urban sociology in the Department of Social Policy, University of Newcastle, England, and is author of *Friday Night, Saturday Night: Youth Cultural Identification in the Post-Industrial City* (Newcastle University 1995) and *The Long Transition: Class, Culture and Youth Training* (Macmillan 1990) and co-editor of *Leisure, Sport and Working Class Cultures: Theory and History* (Garamond, 1988). He is currently conducting an ESRC-funded study on youth cultural identities and nightlife that is due to be published by Routledge in 2003.

JANE JENSON holds a Canada Research Chair in Citizenship and Governance at the Université de Montréal, where she is Professor of

Political Science and Director of the Université de Montréal/McGill University Institute of European Studies. Since June 1999 she has been the Director of the Family Network of Canadian Policy Research Networks, Inc., a policy think tank located in Ottawa. She is also Editor of *Lien social et Politiques,* a social policy journal. She was elected a Fellow of the Royal Society of Canada in 1989. Jenson is the co-author of *Absent Mandate: Canadian Electoral Politics in an Era of Restructuring* and *Crisis, Challenge and Change: Party and Class in Canada.*

ROGER KEIL is Associate Professor and Undergraduate Program Director at the Faculty of Environmental Studies, York University. He is also a member of the graduate faculty of the Department of Political Science at York University.

STEFAN KIPFER is in the PHD program in Political Science at York University and teaches courses in urban politics and social policy in the Faculty of Environmental Studies at York.

FUYUKI KURASAWA is Assistant Professor in the Department of Sociology at York University. He is the author of articles in journals such as *International Sociology, Theory, Culture & Society,* and *Thesis Eleven,* as well as of *The Ethnological Imagination: Western Social Theory and the Cross-Cultural Critique of Modernity* (University of Minnesota Press forthcoming).

LAURA MACDONALD is Associate Professor in the Department of Political Science and the Institute of Political Economy at Carleton University. She is the Director of the Centre on North American Politics and Society in the Faculty of Public Affairs and Management at Carleton. She is the author of *Supporting Civil Society: The Political Impact of Non-Governmental Assistance in Central America,* and numerous articles on democracy, human rights, and civil society in North America and Central America, gender and trade, Canadian foreign economic policy, and the role of civil society in trade agreements. Her current research project concerns the impact of continental economic integration on immigration and border control policies in North America.

WENDY MCKEEN is Assistant Professor at the Maritime School of Social Work, Dalhousie University, Halifax, where she teaches social policy. Her research interests centre on social policy and welfare state politics. She is currently completing a book on the limited influence of feminism on the national child benefits debate in Canada.

RIANNE MAHON is Director of Carleton University's Institute of Political Economy. She is the author of numerous articles on trade unions and on child care in Canada and Sweden and co-editor (with Sonya Michel) of *Child Care Policy at the Crossroads: Gender and Welfare State Restructuring* (Routledge 2002).

ELIZABETH MILLAR is a Pay Equity Consultant with Nelligan, O'Brien and Payne Law Firm and Labour Consulting Group. She recently retired from the Public Service Alliance of Canada, a union representing the majority of federal public service employees, where she served as the Head of the Classification and Equal Pay Group, a team responsible for research, filing, defense and settlement of numerous pay equity complaints. Millar was centrally involved in the groundbreaking $3.5 billion settlement affecting 150,000 current and former clerical and other federal public sector employees.

VINCENT MOSCO is Professor of Communication at Carleton University. He is the author of *The Political Economy of Communication: Rethinking and Renewal* (London: Sage 1996). His most recent book is *Continental Order? Integrating North America for Cyber-Capitalism,* co-edited with Dan Schiller (New York: Rowman and Littlefield 2002).

SUSAN PHILLIPS is Associate Professor, School of Public Policy and Administration at Carleton University and Director of the Centre for Voluntary Sector Research and Development, also located at Carleton. Her research focuses on citizen engagement and the relationships between the state and the voluntary sector in comparative perspective.

ANN PORTER is Assistant Professor of Political Science at York University. Her current research interests include globalization, gender, and the welfare state.

TONY PORTER is Associate Professor of Political Science at McMaster University in Hamilton. He is author of *States, Markets, and Regimes in Global Finance* (Basingstoke, England: Macmillan 1993) and *Technology, Governance and Political Conflict in International Industries* (London and New York: Routledge 2002) and co-editor, with A. Claire Cutler and Virginia Haufler, of *Private Authority in International Affairs* (Albany, NY: State University of New York Press 1999).

DANIEL SALÉE is in the Department of Political Science and Principal of the School of Community and Public Affairs at Concordia University.

VIC SATZEWICH is Professor and Chair of the Department of Sociology, McMaster University, and President of the Canadian Sociology and Anthropology Association. He is the author of *The Ukrainian Diaspora* (London: Routledge 2002), *Racism and the Incorporation of Foreign Labour: Farm Labour Migration to Canada since 1945* (London: Routledge 1991), and co-author, with Terry Wotherspoon, of *First Nations: Race, Class and Gender Relations* (Regina, SK: Canadian Plains Research Centre 2001). He is also editor of *Racism and Social Inequality in Canada* (Toronto: Thompson Educational Publishers, 1998) and *Deconstructing a Nation: Immigration, Multiculturalism and Racism in '90s Canada* (Halifax: Fernwood Press 1992).

JIM STANFORD is an economist with the Canadian Auto Workers union in Toronto.

LEAH F. VOSKO is Canada Research Chair in Feminist Political Economy, School of Social Sciences (Political Science), Joseph E. Atkinson School of Liberal and Professional Studies, York University. She is the author of *Temporary Work: The Gendered Rise of a Precarious Employment Relationship* (University of Toronto Press 2000) and co-editor (with Jim Stanford) of *Challenging the Market: The Struggle to Regulate Work and Income* (McGill-Queen's University Press forthcoming).

MEL WATKINS is Professor Emeritus of Economics and Political Science, University College, University of Toronto, and Immediate Past President of Science for Peace.

LLOYD L. WONG is Associate Professor of Sociology at the University of Calgary and research affiliate with the Prairie Centre of Excellence for Research on Immigration and Integration. His research concerns racism, ethnic entrepreneurship, transnationalism, and citizenship. He has authored several book chapters, the latest of which is in *Communities across Borders: New Immigrants and Transnational Cultures*, edited by P. Kennedy and V. Roudometof. His current research projects include Chinese engineers and the "glass-ceiling."